THE BIG RED ONE TO THE B – 29

**Men and Women from the Fillmore Central
School District Area, Allegany County, New York, in World War II**

**PEARL HARBOR
NORTH AMERICA
NORTH AFRICA
PACIFIC ISLANDS
EUROPE - ASIA
SOUTH AMERICA
AUSTRALIA
TOKYO BAY**

ROBERT N. COLOMBO

International Standard Book Number: 978-0-692-0308-6

Other Publications: To Save the Union – Published 2007 by Heritage Books, Inc, Publishing Division, 65 East Main Street, Westminster, Maryland 21157-5026

Contents

INTRODUCTION

When I got home, I sat down on a rock and cried. I now realized I would make it.

Herbert Leslie Rose, Company B, 26th Signal Construction Battalion, to fellow FCSD area WW II veteran Bernard Arthur Mills, 332nd Bomb Squadron, 94th Bomb Group. Herbert earned five battle stars during his WW II service.

This book is dedicated to: Seaman First Class Albert E. Ferrin,
          Staff Sergeant Gerald B. Gayford,
          Torpedoman First Class Grant A. Vedder, and
          Second Lieutenant David D. Wallace

The courage of these men in combat brought honor to them, their families, and the nation. They died in battle; their remains were never recovered. They will always be remembered by those whom they swore to protect.

The book is also dedicated to the *Northern Allegany Observer,* its publisher, and employees whose journalistic efforts chronicled the history of a small rural area for almost 100 years. Its coverage of the contributions made by that area's men and women in one of our nation's most difficult periods was exemplary. The demise of the *Observer*, and papers like it, shows us that changing times do not always bring progress; that good things are not always replaced with something better.

Many many people helped in the development of this book. Special thanks must go to World War II veteran Bernard A. Mills. Bernard was a fountain of information about veterans and their families. His contributions to this work were enormous. Special thanks also go to veteran Lyle Clarence Brown for his assistance in so many ways, including his suggestions and corrections of a draft of this book, Polly Cockle Miller whose knowledge of the people of the area is unsurpassed, James and Darlene Williams Mowers, Janet Gayford Thomas, Patricia Thomas Ricketts, Hume Historian Rondus Perry Miller and Mrs. Jean Colombo. They endured innumerable telephone calls and e-mails, many times answering with a "What do you need now, Bob?" My friend William T. Salerno also proofread drafts, and provided many important comments. Numerous other people who helped me are acknowledged in Part XIV of the book in the section on the veteran for whom they provided assistance. Finally, special thanks go to the consultants at the National Archives at College Park, MD, without whose help this book would have taken at least 20 years to write.

By 1943 the undisputed leader of the Free World, and the man who would lead the Democracies to Victory in the most savage, killing, and destructive war in World History was President of the United States, Franklin Delano Roosevelt. He was a great, if not the greatest, President in United States History.

But if the Muse of History demanded that one person be named as the individual responsible for saving the civilized world during its darkest hour, that person could only be Winston Spencer Churchill.

"At the request of the Queen and Parliament a 60 by 76-inch polished green-marble slab was placed in Westminster Abbey, the thousand-year- old monument to English history. It is just a few feet inside the great west doors. It reads:

REMEMBER WINSTON CHURCHILL"

From "The Last Lion: Winston Spencer Churchill Defender of the Realm, 1940 – 1965" by William Manchester and Paul Reid.

Underground Cabinet Room where Winston Churchill made decisions regarding the British role in World War II. Photo – A Guide to the Cabinet War Rooms, Clive Steps

President of the United States John F. Kennedy said in 1963 when conferring Honorary United States Citizenship on Sir Winston Churchill that, "his life has shown that no adversary can overcome, and no fear can deter, free men in the defense of freedom".

"I know not with what weapons World War III will be fought, but World War IV will be fought with sticks and stones." Albert Einstein - Einstein spoke a version of this quote in the 1940's. His equation "E = MC (2)" established that nuclear weapons were theoretical possible.

World War II was the most deadly and brutal war in history. Nothing else, war or otherwise, even comes in a close second. There have been wars, disasters, and brutalities, both before and after World War II, which by themselves or as parts of other events, may equal, but never surpass, the same or similar events of World War II. Such other events, in their totality, even when grouped together -- with the possible exception of combining the Stalin purges of the 20th Century, the Black Plague of the 14th Century, and the Influenza epidemic of the late 1910's -- pale in comparison to the absolute total horror that was World War II.

Today we look at genocides, terrorism, and regional wars, and are horrified at the death and mutilation, the suffering, the killing of innocents. Our reaction is outrage. Yet in World War II such horrific events occurred constantly, but on a stage so vast and at a level so huge, they were more than the mind could comprehend. People really didn't believe that a nation could sink so low that it would actually brutally murder at least 11 million innocent human beings, including at least one to one and a half million helpless children, as Hitler's Germany did. People, even today, cannot imagine a nation where, putting to death your enemies and then eating them, for enjoyment, not out of a need to survive, would be acceptable, but for Japan it was.

Today we feel the pain of families who lose a son or daughter, a father or brother, or other relative. We watch as the death tolls mount in the thousands and become irate that we are even fighting a war. Yet in World War II the numbers were so great we weren't even able to grasp them, and so we were left to mourn the few. We do not even know how many died. The estimated range is in the millions. Take your pick - 50 million, 60 million, 70 million. (Historian Max Hastings in his book, *Inferno*, put the number at "at least 60 million. More recent scholarship says 70 or 80 million.") Often even the few were not mourned. There was no family, or even friends, left to mourn them.

This was the war in which many residents of the Fillmore Central School District (FCSD) area participated. Over 60 percent of the male graduates, six female students and four teachers (two males, two females) from Fillmore Central School during the years 1935 to 1945 served in our Armed Forces. These figures do not include men and women from the FCSD area who attended the Houghton Academy, nor do they include those who, for one reason or another, did not finish school. The 1939 class had only 7 males out of a class of 30. Not finishing school was common during those years due to the Great Depression, and then the war.

FCSD's men and women served on six of the seven continents. Men served in every service branch including the Army, Army Air Corps, Navy, Marine Corps, Coast Guard, as well as the Merchant Marine. Howard Kopler of Fillmore earned Merchant Marine decorations for service in the Atlantic War Zone, the Pacific War Zone and the Mediterranean Middle East War Zone. Women from the area served overseas in North Africa, England, Italy, France and Hawaii. One served aboard a hospital ship. They served in the Women's Auxiliary Army Corps, (WAAC), Women's Army Reserve Corps, (WAC), as Army Nurses, the Coast Guard Reserve (SPARS), as WASPS (Women's Air Service Pilots), and the Marine Women's Reserve. A total of 15 women served during the war,

FCSD residents participated in virtually every major invasion of World War II. They were with Big Red One (1st Infantry Division) in North Africa and Sicily. Marlie Hodnett of Fillmore was one of the first (if not the first) men ashore in the Sicily invasion at Gela. They were in the invasions of mainland Italy and Southern France. The FCSD was well represented at Normandy, on land, sea and in the air, including the first waves at deadly Omaha Beach and at Utah Beach. David Hambling identified 20 battles which he considered the 20 most important battles of World War II. Of the 20, four were fought prior to US entry into the war. Four others were fought between Germany and Russia. Of the remaining 12 battles, individuals from the FCSD area participated in 11.

In the Pacific, FCSD area men participated in the island-hopping invasions, including Guadalcanal, Bougainville, Tinian, Saipan, Iwo Jima, Okinawa, and the Philippines, among others. Men from the area were even part of the troops designated to invade Japan, had that been necessary. Their presence was felt at sea where they served on battleships, aircraft carriers, submarines, and everything in between. Ralph Kleinspehn, long-time Fillmore resident was in several engagements, including the Great Marianas Turkey Shoot. Paul Hatch of Centerville won the Silver Star saving the life of a fellow soldier on the hell hole called Bougainville. He later died there. When it was over, several men from the area were aboard ships in Tokyo Bay when the Japanese surrendered. They were part of the occupation forces in both Germany and Japan.

Almond E. Fisher, born in Hume in 1912, earned the Medal of Honor, the second man from the area to do so. George E. Meach, also from Hume, earned the Medal for his actions on September 19, 1864 in the Battle of Winchester, VA during the Civil War.

Today's youth think of World War II as ancient history. In high schools, World War II is barely mentioned. The weapon systems of that era are obsolete and seem tame compared to modern systems to young people. They are both right and wrong. Most of the systems that exist today were introduced during World War II. They are much more advanced and destructive now, but they existed then. One of those weapons ended the war. But Einstein got it right. He understood that any war that relies on the weapon systems that were used in World War II, but which would become even more destructive in the future, would likely destroy civilization. You cannot get worse than World War II and survive. Total world war is obsolete. The question is whether the human race gets it. Einstein apparently was not sure.

Henry L. Stimson, Secretary of War during World War II (the Defense Department did not exist during the war), wrote in his diary in 1945, "We have been compelled to invent and unleash forces of terrible destructiveness. Unless we now develop methods of international life, backed by the spirit of tolerance and kindliness, vis, the spirit of Christianity, sufficient to make international life permanent and kindly and war impossible, we will with another war end our civilization." (Biography of Stimson by Godfrey Hodgson.)

Many of the FCSD men and women served in multiple locations. For the most part, however, I have included information regarding a person's service in a single book part relevant to that service. For a few, I have included information in more than one book part. This was done primarily where an individual served in both the European and Pacific theaters of war, or when the nature of the service merited coverage in more than one part.

The last part of the book is an alphabetical listing of all the men and women who served. It contains a summary of their military service and some basic biographical information. One item summarized is medals earned by each veteran. The medals listed are those that the author knows or believes each veteran earned. Where possible, medals earned were discussed with the veteran. The veterans themselves were seldom sure, and many clearly didn't care about the medals they had earned. Earning medals was not the reason they fought the war. Not one I spoke with knew of the post war (1947) congressionally awarded Bronze Star to men who had also earned the Combat Infantryman Badge. Histories of the war indicate that the only time men asked about medals was when they learned that they received extra points for medals, and those extra points got them home sooner. Where it was not clear if a medal was earned, I have decided to include it as earned. These medals were not given (awarded) to them. They earned them. Determining medals earned was not easy. Military files, where available, are often incomplete, at best.

The lack of files, and time, as well as a lack of cooperation from some individuals and agencies impacted the stories of some veterans. Hopefully, in the future, there will be others who will take on finishing the stories of these men and women when and where necessary.

This book identifies 357 men and women from the FCSD area who served in the military during World War II. It is possible there were a few more. According to the 1940 Census, the entire population for the FCSD area was a little less than 4,000. While a few of the FCSD men and women who served moved to the area after the war, it is clear that a significant percentage of the local 1940 FCSD area adult male population and a surprising number of females served during the war.

The FCSD area is defined as the townships of Hume, Centerville and Granger, and the hamlet of Houghton. It should be noted that some of the men and women from Houghton included in the book attended the Houghton Academy rather than FCS. Some of the veterans from Allen Township which was actually in three school districts are also included. If they attended FCS or had a close relationship to the FCSD area, especially Granger, they are included. The same is true for some residents of Centerville who lived in the township, but may have attended a school other than Fillmore Central.

PART I - IT BEGINS

Pearl Harbor

AIR RAID, PEARL HARBOR. THIS IS NOT A DRILL

"Yesterday, December 7, 1941 - a date which will live in infamy - The United States of America was suddenly and deliberately attacked by naval and air forces of the Empire of Japan." President Franklin Delano Roosevelt - Addressing Congress 12/8/1941

"I fear that all we have done is to awaken a sleeping giant and fill him with a terrible resolve." Japanese Admiral Isoroku Yamamoto - Originator of the attack on Pearl Harbor. This quote is from the movie "Tora Tora Tora." There is a claim that the quote is from Yamamoto's diary, but historians have been unable to locate that exact quote.

In 1941 Hawaii was still a territory of the United States. It had been annexed by the United States on July 4, 1898 following the overthrow of the Hawaiian monarchy. Hawaii did not become the 50th state until August 21, 1959. Despite its territorial status, Hawaii was viewed by most Americans as a foreign country in 1941. Being stationed there was being stationed overseas. It was, however, an overseas assignment that was welcomed by most servicemen.

Pearl Harbor (the name is merely a translation of an earlier Hawaiian language name for "Pearl Waters"), was, and is, a wonderful natural harbor. In 1941 it was the home base of the United States (US) Pacific Fleet. Admiral Isoroku Yamamoto's plans called for destroying, to the maximum extent possible, the US Fleet at Pearl Harbor, especially the aircraft carriers. Commander Minoru Genda developed the initial plans for the attack. Commander Mitsuo Fuchida led the attack. Fuchida sent the famous message "Tora Tora Tora," signifying that the Japanese had achieved compete surprise in the Pearl Harbor attack.

Yamamoto believed his plan would give Japan time to conquer areas in Southeast Asia wanted for expansion purposes, and which contained many of the natural resources Japan needed for its economy and growth. Once that was accomplished, he hoped Japan would enter into a peace agreement with the US. Admiral Yamamoto did not believe that Japan could defeat the US in an all-out war. He had lived in the US and knew the production potential of the country. Once aroused the US would be more than a match for Japan. In this he would be proven correct. As for the rest, the world will never know because, despite the enormous damage at Pearl Harbor and the terrible loss of life, the Pacific Fleet was not destroyed. The US aircraft carriers, prime targets, had departed Pearl Harbor before the attack and were not touched.

Only six months after the attack, four of the six Japanese aircraft carriers (*Akagi*, *Kaga*, *Soryu*, and *Hiryu*) that led the attack on Pearl Harbor were at the bottom of the Pacific Ocean. As for the other two, *Zuikaku* was sunk October 25, 1944, and *Shokaku* on June 19, 1944. Commanders Genda and Fuchida survived the war. Admiral Yamamoto did not.

There is no evidence that anyone from the FCSD area was in Hawaii during the attack on Pearl Harbor.

However, one of the ships damaged during the Pearl Harbor attack was the great battleship, *USS Pennsylvania* (BB-38). It had been one of the first ships to return fire during the attack. The Japanese believed it had been sunk, or at least damaged beyond repair. In fact, by December 20, 1941 it was on its way to San Francisco for repairs. By the end of World War II, *Pennsylvania* had fired more ammunition than any other US ship in history. She retired from battle on August 12, 1945, just days before the end of the war, having been hit, but not sunk. *Pennsylvania* was battle scarred, but unbowed. Only the end of the war prevented her return to battle.

Erwin C. Howden of Fillmore joined the crew of the *Pennsylvania* on October 17, 1942 (probably replacing one of the 68 men killed, wounded, or missing during the Pearl Harbor attack), and he served aboard until the end of the war in 1945. Erwin graduated from FCS in 1939 and was working for Bell Aircraft in Buffalo when he enlisted August 8, 1942. His basic training was at the Great Lakes Naval Training Center in North Chicago, Il. He joined the *Pennsylvania* in San Francisco where it was undergoing a major overhaul. Son Marty remembers that his dad was aboard when the *Pennsylvania* participated in the Aleutians campaign. The NAO reported in October, 1943 that he was assigned to "one of Uncle Sam's battle wagons" soon after his enlistment. The *Pennsylvania* departed for the Aleutians on April 23, 1943. During the Aleutian Campaign she bombarded Holtz Bay and Chicago Harbor. At Attu Island, on May 12, 1943, quick maneuvering enabled the ship to escape a Japanese torpedo. On May 14, it once again pounded Holtz Bay before returning to Seattle for supplies. It then returned to Kiska Island in the Aleutians, but the Japanese had had enough. They had pulled out.

The *Pennsylvania* then headed for Hawaii and from there on to the Gilbert Islands. During this period, it also served as the flagship of Rear Admiral Richmond K. Turner. She bombarded Makin Atoll and Butaritari Island. *Pennsylvania* was near the escort carrier Liscome Bay (ACV-CVE – 56), off Makin Island, when that ship was destroyed by a torpedo. Future Fillmore resident Ralph Kleinspehn was one of the few to survive the sinking of the *Liscome Bay*. The next stop was the Marshall Islands. In January 1944 her guns pounded Kwajalein. In February, it was Eniwetok's turn. On February 18 and 19 she attacked Engebi Island, and on February 20 and 21 her target was Parry Island. When that bombardment ended, there was not a tree still standing. With support from the *Pennsylvania,* landings on all these islands were successful.

After a layover in the New Hebrides in early April, the *Pennsylvania* headed to Australia for a week of rest.

Now came the Marianas. Saipan was first, on June 10, and then Tinian. John Ballard of Fillmore was with the Marines who captured both Saipan and Tinian. Tinian became the home base of the 509th Composite Group, and the B-29 *Enola Gay*. On June 16, Orote Point on Guam was pounded. After re-supplying at Eniwetok (now a US Naval base), it was back to Guam. Again, *Pennsylvania* blasted Orote and the assault beaches. With the beaches secure, she returned to Eniwetok. During the Marianas campaign, the *Pennsylvania* fired more ammunition than any other US warship in history during a single campaign. The NAO reported that one of her officers said, "The old girl shoots so fast, and so much that she looks like she's afire." (The NAO commented, "That may have been one of the reasons why Tokyo radio had many times reported that the *Pennsylvania* had been sunk.") She earned her nickname, "Old Falling Apart," because she expelled so much metal. Erwin told his son Marty that he had been on guard duty once near a battery when the big guns went off. He could not hear for a week.

Pennsylvania now took part in the attack on the Palau Islands in the Western Carolinas, September 12 to 21. On September 15, she pounded Peleliu. Her guns blasted enemy gun emplacements flanking the Red Landing Beach on Angaur Island. Her fire was so accurate and devastating that there was no return fire.

Next was the Philippines. Throughout this operation, *Pennsylvania* was subject to constant air attacks. In addition to the heavy bombardment the ship laid down, she engaged in a major surface battle and remained in the area longer than she stayed in any other battle area of the war. She was the first battleship to enter Leyte Gulf, and the last to leave. On October 18, *Pennsylvania* covered a beach reconnaissance, and on the 20th, the landings at Leyte. On October 26, she took part in the Battle of the Surigao Strait and helped sink two Japanese battleships and three destroyers. On October 26, she assisted in shooting down four Japanese fighters, and then shot down a Japanese bomber making a torpedo run on the ship. On January 4 and 5, 1945, she was attacked by kamikazes as she headed for Lingayen Gulf at Luzon. On January 6, she bombarded Santiago Island, and on the 7th entered the Gulf. From January 8 to 10, *Pennsylvania* provided fire support that destroyed a concentration of Japanese tanks attacking landing troops.

Pennsylvania now retired for repairs and supplies in San Francisco, before heading for Okinawa. In route to Okinawa, she took time out to bombard Wake Island. Anchored in Buckner Bay at Okinawa on August 12, she was hit by a torpedo from a Japanese bomber. Erwin told son Marty that, as a Machinist Mate, he worked in the engine room, and was close to the living compartment room hit by the torpedo. Some 20 men were killed, and ten wounded by the explosion but the *Pennsylvania* survived. *Pennsylvania* participated in the first US battle of the war. She was still afloat at the end. Three days after she was hit, the Japanese city Hiroshima disappeared in an atomic fireball. Three days later, Nagasaki suffered the same fate. The war was over.

Along with other members of the crew, Erwin had helped the *Pennsylvania* play a major role in the destruction of the Japanese Navy and Empire. Like his shipmates, he was eligible to wear a ribbon in honor of the Navy Unit Commendation awarded the Pennsylvania, as well as seven battle stars and several other medals and ribbons.

William J. Stickle of Centerville was in Hawaii within months of the attack. Stickle was eligible to wear the commonly called Pre-Pearl Harbor Medal, since he had joined the military in January 1941. The official name for the Medal is the American Defense Service Medal. It was earned by anyone who had been on active federal service between September 8, 1939 and December 7, 1941. If they were overseas anytime during that period, they were authorized a metal clasp indicating "Foreign Service."

Bill started his service as an enlisted man and took his initial training at Ft. Bragg, NC, where he was assigned to the 9th Signal Corps, 9th Division. In December of 1941, he was ordered to California to train as a flying cadet. After completing his training as a Navigator at Fort Helmet in Sacramento, and being commissioned a Second Lieutenant in August, 1942, he was ordered to Washington State, most likely Ephrata, where he joined the 301st Heavy Bombardment Group. The group was flying B-17s when he arrived, but was very shortly switched to B-24's. Bill's wife of one year, Beula Wells of Fillmore, joined him for a tour of Yellowstone National Park before he reported to his new base.

Bill was now assigned to the 371st Bomb Squadron, 301st Bomb Group. Shortly after he arrived, the group was transferred to Sioux City, Iowa for three weeks of training, probably to familiarize them with the B-24. They then moved to Hamilton Field in California and on November 1 arrived at Hickam Field, Hawaii. The 371st was then stationed at Wheeler Field. The group's assignment was to conduct search and patrol missions over the waters surrounding the Hawaiian Islands. On a mission on December 17, 1942, Bill's plane caught on fire shortly after take-off from Wheeler, exploded and crashed. William and four other crewmen, including the pilot, James H. McClendon, were killed. The War Department letter to his wife announcing his death stated that the crash was not the result of enemy action. The family always believed that the plane was sabotaged, but no hard evidence to that effect has been located.

Stickle was the first FCSD area casualty of World War II.

Harry W. Fairbank was another Fillmore man eligible to wear the Pre-Pearl Harbor Medal. Harry, an adopted son of Fillmore, was born in Maryland as was his father. His Mother was born in England. Harry was a career Army man who served his country in three wars: the border war with Mexico, World War I and World War II. Harry saw considerable combat in WW I. He earned a Purple Heart for a wound received during the Champaign – Marne campaign in 1918, as well as several other medals.

After WW I, and while serving in Panama in the 1920's, Harry made a trip back to the US. While in the US, he met Bernice Redanz, a native of the FCSD area. They were soon married and returned to the Canal Zone where their first child, Evalyn was born. (Another daughter, Effie, graduated from Fillmore High School with the author.) In the early 1930's the family moved to Hawaii, Harry's second tour in what became the Aloha state. Altogether, Harry served seven years in Hawaii. Iceland was next for Harry.

American Defense Service Medal

In addition to Harry Fairbank and William Stickle, several other service men from the FCSD area earned the American Defense Service Medal. They included Paul J. Abbott, Edward J. Amore, William R. Appleford, David M. Babbitt, Barton Burdette Butler, Frank R. Butterfield, Merton E. Byington, Ronald W. Carpenter, Adair W. Common, Herbert T. Darling, Gerald G. Davis, Richard C. Farnsworth, Almond E. Fisher, Lynford S. Fox, Ronald C. Fridley, Forrest L. Gilbert, Thurlow H. Gleason, Charles G. Hodnett, Russell C. Hodnett, Merlin D. James, John V. Jones, Alfred H. Kingsley, Jr. (served with Canadian Army), Roman (NMI) (Ray) Kolokowski, Alvin P. Miller, Arthur C. Miller, Lowell E. Mix, Douglas F. Morris, Carroll C. Phipps, David A. Pitt, Douglas W. Pitt, Charles F. Porter, Lloyd L. Prentice, Robert B. Redman, George A. Rennicks, Gerald W. Rennicks, Floyd K. Roberts, Donald L. Slack, Donald A. Smith, Edward L. Smith, Lyman E. Smith, Sanford I. Smith, Stanley Swales, Harold E. Thayer, Gerald F. Thomas, Roland J. Thomas, Lawrence Treusdell, Anthony R. Vasile, Grant A. Vedder, David D. Wallace, Lowell J. Wilcox, Lyle A. Wilcox, Alfred C. Wilday, Clair N. Williams, and James A. Young, Jr. Of the 55 men who earned the medal, 38 of them entered military service in 1941 and eight in 1940. War clouds were growing and these men responded. Harry Fairbank entered the service way back in 1914, likely anticipating US entry into WW I. The other eight entered in the 1930's likely because they saw opportunities in the military that did not exist in the civilian economy at that time due to the depression.

Iceland

FCSD area men who served in Iceland included Paul J. Abbott, Harry W. Fairbank, John Pattison, Donald L. Slack and Stanley Swales.

As Adolph Hitler swallowed up European countries including Denmark, Great Britain worried that he would also grab Iceland, a sovereign state of Denmark since 1918. Iceland is strategically situated on the air and sea routes between England and the US and Canada. The United States also worried about this possibility. In fact, at one time such a move was considered by Hitler. To avoid this, in 1940 Great Britain peacefully occupied Iceland. By arrangement between Iceland (with heavy diplomatic coaxing) and Great Britain, the US and Iceland entered into a defense agreement in 1941. The US became responsible for the defense of the air and sea lanes going through Iceland.

Paul J. Abbott of Fillmore entered active duty on September 4, 1941. Paul was from Elmira, NY. In the late 1930s he was the agriculture teacher at Fillmore and later at Castile, NY He entered the service from Castile. Paul was a member of the ROTC at Syracuse University and was an active member of the Army Reserves starting in 1930. He served on active duty a part of each year during the 1930s. During this time Paul was an Army Infantry Officer commissioned as a Second Lieutenant on June 9, 1930. He transferred to the Army Air Corps upon entering active duty. He was promoted to First Lieutenant September 4, 1941.

After being called to active duty, Paul attended the Adjutant Generals School in Washington, DC and then was assigned to the 4th Materiel Squadron at Mitchel Field, NY. He was next shipped to Iceland where he served with the 4th Service Squadron, 2nd Service Group, the 375th Service Squadron and Headquarters and Headquarters Squadron of the 2nd Service Group for the next three years. The 2nd Service Squadron was part of the defense of Iceland. It flew P-47 Thunderbolts. Paul served as Squadron Adjutant, Commander and Group Special Service Officer during his time in Iceland. On February 22, 1944 Paul moved to England where he was assigned to Engineering Headquarters of the Ninth Air Force as Assistant Adjutant General. He remained in that position for the balance of the war. His main duties involved the maintenance of Ninth Air Force air fields.

Paul arrived back in the US March 12, 1945. He served at Atlantic City, New Jersey, Tinker Air Field Oklahoma, and Lubbock Field, Texas prior to his discharge February 28, 1946 at Rome Air Field, NY.

Harry Fairbank and the rest of the 2nd Battalion, 5th Engineer Combat Regiment (and other units at various times) were sent to Iceland on September 16, 1941 to prepare airfield and port facilities according to the US/Iceland defense agreement. The British, as well as a US marine unit, had started work on such facilities, but much remained to be done. In the next several months not only were two airfields completed - Meek Field for bombers, and Patterson for fighters - but troop housing, laundries, kitchens, refrigeration units, ice plants and roads were built. Harry's daughter Evalyn remembers stories of his time in Iceland. The winters were brutal, especially the winter of 1941-42. Living conditions were tough as American troops struggled to build permanent quarters. Existing barracks were freezing. Throughout much of the winter there was zero visibility and colored ropes had to be strung in order to guide people from one building to another. There was enormous pressure to finish the airfields, which only intensified after the Japanese attack on Pearl Harbor.

Eventually, some 40,000 US troops were stationed in Iceland, and the sea and air routes to Europe were secured. As the result of a referendum in 1944, in which the Icelandic people voted overwhelmingly yes, Iceland became an independent country with the blessing of still occupied Denmark. The airfields which Harry helped build eventually became Keflavik International Airport. Harry served in Iceland for twenty-two months. German troops remained in Denmark until the end of the war.

When Harry left for Iceland, his family moved to Fillmore, the hometown of his wife Bernice. From that point on the family considered Fillmore home and Harry eventually retired to Fillmore, twice.

Following his return to the US from Iceland, Harry was assigned to Camp Forrest, Tennessee. After a short time there, Harry was ordered to the Army War College in Washington, DC, where he spent the remainder of the war. He was assigned to the Engineer Section, Headquarters, Army Ground Forces under General Lesley J. McNair. Today the Army War College is located on Fort McNair in southwest Washington, DC.

John Pattison of Hume was brought up in the Rochester, NY area. By the early 40's he was working for Virgil Wolfer of Centerville (John is buried in Centerville), and he entered the service from the FCSD area on July 27, 1942. He did not report for duty until August 10, 1942.

It is not known where John took basic training or any technical training. However, given his war time occupation, it is likely that he received some specialized training.

John was assigned to Iceland, and almost certainly to Meeks Air Field. He apparently remained at Meeks for his entire service, ending his service there assigned to Air Transport Command's 1386th Air Base Unit. Initially John was likely part of Air Transport Command's 14th Detachment, assigned to Station 14 in Iceland on August 28, 1943. On August 1, 1944, Station 14 became the 1386th Army Air Force Base Unit.

John's duty assignment in Iceland, according to his write-up at the WW II Memorial, was as a crash boat operator. The 1386th Army Air Base Unit was located in the Naval Air District.

Iceland was a key point on the World War II air and sea routes to Europe. Thousands of aircraft passed through Iceland during the war. Some of them had accidents. Further, there were defense aircraft stationed at the base, which operated daily and also suffered crashes. There were many air crashes and accidents in and around Iceland during the war. Some of these crashes occurred in the sea around Iceland, and there were fatalities. John would have been involved in trying to rescue crews and passengers aboard planes that crashed at sea. John was discharged August 20, 1945, after over three years of service.

Stanley Swales of Fillmore entered the service April 9, 1941 from the state of Pennsylvania. It is likely that he was assigned to Iceland after just a few months of active duty. Any basic training Stanley received would have lasted, at best, no more than a few weeks. It likely would have been provided by the unit to which he was assigned. The first American troops assigned to Iceland (4,100 Marines), as part of the agreement between Britain, Iceland and the United States transferring responsibility for the defense of Iceland to the US, arrived July 5, 1941 from New York, NY and Norfolk, VA. The 33rd Pursuit Squadron arrived August 6. On September 16, 1941 some 6,000 officers and men of the 5th Infantry Division arrived. It is possible/likely that Stanley was one of these men. The NAO reported in November 1942 that Stanley was serving overseas in Iceland. It did not indicate how long he had been there. When he arrived and where he served in Iceland is not known.

During his service in Iceland, he made the acquaintance of Don Slack. While both were from Fillmore, they had never met. They did not meet in Iceland either. All their conversations were over the phone. They were stationed in areas of Iceland totally remote from each other. It is not clear exactly what Stanley's duties were in Iceland.

In July 1943 Stanley returned to the US from Iceland. The 5th Infantry Division was reassigned at about the same time, August, 1943. Stanley returned to the states, the 5th Division moved to England. After a short home leave, Stanley was assigned to Camp Edwards, MA. During his leave Stanley married Miss Pearl G. Blewett of Syracuse. There were a number of activities being carried out at Edwards, and Stanley's assignment is not known. It is possible that he was assigned to the Amphibious Training Command, a major unit at Camp Edwards.

Stanley remained at Edwards for less than a year. In April 1944 he was transferred to Fort Hood, Texas. Fort Hood was a premier training camp for Tank Destroyer Battalions until 1944. In 1944 its focus shifted to training field artillery battalions and the establishment of the Infantry Replacement

11

Training Center. Stanley's final pay record indicates he served with a Detachment to the Veterans Administration Facility at Fort Hood for at least part of his time at Edwards.

Stanley was discharged November 15, 1945 at a separation center in New York as a Sergeant after more than 55 months of service.

PART II - FIGHTING-LEARNING-PREPARING

North Africa

"Never in history has the navy landed an army at the planned time and place. But if you land us anywhere within 50 miles of Fedela and within 1 week of D-Day, I'll go ahead and win." Major General George Patton, November, 1942 – North Africa Invasion.

"The battle is going heavily against us. We've being crushed by the enemy weight…. We are facing very difficult days, perhaps the most difficult a man can undergo."
German Field Marshall Erwin Rommel, November, 1942

The FCSD was well represented in North Africa. At a minimum, the following men and women participated in the North African campaigns: John S. Babbitt, G. Emelene Ballard, Royden Bentley, Gene David Burgess, Burdette H. Byron, Roland C. Dunn, David C. Fiegl, Mabel Elaine Fox, Marlie J. Hodnett, Russell C. Hodnett, Raymond E. Lilly, Roland J. Thomas, Gerald F. Thomas, and Ronald V. Smith. Men from the FCSD participated in the attacks on Casablanca and Oran. FCSD men were also deeply involved in the Tunisian campaign that followed the successful invasions of Algeria and French Morocco. A key port city in Tunisia was Bizerte. American bombers attacked it many times before the arrival of ground troops. Some of those attacks were led by a young American pilot named Paul Tibbets. By the end of the war Tibbets would be world famous for commanding the 509th Composite Group and piloting the plane that dropped the first atomic bomb. Many men and women from the FCSD area passed through Bizerte during the war.

On December 11, 1941, Germany declared war on the United States and the United States acknowledged that a state of war existed between Germany and the United States. Since Germany is several time zones ahead of the United States, its declaration occurred six hours earlier than the US declaration, which was a response to the German announcement.

When the United States entered WW II, the war had been in progress for more than two years. (The official start date for World War II is September 1,1939.) There were a lot of decisions to be made and much catching up to do. One of the first decisions made by President Roosevelt and Great Britain Prime Minister Churchill, along with the top brass of both countries, was that there would be a Europe-first policy. The Japanese would have to wait. The Pacific war was, to a great extent, a naval war unlike any that had ever been fought. The naval war, especially in the Pacific, was mostly fought with airplanes. The great naval task forces were built around aircraft carriers. In many battles, the opposing ships never saw each other. However, the Pacific war also produced savage ground fighting as the Japanese fought to the death of practically every man on island after island.

While there was agreement that there would be a Europe-first strategy, there was initially disagreement on where military operations would start. US leaders and top brass favored a strategy aimed directly at destroying Germany. Churchill wanted to start in North Africa. He considered control of the Mediterranean essential. Many, if not most US leaders were concerned that Churchill was allowing his concern for the British Empire to govern his policy preferences. (This was reinforced by a statement Churchill included in a speech at Mansion House in London on November 11,1942 to wit, "I have not become the King's First Minister to preside over the liquidation of the British Empire.") While the final decision was strategic, it was also practical. President Roosevelt realized that trained troops and the ships needed to get those troops to England, and then to invade Europe, simple did not exist in 1942 or 1943. Except for the Eighth Army Air Force, large scale American forces would first see battle in North Africa, and then, using Churchill's phrase, "the soft underbelly of Europe."

Although US leaders preferred otherwise, the decision to start in North Africa was sound. The US was not prepared, so North Africa was a good learning ground. US troops in North Africa faced armies of three different countries: Vichy France (that portion of France still "governed" by French officials answerable to Hitler), Italy and Germany. Much of the North Africa invasion area was "defended" by Vichy French troops. Hitler had already conquered France, and the French, under an agreement with Hitler, were allowed to govern certain parts of France as well as French territory in North Africa. The "French government" was established in Vichy, thus the name Vichy French. The head of government was Marshal Henri Philippe Petain, a French World War I hero. Vichy France's Naval Forces in North Africa were under the command of Admiral Jean Darlan. It was hoped that the French in North Africa would quickly side with the Allies. Darlan had pledged to never let the French Fleet fall into Hitler's hands. Secret efforts, including a clandestine effort by General Mark Clark, had been undertaken to get the French troops to offer no resistance. In fact, except for Oran, the French did offer little or no resistance, although there was initial resistance at Casablanca. The Italians were more combative. The Germans and General Irwin Rommel's Africa Korps (already suffering from its defeat at El Alamein) were still another matter. They were determined the North Africa invasion would fail. They were to be disappointed. Darlan, in accordance with French military custom felt duty bound to obey the orders of Marshal Petain, who had ordered French forces to resist the invasion. However, when Hitler ordered his troops into Vichy French territory in France, Darlan felt his duty to that government was over. It no longer had any authority, so Darlan ordered a cease fire which was never rescinded. The French fleet was scuttled despite efforts to get Darlan to turn it over to the Allies. Darlan hated the British. Marshal Petain was tried and convicted of treason after the war. He was sentenced to death, but the sentence was later reduced to life in prison. He died in 1951.

(Darlan was a very powerful figure in the Vichy Government. In 1939 he was Admiral of the French Fleet and Chief of Staff of the French Navy. He later became officially, Deputy Leader of Vichy France under Marshal Petain and a little later was simultaneously Minister of Foreign Affairs, Minister of the Interior and Minister of National Defense. He was an egotist distrusted by both Hitler and the British. On December 24, 1942 he was murdered by a French monarchist opposed to the Vichy regime.)

Patton was wrong and right about the Navy. On November 8, 1942 Navy Task Force 34 got him and his men to Africa on time. Unfortunately, confusion then arose over exact landing locations. When the men disembarked, many were at the wrong place. There was also considerable confusion on some beaches, with men being delivered to the wrong landing spots and landing craft crashing into obstacles on shore.

Patton's command was one of three prongs of Operation Torch - the invasion of North Africa. One, the eastern task force, attacked Algiers in Algeria. Another, the central task force, attacked Oran, also in Algeria. The third, under Patten, was itself divided into three prongs: one to attack Mehdia, another Fedela and the third to attack Safi. All these targets were in the vicinity of Casablanca in French Morocco. Taking Algiers was a British-led joint operation. with the 34th Infantry Division represented the U.S. The other landings were American operations. Landings in the Oran area took place November 8, 1942.

The Big Red One

The Oran landings were led by the 1st Infantry Division, the Big Red One, the most famous Infantry Division in the US Army. It fought gallantly in World War I and in World War II it participated in many of the most vicious battles of the war. At Oran it earned its first Arrowhead Assault Badge. It would earn two more, one for the Sicily invasion and another for Normandy where it was part of the first wave of troops to land on bloody Omaha Beach. In addition to two battle stars for Sicily and Algeria-French Morocco, the Division earned battle stars for Tunisia, Normandy, Northern France, the Rhineland, Ardennes-Alsace, and Central Europe. FCSD area members of the 1st Infantry Division included Marlie J. Hodnett, Wesley E. Hopkins, Lyle A. Wilcox, and Lowell J. Wilcox.

FCSD participants in North Africa campaigns included David Gene Burgess, David C. Fiegl, Mabel Elaine Fox, Marlie J. Hodnett and Lowell J. Wilcox.

David Gene Burgess, born in Fillmore November 22, 1920, landed November 8 at Beach X near Cape Figalo, some three miles west of Oran. Dave had only entered the service on July 2, 1942. After

Prisoner of War Medal

a short period of training at Fort Bragg in North Carolina, Dave headed overseas on September 5, first to England, then Scotland, and finally Belfast, Ireland, where he joined Company B, 1st Battalion, 1st Armored Division, 6th Armored Infantry. The 6th was conducting training on the Irish Moors. On October 29, the 6th and Dave headed back to England and then participated in the invasion of North Africa. The Oran landings, which started at 12:30 in the morning, were strongly opposed in certain sections. The 3rd Battalion was mauled by Vichy French forces. Dave's unit was unopposed. When he reached shore, Dave became one of the first soldiers from the FCSD area to earn the prestigious Arrowhead (Assault) Badge. He would not be the last. At 6:00 AM Dave and the rest of Company B (Company B was part of the 1st Battalion) moved out to establish roadblocks near the town of Lourmel. The Company would maintain the road blocks until it rejoined the Battalion on November 14 at a bivouac area west of Tafraoui. On November 22, Dave's 20th birthday, the Battalion began what the Battalion's Operations Report described as, a "routine road march," to join the battle in Tunisia. The road march continued for the next several days.

On December 3, attacks north of Tebourba commenced. Dave's company took up roadblocks astride the key Medjez El Bab Tunis Road, five miles east of Medjez, and at several mountain-passes south of Medjez. The attacks continued December 4th. The Operations Report noted, "We have excellent observation and good defensive terrain, but are badly over-extended as we are out-posting a five-mile front." To partially address this problem, Company B (Dave's company) was ordered to leave its roadblock positions, and guard the battalions southeast (right) flank.

On the 5th both sides moved to improve their positions, but it was obvious that the Germans were preparing to attack. German aircraft, mostly reconnaissance, were in the air all day. The battalion was attacked by intermittent mortar and artillery fire throughout the day. There were casualties.

On the 6th, the Germans attacked in force. While the 1st Battalion's (Company B part of 1st Battalion) Operations Report concentrates on the ground attack, Rick Atkinson in his book, *An Army at Dawn*, states, "Two waves of Stukas hammered the 1st Battalion of the 6th Armored Infantry Regiment." On the ground a vicious battle was taking place. The Operations Report states - "Attack grows in intensity and force. Seven enemy tanks move out into the area between Medjerda River and Co. A left flank. At same time 14 tanks are observed moving in flat lands off Co. A's right flank... Enemy infantry infiltrate thru saddles of ridges... Entire C Company receiving fire from 3 sides... Repeated counterattacks by half-tracks but temporarily relieve situation… Lt. Carter's platoon of Co. B makes successful mounted counterattack on position formerly occupied by Co. A but is unable to hold on as no reserves are available to support him."

The Report goes on to tell of a total of 36 additional German tanks joining the attack. The battalion was simply outgunned. American concern turned to a withdrawal, but a breakthrough by the German tanks cutting across the battalion's rear closed off their ability to do so. However, at that point the German tanks became aware of the advance of American tanks so they broke off the attack on the battalion to concentrate on the tanks. This allowed the battalion to regroup and to execute a somewhat orderly withdrawal to the flat ground to the rear of the American tanks. At that point the Germans decided to break off the entire attack. While forced to withdraw, the battalion had sustained attacks by German aircraft, artillery, mortar, tanks, and infantry; but it had survived. By dark it was is in the process of reorganizing, evacuating the wounded and preparing for the occupation of new defensive positions.

Dave was not a part of this reorganization. He had been badly wounded during the fighting. Unable to withdraw, he was likely discovered by the Germans and became a prisoner of war. (The NAO reported that Dave was captured by Italians, but that seems unlikely given that the Regiments reports had them fighting Germans.) Dave was evacuated to a military hospital in Caserta, Italy, where doctors determined that his left leg was damaged beyond repair. Probably to save his life, it was necessary to amputate the leg. On December 17, 1942, he wrote his parents explaining: "Well, the war is over for me. I could not run fast and they got me." He did not explain, but at that point, he couldn't run at all. He also said that he was being treated well. Caserta was and is the home of a magnificent baroque palace (the Reggia Di Caserta) built for Charles the III of Naples. It rivals Versailles in opulence. The military hospital was on the Palace grounds. On November 3, 1944, it became the home of the US 36th General Hospital and the Palace became Allied Headquarters Italy. By the time the US arrived, the 36th found the hospital building and patients filthy.

By then Dave was already home. When Italy surrendered, he had been transferred, eventually ending up at Stalag 344 near Lamsdorf in Selesia, Czechoslovakia. (After WWII Selesia became part of Poland.) Considering the circumstances, Stalag 344 was about as good as it could get. The medical facilities were among the best of all the Stalags. In fact, while there was a German officer in charge, the staff was entirely made up of captured allied prisoners, including doctors. In addition to physicians and surgeons, there was a neurosurgeon, a psychiatrist, an anesthesiologist and a radiologist. In a letter home, Dave reported that he was fine and getting fat. Prisoners were getting bread and potatoes from the Germans, and everything else they needed from the Red Cross. They did their own cooking. They had plenty of up-to-date reading material and quite a bit of entertainment, self-supplied. There were two POW bands and the men put on occasional shows.

Dave became a candidate for the prisoner exchange program, likely because he was no longer combat able. In June, he was moved to neutral Barcelona, Spain, and then shipped home aboard the Swedish "Mercy Ship" *Gripsholm*, arriving in the states on, incredibly, June 6, 1944. Dave would face many months of rehabilitation, but his war was truly over. Other prisoners at Stalag 344 would not fare that well. As the war ended, they were marched westward to avoid the Russians. Many died from the cold and exhaustion.

On November 22, 1945, his birthday, Dave married Myrtle D. Adams of Wedgefield, South Carolina. It was exactly three years from the day that the 6th Armored Regiment had started for the battlefield of Tunisia. Dave had taken his own "War Log" to battle with him. At some point he had made a single entry in that log. The entry summed up what he, and every historian since, has written and felt about the American troops when they first arrived in North Africa. Dave wrote, "Boy, were we Green!" English troops fighting with US troops put it almost the same. They said "How Green were our Allies."

On November 8,1942, during the Oran landings, something happened that had never occurred before and hasn't occurred since. Fifty-seven Army nurses from the 48th Army Surgical Hospital went ashore with the first wave of invaders. Initial plans called for nurses from the 16th Evacuation Hospital, including Mabel E. Fox of Fillmore, to be part of the first wave of invaders at Salerno, Italy. Due to crowding on the beachhead, the nurses were rescheduled to land later.

David Charles Fiegl of Hume entered the service on January 18, 1944. He reported for duty on February 8, 1944. It is not clear where he served during April, May, and June, but in July he entered a six-month radio and maintenance training program (7/31/1944 to 1/27/1945) at Scott Field, IL. This was the premier radio operator/ maintenance training school in the Army Air Corps. A sign over the entrance to the field proclaimed that "Through these portals pass the best damn radio operators in the world." The six months of training likely made that claim believable. Graduates flew in aircraft and served as operators at command- and-control communications centers in every theater of the war. David's niece, Claudia Kaufman, remembers her uncle telling her that part of his job involved decrypting coded messages.

The NAO reported in March, 1945 that David was home for 15 days visiting his family. The visit likely occurred in February 1945. By March or at the latest April, David was at Morrison Field in West Palm Beach, FL, likely assigned to the 1103rd Army Air Base Service Unit. Personnel documents indicate that David operated airborne transmitting and receiving equipment, sent messages by Morse Code and voice, kept logs of messages received and transmitted, took radio bearings for navigation aids, and made some repairs of his equipment.

Morrison Field served many functions during the war. Early it had participated in Lend Lease operations, in particular the transfer of B-25's to England. It then became a major player in the movement of personnel, supplies and equipment to the major theaters of war, including the European, African, Middle East and Asian theaters. It was also a key starting point for the ferrying of aircraft to these theaters. In conjunction with these activities, it was a major aircraft maintenance center. It had been transferred to the Army Air Force Ferrying Command (later the Air Transport Command (ATC)) on January 19, 1942. In October of 1944, it was designated a permanent airfield as part of the interim United States Air Force. The US Air Force did not gain official final designation until following the war.

When David arrived at Morrison, it still was involved in the above activities, although its primary functions would change shortly as the war ground to an end. David's duties as a radio operator and mechanic were in line with the mission of the base. While his records do not specifically indicate, it is very likely that David flew numerous missions on planes delivering personnel, supplies and/or equipment to various domestic and overseas locations. His niece Claudia Kaufman, said that she understood from conversations with David that he flew on planes which delivered supplies.

Following the war, Morrison became a center for the ATC's Douglas C-54 Sky Master and the C-74 Globe Master transport aircraft. Since David was not discharged until May of 1946, it is possible that he flew in one or both of those planes. His records indicate that he did spend some time overseas from January 24, 1946, to February 13, 1946 at destination AT. While it is not clear what the designation AT stands for, it may have stood for Alexandria in Egypt and Tobruk in Libya.

David's records do not give him credit for earning the European African Middle East (EAME) Theater Medal. His son Dennis is sure that he served some time in North Africa, and the above overseas assignment supports Dennis's recollection. Since the time period for earning the above medal ended March 2, 1946, it appears he may have earned the EAME Theater Medal but maybe lacked the 30 required days in country.

Like almost all World War II veterans David rarely mentioned the war after returning home. He did recount some things to his niece, as mentioned above. His son Dennis said that he brought the war up only once. He recalled an incident during his basic training. Shortly after arriving, the Drill Sergeant required all the men to line up with their backs to the barracks wall. He then requested all of those who preferred not to invest in a war bond to take one step back. When none were able to move, he thanked them for their 100 percent participation in the war bond drive.

During his service, David's records do show that he earned the American Campaign Medal, the Good Conduct Medal, and the World War II Victory Medal.

Mabel Elaine Fox was the daughter of Anna Broadbent of Fillmore. Anna and family moved to Fillmore in 1932. It is not clear how much Mabel lived in Fillmore as by the early 30's she was likely in nurse's training and then at work. On January 15, 1942 she entered military service, although her official civilian resident during most of the 1930's and the war years appears to have been her mother's home in Fillmore. Mabel likely did live with her mother when she returned to the States after the war. The NAO reported that she spent 30 days leave with her mother in February, 1945 and that she attended a meeting of the Fillmore Rotary Club in July 1945. The family, including eighteen-year-old Mabel, were living in Olean in 1930.

Mabel did not take part in the initial North Africa landings, but arrived soon after. In early 1943 she

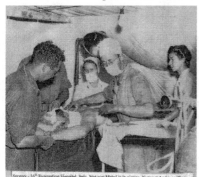
Surgery - 16th Evacuation Hospital, Italy. Not sure Mabel is in picture. National Archives Photo.

wrote her mother about her experiences (excerpts from the letter appeared in the NAO in February, 1943): "You will probably be surprised to learn I am in North Africa. I have been here for some time." She later added: "We lived in a hotel at first; got up at six a.m. and went to the hospital in Army vehicles with helmets, canteens, and mess kits. Still dark out; and it was dark before we got back around nine p.m. Went right to bed in an army cot with my cape rolled up for a pillow. We lived on canned rations, drank no water, took no baths – did not have a bath for three weeks. The water was salty and cold." Regarding her work, "I am in charge of a neurological ward now. The doctor is a peach, and the patients think he's grand." And, "Certainly have learned about war from my patients. I really enjoy my work so much I hate to go off duty." It is not clear to which unit Mabel was assigned at the time of this letter. By no later than August 3, 1943, she was with the 16th Evacuation Hospital and assigned to Surgical Services. The 16th had not landed in North Africa until May 12, 1943. Mabel had likely been overseas, in England first, since mid-1942. She likely arrived in North Africa sometime in late 1942. *Picture, 16th Evacuation Hospital surgery. National Archives. Not sure Mabel is in the picture.*

Lieutenant Fox would spend 28 months overseas. She was part of the Salerno, Italy, invasion force, but the ship she was on (the British hospital ship *HMS Newfoundland*) was sunk by German bombs on Monday, September 13th, 1943 despite the Red Cross painted on the top of the ship. The ship had been in the Gulf of Salerno on the 12th, but had retired to about 20 miles off shore during the night due to heavy air attacks in the Gulf.) Mabel was picked up from a life raft and returned to North

Africa. She was later sent to Italy (the Salerno beachhead again, arriving September 20 on an LCI.) where she would spend the rest of the war with the 16th Evacuation Hospital, working as an orthopedic surgical scrub nurse. Her surgical team performed one of the few operations during WW II that amputated all four extremities of a soldier.

Mabel would spend much of the next 14-15 month at or near the front lines. On several occasions the 16th was the closest evacuation hospital to the front lines. During that time, the hospital was constantly busy, and sometimes under fire, with very little down time. There were times when the causalities were so heavy, that some patients had to be moved to other units. This helped, but the 16th always dealt with the worst causalities. They moved many times. It was moved to Caserta from Salerno (Paestum) in October 1943. In December, Mabel was sent on temporary duty to the Excelsior Grande Alberto Vittoria, in Sorrento. (Likely a rest and recuperation assignment.) Such assignments were numerous for practically all the staff. Mabel was also temporarily assigned to Headquarters in Naples on May 12, 1944. On January 20, the unit received a commendation for its outstanding devotion to duty. In April, they moved to Falciano. The 16th moved on to Anzio in May, 1944, where they were the last evacuation hospital. They dealt with heavy causalities as the Army pushed into Rome. While in Anzio, in mid-June, all personnel were granted a leave to Rome. By June 24, 1944 they were in Montepescali. In July, they were at Ardena; and in August, they were in Vito, ten miles from Florence. Later they moved to Pistoia, about an hour from Florence. During this period, Mabel wrote her mother that she had visited a near-by farm and picked a prime Italian melon. In October, they moved to Firenzuola. There the unit reported the heaviest causalities since Paestum and Vairano. In November, the unit was inundated with torrential rain. Mabel was again sent on temporary duty, this time to the Hotel Anglo Americano in Florence. (This was likely basically for rest and recuperation.) She returned to her unit on December 24. It snowed that same day. On Christmas Day, 1944, she received her promotion to First Lieutenant. On Saturday, January 6, 1945, Mabel was attached to the 7th Replacement Depot for trans-shipment to the US. Although her orders stated this was temporary duty, with the war winding down, Mabel did not return to Europe.

While Mabel's work was dangerous and very heavy most of the time, there were diversions. Numerous USO shows entertained both the patients and the staff. Many Generals visited her unit throughout the war, including General Eisenhower on September 17, 1943 in North Africa. Big name stars also came. On September 1, 1943 in North Africa, they were entertained by Al Jolson. Marlie Hodnett of Fillmore, recovering from his third wound received in Sicily, wrote home that he also saw Jolson in North Africa. Other celebrities included Joe E. Brown, Jascha Heifitz, Al Robinson and Joe Louis.

During her service, Mabel not only treated white and black G.I.s, but also German POWs and Brazilian soldiers.

After being discharged on December 20, 1945, Mabel was recalled by the Army, and served in Korea. She earned, among others, the American Campaign Medal, the European-African-Middle Eastern Campaign Medal and the World War II Victory Medal. She also earned three battle stars, plus, according to the *Unit Citation and Campaign Participation Credit Registrar,* she and her unit earned an Assault Badge for the Salerno landings.

Marlie J. Hodnett of Hume was not part of the initial North Africa invasion force. That was about  the only thing he missed, or, as events unfolded, the only thing that missed him. Upon entering the service in 1942 Marlie was sent to Fort Bragg, NC. It appears he was originally assigned to an artillery unit and at one time was also a truck driver. He ended up as a rifleman with Company F, 16th Infantry Regiment, First Infantry Division - the Big Red One. Arriving as a replacement, Marlie participated in at least eight major engagements during the North Africa campaign. These included Kasserine Pass, some of Longstop Hill, El Guettar, Hill 523, and the battles along the highway to Medjez-El-Bab. At El Guettar the First Division proved its mettle. A 16th Regiment All Personnel Memo dated June 6, 1943 told the story. "In those steep, rocky, treacherous hills, broken by gullies and chasms, the 1st Division fought for four days and nights without rest or relief. Three times the 10th Panzers counterattacked, first with tanks followed by infantry, next with infantry followed by tanks, the third time by infantry infiltration supported by tanks. All three attacks were driven off. On the day of the heaviest attacks the Germans sent in nearly 100 tanks, and the first wave penetrated 1st Division's positions. Cut off from its base, the 16th Regiment stood its ground, as only the best-trained, best disciplined troops will do, until artillery and anti-tank guns drove the tanks back." At Kasserine Pass, a battle that did not go well for the US, the First Division stood out, and the16th Regiment in particular. At one point, the 16th had to counterattack a line that had been left open by the 26th Infantry Regiment. *Picture – Marlie receiving his third Purple Heart.*

During the North African campaign, Marlie was wounded twice, the first probably at El Guettar. The NAO reported that the War Department had notified his wife that he had been wounded on March 29, 1943. There is no information as to the exact nature of that wound, but the NAO also reported that Marlie had just returned to his company when he was wounded for a second time on April 24, probably during the final battle for Tunisia, along the highway to Medjez-El-Bab. This second wound was likely a minor one, as in a letter home, Marlie wrote about the battle for Hill 609 which occurred April 27 to May 1. In his letter, he wrote that they had heard that a million-dollar barrage had been laid down on Hill 609, and that he was sure all of it had passed over his foxhole. Like all soldiers Marlie joked about the situation, saying that it was OK if you could hear the artillery shells, but when you couldn't, you had better get in an ant hole. If a shell landed in your hip pocket, it was guaranteed to tear the lining out. He probably considered the barrage a picnic compared to a later walk through a mine field. Marlie made it through the mine field and Tunisia. The next stop for him was Sicily.

Securing the Air and Sea Routes

While Harry Fairbank and his engineers were busy building airfields and ports in Iceland to secure the air and sea routes in the North Atlantic, efforts were underway to do the same in Central and South America, particularly in Panama and Brazil. The North and South Atlantic routes were the main routes connecting the US to England, North Africa, Europe, and points east during the war, although a Mid-Atlantic route through the Azores was eventually developed. The southern route quickly became the most important. While the development of the convoy system provided greater protection for ships and greater danger to submarines, the ever more sophisticated use of air power proved decisive in securing the air and sea routes. This effort, better known as the "Battle of the Atlantic," was initially, prior to the US entry into the war, about getting food, supplies and materiel to England so it could continue its fight against Hitler. After the US entry, there was a need to send US troops and ships to England and elsewhere to prepare for the European and North Africa invasions. Major players in this effort were Merchant Marines sailors. Their efforts are discussed in Part V. The most vital sea route requiring protection was the Panama Canal.

Men from the FCSD who were involved in air and sea routes operations between South American and Europe and Africa, included David M. Babbitt, Raymond E. Bloomster, William Junior Bucheister, Edward F. Devaney, Merlin D. James, Roman (NMI) "Ray" Kolakowski, Hubert F. McMaster, Douglas F. Morris, Robert B. Redman, Harold D. Rork, Charles Sierra, Lawrence W. Voss, and Ray C. Witter. Douglas F. Morris was another FCSD man who earned the American Defense Medal. He was one of three brothers who served during the war, having entered the service on January 1, 1940. While he was eventually to earn the Air Medal for service in the Pacific theatre, he initially served a year in Panama.

David M. Babbitt of Houghton was one of the FCSD men who entered the military prior to December 7, 1941. He was with an air group and one of thousands of men sent to Natal, Brazil, as part of Operation Rainbow. Dave spent about two years in Brazil. Another FCSD man, Robert F. McMaster, was also there. US soldiers were there to provide refueling and support service for aircraft and allied troops being sent to North Africa. Planes based in Brazil patrolled the Atlantic searching for German submarines and attacking German merchant ships trying to exchange goods with Japan. The southern route to Africa and Europe was vital, and US forces operating along that route provided a particularly valuable war service. In fact, the overall effort was called the "Springboard to Victory." Planes from the Army Air Transport Command also used the Natal base as a stopover on the way to Africa and other points east.

Dave entered the service on September 2, 1941. After some initial training at Fort Niagara, David was sent to Chanute Field in Illinois for 18 weeks of aircraft mechanics training. This was followed by four weeks of specialized P-40 training at the Curtis Wright factory in, of all places, Buffalo. On April 13, 1942, with some seven plus months of training behind him, Dave sailed for Brazil. In his two-years there, during which he likely worked on many types of aircraft, Dave advanced to the rank of Master Sergeant. In April 1944, just prior to his return to the states, Dave managed to squeeze in a trip to Rio de Janeiro. In September, he sailed for the USA.

After a short furlough at home, Dave was assigned to the 4th Operational Training Unit (OTU), Brownsville, TX. His skills were used keeping planes safe for training and for pilots to ferry pursuit planes to the various theaters of war. In January, he moved with the 4th OTU to Greenwood, MS AAF Base. Greenwood was another pilot training base, but here the emphasis was on fighter training, including the P-51, P-47, P-38 and P-63. Some bomber training was also provided on B-17's, and B-26s.

On October 25, 1945, Dave received his discharge at Rome AAF Base in New York, after 50 months of service, including 29 months overseas.

Raymond E. Bloomster of Fillmore, entered the service on September 17, 1942. Following basic training, it is likely that Ray participated in a technical training program in preparation for his service as a supply clerk. These clerks performed various clerical and stock handling duties in connection with receipt, storage, issue, and shipping of general supplies and equipment, usually in an Army warehouse or unit supply section. The clerks also checked incoming and outgoing supplies against items listed on requisitions, invoices, and bills of lading. They also maintained stock records pertaining to such items as amount, kind and value of supplies and equipment received, issued, or expended and balance on hand. Ray's experience as the manager of Market Basket grocery stores certainly was of value to him during his time in the service.

It is not clear where Ray served during the next year and a half. On May 24, 1944 he sailed aboard *LST 552* from New Orleans to the Panama Canal Zone. According to his entry at the World War II Memorial in Washington, DC, he served with the 48th Air Base Squadron as a Supply Clerk at France Field in the Canal Zone. Established in 1918, France was the first military airfield built to protect the Panama Canal. Initially named "Coco Walk Aerodrome", its name was changed in 1918 to honor 1st Lieutenant Howard J. France who had been killed in a hydroplane crash. President Roosevelt visited the field in 1938. It was located on the east coast of Panama near the city of Colon.

Many units were stationed at France field during the war, including the 32nd Pursuit Group, the 24th Pursuit Squadron, the 3rd Bomb Squadron, and the 51st and 52nd Fighter Squadrons. The mission of units stationed at France Field was to protect the Atlanta side of the Panama Canal and to fly anti-submarine missions over the Caribbean. It appears that Ray returned to the United States in late 1945 or early 1946. He was discharged January 28, 1946.

William J. Bucheister (Buchheister) of Houghton entered the service July 8, 1943. Like most men

from the FCSD area who served in the Navy, William took basic training at Sampson Naval Station. His exact assignments during the next six months are not clear. His discharge document indicates that he did not attend any service schools. However, the history of the blimp air services indicate that training was provided to some 3,000-support crew in the Military Airship Crew Training Programs. It is likely that William did receive such training prior to his assignment to an airship squadron in Brazil. He was assigned to "Blimp HEDRON 4" or more formally, Fleet Airship Wing Four. Muster records show him at Naval Air Facility (NAF) Noronho on February 8, 1944. He likely also served at auxiliary Ipitanga Field, Bahia with Detachment 42. William likely worked as blimp ground crew for HEDRON 4 Air Squadron 2. *Picture - US Navy Photo.*

HEDRON stands for Headquarters Squadron. HEDRON 4 had two air squadrons, ZP-41, and ZP-42. Its headquarters were located at Recife and it controlled several auxiliary fields at various times, including Fernando de Noronha, Santa Clara, Maceio, Ipitanga, Carvalles, Vitoria, Amapa, Igarape, Fortaleza and in Rio de Janeiro where it had responsibility for the huge airship hanger built by the Germans for the Graf Zeppelin. William was assigned to at least three different HEDRON 4 bases during his service. He also may have served at Headquarters, Fleet Airship Wing Four at Maceio.

On September 1, 1944 William was promoted to Seaman First Class. Muster records show him transferred to Naval Air Facility 412 (Aratu) where he remained for the balance of his service in Brazil. He was among the first men assigned to Aratu.

Blimp squadrons performed many functions. Most important were convoy escort, locating and attacking submarines and patrols. Other duties included mine laying, mine sweeping, photographic calibration, parachute unit transportation and personnel and cargo transport. The blimps were armed with two 50 caliber machine guns and four 350-pound depth charges. The blimp airship had the best combat readiness rating of all air units, 87%, during the war.

William was transferred to Lido Beach, NY, in May 1945. In July he was home with his wife. It is not clear where he was stationed the balance of his service. He was discharged December 17, 1945.

Edward P. Devaney (Devanney) of Hume entered the service in early to mid-1943. By July 1943, Edward was at Fort Benning in Georgia. It is likely that he took both basic and advanced training at Benning. According to the NAO, Edward was home on furlough in July, 1943. A September, 1945, item in the NAO, reported that he had just returned from 25 months in Trinidad. Given this, it is likely that he arrived in Trinidad circa July-August of 1943. The prime US Army base in Trinidad was Fort Read.

The major US forces in Trinidad were there due to the Lend Lease Agreement with Great Britain. As part of the agreement, the US gained several bases. The principal one in Trinidad was Chaguaramas. Fort Read was primarily Army, but also contained an Army Air Force Field which took up four square miles of Fort Read's 24 square miles. The major activity in Trinidad was protecting air and sea routes to Africa and Europe, particularly against German submarines. However, Fort Read was also a major training base, especially in jungle warfare. The famous Merrill's Marauders were trained there. This training was brutal and realistic. Live ammunition was used. One report stated, likely incorrectly, that as many as four men were killed each day of actual jungle training. While no major attacks were expected, Army personnel did patrol the beaches of Trinidad to protect against unwanted landings by enemy personnel.

Edward returned to the US on September 22, 1945. He was likely discharged in October of 1945. Edward's service files have not been located.

Merlin D. James of Short Tract entered the service April 15, 1941. He took his basic training at Fort Eustis, VA, in anti-aircraft artillery training. Upon completion, in August 1941, Merlin was assigned to Battery G, 9th Coastal Artillery at Fort Andrews. MA. The job for the 9th was protection of Boston Harbor. In 1942, the need for Coastal Artillery units began to decrease. The 9th, Merlin's unit, was phased out in early 1943. By March 1943, all the batteries had been reassigned. Merlin had moved on by that time. The NAO reported in January of 1943 that he was already overseas.

In January of 1944, the NAO reported that Merlin had been in the Army for three years and was now in Miami. It also reported that he had served 17 months at Wideawake Airport on Ascension Island, a key stopover on the Southern Air and Sea Route. A refueling and refreshing stopover, some 25,000 planes landed there during the war. For the first two years of the war, it was the key mid-Atlantic stopover base. When Mallard Field in Dakar, Senegal opened in 1944, multi- engine aircraft were able to make non-stop flights from Natal, Brazil to Dakar; but fighters and other single engine aircraft still stopped at Ascension Island. A major hazard at Ascension was the enormous bird population. It is likely that Merlin was assigned to US Army Composite Force 8012, or to the 1150 Army Air Force Base Unit. A report in a May, 1944 edition of the NAO stated that he served 21 months on Ascension. Given this report, he likely arrived on Ascension around July or August 1942.

Which base he served on, and what he did in Miami is unclear. However, the NAO reported that, even while on Ascension, his mail was routed to him through Miami. So, he may have been assigned to Miami, and merely detached to Ascension for 21 months.

The NAO reported him home on furlough in November of 1944, and that he was stationed at Fort Monroe, VA by May 1945. Fort Monroe was part of the harbor defenses for the Hampton Roads, VA area. It hosted an array of coastal artillery as well as anti-submarine barriers and mine fields.

Merlin likely served as a Military Policeman (MP) on Ascension, in Miami and at Fort Monroe. His information at the World War II Memorial indicates that he was an MP. That information likely came from his discharge document. The NAO reported Merlin home with his discharge in October 1945.

Roman (NMI) "Ray" Kolakowski was an adopted son of Centerville having been born in Buffalo. While he attending several schools, he graduated from Fillmore Central in 1937. He then earned a degree from the College of Agriculture at Cornell University. Throughout his life, Ray was involved in many different activities, but three things were constant - farming, flying airplanes and wood working. Ray lived a very nomadic life, but if there was one place that was home it was the Centerville area of Allegany County, NY. In fact, after 26 years in the Navy he retired to Rushford, Centerville's next-door neighbor.

Ray entered the Navy on May 14, 1941. (His sister Genevieve served with the WAC.) He was in flight training in Jacksonville, Florida, when the Japanese attacked Pearl Harbor and the US entered World War II. Initially assigned as an instructor, in May 1943 Ray was ordered to Lake City, Florida to be trained in flying patrol planes. In the Navy training was a constant. In August, Ray was assigned to Patrol Squadron 7 in Beaufort, SC. The 15-plane squadron flew the PV-2, a two-engine bomber that was used to hunt German submarines. This was just one of the over 35 planes that Ray was to fly during his Navy career. (His son Dave told the author that while Ray said 35 in his memoirs, the actual count was around 60.) Even though Ray was now part of an operational squadron, that squadron's first months of flying were all training flights, focusing on bombing, navigation and instrument flying. (Anxious as he was to become fully operational, Ray knew the training was important. One squadron had lost half of its entire crews and airplanes in its first year of operations due to insufficient training.) Ray's training was topped off when his squadron was sent to the Naval Air Station at Quonset Point, RI for intensive anti-submarine bombing training. Hitting a submarine with a single bomb was unlikely, so the training focused on a process which involved dropping four evenly spaced bombs some forty feet apart.

Ray's group was now ready for combat patrols and was assigned to Floyd Bennett Field in Brooklyn to begin their anti-submarine patrols that protected shipping vital to the war effort. Each patrol lasted from five to seven hours, and the patrols were conducted 24 hours a day. That meant a lot of night flying. It all paid off, however, because the number of ships sunk decreased dramatically as patrol efforts increased. After several months, the squadron was ordered back to Rhode Island where rocket launchers were attached to their planes and pilots were trained in the use of this new weapon. The squadron was then deployed to Elizabeth City, NJ, and then to the Caribbean area. Assignments there included Port of Spain, Trinidad, Zanderey Field, Dutch Guiana, Curacao, and San Juan, PR. Ray flew patrols until March 1945, a total of nineteen months.

In his memoirs, Ray lamented that he was never able to find a German submarine. While on-board radar enabled pilots to search a 20- mile radius, Ray believed that German subs had the ability to locate planes well beyond the 20-mile range and were, in most cases, able to submerge before his squadron could find them. In fact, Ray had only had one suspenseful flight. That occurred when one of his engines started running rough and they were five hundred miles from base. Appropriate preparations were made in case the engine failed, but Ray got back to base without any problems. While Ray was disappointed in not being able to locate a German submarine, Stephen Budiansky in his book, *Blackett's War - The Men Who Defeated the Nazi U-Boats and Brought Science to the Art of Warfare*, presents a strong case that air power proved to be the answer to the U-Boat problem. Airplanes changed the nature of the conflict. The result was, as Budiansky points out, that of the 830 U-Boats that took part in operations during the war, 784 were sunk or captured. Of the 40,000 men who served on those boats, 26,000 were killed and 5,000 taken prisoner.

In 1945 Ray went into training to fly night torpedo planes. The Navy then decided that they had enough torpedo plane pilots; Ray was switched again. This time he was trained for night operations in the plane he had always dreamed of flying, the famous F6F Hellcat. The war ended before his training ended, but Ray would stay in the Navy and rise to the rank of Captain. He was appointed to many key positions, but was especially proud when he received the assignment coveted most by a Naval aviator, Commander of a Carrier Air Group. Other assignments included service on the mighty carrier *USS Forrestal* and on the staff of the Commander in Chief, U.S. Naval Forces, Europe, where he served as the Assistant Chief of Staff for Operations. His duties required that he daily be on top of all naval operations being carried out in Europe

Robert B. Redman was from Allen Township, although the family had long been associated with

Fillmore. Robert served three years in the Army, two years of which were with the coast artillery in Panama. He was one of the first members of a balloon barrage organization. Barrage balloons, first used by the British during World War I, were bags full of gas that was lighter than air. These bags were attached to a large steel cable which could be raised or lowered as the circumstances demanded. The steel cables themselves were a major hazard to attacking fighters. The balloon's purpose was to force attacking aircraft to fly higher. Not only did this make the planes less effective in carrying out their attacks, it made them better targets for both antiaircraft guns and defensive fighter airplanes. *Robert - Family Photo.*

Robert entered the Army on June 27, 1941. He likely was assigned to Camp Davis, NC, where the initial barrage balloon battalions were being organized. In fact, the first such unit, the 301st Coast Artillery Barrage Balloon Battalion was established there on June 1, 1941. Robert was likely assigned to the 301st, since his unit in Panama, the 313th Coast Artillery Barrage Balloon Battalion, was organized in Panama in December of 1941 with cadre from the 301st. Initially, the 313th was assigned to Fort Randolph (Margarita Island) in Panama. By December of 1942 the Battalion was located near Mindi Dairy, (near Colon) with all batteries located within five miles of the headquarters unit.

The 313th was transferred back to the states (Fort Devens, MA.) in December 1943 and January 1944. The NAO reported in January 1944 that Robert was home on leave. After returning from Panama, Robert was stationed at Fort Devens MA where he passed away March 31, 1944. His funeral was held in Fillmore, and he is buried in the Short Tract Cemetery. Keith Knibloe of Fillmore was the bugler at his funeral. The NAO reported, at the time of Robert's funeral, that no information was available as to the cause of Robert's death. The author requested a copy of the Individual Deceased Personnel File (IDPF) for Robert, and was advised that the file could not be found.

The biggest threat to sea routes to and from Europe and Africa was the U-Boat. Primary weapons used by the US to combat that threat were killer destroyer groups and the airplane. FCSD provided men who participated both on the sea and in the air against the German U-Boat threat.

Harold D. Rork enlisted in the Navy on December 15, 1942, but didn't enter active service until February 4, 1943. After eight weeks of basic training at Sampson Naval Station, Harold was transferred to the Naval Training Center in Norman, OK for training as an Aviation Machinist Mate (AMM). His training lasted for 21 weeks, or until September 1943. Harold was then assigned to VR-7 in Miami, Florida. "VR-7" identified a unit that was V (heavier than air), R (used for transport), and 7 (the 7th of this type).

Harold's unit was an R4D unit meaning it primarily provided mechanics service to C-47 aircraft at naval air facilities in Miami, South America, and the Caribbean. While focusing on C-47 planes, the unit likely provided service to several types of aircraft. Aviation Mechanist Mates were aircraft engine mechanics who performed a variety of functions that included inspecting, adjusting, testing, repairing and overhauling aircraft engines and propellers. They were able to perform routine maintenance, prepare aircraft for flight and assist in handling aircraft on the ground. The squadron was stationed at the Miami Municipal Airport which was named after Amelia Earhart. Harold most likely spent several months in Miami. His unit, and others like it were integral to the smooth flow of air and sea traffic in the middle and southern sea and air routes to and from North Africa and Europe.

According to the NAO of February, 1945 Harold was then in San Juan, Puerto Rico. It is likely that he had been there awhile, and was departing San Juan in February. Later NAO reports have him in Cuba for six months, and back in the states by July 1945. In San Juan, he was likely assigned to Air Transport Squadron AT-7. This may mean that he was in San Juan on temporary duty while still officially assigned to VR -7 in Miami. In any event, Harold was surely performing the same duties that he had performed in Miami, and was likely working on the same type of aircraft, C-47s.

In Cuba, it appears Harold was assigned to Detachment No 1, Headquarters Squadron (Hedron), Fleet Air Wing (FAW) - 11 at Guantanamo ('Gitmo") Bay. At Guantanamo, according to his discharge document he was assigned to CASU 26, a carrier aircraft service unit. This was also likely a temporary assignment, and again, he would have been involved in the same activities as in Miami, except this time he may have been servicing carrier aircraft, not just C-47s. On July 2, 1945, according to the daily muster role of the *USS Rehoboth* (AVP 50) he sailed from Cuba to Norfolk, VA for reassignment. The *Rehoboth* was a seaplane tender (provided repair and maintenance service to seaplanes), but was also used to transport personnel. Harold is listed as a passenger aboard the *Rehoboth*. After a leave spent at home with family and friends, as reported in the NAO, he reported to the Naval Air Station a Falmouth, MA. Harold's duties would have remained the same at Falmouth. The aircraft he was servicing however, were involved in patrol and escort duty along the East coast. Since the war was now over, duty at Falmouth would have been more relaxed.

Harold was discharged March 17, 1946.

Charles Sciera of Fillmore was born in Poland in 1907. The Sciera family emigrated to the US in 1914, when Charles was seven years old. An early interest in radio caused Charles to leave his job with the Larkin Company in Buffalo to open his own radio business. In the 1930's, he moved to Fillmore, and his radio business grew and later expanded into television and appliances. On November 2, 1942, Charles enlisted in the Army Air Corps, and Fillmore lost its only radio and television business.

During the next three years, Charles was stationed in numerous locations. He was sent to McClelland Field in Sacramento, CA for basic training. From there he was sent, according to the NAO, to Portland, Oregon. However, his son Mark believes he was next at Pocatello, Idaho, for training as a radio operator. In either case, the NAO received a card from him at that time in which he stated that he thought he would like his new assignment, even though there was snow on the ground. Charles was then

Charlie with friend at Mallard Field, Dakar. Family Photo.

sent to Scott Field, IL, for an intensive course in radio operating and mechanics, to prepare him for duty as a member of a bomber crew. In a letter to the NAO, he reported that, "We had our group pictures taken today, so graduation cannot be far off. It's been stiff going for us boys, and somewhere along the line 15 boys gave up their radio ghost. Chicago is a great town, provided you like them big and sooty. I will be glad to leave it behind me." Before Charles left the area, his son Mark said, he managed to obtain and send him a souvenir St. Louis Cardinal baseball bat. *Picture – Sciera Family Photo.*

Mark believes his dad's next stop was Vancouver, WA. From there he was sent to Smyrna Air Base in Tennessee. In another letter to the NAO, Charles reported that his radio expertise was being put to good use at Smyrna. He was assigned to carpenter work, but also helped put in cement sidewalks. At some point during his travels, Charles was switched from a bomber crew to an Army Airways Communication System Detachment. He sailed from Hampton Road, VA, on May 17, 1944, aboard the *Sea Perch,* for Oran in Algeria. He was assigned to Marrakech, in French Morocco, from May 28, 1944 until April 1945, most likely at Menara Air Field. Seized by allied forces in 1942, Menara was operated during the war by the 1257th Army Air Force Base Unit. In April, Charles was transferred to Dakar in Senegal, and remained there until rotated home in November,1945.

The original air route from Natal to North Africa required several stops. Ascension Island was first, but planes also had to stop in Accra before finally reaching North Africa. Shorter-range aircraft continued to use that route for most of the war. Victories in North Africa opened new territories. By 1944, long range bombers, and other multi-engine aircraft, were able to fly directly from Natal in Brazil to Dakar in Senegal. The US constructed a new airfield, Mallard Field near Dakar, for exactly this purpose. This route reduced the distance to Africa by 1400 miles, and resulted in quicker and safer delivery of supplies and equipment. Charley most likely was stationed at Mallard Field during his time in Dakar.

Both Marrakech and Dakar were major Air Transport Service bases. The NAO reported that Charles was involved in providing radio communications, navigation assistance, and airfield control information for the mass movement of aircraft over North Africa. This would have been true in both Marrakesh and Dakar. Son Mark said he was assigned to the 111th Squadron Transmitting Station during his time in North Africa. He arrived back in Hampton Roads, VA on November 18, 1945, and received his discharge from the service on November 24 at Ft. Dix, NJ.

Lawrence W. Voss of Granger, known as Bing, entered the Army Air Corps on September 3, 1942 although he was not required to report until September 17. He received one month of basic training, apparently in Miami, before reporting to Amarilla Field in Texas, to be trained as an airplane and engine mechanic. He spent almost four months at Amarilla, graduating with high honors in March 1943. Bing was then sent to the Boeing Plant in Seattle, WA for additional training. His records indicate that he was trained to work on "B-17 type heavy bomber aircraft." It is interesting to note however, that both at Amarilla and at the Boeing plant in Seattle men were trained to work on the B-17, and the B-29. It is not known if Bing was trained on both aircraft, but a later assignment indicates he likely worked on both. After completing his training at Boeing, Bing was transferred to Alexandria Army Airfield in Alexandria, LA, where he would serve until September 1944. Alexandria was a training base for both fighter and bomber pilots and crews. While there, he likely worked on several types of aircraft.

Bing's "Separation Qualification Record" summarizes his duties as follows: "Performed duties within the Continental United States and overseas. Served in Caribbean Theater of Operations for about 5 months. Served on the line doing routine servicing, repair, adjustment, maintenance, and inspections of B-17 type heavy bomber aircraft. Performed periodic inspections of aircraft to ascertain seat of malfunction and took necessary measures to rectify same. Served as acting crew chief. Had supervisory control of the men in his crew. Delegated work and inspected results to see that all specifications were met."

On September 6, 1944, Bing was transferred to Cuba. Information on the exact base where he was stationed is not available. However, many wartime activities were being carried out there. Included were anti-submarine patrols and other patrols to secure the air and sea routes from the US to Europe. Another major activity was training for long range navigation over water. Many heavy bomber groups, including B-17, B-24, and B-29 groups were trained there during the war. (Fighter groups also trained there.)

Bing arrived in Cuba on September 6, 1944. While it is clear that he was there to help service heavy bombers, information is lacking which indicates on which type of aircraft he actually worked. An interesting coincidence is that shortly after Bing arrived, B-29s of the 509th Composite Group (the Atomic Bomb group) arrived in Cuba. They were there to train on long-range navigation over water. They would stay until February of 1945. The B-29 which would eventually be named *Enola Gay* was one of those that participated in the exercises in Cuba. Bing was rotated back to the states in January, 1945.

Bing's last assignment was at Peterson Field in Colorado Springs, CO. While the base carried out several different functions, it is likely that Bing was again part of the training of bomber crews that was taking place on the base. He was discharged January 31, 1946, at Lowry Field in Colorado.

Ray C. Witter, according to a March, 1942 edition of the NAO, was the FCS Principal from 1921 to 1923. Ray was originally from Perry, NY, and had served in the Navy as a radio operator during WW I. Ray remained in the Navy Reserve after the war and on June 18, 1942 returned to active duty. At that time, he was the Principal of Silver Creek School, in Chautauqua County.

Ray was initially assigned to a Motor Torpedo Boat (MTB) Squadron in Balboa, Panama. Records show that on July 18, 1942 he departed Norfolk, VA. aboard the *USS Ariel*, and sailed to Panama. There he was "transferred" on July 24 to MTB Flotilla I. Most likely he was assigned to MTB Ron (Squadron) 5. MTB Flotilla 1 was commissioned June 16, 1942 and sent to guard the western end of the Panama Canal. It was stationed at the Naval Base at Balboa which is actually a district of Panama City located at the Pacific entrance to the Canal. The *Ariel* records show that Witter was a RM1c (Radioman first class) at the time. Ron 5 saw no action while stationed at Balboa. About one year later, it was transferred from Panama to the Solomon Islands.

Witter, however, did not go with the squadron to the Pacific. He was promoted to Lieutenant on April 5, 1943 and at about the same time, according to the NAO, he was transferred from the Canal Zone to the Navy Pre-Flight School at the University of North Carolina in Chapel Hill.

The Pre-Flight School had only been established in 1942 and closed in 1945. Witter arrived one year after the arrival of the first cadets. Training was about six months. It had a strenuous schedule, both academically and physically. Classes included aircraft engines, aerology, aircraft identification, Morse code, and even the identification of different cloud patterns. Cadets were required to work on the college farm and to participate in sports. Some of the nation's major sports and political figures participated in the program, including Gerald Ford, the elder George Bush, Paul "Bear" Bryant, and Ted Williams. Lieutenant James Crowley, one of the legendary "Four Houseman" of Norte Dame was also there. Witter was an accomplished athlete, having played semi-pro baseball and professional football.

Witter was likely in administration or an instructor. Morse code would have been a subject in which he was an expert. However, an article, written by one of the cadets said a quite attractive, and distractive, WAVE taught Morse code. Since Witter later served as chief of educational therapy and coordinator of a VA physical medicine rehabilitation center, it is likely Witter was involved in similar activities at Chapel Hill.

Ray was discharged from active-duty September 28, 1945. He remained in the Navy Reserves, rising to the rank of Lieutenant Commander.

Bringing the Wounded Home

At the start of World War II, the US Military had no hospital ships available. It wasn't until June 1943 that the first such ship sailed to North Africa to pick up and return wounded soldiers to the US. Eventually, the Army Transport Service had a total of 24 ships. These military vessels were manned by civilian crews, but had Army medical personnel to care for the sick and wounded soldiers. The Navy eventually had three similar ships. Almost all of the ships were converted passenger liners or troop ships that were given new names. (One ship, the *Marigold* had once bore the name *President Fillmore*.) A total of six Liberty ships were converted to hospital ships. These ships operated under The Hague Convention rules of 1907. Identification markings under these rules proved inadequate so big Red Crosses were added for easier recognition, especially by planes at night. Even then, a few of these unarmed ships were deliberately attacked. (As pointed out earlier, Mable E. Fox was aboard a hospital ship with a Red Cross marking that was deliberately sunk by German aircraft.) Hospital ships really served more as ambulances than hospitals. These vessels were not equipped for extensive medical services, which made the job of the on-board medical personnel extremely trying.

At least one FCSD area military personnel served on a hospital ship, Mildred E. Schmidt.

Mildred E. Schmidt of Granger was born May 6, 1922 to William F. Schmidt and Emma L. Haas. William had emigrated to the US in 1918 from Germany. Mildred was a high achiever her entire life. She was valedictorian of her senior class at Fillmore Central and earned "The Efficiency Award", the highest honor given by her school, the Craig School of Nursing in Sonyea, NY. Mildred was doing postgraduate work in New York City when she decided it was time to join the war effort. She reported for duty on February 1, 1945. At first, she was assigned to Halloran General Hospital on Long Island. By April she had been reassigned to the hospital ship *Aleda E. Lutz*, which made its first trip to Liverpool, England to pick up wounded soldiers on April 18, 1945. (The *Aleda E. Lutz* was named for an Army nurse who had been killed in a plane crash. Nurse Lutz had flown more missions (196), more combat hours (814), and helped treat more soldiers (over 3500) than any other nurse in history. She was awarded the Air Medal with 4 Oak Leaf Clusters and posthumously, the Distinguished Flying Cross.) A total of 765 wounded soldiers were brought home on that first trip. The *Lutz* docked back in the US at Charleston, SC, from where it would continue to operate, May 2, 1945. Mildred was in Charleston preparing for her second trip when President Truman announced Victory in Europe on May 8, 1945. *Picture – Family Photo.*

Millie just before her commissioning as a Second Lieutenant in the Army Nurse's Corps. Hilda Schmidt Gibbons Photo.

The *Lutz* was scheduled to depart on its second trip on May 16, but the voyage had to be delayed for repairs of the fuel and water tanks and the supercharger. Such problems were not uncommon. The *Lutz* was forced to return to port on its third trip for a short period while a faulty freezer was repaired.

On her second trip, from May 26 to June 18, to Cherbourg, France, the *Lutz* brought home 768 patients. Her third trip, also to Cherbourg, lasted from June 28 to July 21, 1945. A total of 754 patients were picked up, but one died on the trip home. The report of her fourth trip dated August 29, 1945, indicates that the *Lutz* sailed from Charleston on August 6. It docked in Cherbourg on August 17 and departed the same day for Southampton, England, where it also docked on August 17. The *Lutz* departed there on August 19 and arrived back in the states in New York City on August 29. The *Lutz* had performed double duty on this trip. On the way over it returned 748 German prisoners of war back to Europe.

Then it picked up 757 wounded Americans and returned them to the US. Mildred wrote her mother while at sea on August 9, 1945. She confided that all she had to do was to be on duty. She did not have to actually work because they were taking German POWS back to Europe, and the prisoners were doing all the work. As Mildred put it, "Boy -- We are really making them work, and it is good enough for them." She continued the letter on August 10 telling her mother that they had just heard a rumor that the war was over. She did not put too much credence in the rumor. She added that another rumor was that they would be returning to New York rather than Charleston. On the 12th she added a footnote: "12th I hear the war's over - Hurray!" This time she believed the rumor, although it would be a few days before the official announcement. (Mildred was referring to the war in the Pacific, and thus the end of World War II.)

USAHS *Aleda E. Lutz* arriving New York City Harbor, likely on August 29, 1945 with Mildred Schmidt aboard.

US Army Photo - Archives

According to Mildred's sister Hilda, during the trip the prisoners, speaking German, began making snide comments about the US. Mildred, whose family spoke German at home, understood every word and lit into the prisoners. There were no more snide comments the rest of the trip. (The October 25, 1944 edition of the 179th Infantry Regiment's Beachhead News, reported the following. A German POW in New Mexico remarked that "Hitler had told them that they would march across the US. I did not think he meant like this - sowing grain and chopping cotton along the way.") Hilda also related that her dad, William, who was born in Germany, had been listening to Hitler via short wave when he first took power. During one of Hitler's rants, her father turned the radio off and said to the family, "That fool will ruin that country." He never listened again. Ironically his short-wave radio was later seized by federal agents, since William had not become a US citizen, and was registered as an enemy alien. That classification was applicable to any foreign-born individual who had not been naturalized and whose country of birth was at war with the US.

During this fourth trip, there was a communication from the Pentagon requesting that USAFET, Paris, order the *Lutz* to proceed to Marseilles, after dropping off the POWs in Cherbourg, to pick up a "full load of American patients at Marseilles." A decision must have been made not to follow through on this request since the official August 29, 1945 report, dated the same day the Lutz arrived back in NY, says that the *Lutz* picked up its patients in Southampton.

There was also a near suicide. About one quarter to one third of the patients on each trip were suffering mental emotional stress. In the language of the day, they were suffering from "battle fatigue." On this last trip one of the patients jumped overboard. Alert personnel were able to stop the ship and to rescue the patient before he drowned.

The *Lutz* was later transferred to the Pacific. It sailed from New York to Hawaii on October 26, 1945 (trip 5) arriving November 21, 1945. Mildred was aboard in Hawaii where it was being refitted when it received orders to return to New York. On the return trip, it carried about 40 patients, but no nurses, all of whom must have remained in Hawaii.

On its four trips to Europe, the *Lutz* had a complement of 42 nurses. That worked out to about one nurse for every 7 patients. The *Lutz* also carried Army enlisted personnel who assisted the nurses. There were also 20-22 officers aboard, but it is not clear how many were medical personnel. Based on the initial plans for the ships complement, it is possible that up to 20 were medical personnel. The *Lutz* was manned by a civilian crew, as were all the Army's hospital ships. One thing is for sure. The patients were well fed. For the 768 patients brought home on trip 2, just the meat order was as follows: 1000 lbs of beef tenderloin, 1000 lbs of Boston pork, 3000 lbs of turkey, 1000 lbs of spare ribs, 2000 lbs of pork loin, 2000 lbs of lamb, 2000 lbs of sweet ham, 200 lbs of frozen shrimp, and 2000 lbs of chicken. Apparently, shrimp was not in demand.

Mildred remained in the service and rose to the rank of Captain. She was on reserve status for a short period while earning her Master's degree in Nursing at the University of Colorado in Boulder. In 1952, while serving in Fairbanks, Alaska, Mildred, and some friends hired a plane for a sightseeing trip. The plane crashed June 15, 1952 and all aboard were killed. Mildred's body was transported back to Fillmore for burial. Her brother, Air Force Corporal John R. Schmidt, released from duty in Korea, served as Honor Guard. Mildred was buried in Fillmore with full Military Honors.

Hilda Louise Schmidt (Gibbons) of Granger, sister of Mildred, had planned to follow her sister into the service. Hilda was a Cadet Nurse at the Craig School of Nursing in Sonyea, NY when the war ended. She was in a program where the government paid for both her books and uniform, which she only wore off duty. For this she had to commit to two years of service following graduation. Hilda said that once the war ended, the Army just forgot about the Cadet Nurses.

Hilda might have served as an Army nurse, except that the Craig School had an entrance age requirement of 17. Hilda had graduated from Fillmore Central at age 16 in 1941 and had to wait a year before entering nursing school. She spent the year working as a baby sitter in Mt. Morris, NY. Without the age requirement, she would have graduated from the nursing school in 1944 instead of 1945.

The Atlantic Fleet

Besides patrols conducted by destroyers and aircraft to combat submarine activity on the Atlantic Sea routes, the Atlanta Fleet also provided destroyer escorts for shipping convoys and other missions.

Men and women from the FCSD area who served with the Atlantic Fleet included Lloyd A. Carmer, William A. Curry, Willis A. Hayes, Frank A. Lowe, Alanson C. Papke, Robert W.E. Schultz, Howard J. Wilcox, and Alfred C. Wilday.

William A. Curry of Short Tract entered the service in March of 1943. After completing basic training at the Sampson Naval Training Center in Geneva, NY, William (who was Bill to everybody he knew), according to the NAO, was sent to a baker's school in Noroton Heights, CT. His career as a baker was short lived. By October, again according to the NAO, he was assigned to Motor Torpedo Boat training in Portsmouth, RI. During his training, Bill was considered a "Striker." A Navy Striker was a non-rated person working for promotion toward a specific third-class rating. The Navy eventually determined that service aboard PT boats was not the best career move for Bill.

By November 1943, Bill was at the Fargo Receiving Station in Boston, where he was assigned to the *USS Guinevere (IX 67)* January 19, 1944. The *Guinevere* was one of several three-mast Auxiliary Schooners assigned to the Atlantic Fleet. Armed with one 40 mm, and four 20 mm guns, two depth charge tracks with 300-pound depth charges and two rocket launches, the *Guinevere* conducted sonar searches in mid-Atlantic under full sail. (*Guinevere* also had two 300 horsepower diesel engines and could make 12 and a half knots.) The patrols were primarily near Newfoundland and Labrador, but also at times, as far as Iceland. These schooners had a big advantage, in theory, when conducting submarine searches. Under sail, enemy submarines could not detect them electronically. Therefore, they had a better chance of detecting the subs before they could submerge. The *Guinevere* also, apparently prior to Bill joining the crew, conducted escort services for various convoys heading for Europe. It would travel 30 miles off one flank of the convoy searching for submarines. At mid-ocean the convoy would be turned over to British and Canadian ships and the US escorts, including the *Guinevere* would return to the US. Bill remained aboard the *Guinevere* until August 18, 1944, when he was transferred back to the Fargo Receiving Station. He was next assigned to the Mine Test Facility at Provincetown, MA. The facility was focused on tested various types of mines. It is not clear what Bill's actual assignment was at Provincetown but he clearly was working toward a different rating. On June 8, 1945, Bill was promoted to Motor Machinist Mate 3rd class. Bill held this rating until he was discharged on April 5, 1946.

Bill was one of the most liked men in the area, and a genuine free spirit. He always had a smile and was not one to get bogged down by trivial matters. (That was likely the reason he twice was charged with being AWOL for being a few hours late reporting back to base after a leave.) He played baseball for the Fillmore nine, and one day he broke the little finger on his right hand. He never bothered to have it fixed, saying to the author, and others I am sure, that it never bothered him, so why bother it. Bent in three different directions, the crooked finger stayed with him for the rest of his life.

Frank Austin (Austy) Lowe entered the service on July 7, 1943. After basic training at Sampson Naval Training Station, NY, and technical training in Memphis, TN, Austy was stationed in Hollywood, Fl. His occupation was as an aviation ordnance man, responsible for arming aircraft. By June 1944, he was at the Naval Receiving Station in Norfolk, VA, and on June 2, he boarded the escort aircraft carrier, *USS Croatan (CVE 25)*. He was assigned to Composite Squadron VC 95, the carriers air arm.

The *Croatan* was the centerpiece of a task group whose job was to hunt and kill enemy submarines. During this patrol, which lasted from June to July 22, 1944, the planes and ships of the task group found and destroyed two enemy submarines. On June 10, it sunk U- Boat 490 (and picked up 60 survivors); and on July 3, the *Croatan's* planes and escort destroyers sank U Boat 154. VC 95 and Frank, disembarked from the *Croatan* on July 22, 1944. Frank apparently spent the next three months in Norfolk.

On October 19, 1944, Frank, and VC 95, boarded the escort carrier *USS Bogue (CVE 9)*. The *Bogue* spent the next several months operating training missions out of Bermuda, and Quonset Point, RI. Then it returned to Norfolk, where Frank and VC 95 disembarked on February 7, 1945. The NAO reported that Frank was home in February visiting friends and relatives in Fillmore and Angelica.

On March 27, Frank embarked on his third patrol, this time aboard the escort carrier *USS Mission Bay (CVE 59)*. The *Mission Bay* had just returned from a very special mission. Near Gibraltar it had joined the Task Group escorting President Roosevelt back from the Yalta conference.

Following that assignment, the *Mission Bay*, along with Frank and the rest of VC 95, became part of "Operation Teardrop." Intelligence reports were suggesting that German U Boats had been ordered to attack New York City with V1 Flying Bombs, and V 2 missiles as part of a last-gasp effort to turn the war around. Several of the best submarines in the German Navy were assigned to the effort. None of them was successful. Most of these German submarines were sunk. The rest surrendered. The operation lasted from March 29 to May 14. From the 14th until June 5, the *Mission Bay* cruised off the east coast training pilots. It then returned to Norfolk where Frank disembarked on June 5.

In June, the NAO reported that Frank had returned to the US after eleven months of duty with a Navy aviation squadron. (Actually, Frank was with VC 95 from at least June 2, 1944, until at least June 13, 1945.) The NAO report said he was wearing both the American Campaign Medal, and the European African Middle East Theater Medal. On June 27, Frank was transferred to the recruiting station in Buffalo (where he had entered the service) for further transfer to the NATTC in Memphis. There he was to be evaluated for a further assignment. Frank would not be discharged until September 14, 1946.

Alanson C. Papke of Hume served aboard the destroyer escort *USS Pennewill* as an electrician. He had attended the Navy's electrician's training program at Purdue University, graduating in August of 1943. The *Pennewill* carried out its escort duties as part of Task Group 42.2, up until April of 1944. In November, the *Pennewill* provided escort service from Trinidad to Recife, Brazil, for Convoy TJ-15. From December 25 thru 27, 1943 it escorted the US Army transport, *State of Maryland* from Trinidad to San Juan, Puerto Rico. During January 21 and 22, 1944, it escorted the British tanker *SS Destiny* from Recife, Brazil to its rendezvous with Task Group 41.4. It then conducted patrols off the coast of Brazil, with the light cruiser *USS Memphis (CL-13)*, for several months. In August of 1944, the *Pennewill* was turned over to Brazil and Alanson was reassigned.

His new assignment was the brand-new *USS Knudson (APD-101)*, a high-speed transport, which was commissioned in November of 1944, and left for the Pacific on November 30. When it sailed, it had underwater demolition team 19 aboard. It stopped at Eniwetok and Ulithi Atoll to prepare for operations in the Ryukyu Islands. During the period, March 25 to 30, it conducted reconnaissance and demolition operations at four islands: Kuba Shima, Aka Shima, Keise Shima and Geruma Shima. On March 26, while serving as an antisubmarine screen, it was attacked by a Japanese bomber. *Knudson's* gunners shot the bomber down after two of its bombs just missed the ship.

Knudson now prepared for the Okinawa invasion. As the landings took place on April 1, 1945, the *Knudson* conducted antisubmarine patrols. These patrols continued for the next two weeks, as the battle for Okinawa raged. On April 14, it was tasked with escorting battleship, *USS Nevada*, to Guam. It then escorted the heavy cruiser *USS Portland* to Okinawa on May 5. The NAO reported in May that Alanson had run into his uncle, Royce Papke, who was also serving in the Navy, when his ship docked for a few hours at one of the islands. It is likely that this meeting took place on Guam, before the *Knudsen* returned to Okinawa with the *Portland (CA-33)*. At Okinawa, it resumed screening activities, helping to repel Japanese fighter attacks until June 15, 1945, when it sailed to Leyte in the Philippines. It operated in Northern Philippine waters from June 18 until July 4, 1945. It then headed back to Okinawa, to escort an LST convoy filled with tanks. From there it headed to San Diego via Guam, Eniwetok, and Pearl Harbor. Arriving at San Diego on August 5, it departed for Tokyo Bay on August 16 to become part of the occupation forces. The *Knudsen* returned to San Diego, October 11, 1945 but sailed across the Pacific again on October 30. Her job now was to transport men and cargo among the Marshall, Mariana, Admiralty, and Philippine Islands. It appears that Alanson left the *Knudsen* in early February, in the Philippines (probably at Subic Bay), and returned home aboard the attack transport, *USS Marvin H. McIntyre*, arriving in San Francisco March 3, 1946. By March 12 he was at Sampson Naval Base, where he was discharged. Alanson was one of the few men from the FCSD area to earn Navy Operations Medals from two theaters of the war.

Howard J. Wilcox of Centerville was one of four bothers (Virgil, Lyle and Lowell being the others) who served in the military during World War II. The only other family with four members who served was the Thayer family. Howard entered the Navy on June 1, 1943. Like others from the area, he likely took his basic training at Sampson Naval Training Station. On October 10, 1943, Howard boarded the *USS Rich* (DE 695), a destroyer escort, in Norfolk, VA. At the time the *Rich* was performing coastal escort and patrol duties along the eastern seaboard. For some reason, he was transferred to the Boston Naval Receiving Station on November 26, 1943, and then on February 9, 1944 he rejoined the *Rich* from the New York City Receiving Station. Howard may have been sick or on leave or both during the 10 weeks between November 27, 1943 and February 8, 1944. Between February and May 10, 1944, the *Rich* made three round trips to Europe, performing trans-Atlantic escort services.

Its first trip was as part of Task Force 69. The *Rich* left New York Harbor February 27, 1944 escorting Convoy UT 9. It arrived in Lisahally, Northern Ireland on Thursday, March 9. While there, the *Rich* conducted tactical exercises on March 14. It sailed, with the Task Force, on its return trip on March 15, escorting Convoy TU 9 to NY, arriving on Saturday March 25. Howard sailed with the *Rich* on his second (and the *Rich's* third) trans-Atlantic trip on Wednesday April 4, 1944 from New York harbor. The *Rich* was part of Destroyer Division 30 escorting Convoy TU 9. It arrived on April 15, again at Lisahally, Northern Ireland. During the trip over, on April 8, a possible torpedo wake was spotted and the "all hands to battle stations" was sounded. The *Rich* left the convoy to investigate, but found no enemy vessels. It sailed for home again on April 20, escorting Convoy TU 11. It arrived back in early May. During the return trip, the *Rich* rendezvoused with the *USS George Washington (ID-3018)* to pick up mail. It also served as a target for a radar tracking drill. It is likely that the convoys escorted by the *Rich* and other ships were delivering supplies and/or men for the European invasion.

The *Rich* must have returned to Norfolk following its third trip (Howards second), since on May 17, 1944, according to muster records, Howard was received aboard the *USS Maumee* (AO 2), a fuel ship, from the Norfolk Receiving Station. The *Maumee* had recently returned from a trans-Atlantic run to Northern Ireland and Britain. (As a result of this transfer, Howard missed the Normandy invasion, as the *USS Rich* returned to England, and became part of the D-Day invasion fleet. It was sunk June 8, 1944 by underwater explosions off Utah Beach.) The *Maumee* muster records of June 15, 1944, report Howard as a "straggler" as of May 29, 1944. His records were transferred to the Norfolk Receiving Station, and the *Maumee* returned to refueling duties along the east coast.

Howard's record for the next year is not clear. He likely was AWOL for part of that period. He also likely was court-martialed and may have served some time. This event did not have a permanent effect on his career, as he ended his service as a Seaman Second Class and received an Honorable Discharge.

On May 28, 1945, Howard reported aboard the *USS Bogue (CVE 9)* an escort aircraft carrier, in Norfolk. The *Bogue* sailed to San Diego, arriving July 3, 1945, and then, on July 24, 1945, headed for Adak, Alaska, via Guam. It was at sea when the Hiroshima and Nagasaki atomic bombs ended the war. The *Bogue* stayed in Adak from August 19 until September 8, the date of the official surrender of Japan. The *Bogue* was then assigned to "Operation Magic Carpet," returning servicemen from the Pacific war zone to the US. Howard was discharged in April of 1946.

Alfred C, Wilday of Centerville was a Navy veteran even before the start of World War II. He originally enlisted on February 13, 1935, and reenlisted in February 1939, May 1941, and perhaps October or November 1943. Alfred served in both the Atlantic and the Pacific on several ships, and at submarine repair bases in the Zone of the Interior (ZI). It is not clear where he served during all of his first enlistment, but by the late 1930's he was aboard the *USS Detroit* (CE 8), a light cruiser. Its home port was San Diego, and its duties included participating in exercises along the West Coast, as well as in Alaskan and Hawaiian waters. During this period, the *Detroit* was part of a Destroyer Squadron Battle Force, and the *Detroit*, for at least part of the time, was the flagship of the Commander of the Battle Force.

When Alfred reenlisted in 1939, apparently in Norfolk, VA, he was transferred to the *USS Melville (AD-2)* first boarding on February 6, 1939. The *Melville* was a Destroyer Tender at the time he boarded, Alfred was listed as a Torpedoman Mate 3rd Class. As such, Alfred would have been responsible for maintaining and repairing torpedoes, the torpedo tubes, and the launching equipment. This likely also included test firing aboard ship. The duties were essentially the same for both surface ships which carried torpedoes and for submarines. Alfred served as a Torpedoman's Mate for the balance of the war. He spent some two years, four months aboard the *Melville*. The *Melville* was in the Caribbean when Alfred went aboard, but, as the threat of war grew, the ship was recalled to Norfolk, where it operated with patrol forces of the US Fleet. On February 1, 1941, it was transferred from the US Fleet, back to the Atlantic Fleet. It was sent first to Guantanamo Bay, Cuba, and then to Culebra, Puerto Rico where the crew underwent intensive training. It then spent three weeks in Casco Bay, ME performing supply duties. At this point, Alfred's second enlistment was up. He reenlisted in May and was assigned to the *USS Antaeus (AG-67)*, a submarine tender. He boarded *Antaeus* June 20, 1941. He would only spend some 15 months aboard the *Antaeus*, most of that time in the Caribbean, taking part in training exercises, and providing repair services to submarines on patrol in the Caribbean. On September 21, 1942, he was transferred to the submarine base at New London, CT.

The New London Submarine Base was located at Groton, CT. But its main offices were in New London, thus the name. It was, and is, the primary Navy Submarine Base in the world. Its various nicknames, including "Home of the Submarine Force", and "Submarine Capital of the World", attest to its importance. Albert served at New London from September 1942 until September 1944. According to the NAO, he reenlisted for the fourth time in October or November 1944 while at New London. In September, according to the NAO, Albert was transferred to Mare Island, CA, the premier submarine base on the West Coast, located on San Francisco Bay. At both New London and Mare Island, Alfred continued to perform his Torpedoman Mate duties. He was then transferred to the *USS Bushnell (AS 15)*, a submarine tender.

USS Bushnell, muster records for September 1, 1945 show that, on August 25 1945, Alfred was promoted to Torpedoman Mate First Class. It is likely that Alfred joined the *Bushnell* in San Diego where it was performing repair work for submarines from September to October, 1945. In January 1946, the *Bushnell* sailed for Guam to perform occupation duties. In April 1946, it sailed to Pearl Harbor and became part of a submarine squadron.

PART III - THE SOFT UNDERBELLY

Sicily

"I want you to remember that no bastard ever won a war by dying for his country. He won by making the other dumb bastard die for his country." 1944 speech to Third Army. General George C. Patton III

"No amphibious attack in history has approached this one in size. Along miles of coast line there were hundreds of vessels and small boats ----" 1943 – Allied landings *at Sicily.*
General Dwight D. Eisenhower

Representing the FCSD at Sicily were Marlie J. Hodnett, Carroll S. Phipps, Floyd K. Roberts, Donald B. Smith, Melvin L. Slocum, Gerald F. Thomas, and Roland J. Thomas.

While there is no absolute proof that anyone from the FCSD area ever led an invasion, the chances are very high **Marlie Hodnett** of Fillmore, did or came awfully close to, leading the invasion of Sicily at Gela. There is no question that the 16th Infantry Regiment (Marlie's regiment) of the First Infantry Division led the invasion of Sicily at Gela. And, in a letter home to his wife Shirley, Marlie stated that he was one of the first two men off the boat at Gela as that was his job. Like other WW II veterans Marlie never spoke about the war. His son Gary said that he mentioned it just once to him. They were cutting bushes outside the house and Marlie casually mentioned that when he landed at Gela the only thing he had when he left the landing craft was a pair of barbed wire cutters. That undoubtedly was the job of the first two men off the boat. It also earned Marlie the prized Arrowhead Badge. (The Sicily invasion was the largest US amphibious invasion of the war. Eight divisions with 175,000 men landed the first day. At Normandy, five divisions and three armored brigades with 150,000 men landed on June 6th.)

Sicily was the end of the war for Marlie. On July 11, 1943 at Gela, he was wounded for the third and final time. This one was serious; a large piece of shrapnel to the hip. He was evacuated to North Africa, where he spent considerable time in the hospital recuperating. It did have its benefits, however. Marlie wrote his wife Shirley that he got to meet Al Jolson. He was finally shipped home on June 2, 1944 having spent almost 20 months overseas, a good part of it in combat.

Marlie earned numerous medals, many of which, I suspect, he never received (as was the experience of many G.I.s). For instance, his three wounds entitled him to three Purple Hearts. He only received two. Also, as far as is known, he also never received the medal most prized by infantrymen, the Combat Infantryman Badge (CIB). There is zero question that he met the requirements for earning this badge. While recovering from his last wound, by chance, Marlie had an opportunity to see his service record. He wrote home that it credited him with eight major battles, and that he was entitled to more ribbons and medals "which I probably won't get until it's all over with and me home with a family." As far as the family can tell, he never got those decorations at all. That includes the Bronze Star awarded, after the war by Congress, to all men who earned the CIB. That is probably because his records do not show he earned the CIB.

After being rotated back to the states, Marlie primarily worked in an Army Post Office in New York City. Keeping the mail flowing was a critical function during the war as it was a major morale factor. Practically every letter written by a G.I. reminded the recipient to keep writing. From time-to-time Marlie was also detailed to other duties, at one time helping to care for wounded soldiers on a hospital troop train.

Despite all of this, Marlie would always be famous in Fillmore, a baseball crazy town, for having pitched a perfect no hit no run game in his last appearance for the Fillmore nine before leaving for the service. The uniform he wore that day still hangs in the local museum. The author is Marlie's great nephew. He once got to wear Marlie's uniform when he was about four. Maybe "wear" is not the right word. Marlie's second wound was on April 24, the birthdate of his great nephew.

Donald B. Smith of Hume entered the service March 4, 1941. He was assigned to the Headquarters Battalion of the 62nd Coast Artillery at Fort Totten, NY. Except for various maneuvers, Donald was to remain at Fort Totten until the 62nd was shipped overseas on August 29, 1942. The 62nd was part of the North Africa invasion force. Shipped with Donald was Roland Thomas, also from the FCSD area. Donald and Roland had entered the service on the same day, and both were assigned to the 62nd Coast Artillery.

Donald and the 62nd participated in the entire North African campaign, and were part of the initial landings at Oran, Algeria. The NAO reported that Donald had written his parents that he had witnessed some of the great air battles of the Mediterranean campaign. By June, Donald had moved to Tunisia. In Oran, the 62nd had been initially concerned with the protection of the shipping ports against enemy air attacks. Later it defended airfields. In Algeria, it was primarily concerned with protecting the staging areas to be used for future invasions, especially Sicily and Italy. In July, the 62nd participated in the initial landings at Licata, Sicily. Donald served with the 62nd throughout the entire Sicily campaign. His FCSD area buddy, Roland Thomas, also remained with the battalion during this period. In fact, Roland wrote home that, "I see Donald frequently. He was inducted into the Army the same day I was, and sent to the same camp back in the states. We have been together ever since. Makes you feel lots better to have someone around from your home with you."

With victory in Sicily however, that relationship ended. The Allied and US dominance in the air was reducing the need for many anti-aircraft units. In November, on Sicily, the 62nd was disbanded. Roland was transferred to the 24th Infantry Regiment Artillery and Donald was rotated back to the states in December. Donald had earned three battle stars - Algeria, Tunisia, and Sicily. His initial duty station back home was Camp Stewart, Georgia. Stewart was primarily an anti-aircraft training center. (It also later became a POW camp for German and Italian men captured during the North African campaign.) Donald likely became an instructor. He had been promoted to First Sergeant in March 1943. During his assignment at Stewart, Donald was one of five battle tested Sergeants to participate in the 4th War Loan rally in Georgia. He was even written up in the Savannah, Georgia Press.

In May 1944, Donald was transferred to Camp Campbell, KY. This was a short-term assignment as, even including a furlough he received, he was only there six months. Campbell was another training base, and at the time of Donald's tour, was training men from the 20th, 14th and 12th Armored Divisions, as well as the 26th Infantry Division and Headquarters IV Armored Corps. By January 1945, Donald was at Camp Wheeler, Georgia. Wheeler was an infantry replacement training center. Recruits received basic and advanced individual training to replace combat casualties. Donald was discharged September 29, 1945.

Italy

There were three strategic goals behind the invasion of Italy. They were to: (1) gain total control of the Mediterranean, (2) force Italy to withdraw from the war, and (3) keep pressure on the Germans while preparations were being made for the cross-channel invasion of France. Capturing Italy would also provide bases from which the Allies' Air Forces could attack German sources of supply and the German industrial heartland. All these objectives were achieved. The price was high, especially during the disaster attempting to cross the Rapido River. When the Allies forced Italy to surrender on September 2, 1943 (whereupon Italy immediately switched sides and declared war on Germany) Hitler moved 16 German divisions into Italy. The "soft underbelly" which never really existed anyway, was no longer even mentioned. There were two invasions of mainland Italy. The first was at Salerno and the second at Anzio. Men and women from the FCSD area participated in both. German General Alfred Kesselring, in charge of German forces in Italy, later admitted that had the Allies invaded at Rome instead of Salerno and Anzio, he would have had to pull all of his forces out of Southern Italy. Rome would have been liberated in late 1943 instead of June 1944. A lot of lives would have been saved, at least in Italy. The big question is whether this would have resulted in German divisions in Italy being moved to Normandy, or at least being in a better position to participate and attempt to repel the Normandy landings.

The FCSD area was ably represented in the battles for Italy. At least the following men and women all served in Italy in some capacity during the Italian campaigns: G. Emelene Ballard, Warren H. Bennett, Royden F. Bentley, Leonard O. Blakeslee, Franklin L. Brown, Ronald W. Carpenter, Lloyd D. Clark, Lorne F. Collver, Roland C. Dunn, Herbert R. Foster, Mabel E. Fox, Donald R. Haskins, Russell C. Hodnett, Allen L. Isham, Raymond E. Lilly, Lowell E. Mix. William B. Parker, Raymond I. Peck, Carroll S. Phipps, Milton C. Rathbun, Evan R. Ricketts, Albert A. Roth, Melvin S. Slocum, Royal S. (Roy) Strait, Roland J. Thomas, Robert L. Van Name, Kent M. Weaver, Kenneth A. Williams, and Warren M. Woolsey. Allen L. "Pat" Isham of Houghton earned the Silver Star there. He also died there.

While it is known that the following men served in Italy, in most cases it is not known in what units they served, the exact time period they served there and the specific battles in which they may have participated. The personal files for these men were apparently destroyed in the July 12, 1973 St. Louis National Personnel Records Center fire which destroyed some 16 to 18 million World War II files for men who served in the Army and Army Air Force during the war. The cause of the fire was never officially determined. A custodian admitted that he had been smoking in the fire room and put out his cigarette on a cabinet. He assumed that was the cause. The fire roared for four days before officially contained. Records were lost due to the fire and the enormous amount of water needed to put out the fire. No copies of the records existed. The records Center has done everything possible since then to reconstruct the lost files.

Ronald W. Carpenter of Fillmore entered the Enlisted Reserve Corps (ERC) on March 12, 1941 and served ten months nine days as an enlisted reserve during 1941. At least seven of those months were possibly served with the 96th Coastal Artillery according to his induction document. His discharge record indicates that he served an additional three months and nine days with, probably, the 2nd or 9th Coastal Artillery. For this service he likely earned the American Defense Medal. The earning of this medal is not recorded on his scorched discharged document which is one of the few things that remains from his personnel file which was destroyed in the St. Louis fire. In this book, it is acknowledged that he earned the Defense Medal. The NAO reported in April 1941 that Ronald, formerly of Fillmore, was assigned to Company C of the 7th Medical Training Battalion at Camp Lee, VA. He was discharged for the first time on about January 21, 1942. His service with the Coastal Artillery may have been as a medical technician.

Finally, on January 19. 1942 he entered the service for the duration of the war plus six months. His discharge document called this a "Recall." He reported to Fort Niagara, New York to be inducted.

No information on Ronald's activities during the period 1/19/42 to 4/29/43 have been located. On April 29, 1943 Ronald was shipped to the Mediterranean Theater of operations. He arrived May 11, 1943. He served, likely with a medical battalion, during his stay in Italy. His discharge document indicates he served with Company D, 366th Medical Battalion. His discharge record also indicates that he earned the Rome-Arno Campaign Medal. The campaign took place during the period January 22, 1944 until September 9, 1944. Other documents indicate that the 366th was attached to the 66th Infantry Division. That Division did not earn the Rome-Arno campaign medal which means Ronald was with a different medical unit at the time of the campaign. This is reinforced by the fact that Ronald's records also show that he earned the Rhineland Campaign Medal. The 66th did not participate in the Rhineland Campaign. The 66th was not activated until April 15, 1943 in Camp Blanding, FL. It did not serve in Italy.

It arrived in England December 12, 1944 and served in Northern France until May 14, 1945. It was then assigned to occupation duties in Koblenz, Germany. It is likely that Ronald joined the 366th Medical Battalion which was part of the 66th, in Koblenz. The 66th was shipped back to the states starting on October 27, 1945. Ronald's record show he was shipped home October 31, 1945.

Ronald's discharge document does not reflect that he received the Northern France Campaign Battle Star. Nor does it reflect the Army Occupation Medal with Germany Clasp. The 66th did perform occupation duties in the Koblenz area of Germany for a short period in May. It appears that Ronald should have received the occupation medal. In late May the Division moved to Marseille, Arles, and St. Victoret, France to stage for the Pacific. A history of the 66th indicates that the 366th was with it performing their usual duties during this period. The 66th was assigned to staffing the three staging areas while decisions were made regarding troop movements to the Pacific. The war ended before any decision regarding the 66th could be made. Part of the 66th sailed for home in late October. Ronald was among those men. His discharge document indicates he sailed for the US on October 31, 1945 and arrived November 11, 1945. He was discharged November 19, 1945 at Fort Dix, NJ.

Ronald's records list his Military Occupation Specialty as 861 (Surgical Technician). The duties of a surgical technician called for performing a variety of nonprofessional surgical and medical duties in rendering surgical care and treatment to patients. This included preparing operating rooms and surgical equipment for use, cleaning and washing equipment, and sterilizing linen, equipment and instruments. Other duties involved assisting operating personnel, preparing patients for operation, assisting in the administration of hypodermic injections and anesthetics, and handing instruments and materials to the surgeon. He also assisted in transporting patients, giving first aids, changing dressing and bandages, treating minor cuts, etc., and post operative treatment of patients.

Lorne F. Collver of Fillmore entered the service on March 5, 1943. His records were destroyed in the St. Louis personnel records fire. However, a good deal of his service is available from other sources. Lorne family moved to Fillmore in the early 1940's. Fillmore was his home town during his service years and for some time after the war. An item in the NAO even tells us that his parents lived on West Main Street. Another article reports that Lorne served with a 15th Air Force service crew and spent two years overseas, with three months in North Africa and the balance in Italy. It also mentioned that he was a direct descendant of Reverend Jabez Coller, a presbyterian bishop, and friend of George Washington.

Lorne likely spent some two to three months in basic training and, giving his military occupation, some additional time, maybe three to four months, in occupational training. Since he was overseas for about two years and arrived back in the states in August 1945, it is likely that he arrived in North Africa sometime in late 1943. It is not known his exact assignment in North Africa, but it may have been with the 12th Air Force. It is also possible he did not have a permanent assignment during that three-month period. He later served with the 15th Air Force which was not activated until November 1, 1943 in Tunis, Tunisia. In fact, he may have been assigned to the 15th at the time of its activation or shortly thereafter and moved with the Force to Italy.

His Discharge Certificate, a copy of which did survive the fire, indicates that he served with Headquarters Squadron and Base Service Squadron of the 540th Air Service Group. Air Service Groups, originally organized to service B-29 groups, were apparently not established until November 1944. Previously they were just service groups and Lorne was likely assigned to such a group. As such he would have been part of a crew servicing a 15th Air Force Bomb Group. The Air Service Groups performed the same duties but were responsible for operating a service center for two air groups rather than one. It is not known to which base Lorne was assigned.

The NAO reported in April 1944 that Lorne had finally arranged a meeting with his cousin Technical Sergeant Wilbur Webb of Buffalo at Wilbur's camp. Lorne completed his service as a Private First Class. He returned to the US in July of 1945 and was home on a 30-day furlough in August. He was discharged October 30, 1945 at Drew Field, Florida.

Lyman E. Smith of Allen, a 1934 graduate of Fillmore Central, entered the service on March 19, 1941. The NAO reported in February 1941, that he was stationed at Camp Lee, VA. Camp Lee was a Quartermaster Replacement Training Center. It had started operations as such in February 1941. The NAO also reported that Lyman was being transferred to Fort Jackson, SC. In January 1942 NAO reported that Lyman was home on leave, that he was still stationed at Fort Jackson and that he had been promoted to Corporal. It is likely that he was permanent staff at the Fort. In May Lyman was again home on leave and NAO reported that he was being transferred to a camp near Augusta, Ga. Another report that same month indicated that he was at Camp Gordon. In May 1945, the same month Lyman was transferred to Camp Gordon, the 549th Quartermaster Company was activated at Camp Gordon. Lyman likely went through Quartermaster training while at Camp Lee in Virginia.

Like most World War II veterans, Lyman personnel file was destroyed in the St. Louis fire of 1973. Some 17 million records were destroyed. No cause for the fire has ever been officially determined. His final pay record is available and does provide a few items of information.

The NAO reported that Lyman was home from Italy on furlough in May of 1945. A further article in June reported that he had been granted an honorary discharge as a Staff Sergeant, had served for four years with 30 months overseas with the Fifth Army, and had earned two battle stars. His final pay record shows that he was assigned to and arrived at the Lake Placid Club on May 28, 1945. The Club was for G.I.s returning from overseas. It provided them a chance to go boating play tennis and golf, go for bike rides and sight see before returning home. He was discharged at Fort Dix on June 4, 1945.

These remaining records do not, however, contain vital information about his service. That information would include the unit he served with overseas, his military occupation and duties, and the locations and military actions in which he participated. Since his last known location was Camp Gordon in May 1942, he could have participated in any or all the Italian campaigns. The NAO said in June 1945 that he participated in only two campaigns. However, the June 1945 NAO item said he served 30 months overseas. Since he returned at the end of May 1945, 30 months back from that would have him overseas around December 1942 or January 1943. That June NAO entry also said he served with the Fifth Army.

Kenneth A. Williams of Centerville entered the service on November 11, 1942. Ken's files were destroyed in the St. Louis fire and except for a few items published in the NAO, very little is known about his service. There is no information regarding his service in the US. An item published in a December issue of the NAO reported that he had bought some sweaters for three Italian children. In January he wrote home that he had received the Christmas packages, probably from the Junior Red Cross unit in Centerville. That NAO article also included the Initials MP beside his name probably indicating that he was serving with the Military Police. His final pay record indicates that he arrived back in the US on August 31, 1945. This is also mentioned in the NAO. An article in September reported that he was home in Centerville with his family on a 30-day furlough. In October another article reported that he had returned to Fort Knox after 45 days of leave. This was probably the September leave extended for another 15 days. He was discharged at Fort Dix, NJ on October 30, 1945.

Salerno

The initial landings on mainland Italy took place at Salerno at one in the morning, September 9, 1943. Only hours earlier on September 8, Italy had surrendered. In less than a year, two of the three opponents that Allied soldiers had faced during the invasion of North Africa were out of the war. Italy and the Vichy French. (Free French forces fought with the Allies from the beginning.) That still left the most formidable foe, Germany. (Also supporting Germany were Hungary, Romania, Bulgaria, Slovakia, and Croatia.)

Generva Emelene Ballard, who went by Emelene, was a native of Fillmore's neighbor, Rushford, but worked in both the Houghton Infirmary and the Fillmore Hospital. Her father was a physician. She was an early member of the 23rd General Hospital, having joined the unit on October 28, 1942. The 23rd was sponsored by the Buffalo General Hospital which provided both staff and funding. The Nurses for the 23rd were recruited from the Buffalo area, which included the FCSD area. The 23rd had been activated July 15, 1942 and training took place at Fort Meade, MD until July 13, 1943. The unit was then sent to Camp Patrick Henry in Virginia on July 18, 1943. They sailed from Pier 6 in Hampton Roads, VA, on July 30, for North Africa, aboard the *Empress of Scotland*. The ship had been renamed for the war. Its original name had been *Empress of Japan*.

Wherever the men went during World War II, nurses either went with them, or were close behind. Emelene arrived at Casablanca, in French Morocco on August 6, 1943, after having spent a week at sea. On August 3^{rd,} aboard ship they published the 26th and last edition of the unit newsletter, *Tattler*. It was called the "Ocean Edition." They immediately set up a camp, called Don B. Passage, just outside of Casablanca. They initially slept on the ground. By September 16th they were on their way to Oran, where they stayed for about a month. On October 23rd, they boarded the *Orontes* and headed for Italy. They arrived at Naples on October 28th. They moved into the Mostra Fair Grounds an area that had been built as a medical center. It had been heavily bombed. The least damaged buildings were used for the hospital, with materials from the more damaged ones used for repairs. The first patients arrived November 17, 1943. They operated there until September 20, 1944. During this period Emelene earned her first two battle stars for the Naples-Foggia and Rome Arno Campaigns.

The 23rd was initially a 1,000-bed hospital. In May of 1944 it was increased to a 2,000-bed hospital. It eventually had 3,200- beds. On May 17, 1944, it held a dinner/dance party to celebrate its first six months of operations. During that period as a 1,000-bed hospital, it had served over 11,700 patients. In June of 1944, Irving Berlin and his show, "This is the Army," played at the Medical Center. On June 6, 1944, Berlin visited the hospital wards. It is not known what time Berlin was in the wards, but there is no doubt that the invasion of France was occurring while he was there. On June 4, 182 patients were admitted to the hospital. In July the hospital averaged each day over 2,300 patients.

In September wounded soldiers from the invasion of Southern France arrived. On October 18, 1944, the 23rd was moved to France. It opened there in Vittel on November 15th. During this period the hospital personnel were quartered at the Continental Hotel. When they first arrived, the Hotel was without beds or any type of furniture. Interestingly, the nurses were quartered on the top floors, the enlisted personnel on the bottom, and the male officers in between. Some would have thought the nurses safer if the men and officers had been reversed.

There was not much time to think about it, as wounded from the Battle of the Bulge begin arriving as did those from the much nearer Colmar Pocket battle, SW of Vittel. At one point, with the fighting near, the Army considered arming the doctors, but they were no arms available, and most of the medical officers did not know how to use them anyway. Their time in Vittel was a lot less intense than their time in Italy.

Nevertheless, they cared for over 11,600 patients prior to the end of the war on May 8, 1945. The unit was split up following war's end, but most members moved to Paris and occupied the "L'Hospital de la Pitie." The unit's personnel were then discharged in stages with the last group being transported home in mid-November, on a Liberty ship from Marseilles. The 23rd had landed at Marseilles when they arrived in France back in October, 1944. They had come full circle. Emelene was discharged on February 6, 1946.

Warren H. Bennett of Hume enrolled in the service September 3, 1942, but he did not enter active duty until the 17th. The Journal for the 532nd Anti-Aircraft Automatic Weapons Battalion states the following; "Sept. 25, 1942 - 289 enlisted men arrived this Hq. from Hq.1213th Reception Center, Fort Niagara, N.Y." It is likely that one of those men was Warren. The reason for this is that Warren's discharge records show that he was awarded the Combat Infantry Badge by General Order No. 10 (1 April 1945) issued by Headquarters, 473rd Infantry Regiment. It further shows that Warren was a member of Company E of the 473rd. Company E would have been part of the 2nd Battalion. of the 473rd. A Narrative Report of the 532nd Battalion (dated 15 January 1945) states that "On January 14, 1945, orders were received for the disbandment of the 532nd AAA - AWBN and its personnel became members of the 2nd Battalion 473rd Infantry Regiment."

The 532nd was organized at Fort Bliss in July 1942. As indicated above, Warren entered active service on September 17, and it was likely with the 532nd at Fort Bliss. There he would have participated in training until the 532nd sailed for North Africa on February 28,1943. The battalion arrived in Casablanca on March 9. By late March they were in Tunisia. There it served in several locations to provide anti-aircraft protection against enemy air attacks. (The batteries were assigned to individual airfields.) On November 8, the battalion sailed from Bizerte, Tunisia, arriving at Bagnoli (Naples), Italy on November 11. Throughout the balance of 1943, the batteries of the Battalion were again assigned to various locations to support different (usually Army) units. During this period, the batteries engaged in several battles against enemy aircraft, primarily German ME-109's and FW -190's.

Beginning in 1944 however, the 532nd was used primarily in support of ground troops, including the 36th Infantry Division, the 19th Combat Engineers, and the British 12th Brigade. It participated in most of the major battles of that period, including the Rapido River crossings, the attacks on Monte Cassino and the advance into Rome. In March, its commander, Lt. Col. Coyne wrote "…we have been front line troops for five solid months with no rest." In May, the final move to capture Rome began, and the 532nd entered Rome, victoriously, on June 5, 1945. This major event received only one day of major coverage, as the next day, June 6, 1944, the most important invasion in history took place at Normandy. During this period, the Allied Air Forces, and the anti-aircraft batteries were destroying the German Air Force. The Germans were becoming less and less able to mount credible air attacks. The Normandy landings and the advance across northern France also were taking its toll. The result was that many anti-aircraft units were no longer needed. The move north continued as the 532nd moved through, among others, Cecina, Florence, Viareggio and into Bologna; but the 532nd was now assigned to Task Force 45, which was the first step in its transition to an Infantry unit.

In January of 1945 a decision was made to inactivate the 532nd Anti-Aircraft Battalion. The men of the 532nd now became the 2nd Battalion of the 473rd Infantry Regiment. Warren had already earned four battle stars serving with the 532nd (Tunisia, Naples-Foggia, Rome-Arno, and Northern Apennines). He would earn another with his new outfit.

The 473rd was formed at Montecatini, Italy on January 15, 1945.Warren was assigned to Company E, 2nd Battalion. For the next 30 days, they underwent training as combat infantrymen. On February 15, they entered combat at Cutigliano. Initially they conducted numerous patrols. On the 23rd, the Regiment was attached to the famous black 92nd Infantry Division. They then moved into the Serchio Valley. They were constantly defending their gains as they continued to move forward. During March, the Battalion carried out 202 patrols. These were long tiring patrols against Germany's 286th Infantry Regiment at Monte Del Olmo, Monte L'uccelliera and others. On April 7, the 2nd Battalion attacked Stretoria Hill, a position which dominated Highway 1. The battle to drive the Germans from the Gothic Line (called the Green Line by the US) had begun. The Gothic Line was the final main German defensive line in Italy. It stretched from south of La Spezia on west coast of Italy, through the Apennine Mountains to an area between Pesaro and Ravenna on the east coast. The 2nd Battalion attacked uphill from Carrana. During this attack the 473rd suffered 50 men killed and some 200 wounded. One of the wounded was Warren. He had not only earned his fifth battle star he now had a Purple Heart.

Warren ended up in the hospital following the engagement. His parents received word of his wound shortly thereafter. They said it was the first word they had received since January, which is an indication of the intensity of the campaign in which the 473rd was engaged. The NAO reported that Warren was back with his company by June. But it is likely that he was assigned to a new Regiment at this time, as his discharge record shows that he was serving with Company L, 349th Infantry Regiment when discharged. The 349th returned to the US on September 10, and Warren's discharge record indicates that he also sailed for home that same day, arriving September 17. He was discharged on September 26, 1945.

Allen Leroy (Pat) Isham of Houghton was born on St. Patrick's Day (thus the Pat), March 17, 1916. By 1943 Pat was a rifleman with the 141st Infantry Regiment of the 36th Infantry Division. German General Heinz William Guderian, at the end of World War II, in his Order of Battle, rated the 141st Infantry as the second most effective of all allied forces. Part of that effectiveness was surely due to Pat Isham.

Pat joined the 36th Division in North Africa as a replacement. On September 9, 1943, he earned his first Arrowhead Badge when he landed with the Division at Salerno, as part of Operation Avalanche. This was accomplished despite intense German resistance. The Germans commanded the high ground and were able to shoot down on the invaded forces. To get ashore the men cut paths through mine fields and barbed wire. There were artillery pieces (88's) on the ridges and tanks on the flats. The Germans launched an armored counterattack just after the landing. Pat's regiment, the 141st, in a bitter and bloody hand-to-hand battle, repelled the German attack. The landing was secured and the 36th moved rapidly inland. They were able to secure the area from Agropoli to Altavilla, although they were forced to twice take Altavilla. The small pamphlet, "The Story of the 36th Infantry Division" summed it up. "Guts, firepower and teamwork decided the battle of Salerno that day." *Picture – Pat on leave in Cassini, Italy. Family photo.*

By November 15, 1943, against an enemy which held strong defensive positions and despite the severe winter weather, they captured Mount Maggiore (named Million Dollar Mountain after the enormous artillery barrage leveled on the mountain), Monte Lungo and the village of San Pietro. In early January and February, they attempted to secure a bridgehead across the Rapido River, but were unable to do so. There were too many mines, too many good observation posts, and the cross fire was murderous.

It was during this advance that Allen L. "Pat" Isham earned his Silver Star. General Order No. 230 dated July 8, 1944 tells the story. Section I of the Order is titled "Posthumous Award of the Silver Star." Under Allen L. Isham it reads "…for gallantry in action 2-4 February 1944 in the vicinity of Cassino, Italy. Volunteering on three successive nights to make dangerous reconnaissance patrols of the enemy held bank of the Rapido River, Staff Sergeant Isham courageously crossed the treacherous waters and skillfully obtained invaluable information of enemy emplacements, strength, and disposition. Constantly exposed to enemy fire and repeatedly risking discovery by the hostile troops, he completed a thorough reconnaissance of the area where severe casualties had already been sustained; and his information contributed materially to later operations in this sector." The award was made posthumously because, by the time the order was issued in July, Pat had been killed in action.

Before being withdrawn from the line for some rest and recuperation on March 12, 1944, the 36th assisted in the attack on Monte Cassino.

On May 22, they landed on the Anzio beachhead to assist in Operation Diadem. The Allies had been stuck in Anzio since the invasion forces landed on January 22. On May 23, they broke out and the race to Rome was on. The 141st Infantry captured Valletri on June 1. The Division's pamphlet quotes Eric Sevareid of the Columbia Broadcasting System as follows: "This action turned the key to the city of Rome and handed it to Gen. Mark Clark," On June 5th the division and Pat entered Rome. For one day, this was the biggest news of the war. The next day, June 6th, the Normandy invasion occurred.

The 36th did not stop long in Rome. It continued to push north and, despite facing fierce German resistance, captured Magliano and Grossetto. By June 26th it had captured Pombino. Pat did not make it to Pombino. Near Rome, on June 22nd he was climbing into a jeep and was hit by a piece of shrapnel. He died that same day.

One of Pat's many friends, Maynard C. Rapella, wrote his wife, Chrystal, following his death. The letter is dated July 23, 1944. In part, he wrote: "Pat and I came through the entire Italian campaign together. We first met in Africa where he joined our outfit. We saw our first combat together when we landed on the Italian beaches nearly a year ago. Since that time, we have tasted the bitterness and hardships of a soldier's life in battle. We fought all winter long in the cold mountain ranges of Italy and in the muddy wasteland around Cassino. We blasted the Germans from their strongholds before Rome and chased them many miles beyond. It was ten months of bitter fighting." Maynard then went on expressing the deep sentiments of the combat veteran for his buddies. "Pat and I were closer to each other than just mere friends. We were comrades in battle, and we shared the fears and hopes and tiny pleasures which the war gave us. We lived in a world of fear and bitter struggles." He then expressed in his own way the feeling that so many combat veterans have when a buddy dies and they live. "We were a part of each other, not to be separated even by death. I came to believe in him righteously. I even believed that he was a man who could not die. His will to live was so strong. Then it seemed so strange for him to die alone, while I lived yet. For we had been accustomed to share everything together, barring nothing." Maynard closed by assuring Chrystal of Pat's love. "There is one more thing you should know. Throughout the many months over here and the frequent temptations, he remained true to you, Mrs. Isham. For he had so much to return home to. His life was centered around you." Maynard survived the war.

Pat had married Crystal Marie Burr on June 13, 1942, shortly before his entry into the service. While overseas, he met Harold L. Michael from Niagara Falls, and they soon realized that they had played professional baseball against each other. They became fast friends. After returning home from the war, Harold wrote to Crystal Isham about his friend Pat. In his second letter, he wrote about Pat's death. Like Maynard, Harold had a hard time accepting that something had happened to Pat. He wrote, "I could not imagine Allen being hurt. He'd been around so long that it just didn't seem right without him.". Crystal and Harold exchanged letters for a time and then finally met. In 1953 they were married. Crystal said that they had two sons and 30 wonderfully happy years of marriage.

Evan R. Ricketts of Granger entered the service on April 2, 1942. By September 1942 he was at Harding Field located near Baton Rouge, LA. He had been there since he entered the service according to a letter he wrote to the NAO in December. By September he had already been promoted to Sergeant. Evan also mentioned in his December letter that he was a personnel administrative clerk. (Like most others, Evan's personnel file was destroyed by the fire at the Records Center in St. Louis. Therefore, Evans service is based primarily on reports from the NAO and on other historical information.)

In April 1943 NAO received another letter from Evan. He was now in Tunisia, North Africa. He again mentioned how much he liked the paper. A June 1945 entry in the NAO made clear that by April of 1943 Evan was no longer in administration. He was now part of an Air Service Squadron whose job was to service the big bombers who were busy destroying the ability of the Third Reich to wage war. Since it was early in the war, this was not an easy job. The need was great for daily missions. The availability of bombers was limited. The Nazis still had massive air power. Their Air Force was still close to if not, for the time being, the best Air Force in the world. The Allies losses were high, but so were the Germans. The Tunisian Campaign was still in progress. It did not officially end until May 13, 1943. Evan likely earned a Battle Star for the Tunisian Campaign.

Another article in the NAO mentioned that Evan had participated in the North African, Sicilian and Italian campaigns. As a member of a bomber unit, it is likely that Evan participated in the Sicilian campaign from North Africa. The Sicilian Campaign lasted from July 9, 1943 to August 17,1943. It is likely that Evan earned another Battle Star for the Sicilian Campaign.

In February 1944 Evan wrote that he was in Italy and been transferred to a different squadron. It is assumed that he remained with the same bomb group. His duties did remain the same. A June 1945 entry in the NAO reported that during this time Evan's Air Service Squadron had earned a Meritorious Service Award. The award recognized that during the hectic days when large-scale daily missions were an absolute strategic necessity, the men of his squadron had worked untiringly to keep an exceedingly high percentage of bombers on operational status. Their efforts had made it possible for US aircraft to deliver hard blows to Nazi supply lines and industrial targets.

Evan did not return home until August 1945. His arrival date in Italy is not known. It is likely that Evan received battle credit for most if not all the Italian campaigns. He may also have received credit for other European campaigns such as Rhineland and Central Europe. Evan was discharged September 5, 1945.

Anzio

Anzio was originally known as Antium. Two Roman Emperors, Caligula, a megalomaniac, and Nero, who had his mother murdered, were both born there.

Hell's Half-Acre - The Anzio Beachhead
Name given by the soldiers and nurses who were there - From the book, "And If I Perish"

"The nurses worked with the doctors and in the operating rooms through bombardment of all kinds, day and night. It seems to me that they were among the real heroes of Anzio."
General Mark Clark. From the book, "And If I Perish."

Anyone who thinks women cannot perform under combat conditions should read, "And If I Perish" The Author

"Rear echelon commanders" did not exist at Anzio – everyone on or off shore was within range of enemy fire."
From "And If I Perish" by Evelyn M. Monahan and Rosemary Neidel-Greenlee

Franklin L. Brown of Fillmore entered the service on September 4, 1942 although he may not have started training until September 18. Like most World War II Army veterans, his records were destroyed in the St. Louis fire. As a result, the National Personnel Records Center in St. Louis has only been able to provide limited information. This information is contained on his final pay voucher and two summary medical reports. An item in the NAO in June 1945 indicates that he served in Italy.

The medical reports indicate that Franklin likely started his service as a member of a Coastal Artillery unit. He may have also, for a short period, been assigned to an airborne unit. It appears that he spent most of his time in the service with an anti-aircraft (AA) unit.

While he may have gone overseas with an AA unit, it is also possible that he was a replacement for an AA unit that went overseas possibly as early as 1942. However, based on the available information, he likely was shipped overseas in 1943 or even early 1944. The first entry in the NAO that indicates he was overseas was published in May 1944.

The NAO reported in that May 1944 entry that, based on a letter he wrote his mother, he had been wounded in battle. The summary medical report indicates that he was wounded in April, 1944 both in the head and foot. The two wounds were caused by artillery shell fragments. He was treated at a Station Hospital. He was there for 81 days and was unable to return to duty until July, 1944. The only US campaign active during that time period in Italy was the Anzio Campaign. While he could have been wounded in several different locations, chances are it was during one of the vicious battles raging as American forces attempted to break out of the Anzio area. By the time he returned to duty in July, the Anzio Campaign was over and the American Army had entered Rome. He still likely participated in the Rome-Arno Campaign as that lasted until September 9, 1944.

He also likely participated in the North Apennines Campaign. That campaign took place during the period September 10, 1944 until April 4, 1945. A second medical report on Franklin reports him being treated for an unspecified injury (or sickness) in November, 1944. It was likely a minor problem. The report contains minimal information but does indicates that he did not stay in the hospital.

The last major campaign of the Italian phase of the war was the Po Valley Campaign. It lasted from April 5, 1945 until May 8, 1945. Franklin's final payment voucher states he arrived back in the US on June 2, 1945. Therefore, it is possible but unlikely that he participated in the Po Valley Campaign. By this time there were not a lot of enemy planes left to be shot down.

The final pay voucher appears to indicate that Franklin was discharged on June 30, 1945 although the voucher also states that the men receiving their final pay were discharged June 13, 1945. The June 13 date is more likely the correct date as the NAO reported in June 1945 that he was honorably discharged on May 13,1945. Since he did not arrive in the US until June 2, it is likely that the NAO reported the wrong month and he was discharged on June 13, 1945. The discharge occurred at Fort Dix, NJ.

Milton C. Rathbun of Houghton was one of the soldiers there. Whether he helped name Anzio beach "Hell's Half Acre" is not known.

Milton, a 1935 FCS graduate, joined the US Army January 22, 1942, one of the first men to enter the service after the attack on Pearl Harbor. He served in three different armies (5th Army, 7th Army and 3rd Army) during his enlistment, and fought his way through Italy, France and Germany. By July 1945, Milton was in Munich, Germany, one of the birthplaces of the Nazi movement. There was no one around claiming to be a Nazi by the time Milton and the American Army got there.

Milton served with the 645th Tank Destroyer Battalion. It is not certain when Milton joined the 645th. It appears that he took his basic training at Fort Devens in Massachusetts. The 645th was activated December 15, 1941 at Fort Berkeley, TX. The NAO reported that Milton went overseas in April of 1943, and the 645th sailed from Norfolk, VA in April, arriving in Oran, Algeria on May 11, 1943. Milton almost surely was with the Battalion at that time. The NAO also reported in July, 1945 that he had spent over two years overseas in a tank destroyer battalion. The 645th spent two months in North Africa before sailing for Italy, landing at Salerno (Paestum) on September 9th. This was the first of some 605 days the Battalion would serve in combat. The Battalion was supporting the 36th Infantry Division at that time. The battalion pushed forward to Benevento, crossed the Volturno River, and climbed the mountains above Venafro. During this push the battalion was supporting the 45th Infantry Division. They then received a short break before landing with the 45th at Anzio. Anzio would prove to be a hell hole. The 45th and the 645th would spend four months there, crammed into a pocket of some 100 square miles with the rest of the Allies forces. There were constantly under attack from German artillery and planes that commanded more favorable positions. In May, the breakout occurred and the rush was on to Rome, which was captured June 5, 1944. The headlines of the capture lasted one day. D-Day at Normandy occurred June 6th.

The 645th did not have time to ponder this event. With Rome captured they were pulled out of the line for more amphibious training. During this period, General Order No 1, dated June 15, 1944 awarded Milton his Good Conduct Medal. On August 15, 1944, the 645th landed near Saint Maxime in France during the Southern France invasion. With this landing, Milton, and others in the 645th Battalion earned their third Assault Badge. Still supporting the 45th Infantry Division, they headed north through the Vosges Mountains. As mentioned elsewhere, many experts considered a winter offensive through the Vosges Mountains unlikely to succeed. The experts were wrong. Despite stiff defenses (the Germans were fighting furiously defending their homeland) cold and snow, the 45th fought its way into Germany, and assaulted the Siegfried line. The advance was then halted as they were forced to confront the German "Nordwind" winter offensive.

The German offensive was beaten back and, in the spring, the 645th once again resumed its relentless drive into the German heartland. It also converting from the M10 tank (3-inch guns) to the M36 (90 mm guns). Breaching the Siegfried line at Homburg, they crossed the Rhine at Mainz and roared through Mannheim, Bamberg, Harr, and Nurnberg. On May 7, they crossed the Blue Danube and helped take Munich, another birthplace of the Nazi party.

The battalion served as part of the occupation forces in Munich and Dachau from May 2 to September 29. Milton appears to have been rotated home a little earlier than the battalion, and was discharged September 29, 1945.

Up The Boot

Royden F. Bentley of Granger enlisted in the service May 25, 1943, but he did not enter until June 8th. It is not clear where Royden was assigned during his first six months. He likely went through basic training and then maybe some technical training. Since he worked for the US Postal Service prior to entering the service, he may have been directly assigned to the US Army Mail Service following basic. Whatever his initial assignments, by December 1943 he was on his way to North Africa. It is not clear to which unit, if any, Royden was assigned during his first months of service in North Africa, but he eventually was assigned to the 20th Base Post Office, probably in April of 1944.

The 20th was activated on April 25, 1944, in Algiers and it is likely that Royden was assigned at that time. Items in the NAO reported that Royden was in Naples, Italy by June of 1944, and the 20th did move, via Oran, to Naples on June 15, 1944. The History of the 20th Base Post Office indicates that PFC Bentley was in the 182nd Station Hospital in Naples in July 1944. This was during the height of the Rome-Arno campaign, and records indicate that the 20th did receive credit for participating in that campaign.

However, it does not appear that the 20th set up formal operations although it did participate in mail delivery activities. Royden wrote home saying that the weather in Naples was great and that he had gone swimming several times. He also got to see Mount Vesuvius while it was smoking.

In July Royden sent a copy of the Mediterranean issue of the *"Stars and Stripes"* to the NAO. (It took two months for the paper to arrive.) He also related that he had been promoted to Private First Class. The history of the 20th indicates he was a PFC when he was in the hospital in July. It is likely during this time that the 20th was preparing for a further move. In September 1944 the 20th did move to St. Tropez in southern France, arriving on September 9. It then moved quickly to Marseilles. The 20th history indicates that this was the first time that the 20th had functioned as a unit since its organization. This move was part of the invasion of Southern France, for which the 20th also received credit. Assuming Royden was with the initial 20th staff to arrive in France on September 9, he would have received credit for the campaign and earned his second battle star. The 20th also received credit for the Rhineland Campaign, earning Royden his third battle star.

The 20th now went about the business of setting up a Post Office, while at the same time receiving, sorting and delivering vast quantities of mail, packages and other services. It hauled mail to Poligny, Vesoul, Lyon, and Nice, while still setting up the post office in a bombed-out building that was once part of the French Post Office system. Their living quarters were in a bombed out former shipyard company building. They were also involved in repairing the facilities as they carried out their postal duties. Those duties were enormous. They included sitting up incoming and outgoing mail, handling mail for units not yet in France but whose mail had been forwarded, an official mail section, a pouch section (first class mail), a section for units in the vicinity of the post office or who were passing through staging sites in the area. There was also a section for mail to the states and a parcel post section. The finance section became operational on September 20 and in the first four and one-half hours 45,000 money orders worth two and one-half million dollars were issued. The transportation section was so busy (outgoing and bulk mail) that they had to use 100 German prisoners each day to meet the demand. During Christmas, local units had to supply men to assist with the workload. In November, they got the V Mail Section working. The V Mail added greatly to the work load and the technical expertise required, but saved enormous amounts of space. In December, the 20th received 901 rolls of film which contained 1,148,619 letters.

In April of 1945, Royden was detailed to a post office in Antwerp, Belgium where he spent six months. In October, he was returned to the 20th in Marseilles and rotated home. He was discharged November 18, 1945.

Leonard O. Blakeslee of Centerville entered the service February 13, 1943. Leonard served the next two and a half years in the Zone of Interior. While the bases he served on have not been identified, it is likely, following basic training, that he did serve in the Quartermaster Corps with a Salvage Unit.

On June 14, 1945, according to his discharge document, he sailed for the Mediterranean Theater of Operation (MTO) where he was assigned to the 218th Quartermaster Salvage and Repair Company. The company was located at Depot Q-5N55 in Naples. He arrived in Italy on June 25, 1945 and at the depot on July 1, 1945. The 218th history indicates two enlisted men joined the company that day and one of them was likely Leonard.

The 218th was the first Salvage and Repair unit in the MTO area. It was first assigned to North Africa, where among other areas, it served in Oran, Algeria. On January 1, 1945 it moved from Oran to Taranto, Italy and then to Naples on January 8, 1945. There it took over all operations at Salvage Depot Q-5N55.

Those operations primarily involved salvaging and repairing shoes, clothing and textiles, but also tents, canvas cots, webbing equipment, typewrites, adding machines, and other business machines. It operated a reclamation shop to reclaim usable products and materiel. In addition, it was charged with training and managing Italians as salvage workers, and utilizing them in the company's work.

Leonard served as a salvage technician. As such he may have been primarily involved in gathering all types of salvage materials rather than repairing such items. The Army definition of a salvage technician provides that the technician assists in the collection, classification, and disposition of salvageable material and equipment. The technician classifies salvage with respect to the supply service originally issuing each item of equipment, determines salvage value, and separates salvage into repairable and non-repairable, critical, and non-critical, ferrous and nonferrous materials.

The war in Italy was officially over when Leonard arrived in the country. The last American campaign, the Po Valley Campaign, officially ended May 8, 1945. Leonard arrived back in the US on March 1, 1946. He was discharged March 6, 1946 at Fort Dix, NJ.

Lloyd D. Clark of Hume was a member of the 338th Field Artillery Battalion, 88th Infantry Division, one of the most distinguished Field Artillery Units of WW II. The Battalion had sailed, with the Division, to North Africa on December 15, 1943. By February 4, 1944 it was on its way from Oran to Naples, Italy. From its landing in Naples until the end of the war in May 1945, the Division would spend some 344 days in combat. It would participate in three different campaigns (Rome-Arno, North Apennines, and the Po Valley) earning three Battle Stars. It would be recognized for its outstanding work in central Italy by the French Government, no less, which awarded the Division the French Croix de Guerre with Palm. It battled and defeated the German 71st and 94th Divisions at the Gustav Line.

Praise of the work of the Field Artillery, of which Lloyd was a part, was common. On July 12, 1944 during a horrific battle in the Villamagna area of Italy, for instance, the Commander of 1st Infantry Battalion sent a message saying, "Magnificent Artillery Support. Best I have Even Seen." The Commanding Officer of the 2nd Battalion, 350th Infantry Regiment also lauded the Artillery. His message read, "Beautiful Support. With that kind of support, we can go anywhere."

Lloyd D. Clark proved over and over that he was as good as the Battalion. During a savage battle on July 12, enemy artillery hit the gas tank of an ammunition truck. A blazing fire threatened to explode the ammunition on the truck and endanger the entire battalion. Several men, including Lloyd, without regard to their personal safety, proceeded to unload the ammunition from the truck even as the flames licked at the ammunition cases. Several of the men later had to be evacuated to hospitals. All the men, including Lloyd, received a Commendation Letter from Brigadier General Kurtz, Commanding General, Division Artillery.

In August, Lloyd was wounded in action and earned a Purple Heart. His Artillery Battalion was engaged in a slug fest with German artillery a few miles east of Firenzuola on the Santerno River. On the 23rd, the entire battalion was shelled and several men including Lloyd were wounded. Lloyd was treated for his wound by the 12th General Hospital. The NAO reported that Lloyd had been slightly wounded in action on September 24th, but the Battalion's history reports him wounded in August.

Lloyd had already proved his courage prior to his Purple Heart as described above. On June 2nd, the Battalion was positioned on Highway 6, opposite Rocca Priora. Lloyd and three other men volunteered to serve as observers, thereby endangering their lives. For this they were awarded the Bronze Star for Valor. The Bronze Star citation for this action reads as follows:

"On 2 June 1944, the above-named enlisted men voluntarily occupied an observation post and radio relay  station on Mount Daddo, Italy. While in position, the above-name men came under direct small arms fire. Their voluntary action with disregard for personal safety enabled the battalion to maintain the close liaison essential to a direct support battalion and contributed materially to the flow of information vital to the operations and the division. Their actions reflect the highest tradition of the service." *The above photograph shows Lt. Colonel Richard P. Lively, Battalion Commander, awarding Lloyd and his fellow volunteers their Bronze Stars. Lloyd is the third soldier from the right in the photo. (Military photo)*

Like all good soldiers, it is likely that Lloyd was most proud of his Good Conduct Medal. His was for fidelity, efficiency and exemplary behavior during the Italian Campaign, according to the NAO. Given his performance under fire, citing him for "exemplary behavior" may have understated things just a little. It appears that Lloyd was discharged in November 1945.

Roland C. Dunn of Granger entered the service November 4, 1942. The NAO reported in January, 1943, that he was at Fort Riley, KS. It is likely that he left Fort Riley in January and moved to Fort Carson, MI. There was military police training at Fort Riley, and Roland was to spend his service years as a military policeman; it is likely that he received his basic training at Riley. At Fort Carson, he joined up with the unit he would serve with, the 794th Military Police Battalion, and went through extensive military police training. The 794th was formed at Carson, and the training included everything from military law, courtesy, discipline, judo (important for self-protection and for making arrests without undo violence), weapons disassembly and assembly, and gas drills. They even practiced traffic control. There were ample opportunities for social activities, both on the base and in the nearby towns (Battle Creek and Kalamazoo), but the training was intense. On February 22, they departed for Fort Dix. While they expected to be shipped overseas immediately, it was the usual military hurry up and wait. They did not ship out until March 19, and didn't arrive in Arzew, North Africa until April 14. They had sailed aboard LSTs 306, and 335. The NAO reported in May that Roland had safely arrived overseas.

Their first duty assignment was Casablanca, where they relieved the 101st Military Police. Duties included static and walking guard duty, along with motor and motorcycle patrols. They conducted frequent raids on black market operations, recovering everything from nails to trucks. They investigated bombings, drownings and other non-battle deaths, and tracked down deserters. This at times included British soldiers. There was also escort service for POWs, convoys, and protection of prominent or political personnel. During Roland's time in North Africa, this included both General Mark Clark, and General Charles De Gaulle. The most strenuous and nerve-racking job was at the Military Police Station. The noise was constant, from typewriters (pounding out reports, forms on everything, letters, and statistics.) and phones, to drunks yelling. It was always full of offenders, both military and civilians. One of their jobs was to stop civilians from taking advantage of the soldiers. Maybe the most dangerous job was handling drunks. Mobs of drunks would beat up the military police. On one occasion, a drunken soldier with a knife almost killed one of the men in Company A.

On September 22, 1943, they were assigned to the Military Railroad Service, a duty that would occupy them for the balance of the war. Their first assignment was in Algiers. They were shipped there in a train on December 2. A WAC detachment was also aboard. There was almost a riot when volunteers were solicited as guards for the WAC car.

In late March 1944 the Battalion sailed aboard the British ship *V.M. Derbyshire* from Oran to Naples. It then moved by train and by truck to its new base, Casa Giove, near Caserta, Italy. Its job remained the same: to guard all the equipment and supplies in the railroad yards and along the many miles of Allied railroad. Roland's company was specifically responsible for the railroad arteries from the town of Aversa to the front lines, as well as the large Aversa yards. The NAO reported that Roland had written that shortly after arriving in Italy he had run into Glenn Williams of Centerville. It was the first time he had met up with someone from home since he had entered the service.

Headquarters, 749th Military Police Battalion General Order No. 5, dated May 18, 1944, announced that Roland had been awarded the Good Conduct Medal. Of all their medals, the FCSD area men seemed most proud of their Good Conduct Medals.

The Battalion was now essentially working for the Military Railroad Service (MRS). The MRS was over-burdened and their communication system was virtually nonexistence. The Military Police had an excellent communications system. Agreement was reached whereby the Military Police Battalion would provide communication services for the MRS. The big push to Rome was on, and in June of 1944 TNT was discovered in the Aversa yards. Sabotage became a constant problem. By June 30, the rail route to Rome was open. Men from the 794th provided protection on the first run from Naples into Rome. It does not appear that Roland was on this trip. The train arrived in Rome on July 4th. The battalion was now providing static guard service in Rome. That lasted only until late September, when the battalion was shipped to southern France on October 1st. During this period the NAO reported that Roland was recovering from a case of malaria. Nevertheless, he made the trip to France. Company A was stationed in Lyon, and assigned to guard Lines 10 and 11, Grenoble to Bourg, and Bourg to Dole. By November, the Battalion was guarding all trains, American and French. The Battalion also became friends with Free French Forces in the area. The French commander sent a letter thanking the 749th for its assistance and kindness. The last paragraph reads, "Let the present letter be a token of Franco-American Friendship for the present, and for the days to come, after the war, when our arms have won victory over the Nazi barbarity."

December 1944 started sadly when one of the men was killed in a train accident. Others were injured. But the trains were running, in ever increasing numbers, as the Allies swept across France. The men held American-style Christmas parties with special passes and an excellent dinner. Gifts, everything from kids toys to alarm clocks, were handed out. The NAO reported in January that Roland had written thanking the Junior Red Cross and the Rotary Club for the Christmas boxes they had sent. He also thanked his friends who had sent cards.

The 794th continued to provide its protective services in 1945, in both France and Germany. During late 1944, and the first three months of 1945, the Battalion and Roland, earned their fourth and final battle star during the Rhineland Campaign. Roland would remain in Europe for most of 1945. When he was finally discharged November 4, 1945, he had spent exactly three years in the service, with all but five months of it overseas.

William B. Parker of Hume is remembered by friends and family as a hard-working, fun-loving guy. Bernard Mills remembered the first day Bill opened a checking account at the State Bank of Fillmore. He immediately went across Main Street to Watson's Drug Store and purchased a five-cent candy bar, and paid for it with a check.

Bill was pretty good with a rifle. During basic training at Fort McClellan, AL, he astounded his instructors by scoring 200 out of 200 on the shooting range, easily earning his sharp shooting badge. Many of his instructors, according to the NAO, had considered such a score impossible.

By December 1944, Bill was on his way to Italy. There he was assigned to the newly formed 473rd Infantry Regiment. The 473rd was created in January of 1944 out of the 2nd Armored Group, primarily the 434th, 435th, 532nd, and 900th Anti-Aircraft Artillery Automatic Weapons Battalions, and new replacements like Bill. Anti-Aircraft Battalions were being converted to infantry since they were no longer needed for anti-aircraft duty.

On February 21, 1945, the 473rd was attached to the famous, primarily black, 92nd Infantry Division. Another regiment assigned to the 92nd was the all Japanese-American 442nd Infantry Regiment, the most decorated regiment of the war.

The 473rd was committed to battle on February 14, 1945. It was attached to the 92nd on February 23, and remained with the division until May 12, 1945. It engaged in bitter fighting as it fought its way north through Cutigliano, the Serchio Valley, Massa, the Gothic Line, Sarzana, and Genoa. The fighting was fierce. During just the period April 13 to April 18, the regiment suffered 250 casualties. By that time the 473rd had helped capture Genoa, it had taken over 11,000 prisoners. At Genoa, the German Colonel controlling the Monte Mora area arrogantly tried to bargain with the regiment. He agreed to not fire on Genoa and the US troops provided he and his men were left alone in their fort. Instead, land, sea and air attacks were quickly organized. The German Colonel surrendered his men and his position. In just seven months, the 473rd had been formed, trained, and fought in the decisive battles for Italy. The Germans in Italy surrendered on May 2nd. The 473rd was deactivated in August.

Bill served in Italy until the deactivation, some three months following the end of the war. His sister Dolores remembers that he served as a Military Policeman guarding prisoners of war during part of this time, probably after the German surrender. He even sent her a post card with a picture of Mussolini on it. Giving his sharp shooting skills, it is unlikely that many POWs tried to escape, and even more likely that they did not get too far if they did try.

Bill returned to the states in mid-August 1945. He had flown some 7,500 miles from Italy through Casablanca in Africa, to South America and finally Miami in five days to get home. He heard the news of the Japanese surrender just prior to touching down in Miami. Bill served with the Military Police in Buffalo after returning. Home on leave in December 1945, he was discharged that same month.

Raymond I. Peck of Short Tract entered the service on March 11, 1943. He likely took his basic training and any advanced training at Camp Shelby, MS. In two weeks less than six months after induction, October 4, 1943, he was aboard a troopship heading for the war in Italy. He arrived October 21, 1943. Shortly thereafter, he was assigned to the 15th Infantry Regiment, 3rd Infantry Division. The 15th was one of the first units to arrive in the Mediterranean area and had already been in combat in North Africa, Sicily and Italy by the time Raymond arrived. He likely joined the 15th in mid-November at the Gustav line where the 15th had just been relieved after months of combat. The next month was spent in training and then the Regiment with Raymond headed back into battle. The NAO reported in January, 1944 that he was in Italy and had been in combat.

On January 22, the 15th landed at Nettuno, Italy and on the 22nd participated in a major battle at Cisterna. Cisterna was a bloody mess that eventually involved hand-to-hand combat. It was also part of the Anzio Campaign. The Regiment received a battle star for this campaign but Raymond's discharge document does not indicate he received the Anzio battle star. This is clearly an oversight since his records do indicate that he was wounded in battle on February 8 at Cisterna. He was hit by artillery shrapnel, was treated at an aid- station and returned to the battle. His record indicates that he received a Purple Heart for this action.

On February 29 the regiment faced the brunt of and repelled an all-out German attack which caused the German's heavy casualties. In April, the Regiment was still stuck at Anzio. Raymond, on a work detail slipped and badly twisted his back. This time he ended up in a hospital for 30 days. An April 1944 item in the NAO has Raymond assigned to an anti-tank unit. His hospital records list him as infantry and he did earn the Combat Infantry Badge. (In addition, the 15th Regiment received a Distinguished Unit Award, the French Fourragere, for its actions at the Colmar Pocket from January 22 to February 6, 1945. Raymond's records show that he shared in this award. (Another Distinguished Unit Award, this time just for the Anti-Tank Company, does not appear on his records.)

The Regiment was one of the leaders when, on May 23, 1944, the Allied forces finally forced their way off the Anzio beaches and headed for Rome. The 15th cut Highway 6, the main German supply line, leaving them no option but to retreat. On the way to Rome the 15th took on the elite Hermann Goeing Division that they had previously met in Sicily. This time they trashed it. On June 5, 1944 Rome fell to the Allies. The celebration lasted one day. On June 6, 1944 the Allies landed at Normandy.

The 15th garrisoned Rome for a short period and then were withdrawn to begin amphibious training. On August 15, 1944 it landed at San Tropez as part of the Southern France invasion. It quickly headed east toward Germany. Taking town after town it also finished off a German infantry division. In late September it headed into the Voges Mountains to be part of the forces which destroyed the old belief that no army could fight their way through those mountains, especially in winter. They led one drive and then were pulled out to start another one on a different route, this one further north and through snow, rain and freezing temperatures. It smashed its way through the German winter line to the Meurthe River. On November 20 it crossed the Meurthe at night without the Germans even knowing. In the morning, they smashed the German defenses and again headed east. By November 26 they were through the mountains overlooking the Rhine Plain. They were the first American unit in history to fight their way to the Rhine through the Voges Mountains. It had taken them two months to trash a long held military belief. Their guns were now trained on what remained of Hitler's Third Reich.

They stopped their advance at this point to help clear the Colmar pocket for which, as pointed out earlier they earned the French Fourragere. It was another bloody battle, but the pocket was secured and the Regiment now headed into Germany. They smashed through the Siegfried Line, crossed the Rhine and captured more towns. In April in what turned out to a fierce block by block battle they took Nurnberg. Augsburg and Munich. The Third Reich no longer existed.

The NAO reported Raymond home in November. He had arrived back in the states on November 13, 1945, visited the area and then was discharged on November 19, 1945 at Fort Dix. The 15th Infantry did not return home until September 1946. At some point, maybe in May 1945 Raymond was transferred to the 216th AAA Battalion and apparently shipped home with that unit. This is possible since Raymond was in the hospital in May with a bacterial skin infection and a decision may have been made when he was released to ship him home rather than back to his regiment.

As previously indicated Raymond's records do not show that he earned a battle star for Anzio. He obviously did since he was wounded there. The records also do not show a star for Rome-Arno. The time period for that award is January 9 to September 9, 1944. There is nothing to indicate that Raymond was not with the 15th during that period. His records also show he received credit for the 15th Distinguished Unit Award for the period January 22 to February 6, 1945. Therefore, it is likely that he did in fact earn the Rome-Arno battle star and it was accidentally omitted from his records.

Audie L. Murphy, cited as the most decorated soldier of World War II, served with the 15th Infantry Regiment. General Eisenhower and General Arnold also serve with the 15th early in their military careers.

Carroll S. Phipps was born in Granger, lived in Pennsylvania, and enlisted at Media, PA on December 10, 1941, three days after Pearl Harbor. He was one of the first men to volunteer after Pearl Harbor. It appears he took his basic training at Fort Meade, MD. According to his Pennsylvania Compensation World War II Application he served in the United States from December 10, 1941 until October 5, 1944. He was then shipped overseas where, according to the NAO he joined the 45th Infantry Division. The 45th had been overseas since June of 1943, first in North Africa, then Sicily and finally Italy where Carroll joined the Division around December 23, 1944 probably at Rambillors. The 45th had seen a lot of combat by the time Carroll arrived. It was to see a lot more. With Carroll aboard it attacked forts north of Metzig blocking German access to the plains of Alsace. It then crossed the Eintzel River and pushed through the famed but ineffective Maginot Line. The German last gasp winter offensive was now on and the 45th held its line for the balance of the winter. During this break it was reassigned to VI Corps. As spring arrived it was reassigned again, this time to XV Corps for the final push into Germany. It now again smashed through the Siegfried Line, a still ineffective line as far as holding back the American Army was concerned, on March 17. On March 21 it took Hamburg, a city that had suffered massive bombing raids. A major industrial center, Hamburg had ships, U-Boat pens, and oil refineries that the Allies were determined to destroy. Following Hamburg, the 45th crossed the Rhine and took Aschaffenburg and Nuremburg. It now crossed the Danube and liberated 32,000 prisoners at the Dachau death camp. It then captured Munich which it held and occupied for the balance of the war. As a result of its capture of Dachau, the 45th and Carroll are recognized as Liberators by the Holocaust Museum. The 45th was originally slated to be sent to the Pacific but that proved unnecessary, after the atomic bombs were dropped.

On September 12, 1945, Carroll returned to the states. He was discharged November 12, 19 at Camp Boone, Texas. Carroll earned three battle stars while serving with the 45th, Rhineland, Ardennes - Alsace and Central Europe.

Albert A. Roth of Houghton entered the service on September 3, 1942. He was immediately assigned to the 532nd Coast Artillery Battalion at Fort Bliss, TX. His address at Fort Bliss indicates he was assigned to Battery B. He may have been assigned to Headquarters Battery, or was transferred there at some point since the 532nd Journal shows that he was transferred from Headquarters Battery to Battery A on September 1, 1943. The battalion went through extensive training at Fort Bliss before being moved overseas on February 27, 1943. It arrived in Casablanca, French Morocco on March 9, 1943. It bivouacked just outside Casablanca waiting for its equipment, performing ship unloading duties to pass the time. A separate ship carrying their original equipment had been sunk by a German U-Boat on the trip overseas, so they had to wait for replacement equipment. The battalion itself was now designated the 532nd Anti-Aircraft Automatic Weapons Battalion.

Once armed they were moved into action. They provided anti-aircraft defenses for airfields in Montesquieu and Sedrata, Algeria from April 23 until June 28. They then took up positions to defend other airfields. From July 22 until they moved to Italy on October 28, they defended airfields at Protville and La Sebala, Tunisia. Arriving in Bagnoli, Italy (near Naples), on November 8, 1943, the 532nd was assigned to defend several different possible targets. These included ration and gasoline dumps near Teano and Venafro as well as Highways 6, 48 and 7. They also provided cover for troops and field artillery units. On January 20, 1944, they were assigned to support the crucial but unsuccessful Rapido River crossing near San Angelo. On March 11, the battalion moved to Sessa, Italy. It would remain in Sessa until it moved to Montecatini, Italy where it was disbanded January 14, 1945. It was credited, among other awards, with downing two confirmed Me-109's and 2 "probable's," (planes likely shot down, but unconfirmed.) It earned four battle stars.

It is likely that Albert served with the unit until it was disbanded. A July 2, 1944 entry in the 532nd Journal states that he had been "placed on TD (temporary duty) with Fifth Army Broadway Bill's Restaurant effective 22 July 1944." It is likely that the restaurant was located at one of the rest areas for combat veterans. Apparently, men from combat units were assigned duties at such rest areas from time to time. Albert, according to his entry at the World War II Memorial, was officially transferred at some point to the 2633rd Service Company. He was assigned as a sales clerk/cashier. His experience at Broadway Bill's may have been the reason he was assigned to a service company when his anti-aircraft battalion was disbanded. The NAO reported that Albert was discharged in September of 1945

Gerald F, Saunders of Hume entered the service January 4, 1943. The family moved to the Fillmore area in early 1940. It appears they may have had a place in Higgins. Gerald, called Jerry, post-war married June Haskins of Centerville. He was initially stationed at Army Basic Training Center in Miami Beach. By March 1943 he was at Scott Field, IL where he was promoted to Private First Class. By May 1943 he was still at Scott Field according to the NAO. It appears that he was permanent party at Scott as his discharge papers do not show any training for him at that location. The NAO reported him still stationed there when his parents met him in Buffalo when he had a few hours leave on Mother's Day.

By October 1943 he had been transferred to Lowry Field in Colorado. His discharge paper show that he received aircraft armaments training at Lowry. His papers also show that he attended the aerial gunnery school in Fort Myer, Florida. The airplane armorer's course at Lowry trained personnel to perform first and second echelon maintenance on all armament except bomb sights, remote control turret systems and related sights. Gerald spent about six months at Lowry. On July 10, 1944 he sailed for the Mediterranean Theater, arriving July 21,1944. At some point he was assigned to the 12th Air Force's 84th Bomb Squadron, 47th Bomb Group. He likely joined the 84th on Corsica where it had been stationed since July 15th.

The 84th was a battle-hardened group having been overseas since mid-1942. It had flown anti-submarine missions before leaving the states and had already earned battle stars for the Algeria-French Morocco, Tunisia, Sicily, Naples-Foggia, and Anzio Campaigns. It would earn four more in which Jerry would share for Rome Arno, Southern France, North Apennines, and Po Valley. It had starting flying night intruder missions in July 1944 as part of the Rome-Arno Campaign. It supported the Southern France invasion both from Corsica and Salon, France where it was located from September 5 until September 21, 1944. By September 23 it was at Follonica Air Field, Italy where it remained until October 4 when it moved to Rosignano Air Field, Italy. By January 2,1945 it was at Grosseto where it remained until June 22,1945 when it arrived in Pisa, Italy.

From its base at Follonica it joined the just started Northern Apennines Campaign. Its primary mission during this campaign was to attack German communications in northern Italy. The Germans last gasp in Italy was the Po Valley. It was also the last campaign of the war in Italy. The 84th earned its second Distinguished Unit Citation, and Jerry earned his first, during this campaign. During the period April 21 to April 24, in extremely bad weather over the mountainous regions of Northern Italy, the 84th, as well as the rest of the 47th Bomb Group, for 60 straight hours attacked and destroyed enemy transportation in the Po Valley. The result was chaos. It doomed the chances for any type of an organized retreat for the Germans troops.

During this period, the Squadron flew the A-20G until January 1945 when it received some A-26C's. Jerry's Military Occupation Code, 612 per his discharge with a title of Armorer Gunner, provided that his duties involved inspecting, repairing, and maintaining all aircraft armament, including bomb release mechanisms, airplane canons, machine guns, and auxiliary equipment. However, his discharge also indicates that he earned the Air Crew Member Badge (Wings) and that he earned three Air Medals. The

Aircrew Badge was awarded to personnel who served as aircrew members on military aircraft. During World War II, the award criteria for the Air Medal varied all over the place depending on the theater of operations. However, it always involved type of aircraft flown and missions accomplished. In European operations it also considered that the airspace was enemy controlled in many locations and that heavy air defenses were encountered. Since Jerry received three Air Medals it is obvious that he participated in several combat missions. One criterium provided for the award of an Air Medal for every five combat missions. Records on missions flown by the 84th were not available for review.

Jerry returned to the states on June 23, 1945 arriving July 9. The NAO reported him home on a 30-day furlough in July 1945. He was discharged October 11, 1945 at Seymour Johnson Field, NC.

Kent M. Weaver of Hume was a student at Cornell University when he entered the service on March 21, 1944. After four months of basic training at Camp Wheeler in Georgia, and three months of advanced training at Camp Meade in Maryland, Kent was ready for a different type of education. He was now a full-fledged infantryman and would soon join Company D, 133rd Infantry Regiment, 34th Infantry Division.

On September 23, 1944, he sailed aboard the Queen Elizabeth from NYC to Scotland arriving the first of October. He later moved to France. On October 30, he flew to Italy where as a replacement, he was assigned to Company D. He likely arrived just as the bloody battle in the Mount Belmonte area was ending. He may have been and likely was a replacement for one of the men killed in the battle. He was joining a regiment and division that had a rich combat history. It had already earned three battle streamers (Naples - Foggia, Rome-Arno, and Tunisia). During Kent's tour with the division and regiment it would earn two more, North Apennines and Po Valley). With winter underway, the 133rd and Kent, began several months in an active defense of its area. This defense would last until the spring.

During the next five months, in bitter cold and many snow storms, the regiment was under constant artillery and mortar attacks. Occasionally there were air attacks. Primarily the regiment conducted constant combat patrols. As the winter progressed, the frequency and intensity of the patrols increased. There were also attacks on various German positions. To break up the winter, some men were lucky enough to receive passes to visit Florence and the rest and recreation facilities at Montecatini Terme. The entire 133rd Regiment spent a week there in November. General George Marshall also visited the 133rd and on February 21, 1945, personally awarded medals earned by several men.

As the snow melted and the weather got warmer, the 133rd and other units exploded out of their winter defenses and smashed their way 420 miles across the Po Valley helping to destroy nine German and three Italian Fascist Divisions. On May 2 the Germans surrendered unconditionally.

With the war over, the 133rd and other units started rotating many of its veterans back to the states. Kent, as a relative newcomer, did not have the points to be rotated home. Instead, he, along with 1,888 other men from the 133rd were transferred to Company D, 349th Infantry Regiment, 88th Infantry Division in October.

The 349th was engaged in occupation duties when Kent arrived. Their primary duties were guarding and processing German POWs and friendly foreign nationals. In December Company D of the 349th was assigned to the United Nations designated Free Territory of Trieste. The area was an independent territory between Northern Europe and Yugoslavia facing the north part of the Adriatic Sea. It was originally Italian territory and then part of Austria. The Treaty of Rapallo in 1920 returned the territory to Italy. After the war both Russia and Tito of Yugoslavia tried to annex the area. The troops sent to guarantee its independence were primarily garrisoned in Gorizia, Canaro, and Trieste. Kent and the 349th were in

Trieste. In February Kent was sent to a replacement depot. He was rotated back to the states in early February and discharged at Fort Dix February 13, 1946.

Motor Torpedo Boats

Motor Torpedo Boats, or as they are more commonly known, PT Boats, rank among the glamour weapons of WW II. At least that is the image they hold today. That image is due to both fact and fiction. The John Wayne fiction movie "They Were Expendable" had a major impact on the public's positive perception of PT Boats. More importantly, one of the episodes in that movie is the true rescue of General Douglas MacArthur and his family from the Philippines. MacArthur and his family were rescued by PT Boats. The Commander of the boats that rescued MacArthur was John D. Bulkeley. He was awarded the Medal of Honor for leading the rescue. President John F. Kennedy was also commander of a PT Boat. Serving on PT boats was dangerous. The popular image, and one advanced by the movie, was of the boats speeding in against a Japanese warship, launching its torpedoes and speeding away. In reality the wooden hulk ships could be destroyed even by a close miss from the guns of an enemy ship. MT boats would more often sneak in as close as possible, launch their torpedoes and then quickly depart.

The above examples all took place in the Pacific, and we tend to think of PT Boats as operating solely in the Pacific. In fact, they were in operation in most other theaters of WW II, including the Mediterranean.

Albert Eugene Ferrin of Centerville went to war on a PT Boat in the Mediterranean. He was a Gunner's Mate on PT-307. Albert, who went by Eugene or Gene, was a member of Motor Torpedo Boat Squadron 22, Eighth Fleet, commanded by Lt. Commander Richard J. Dressling. The Squadron, known as "RON 22," operated under British Coastal forces and saw action along the northwest coast of Italy and the southern coast of France. They were based on Bastia, Corsica, and later at St. Tropez, France. RON 22 was equipped with the Higgins-built PT Boat, the most rugged of the three types of PT boats built during the war. The squadron participated in the invasion of Elba on June 18, 1944, although it is likely that Gene had not yet arrived from the US. The squadron also likely participated in the Southern France invasion in September of 1944. A letter from Lt. Commander Dressling to Gene's parents indicates that Gene and RON 22 were involved in that invasion, and that Gene was with the squadron when it moved from Corsica to southern France.

On December 8, 1944, PT-307 was conducting a patrol off the Italian coast. A heavy swell engulfed the boat when it was about five miles off the coast of Leghorn, Italy. The swell smashed the men around the boat and three were injured. Two others, including Gene, were washed overboard. (The other man washed overboard was Lt. (JG) Paul Frank Fidler.) His shipmates reported that Gene's head was slammed into the torpedo tube as he went overboard and that he likely was unconscious when he hit the water. Searches were conducted by both PT 307, and later, by planes and other ships. Neither man was found. The official casualty report states that Gene was washed overboard by a heavy swell. His loss was in the line of duty and was not due to his own misconduct. His remains were never recovered.

There are only nine known World War II PT Boats still in existence. Two of those, PT-305 and 309, served with RON 22. PT- 305 is in the National WW II Museum in New Orleans and the other, RON 309, is in the National Museum of the Pacific War in Fredericksburg, TX. It appears that many of the boats were named by their crews, just like most airplanes. PT-305 in New Orleans, apparently had several names, including "Half Hitch', "Barfly" and "Sudden Jerk." PT- 309, commanded by Lt. Commander Dressling, was nicknamed "Frankie." Apparently, Dressling ran into Frank Sinatra in a bar in New York City before going overseas, and decided to name his boat after him.

It is not known if PT-307 had a nickname. Lt. Commander Dressling wrote Gene's parents, saying in part: "Your son died fighting for the freedom of all peoples from tyranny and for lasting peace in the world. If you could see how happy the people of France are to be liberated as your son and I have, you would be very proud of the work your son has done." (NAO 2/1945). I am sure Mr. & Mrs. Ferrin were proud of Gene, without seeing the liberated people of France. There is a memorial headstone for Albert Eugene Ferrin in Freedom Cemetery, Freedom, NY. He is also memorialized at the Florence American Cemetery in Via Cassia, Italy. Eugene's brother Bob was a classmate of the author.

15th Air Force

"I could never be so lucky again". General Jimmy Doolittle – from his 1991 autobiography.

The first commander of the 15th Air Force was Jimmy Doolittle. Doolittle led the famous surprise raid on Japan in 1942. He later made the above remark. In 1942 he had only a few B-25B's with minimum bomb loads to attack Japanese targets. In Italy, he had an entire Air Force and they made their own luck. The primary job of the 15th was to attack and destroy the oil refineries of eastern Europe, primarily Ploesti in Romania, but also synthetic oil plants in Silesia and Poland; to attack and destroy aircraft production, primarily in Wiener Neustadt and Regensburg in Germany; to attack and destroy, behind the lines, Axis communication and transportation systems in Italy, Austria, Germany, and German controlled territories; and to attack and destroy Axis ground forces. This latter included attacks at Salerno, Anzio, and Cassino as well as other attacks during World War II campaigns.

The FCSD area was well represented in the 15th Air Force in Italy. Donald R. Haskins, Ray E. Lilly, Lowell E. Mix, Melvin S. Slocum, Royal S. Strait, Robert L. Van Name and Warren M. Woolsey all served with the 15th.

Donald Robert Haskins of Centerville enlisted in the Army on July 1, 1942. Almost immediately he

Bronze Star Medal

wrote the *Northern Allegany Observer* wanting to boost the morale of those he left behind. In part. he wrote, "We have a great fight ahead of us -- not only on the battlefield, but right at home. We must all work together in order to do a good job. It may seem hard at times, but in these times, we must not fall-down on the job. We must stand erect, head up, grit our teeth and go into it fighting like the men and women we are. We must make our country a good place to live in and to raise our children in. None of us would like to live under Hitler's rule, so we must not fall along the way. We must keep on going and make it what we want it to be. You may think it is hard to lose your loved ones. It is just as hard for us. We are willing to give our lives to make a better country for the rest of you to live in and raise your children under better conditions."

After extensive training at Buckley Field, Colorado, Gowan Field, ID, Bruning Air Base NE and Kearns, UT, Donald was ordered to Muroc Field, CA from where he and the rest of the 456th Bomb Group would depart for Italy. The 456th arrived in Italy during December of 1943 and January of 1944. It would fly its first mission in February 1944. Donald flew to Italy on one of the Groups B-24's.

As Armament Chief for the 746 Bomb Squadron, Donald had to make sure that the armaments of the big Liberator bombers were in perfect condition for every mission. This specifically meant that the bomber's turrets, all its guns, its bomb racks, the automatic pilot, the bomb sights, and the chemical warfare equipment were all functioning properly. His duties also included the loading of the bombs.

All of this effort enabled the 456th to carry out devastating attacks on occupied Europe. The group flew over 100 missions during the war. It attacked marshalling yards, aircraft factories, railroad bridges, airdromes, oil refineries and storage facilities, locomotive works, and viaducts. It also flew missions supporting the US Fifth Army and the British Eighth Army, attacking gun positions, bridges, roads, and rail lines. After the war, it transported supplies to airfields in northern Italy.

Fifteenth Air Force targets were located throughout Europe, including Italy, Austria, Rumania, France, Germany, Czechoslovakia, Hungary, and the Balkans.

The work of the 456th did not go unnoticed. This Group was awarded two Presidential Distinguished Unit citations: one for an attack on Neustadt, Austria and the other for a raid on Budapest, Hungary. These awards recognized the contributions of all the men of the group in the success of the missions. In fact, the award for the Neustadt mission specifically stated, "Ground personnel worked feverishly, enthusiastically and with untiring intensity to get all type B-24 aircraft in the best mechanical condition to ensure the success of the operation."

Throughout the war, Donald continued to write to the *Observer*. In April 1944 the Observer reported that he had spent five days in a rest camp in Italy. That same month Donald wrote about flying past the volcano Vesuvius. He reported smoke was coming out of it and that had the day been clearer, it would have been a beautiful sight. In the same letter, he mentioned that Bob Van Name, another FCDS soldier, was visiting and had gone for ice cream (somewhere). Donald reported the ice cream had tasted "really good."

In June, he wrote that his outfit had adopted a small Italian boy about five or six years old. He was quite smart and had learned quite a bit of English. He could sing "Poppy Song" and "Pistol Packin' Mama."The 456th Bomb Group returned to the US in September of 1945, and Donald was discharged September 13th.

Ray E. Lilly entered the service on April 2, 1942. Ray was born and raised in Angelica. Following the war Ray made a career working for the Rochester Gas & Electric Company in its Fillmore office. Based on a report in the NAO in August 1945, it is likely that Ray was overseas by no later than July 1942. His wife, Winona Bennett, advised that he served as ground crew first with a P-38 Fighter Group in England, then North Africa and finally Italy. She also indicated that she believes he arrived overseas in July, 1942.

Ray working on a P-38 and having fun at the same time.

It appears that Ray had little if any basic training. Given the time between his entrance into the service and his shipment overseas, it appears possible and likely that he was assigned to P-38 maintenance, armaments and/or support training immediately. It is possible that such training took place at Twenty-Nine Palms Army Airfield in California. Twenty-Nine Palms was one of the few, if not the only location, where P-38 maintenance training was provided at this early point in the war.

Information on the exact group to which Ray was assigned has not been located. However, there were three P-38 fighter groups that moved overseas during the mid-1942 time period - the 1st ,14th and 82nd Fighter Groups. Ray probably was assigned to one of these, most likely the 1st Fighter Group as it arrived in England in June and July, 1942. The 1st was assigned to the 8th Air Force while in England and flew its first combat missions in August. These missions were against various targets in France.

By November 13, 1942, the group had been moved to Algeria, North Africa. It remained there a year, escorting bombers to various targets and providing air coverage for ground operations as part of the 12th Air Force. In November 1943 the group moved to Italy. Initially it was based at several different airfields.

By January 1944 it had settled at Salsola Air Field, part of the complex of airfields in the Foggia area. Ironically, during its stay in North Africa the group had flown missions attacking the Foggia airfields.

In Salsola the group primarily flew escort missions protecting bombers. These missions attacked targets in Italy, France, Germany, Czechoslovakia, Austria, Hungary, Bulgaria, Rumania, Yugoslavia, and Greece. Ray and the other maintenance men made sure the planes flown by the pilots of the 1st were as safe as possible on these deadly missions. By early 1945 targets were becoming scarce.

As the war wound down, the Group flew one last dramatic mission. It escorted the American and British delegations to the Yalta Conference (February 4 – 11, 1945). A total of 61 aircraft escorted the ships and planes carrying President Roosevelt. The 1st Fighter Group earned three Distinguished Unit Citations and 17 battle stars.

The NAO reported in August 1945 that Ray had spent a 30-day furlough in the Fillmore area. Based on his final pay record, he returned to Greensboro Air Force Base in North Carolina following his furlough. He was then transferred to Fort Dix, NJ on September 13, 1945 and was discharged on September 30, 1945.

Lowell E. Mix of Hume first entered the service in 1938 after graduating from Friendship Central High

School. He had spent most of the first 15 years of his life in Hume. When his mother died, he first went to live with relatives in Attica, NY, then with other relatives in Friendship. Lowell served with the Medical Department at a hospital on Fort Totten, NY during what would be his first enlistment, rising to the rank of Sergeant. It was during this enlistment that he earned his first medal. On May 8, 1941, Lowell and four other men saved a fellow soldier from drowning. The soldier was boating about 50 yards from shore in Little Neck Bay when an accident occurred in the rough water. The man fell overboard and was near death when Lowell and the other men, swimming from the shore, rescued him. He was brought ashore unconscious, and was revived by artificial respiration. Lowell and the others were awarded the Soldiers Medal. In October of 1941, Lowell left the service. *Picture – Soldier's Medal.*

In October 1942 Lowell decided it was time to return to military service, but this time as a pilot. He therefore took and passed the exam required to enter flight training. He trained at Maxwell Field, AL, Greenville Air Field, MS, Tyndall Field, FL, a base in Illinois, and finally Davis-Monthan Air Field in Arizona. By late 1943, he was on his way to North Africa to join the 98th Bombardment Group, a heavy bomber group. He was assigned to the 344th Bomb Squadron.

Lowell told his wife Viola Buzzard Mix, whom he met in Friendship, that he flew 52 missions, but was only credited for 50. Records indicate that he flew 33 combat mission, although he may not have received credit for all 33. That may be because records show that at least once his plane turned back for mechanical problems, and a couple of times conditions preventing them from dropping their bombs. Viola said that he also flew some mail runs, and other non-combat missions.

Lowell's combat missions were over Italy, Austria, Germany, Romania, France, Yugoslavia, Bulgaria, Hungary, and Czechoslovakia. The largest number of missions was flown against Italian targets, in support of the Naples-Foggia and Rome-Arno campaigns. Other missions supported the Air Offensive Europe Campaign. The plurality of missions was flown against marshalling yards. They also attacked airdromes, aircraft production plants, oil refineries, railroad bridges, harbors, shipping, and a communication center. One mission was to the famous Brenner Pass. The purpose was to stop and/or hinder the supplies coming through the pass to the German Army. On most missions, Lowell flew as the co-pilot, but on July 12, 1944 to Theoule, France, July 13 to Brescia, Italy, and July 19 to Neuberg, Germany, he was the pilot. His first combat mission was on February 4, 1944 when the 344th attacked the marshalling yards at Ferrara, Italy. His last, on July 20, 1944 was to Freidrichshafen, Germany, where they knocked out an aircraft factory. Intense flak during that mission left holes in the plane's nose and left wing, and an aileron was shot off.

On virtually every mission, they faced anti-aircraft fire, most times, intense and accurate. Enemy fighters rose up to battle them on numerous occasions. But danger also came from other places. On March 30, 1944, while attacking the marshalling yards at Sofia, Bulgaria, Lowell's pilot, Captain Jerome J. Casper, was wounded when an empty shell casing from the plane in front of them crashed through the cockpit window. There was intense flak on that mission, but they left the city in flames. On the May 17 mission to attack the harbor at San Stefano, Italy, flak damaged their hydraulic fluid line. On June 26, when attacking the marshalling yards at Schwechat, Austria, they also faced intense flak, and were attacked by a German ME 109. The bombardier was hit in the eye, nose, and hand. The nose gunner was wounded in his cheek and left leg. A six-inch hole was blown out of the left flap. The radio was jammed on channel A for six hours. The heaviest flak was at Munich where they attacked the marshalling yards, and at Ploesti, where, on April 5, they attacked the marshalling yards and on April 24, when they attacked both the marshalling yards and oil refineries. On the April 5 mission, they reported many fighters, estimated from 50 to 100, including FW 190s, ME 210s, and 110s. Ball turret Albert Rattay claimed two shot-down and one probable that day.

Lowell returned to the states in August of 1944 having completed his tour of duty. He remained in the service until November of 1948. His wife Viola said that he decided to leave the service when he was notified that he was to be assigned to a remote Asian post where it would be difficult for his family.

Lowell's missions were 2/14/44 - Ferrara, Italy; 3/18/44 - Gorizia, Italy; 3/19/44 - Steyr, Austria; 3/30/44 - Sofia, Bulgaria; 4/2/44 - Steyr, Austria; 4/3/44 - Budapest, Hungary; 4/5/44 - Ploesti, Rumania; 4/15/44 - Bucharest, Rumania; 4/16/44 - Brasou; - 4/20/44 - Mestre, Italy; 4/23/44 - Schwechat, Austria; 4/24/44 - Ploesti, Rumania; 4/29/44 - Toulon, France; - 4/30/44 - Alessandria, Italy; 5/2/44 - Castle Maggiore, Italy; 5/7/44 - Bucharest, Rumania; 5/17/44 - San Stefan, Italy; 5/19/44 - Spezia, Italy; 5/22/44 - Porto d'Ascoli, Italy;   5/25/44 - Monfalcone, Italy; 5/26/44 - Nice, France; 6/9/44 - Munich, Germany; 6/10/44 - Trieste, Italy; 6/16/44 - Bratislava, Czechoslovakia; 6/22/44 - Udine, Italy; 6/25/44 - Toulon, France; 6/26/44 - Schwechat, Austria; 6/30/44 - Zagreb, Yugoslavia; 7/8/44 - Markersdorf, Austria; 7/12/44 - Theoule, France; 7/13/44 - Brescia, Italy; 7/19/44 - Neuberg, Germany; 7/20/44 - Freidrichshafen, Germany.

Melvin S. Slocum originally of Farmersville and Centerville, moved to the Hume area in the early 1940's. One year and three days after the attack on Pearl Harbor, Melvin entered the Army Air Corps. After basic training, in April 1943, he was transferred to Army Air Corps Radio and Communications School in Sioux Falls, South Dakota. In November 1943, he was moved to the Las Vegas Army Air Field for flexible air gunnery training. Following a leave in December of 1943, he moved to the Columbia, SC Army Air Field for B-25 Mitchell medium bomber crew and replacement training.

By May of 1944 he was in Africa, and shortly thereafter joined the 340th B-25 Bomb Group, at Alesan Airfield on Corsica, as a Radio Operator/ Gunner. (The 340th flew all its mission from Corsica during Melvin's time with the Group.) By at least May 18, 1944 he had joined the shooting war. He flew what was likely his first mission with the 486th Bomb Squadron that day. The target was the railroad bridge at Arezzo, Italy. He flew that mission with the R.W. Pike crew. British Spitfires accompanied the bombers on the mission, as they did on virtually all missions. Before the war was over, Melvin flew at least 56 additional missions. (There was also a mission where his crew was the alternative crew. It is not known

61

if they flew a mission that day.) Some 29 of the 56 other missions were flown with the Lieutenant (Lt) R.W. Middlekauff crew. Another 26 were flown with the first permanent crew he was assigned to, the Lt. K. G. Anderson crew. On May 27, 1944, June 5 and September 3, Melvin's crew flew 2 missions each day. His last mission was New Year's Day, January 1, 1945. The group attacked the Palazzolo, Italy railroad bridge that day.

On most of its missions the 340th Bomb Group attacked railroad and regular road bridges. But there were many other targets, including, fuel dumps, gun positions, ammunition dumps, repair facilities (trucks and tanks) troop positions, troop bivouac sites, supply areas, and viaducts. On a mission on May 31, 1944, Melvin's squadron attacked the town of Grotta Ferrata. Their purpose was to create a roadblock. On June 6, 1944, D Day, as the Normandy invasion began, Melvin's crew attacked the road bridge at Orvieto. On October 10, they dropped chaff at Casa Leccio while the rest of the squadron attacked troop bivouac and stores areas. The purpose of the chaff was to interfere with the accuracy of German anti-aircraft guns. (By this time in the war, Italy had surrendered, and the US was fighting only German troops in Italy.) On December 31, 1944, Melvin's crew again dropped chaff, but also took photos of the attack at Calliano.

On August 15, 1944, Melvin's crew participated in the invasion of Southern France by attacking gun positions at Frejus, France. The NAO reported in July 1944 that Melvin had been wounded by anti-aircraft fire while they were attacking supply installations. This was likely on July 3, 1944 while attacking fuel dumps at Ponte Lagoscuro, Italy. Following that mission, Melvin did not fly again until the August 15 invasion of Southern France mission. On September 23, 1944, the 340th helped sink the Italian cruiser *Taranto* in La Spezia harbor. The sinking bottled up the harbor, and the group received a distinguished unit citation for its action. That day Melvin's squadron attacked the railroad bridge at Piazzola, but the entire group was recognized by the September 23 citation. Both future Mercury 7 astronaut Donald "Deke" Slayton and *Catch 22* author Joseph Heller served with the 340th Bomb Group. Slayton served in the 486th Bomb Squadron, the same as Melvin, but no missions have been identified where they flew together. Heller was a bombardier with the 488th Squadron.

By March 1945 Melvin was back in western New York on furlough. He was discharged in August 1945 at Seymour Johnson Air Field in North Carolina.

Royal S. Strait, who lived in the village of Fillmore and whose dad Seymour worked for the town of Fillmore in the 1930's (his sister Ellen graduated from FCS in 1928) flew 35 missions (all in B-17s) with the 49th Bomb Squadron (Heavy), 2nd Bomb Group, 5th Bomb Wing, 15th Air Force, out of Amendelo Airfield, Foggia, Italy. (Fiorello LaGuardia, who was Mayor of New York City from 1934 to 1945, and many other US airman took their training in the US Air Force at Foggia during World War I, in accordance with an arrangement between the US and Italian governments. At the time, La Guardia was already a member of Congress. Foggia, by coincidence, was the ancestral home of his father.)

The 2nd Bomb Group, famous as the "2nd to None Group", flew some of the toughest missions of the 15th Air Force, including two to the Ploesti oil fields in Romania. Roy's first mission was to Verona, Italy on July 13, 1944. His last mission, 126 days later, was to Munich, Germany on November 16, 1944. (The grandmother of a friend of the author lived in Munich during the bombing. The author was introduced to her 50 years after the war. Her grandson introduced me and mentioned that I just returned from a visit to Germany, including Munich. The first words out of her mouth were how terrible the bombing had been.) Given the number of missions and the time span, it meant Roy averaged a mission every three and one-half days, or twice a week for four months.

Roy few as co-pilot on 30 of his missions and on the other five he was the navigator. Ten of his co-pilot missions were with the William Bedgood crew. All five missions as navigator were with different crews.

One mission to Hungary had to return early, probably due to mechanical problems. Two of the missions were in support of "Operation Dragoon" the invasion of Southern France. Somewhat unusual, the B-17 flown by the William R. Bedgood crew apparently was not named. However, some of the planes Roy flew in on other missions had rather colorful names, including the "Tuff Titt," the "Bataan Avenger," and the "Flying Latrine."

Five of Roy's missions were to Blechhammer, Germany. Blechhammer was one of the four main areas in Germany producing synthetic oil. Some 7,000 tons of bombs were dropped on the plants there. In addition to Italy, France, Romania, and Germany, Roy made trips to Hungary, Austria, Greece, Czechoslovakia, and Yugoslavia. The 15th was very ecumenical with its bomb loads.

Combat Missions flown by Roy Strait: 7/13/44, Verona, IT, 7/19/44, Munich, GE - 7/20/44, Memmingen, GE - 7/25/44, Linz, AU - 7/27/44, Budapest, HU - 7/31/44, Ploesti, RO - 8/2/44, Portes les Valence, - 8/7/44, Blechhammer, GE - 8/9/44, Gyor, HU - 8/13/44, Genoa, IT - 8/15/44 - Landing Beach, FR (Invasion of Southern France) - 8/18/44. Ploesti, RO - 8/24/44, Pardubice, CZ - 8/27/44, Blechhammer, GE - 8/28/44 , Vienna, AU - 8/29/44, Moravska Ostrave, CZ - 9/3/44, Sava RR Bridge, YU - 9/4/44, Genoa, IT - 9/5/44, Budapest, HU - 9/6/44, Oradea, RU - 9/13/44, Blechhammer, GE - 9/15/44, Athens, GR - 9/17/44,   Budapest, HU - 0/20/44, Budapest, HU - 9/21/44 - Debrecen, HU (early return, aircraft malfunction) - 9/22/44, Munich, GE - 9/23/44, Brux, CZ - 10/13/44, Blechhammer, GE - 10/14/44, Blechhammer, GE - 10/20/44, Brux, CZ - 11/1/44, Vienna, AU - 11/6/44, Vienna, AU - 11/7/44, Maribor, YU - 11/12/44, Blechhammer, GE - 11/16/44, Munich, GE.

Robert L. (Bob) Van Name of Hume entered the service on September 17, 1942. It is not known where he took his basic training but by December 1942 he was at Seymour-Johnson Field in North Carolina being trained as a B-24 Liberator Bomber mechanic. The initial training took about five months. In April 1943 he was moved to Chanute Field in Illinois. It is likely that he was trained on radio repair at Chanute. It is not known where he was trained next, but many B-24 mechanics received hydraulics training at Ypsilanti, Michigan and/or spend time at an aerial gunnery facility. It is likely that he spent most of 1943 in training. In December 1943 he was transferred to Italy with the 456th Bomb Group. He would spend the rest of the war at Stornara Field near Foggia, Italy. Also serving with the 456th was Donald Haskins, a friend of Bob's from the FCSD area.

Donald was assigned to the 746th Bomb Squadron. Bob was assigned to either the 744th, 745th or 747th Bomb Squadron. The NAO reported that they often got together to read the newspaper which usually arrived three or four at a time. They also reported that they read each-others mail. On one occasion when Bob visited, Don wrote that he brought some ice cream and they had a fun evening reading and eating.

The 456th participated in 10 different World War II campaigns earning 10 battle stars. The group also earned two distinguished unit (DCU) citations, one for a mission to Neustadt, Austria and the other for a mission to Budapest Hungary. It flew bombing missions against enemy airfields, factories, refineries, viaducts and railroads in Italy, France, Germany, Czechoslovakia, Rumania, Hungary, Austria, and the Balkans. The citation for one of the DCUs included an acknowledgement of the efforts of the ground crew. It read, "Ground personnel worked feverishly, enthusiastically and with untiring intensity to get all type B-24 aircraft in the best mechanical condition to ensure the success of the operation." The 456th achieved the highest rate (over 83%) of aircraft availability for combat missions in its Bomb Wing, the 304th. It lost 117 aircraft during the war, and many more were damaged and repaired by the ground crews to fly more combat missions.

The NAO reported in August 1945 that Bob was back from overseas and enjoying a 30-day leave. He reported to Fort Dix at the end of his leave where he was discharged on September 30, 1945.

Warren Morris Woolsey was a student at Houghton College when the war started. He had moved to Houghton in 1923 at the age of one with his parents. In 1942, Warren became an Air Cadet, but was assured he would be able to finish his education before being inducted. That almost worked out, Instead, he was called to active service in February 1943. He nevertheless received his degree in June 1943. By June, however, Warren was part way through his Army Air Force Training. He had completed his basic training at Atlantic City, NJ, and his basic academics at Norwich, VT, and was in Nashville, TN. He was at the point where he had to select his "job." Warren wanted to be a navigator, but the Air Force felt he would make a good pilot. They agreed to disagree and he became a bombardier. He quickly went through gunnery training in Las Vegas, NV and then bombardier training at Deming, NM. At Tucson, AZ, (Davis Monthan Air Field) the air crews were formed and learned to work together. He became part of the George Wilson B-24 Liberator crew. He would serve as bombardier and armaments officer.

In August 1944 the crew was shipped to Grottaglie Army Air Base, near Taranto in southern Italy, first on a made over freighter to Naples, and then by truck to the base. They were a replacement crew so they did not get to fly over in their own plane. Warren was now part of the 15th Air Force, 47th Bomb Wing, 449th Bomb Group (Heavy), 717th Bomb Squadron.

The 449th Bomb Group saw a lot of combat, as reflected in the number of campaigns in which it participated. During some 475 days of combat, it flew 254 combat missions. It attacked oil production, including the key refineries in Ploesti, Rumania which provided 30 percent of the Third Reich's oil, as well as synthetic oil plants in Silesia and Poland; flew missions designed to cut communications lines; disrupt transportation (road junctions and railroad marshalling yards) and the movement of ground forces; and helped destroy the German air force, both in the air and on the ground, including raids against aircraft production in Weiner Neustadt and Regensburg. Warren's group participated in "Big Week," flying three missions. On February 22, 1944, it attacked a ME 109 manufacturing complex at Regensburg. On February 23 it blasted a ball bearing factory in Austria, and on the 25th it went back to Regensburg. Warren and his crew arrived too late to participate in "Big Week." but it did take part in many dangerous and tough missions.

Warren completed 30 missions during his tour. He told The Fillmore History Club, that his flights were mostly to northern Italy, German-occupied Austria, and southern Germany. The closest his crew came to disaster was on Christmas Day, 1944. The mission was to Innsbruck to attack transportation lines, or, in the words of the report of the mission, "Innsbruck Main M/Y South Choke Point." Over the Brenner Pass (between Italy and Germany) Warren's plane was hit by a heavy concentration of flak. The waist gunner lost consciousness when his oxygen hose was cut. They survived but another plane was lost on that mission.

Warren's tour ended at the same time the war in Europe ended. He returned to the US in May 1945 flying, as he told the History Club, in a war weary B-24. After a short leave, he spent the remainder of his service as an information and education officer in Atlantic City. He was discharged October 14, 1945. Listed below are 23 of Warren's 30 missions. The other 7 have not been identified. Warren's missions: 12/19/1944, Rosenheim, Germany, Marshalling Yards - 12/20/1944, Freilassing, Germany, Locomotive Depot - 12/25/1944, Instruction Main, Austria, Marshalling Yards - 1/8/1945, Linz, Austria, Marshalling Yards - 2/7/1945, Moosbierbaum, Austria, Oil Refinery - 3/2/45, Bresia, Italy, Marshalling Yard - 3/9/1945, Maribor, Yugoslavia, Locomotive Depot - 3/13/1945, Regensburg, Germany, Marshalling Yards - 3/14/1945, Zagreb, Yugoslavia, Marshalling Yards - 3/16/1945, Weiner-Neustadt, Austria, Marshalling Yards - 3/20/1945, Steyr, Austria, St. Valentin Tank Works, 4/2/1945, Slum River Bridge, Austria - 4/6/1945, Verona, Italy, Porto Nuova Marshalling Yards - 4/7/1945, Campo di Trens, Italy, Railroad Bridge - 4/9/1945, Lugo, Italy, Area "Apple" Troop Concentration - 4/10/1945, Lugo, Italy,

Area "Baker" Troop Concentration - 4/16/1945, Bologna, Italy, Ground Support - 4/17/1945, Bologna, Italy, Ground Support - 4/19/1945, Aviso, Italy, Diversion Railroad Bridge - 4/20/1945, Mairhof, Austria, Railroad Bridge – 4/23/1945, Legnago, Italy, Railroad Bridge – 4/24/1945, San Ambrogio, Italy, Marshalling Yard – 4/26/1945, Casarsa, Italy, Ammunition Storage Dump.

PART IV - FIGHTING ALONE

"From Berlin and Rome to Tokyo we have been described as a nation of weaklings and playboys who have British, Russia and Chinese soldiers to do our fighting for us. Let them repeat that now. Let them tell that to General MacArthur and his men. Let them tell that to the soldiers who are today fighting hard in far waters of the Pacific. Let them tell that to the boys in the Flying Fortresses.... LET THEM TELL THAT TO THE MARINES!" President Franklin D. Roosevelt Fireside Chat, 2/23/1942

The Europe-First Policy left the US Army and Naval forces virtually alone in the Pacific. There was able assistance from New Zealand, the Australians, Philippine forces, the Canadians and Chinese, as well as some British forces. It was, however, a war fought in the air by Army bombers and Navy and Marine fighter and bomber pilots, and on the ground by Marines and Army grunts. Army Air Corps participation would become decisive after the capture of islands big enough for air fields, and the arrival of the B-29. The two principal commanders were General Douglas MacArthur in the South Pacific and Admiral Chester H. Nimitz in the Central Pacific. And, despite the Europe First Policy, the Pacific Theater continued to receive most of the arms and materiel produced during the first year of the US participation in the war. Prime Minister Churchill was aware of this and was worried that Chief of Naval Operations Admiral Ernest King would convince President Roosevelt to switch to first defeating the Japanese. King strongly supported such a position. Churchill feared such a change could result in the US deciding to reach a truce with Germany once Japan was defeated.

Aleutians Campaign

"I believe that in the future, whoever holds Alaska will hold the world. I think it is the most strategic place in the world." General Billy Mitchell to Congress 1935

It is called the "Forgotten Battle." It occurred in the same time period as the Battle of Midway, the great sea battle that is considered the turning point of the Pacific War. In fact, many believe that the Japanese attacks in the Aleutians were merely a diversion, designed to distract the US from the attack on Midway Island. Others believe, like Billy Mitchell, that both the Japanese and the United States understood the strategic value of the area, and the danger posed to the United States should the Japanese gain control there. They would have had the ability to attack the continental US with land-based airplanes. The United States knew that with such bases, the Japanese could challenge the US for control of the Pacific Great Circle Routes. The bases would also provide protection for the northern flank of the Japanese Empire.

The US was caught off guard, when, on June 3, 1942, the Japanese attacked Dutch Harbor, and then the island of Kiska on the 6th. They seized the undefended island of Attu on June 7. The raid on Dutch Harbor cost 100 Americans their lives. The US quickly prepared to drive the Japanese from the area, but harsh weather conditions impacted the ability to do so. The US was able to contain the situation. With superior air power based in Alaska, and greater naval forces, it was able to discourage and prevent the landing of any additional forces. In fact, the Japanese were limited to re-supplying by submarine those already there. It would, however, be May of 1943 before the US retook Attu Island. Orson D. Beardslee, Erwin Howden and Harry A. Schuknecht of Hume represented the FCSD area in the Aleutians.

Orson D. Beardslee of Hume, entered the service on March 3, 1942 at Fort Niagara. He took basic training at Fort Lewis in Washington. By July 19, 1942, only four months after entering the service, he was on a ship heading for the Aleutians as part of the 165th Field Artillery Battalion. He would not get back to the US until May 24, 1944, some 22 months later. The job of the 165th was to provide artillery support for the 159th Infantry Regiment. At the time, the 159th was assigned to the 7th Infantry Division. Orson was a Gun Crewman/Cannoneer with Battery C, which fired the tractor (truck) drawn 155 mm howitzer. During World War II, field artillery units provided surface to surface long range indirect fire in support of ground troops. Their mission was to destroy, neutralize, or suppress the enemy by canon, rocket, and missile fire. They were considered the "King of Battle." During the war, the field artillery was the single highest casualty-producing weapons system on any battlefield.

In May, 1943, the US was finally ready to drive the Japanese from the Aleutians. The 159th was a main component in that effort, but the 17th Infantry Regiment was the spearhead. An intense battle took place on the cold tundra of Attu Island against strong Japanese resistance. The final act was played out at Chichagof Harbor, where the Japanese invaders were totally wiped out after making one last desperate suicide bayonet charge. Such charges were to repeated again-and-again on several Pacific Islands.

The 159th Regiment (and thus the 165th, Orson's Battalion) was not used during the battle. Their disappointment is reflected in a General Order (G.O.) No 2 dated 7/31/1943, written by their Commanding Officer, Lieutenant Colonel Thomas A. Poole. In part, he wrote, "Today marks the completion of a year's service in Alaska. The year has been in many ways a disappointment to most of us. We seem to be marking time; action against the Japanese seemed so near when we landed, but has not materialized …" He went on to say that they had much to be proud of. They had done the hard, dirty work that had to be done, and they had done it without complaint. He expressed pride in the men and looked forward to the future, one in which they could hope to engage the Japanese.

By at least January of 1944, the 165th was stationed at Camp Earle on Attu. It had moved there from Dutch Harbor, on Unalaska. But Orson had earned his first battle star for his participation in the Aleutian campaign. While they may have done the dirty work, it was, as Lt. Col. Poole had said, work that had to be done. A little more than a month before he returned to the states, General Order No. 7, dated April 8, 1944 awarded Orson his Good Conduct Medal.

With Attu back in US hands, the small Japanese contingent on Kiska quietly departed without a battle. Orson and his unit would remain at Camp Earle on Attu until transferring back to the states on May 10, 1944, landing in Seattle on the 24th. From Seattle, they were shipped first to Fort Lawton, WA, and then, on May 30, to Camp Gruber, OK. They were assigned to the Replacement and School Command where likely they were used to instruct field artillery trainees. Lt. Col. Poole had mentioned in his July 31 G.O., that some of them would likely be used as instructors back in the states. The NAO reported Orson home on a 25-day furlough in June, before reporting to Gruber.

The great mystery writer Dashiel Hammett, author of *The Maltese Falcon* and *The Thin Man*, served in the Aleutians at the same time as Orson. The movie *The Maltese Falcon* had come out in 1941, the year before both he and Orson ended up in the Aleutians. On August 26, Orson and the 165th moved to Camp Hood, TX, another major training base.

Orson, however, was not destined to spend the rest of the war in the states. In December 1944, his unit moved to Fort Bragg in North Carolina. In March, they moved to Camp Shelby, MS. By July, they were on their way to the Philippines. Here Orson earned his second battle star by participating in the windup of the Southern Philippines campaign, which officially lasted until July 4, 1945, but actually-lasted until September 1945. During his stay in the Philippines, he served on Luzon and in Manila. For his service in the Philippines, Orson earned the Philippine Liberation Medal. He arrived back in the states December 16, 1945. That month the NAO reported that he had been promoted to Sergeant, and that he was to report to Fort Knox, KY for his discharge. He was officially discharged December 28, 1945.

Harry A. Schuknecht of Hume entered the service October 29, 1942. After basic training at St. Petersburg, FL, the NAO reported Harry was transferred, in January 1943 to a camp near Salt Lake City, UT. The base was likely Kearns Army Air Base. In a February 1943 issue, the NAO reported him at

Kearns. At that time, Kearns was both a replacement training center and a replacement depot. That same month, February, 1943, he was likely transferred to Alaska, where he became part of the 11th Air Force (in 1945, the 11th became the Alaskan Air Command). Harry would spend 33 of his 37 months of service in the Army Air Corps in Alaska and the Aleutians.

It is likely that he initially served at Elmendorf Air Field near Anchorage. There were other airfields in Alaska at the time, but Elmendorf was the major airfield, and Harry was not stationed in Alaska for his entire tour. He also served in the Aleutians, and there were numerous airfields there during the war. It is not known to which one he was assigned. The most likely assignments were Attu, Kiska, Shemya and Alexai fields. His military occupation is also not known. Based on his post war employment as a long-haul truck driver, he may have been a truck driver in the service.

Harry earned a battle star there for his participation in the Aleutians Campaign. The Japanese capture of Attu and Kiska islands in June 1942 caught the US by surprise. Weather and logistics delayed a response. However, beginning with an attack on Attu on May 11, 1943, the US quickly recaptured both islands. Attu was first and was a blood bath. The final battle was a surprise Japanese banzai attack on May 29, 1943. In what ended as hand-to-hand warfare, practically all the Japanese remaining on the island were killed. It is known as the "Forgotten Battle" as the Guadalcanal Campaign was taking place at the same time. After a three-week naval bombardment, the island of Kiska was attacked on August 15, 1943. The Japanese were gone, evacuated by submarines which had been re-suppling the troops due to the inability of the Japanese Navy to break through a US blockade.

As mentioned earlier, there is still debate as to the reason for the Japanese seizure of the islands. Some believe it was a divisionary attack for their June, 1942 attack of Midway Island. Others believe that it was a strategic decision and the goal was to protect the northern flank of Japan, and to be able to establish air fields for attacks on the US homeland by ground-based aircraft.

Harry was discharged November 9, 1945 at Fort Dix, NJ.

Australia

Many of the FCSD area men who served in the Pacific passed through Australia at some point. A few were stationed there for significant time periods in the performance of their duties.

Elmer A. Babcock of Houghton entered the service on November 3, 1942. It is not clear where Elmer took his basic training, but it is likely that he was assigned to an infantry training center as his final pay record indicates he did receive combat infantry pay. Elmer's personnel record file at the Military Personnel Records Center in St. Louis, Missouri, like so many others, was destroyed in a fire on July 12, 1973. Therefore, there is little information on where and when Elmer served and what exactly were his duties. Items in the NAO, and his final pay records offer some clues. In addition to his pay for combat infantry duty, his pay record indicates that he served with a combat infantry unit. Reports in the NAO indicate that he arrived in Australia in February 1943.

There were two US Army divisions which served in Australia during or around February 1942, the 32nd and 41st Infantry Divisions. It is likely that Elmer was assigned to one of these divisions. It is unclear which as Elmer's determinable overseas history is basically consistent with the history of both divisions, due to the activities of especially the regiments of those divisions. It appears most likely that he served with the 32nd, although no proof of that has been located. The 32nd was in Australia by April/May 1942. It then served in New Guinea from September 1942 until March 1943 when it returned to Australia. Elmer had arrived in Australia circa February 1943. The 41st first arrived in Australia in May 1942, but by the time Elmer arrived was in combat in New Guinea. While it is possible that he was sent to New Guinea to join the 41st, it appears more likely that he was assigned to the 32nd which arrived back in Australia, as indicate above, less than two months after Elmer's arrival. The 32nd had suffered significant casualties in New Guinea. Despite these similarities, there is one issue that raises a question as to whether he served with either division.

A November 1945 entry in the NAO points out that, Elmer served two and a half years in Australia, New Guinea, and the Philippines. Both the 32nd and the 41st served in all three locations. The NAO reported in October that Elmer was on his way home from the Pacific. He arrived October 19 and was discharged October 27, 1945. In September, 1945 the 41st Infantry Division was in Japan commencing its occupation duties. The 32nd Infantry Division moved to Japan during the period September 25 to October 13, 1945. Given that Elmer arrived home in October, it raises the possibilities that Elmer was rotated home at the time the divisions were transferred to Japan for occupation duties. Since Elmer only entered the service in November of 1942, and since both divisions were overseas before Elmer entered the service, it does not seem logical that he would have been shipped home prior to the other men in either division. There is no indication of illness or combat injury.

Both divisions saw considerable combat. The 32nd earned battle stars for the New Guinea, Leyte, Luzon and Southern Philippines campaigns during Elmer's time period. The 41st earned stars for Luzon and the Southern Philippines campaigns during the period in which Elmer could have served with the division. There is also the possibility that Elmer served with an independent unit.

Lowell B. Fox of Houghton entered the service August 27, 1943. He was a math teacher in Attica at the time. Lowell spent a month in basic training and then likely spent some time in training to become a Geodetic Computer specialist. He served his entire time in the service working in that specialty. A geodetic computer specialist performed mathematical computations, using logarithmic and natural function tables in the construction of topographical maps or charts. The work included: 1. calculating latitude, longitude, angles, and areas from held notes made by survey parties; 2. Computing positions from triangulation or primary traverse, stellar or solar observation notes; and 3. Computing intersections, point locations and coordinates. It also included computing intersections, point locations and coordinates. Equipment used included drafting instruments and calculating machines. The Geodetic Computer also had to compute azimuth and position from solar or stellar observations, make involved arithmetic and algebraic computations and have general knowledge of drafting, including mechanical drawing, geometric constructions lettering and conventional symbols used in topography and surveying. He worked with the Corps of Engineers. His background in math was obviously a major aid in his military assignment. The work done by men like Lowell produced the charts, maps and other information that was used by planners and combat personnel during the many conflicts of the war.

Lowell shipped overseas on March 12, 1944 arriving in Australia on March 29, 1944. It is not clear to which unit Lowell was initially assigned. Items in the NAO indicate that during his service in Australia Lowell was stationed in Melbourne.

Lowell was eventually assigned to the 1632nd Photomapping Platoon. He served for a year in Melbourne. He returned to the United States on September 2, 1945 arriving September 21, 1945. He was discharged September 30, 1945 at Fort Dix, New Jersey.

Paul T. McCarty of Houghton entered the service on July 11, 1943. It is not known where he took his basic training or what technical school he attended. It is presumed that he attended a technical school since his military occupation involved the repair of radios and similar equipment. Paul served with Signal Service units during his service. H was a high school math and science teacher prior to the war.

Information is also not available on when Paul shipped overseas. However, given the units he served with, he clearly was a replacement since the original unit from which the subsequent units were formed did ship overseas prior to Paul entering the service. Paul's write-up at the World War II Memorial in DC says that he was assigned to Detachment 3, 4025th Signal Service Group. The 4025th was not activated until June 1, 1945 in Australia. Detachment 3 of the 4025th was previously Detachment #3 of the 997th Signal Service Battalion. Detachment 3 originally was part of the 832nd Signal Service Battalion. The 832nd which had been formed from Detachment 3 of the 832nd Signal Service Battalion which had been formed September 27, 1944 from Detachment 3 of the 832nd Signal Corps Battalion which had been formed from the original 832nd Signal Service Battalion on September 6, 1944 at Camp Veronal, Area 3, Brisbane, Queensland, Australia. The 832nd Signal Service Battalion was originally the 832nd Signal Service Company which had been activated July 7, 1943 at Camp Moorocka, Brisbane, Australia prior to Paul entry into the Army. Very complicated. Due to a lack of documents more information on Paul is not currently available.

Paul's World War II Memorial posting also says that he was a Radio Repairman Fixed Station 649, New Guinea. That designation would have been true whether he was in New Guinea or Australia. Since the 4025th was activated in Australia, it is likely the reference was to Australia. In fact, the 4025th mission statement read "To furnish personnel for the operational control of administrative signal community systems located within the area. All personnel under control of the signal officer (APO 923)." At that time APO meant the signal service located in Brisbane, Queensland, Australia.

"We shall never forget that it was our submarines that held the line against the enemy while our fleets replaced losses and repaired wounds." Admiral Chester A. Nimitz – per US Naval Historic Division, US Navy

(Admiral Nimitz assumed command of the US Pacific Fleet on December 31, 1941, aboard the submarine *USS Grayling*. Nimitz always considered himself a submariner. He considered the failure of the Japanese to destroy or damage our submarines and supporting equipment one of their biggest mistakes at Pearl Harbor.)

"I saw the submariners, the way they stood apart and silent, watching their pigboats with loving eyes. I admired the PT boys, and I often wondered how the aviators had the courage to go out day after day and I forgave their boasting. But the submariners! In the entire Navy, they stand alone." James Michener *Tales of the South Pacific*- Originally published 1/28/1947.

In the aftermath of Pearl Harbor there was one weapon in the US Navy that could respond immediately, and that was the submarine. And it did. It went after the Japanese whenever and wherever. By the end of the war, among other things, submariners had sunk 75 percent of the Japanese merchant marine shipping.

Grant A. Vedder, a 1936 graduate of Fillmore Central and another holder of the Pre-Pearl Harbor Medal joined the Navy December 29, 1936. When he reenlisted in 1940, Grant was assigned to the *USS Grampus*, where he served as a Torpedoman Mate First Class. He had previously served aboard the *USS Richmond*.

The *Grampus* was in dry dock undergoing an overhaul on December 7, 1941. By December 22, it was on its way to the Pacific where it would be based first at Pearl Harbor and later in Australia. On February 8, 1942, it sailed on its first patrol. Its mission was to sink any Japanese ships it found and to reconnoiter Kwajalein and Wotje Atolls. On this patrol the *Grampus* found and sank an 8000-ton Japanese merchant ship and a 10,000-ton tanker. Given Grant's job, it is possible, and likely, that he helped launch the torpedoes that sank the Japanese ships. Over the next 10 months the *Grampus* would carry out four more patrols. The second and third patrols were along the coasts of Luzon and Mindoro in the Philippines.

Heavy rains during those patrols resulted in poor visibility limiting her activities. The after-action reports for these patrols show mostly positions reports day after day. While she sailed from Pearl on her second patrol the *Grampus* returned to her new home, Fremantle, Australia. She would sail from and return to Fremantle on her third patrol. The *Grampus* conducted attacks during its third patrol. The after-action report states that in one case she fired three torpedoes and one passed directly under the target, but did not explode. The *Grampus* commanding officer, Lt Commander Edward S. Hutchinson, reported that he could not understand the torpedoes failure to explode.

It appears Hutchinson was an outstanding commander. He analyzed carefully every part of every patrol, and was faithful in reporting what he perceived to be his mistakes, and what he believed were problems he was not positioned to address. In one he reported he had not been aggressive enough in carrying out an attack. In another, he reported he had not taken the proper position for an attack. In still a third he reported that internal ship communications had allowed a ship they were attacking to escape. He also pointed out that missions to a particular area were being dispatched at the wrong time, causing them to arrive at their destination at an inopportune time of the day. Even the ship's design did not escape his eye. He reported that the hatch to the conning tower was even with the deck allowing water to pour into the ship every time it was opened after being submerged. The water flow hindered the men's actions. His superiors, responsible for analyzing every action carried out on each patrol, always agreed with his observations, even his self-criticisms, but also pointed out that this was a man who was constantly thinking about everything.

Before departing on her fourth patrol, the *Grampus* moved to a new home base at Brisbane, Australia. Her fourth patrol, from and back to Brisbane, began on October 2, 1942, during the height of the battle for Guadalcanal. Grampus new orders were to conduct unrestricted warfare. She was also on a special mission to deliver four coast watchers to the islands of Vella Lavella (part of the New Georgia Islands) and Choiseul (largest island of the Choiseul Province) in the Solomon Islands. She successfully completed that part of her mission delivering Sub Lieutenants Josselyn and Keenan to Vella Lavella and Sub Lieutenant Wadell and Sergeant Seton to Choiseul. *Grampus* also reported that she saw four cruisers and 79 destroyers in five different convoys on this patrol. She conducted a series of attacks. On October 8, she scored a direct hit on the Japanese light cruiser *Yura*, but the torpedo failed to explode. During this patrol, the *Grampus* was also attacked by Japanese destroyers and survived a reported 104 depth charges. Commander Hutchinson reported that, while he did not see them sink, he was sure the *Grampus* sank two destroyers, one an *Amagiri* Class near New Georgia, and the other an *Asashio* Class near Kolobangara Island.

Grampus left on her fifth patrol and 5th of 1942 on December 14. She was to patrol Japanese access routes. Her orders again called for unrestricted warfare. She made 41 contacts and conducted five attacks, including two night time attacks. The *Grampus* claimed 3 ships sunk and one damaged on this patrol.

On February 11, 1943, the *Grampus* departed Brisbane on her sixth and final patrol, in company with the submarine *USS Grayback*. This patrol took her to the Blackett Strait area, again near the Solomon Islands. The *Grayback* reported last seeing the *Grampus* on March 4. On March 5, the Japanese destroyers *Minegumo* and *Murasame* conducted an attack near Kolombangara Island. The next day a large oil slick was seen in the area. Given this information and the fact that the *Grampus* was never heard from again, the Navy declared the *Grampus* lost and sunk on March 5, 1943. The same day the oil slick was spotted, March 6, 1943, the Battle of Blackett Strait took place. Both the Japanese destroyers credited with sinking the *Grampus* were sunk during that battle. Five months later, on August 2, 1943, a PT boat under the command of future President John F. Kennedy was sunk in Blackett Strait. The Australian coast watcher, Arthur Reginald Evans, who helped save Kennedy and his crew, was stationed on Kolombangara and may even have seen the two Japanese destroyers that sank the *Grampus*.

Grant was posthumously awarded the Purple Heart and the Submarine Combat Patrol Insignia. The Purple Heart, in Grant's situation, was awarded in the name of the President of the United States. This was true for all persons serving with the Navy since December 6, 1941 who were killed in action. The Submarine Combat Patrol Insignia was awarded to US Navy officers and men who, after December 7, 1941 completed one or more patrols during which time their submarine sunk or assisted in sinking at least one enemy vessel, or completed a mission of comparable importance. Grant qualified on both counts. His commendation reads in part, "As Torpedoman's Mate first class of the *U.S.S. Grampus*, Grant A. Vedder's performance of duty materially contributed to the success of his vessel against the enemy. The Commander, Pacific Fleet, forwards this commendation in recognition of the splendid performance of duty, which was in keeping with the highest traditions of the Naval Service."

Submariners consider the *Grampus*, Grant, and his shipmates to be on Eternal Patrol.

The Pacific Fleet

Under Admiral Chester Nimitz, the US Pacific Fleet became the most powerful naval force the world had ever known.

Donald L. Slack of Fillmore was a part of that fleet. Don had entered the service in January of 1940. After basic training, likely at the Great Lakes Naval Training Center. Don was assigned to the *USS Denebola*, a destroyer tender, reporting aboard on April 4, 1940. The *Denebola* had just been re-commissioned on April 1, and it is not clear what duties Don performed. The *Denebola*, during the pre-war period, served as the flagship for the Atlantic Fleet destroyer commander. It later played a role in preparing for and transferring destroyers to the British under the provisions of the lend-lease agreement, and part of Don's duties were likely related to that agreement.

It is not clear how long Don served aboard the *Denebola*, but on October 1, 1941 he was received aboard the *USS Relief* from Advance Aviation Base "A", Naval Air Station, Norfolk, VA. He was being transferred to Iceland. There Don worked in communications as a Yeoman. During this period, he struck up a friendship with fellow FCSD area and US Army man Stanley Swales. They had not known each other in Fillmore, and did not meet in Iceland. They only communicated over the telephone.

In December of 1942 Don was transferred from Iceland on the *USS Pleiades* to Quonset Point, RI, for further transfer to the *USS Lexington*. According to the *Lexington's* March 31, 1943 Muster Record, he was received aboard the *Lexington* on March 20, 1943. However, the *Lexington's* June 2, 1943 Muster indicates that he was AWOL (Away Without Leave) for some time, and that he surrendered to the Navy Receiving Station in Boston on May 18, 1943. The Muster for June 30, shows that he received a Deck Court Martial on April 7, 1943. That court martial must have been in absentia, since apparently, he was not aboard on April 7, assuming the June 30 muster roll is correct, and he did not report to the Boston Naval Receiving Station until May 18. His absence may have been related to his recent marriage. The NAO reported that he was in Fillmore in March for a short time with his new wife, whom he had married on March 18.

It does not appear that the offenses tried by a deck court martial were considered major offenses. The punishments were relatively minor, with the most severe being a reduction in rank. Based on later musters, which include sailor's rank, it does not appear that Don was reduced in rank. In fact, by no later than May of 1944, he had been promoted to Yeoman First Class. Don was aboard the *Lexington* when it sailed for the Pacific. Over the next year and a half, aboard three different ships, Don would participate in several of the major WW II battles in the Pacific.

Aboard the *Lexington,* Don served on the staff of Admiral Richmond K. Turner, Commander of the 5th Amphibious Force, Pacific Fleet. The *Lexington* arrived at Pearl Harbor on August 9, 1943. A month later it took part in the raid on Tarawa, and in October participated in the raid on Wake Island. For this campaign, Don earned his first battle star. On October 25, Admiral Turner's command was transferred to the *USS Pennsylvania.* Don was part of the transfer. Irwin Howden of the FCSD area was aboard the *Pennsylvania,* but it is not known if they knew each other.

During his service aboard the *Pennsylvania* Don earned two more battle stars for the invasion of the Gilbert Islands (Makin Atoll, Batarian Island) in December 1943 and the Marshall Islands (Kwajalein, Ongebi, Parag) in January/February 1944.

In May, Don was transferred again, this time to the *USS Rocky Mount.* The *Rocky Mount* was a specially equipped command and communications ship that served as Admiral's Turner's flagship. The *Rocky Mount,* and Don, earned battle stars for the Mariana's (Saipan, Guam, Tinian) invasion, and the assault on Leyte as part of the Philippine invasion. Don now had five battle stars.

The NAO reported in December of 1944 that Don was home on a 25-day furlough. He reported to a base in California for training at the end of his furlough, according to NAO. On May 29, 1945, he reported aboard the *USS Biddle,* and headed back to the war. By July 5, the *Biddle* was in Hawaii, sailing from there on July 15. It was at Eniwetok on July 25, and Leyte on July 28. It sailed from Leyte on August 4 with casualties. After a stop at Ulithi Atoll on August 8, it headed home, and was at sea when the Japanese surrendered. It arrived at San Pedro, CA on August 26.

Don remained in the Navy and enjoyed some more rather unique experiences. On April 13, 1946 Don boarded the *USS Wharton.* Later that spring, the *Wharton,* and Don, participated in Operation Crossroads, the Bikini Atoll atomic bomb tests. The *Wharton* transported observers to the tests. Don was at least the third FCSD area veteran to be at those tests, the others being Wells Knibloe and Francis Morris. The *Wharton* also participated in post war occupational activities, visiting Yokohama and Sasebo in Japan, and Shanghai in China. As a result, the *Wharton,* and Don, earned the Navy Occupational Service Medal. In 1947, Don was assigned to the US Naval Academy at Annapolis, MD, where he participated in two summer cruises for the academy midshipmen.

Richard J. Wilson of Hume volunteered for the service on July 2, 1943. That same month, the NAO reported that the Selective Service Bureau had announced that induction of students 18 or 19 years old could be postponed until the end of their academic year. (Richard was 18 at the time.) He took basic training at Sampson Naval Training Station and completed it in September 1943. After a home leave, according to the NAO, Richard served several months in the southwest Pacific aboard an LST (Landing Ship Tank) as part of the Pacific Fleet. This service apparently lasted five to six months. Throughout his service, Richard served as a Water Tender, rising to the rank of WT2c. His duties primarily involved tending to the fires and boilers in the engine room.

On March 9, 1944, he reported aboard LST 653 in Panama City, Florida. He was home on leave in May of 1944. He then reported back aboard LST 653 where he would remain until March of 1946. During this time the 653 was on duty along the east coast., including Little Creek, VA and the Chesapeake Bay. Various training activities were conducted and trainees transported during this period. In August 1945, LST 653 headed to China. It was credited with performing occupation duties there during the period September 2 to November 18, 1945 and December 23, 1945 to February 3, 1946. On February 3, *LST 653* was de-commissioned. On March 16, 1946, Dick boarded *LST 729.* He was temporarily assigned to *USS Stentor* on March 27, 1946. The *Stentor* was a landing craft repair ship which arrived in China on

December 22, 1945 and remained there until October 6, 1946. Richard returned to the United States in May and was discharged June 1, 1946.

The Great Sea Battles

The Battle of Leyte Gulf (October 23-26, 1944) was, according to some historians, one of the six great sea battles fought in the Pacific during World War II. It was the only one fought by surface vessels. The other great sea battles of the Pacific War were Naval battles fought by airplanes. The surface ships never saw each other. These battles included Pearl Harbor (December 7, 1941), Coral Sea (May 7-8, 1942), Midway (June 4-6, 1942), Philippine Sea, which included the Great Turkey Shoot (June 19-20/1944), and Okinawa (March 26 – April 30, 1945). At Okinawa, the Japanese super battleship *Yamato* was sunk by US Navy airplanes. Some historians, and others, consider the sea battles of Guadalcanal (January 12-15, 1942), and the Solomon Islands as great sea battles. (The Solomon Islands were a series of sea battles fought as the Japanese tried to keep Guadalcanal re-supplied. They took place in "The Slot" some 300 miles between Bougainville to the northwest, and Guadalcanal to the southeast. Following the Solomon Islands battle of Santa Cruz, on October 26, 1942, the USS Enterprise (The Big E), although damaged, was the only US aircraft carrier still operational in the entire Pacific Theater. This prompted the remark quoted below in the section on Eugene Eldridge.)

To the author's knowledge, no one from the FCSD area was involved in the great sea battles at Pearl Harbor (the USS Pennsylvania was there, but Erwin C. Howden and Donald L. Slack of the FCSD area were not yet aboard), Coral Sea and Midway. The FCSD area was ably represented at the other three.

Eugene R. Eldridge and Ralph Kleinspehn, Jr. participated in the Philippine Sea Battle. Walter D. Makowski participated in the battles of Leyte Gulf and the Philippine Sea. Laurence A. Sweet participated at Okinawa.

Eugene R. Eldridge of Granger served aboard the heavy cruiser *USS Canberra*, a ship that originally was to be named the *USS Pittsburgh*. Its name was changed to honor the Royal Australian cruiser *Canberra* which was sunk during the Battle of Savo Island. Launched April 19, 1942, it was commissioned October 14, 1943. Eugene boarded the *Canberra* that same day. Eugene had gone through Officer's Candidate Training at Noroton Heights, CT.

The *Canberra* left Boston in January of 1944 to enter the war. It joined Task Force 58 in mid-February. On March 31 - April 1, the *Canberra* provided bombardment support during the Battle of Eniwetok Island. During the next seven months, it participated in raids and battles at Palau, Yap, Ulithi, Woleai, Hollandia, Wakde, Truk, Satawan, Marcus Island, Wake Island, Marianas Islands, Palau, Philippines, Bonin Islands, Palau again, the Philippine Islands again during the Moretai landings, Okinawa, and Taiwan.

The *Canberra* was part of the *Yorktown* carrier task group during April, for raids on Palau, Yap, Ulithi, and Woleai. This was a brand-new *Yorktown*, replacing the *Yorktown* sunk at the Battle of Midway. In late April *Canberra* joined up with the *USS Enterprise* (The Big E) task group for attacks on Truk. The mighty *Enterprise* was the most famous World War II aircraft carrier. At one point in 1942, someone remarked that the only thing that stands between the Japanese Empire and the west coast of the United States is the *USS Enterprise*. It was enough. During the Truk attack, *Canberra* was detached to shell the Japanese airfield at Satawan. In May she participated in raids on Markus and Wake Islands. In June, she was involved in the Marianas operations and participated in the great Philippine Sea battle. She also shelled Japanese bases in the Bonin Islands. In August and September, she performed raids on Palau and the Philippines, supporting the Morotai landings. In October of 1944, now part of Task Force 38, she participated in raids on Okinawa and Taiwan, in preparation for the Leyte landings. At Leyte, the US Navy demolished the Japanese Fleet, or what was left of it. Four Japanese carriers, three battleships, ten cruisers, and nine destroyers were sunk.

On October 13, 1944, an air-dropped torpedo hit the cruiser below her armor plate. The *Canberra* was about 90 miles off the coast of Formosa at the time. The explosion killed 23 men. Another man died later trying to make repairs to the ship. The Canberra was towed to Ulithi for temporary repairs. She then proceeded to Boston under her own power for permanent repairs. She was back on the west coast by October 1945. The NAO reported that Eugene and his wife were in the Fillmore area for a few days in March and April. The *Canberra* earned seven battle stars during the war.

Task Force 58 later became Task Force 38. The number of the task force was changed depending on who was the area commander. When Admiral Raymond Spruance was in charge it was 58 in the Fifth Fleet. When Admiral "Bull" Halsey was in charge it was 38 in the Third Fleet. In 1945 the Task Force itself, under the command of Admiral Marc Mitscher, would become the mightiest task force ever assembled.

Eugene left the *Canberra* October 30, 1945 in Baltimore to report to the Intake Separation Center in Washington, DC, where he was released from active duty.

Ralph Kleinspehn, Jr. arrived in Fillmore in 1948 and was a fixture at the central school until his retirement in 1980, serving as everything from coach of all sports to Physical Education Director, from English teacher to Social Studies teacher, from Elementary School Principal to School Vice Principal. Ralph was the author's high school soccer, basketball, and baseball coach for three years, and like all his players, I greatly admired and respected him. I called him "Coach" his entire life.

Ralph was also a WW II combat veteran of the Pacific, having served on three different escort aircraft carriers. He first served on the *USS Liscome Bay,* which took part in the capture of Tarawa. Following the battle, the *Liscome Bay* was struck and sunk by a Japanese torpedo off Makin Island in the Gilbert Islands. Only 272 men, including Ralph, were saved out of a crew of 916. The *Liscome Bay* earned a Battle Star for its work at Tarawa.

One of Ralph's shipmates who was lost was Navy Cross winner Doris "Dorie" Miller from Waco, TX, the first African American to earn the Navy Cross. Dorie had been aboard the *West Virginia* at Pearl Harbor. When the attack occurred, he found his combat station, the amidship antiaircraft battery, wrecked. He went on deck and moved wounded sailors, including the mortally wounded Captain of the ship, to safety. Then, even though he had no training, he manned a machine gun and fired at the attacking planes until ordered to abandon ship. Dorie always believed he got one of the attackers.

Ralph was next assigned to the escort carrier *Nehenta Bay*. The main job of the escort carriers was to deliver planes and men to the fast carriers and transport wounded men back to safe harbors. Most times, obviously, the escorts also participated in the battles, as evidenced by the fact that the *Nehenta Bay* earned seven Battle Stars. Ralph made several trips to the war zone aboard the *Nehenta* before being accepted into the Navy V-12 program. During his V-12 program, he studied at Chapel Hill, NC, and Fort Schuyler, NY. He was awarded his Navy commission on July 3, 1945. It is likely that his last trip before entering the V-12 program was to the Philippines, where the *Nehenta* would have participated in the wind-up of the Battle of the Philippine Sea and the "Great Marianas Turkey Shoot." The latter was so named because at least 429 Japanese planes were shot down compared to 29 for the US. The planes lost created a burden for Japanese industry, but even more important was the loss of their elite pilots. The Japanese had loss a major portion of the cream of their flyers at Midway. The Turkey Shoot, in many ways, was the result of the loss of those pilots. The Japanese lost four carriers at Midway. They lost three more at the Battle of the Philippine Sea. Japanese industry was not able to replace those carriers.

After earning his commission, Ralph returned to the war in late July 1945, this time aboard the escort carrier *USS Nassau*. The *Nassau* performed escort duties until the end of the war. Ralph remained in the Naval Reserve after the war and rose to the rank of Lieutenant Commander.

Walter D. Makowski of Centerville entered the service on February 22, 1943. During the next 10 months, he went through basic training at the Sampson Naval Training Station, and then attended gunners mate training, also at Sampson. He then took advanced gunner training at a Naval Training School in San Francisco. It appears that he then attended the Submarine Chaser Training School at Terminal Island (SCTC), CA. as the muster records for the *USS Harris* indicate that he was transferred to the *Harris* from the SCTC. Since he first boarded the *Harris*, an attack transport, April 15, 1944, this would account for the five months between the completion of his training at Sampson and training in San Francisco. His records indicate he spent 16 weeks at Sampson, and 12 weeks in San Francisco. When Walter joined her, the *Harris* was already a combat veteran, having earned battle stars for its participation in the Aleutians Operations, the Gilbert Island Operations, and the Marshall Islands Operations. Walter did not have to worry. That was only three battle stars. The *Harris* would earn five more with Walter aboard.

The *Harris* was an exceptional ship. She had gone through a series of incarnations, including a stint as *USS President Grant*, during which she won a race against the *Empress of Russia*. She had survived one of the biggest typhoons in history (winds of 167 mph), even though 35 other ships were lost. And, during her cargo days as a merchant ship she had traveled to many places that she would visit again as the *USS Harris*. During those earlier trips, she would have needed permission to enter harbors. As the *Harris,* she would not even ask for permission.

When Walter first boarded the *Harris* on April 15, 1944 in San Francisco, she had been there for repairs since February 22, 1944. From San Francisco, she sailed to Hawaii, but then returned to San Pedro, CA, for additional work.

As a Gunner's Mate aboard the *Harris,* Walter duties would have included taking charge of a gun and its crew. He would have had to be able to assemble and fire all types of guns aboard ship. He would have had to know how to handle all shipboard ammunition, including mines and depth charges.

In June 1944, the *Harris* was part of the Saipan invasion force. She carried cargo and elements of the 7th Marine Division. For four days, from June 16 to June 20, as the battle raged, she disembarked her men and cargo. She then embarked 300 wounded men and sailed to Pearl Harbor. Walter had earned his first battle star.

In mid-September 1944, the *Harris* next took part in the Western Caroline Islands Operation. She conducted a diversionary landing at Babelthuap Island while the main force attacked Peleliu. She then joined the rest of the force at Angaur Island. However, her troops were reserves, and it turned out they were not needed. By September 23, 1944, she was at Ulithi where she put troops ashore to occupy the atoll.

The *Harris* now prepared for the Philippines, where she participated in the battle of Leyte Gulf. From October 20 to October 28, she performed duties in the gulf supporting the invasion. On the 28th she took survivors to Guam.

The *Harris* was not finished with the Philippines. On December 21, she rendezvoused with assault forces steaming toward Lingayen Gulf. During this trip, she and others were under heavy air attack from the Japanese. The gunners, including Walter, were extremely busy, according to reports. She disembarked troops under a heavy smoke screen as the battle of Luzon accelerated. The Philippine operations earned Walter his third and fourth battle stars.

Now came number five, Okinawa. The *Harris* was part of the southern task force. On April 1, invasion-day, his group was hit by fierce Japanese air attacks, including kamikaze attacks. Ships all around the *Harris* were hit, but it escaped and finished unloading on April 3.

On April 6, the *Harris* sailed for Pearl and then to the west coast. Boarding fresh troops, she returned to Okinawa on May 28, 1945. She continued to move troops, and was on her way to Ulithi in August when the war ended. Picking up occupation troops in the Philippines, she headed for Japan, arriving September 8 at Yokohama. On another voyage she took troops from the 77th Infantry Division to Hokkaido. On a third occupation trip, she took a construction battalion to Tientsin, China. She then headed home, reaching Boston via San Francisco and the Panama Canal on February 2, 1946. Walter was discharged February 10, 1946 at Sampson Naval Training Station in New York.

Laurence A. Sweet of Centerville (the 1940 Census shows him living in Centerville with his uncle Seth Jones) was accepted in the Navy September 15, 1943. He was 16 in 1940 and working as a farm laborer. His Naval ship personnel records list his home town as Houghton (probably a Post Office address.). For most of the next year, Laurence would be in training, first basic training at Sampson Naval Training Station and then as a hospital apprentice.

During World War II, hospital apprentices had to undergo an elaborate examination to determine their qualifications to perform the duties of the job. If qualified they were generally appointed as Hospital Apprentice First Class. Their primary duty was to act as nurses in charge of hospital wards. They also acted as assistants in dispensaries and in operating rooms. They were called upon to perform as special nurses in critical cases. On board ship, they performed the bulk of all nursing work.

Laurence would eventually be assigned to and go to war on the aircraft carrier *USS Bennington*. He boarded the *Bennington* the day it was commissioned, August 6, 1944.The *Bennington*, an *Essex* Class carrier, was the second Naval ship named for the Revolutionary War battle of Bennington, VT. Named for a battle, it would not be battle shy. It sailed for the Pacific on January 8, 1945, with Laurence aboard. Its route took it to Pearl Harbor and then Ulithi Atoll in the western Caroline Islands, where it became part of legendary Task Force 58. In February, it earned its first battle star by participating in the initial strikes against Iwo Jima. Beginning in March it participated in raids against Okinawa. It was during the Okinawa Gunto operation that the *Bennington* earned its second battle star, playing a role in the last great sea battle of World War II. During this sea battle, against a Japanese task force in the East China Sea, the mightiest battleship ever built, the Japanese ship *Yamato,* was sunk. Planes from the *Bennington* participated in that battle. The Yamato was the flagship of Admiral Isoroku Yamamoto from its commissioning until Yamamoto's death.

In early June, 1945, the *Bennington* suffered its only damage. It was hit by a typhoon off Okinawa. The storm buckled the *Bennington's* forward flight deck. It retired to Leyte in the Philippines for repairs. By July 1, it was again at sea. In July and August, it earned its third battle star for participation in Third Fleet aerial operations against Japan. After the war ended, it would continue to operate in the Western Pacific as part of the occupation forces, until late October 1945. Its planes were part of the September 8, 1945 fly over of Tokyo and the *USS Missouri* during the surrender ceremonies officially ending World War II. It returned to the states in November 1945.

The *Bennington* escaped the war with no battle damage. Several shot-up planes crashed on the flight deck however, and it is likely Laurence participated in treating men injured in these crashes. Laurence would have also helped treat men who reported for sick call. He was promoted to Pharmacist's Mate while at sea. Pharmacist mates are petty officers who, under the direction of medical officers, administer medical assistance, treatment, and services. Aboard a ship like the Bennington, they would serve in the sick bay or the dispensary. Through experience, or training, pharmacist mates often became medical technicians.

The Pacific Islands

"Our citizens can now rejoice that a momentous victory is in the making. Perhaps we can be forgiven if we claim we are about midway to our objective." Admiral Chester Nimitz June, 1942 – Following the successful Battle at Midway.

The overwhelming American victory at Midway was the first major step back. Given the total evil that the Allies were fighting, it is probably not an exaggeration to say that it too was (stealing Neil Armstrong's words upon landing on the moon) a "giant step for mankind." From Midway on, the United States was fighting an offensive war in the Pacific; and it was fighting it with only one arm. As stated earlier, the US did receive critical assistance from the British, Australians, New Zealanders, Canadians, and even China in the Pacific. However, the major powers, including the other arm of the US, were busy in Europe. The overall war policy was "Germany first."

To people of a certain generation and age and those who have carefully studied history, the names themselves send chills down your back and bring back images of horror, unimaginable suffering, death, and mutilation. On the Pacific Islands it was kill or be killed. The Japanese did not surrender. If giving a choice between attacking some of those islands or going to Hell, some may have chosen Hell. Just reciting the names is gut wrenching: Aleutian Islands! Guadalcanal! Wake Island! Bougainville! Tarawa! Kwajalein Atoll! Eniwetok! Hollandia! New Guinea! Saipan! Tinian! Guam! Peleliu (Palau)! Philippines! Iwo Jima.! Okinawa! Except for the Philippines, these were locations most Americans had never heard of, but afterwards would never forget. To win World War II in the Pacific the US had to drive the Japanese from each one of these hells on earth. While a strategy of island hopping was employed, and many islands were "hopped" over, leaving the Japanese to rot on the vine if you will, the above islands could not be skipped. Except for Wake Island, someone from the FCSD area participated in every one of those battles. They also served on other islands where no battles took place, including the Galapagos Islands, Falapop, Ulithi Islands, Espiritu Santos, and Johnston Atoll.

Hawaii – (US Territory)

Very few World War II military personnel, including it appears, all FCSD military personnel, served in the Pacific without at least passing through Hawaii. A few served their entire time overseas in Hawaii. The latter included Leslie R. Beach, Clifford D. Cooley (although he flew missions to several other areas), Faith G. Paine, Sherman C. Robinson Jr (although as part of a CASU crew, he was assigned to other locations for duty assignments and then returned to Hawaii), Howard F. Redmond and Wayne C. Sylor, Jr.

Leslie R. Beach of Houghton entered the Navy August 21, 1944. Like many others, his first stop was Sampson Naval base for nine weeks of basic training. Upon completion he headed to Bainbridge, MD for 19 weeks of radioman training. This was followed by another nine weeks of training at a radio school in Washington, DC. It is likely that Leslie completed his training in June or July of 1945. An August 1945 edition of the NAO reported that he had been a guest of the Fillmore Rotary Club.

It is likely that his leave at this point was the normal leave most service people received just prior to going overseas. Leslie was assigned to the Supplementary Radio Station in Wahiawa, Hawaii. The station was the most important one in Hawaii. It had been constructed in 1941 and 1942, and was located just 21 miles from downtown Honolulu. It was a new generation station and would prove to be extremely effective. One great advantage over the then existing stations was that it was in an easily protected area. Most importantly, it was in an area where reception was excellent. Other units were also quickly moved to the new area. This included a security group unit, and a Communications Security Unit. Its purpose was to assist in a program of cryptographic security, message traffic control and security traffic analysis.

Leslie worked as a Radioman at the radio station during his time in Hawaii, but it is not clear how long he stayed in Hawaii. He was discharged August 5, 1946.

Clifford D. Cooley of Centerville joined the military on September 7, 1942, but entered into active service January 3, 1943. Clifford, who used his middle name Delos, prepared for his military career by enrolling in a Cadet flying program at the Buffalo, NY airport from September 7 thru November 8, 1942. He trained in a Cub J-3 at Buffalo. His training as a Naval aviator, however, was much more extensive. His first station was Chapel Hill, NC where, as a Seaman Second Class, for 10 months he went through the Cadet Training Program. He also attended Officer's Candidate Training at Chapel Hill. He then moved on to Corpus Christie, TX for basic instruction school. He also attended the VPB instruction school. Overall, his training included instruction on a N3N nicknamed the "Yellow Peril", the SNV, the Navy version of the Army BT-15 Valiant Trainer, PBY 3 and 5, a Patrol Bomber build by Consolidated Aircraft, and the SNB, a two engine Beechcraft Airplane used for training. His training on PBYs took place at Naval Air Station, Corpus Christie.

Delos' first assignment, as a Flight Instructor, was to Squadron VN 18D8-B in Atlanta. He served there from March to May of 1945. He was then assigned to Air Transport Squadron VR - 11 in Hawaii. (V for heavier than air, R for transport). When Delos arrived in Hawaii, VR – 11 was stationed at Hickam Air Force Base.

In Hawaii, Delos became part of the war against Japan. He arrived at Pearl Harbor at the end of June, and flew his first mission on July 28, 1945. He flew the Navy R5D (the Army C-54) for the Navy Air Transport Service. The Service was responsible for transporting passengers and air cargo, including mail, to vital war zones. Delos would fly six more missions prior to the official end of the war, and an additional six after the war ended.

Delos' trips were to Kwajalein (designation king), Guam, Salamo, Papua, NG (designation sam), Manus Island (designation mas), Johnston Island (designation joh), and Honolulu (designation hul). The World War II Memorial states that Delos earned one battle star during the war. It appears that this may have been related to a trip to Papua, NG in late July. The Papua Campaign lasted from 1942 until the end of the war.

Following his discharge on November 6, 1945, Delos received a letter from Secretary of the Navy, James Forrestal. In part, the letter said: "You have served in the greatest Navy in the world. It crushed two enemy fleets at once, receiving their surrender only four months apart; it brought our land-based air power within bombing range of the enemy, and set our ground armies on the beachheads of final victory; it performed the multitude of tasks necessary to support these military operations." "No other Navy at any time has done so much. Congratulations – Thanks. Good luck in your civilian life."

Gerald G. Davis of Centerville entered the service on August 25, 1941. It is not known where he took his basic training. It is likely that he was immediately assigned to Fort McClellan and there assigned to the 27th Infantry Division. The Division was training there at the time. The 27th was the first division transferred from the states to Hawaii following the attack on Pearl Harbor. Gerald's discharge document indicates that he left for overseas on March 10, 1942. The NAO reported upon his return to the states that he had been stationed in Hawaii. His discharge document also notes that he arrived at his overseas assignment on March 17, 1942.

Various elements of the 27th Division sailed for Hawaii in the early days of March 1942. On March 10th two ships (*Aquitania* and *Lurline*) sailed from San Francisco with several of the 27th Division's units, including the 105th Infantry Regiment less the 2nd and 3rd battalions. The 105th was likely aboard the *Aquitania*. (The 1st Battalion of the 106th Infantry Regiment was also aboard the *Aquitania*.) The ships arrived in Hawaii on March 15th and the Lurline docked at Hilo on the "Big Island" Hawaii. The docks at Hilo were too small for the *Aquitania* and it docked at Honolulu. The troops aboard the *Aquitania* were transshipped aboard the *SS Republic* on March 16 landing at Hilo on March 17, 1942. Gerald's discharge document shows that he arrived overseas on March 17th.

It is not known what Gerald's Army Military Occupation Specialty (MOS) was during his tour in Hawaii. It is likely, given the MOS listed on his discharge document, that he worked in administration and/or personnel issues. This is also consistent with his civilian background as a school teacher. Gerald served in Hawaii for almost a year. He then returned to the mainland. Why he returned to the states is not known. The 27th Infantry Division served honorably in many battles in the Pacific throughout the war. However, in Hawaii the 27th underwent a major reorganization becoming a triangular division. This did result in some men becoming excess. The History of the 106th Infantry Regiment states that, among others, men of the Regimental Headquarters Company cadre were transferred back to the states in February 1943. Gerald left Hawaii February 20, 1943, arrived back in the states February 28th.

The NAO reported in March 1943 that he had returned to the states from a year's service in Hawaii. His Mother met him in Rochester, NY. The NAO reported further that during his furlough he spent time with his Aunt Mary L. Clark of Houghton.

It is not clear where Gerald served next. His discharge record indicates he was awarded the Good Conduct Medal in 1943 by General Order Number 118 II Army Corps. That document has not been located. Further the II Army Corps was in the European theater at the time.

More likely Gerald was assigned to the Headquarters, Army Ground Forces, upon his return from Hawaii. His discharge document indicates his last military assignment was Headquarters and Headquarters Company, Army Ground Forces. The Army Ground Forces Headquarters was located at the Army War College (later the Army-Navy Staff College) on Fort Humphreys in southeast Washington, DC. The Commander of the AGF was Lieutenant General Lesley J. McNair. McNair was killed near Saint-Lo, France on July 25, 1944. Fort Humphreys was renamed for General McNair in 1948. The Army-Navy Staff College became the National War College in 1946 and the National Defense University in 1976.

The discharge document listed Gerald's MOS as Personal Affairs Consultant. His duties included, among others, interviewing military personnel concerning their personal and financial affairs as well as disseminating information, rendering advice, and giving assistance to military personnel and their dependents and beneficiaries and dependents of deceased or missing personnel.

The NAO reported that Gerald was discharged November 5,1945 at Fort Bragg, NC.

"They (women Marines) don't have a nickname, and they don't need one. They get their basic training in a Marine atmosphere, at a Marine post. They inherit the traditions of the Marines. They are Marines." Marine Lieutenant General Thomas Holcomb 1943.

Faith Geraldine Paine of Houghton was a Marine, having enlisted in the Marine Corps Women's

Reserve on November 6, 1943. While they were Marines, the women were assigned to the Division of Reserve and were generally called reservists. As with the other services, they were there to free up men for combat. *Picture - Marine Corps Good Conduct Medal which it is believed Faith earned during her service.*

Faith arrived shortly after the basic training for females was switched from Hunter College in New York City, to Camp Lejeune, North Carolina. While the activities at Hunter (general processing, medical exams, wearing of uniforms, classification tests, abilities assessment, orientation classes, work experience, close order drill, and others [reveille was at 05:45]) were continued, more standard Marine training was added at Lejeune. Weapon demonstrations for guns of all sorts were made a part of the curricula, as was hand-to- hand combat, and the use of mortars, bazookas, and flame throwers. Instruction was provided in using amtracs and landing craft. The Women Marines were the only females in World War II to receive combat training during boot camp. Faith was likely quite at home in the physical atmosphere of the Marine Corps. In college, she had played basketball, volleyball, and tennis.

Following basic training, in April 1944 Faith was assigned to the Marine Corps Institute at the Marine Barracks in Washington, DC. The Institute facilitated the training and instruction for individual marines. Its basic function was the development and maintenance of a curriculum of Marine Corps education. Faith was listed as an instructor with a specialty code of 659, which meant she could be assigned to a variety of subject areas. She served at the Institute until January of 1945 when she was transferred to Hawaii. Initially, she was assigned to Company A of the Marine Corps Women's Reserve Battalion of the Marine Garrison Force at Pearl Harbor. Later she was assigned to the Headquarters Company at the same location. The Muster Records for April 30, 1945, show Faith was working as a Statistical Clerk, in the Personnel Office of Headquarters, Fleet Marine Force, Pacific. Faith served in Hawaii until the end of 1945 when she was transferred to Henderson Hall in Arlington, VA for reassignment. She was then ordered back to the Marine Corps Institute in Washington, DC. Faith was discharged January 4, 1946, but rejoined the Corps the same day. She was again assigned to Henderson Hall. Muster rolls as late as July 1952 show her on duty with a rank of Sergeant. The April 1952 Muster Roll shows her located in Philadelphia. She worked as a recruiter until May 22 when she was discharged.

Howard F. Redmond of Fillmore entered the service on June 3, 1942. After basic training, Howard attended a four-week Auto Equipment Training program at Fort Monmouth, New Jersey. He apparently then was assigned to Drew Field near Tampa, Florida, where he served until approximately June 1944. Drew Field was a training base, and Howard likely was permanent personnel on the base. He then was ordered to Hawaii, where his son David believes he served the balance of the war. On the Allegany County War Service record that he completed Howard wrote that he served in the Asiatic Pacific Theater which would have included Hawaii. The NAO reported in August, 1944 that he was located "somewhere in the Pacific," and in August, 1945 reported that he had served in the Pacific theater of operations.

David told the author that his dad served with the 1714th Signal Corps Company as a truck driver. That is likely the unit in which he last served. However, the 1714th was not activated until January 20, 1945, at Fort Lawton, WA. Howard was in Hawaii by June or July 1944.

He may have been, and likely was, originally assigned to the 1701st Signal Service Battalion, which was activated in July, 1944 in Hawaii. A report in the files of the 1701st states that 80 enlisted men from the 1701st (and its 1702nd, 1703rd, and 1704th companies) were assigned to the 1714th Battalion in January 1945. Interestingly, the 1702nd, and 1703rd, company men remained on detachment with the 3117th and 3181st Signal Service Battalions elsewhere in the Pacific, even though they were at that point officially assigned to the 1714th. The 1701st Battalion men presumably remained in Hawaii with the 1714th, which was stationed at Bellows Field, and it is assumed that Howard was with the 1701st. The 1714th had a unique assignment. It was to train, equip and ready for shipment detachments to function as or with Joint Communication Centers throughout the Pacific theater. In Hawaii, this would have included transporting the men and equipment among the various communications centers on the island. The 1701st Battalion was composed of men performing the duties that the 1714th would later train men to perform. Their experience in performing the functions was likely the reason they were chosen to train future units.

Detachments 1, 2 and 3 of the 1714th earned the Okinawa Battle Star. Since it is likely Howard was in Hawaii with the main unit, he did not qualify for the Battle Star. The 1714th also earned the Army Occupation Medal for Japan. Again, Howard was not eligible since he was home and discharged by August 3, 1945. The period of eligibility for the Occupation Medal was September 15, 1945 to January 5, 1946. Howard may have been shipped home earlier than some others since he arrived overseas earlier, and thus had accumulated more of the points needed for shipment home.

Sherman C. Robinson Jr of Hume entered the service December 12, 1944 at Buffalo, NY. He took his basic training at Sampson Naval Base. The NAO reported that he and Howard Ricketts entered the service the same day. They completed training at the same time and the NAO reported Sherman home visiting his parents in February.

He received advanced training at the Ordnance School in Norman, OK. The NAO reported that he was "delighted with the country climate" in Norman. He graduated from the Naval Air Technical Training Center (NATTC) in Norman on July 28, 1945 according to the NAO. He was promoted to Seaman First Class at Norman. By this time the war in Europe was over. He was then transferred, probably in August, to Camp Elliott, CA located a few miles from San Diego where he went through ordnance crew training as part of CASU 5 (Carrier Air Service Unit). CASUs were ordnance teams that were sent to various locations to service combat planes. While there was an evolution during the war in service carrier aircraft units, especially by the time Sherman arrived, units were not being assigned to a particular air group, but were moved quickly to wherever they were needed. CASU 5 was apparently a training unit. Sherman spent some time in San Diego, probably assigned to shore duty. He was still in San Diego in December when he visited his parents in Hume, although that same month the NAO reported that he was "out on the broad Pacific. The war in the Pacific was over by December having ended officially in September.

From San Diego Sherman was transferred to Hawaii where he was assigned to CASU 32 (Ecenpac – East Central Pacific) which serviced carrier air groups in Central Pacific locations. Sherman was classified as an aviation ordnanceman for Navy bombers flying off aircraft carriers. CASU 32 was initially based at Kahului (north shore of Maui), Hawaii but, as indicated above, did move around as needed. Shermans discharge document indicates he did see some sea service but there is no information as to how much and where and which carrier groups were serviced.

He did earn the Asiatic Pacific Theater Medal. It is not known when he returned to the states. He was discharged July 25, 1946.

Wayne C. Sylor Jr of Granger entered the service March 3, 1943. After completing basic training at Fort Dix, NJ, he was transferred to Miami, Fl. There the Army Air Corps made good use of his airplane mechanics skills by assigning him to guard duty at a swanky officer's club. By May 1943, he was in training at Kansas City. The NAO reported him home on leave in October. Wayne returned to Kansas City, but was immediately transferred to Kelly Field, San Antonio, Texas where he worked on overhauling aircraft engines. A letter home appearing in the January 1944 NAO reported he had been transferred to the Packard Plant in Detroit, where he was assigned to the mechanic's engineer program.

In the same letter, he thanked the local Junior Red Cross group for the Christmas packages they had sent him. The program in Detroit was involved in one of the most important works of the war. The decision had been made to adjust the Rolls-Royce Merlin engines so that they could be installed in the P -51 fighter plane. Once completed the P-51, which up to then had been a so-so fighter due to underpowered engines, became one of, if not the best, fighter plane of World War II. Along with the P-47 and P-38, and others, it helped eliminate the Luftwaffe from the skies over Europe. The new engines also made it possible for the P-51 to accompany allied bombers all the way to targets in deepest Germany, something no other fighter could do. These advances make possible General Eisenhower's statement on D Day that if the men heard planes over the beaches of Normandy, they did not even have to look up. The planes would be ours. It was close to true.

Wayne remained at Kelly Field until the fall of 1944 when, likely in September, he was transferred to Hawaii. While at Kelly he had learned the lament of all soldiers stationed in Texas. "You could stand in mud up to your ankles while a dust storm blew in your face." The author heard a version of that while stationed at Wichita Falls, TX in the late 50's. There it went that, "You could stand up to your ankles in Texas mud while dust from Oklahoma blew in your face,"

Wayne was part of a squadron at Kelly that was designated for overseas deployment. They were headed for Guadalcanal, where periodic fighting was still in progress. They shipped from San Diego on an old Dutch freighter. Wayne told his son that his bunk was right above the propeller, and that under certain conditions such as storms, it made a terrible racket. When they stopped in Hawaii, Wayne was offered a vacant post which had recently become available. He immediately accepted it. He spent the rest of the war, repairing and overhauling aircraft engines in Hawaii.

He told his son Eric that the biggest danger there was from pilots trying to show off but ending up crashing their planes. There was also danger from carelessness. One day a sloppy mechanic working on a plane directly across from the one Wayne was working on, opened a machine gun without checking the magazine. The gun was loaded, the safety was off, and bullets flew just inches over Wayne's head. Many men died during the war from such careless acts.

When the men started returning home through Hawaii after the war, Wayne, like Howard Ricketts on Okinawa. sat up a small business. He sold sandwiches and made a nice buck. This entrepreneurship speaks well of the education the men received at FCS.

Johnston Atoll (US Territory) - 1941

By 1941 Johnston Island had been under the control of the US Military for 70 years. It was primarily used by Navy seaplanes and submarines on patrol. In 1941 a runway was built and was operational by December 7, 1941. The runway was lengthened in 1943. On December 15, 1941, and again on December 22 and 23, the Atoll was shelled by Japanese submarines. No American personnel were killed or injured, but some buildings were hit. There was no other action at Johnson Island during the war.

Frederick J. Kruppner of Hume was apparently the only man from the FCSD area who served on Johnston Island, although others may have landed there.

Frederick was inducted into the service in August 3, 1942. Following basic training, he was transferred to the Strother Flight Training School in Winfield, KS. Strother was part of the Central Flying Command, and its job was to help train fighter pilots. When Frederick arrived, it was just commencing operations, and he was likely assigned to the 332nd Aviation Squadron. Giving his later assignment as a Field Lighter (according to the NAO) it is possible that he was involved in the control of planes taking off and landing at Strother. Since this was a newly operational base, and training was started before the runway was ready (initially planes were taking off and landing using the ramp), the whole process required everyone to be extra careful.

On June 1, 1944, the training function at Strother ended. The NAO reported at that time that Frederick was on his way overseas. In August, his parents notified the NAO that Frederick had written saying he was safely in Hawaii. He likely arrived at Johnston Island that month, (Johnston Island is one of four small islands that make up Johnston Atoll, one of the most isolated atolls in the world.)

It was a true hardship site, originally developed as a seaplane base and run by the Navy. During the war, fresh water was a constant problem, and portable refrigerators had to be used to preserve food. Thousands of birds used the island, so bird dung was another major problem.

However, Johnson Island was an indispensable link in the air route between Hawaii (4 hours away) and points east, including Tarawa, Majuro, Kwajalein, Marshall Islands, Guam, Tinian, the Philippines (8 hours distance), and other key islands. The Army Air Transport Command started using the base in February 1944, and Frederick was part of the build-up of Army Air Force personnel sent to the island to keep the planes moving. Tactical aircraft also started using the island for refueling and rest. And it became a major refueling stop for planes evacuating wounded personnel. All of this was in addition to the Navy seaplanes and submarines which had been using the island all along. Frederick returned home and was discharged on December 15,1945.

Wake Island (US Territory) – Japan Invasion and Capture, December 11 to 23, 1941

There is no indication that anyone from the FCSD area was at Wake Island when it was captured by the Japanese. However, Kirby Ludwick, brother of Helen Greer (wife of Thomas who owned the Fillmore Hotel) was there. Ludwick, a Naval Boatswain's Mate, was taken prisoner. He was liberated three years and eight months later in Shanghai, China. The US did not regain control of Wake until September 1945.

Galapagos Islands (Ecuador) – 1941 to 1946

In 1941 the United States and Ecuador entered into an informal agreement whereby the US could establish bases in the Galapagos Islands. Both the Army and the Navy eventually did so, although there was confusion regarding the island on which the bases were located. Initially it was believed they were located on Seymour Island. It was later determined the bases were built on Baltra Island, the Navy on one end and the Army on the other. The bases provided protection for the Panama Canal, guarded against U-Boats, and served as a refueling station for Navy aircraft. First Lady Eleanor Roosevelt visited the Galapagos from March 31 to April 2, 1944.

Richard L. Allen was born in Pennsylvania, but by the early 1940's was working for the Rochester Gas and Electric Company's office in Fillmore. On January 4, 1943, Dick became part of the US Navy as an aviation cadet. The NAO reported in September 1944 that Dick was in Fillmore with his wife and had just completed his training at Pensacola. He received his commission August 1, 1944, and likely was in Fillmore in August prior to shipping overseas.

To obtain his wings, Dick had to go through an extended period of training. This included pre-flight and primary training. Navy policy also required two four-month semesters of academic training before even entering pre-flight. Dick did attend Alfred Agricultural and Tech College. It is not clear when, but it likely was following his graduation from high school in New Jersey, and the two-years there satisfied the Navy's requirements for academic training. He then attended both pre-flight and primary training at Pensacola, Fl at the end of which he received his commission as an Ensign in the Navy.

His discharge record indicates that he attended the NAS at Quonset Point, RI. Quonset Point provided advanced training in anti-submarine warfare and use of radar. He spent 24 weeks at Quonset Point. His records also indicate he attended an "Asdevlant" (Anti-Submarine Development Detachment Atlantic Fleet) course in Anti-Sub warfare. Asdevlant's purpose was to test and develop anti-submarine equipment and tactics for its use.

Dick was then assigned to the NAS in Elizabeth City, NC. Navy aircraft stationed at Elizabeth City carried out anti-submarine patrols, search sweeps and convoy protection in the central portion of the East coast. From there it appears that Dick was assigned to the NAS in Coco Solo, Canal Zone. He likely was assigned to VPB-1 Squadron. On October 20, 1944, VPB-1 was transferred to the Galapagos. His discharge record indicates that the Galapagos is in the Pacific Ocean. However, his records do not show that he received the Asiatic Pacific Theater Medal. In the Galapagos, the squadron flew six patrol tracts daily. One track, north-south, was flown from the Canal Zone to the Galapagos. A second, the east-west track, was from the Galapagos to Corinto. A third track would have been from Corinto to Coco Solo. The reverse of these tracks likely constituted the remaining three tracks. The flights were designed to protect the Panama Canal, especially against submarines.

On February 19, 1945, VPB-1 was transferred back to Coco Solo. The history of VPB-1 indicates that officers and enlisted men of the squadron were detached and returned to NAS, San Diego. There is no evidence that Richard served in San Diego at the end of his service. He may have remained at Coco Solo when the squadron transferred to San Diego and was de-established. Dick was discharged on October 29, 1945. He remained in the Naval Reserves until October 21, 1954.

Aleutian Islands - June 2, 1942 - August 24, 1943

Erwin C. Howden and Harry A. Schuknecht from the FCSD area participated in the Aleutians Campaign. (Erwin's history is covered in Part I, Pearl Harbor section and Harry's in the Aleutians section above.)

Solomon Islands - Guadalcanal (Under British rule)- August 7, 1942

"Goddam it, you'll never get a Purple Heart hiding in a fox hole! Follow me!" Captain Henry P. "Jim" Crowe 1/13/1943 – Battle of Guadalcanal. Jim earned the Silver and Bronze Stars on Guadalcanal. Fought in four wars – WWI, Banana Wars, WWII, Korea.

Guadalcanal was first invaded August 7, 1942. On August 8, the Marines captured the big prize on the Island - Henderson Field. However, it would not be until February 1943 that the Japanese were finally driven from the island. John D. Ballard of Centerville was there. So was John D. Redman of Allen.

In March 1942, 25 young men turned out for the start of baseball practice at Fillmore Central School. Eighteen of those men would honorably serve their country during World War II. Two of them, Eugene Ferrin and Paul Hatch, would die. One of the young men, John Daniel Ballard, took part in some of the bloodiest battles of the war in the Pacific.

John D. Ballard entered the Marine Corps in November of 1942. He took basic training at Parris Island, NC. He then received further training at Camp Lejeune, NC. John qualified in three specialties at the end of this training, light machine gun crewman, rifleman, and mortar crewman. His primary duty assignment would be as light machinegun crewman. Without receiving any home leave, he was ordered to San Diego, CA, and on January 16, 1943, shipped out to the Pacific. By late January he had joined the rest of the 2nd Marine Division on Guadalcanal. That Division participated in the capture and defense of Guadalcanal.

When John got there, the so called "mopping up" phase was in progress. It was the last US offensive operation on Guadalcanal from Kokumbono to Cape Esperance. John spoke to his family about this type of operation. He said that many people think of "mopping up" as an easy operation. It was anything but. It was difficult and extremely dangerous. The Japanese were dug into their bunkers and into the many caves on the island. When situations became tough, they were not above using the local natives as shields. The Marines would move back and forth systematically, flushing the Japanese from their hiding places. All the time they had to be aware of Japanese snipers, who would climb the trees and shoot down on the men. The island was finally declared taken on February 8th. The famous book by Leon Uris, and World War II movie, *Battle Cry,* addressed the danger and hardship of the "mopping up" operation on Guadalcanal. Uris was a member of the 6th Marine Regiment, in which John served. His book covers the entire history of John and the 6th Marines in World War II. John had earned his first battle star. John's next stop would be Tarawa.

Espiritu Santos - New Hebrides Archipelago (Joint British- French Rule) - December, 1942

Espiritu Santos was never captured by the Japanese. It served as a military supply and support base, a naval harbor, and an air field. The famous Black Sheep Squadron led by Pappy Boyington operated out of Espiritu Santos for a time. Espiritu also served as the main locale for James Michener's book *Tales of the South Pacific.* Michener served on Espiritu Santos for some time. Eleanor Roosevelt visited the island in 1943.

James G. Ringelberg of Granger spent almost 13 months on the island with Marine Squadron VMD 154, a Marine photographic squadron. James was an airplane engine mechanic. He had entered the service on January 30, 1942. After basic training at Parris Island, SC he was transferred to Training Squadron 4 of the Marine Aviation Detachment at the Naval Air Station in Jacksonville, Fl. He likely went through his engine mechanic training at Jacksonville over the next several months. Muster rolls show him in Jacksonville by at least April 1942. By October he was in San Diego assigned to a SAR (Search and Rescue) squadron. It is likely that he was there only a short time. A February 1943 muster record shows him serving with VMD 154, which at the time was on Espiritu Santos. VMD 154 had sailed for Espiritu in October and December 1942. James almost surely was with the part of the squadron which sailed in December.

By February 1943, the squadron was operational, and between February and December flew over 300 missions. The unit flew PB4Y-1's which were converted B-26's. They operated out of both Espiritu Santos and Guadalcanal, with Espiritu Santos the main base. The photographs provided key information used by the military during the assaults on Bougainville, New Georgia, Guadalcanal, Truk and the Solomon Islands. Despite its many missions, VDM 154 never lost a plane to enemy action, and only one plane overall. It crashed on take-off. VDM's missions required flying long hours over open water and Japanese controlled islands under tricky weather conditions. This record speaks well for the skills of both the pilots and the maintenance crews. Living conditions at Camp Elrod, their base camp on Espiritu, left a lot to be desired. Both malaria and dysentery were problems, and there were many night raids by Japanese fighters. VMD 154 was rotated home at the end of 1943. James was on Espiritu Santos when Eleanor Roosevelt visited. It is not known if he got to see or meet her.

James likely sailed for home with the main body of the squadron in December aboard the U*SS Matsonia.* They arrived in San Francisco on January 19, 1944. He was assigned to Camp Kearney, CA, although the NAO, in March reported him home on leave, probably in February. He returned to Kearney after his leave but transfer orders dated March 7, 1944, ordered him to Cherry Point, NC to be part of a cadre for the formation of two new photographic squadrons, 354 and 954. The orders list his occupation as AMM (Aviation Machinist Mate). James remained at Cherry Point for several months, but by no later than July

1945, muster records show him back on the west coast assigned to Detachment 7 of the CASU (Marine Carrier Aircraft Service Unit). The CASU was a roving band of mechanics who served as Combat Air Support Units. James served with this unit in both San Diego and San Francisco according to muster rolls. By October of 1945 he was back at Cherry Point, NC where he was discharged October 31, 1945.

VMD 154 earned two battle stars, likely for the Guadalcanal and Solomon's campaigns. It also earned a Presidential Unit Citation for the Guadalcanal campaign.

New Guinea (Part Australia, Part Holland) – January 24, 1943 – December 31, 1944

The following FCSD area men all served at one point or another on New Guinea, or aboard ship at New Guinea: Elmer Babcock, Clifford H. Beardsley, James Gilbert Bloomster, Roy N. Byington, Arnold H. Eldridge, Horace N. Emmons, William C. Gelser, J. Russell Gillette, Milford M. Hatch, Paul T. McCarty, Douglas F. Morris, Herbert H. Thayer, Frank W. Wolfe Jr, and James A. Young, Jr.

New Guinea is a large land mass just north of Australia. During World War II its location made it strategically important. The island itself was divided into three territories, Dutch New Guinea to the west, the Territory of New Guinea (Australia) in the northeast and the Territory of Papua (Independent) in the southeast. The Japanese controlled the key port of Rabaul in Dutch New Guinea. Fighting over New Guinea started in 1942, and, in some areas, lasted until 1945. Key Naval battles were fought in the seas around New Guinea. In the east were the key ports of Port Moresby and Oro Bay, controlled by the allies.

Gil poses atop an armored vehicle on New Guinea.
Melanie Bloomster Samsel Photo.

James Gilbert (Gil) Bloomster of Fillmore arrived in New Guinea July 28, 1943 along with the rest of the 491st Port Battalion. The job of the 491st was to manage the port at Oro Bay. Gil would remain at Oro Bay until October of 1945 when the Battalion was rotated home, except for an emergency leave he was granted (arranged by the Red Cross) to visit his critically ill wife Onalee in September 1944. Ironically, Onalee's brother Ray Yeager was severely injured in his war time factory at home, while her husband Gil suffered no injuries in his job in the Pacific war zone. The 491st sailed for New Guinea July 1, 1943 from San Francisco. It arrived just after a major attack by the Japanese in which two US ships were sunk. Oro Bay served as a staging area for Army campaigns and Naval operations during the remainder of the war. *Picture – Gil atop armored vehicle in New Guinea. Family Photo.*

Gil was inducted into the service in March of 1943. He received his training with the rest of the Battalion at Indiana Gap Military Reservation in Southern Pennsylvania. In mid-May 1943 the Battalion was shipped to California where training continued at docks in San Francisco and Oakland. On July 1, they were shipped to New Guinea, arriving July 17. Gil served as an administrative clerk during his 30 months at Oro Bay.

Many of Gil's letters to his wife Onalee survive. Three days after arriving, he wrote a V letter to her. He told Onalee that V letters were supposed to get through faster. The letter made mention of several things, but two stood out. He missed her, and he wanted her to write.

A few months after his arrival Gil wrote a letter to the FCSD community that was published by the NAO. In part he wrote, "Somewhere in the Southwest Pacific, Nov. 17, 1943. There are so many people in and around our community to whom I would like to send a greeting card personally, but due to the extra burden placed on the mail, and because of the lack of greeting cards at our disposal, I find I am unable to do, so may I take this informal opportunity to wish you a Merry Christmas and a Happy New Year."

He went on to praise the citizens of the community for their friendliness, their concern for others, their willingness to share the sorrow and grief of others, their liberal contributions to charity and their patriotism. He then spoke of his current situation. "I have never harbored the thought of spending innumerable months in the tropics. The heat is intense, which at first caused much discomfit; however, after a short time we became acclimated to it. The rain is forever descending in torrents upon us, leaving in its wake, mud almost knee deep. Transportation is at a standstill except for the jeep's tenacity for traversing the deepest mire. The sun is soon sending its most brilliant rays from the heavens and in a short interval the ravages of the storm disappear." He went on about the scenery, the peaceful waters, the blended hues of the sunset, ranging from a brilliant orange to a violent red, all with a background of blue. Still, he concluded, he preferred the idiosyncrasies of New York. He then dealt with the war. "I have distinct recollections of the grumbling we all did at the advent of rationing. We were wont to exclaim over the imagined violation of our rights as a free people and make dire threats of rebellion. This trend of thought has fortunately changed and it is now evident everyone has his shoulder to the wheel, gladly depriving himself so that freedom may reign. Since entering the armed forces, I have been confronted with the necessity of rationing. Transportation of munitions and foodstuffs to the front relies on the gasoline you are doing without." He concluded his letter by saying, "The spirit in which the people have accepted these restrictions causes us to believe their heart and soul are in this to the finish, so our faith in Humanity is thus restored."

That last sentence reflected a feeling and a concern in many letters home. The men and women involved in carrying out the war wanted to be sure the folks back home were with them.

Gil apparently wrote two letters on the 17th. The first one discussed a USO show he had attended the previous night. It had been held despite a torrential rainstorm. The stars were Gary Cooper, Una Merkel, and Phyllis Brooks. Gil's commanding officer was Merkel's godfather. He was very impressed with Cooper, who recited Lou Gehrig's farewell address at Yankee Stadium. Cooper had played Gehrig in the 1941 movie, "Pride of the Yankees." Gil managed to get autographs from all three, and sent them off to Onalee.

Another letter in December reflected boredom. He had been in the service nine months and it seemed like nine years. They were now playing Chinese checkers for money. He had made a lamp so that he could read at night without disturbing anyone else. The weather was a little cooler. He was feeling a little homesick. Having nothing else to do, they had composed a weekly newsletter, named, "The Brainstorm." He sent her a copy. The big item was the importance of Port Battalions. Without the supplies provided by these battalions, the war could not be won.

In February, he again wrote about mail. He had not gotten any. (It finally came while he was writing the letter.) They had seen another show the night before, put on by Special Services. The stars were Curly Miller and Lanny Ross. It was held in their new 800-seat roofed stadium that he had mentioned in a previous letter. They no longer had to worry about rain. He again managed to get autographs which he sent home. They had also seen the western, *In Old Oklahoma,* earlier in the week. It was pretty good. No rustling for a change. He then mentioned it was time to wash his clothes. He had put it off as-long as he could. In an earlier letter he had told Onalee he wished she was there so she could wash his clothes.

In March 1944, more USO stars - Jean Darrell, Helen Talbot, and Red Don Barry. They posed for pictures, but he forgot to get autographs. He mentioned he had a cold, but it was gone. He started with the fact that he had not received any letters for three days. On March 9, 1944, Easter Sunday, he wrote again. he had been to church twice. The choir was made up of some nurses and a few GIs. He was sending a roll of exposed film and wanted a couple of pictures back. He hoped he would be home by next Easter, but was not hopeful. That line was one of the few times Gil referred to the war, even indirectly, in his letters. Gil returned home in August and was discharged in November 1945.

Roy N. Byington of Centerville entered the service January 12, 1943. Roy's final pay record indicates that he was part of the Army Service Forces. The entry in the Previous Organization section of the pay record reads "A.P.O. #318." Other documents indicate that APO 318 served the 155th Infantry Regiment during at least part of its time in New Guinea. The 155th Infantry was part of the 31st Infantry Division during the war. APO 318 was also used in the Philippines and the 155th also served there. The Unit Citation and Campaign Participation Credit Register indicates that the 155th earned Battle Stars for both the New Guinea and Southern Philippines campaigns.

Historical records for the 155th Infantry indicate that the regiment participated in major battles in the Wakde-Sarvai area and Morotai Islands as part of the New Guinea campaign. It also participated in the Mindanao battle in the Southern Philippines campaign. The 155th also earned an Assault Badge for the Morotai Island battle on September 15, 1944. Assuming Roy did serve with the 155th Infantry, he would have earned both Battle Stars as well as the Assault Badge. He would have been part of the Philippine Unit Citation awarded by the Government of the Philippines for the unit's actions during the period October 17, 1944 to July 4, 1945.

It is not known in what occupation Roy worked during his service. Given his post war occupation as a truck driver, it is possible that he worked in the same occupation during his service, perhaps as part of the Transportation Corps.

Roy was discharged January 23, 1946 at Camp Atterbury, IN.

Milford M. Hatch of Centerville entered the US Army on May 18, 1945. Milford took his initial training at Fort Leonard Wood in Missouri. He received further training at Fort Jackson in South Carolina. By December 6, 1945 he was in-route to Dutch New Guinea where he would remain until June 11, 1946. Milton served as the labor foreman in the Engineer Battalion Headquarters Service Squadron.

Douglas F. Morris of Centerville entered the service on January 30, 1940. Like others he earned the American Defense Medal for his service prior to December 7, 1941. It is not known where Douglas received his basic training, but by April of 1940, according to the 1940 Census, he was stationed at Mitchell Field in Nassau County, NY. At the time of the census, April 1940, Douglas was only 18 years old, despite having graduated from FCS in 1938, and attending college in 1939. He was a Private. Over the next year, Douglas earned more promotions and by September 1941 was an Airman Second Class. That December, following the Japanese attack on Pearl Harbor, Douglas was shipped to an air base in Panama. Douglas sailed from New York to Charleston, SC aboard the *USS* Kent (APA 217) attack transport, where he likely changed ships. Records for the *Kent* indicate that the ship did not sail to Panama from Charleston.

Douglas's military occupation is not known. However, Mitchell Field was the home of the Air Defense Command. Following the Pearl Harbor attack, the air defense of the Panama Canal became one of many top priorities. Douglas, as a member of the US Army Air Corps was likely assigned to one of the US Air Bases in western Panama. The major air base at that time in Panama was Howard Air Force Base, located about six miles from Balboa, Panama near the Pacific entrance to the Canal. Douglas served in Panama until November 22, 1942. By the time he departed he had been promoted to Sergeant.

By December, 1942 he was home on furlough. He likely was then assigned to the Greensboro Training Center in North Carolina. Basic Training Center No. 10 opened at Greensboro on March 1, 1943. The

Center's purpose was to train crewmen for the air war. The training lasted four to six weeks. In May or June of 1943, he took a reduction in rank from Staff Sergeant (promoted to in June of 1943) to Private in order to accept an assignment with the Army Specialized Training Program (ASTP). He entered an engineering program at Syracuse University. The program lasted six months. In November 1943, according to the NAO, he returned to Greensboro, NC for reassignment. He likely was then assigned to an advanced training center for air crewmen. That was the normal procedure for those men who completed the initial training at Greensboro.

On October 15, 1944 Douglas sailed aboard the *USS Admiralty Islands (CVE 99)* escort aircraft carrier for New Guinea. The ship was carrying replacement planes and personnel. On New Guinea, Douglas became an airplane crewmember. Flying combat missions with his crew, Douglas, among other decorations, earned the Air Medal before the end of the war. A letter signed by General George C. Kenny, Commander of the Far East Air Forces, stated that Douglas had earned the Medal for meritorious achievement while participating in aerial flights in the Pacific area from February 15, 1945 to April 2, 1945.

General Kenny was an expert on aerial combat. In a dispute with a top aide to General MacArthur, Kenny had picked up a blank sheet of paper and made a dot in the center with a pencil. Then speaking loud enough so that MacArthur, who was in the next room, could hear, he pointed to the paper and informed the aide that the dot represented what the aide knew about air power. The rest of the paper was what he knew.

Solomon Islands - New Georgia (British Rule) – June 17, 1943 - August 23, 1943

John D. Redman Jr. served with the Marine 9th Defense Battalion, Fleet Marine Forces during the New Georgia Operations.

John D. Redman Jr. entered the Marine Corps on January 31, 1942. The Redman family had been a part of the Allen community since at least 1900 and John was born there. By the time John entered the service the family had moved to Buffalo although they still owned and visited frequently their farm house in Allen. John likely started school in the Fillmore Central School system and is buried in the Short Tract cemetery.

John took his basic training at the famous Quantico Marine training base. According to the NAO, he was assigned to Companies A and then E, Training Center, Marine Barracks. Upon completing his basic, July muster records show that he was assigned to Special Weapons Group, Ninth Defense Battalion, Fleet Marine Force (FMF). That same month John was charged with being AWOL from 6:00 AM June 26, 1942 until July 6, 1942. He was sentenced to three months confinement at the Marine Barracks in Norfolk, VA.

Upon his release (actual time served is not known) John rejoined his unit in Cuba where it had been transferred in July. His unit was in Cuba to help defend the Guantanamo Naval Base. In December the 9th Defense Battalion moved to Guadalcanal to reinforce US air defenses. The Guadalcanal Campaign (Operation Watchtower) which had begun August 7, 1942 lasted until February 9, 1943. John was a member of a machine gun crew and would remain so throughout the war. The duties of crew members included loading, aiming, firing, and maintaining an antiaircraft machine gun such as the .50 caliber or 20mm. He could and likely did perform other relevant duties during his career, including supervisory duties pertaining to the control, coordination, and tactical employment of one or more antiaircraft machine guns and their crew members.

In January, 1943 as the Guadalcanal Campaign approached its end, the 9th Defense Battalion started preparations for its next operation. John's unit was redesignated as the Special Weapons Group, 9th Defense Battalion, FMF. The Battalion was to support the invasion of New Georgia. The goal was to capture or isolate the major Japanese fortress at Rabaul. The 9th was assigned to the island of Rendova which was close to New Georgia, and from which its guns could provide antiaircraft support for the invasion force. It moved to Rendova in June 1943. Future President John F. Kennedy arrived at Rendova shortly after the 9th Battalion. While it is unlikely that John met Kennedy, they did serve on Rendova at the same time and both participated in the New Georgia campaign.

The 9th moved to New Georgia in October 1943. The major battles for Munda (early July), Kolombangara (July 12 and 13) and Vella Gulf (August 6) had forced the Japanese into a defensive position at Rabaul and a decision was made to just bypass them and leave them there. The Battle of Vella Gulf was a major US victory and ended the Japanese attempts to reinforce their forces on New Georgia. Another two months were needed to fully secure the island but the 9th began planning for its next engagement.

That engagement would be the second battle of Guam. The Japanese had captured the island in 1941 and now the US was determined to retake it. John's 9th Defense Battalion was part of the invasion force. They landed on D-Day, July 21, 1944. The fighting was fierce. Like almost all the Pacific Islands the Japanese fought to virtually the last man. The Japanese defense plan was comparable to ones used at other islands with interlocking tunnels. In the end it is estimated that of 19,000 defenders, some 18,000 died. This included the two major Japanese commanders. Lt. General Takeshi Takashina was killed in action on July 28. Lt. General Hideyoshi Obato committed suicide on August 8, 1944. The island was declared secure on August 10. A few Japanese soldiers escaped to the mountainous regions of the island. All except one surrendered eventually. One soldier held out until 1972.

John's war was over. He now had three Battle Stars. In addition, the battalion was awarded the Navy Unit Commendation for its service in action at Guadalcanal, Rendova, New Georgia and Guam. While the 9th did not return to the states until 1946, muster records show that John returned November 1944. He served another year, part of the time with a Guard Company at the Marine Barracks in Yorktown, VA and part with a Special Training Regiment at Camp Lejeune, SC. He eventually was transferred to the US Naval Hospital in San Diego in January 1946 for some reason, and then, that same month, to Marine Barracks in Bainbridge MD where he was discharged as a Corporal on February 1, 1946.

Solomon Islands – Bougainville (British rule) - November 1, 1943

Bougainville was already famous before the Marines invaded on November 1, 1943. On April 18, 1943, based on secret intercepted information, Army P-38's carried out the most precise aerial ambush of the war. They found the plane carrying Japanese Admiral Isoroku Yamamoto and shot it down, thus killing the most famous, and likely most capable, Admiral in the Japanese Navy. He was the man responsible for the attack on Pearl Harbor. After much controversy and many years, First Lieutenant Rex T. Barber was credited with shooting down Yamamoto's plane.

One of the most prestigious awards, and many would say the most prestigious award, a Fillmore High School student can receive is the Paul Hatch Award. That has been true now for over 70 years. The namesake of that award, a 1942 graduate of Fillmore Central, was born and grew up in Higgins. An outstanding athletic, Paul was also an outstanding young man and the award recognizes both those aspects of his character. A superior student, Paul had a perfect attendance record during his 12 years of school. His senior year he earned a leadership award, was president of the Future Farmers of America, and was sports editor of the school newspaper. He won the honor letter in recognition of his athletic ability and sportsmanship that year.

On March 19, 1944, **Paul Story Hatch**, like Admiral Yamamoto before him, died on Bougainville. Like everything else about his life, Paul's death was not ordinary.

Paul was inducted into the service on January 4, 1943. He entered April 8, 1943. His basic training was

Silver Star Medal

at Jefferson Barracks in Missouri. He was later ordered to San Francisco. He joined the 129th Infantry Regiment (Company A) as a replacement in October while it was on Guadalcanal preparing for the Bougainville invasion. (A letter to Paul's mother written in 1946 by a W.W. Stover claimed Paul joined the Battalion (of the 129th Regiment) when it was in the New Hebrides Islands, but Paul would not have been overseas when the 129th was at that location. The NAO reported that he was shipped overseas in October 1943. The 129th was at Guadalcanal in April of 1943, then it was in New Georgia and then it was shipped back to Guadalcanal in September 1943. So, it is likely that Paul joined the Regiment on Guadalcanal prior to the Bougainville invasion.

The 129th was an Illinois National Guard unit and originally was part of the 33rd Infantry Division. On July 31, 1943 it was detached to the 37th Infantry Division. The Division helped fortify Fiji and then was shipped to Guadalcanal for more training. The Division then saw action in New Georgia before being sent back to Guadalcanal in September for R&R. It arrived on Bougainville during the period November 4-11, 1943. Bougainville was invaded near Cape Torokina (mid island) on November 1 by the 3rd Marine Division (First Marine Amphibious Corps). A perimeter had been established containing the key fighter and bomber bases at Piva. By mid-December most of the Marines had been withdrawn and the 37th, and the American Division, had taken their place. The 37th was assigned to the western beachhead section. Its job was to expand the sector, build roads and bridges, and carry out extensive patrol activities.

In February during one of those patrols, Paul earned the Silver Star. His citation reads, "For gallantry in action when he helped save a wounded comrade from falling into the hands of the enemy at Bougainville, Solomon Islands on February 19, 1944. Private Hatch crawled and ran seventy-five yards through enemy fire and over rugged terrain to reach the casualty and drag him from his exposed position. Sniper fire drove the rescuers with their helpless casualty into a river, where the swift current swept them downstream for fifty yards before they could escape and carry the wounded man to safety."

A fuller explanation of the rescue was contained in a letter to Paul's mother written by his commanding officer, Lieutenant Colonel Frank J. Middleberg. Col. Middleberg wrote, "I witnessed his courage and bravery at Bougainville when he and Bob Klase rescued a wounded man in the face of grave peril to their own lives. "On the afternoon of Feb. 14th our patrol made contact with an enemy detachment. In the ensuring fire-fight several members of our patrol were injured and due to unfavorable terrain, we were forced to withdraw. The route of withdrawal was over a narrow rocky trail on the side of a steep bluff overlooking the swift flowing Favorma River. This ground was exposed to enemy fire and therefore when we all made it back safely, we considered ourselves lucky. But on moving back it was discovered that one of our wounded comrades was still lying where he had fallen, helplessly exposed to Jap gunfire and savagery. Without hesitation Paul and Bob Klase volunteered to bring this man back. Using every trick and maneuver taught them in training they shied away from the exposed trail and proceeded to inch their way upstream against the rushing current of the river. Finally, they made it to the upper bank. Here they crawled on their stomachs up to the top and the exposed ground. And then under fire from Jap riflemen your son went forward on his stomach up to the wounded man, grabbed him and laboriously dragged him back to the shelter of the bank. In returning they decided the river would be the better route. This was indeed dangerous for despite the chances of getting hit by enemy fire and the slow progress necessitated by the weight of the injured man, a single slip in the turbulent waters meant drowning or smashed bones and the loss of the injured man. But they finally made it back to the lower bank without mishap. The wounded man was injured severely in the face and was unable to walk. So, your son ripped off his drenched jacket and by placing two tree branches through the sleeves created a sitting litter... "It was due entirely to your son's great courage and fearlessness that the wounded man was saved." Col. Middleberg also wrote that Paul, shirtless and wet, spent a very cold night in the jungle without a single complaint.

The man saved by Paul and Bob Klase was Otto Joseph Boerner of Robstown, Texas. Boerner had been hit twice by rifle fire, once in the jaw but also in the arm, breaking the bone. Another member of the patrol did not make it back. He was also wounded, and when his body was located the next day, he had been bayoneted to death. Otto J. Boerner survived that day. When he died in 2008, he was survived by his wife, two sons, one daughter, 12 grandchildren, 17 great grandchildren, and two great-great grandchildren. In a very real sense, Paul saved not one, but 35 lives that day.

Paul did not live to personally receive his Silver Star. On March 19, 1944, he was leading a mortar squad on another patrol. He stepped on a mine and was killed almost instantly. The Silver Star was presented to Paul's mother in a ceremony at her daughter's home in Fillmore. Paul was originally buried in the Military Cemetery on Bougainville. In 1948 his remains were removed to Fillmore. He now rests there in Pine Grove Cemetery. Paul was 19 years old when he died on Bougainville.

Rabaul, New Britain, Papua, New Guinea, Philippines - January 1943 to July 1945

Herbert H. Thayer entered the service on July 2, 1942. A February 1944 NAO issue reported that Herbert had been overseas in Australia and New Guinea for 15 months. Given that, he likely was transferred overseas sometime in November or December 1942. NAO had reported in an October 1942 edition that he was "somewhere in the world." In a November 1943 issue, the NAO reported him stationed at an Army Air Base in Australia. The February 1944 edition also reported that he had just had his first furlough and had spent it in a large city in Australia. He served as a Truck Driver for an air service squadron.

Herbert's World War II Memorial entry says he served with the 6th Technical Squadron. That squadron was possibly assigned to the 374th Troop Carrier Group. The 374th was activated in Australia on November 12, 1942. It participated in most of the very long New Guinea campaign and earned three Distinguished Unit Citations for its efforts during the Papuan campaign. It also participated in the Bismarck Archipelago Campaign, the Luzon Campaign, the Southern Philippines Campaign, and several others. However, Herbert and his unit, the 6th Technical Squadron, may have been assigned to some other air group.

In March 1945 the NAO reported that he had been promoted to Corporal and was with the Army Air Corps in New Guinea. Given that his World War II Memorial entry indicates that he earned battle stars for both the Luzon and Southern Philippines campaigns, he likely was also stationed in the Philippines for some time in the summer and/or fall of 1945.

Herbert's citation at the World War II Memorial lists four campaigns in which he participated. One was Papua, New Guinea (January 24, 1943 to December 31, 1944). The other three were the Bismarck Archipelago (June 15, 1943 to May 1, 1944), Luzon (December 12, 1944 to April 1, 1945) and Southern Philippines (February 7, 1945 to July 4, 1945).

The Bismarck Archipelago is located just northeast of New Guinea. The main island is New Britain, and its major city is Rabaul. The Japanese seized Rabaul in early 1942. The original plan to recapture Rabaul, code named "Cartwheel" ended in a stalemate. Other parts of the plan proceeded on schedule. The second plan to take Rabaul (Elkton III) also was not decisive. In executing this plan, the Allies soon recognized that the Japanese had created an almost impregnable fortress at Rabaul. A decision was made to simply by-pass it after it was basically neutralized by air-power. Rabaul was left, as they say, to wither on the vine.

The Papua, New Guinea Campaign began with the air neutralization of Rabaul. The Allies then leapfrogged Wewak and Honsa Bay on the northern coast of New Guinea. Both Wewak and Honsa Bay were also left to wither on the vine. Attacks were then conducted against Aitape and Hollandia on the New Guinea northern coast. Both attacks caught the Japanese completely by surprise, and, in addition to the towns, resulted in the capture of two important bomber bases. More important it cleared the way for the invasion of the Philippines. The final phase of the plan called for the dangerous job of mop-up of Japanese troops. This was primarily undertaken by Australian troops.

The battle for the Philippines began at Leyte on October 20, 1944. General Douglas MacArthur waded ashore a few hours after the initial attack. In a prepared speech he said, in part, "People of the Philippines: I have returned…" With those words he redeemed his promise made some two years earlier when, after being force to flee Corregidor, he promised, "I Shall Return." Senior staff in Washington had requested him to revise his statement to say, "We Shall Return." He ignored the request. Next came the invasion of Mindoro. MacArthur had planned to be aboard the *USS Nashville (CL 43)* cruiser as part of the invasion force. His staff talked him out of it due to the danger of Japanese planes and the lack of land-based US air cover. The *Nashville* was struck by a Kamikaze and 133 men were killed. But Mindoro was taken which cleared the way to Luzon.

The invasion of Luzon commenced on January 9, 1945. It did not officially end until August 15, 1945. MacArthur ridiculed Sixth Army estimates of over 234,000 enemy troops. The actual total was closer to 287,000. The primary objectives were first, the port of Manila and second, the air base at Clark Field. The fighting was vicious. Except in emergencies, MacArthur placed humanitarian concerns above military needs. This included prohibiting the use of air strikes and restricting the traffic of civilians out of Manila to spare the civilian population. Nevertheless, thousands of Filipinos died in the cross fire between the opposing forces and from Japanese massacres. The capture of Manila and Clark Field took three weeks. For his personal bravery during this campaign MacArthur was awarded his third Distinguished Service Cross. MacArthur would go on to earn additional honors especially for his liberal, effective, and thoughtful management of Japan following the war. However, his reputation suffered severe damage later when it was learned that he had accepted $500,000 dollars from President Queson of the Philippines for his "pre-war service."

The Southern Philippines Campaign was one that was undertook by MacArthur practically on his own. MacArthur firmly believed that his promise to return meant the total liberation of the Philippines, and he was determined to continue until that goal was achieved. The campaign itself involved a series of landings on such islands as Palawan, Mindanao, Danay, Cebu, Negros, and a few others. Several invasion forces faced little or no opposition. In others there was resistance, none of which would change the outcome. On July 5, 1945 MacArthur announced the total liberation of the Philippines. It was essentially true although Japanese forces resisting the Allies were considerably greater than the 4,000 MacArthur claimed were still alive. Japanese General Tomoyuki Yamashita moved his forces into the mountains of central and northern Luzon. As a result, despite MacArthur's desire, liberation of the entire Philippine population was never achieved during the war. After the end of the war, at the order of the Japanese Emperor, Yamashita and 100,000 of his men finally surrendered. In July MacArthur was awarded his fourth Distinguished Service Medal.

MacArthur received many awards and acknowledgements for his military service especially his World War II service. The two he treasured most were awarded by the Congress of the Philippines. Both were in letters from the Congress and the first granted him honorary citizenship to the Philippines. The second informed him that his name would be carried in perpetuity on the company rolls of the Philippine Army, and at parade roll calls when his name is called, the senior non-commissioned officer present shall answer "Present in spirit." During his lifetime MacArthur was also accorded a guard of honor composed of twelve men of the Philippine Army.

President Roosevelt and General MacArthur were not the best of friends. Nevertheless, Roosevelt made it clear that he wanted MacArthur to become the Supreme Allied Commander of the occupation forces in Japan. Harry Truman, upon becoming President, honored Roosevelt's wish and appointed MacArthur. As Supreme Commander MacArthur countersigned the Japanese surrender document aboard the USS Missouri on September 2, 1945.

While Herbert H. Thayer's World War II Memorial entry indicates he earned four battle stars, he may have earned more. Most of the combat and other groups to which his unit may have been attached did earn several more battle stars and he likely would have been eligible for these additional medals. In addition, if he was in fact attached to the 374th he would also have earned the Distinguished Unit Citations mentioned above for the 374th. If attached to another group he would have earned any unit citations awarded that group.

Finally, his World War II Memorial entry indicates he earned two US battle stars for the Luzon and Southern Philippines campaigns. Given this it is possible that he also earned the Philippine Liberation Medal with two bronze stars awarded by the Government of the Philippines. The Liberation Medal was awarded to US military personnel for any one of four distinct reasons. Herbert likely could have qualified if he served in the Philippine Islands for not less than 30 days during the authorization period which ran from October 17, 1944 to September 3, 1945. Since the NAO reported Herbert in New Guinea in March 1945, it is possible that his service squadron never actually served in the Philippines although the air group to which they were assigned did participate in the Luzon and Southern Philippines campaigns which qualified him for the American awarded bronze battle stars. As indicated above, he would have also received two bronze stars with the Philippine Liberation Medal from the Philippine government for the Luzon and Southern Philippines campaigns assuming his squadron did serve in the Philippines for at least 30 days. The 374th Troop Carrier Group did serve in the Philippines at Nielson Field on Luzon for a year beginning May 28, 1945. If his squadron was attached to the 374th and was at Nielson for at least 30 days he would have earned the medals and battle stars mentioned above.

The NAO reported in October 1945 that Herbert's parents received a telegram from him saying he had just arrived back in the states and that he would soon see them. He was discharged October 13, 1945.

Gilbert Islands (Japanese Mandated Islands) - Tarawa - November 20 - 29, 1943

"Casualties - many; percentage of dead - not known; combat efficiency - we are winning."
Colonel David M. Shoup – Battle of Tarawa 1945 – David M. Shoup went on to earn the Medal of Honor, attain the rank of General, and become the 22nd Commandant of the Marine Corps.

"There was one thing that won that battle Holland, and that was the supreme courage of the Marines. The prisoners tell us that what broke their morale was not the bombing, not the naval gunfire, but the sight of marines who kept coming ashore in spite of their machine gun fire." Julian Smith to 2nd Marine Division Commander Holland Smith. From Robert Sherwood's book, *Tarawa.*

"Surely...they would all be dead by now. "War Correspondent Robert Sherrod who was at Tarawa, responding to the incredible bombardment laid down by the Navy.

They were not all dead, not yet. Tarawa was a bloody hell hole. There were over 4,200 Japanese on the island. It took the Marines two days to break off the beach, even with reinforcements. When it ended, there were 17 Japanese left alive. FCSD area men who participated in the Battle of Tarawa included John D. Ballard and Ralph Kleinspehn Jr.

John Daniel Ballard was a sophomore when he tried out for the FCS baseball team in March 1942. By November 1942, he was a Marine, taking his basic training at Parris Island, North Carolina.

On January 16, 1943, John left San Diego, CA to join the Sixth Marines, 2nd Marine Division. By late January, he was on Guadalcanal, as discussed above. In a letter to his parents, reported in the NAO in May 1943, John remarked that he had been on Guadalcanal and American Samoa.

Following Guadalcanal, the 2nd Division spent the summer and fall on Samoa, preparing for the invasion of Tarawa. His family said that John spoke often and fondly of his time on Samoa. He met many of the local inhabitants and was even invited to join a tribal dance. The Samoa women were often hired to clean the men's clothes. John said that, since they beat them clean on riverside rocks, many shirt buttons were broken.

The Battle of Tarawa took place November 4 to December 4, 1943. The 2nd Marine Division earned a Presidential Unit Citation for its performance on Tarawa during the period November 20 to 24. The citation reads: "For outstanding performance in combat during the seizure and occupation of the Japanese-held Atoll of Tarawa, Gilbert Islands, November 20 to 24, 1943. Forced by the treacherous coral reefs to disembark from their landing craft hundreds of yards off the beach, the Second Marine Division (Reinforced) became a highly vulnerable target for devastating Japanese fire. Dauntlessly advancing despite rapidly mounting losses, the Marines fought a gallant battle against crushing odds, clearing the limited beachheads of snipers and machine guns, reducing powerfully fortified enemy positions and annihilating the fanatically determined and strongly entrenched Japanese forces. By the successful occupation of Tarawa, the Second Marine Division (Reinforced) has provided our forces with highly strategic and important air and land bases from which to continue future operations against the enemy; by the valiant fighting spirit of these men, their heroic fortitude under punishing fire and their relentless perseverance in waging this epic battle in the Central Pacific, they have upheld the finest traditions of the United States Naval Service. For the President. James Forrestal, Secretary of the Navy."

The next stop for John and the 2nd Marines was Saipan. Saipan was another of the islands that the US felt it had to take out on its way back to the Philippines, and then to the Japanese home islands.

Bismarck Archipelago – December 15, 1943 – November 27, 1944

Mark K. Washburn of Centerville entered the service on October 5, 1942. Mark served a total of 39  months, earned several medals, and participated in three crucial Pacific campaigns. After basic training, Mark attended an advanced individual training program as an Army Radar Operator, most likely at Murphy Field at Hobo Sound in Florida. After training, he was ordered to join the shooting war in the Pacific.

Mark's job was Military Occupational Specialty 514. Working as a member of a team, he assisted in assembling and disassembling mobile or fixed ground radar equipment (designated set) and operated it by manipulating tuning or operating controls while observing readings or oscilloscopes. He had to plot and read both polar and rectangular coordinated and converted polar coordinates into rectangular coordinates. By the end of the war Mark was the Chief Radar Operator. *Picture shows a SCR-268 radar unit of the type that Mark worked on during his service. Unit book photo – National Archives.*

Mark sailed for the Pacific war on October 6, 1943 probably aboard the *USS General John Pope* (AP 110) troop transport. He arrived, with his unit Battery C, 237th Anti-Aircraft Artillery Searchlight Battalion at Milne Bay, New Guinea on November 4, 1943. Battery C remained at Milne Bay until early March. They participated in numerous activities outside their regular assignments including helping to construct three hospitals, and an engineer depot. They also worked on the docks and an ordnance assembly line.

The unit then moved to Oro Bay arriving March 4. Mark was now part of the Admiralty Island Campaign. His unit was assigned the mission of providing illumination of targets for anti-aircraft guns and illuminating targets for fighter pilots. They also placed lights to act as homing beacons for remote landing strips and to illuminate hostile vessels at sea.

On March 22, aboard the *SS Brander Matthews*, Battery C moved to Los Negros landing on Red Beach. By March 29 lights had been established at both ends of Red Beach. Lights were established in several locations not only for defense purposes but also to aid in night work. Battery C remained in its tactical position at Los Negros through the first quarter of 1944. During the second quarter, Battery C also remained at Los Negros and continued to participate in the defense of its area.

During the 3rd quarter of 1944 Battery C continued as part of the antiaircraft defense of its area. At the end of the third quarter Battery C was alerted for movement. It was heading for the Philippines. During its entire service, all the Batteries of the 237th were constantly being reassigned to different organizations in order to provide the best support for the invading troops and to provide the best defense against counterattacks once the US forces gained control of its objectives. As an example, as it moved to the Philippines, Battalion C was relieved from attachment to the 14th AA Command and attached to the Sixth Army. Battery C was the first unit of the 237th to enter combat in the Philippines.

Battery C was next assigned to the invasion of Leyte Island. Its mission was to initially provide spread-beam illumination against low-flying aircraft until additional equipment arrived and made illumination of high-flying aircraft possible. One of its sections was assigned to protect Cancabato Bay against possible counter-attacks by water borne forces. It also carried out experiments to illuminate front-line enemy troops.

The 237th earned a Battle Star for its participation in the Leyte campaign. However, Mark's discharge document does not indicate that he earned the Leyte Battle Star. This does not appear to be a mistake or oversite as apparently Mark understood or believed he had not earned this medal. Minutes of the January 18, 2011 meeting of the Wyoming County Board of Supervisors, at which Mark led the Pledge of Allegiance, noted that Mark served as a Radar Operator and participated in the Bismarck Archipelago, New Guinea, and the Southern Philippines Campaigns. It is assumed that Mark provided this information. However, it is possible that Mark relied on his discharge document and was not aware of all the individual campaigns in which he had actually participated.

In October Battery C moved to San Pedro Bay. It arrived there on October 20. The first wave of assault troops landed at 1000 hours that same day. The unit was under attack by Japanese aircraft during the unloading of its equipment. During this period through December 25, 1943 there was constant action. Reports indicate that two enemy aircraft were destroyed, another two were shot down by automatic weapons while illuminated by searchlights and 95 more aircraft were illuminated. There were 125 air raids and 80 homing missions. Several men suffered combat injuries. One man earned a Bronze Star Medal for Meritorious Achievement. At the end of 1944 Battery C was still assigned to the tactical air defense of Leyte Island.

For most of the first quarter of 1945, Battery C remained at San Pedro Bay as part of the defense of Leyte Island. There were thirty red alerts and 18 air raids during this period. Near the end of the quarter, Battery C was moved to Tacloban to be part of the defense of that area. It participated in a special training station of one week on setting up, operating, and maintaining Searchlight 268, the most powerful searchlight then in use.

During the second quarter Battery C continued to provide defensive support. It participated in five low altitude tracking missions. On the 12th it marched in a victory parade. On August 14 Battery C was alerted for movement. It is likely that this alert was connected to the planned invasion of Japan. The next day the Japanese surrendered. The war was over.

Mark returned to the states on November 30, 1945 arriving December 20, 1945. He was discharged January 4, 1946 at Fort Dix, NJ. As previously noted, Mark did not receive a Battle Star for the Leyte Campaign. The 237th Searchlight Battalion did receive the medal. The history of Battery C clearly indicates that it participated in the campaign. It was part of the invasion force. It is possible that Mark was not with Battery C during the Leyte Campaign. No evidence has been identified to support that possibility. Therefore, I have included the Leyte Battle Star as part of Mark's decorations.

Frank W. Wolfe Jr. entered the service on November 7, 1942. Prior to entry, he had officially served with the New York National Guard from January 20, 1942 until December 1, 1942. Frank was initially assigned to Fort Eustis, VA which was a Coast Artillery Replacement Training Center at the time. It is not clear when Frank was assigned to his combat unit, the 470th Anti-Aircraft Artillery Automatic Weapons (470th AAA AW) unit, but it likely occurred in late 1942 or early 1943. The unit was formed October 15, 1942 at Camp Davis, NC and the men assigned to it began arriving in November, 1942. The 470th history notes that most of the men had not even had basic training when they arrived. By late February the 470th was at Fort Fisher, NC and undergoing extensive training. On August 4, 1943 the 470th moved to Camp Stoneman, CA and on August 29 it sailed for the war aboard the USS *President Grant (AP 29)* troop transport. Its first stop was Brisbane, Australia. On October 29, 1943 it sailed for New Guinea aboard the USS *Thomas Jefferson (AP 30)* troop transport. Batteries C and D were disembarked at Milne Bay on November 1. The balance of the unit, including Frank who was assigned to Headquarters Battery were moved to Woodlark Island arriving November 28. The 470th replaced the 12th Marine Defense Battalion. They withstood their first bombing January 13, 1944. During this period

Frank's medical report indicates that sometime in November 1943 he was wounded by shrapnel in the right wrist. He was treated by the 470th Aid Station and for some reason, apparently, was never awarded the Purple Heart to which he was entitled. A Purple Heart has been included in his list of medals in Part XIV of this book, as under the rules he clearly earned the medal.

On March 18 they were moved to Finschhafen aboard the *SS Thomas Cooley* Liberty Ship Troops/Cargo. Since all the remaining gasoline at Woodlark as well as available aerial bombs were also aboard the men renamed the ship the "Brooklyn Bombshell." At Finschhafen the unit was equipped with M-51 quadruple machine guns in addition to their regular weapons. Batteries C and D also rejoined the unit. In August 1944 the unit was visited by General Walter Krueger, Commander of the 6th US Army, to which the 470th was assigned.

The 470th now became part of the Luzon invasion force. On January 5, 1944, the ships were attacked by airplanes and submarines. LST 486 with the Headquarters and Headquarters Battery aboard were attacked by a kamikaze. It was shot down before hitting the LST. When they landed on January 9, 1944, Frank and the battalion earned their first Assault Badge. The Headquarters was established at San Fabian. During the first four days they were bombarded by heavy mortar and artillery fire. During the first six weeks there were 31 red alerts. At the end of the year, the battalion was notified that they had been the 10th most effective unit with 15 enemy planes shot down.

On February 19, 1945 Headquarters and Headquarters Battalion were attached to the 8th Army, 40th Infantry Division. They were now part of the Visayan Campaign for the Southern Philippine's invasion. On March 4 they moved to Panay Island and on the 21st to the vicinity of Iloilo City. On April 23 they moved to Negroes Occidental for artillery reinforcement for the 40th Infantry Division. A Commendation letter from Major General Rapp Brush summarized their contributions to the campaign.

"To Commanding Officer, 470th AAA Gun Battalion, APO 40. 1. Upon conclusion of the Negros Operation I desire to express to you and to your officers and men my personal appreciation and official commendation for the efficiency with which the 470th AAA Gun Battalion has accomplished its mission. 2. Due to the absence of enemy air (power) the battalion was called upon to depart from its normal mission and to assume the role of artillery in support of ground troops against terrestrial targets. All personnel displayed a quick mastery of the essentials of terrestrial fire control. The 40mm and multiple 50 caliber fire gave devasting support to our advancing troops. The support of the 470th AAA Gun Battalion was a material contribution to the success of the operation as a whole. Rapp Brush Major General, USA Commanding." On May 31 the unit moved to Pulupandan for training in water movement.

In August it began official preparations for the invasion of Japan. A few days later Hiroshima and Nagasaki were bombed and Frank's war was over. He sailed for home on October 3, 1945, arriving October 22. The NAO reported that he called his wife from Seattle to tell her he was back in the states and would be home in a few days. He was discharged October 29, 1945 at Fort Dix, NJ. Frank had earned the American Campaign Medal, the Asiatic Pacific Campaign Medal, the Good Conduct Medal, a Purple Heart (unofficially), a Philippines Liberation Medal, the World War II Victory Medal, a Philippine Presidential Unit Citation (awarded to the unit but all men received credit), an Assault Badge, and four battle stars.

One of the battle stars earned by Frank was for the Bismarck Archipelago Campaign. Actually, only Batteries C and D from the 470th participated in the campaign, although the entire Battalion received a battle star. Batteries C and D did receive an Assault Badge for the invasion at Aware. Frank's youngest daughter was a classmate of the author at FCS for a couple of years.

Marshall Islands (Germany, controlled by Japan) - Kwajalein - January 30 - February 4, 1944

"The entire island looked as if it had been picked up to 20,000 feet and then dropped."
US Army History - commenting on the bombing of Kwajalein Island.

Robert Homer (Bob) Speicher, Jr. of Fillmore entered the Marine Corps in July 1942. He was living in Lockport, NY at the time. He became a farmer in the Fillmore area after the war, and lived the rest of his life there.

Bob had two specialties as a marine, automatic rifleman and demolition expert. He was very good at both. Once he arrived overseas, it did not take him long to prove both his expertise, and his courage. Like most Marines, Bob took his basic training at Parris Island, NC, and advance training at Camp Lejeune, NC. He was then ordered to Camp Pendleton, Oceanside, CA for specialized training with the 20th Marine Engineer Battalion. While he was at Pendleton, the 4th Marine Division was formed by bringing together units from other organizations.

On January 13, 1944, the Division sailed from San Diego for Kwajalein Atoll. The 4th became the first division to be shipped directly into battle from the United States. During the next 13 months, the division would participate in four amphibious landings on Japanese strongholds in the Central Pacific. It would emerge victorious from each.

The 4th Marines attacked two islands, Roi and Namur, at the north end of the Kwajalein Atoll. Another attack was occurring at the same time on the southern part of the Atoll. There were some 3,500 defenders in the north. Only 51 survived. The key objectives were airfields, which were the main protection for the Atoll. The main airfield was captured the first day. The biggest damage suffered by the Marines was when a demolition team tossed an explosive charge into a bunker. It ignited torpedo warhead magazines stored in the bunker, and 20 marines were killed. By February 4, the Atoll was secure. Kwajalein would be used as a supply and repair base by the US for the rest of the war. The NAO reported in March 1944, that Bob, commenting on the battle, merely said, "We found plenty of work here." He also commented that he assisted in unloading ammunition and supplies. Bob had earned the first of four battle stars. His next stop was Saipan.

Marshall Islands - Eniwetok - February 17 - March 2, 1944

Leroy Thayer was part of the invasion force at Eniwetok aboard the *USS Dione* and later at Ulithi aboard the *USS Piedmont* (See Ulithi section below.)

Leroy W. Thayer of Fillmore graduated from FCS in 1941. He entered the Navy April 1, 1943, in Buffalo and was sent to Sampson Naval Training Station for his basic training. After technical school, Leroy was assigned to the *USS Dionne*, (DE 261) a destroyer escort designed to protect ships against submarines and air attacks. He boarded the *Dionne* September 18, 1943, as a Fireman first class. In this capacity, Leroy duties could have included firing the boilers, maintaining fire room equipment, and operating the ships engines. Giving his later duties, it is likely that he was operating the boat engines aboard the *Dionne*. The *Dionne* sailed from Boston on September 7 to conduct training. On October 12, it headed for the Pacific. Once there it was assigned to night radar picket duty. On November 15 it sortied for the invasion of the Gilbert Islands, and performed screening duties for a group of tankers. During this period, the *Dionne* and Leroy, earned their first battle stars. *Dionne* returned to Pearl Harbor January 12, 1944. From February 4 to March 1, 1944, the *Dionne* served in the Marshall Islands operations, escorting convoys, and serving as harbor guard at Eniwetok. Leroy now had his second battle star. The *Dionne* returned to Mare Island, CA for an overhaul. During this period, Leroy visited his parents.

In May 1944 Leroy was transferred from the Dionne to the *USS Piedmont* (AD 17), a destroyer tender. The *Piedmont* sailed from Tampa, FL on March 6, 1945 for Pearl Harbor. Within 24 hours after arrival, it had taken its first destroyer alongside for repairs. Leroy was now a motor machinist mate 3c, and as such, was responsible for operating, maintaining, adjusting, and repairing diesel and gasoline engines. He also adjusted and overhauled the engines and its parts. The *Piedmont* spent April and part of May at Pearl, helping to prepare for the Marianas campaign. Leroy boarded the *Piedmont* in Eniwetok.

Leroy served as a Machinists Mate First Class. In September 1944, the P*iedmont* sailed with the fleet to the southwest Pacific to prepare for the Philippine invasion.

By mid-June the *Piedmont* was back at Eniwetok. The Marianas campaign was in full force and every job was a race against time. The work was more difficult now, because, at Eniwetok, shore facilities were not available.

In November, she was anchored in Seeadler Harbor, Manus Island, Admiralty Islands when the *USS Mount Hood* exploded. The ship literally just disappeared, with virtually no trace left. The *USS Mindanao*, anchored between *Piedmont* and *Mount Hood* was severely damaged. One sailor aboard *Piedmont* was killed by a five-inch shell. He was hurled through the air by the blast. Two other bombs hit the *Piedmont* but did not explode, and it escaped with minimum damage. Some 350 men aboard *Hood* were killed. Only 18 men who were ashore that day survived. Some 82 men topside aboard *Mindanao* were also killed. No cause for the explosion was ever determined. The largest remaining piece of the ship was only 16 by ten feet. (See Ulithi section for the rest of Leroy's story.)

Hollandia - Dutch New Guinea – April 21-24, 1944

William C. Gelser of Granger served with the 79th Engineer Combat Battalion. He entered the service January 11, 1943. After basic training he was assigned to the Battalion as a truck driver. At that time, the Battalion was stationed at Fort Riley in Kansas. In July, the Battalion was in Tennessee, participating in maneuvers designed to prepare them for invasions. In October 1943 they were at Camp Forest, TN for more training. Foot marches to prepare them physically were conducted. They also received training on various types of booby traps, as well as constructing and repairing bridges, fences, and roads.

By January of 1944, the Battalion was at Camp Stoneman in California. On the 15th, they boarded the *USS Cape Mendocino (APA 100)* attack transport and on the 16th, they sailed for the Pacific. William (Bill) was initiated into the "Order of the Shellbacks" when the *Mendocino* crossed the Equator on January 24, 1944. On January 30, they crossed the International Dateline, losing a day. On February 8, they arrived in Milne Bay, New Guinea, dropping off some important mail for the troops. They then proceeded to Goodenough in New Guinea, where they disembarked. On March 3, the Battalion moved to Cape Cretin, New Guinea.

On April 19-20, the Battalion sailed for Hollandia, in Dutch New Guinea, as part of Operation Reckless, the seizure of the major Japanese air base there. As part of this operation, the 79th constructed a road from "Pancake Hill" to a junction on the Hollandia-Pim Road. They also widened and did maintenance on the Pim-Airport Road. Operation Reckless was a success, and greatly aided in securing New Guinea. It was also a major step toward the invasion of the Philippines. The 79th received a Letter of Commendation for their work at Hollandia. They were now based at New Hollandia, and they were put to work building docks and approaches to docks. They operated a sawmill and started building the 51st General Hospital.

They also built 12 station hospitals and completed a staging area for nurses. In November they completed the 51st Hospital, laid a water line completing a central water system for the hospital and built a division staging area. They had helped transform New Guinea from a jungle hole to a major Pacific US military base.

On November 20, they commenced training for the invasion of the Philippines. The 79th was part of the Luzon invasion force. According to Battalion files, they were aboard LST 483. They arrived in the Lingayen Gulf on January 11, 1945 and disembarked on the 12th, two days following the initial landings. They immediately established a bivouac near San Fabian. They were constantly on the move, however. Their job was to support the combat troops, and that was not possible from a single point. They built and repaired bridges, roads, and culverts. The rapid advance required bridges across the many Philippine rivers. In January, they built a 50-foot Bailey bridge over the Calascio. They were under fire during almost the entire period. In March, they built a 230-foot Bailey bridge over the Angat River, a 789 double-single bridge over the Talavera River, and a 300-foot one over the Licah River. In May, they rebuilt the San Jose Railroad Station, a Signal Corps warehouse, and the 36th Evacuation Hospital. In June, they built three field hospitals and a sawmill. In August, they moved into San Jose and Santa Fe. The work continued with revetments, culverts, and drainage ditches. And it was carried out under fire. Two of the men were shot up at that time.

The work continued even after the Philippines were taken, and even after the war was ended, although they no longer had to worry about being shot. They constructed a huge storage facility and repaired the Rizal Memorial Sport Facility. The facility, located in Manila and named after Philippine national hero, Jose Rizal, had been practically destroyed by the war. The 79th made major repairs to ball fields, swimming pools and track facilities. The history of the 79th says it was used for the "Armed Forces Olympics."

Bill also found time during this period to write to the *Northern Allegany Observer*. In August, 1945, the paper published an excerpt from a letter he wrote them. It said, "If it were not for your paper, I wouldn't know what is happening to all the young people I used to go to school with." Bill was finally rotated home near the end of 1945, and was discharged in January of 1946.

Marianas Islands - Saipan - June 15, 1944

"It was the decisive battle of the Pacific offensive. It opened the way to the Japanese homeland." Marine Corps General Holland Smith

"Don't Give Them a Damn Inch" Lt. Colonel William P. O'Brien responding to a suicidal attack ordered by the Imperial Japanese Headquarters in which each Japanese was to commit suicide, but to kill seven Americans in doing so. Colonel O'Brien was killed during the attack. Battle form Saipan.

FCSD area men who served on Saipan included Robert G. Aldrich, John D. Ballard, Richard H. Fuller, Peter J. Kaszynski, Robert H. Speicher, Jr., George R. Wells, and Leonard A. Wood.

John Ballard of Centerville wrote, "We have now taken Japan's most wealthy island, Saipan. I am now sitting aboard the remains of an old Jap freighter and can see the island. There is still the steady hammer of machine guns and flares light up the night, but the island is ours. They are just wiping up. I was hit with a Jap shell, not direct though; it exploded about a foot away from me and flying pieces hit me in the head, not seriously. Do not forget, 'the Marines have landed and have the situation well in hand'." Letter from John Ballard to his parents published in the NAO July, 1944. John had not been seriously wounded, according to him. In fact, he had been battered and temporarily blinded. To a Marine like John, that was not serious. He had his Purple Heart sent home to his parents.

To John, Saipan was another island on the sea route to Japan. He had already helped in the deadly mop up of Guadalcanal, engaged in more training on British Samoa, and participated in the blood bath of Tarawa. Saipan was just the next stop. However, Second Division Commander Holland Smith, and many others, felt that Saipan was the decisive battle of the Pacific offensive. It not only cleared the way to the Japanese homeland; it brought about significant changes in the Japanese government.

The Battle of Saipan lasted from June 15 until July 9, 1944. Some 30,000 Japanese died on Saipan. The last to die were some 4,000 to 5,000 men who carried out a suicidal banzai charge. The fight lasted 15 hours, and part of it was hand to hand fighting. The savagery of the fighting on the island is reflected in the names the men gave to various locations - Hell's Pocket, Purple Heart Ridge, Death Valley.

The fight in which John was wounded took place July 1, 1944. John had been on the front line for two weeks. He was in his foxhole with a buddy, when a mortar shell exploded in the foxhole. John was thrown clear, landing face down outside the foxhole. Red-hot shrapnel fell on him, burning the back of his head, neck, arms, and legs. The glare of the explosion caused temporary blindness. His buddy was killed instantly. John was taken to a field hospital for treatment. The blindness lasted about five hours. He had been in the hospital ten days when he heard his outfit was moving out. He simply got up, put his clothes on, and left to rejoin his outfit.

John and the 2nd Marines now focused on Tinian. It would be from Tinian that a single B-29 would fly a mission that ushered in a new age in the history of what we call civilization.

Peter Joseph Kaszynski of Centerville entered the service March 2, 1942. After two months of basic training, Peter sailed for the Pacific on May 9, 1942. He would not return to the US until November 11, 1945. His records indicate that he served as a heavy artillery crewman, specifically manning a machine gun. His records also indicate that he concurrently worked as a utility repairman doing maintenance work, mostly as a carpenter. The work included erecting buildings and mess halls and repairing wooden structures, and likely occurred prior to his unit, apparently Battery B of the 178th Coastal Artillery Battalion, entering combat. Some of this work likely occurred on Hawaii, but may have occurred elsewhere also. His records show that he earned battle stars for both the Eastern Mandates Campaign and the Western Pacific Campaign. The Eastern Mandates Campaign (Mille, Maloelap, and Wotje Islands - all part of the Marshall Islands) lasted from December 7, 1943 until June 14, 1944. The Western Pacific Campaign (Saipan and Guam Islands - both part of the Mariana Islands) lasted from April 17, 1944 until September 2, 1945. Saipan was one of the most important and brutal battles of the Pacific war. Peter returned to the states on October 25, 1945 arriving November 11th. He was discharged as a Corporal on November 11, 1945.

Peter's discharge document indicates that he received the European, African, Middle East Theater Medal. That likely was a mistake as there is no information which shows that he served any time in that theater of war. He did earn, at a minimum, the Asiatic Pacific Theater Medal the Good Conduct Medal, two battle stars and the World War II Victory Medal.

(Following World War I, the League of Nations passed the South Seas Mandate. This action transferred control of the mandated island (Palau, Northern Marianas, Federated States of Micronesia, and the Marshall Islands) from Germany to Japan. All were captured by the US during WW II and then became the Trust Territories of the Pacific Islands governed by the US. In 1978 all but Palau became independent states. Palau became independent in 1994. The author was directly involved in one aspect of the process making these areas independent states.)

Robert Homer Speicher earned his first Bronze Star on Saipan. His citation reads, "For meritorious achievement while serving as a Member of a Pioneer Platoon of Company D, Second Battalion, Twentieth Marines (Engineer), Fourth Marine Division, during action against enemy Japanese forces on Saipan, Marianas Island, 15 June 1944. Undeterred by enemy mortar and artillery fire in his section, Sergeant Speicher repeatedly set off demolition charges to cut down trees which obstructed an artillery battery's field of fire. Sergeant Speicher contributed materially to the success of his platoon and upheld the highest traditions of the United States Naval Services."

The battle was also marked by the mass suicide of civilians. This occurred when Japanese Emperor Hirohito issued an order promising afterlife glory to all civilians who committed suicide. The order was an attempt to keep the civilians from surrendering. Emperor Hirohito believed such surrenders would constitute a loss of face for Japan and would discourage the mainline population. Later, the Japanese tried to claim the order was forged. This was part of the rehabilitation of Hirohito's reputation that also included claims that he had never been a big supporter of the war. It was all nonsense. History has basically let Hirohito off the hook for his support of Japanese aggression in the 1930's and 40's.

Top Japanese commanders on Saipan committed suicide as a result of the defeat, including Japanese Naval Forces Commander Vice Admiral Chuichi Nagumo. Nagumo had led the attack on Pearl Harbor. The defeat also forced the resignation of Japanese Prime Minister Hideki Tojo and his entire cabinet.

The capture of Saipan represented a sea change. The B-29 could now attack the Japanese mainland from Saipan air bases. Four months after its capture, 100 B-29's based on Saipan attacked Tokyo. Bob had not only earned his first Bronze Star he had also earned his second Battle Star.

Marianas Islands - Guam - July 21, 1944
FCSD men who served on Guam included Peter J. Kaszynski, Ralph L. Phipps, Robert H. Speicher Jr., Evar G. Swanson, and George Wells.

Ralph LaRue Phipps was born in Fillmore (some records say Rochester) on February 26, 1910. He enlisted on November 23, 1942 but did not enter active duty with the US Navy until January 17, 1943. He was assigned to the Seabees. He may even have been recruited by the Seabees. During the early part of World War II, Seabees were recruited from the construction trades. The Seabees were looking for men with both the right skills and experience. The average age of the early recruits was 37. Ralph was in his early 30's at the time. Like several other men from the FCSD area, he became an instructor. This was consistent with the military's need for men with both skills and the ability to teach and instruct other men in those skills.

Ralph was sent to Camp Endicott in Davisville, RI. (He apparently was stationed at both Camp Thomas and Camp Endicott at Davisville. However, Camp Thomas was basically a receiving station, so his stay there was probably short.) The Naval Construction Training Center was at Camp Endicott, and Ralph was stationed there for about two years. The Camp had only become operational in June of 1942, and the Navy Construction Training Center was not opened until August. Ralph was among the early instructors assigned to the camp. The NAO, which carried several mentions of Ralph, indicated that his specialty was CM, or construction mechanic. The 1930 Census showed Ralph's occupation as electrical supplies salesman. Ralph wrote to the NAO, both thanking it for copies of the paper and providing other news. On one occasion, he mentioned that he had been walking down the road and had run into Hank Miller and Richard Farnsworth from Fillmore. The three of them went to a New York Giants baseball game. In July 1944, he visited Fillmore.

In September 1944, Ralph was transferred to Camp Parks in California. Camp Parks was a Seabees training and replacement center. It was home for Seabees returning from the Pacific. (Most Seabees served in the Pacific. They built air strips, bridges, roads, and living and storage facilities.) Camp Parks provided medical treatment, training, and reorganization services. It also prepared returning battalions for second tours in the Pacific. Ralph may have been assigned to the retraining activities, at least for a while. He was transferred to Guam in the final months of 1944 and assigned to the 49th Naval Construction Battalion.

The 49th was part of the 5th Naval Construction Brigade located on Guam. Ralph would have served with the 49th until about July 1945 when it was inactivated. The Battalion continued to perform its normal duties with more emphasis on post war needs. In June all the men were transferred to the 134th Construction Battalion also located on Guam. The 134th was only activated on June 1, 1945. It was inactivated on October 30, 1945. Ralph was likely rotated back to the states at that time. He was discharged November 9, 1945 at Sampson Naval Station.

Evar G. Swanson was known to everyone as "Benk." He had earned the nickname as a youth. Evar was of Swedish descent, and when he was young, the men working with his father used to give him pennies. He would put them in his mouth and then run home. The men began calling him "Benk," which is Swedish for bank.

Mrs. Frances Gilbert Wiles related that story to the author and wrote the following about Evar. "On 1 August 1930, he married my older sister. They had no children, but my father died that month and they took my mother, my older brother, and me to live with them in Elmira, NY. I lived with them until I got married on September 6, 1938. That is how I got to Fillmore in 1933. (Note: Evar took a job with the Rochester Gas & Electric Company in Fillmore in 1933.) He was very good to our family." All the evidence indicates that everyone who met him thought Evar G. Swanson was a very good man.

Upon entering the Navy in 1943, Benk was assigned to the Brooklyn Navy Yard as a supervisor in the electrical department. He was quickly promoted to more demanding positions. His work there earned him a letter of commendation from Admiral Monroe Kelly. Kelly wrote in part, "His efforts and advise were invaluable and no problem was too small to command his attention. It is through efforts of men like this that the Navy of the U.S. is the best equipped and best fighting fleet in the world."

In February 1944, the NAO reported that Evar wrote that he and his wife had been fortunate to attend the launching of one of our newest battlewagons. That battlewagon was likely the battleship "Big Mo", the mighty *USS Missouri* (BB 62) battleship. It was launched at the Brooklyn Naval Yard on January 29, 1944. The ship was christened by Margaret Truman, the daughter of then Vice President Harry Truman. The Missouri would go on to earn 11 battle stars during its illustrative career. On its deck, General Douglas MacArthur would accept the unconditional surrender of Japan to end WW II. It is likely that Evar supervised much of the work (especially electrical work, his specialty) on the *Missouri* in his capacity as Planning Officer for Construction. It was later that year (1944) that Admiral Kelly commended Evar for his outstanding work.

Evar also served with the Pacific Fleet and was stationed on Guam in late 1945.

Marianas Islands - Tinian - July 24, 1944

"Into the air the secret rose,
Where they're going nobody knows,
Tomorrow they'll return again,
But we'll never know where they're been,
Don't ask about results or such,
"Unless you want to get in Dutch,
But take it from one who is sure of the score,
The 509th is winning the war."

Poem written by a company clerk on Tinian about the 509th Composite Group, the atomic bomb group. By mid-June, 1945 the entire group was at Tinian, but was not participating in regular combat activities. Due to this, some friction did develop between the 509th and other units on the base. After Hiroshima, that changed. The rest of the men now knew the 509th secret, and that the war was over.
Unit History Book – National Archives.

The following FCSD area men served on Tinian during the war: John D. Ballard, Grover Alfred Bates, Vernon A. Closser III, Ralph L. Common, Robert H. Speicher, Jr., and George R. Wells.

In his article, *Amphibious Blitzkrieg at Tinian*, Joseph Alexander describes the capture of Tinian by the 2nd and 4th Marine Divisions. He argues that it was one of, if not the most, successful invasions of the war in the Pacific. Alexander asserts "No island seized produced greater strategic dividends at less cost." The Japanese had expected a full-scale landing at Tinian Town, and the US invasion armada appeared set to carry out just such an attack. However, it was all a ruse. A lightning-quick landing on July 24th by the 4th Marines Division, on the northern tip of Tinian, was carried out while the Japanese massed to repel the anticipated Tinian Town invasion."

John D. Ballard of Centerville and the 2nd Marine Division were aboard the ships faking the invasion at Tinian Town. The 2nd Division landed the next morning and joined with the 4th in clearing the island. It was the 2nd Marine Division that fought the last decisive encounter on the southern tip of Tinian. It is called the Battle of the Plateaus, and it lasted three days. The island was declared secure August 1st. It was not. A Japanese suicide attack against 3rd Battalion, 6th Marines, 2nd Marine Division resulted in the death of 6th Marine Commander, Lt. Colonel John W. Easley. The attack failed. At least 6,000 Japanese died on the island. Only 313 prisoners were taken. A few managed to escape to Aguijan Island, off the SW coast of Tinian. They were basically ignored and finally surrendered September 4, 1945. One Japanese soldier, Murata Susuma, was not captured until 1953. The Marines had Tinian.

During the battle for Tinian, napalm was used for the first time. It would prove to be a deadly, horrifying weapon.

American Seabees now converged on the island. In virtually no time they turned the flat terrain of the island into six huge runways, each 8,500 feet long. (Just six years earlier in 1939, La Guardia Airport was completed with the longest runway in the world – 6,000 feet.) Tinian became the largest B-29 base in the world. John Ballard had earned his fourth battle star. There was one to go.

Grover A. Bates was from Elmira, NY. He was in Fillmore in the early 1930's as a member of the FCS training class of 1932. He entered the US Marines on September 30, 1942, and took his basic training at Parris Island, SC. He then attended Officers Candidate School at Quantico, VA. He graduated as a Second Lieutenant in March of 1943. It is likely that he was then shipped overseas to New Zealand where he joined the Second Marine Division, Tenth Marines, Third Battalion. He and others likely replaced men lost on Guadalcanal.

By the time Grover, who went by G. Alfred, joined the Second Marines, it was already a battle-hardened outfit, having participated in the capture of Guadalcanal. Grover arrived just in time for Tarawa. It was a bloodbath. Almost 900 Marines were killed. Of some 5,500 defenders, only some 150 survived. Marine General Holland Smith, speaking after the battle, stated that the atoll was not worth the cost. Nevertheless, everyone agreed that the front door to Japan had been blown away. The US would fight the rest of the war on the Japanese home field. It would not prove to be an advantage for the Japanese.

The Second Marine Division was awarded a Presidential Unit Citation for the Tarawa Atoll Operation. It provided: "For outstanding performance in combat during the seizure and occupation of the Japanese-held Atoll of Tarawa, Gilbert Islands, November 20 to 24, 1943. Forced by the treacherous coral reefs to disembath from their landing craft hundreds of yards off the beach, the Second Marine Division (Reinformed) became a highly vulnerable target for devasting Japanese fire. Dauntlessly advancing in spite of rapidly mounting losses, the Marines fought a gallant battle against crushing odds, clearing the limited beachheads of snipers and machine guns, reducing powerfully fortified enemy positions and completely annihilating the fanatically determined and strongly entrenched enemy positions. By the successful occupation of Tarawa, the Second Marine Division (Reinforced) has provided our forces with highly strategic and important air and land bases from which to continue future operations against the enemy; by the valiant fighting spirit of these men, their heroic fortitude under punishing fire and their relentless perseverance in waging this epic battle in the Central Pacific, they have upheld the finest traditions of the United States Naval Service."

John Ballard of Fillmore was also at Tarawa. Both Grover and John, then moved onto Saipan. As mentioned, Saipan, to many, was one of the battles that decided the war in the Pacific. That battle is discussed in the John Ballard write-up in the Saipan section above.

The nest stop for the Division was Tinian. Its capture provided the US with an island airfield from which to destroy Japan with air power. Grover served as an Artillery Observer with the Tenth Marines, which was a field artillery unit. In the battle for the island, Grover earned a Silver Star. His citation reads: "The President of the United States of America takes pleasure in presenting the Silver Star to Second Lieutenant Grover A. Bates (MCSN: O-20616), United States Marine Corps Reserve, for conspicuous gallantry and intrepidity as an Artillery Forward Observer, attached to the Third Battalion, Tenth Marines, Second Marine Battalion during action against enemy Japanese forces on Tinian, Marianas Islands, 27 July 1944. Although his observation was limited by wooded and hilly terrain, Second Lieutenant Bates proceeded with the infantry assault echelon until they reached a radio tower. With a detail of two men, he climbed the radio tower under heavy enemy small arms fire and, for approximately one and a half hours, directed effective artillery fire from his vantage point. His cool courage, fighting spirit and devotion to duty were in keeping with the highest traditions of the United States Naval Forces. Commanding General, Fleet Marine Force Pacific."

Grover now headed with the Second Division to Okinawa where the Division served as floating reserve during the invasion. Some elements of the Division did participate, but it is not known if Grover was part of any of those elements. The Division and Grover ended their war service by performing occupation duties in Nagasaki, Japan. They arrived in Nagasaki just 25 days after the atomic explosion that destroyed most of the city. Grover was discharged April 9, 1946.

Ralph L. Common of Fillmore entered the service on November 3, 1942. The NAO reported in December that Ralph was stationed at Camp Stockton, California. It appears that at that time Stockton was primarily a German Prisoner of War camp. Since he had only entered the service in November, it appears that his assignment to Stockton was possible an emergency and temporary assignment as a POW guard. By January 1943 he was at Miami Beach, Florida likely in basic training. In March he was transferred to Lowry Field, Colorado where he likely went through armaments training. From there, in October 1943, he was ordered to Pratt Air Base in Kansas. There he likely went through his final training as an Armorer for a B-29. Armorers performed first and secondary maintenance on all B-29 armaments as well as loading bombs and ammunition. Ralph likely participated in the "Battle of Kansas" the effort to modify the B-29 to get it ready for combat duty.

In July 1944 the NAO reported that Ralph's parents, after not hearing from him for six months, received a letter informing them that he was now in India and was serving as an armorer in a B-29 squadron. It is likely that Ralph was with the 40th Bomb Group. It had trained at Pratt during the period July 1, 1943 to March 12, 1944. It was then transferred to Chakulia, India. Ralph may have been, and likely was, shipped to India aboard the *SS Champollion.* The *Champollion* carried the 1st and 3rd maintenance squadrons to India. It anchored in Bombay Harbor on April 1, 1944. After a short acclimation period, the squadrons arrived at Chakulia on April 15. The 2nd and 4th squadrons had arrived at Bombay on April 4 and at Chakulia April 8. It is not known to which 40th Bomb Group squadron Ralph was assigned.

In December 1944 Ralph was moved to China. The 40th Bomb Group continued to fly missions from India, but also now flew some from Hsinghing in China. This lasted for approximately four months at which time the entire group was transferred to Tinian. Tinian, the largest B-29 base in the world was the heart of the B-29 attacks on mainland Japan. It was from Tinian that a B-29 flown by Colonel Paul Tibbetts would fly to Japan and drop the atomic bomb that would convince the Japanese war lords that the war was over.

The B-29 was eventually the mightiest bomber of World War II. However, it was committed to battle before all the kinks were worked out. As a result, changes were constant in the first months of combat. Maintenance men like Ralph had to deal with the problems and the corrections. Eventually the kinks were solved and after the arrival of General Curtis LeMay from the European war, another big change was made. LeMay switched the attacks from high altitude conventional bombing to low level incendiary raids. The impact of this can be seen in the results of three raids over Japan in early March. On March 9th 16 square miles of Tokyo were destroyed by incendiaries; on the night of March 11-12 two square miles of Kobe disappeared; and on the night of March 19-20 three square miles of Nagoya went up in flames. Many other Japanese cities suffered similar fates, until atomic bombs destroyed Hiroshima and Nagasaki.

Ralph served 22 of his 37 months in the service overseas. He returned to the states on November 2, 1945 and was discharged November 15. Ralph later reenlisted and made the Air Force his career.

Robert H. Speicher of the FCSD area was with the 4th Marines that pulled off the surprise landing on the northern coast of Tinian. With the Japanese prepared for a landing at Tinian Town, Bob had probably the easiest landing of his combat tour. Since the Japanese had massed to defend at Tinian Town, there was apparently no demand for Bob's specialty: disarming mines, bombs, and other unexploded ordnances. But Bob likely was involved in the major battle the night of July 24th. The Japanese, recognizing that they had been duped, rushed as many troops as possible to the northern tip area. They attacked overnight, attempting to drive the marines back into the Pacific Ocean. A vicious battle ensued. Some historians consider this overnight battle as The Battle for Tinian. The Marines held. The NAO reported that Bob sent home a silk flag that he received when Tinian was captured, along with various pieces of Japanese paper money. Bob had earned his third battle star.

George R. Wells of Houghton told the Fillmore History Club that he was playing golf at Silver Lake in Perry, NY on Sunday morning, December 7, 1941. He was a student at Houghton College. In January of 1942, George enlisted in the US Navy. The Navy allowed him to continue his studies at Houghton until the middle of 1943, when he was called up. However, that fall he was sent to Dartmouth College in New Hampshire, and during the spring and summer of 1944 attended Columbia University in New York City. He was taught a lot of math and navigation at the two schools.

In the fall of 1944, George was shipped to Hawaii, and assigned to an LST (Landing Ship Tank), on which he would go to war. During the next year, George made stops at Saipan, Guam, and Tinian. His primary duties during this period were as Navigation Officer, however, he told the Fillmore History Club that, while in the Saipan area, he was called upon to serve as a male nurse. At one location, he was the only officer aboard the LST when the harbor area was shaken by explosions. He immediately ordered, and navigated, the ship out to open sea to avoid possible damage.

His ship was at Guam when the war ended, and he was given a 30-day leave to go home and marry his fiance. He then reported to Coronado Island near San Diego, where he attended another navigation school. He spent about three months at the school, and in January was shipped to China. On January 17, 1946, in the anchorage area of Mole Pier, Taku, China, he reported aboard LCS (L) (3) 103 as Executive and Gunnery Officer. Later that year the *103*, a Landing Craft Support ship which was now equipped with rocket launchers, moved to the harbor in Kunsan, Korea, and did a geodetical survey. George was transferred, via Pearl Harbor, to Portland, Oregon, where he received his discharge in August 1946. George told the Fillmore History Club that he was very thankful that, during his years of service, he never had to kill anyone.

LST 103 served on in the Navy until 1953 when it was loaned to the Japanese government. They renamed it *Yaguruma*.

Palau Islands – September 15, 1944 – December 1, 1944

The primary targets in the Palau Island groups were Peleliu, Angaur, and Ngesebus. The prizes, as was true with most of the Pacific Islands, were airfields. Control of the airfields meant the Japanese could not use them to attack American forces, and the US could use them to attack not only Japanese forces, but the Japanese mainland.

Charles R. Fiegl of Centerville arrived at Palau in January of 1945, aboard *LCI (Landing Craft Infantry) 867*. He had entered the Navy in January of 1944 at the Sampson, NY Naval Training Station. After basic he remained at Sampson for two months of quartermaster training. One of the things that stuck in his mind was how cold it was at Sampson. Charles also remembers boxing in a "smoker" one night. On the same program was Don Rickles, listed as a comedian. (A "smoker" was and is an evening of entertainment put on by a group of associates, in this case apprentice seamen. The performances can vary from song and dance to comedy. In the military, boxing matches were usually included. The "smoker" originated at Cambridge University in England in 1883. One of its early performances included a cricket match.)

After Sampson, Charles was ordered to Solomons, MD. (Solomons, MD is an island, but is part of Calvert County, MD.) Here he received amphibious training. Amphibious training consisted of everything from basic seamanship and boat handling to small arms practice, mechanics and gunnery practice night and day. The training many times included putting on full packs and weapons and making practice beach landings. Specialized training included such activities as bringing wounded men aboard. Charles' ship's crew was also assembled at Solomons, and then sent, as a unit, to New York City. There, in June, they picked up their ship, *LCI 867*. Charles remained with *LST 867* until May of 1946, working in both navigation and signal operations.

At Palau, his squadron was constantly on patrol. Their job was to guard against any counterattacks by the Japanese. He particularly remembers the LCI picket lines at Peleliu and Angaur. They patrolled, usually in groups of ten, day and night, to protect the islands, and especially the airfields. Huge searchlights were employed at night. While the US held the key islands, Charles said that the Japanese still controlled the 80 or so islands to the north. Charles remained at Palau with *867* until the end of the war. It then remained in the area as part of the occupational forces until April of 1946. During this time, they went into Japanese territory to release and repatriate prisoners from India who had been held since the fall of Singapore (February, 1942). They picked up American personnel and took them to Saipan and Guam for further shipment to the US.

Charles went to Brockport State in NY after the war, and while there played for the school's first football team. One of their games was against Sampson, now an Air Force training base. The game was played on the same field he had drilled on during his quartermaster training.

Ulithi Islands - Caroline Islands - September 23, 1944

The US occupied Falapop Island in the Ulithi Islands on September 23, 1944. The Ulithis had been used by the Japanese for a radio and weather station, and the lagoon as an anchorage. As US pressure mounted in 1944, they abandoned the islands. Ulithi, for the last year of the war, was a major staging area for the US Fleet, and the largest and most active naval base on the planet.

Leroy W. Thayer, as previously mentioned above, graduated from FCS in June 1941. During his Naval career, Leroy visited numerous Pacific Islands, from Hawaii to Japan. Eniwetok, however, as explained above, was home base during a good part of his Pacific career.

In early January, *Piedmont* headed to Ulithi, which would be its home for most of the rest of the war, except for a short stay at the Leyte Naval Base in the Philippine Islands. Now part of Service Squadron 10, it prepared for its biggest effort of the war. For the next four months, through April, the *Piedmont* was constantly at work servicing ships from the invasions of Lingayen Gulf, Iwo Jima, and Okinawa. It averaged 1,000 completed job orders and almost 100,000 man-hours of work each month. The most battle-damaged ship she serviced was the *USS Hazelwood*, which had suffered a direct hit by a bomb. When *Hazelwood* arrived for repairs, there were still dead bodies aboard, which had to be cut out of the tangled wreckage.

Piedmont then headed for Leyte in the Philippines, where it put in for rest and repairs during May and June, before heading to Eniwetok on the 30th. At Eniwetok, it prepared for the return of the Pacific fleet, and the preparation for the probable invasion of Japan. The B-29 *Enola Gay* ended any need for an invasion. The *Piedmont* was at Ulithi when the war ended.

Piedmont was selected to move into Tokyo Bay with the first naval units. She sailed August 16th and on August 28, she dropped her anchor in Sagami Wan, Honshu, Japan and on the 30th, moved into Tokyo Harbor. The next day she moored at the Yokosuka Naval Base just outside of Tokyo Bay. Leroy and the rest of the crew of the *Piedmont* were there to celebrate the official end of the war on September 8, when the Japanese signed the terms of unconditional surrender aboard the *USS Missouri* in Tokyo Bay. The *Piedmont* continued its occupation duties until March 1946.

She served with the occupation forces, providing provisions and clothing to the landing force, and to released POWs until sailing home in 1946. *Piedmont* arrived at Alameda, CA on March 15, 1946.

The Philippine Islands - October 20, 1944

"I Shall Return!" General Douglas MacArthur when ordered to leave the Philippines by President Roosevelt to avoid being captured by the Japanese. He had been ordered to say, "We Shall Return."

"I Have Returned!" General Douglas MacArthur upon his return to the Philippines in 1944.

MacArthur was not alone when he returned. Several of the men with him, immediately or eventually, were from the FCSD area. They included Mark Armstrong, Clifford H. Beardsley, Fred L. Beardsley, Orson D. Beardsley, Warren E. Beardsley, Lionel R. Briggs, Glenn E. Burgess Jr., Barton Burdette Butler, John W. Collopy, Curtis John Common, Arnold H. Eldridge, Horace N. Emmons, Lowell B. Fancher, Lowell B. Fox, Lynford S. Fox, William C. Gelser, John Russell Gillette, Manfred C. Griggs, Erwin C. Howden, Walter Donald Makowski, Robert F. Miller, Douglas G. Morris, Alanson C. Papke, Robert S. Preston, Alton A. Sylor, John L. Thomas, Roy G. Tillinghast, Hugh H. Van Buskirk, Mark K. Washburn, Harold Wesley Wass, Frank W. Wolfe Jr, and James A. Young.

Mark L. Armstrong of Houghton entered the service on June 8, 1942 after graduating from Houghton College. It is likely that he spent the next 120 days as an Apprentice Seaman, first at a Naval Indoctrination School for 30 days, and then 90 days at an Officers Candidate School. During this training, he would have attended classes on ordnance, gunnery, seamanship, navigation, and engineering. At the completion of this training, he was commissioned an Ensign in the US Navy.

His activities for the next six months are not clear, but on March 26, 1943, he boarded the minesweeper *USS Palmer* (DMS-5). The *Palmer* was already a battle-tested ship, having participated in the North Africa invasion at Fedala, French Morocco. At the time Mark boarded, the *Palmer* was performing escort duty, primarily in the Northwest Atlantic and Caribbean routes. In late 1943 it sailed to the west coast and on January 23, 1944, sailed for Kwajalein as part of the invasion assault force.

The attack at Kwajalein was the first of four major battles in which Mark would participate. In June, two days prior to the invasion, the *Palmer* made a sweep of the landing areas and then screened transports during the landings at Saipan. After successfully completing this assignment, *Palmer* was assigned to provide screening duty for ships heading to Eniwetok. As a result, it missed the Battle of the Philippine Sea. By June 22 it was back at Saipan, performing screening duties until July 8, 1944. On July 22 it was at Guam, screening transports off Apra for five days. Since this was part of the Marianas Operation, as was Saipan, the *Palmer* and Mark did not get credit for a separate battle star.

After Guam, the *Palmer* retuned to Pearl Harbor to prepare for the invasion of the Philippines. On October 17, it arrived at Leyte Gulf, and swept both the main channels and transport areas searching for mines. Later it performed escort service, conducting transports through swept channels. It also made a minesweeping run through the Surigao Strait. *Palmer* then headed for Manus Island to prepare for the second battle of the Philippines, Lingayen Gulf.

Starting on December 23, at Lingayen, the *Palmer* was assigned the same duties it had performed at Leyte. The vessel was constantly harassed by Japanese ships and planes. On January 7, 1945, it was within the Gulf performing a minesweeping operation. A violent knocking in the port turbine engine caused the ship's captain to shut down the engine. The *Palmer* left the formation and began to recover its minesweeping gear. It then rejoined its formation as the ships were departing the Gulf. At about 6:30 p.m., low flying aircraft were identified by radar. A Japanese Yokosuka P1Y Ginga (Galaxy) Navy two engine Bomber (US code name Frances) attacked the *Palmer*. The *Palmer* commenced firing, but two of its 20mm guns jammed while the 3" guns put up a steady stream of fire. Although a later report called the gunnery ineffective, it also noted that the Ginga was burning as it approached the *Palmer*. Two bombs hit the port side causing a huge fire. The *Palmer* sank in six minutes. Two men were dead, 26 were missing and 28, including Mark, were wounded. The Ginga was shot down by other ships in the formation. The Yokasuka P1Y type aircraft would be used for kamikaze missions at Okinawa.

Palmer's men were all rescued by other ships in the formation. One of those rescued later died and was buried at sea. Mark suffered second-degree burns in both upper extremities according to the medical report.

In February, the NAO published part of a V mail letter from Mark to his father. From his hospital, he wrote: "Don't let anything you read disturb you. I am safe and having a good rest, am quite sure to see you this spring." By March Mark was home for a 30-day leave. He then reported for shore duty at Pearl Harbor, where he remained for the balance of the war. In November 1945, he reported to New York City, where he received his discharge on November 26th. Mark remained in the Naval Reserves until October 13, 1953.

Mark served as both an Ensign and a Lieutenant (JG) aboard the *Palmer*. According to the ship's log, his duty assignment as a Lieutenant (JG) was Assistant First Lieutenant.

Clifford H. Beardsley of Hume entered the Army on February 3, 1943. After completing basic training, Clifford was assigned to bases in the US for the next 15 months. On August 17, 1944, he was shipped to the Asiatic Pacific Theater of War as a replacement. He arrived in New Guinea on September 6th. There he was assigned to the 27th Engineer Construction Battalion. The 27th had been shipped overseas in January of 1944. By April it was involved in the New Guinea campaign and had been part of the initial assault forces at Noemfoor Island. Clifford earned his first Battle Star for his participation in the New Guinea campaign. That campaign lasted until December 31, 1944, but the 27th was pulled from New Guinea to become part of the forces attacking the Southern Philippines.

The 27th Headquarters and Service Company, to which Clifford was assigned according to the official history (The 27th History has Clifford middle initial as P.) landed at White Beach on Leyte October 22nd, some five days after the initial attack. Clifford was likely part of that landing. During the Leyte campaign, the 27th built a supply dump at Pinamopoan, the Causara-Pinamopoan road, performed maintenance on other roads, built part of a causeway from Culasian Point to the beach, and assisted the 3rd Engineers lay a plank runway at the Tacloban Airdrome. They also constructed a sawmill and medical facilities. As a power shovel operator, Clifford would have been prominently involved in all these construction projects.

The 27th now headed to Luzon where it, and Clifford, were about to earn their third battle star. On Luzon, they built more roads, including a key road from Olongapo to Pinalumbian through a zig zag-pass. This construction opened a road to the Luzon Plain. They also built several bridges including one over the Santa River and the Marikina Bridge near Manila.

The 27th remained in the Philippines until the end of the war. On September 29, 1945, it arrived in Wakayama Bay, Osaka, Japan. On October 6, it moved to Nagoya, Japan as part of the occupation forces. At Nagoya its camp was a former Japanese arsenal. One of its main duties was to build the 11th Replacement Depot at a Japanese Naval Air Station in Okazaki. Many of the American forces in Japan were processed home through this station.

Clifford arrived back in the US on January 3, 1946, and was discharged January 14 at Fort Knox, KY.

Fred L. Beardsley entered the service February 29, 1944. He took his basic training at the Great Lakes Naval Training Station in Illinois and then proceeded to Williamsburg, VA where he received training at the US Navy Construction Training Center. After five months of training, plus a pre-overseas furlough, Fred boarded the troop transport *General John Pope* on August 14, 1944. On August 29, 1944 Fred was debarked at Milne Bay in Papua, New Guinea. From there he was forwarded to Navy Base 3505 on Biak Island in New Guinea.

Fred rose to the rank of Seaman First Class his first 21 months of service. During this period, he likely served in several different occupations. Such assignments would have a been a way of both working and learning skills for advancement to a specific skilled occupation through on-the-job training. However, giving his background at the construction training center in Williamsburg, he most likely focused on the construction trades. His duties may have included installation of wiring and/or operating heavy equipment. It is possible that Fred earned a Western New Guinea Operations battle star for his work on Biak

Following his service on Biak, Fred was moved to Naval Station 3142 (likely Subic Bay) near Manila. He likely continued to perform duties like or the same as those he performed at Biak, depending on the date of his transfer from Biak to Manila. By late January 1945 the Navy was in the process of reactivating the Subic Bay Naval Base, which the Japanese had captured in 1942. Much needed to be done, including the building, and repairing of bridges, buildings port facilities, constructing a communications center, clearings for barracks, and installing a facility for a ship storage unit. Fred possessed the necessary skills to participate in all these activities. Fred also earned a battle star for the Luzon operations.

On October 10, 1945 Fred was moved from Manila to Navy Station 3964 (Tacloban, Leyte) for further transfer to United States. He was discharged at Sampson Naval Training Station on November 19, 1945.

Warren E. Beardsley of Hume boarded the seaplane tender *USS Currituck* (AV 7) June 26, 1944. He had entered the service November 17, 1943, in Buffalo and had taken his basic training at Sampson Naval Training Station. By January 1944, per the NAO, he had completed basic and was home on leave. Before reporting to the *Currituck*, he received some additional training. Warren reported aboard as a F2c (Fireman Second Class.) As such, he fired, operated, and maintained the ships boilers and pumps and communicated with other ship divisions as necessary. He would be discharged as a Machinist's Mate Third Class. Machinists Mates worked with the many and myriad machinery aboard ships.

Traveling through the Panama Canal, the *Currituck* picked up passengers at the Pacific port of Balboa, before headed to Manus. Here it debarked its passengers and then headed for the Philippines, with a short stop at Mios Woendi Island to unload cargo. It was carrying both men and airplane parts for the *USS Tangier* (AV 8.)

The *Currituck* was now ready for war. On November 11, it arrived at San Pedro Bay in the Philippines, where it tended seaplanes flying missions during the invasion at Leyte Gulf. It remained there until January 5, earning its first battle star. It departed Leyte on January 6, 1945, for Lingayen Gulf, where it participated in the initial Luzon landings and earned its second battle star. It tended airplanes and directed seaplane search and rescue operations until February 5, when it returned to Leyte. It then sailed on to Manila. Here, crew of the *Currituck* participated in the inspection of captured Japanese vessels. It is not known if Warren (who went by his middle name Elmer, or by Mike, a nick name given to him by his navy boxing coach) was a member of these boarding parties. In late April and early May, it provided maintenance services to the 76th Wing of the Royal Australian Air Force. Moving back to Lingayen Gulf, it maintained a base for seaplanes conducting night patrols. It sailed to Okinawa on August 30.

From Okinawa the *Currituck* sailed to China, supporting reoccupation of the Chinese mainland. It provided tender service at Shanghai, Tsingtao, and Taku in China, and at Jinson (Inchon), Korea. On October 28th *Currituck* returned to Okinawa and then sailed for San Francisco on December 9th. Warren left the *Currituck* May 14, 1945 at Lido Beach, NY.

Glenn E. Burgess of Fillmore entered the service July 24, 1944. He went through basic training at Fort Warren, WY. His next assignment was Camp Robinson, AR. Robinson was basically a combat replacement training center. Men were trained for combat regardless of Army occupational specialty. In late December or early January, Glenn injured his eardrum in a fall. He was given a seven-day furlough, and then returned to Camp Robinson. The NAO reported in March that he had arrived safely overseas in the South Pacific area. He may have sailed from San Francisco on February 14, 1945 with the 737th Railroad Operating Battalion, since he served with that Battalion in the Philippines. The Battalion arrived in Manila on March 26, 1945. It began operations on April 1, 1945. Like all Railroad Operating Battalions, the 337th was sponsored by a US railroad company. The 337th was sponsored by the New York Central Railroad.

The primary purpose of the battalion was maintenance of the railroad and the rolling stock in its assigned area. The men in Company C served as train operators. Trains were both diesel and steam. Glenn worked with Headquarters Company. The company was used for signaling, dispatching, and supplying their section of the railroad. Glenn worked as a station agent and a telegraph operator. Their initial office was a railroad car at the Tarlac Railroad Station. The battalion very shortly moved to a nearby Standard Oil Company service station. The battalion did come under fire from time to time, primarily from enemy stragglers. Two men from the 337th were killed.

In May 1945, Glenn hitchhiked some 200 miles to meet up with his brother-in-law Arnold Eldridge. They managed to spend three days together (May 8, 9 and 10). The NAO reported in November of 1945 that Glenn was in Korea. He was discharged in the US on December 29, 1945. Glenn earned the Luzon Battle Star and the Navy Occupation Medal, Korean Clasp.

Barton Burdette Butler of Centerville entered the service 10/15/1940. Barton records were destroyed in the St. Louis fire so little is known about his service. He was originally assigned to likely the 11th Coast Artillery unit. Later, like many men in the Coast Artillery, he was transferred to a Field Artillery Battalion, possibly the 655th. He eventually was stationed in the Philippines. It is not known in which campaigns he participated. At some point he suffered a broken ankle, likely in Portsmouth, New Hampshire. He was discharged December 0, 1945. At a minimum he earned the American Defense Medal, the American Campaign Medal, the Asiatic Pacific Campaign Medal, and the World War II Victory Medal. Given the time span for his service in the Philippines, he almost surely earned a battle star for one of the Philippine campaigns.

Roy N. Byington of Centerville entered the service 1/12/1943. As with many, Roy's personnel records were destroyed in the St. Louis fire. Apparently the only still existing record is his final pay record. That record provides minimum information. The most important was that he served at APO 318. Someone also wrote 155 Infantry on the document. APO 318 was used in at least New Guinea and the Philippines during the war. The 155th Infantry Regiment was part of the 31st Infantry Division. That Division was shipped overseas in March 1944. It saw extensive action in New Guinea and the Philippines earning battle stars for New Guinea, plus an arrowhead, and Southern Philippines campaigns It also earned a Philippine Presidential Unit Citation. The Regiment was shipped home in probably November 1945. It was inactivated December 12, 1945. Roy arrived back in the states on January 17, 1946 and was discharged January 23, 1946. This indicates at a minimum that Roy was transferred to another unit at some point, assuming he was initially assigned to the 155th Division.

Curtis John Crandall, Jr. of Houghton was named John Curtis Crandall after his father, but the Doctor, Robert H. Lyman, who also served in World War II, recorded the name on the birth certificate as Curtis John. Friends called him Jack. According to his memoirs, following college at Houghton, John became a history teacher at Fillmore Central. At the conclusion of the 1941-1942 school year, he entered the Navy V-7 program. His program ran four months at Notre Dame University before he became a commissioned officer.

At the conclusion of his training, Curtis was assigned to *LCI (L) 430*, which was a Landing Craft Infantry (Large) with hull number 430. This relatively small amphibious vessel was launched June 16, 1943, and commissioned July 13, 1944. Curtis served as Executive Officer, Navigator and Commander at different times during his duty aboard the *430*. According to the ship's Deck Log, by December of 1943, the 430 was in Australia. It remained in the Southwest Pacific for the remainder of the war, operating in waters around Hollandia, Western New Guinea, and the Philippines. The *430* primarily transported troops, cargo and, of course, mail. During operations, it made smoke for cover for itself and other ships. It received three battle stars for participation in Hollandia (Hollandia Operations), Morotai Landings (Western New Guinea Operations), and Nasugu (Manila Bay-Bicolo Operations).

In all three operations, it is likely that the *430* landed invasion troops. The landing at Hollandia took place on April 22, 1944. The invasion force had taken evasive actions in approaching the landing area, thus confusing the enemy. The landings went off without a problem, although the beach at Tanahmerah Bay was determined to be unsuitable. Following the landing of the initial forces, additional troops were landed elsewhere. The landings at Humboldt Bay were also successful, and by April 26 the objective (capture of two airfields) had been achieved. On September 14, the *430* landed troops on the SE corner of Morotai. The area was secured in two weeks although Japanese forces remained on Morotai until the end of the war. Two airfields and naval facilities, especially for PT Boats, were captured and later played key roles in the invasion of the Philippines. On January 31, 1945, the *430* landed troops at Nasugbu in southern Luzon. This was part of the battle for Luzon and Manila. At Nasugbu, the troops were unopposed and were totally embraced by the local populations.

In his memoirs, Curtis talked about being hit by a typhoon at San Pedro Bay. The *430* managed to reach open waters, and suffered only *a* big scare and a broken mast. Other ships did not fare as well. There was a typhoon that hit the Philippines around November 8, and it is possible the November 8 typhoon was the one referred to by Curtis. He also discussed a *Kamikaze* attack on the *430*. The LCI came under air attack on several occasions during the war. The Japanese resorted to *Kamikazes* for the first time on October 25, 1944 in the Philippines. Curtis' narrative evoked the terror of such an attack, and the marksmanship of the gunners on the *430* who managed to destroy the *Kamikaze* attacking the ship.

On April 16, 1945, Curtis turned over command of the *430* to Executive Officer James Hartman.

Arnold H. (Pat) Eldridge of Fillmore entered the service March 1, 1943, at Fort Niagara, NY, according to his Allegany County War Service Record. For the next three months Pat was stationed at Fort Indiantown Gap, PA. There he was trained in both basic military skills, as well as technical training for work with an Army port battalion. A 1943 *Philadelphia Inquirer* article described the training, which was likened to visiting a wartime port. There was a wharf front, complete with quay, warehouse, rail sidings, and a couple of mock up Liberty ships, all miles from any ocean. Another article said one of the training ships was named *USS Neversail.*

A notice in the June 1943 NAO reported that Pat was on his way to the West Coast. At the same time, the 242nd Port Battalion was being established in California. It is possible that Arnold joined the 242nd at Camp Anza in Arlington, CA, in June or July. For sure he was with the unit when it sailed from San

Francisco to Sydney, Australia on September 25, 1943. On his Allegany County War Service Record, Arnold reports he sailed for Australia on September 25 aboard the *USS West Point*. Arriving in Sydney on October 10, the 242nd spent the next month stationed in numerous camps before flying to New Guinea on November 4, 1943. On the 5th, they arrived at Lae, New Guinea where they would spend the next 14 months. During his stay Arnold managed to send home a captured Japanese flag.

In March 1945 the 242nd moved to the Philippines. Arriving in Manila, they found they were to be billeted in a cigar factory. On April 17 they moved out of the cigar factory to the South Harbor district, where they once again were billeted in tents. One of their first jobs was to build facilities to make their camp more live-able. This included a shower, an orderly room, latrine, supply room and shop building. Their primary assignment, however, was Pier 7 where they were responsible for supervising civilian stevedores. It was their first time working with civilians. During the next few months, while 80 men were assigned as fork lift operators, the rest continued as instructors, pier superintendents and office workers. Arnold's primary assignment during his service was as a winch operator.

By July, the men were working 12-hour shifts at the South Harbor. The lack of time off began to take a toll. During this period, two enlisted men received the Bronze Star for Meritorious Service. The unit's historical summary describes August as "Without a doubt, the most exciting of any one month that this organization has ever experienced." The Japanese had surrendered. By mid-month the 242nd were alerted for a move to Japan to be part of the occupation force. After a stop in Tateyama, they were assigned to Yokohama. There they worked as checkers in warehouses, forklift operators, mechanics, Japanese labor supervisors, clerical workers, and crane operators. Arnold sailed for home on December 10, 1945.

Among other awards, Arnold earned battle stars for New Guinea, Luzon, and Leyte. He also earned the Army Occupation Medal with Japan Clasp.

Horace N. Emmons of Houghton moved to the FCS area in 1963. Born in Maine, Horace was drafted May 25, 1943 at Portland, and entered the service on June 8, 1943. He took basic training at Camp Wheeler in Georgia, and then was shipped to California for further shipment to the Pacific Theater. In an interview with the Fillmore History Club, Horace indicated that he was initially shipped to New Caledonia, probably in October 1943. He then was sent to New Zealand, to the 3rd Infantry Division. The Division was in New Zealand at that time for rest and recreation following combat tours in New Guinea and the Northern Solomons. The division was in New Zealand from March 10, 1944 to July 10, 1944. The Division and Horace, were then sent to British New Guinea to prepare for the invasion of the Philippine Islands. Horace was assigned to Company F, 2nd Battalion, 172nd Infantry Regiment. The Division was in New Guinea from July 23, 1944, 1945 to December 22, 1944.

The landing force faced strong resistance with Japanese *Kamikazes* attacking the landing ships. Once ashore, however, US forces advanced rapidly. Only upon reaching Clark Air Force base did the opposition stiffen. After punching their way through, the 6th Army, of which the 172nd was a part, advanced on Manila. Here General Yamashita ordered bridges and other approaches to the city destroyed, but his order only delayed the inevitable. American forces smashed their way into Manila and MacArthur's pledge to return had been fulfilled. Horace and the 172nd had played their part.

The 2nd Battalion, Horace's unit, led the 172nd invasion forces ashore at Lingayen Gulf on January 9, 1945. During the Luzon campaign the 2nd Battalion, and the entire 172nd Infantry Regiment performed in an exemplary manner. After landing the 2nd Battalion was ordered to move east across the foothills of the main mountain ridgeline in a flanking movement into the Apangat River Valley and then north to secure the National Highway. The battle to clear the Japanese from the Philippines would not officially end until July 4, 1945. The 3rd Division's final mission was to search out remnants of the Japanese force, drive them from the Ipo area and capture and destroy them. General Walter Krueger, commanding general of the 6th Army, recognized their contribution when he gave special recognition to the 172nd for the capture of the Ipo Dam, the main source of water for Manila. During the Luzon Campaign, the 6th Army killed more than 200,000 Japanese. Some 10,000 Americans were killed in action.

The 3rd Infantry Division was now transferred to Japan to perform occupation duties. It departed Manila harbor in early September and arrived in Yokohama September 13, 1945. Initially it was assigned to Miizu Ghana Airfield near Kumagaya in Honshu. Its job was to conduct reconnaissance and to demobilize the Japanese soldiers in the area. On September 16-17, it was moved to Irumagawa Airfield where it performed the same duties. It was relieved of its duties in late September.

Horace served as a rifleman and supply sergeant, and worked in the kitchen and hospital during his almost 32 months of service.

Lowell B. Fancher of Houghton arrived at Palo Leyte on February 24, 1945. He was part of a replacement group of 1500 men aboard the *USS Fond du Lac* (APA 166) attack transport. His trip to the Philippines had taken him to or by places that had now become famous, or in some cases, infamous, to most Americans: Hawaii, New Hebrides Islands, Coral Sea, Australia, Guadalcanal, New Guinea, and Leyte Gulf. Lowell was with the 167th Field Artillery Battalion, assigned to the 41st Infantry Division. He would remain so until the end of the Philippines campaign, landing on Porto Prince on March 6 and Zamboanga City March 28, 1945. Zamboanga City had been the defense headquarters of Japanese Vice Admiral Skugiy Marokuzo and Rear Admiral Naosaburo Irifune until ousted in 1945.

The following story about Lowell appeared in Richard L. Wing's book, *A Vine of Gods Own Planting: A History of Houghton College from Its Beginnings Through 1972*. ".... Lowell volunteered for the draft even before he graduated from high school. His army combat service began in the Philippines, and there on the island of Mindanao he managed to get behind enemy lines while on a banana-gathering expedition. He and some others had gone to a nearby river to get cleaned up, and then wandered into a banana grove to pick bananas for the company's kitchen. After being chased by a wild boar, he got disoriented and as darkness fell, he realized he was lost. He spotted a tiny fire and drew near, only to discover the men were speaking Japanese. As he headed the other way, up and down a small mountain, American artillery fire passed low overhead, giving him a general bearing for his home base. Later, as dawn was nearing, he crept up a slope, unchallenged, between two American machine-gun outposts. At last, back in his own camp, Lowell learned that the final slope he had navigated had been mined."

Lowell would later serve ten months in Japan with US occupation forces. Cities in which he carried out occupation duties included Kobe, Osaka, Kuri, Nagoya, Kyoto, Yokohama, and Tokyo. While in Kobe, Lowell had an experience, covered later in this book, which would seriously impact him in later life.

John R. (Russ) Gillette of Fillmore, known as Russ, entered the military November 4, 1942. Russ was assigned to the Army Air Corps Training Center Number 7 at Atlantic City, NJ. The trainees were housed in the city's hotels, and the Convention Hall served as headquarters. The main hall was used for mass exercises and physical training. One of the features of the Atlantic City training was an emphasis on basic education. Unfortunately, almost all the center records were destroyed after the war, and thus no records of the training regimen exist. Russ did spend about three months at Atlantic City and graduated in late June or early July. He was then transferred to South Dakota for radio training. He spent some three months at the Sioux Fall Air Base in Tomah. The Tomah Technical School provided training in radio interception techniques, radio maintenance and radio operations. In May 1943, Russ sent a copy of the base newspaper *Interceptor* to NAO. By July, having finished his initial radio training, he was forwarded to the Jefferson Barracks in Missouri, likely for more advanced training. While at Jefferson, he received his last home leave before being shipped overseas.

In December 1943, the NAO reported that Russ had arrived in Australia. He was now assigned to the 8th Fighter Group, 38th Fighter Squadron. He spent vary little time in Australia. In a letter home, dated January 12, 1944, he wrote that he was in New Guinea, and for the last two weeks had suffered through a bad sunburn. Given the timing it is likely he arrived in New Guinea sometime in December.

The 8th Fighter Group, including the 36th Fighter Squadron, entered combat in April 1943, just as Russ was entering into his radio training. The Group performed three basic missions during the war, providing cover for allied landings, escorting bombers, and attacking enemy forces. These efforts specifically included supporting Marine Corps landings at Cape Gloucester, attacking enemy shipping, flying cover for convoys, flying long-range escort and attack missions including Borneo, Ceram, and the southern .Philippines, covering the landings at Lingayen Gulf, supporting ground troops on Luzon, escorting bombers to targets on the Asian mainland and Formosa, and attacking air fields and railroads in Japan. During the war, the 38th flew the P-40 Warhawk, the P-39 Airacobra, the P-47 Thunderbolt, and the P-38 Lightning. Russ would have had to be knowledgeable with the radio operations in all the above aircraft. He and the 38th moved several times during the war, serving on at least three fields on New Guinea (Finschhafen, Port Moresby, Nadzab), Cape Gloucester on New Britain, Owi on the Schouten Islands, Wama in the Dutch East Indies, McGuire Field in San Jose, Mindoro, P.I., Ie Shima, Okinawa, and Fukuoka, Japan. In addition to participating in seven campaigns, the 36th earned two Presidential Unit Citations.

Russ wrote home frequently, and his parents shared much of his information with the NAO. In an August 3, 1944 letter, he mentioned that they had been moving around a lot. There was no question about that. In October, he wrote of his time in the Dutch East Indies. They had to dig foxholes in the coral rock. Instead of shovels, they used dynamite. One positive was that they had lots of fruit to eat. In December 1944, he wrote about participating in the invasion at Leyte. In August 1945, on Ie Shima, Okinawa, he wrote about visited the monument to the famous reporter Ernie Pyle, who had been killed there earlier that year. He also wrote that he seen the Japanese envoys who landed on Ie Shima en route to the Philippines to discuss the terms of surrender. Russ observed that they were flying in the famous Japanese "Betty Bomber." He noted that he had seen them before, including many that were shot down.

Russ rotated home in December of 1945.

Manfred C. Griggs of Hume was married with three children when he entered the service on March 23, 1944. Manny, as he was known, took his basic training at Sampson Naval Training Station. He was next assigned to the Brooklyn Naval Yard (likely at the receiving station) for assignment. The NAO reported him home on leave in September of 1944. It reported that he was returning to New York City, probably Brooklyn, and was about to go overseas. Instead, his next assignment was to the Great Lakes Naval Training Center near Chicago. From there, again according to NAO, in December 1944, or January 1945, he was transferred to New Orleans. This was likely to the receiving station there for further assignment. He was there no more than two months, and probably much less, when he was transferred to Norfolk, VA. The NAO reports him home on leave from Norfolk in March 1945. In May, his wife met him for a few vacation days in Washington, DC. Despite his constant travels, Manny was now a Seaman 2c.

According to his record at the World War II Memorial; Manny was in amphibious training at Camp Bradford in Norfolk for at least part of his time there. Giving his later assignment to a landing craft repair ship, it is likely that he was receiving special training related to the repair of landing craft during this period, quite possibly in preparation for an eventual invasion of Japan.

In probably late May, Manny was once again at home, but this was clearly just prior to shipping out. He boarded the brand-new landing craft repair ship *USS Pentheus (*ARL 20) on June 7, 1945, in Norfolk.

The *Pentheus* sailed for the Panama Canal, and the Pacific, on June 15, 1945. It was heading for the big Naval base at Subic Bay, Philippines, where it arrived on October 17, 1945. When the *Pentheus* left Norfolk, the war in the Pacific was still raging, and plans were moving ahead for the invasion of the Japanese homeland. While no one aboard the *Pentheus* knew it at the time, during their voyage the entire world changed. A new age, the Atomic Age, was ushered in by a B-29 named the Enola Gay, and its crew.

By the time the *Pentheus* arrived at Subic Bay, the war was over. There was still plenty to do, however, and the *Pentheus* spent the next several months repairing ships at Subic Bay. The *Pentheus* muster rolls indicate that Manny, and several others, left the ship at Tacloban in the Philippines on October 14, 1945. These muster rolls indicate that they were to be transported back to the states for demobilization. The *Pentheus* itself was not far behind. It left the Philippines in January 1946 and was decommissioned in April 1946.

Manny was discharged as a Seaman First Class at Lido Beach, NY, November 14, 1945.

Robert S. Preston of Hume, according to the NAO, was accepted into the service in December of 1943 (12/22/1943 per the Veterans Affairs BIRL Death File). After completing his basic training at Sampson Naval Training Station, the NAO reported in March 1945 that he was transferred to the Naval Air Corps in Jacksonville, FL, to study radio operations and naval gunnery. In June 1944 he wrote a letter to the NAO, saying that he was at the largest Naval Air Base in the US and that the base had fine recreational facilities, good living quarters, and a large air-conditioned auditorium. (Jacksonville was one of the three largest naval bases in the world at the time). He wrote home in July, saying that he had completed his radio training on July 15, was now a Seaman First Class, and was headed to two weeks of radar training, after which he would head for gunnery school and be assigned to an operational squadron. He also had managed to acquire a southern drawl. By November, Robert was in a PBM squadron at Banana River, FL, and expected to receive his Petty Officer rating shortly. His training was nearly complete, and he would be receiving his wings as a combat air crewman. He also wrote that he had sweated out a recent hurricane, his first, in a truck cab at the base. He preferred not to do it again. Soon after the November letter, Robert was apparently transferred to the West Coast, as the NAO reported in February, 1945, that he was home visiting his parents, and would be returning to San Diego, CA.

From San Diego, it is likely that Robert was sent to Hawaii. The WW II Memorial indicates that he served with both Patrol Bombing Squadrons VPB-100, and VPB-17. VPB-100 was stationed in Hawaii at that time, and did provide training for men being assigned to other combat squadrons in the Pacific. Bob likely went through a month of training in Hawaii in December of 1944 before joining VPB-17, probably in January, 1945.

VPB-17 was a patrol bomber squadron that performed numerous duties. Its primary duties involved patrols looking for Japanese submarines as well as "Dumbo" missions (search and rescue missions), to locate and rescue downed pilots and crews. However, such squadrons also transported cargo and passengers, flew reconnaissance and photographic missions, made mail runs, transported freed POWs, wounded personnel, and Japanese POWs. It carried out special missions covering wounded war ships as they traveled to repair locations, covered troop convoys, and conducted bombing raids on important targets. These missions included attacks on Iloila, San Carlos, Panay, Zamboanga, Davor, Mindanao, Cebu, Negros, Legaspi, and Luzon. Bob likely participated in several of these missions. Occasionally they were assigned to accompany Marine, Army, or Navy combat missions in order to quickly rescue downed fliers. Bob was certainly on many of those missions. The War Diaries for the squadron reports numerous rescues of downed airmen. There were also missions for the Allied Intelligence Bureau which involved flying personnel and supplies from Morotai to the coast of North Borneo.

The squadron was assigned to numerous locations during the war. These included Saipan, Ulithi, Palau, Leyte, Luzon, and Palawan. Often, they served in the same location more than once. At each location and each time, they were also assigned to navy tenders for support purposes. These seaplane tender ships included the *USS Hamlin* (AV 15), *USS Kenneth Whiting* (AV 14), *USS Orca* (AV 49), *USS Pocchoke and USS Currituck.)* Warren Beardsley, also from Hume, served on the *Currituck*, but it is not known if they knew each other or even if they knew they were on the same ship.

At war's end, the squadron was assigned first to Jinsen (Inchon), Korea, and then to Shanghai, China. It was charged with various duties such as currier flights, and transporting mail and personnel. In Korea, it would have been engaged in occupation duties. The NAO reported Robert home on leave in December 1945, and mentioned that he had been in Shanghai. He was discharged in January, 1946.

For his service, it is likely that Robert earned the following medals - American Campaign Medal, Asiatic Pacific Campaign Medal, World War II Victory Medal, China Service Medal, Navy Occupation Medal (for service in Korea), Philippine Liberation Medal, and likely battle stars for both Leyte and Luzon. The squadron likely also received the Philippine Liberation Medal with possible two battle stars.

Alton A. Sylor of Allen originally entered the service in 1942 at age 16. Underage, he was soon released. On September 27, 1943, he was officially accepted. Following seven weeks of basic training and then 16 more weeks in an electrician's mate training course at Sampson Naval Training Station, NY, he was transferred to Camp Bradford, VA. There he went through eight weeks of crew training for service on a Landing Ship Tank (LSD). From Virginia, he was sent to Boston, where following one week in a Motion Picture training class, he boarded *LST 1029* on July 13, 1944 at the Boston Naval Yard. After a couple of East Coast sailings, including one to Guantanamo, Cuba, the *1029* sailed through the Panama Canal to San Diego. Next was a voyage to Pearl Harbor, where it unloaded troops that had boarded at San Diego.

On October 17, *LSD 1029* loaded men and equipment from the Third Marine Aircraft Wing and sailed for the Russell Islands. This was only the first stop of many as the *1029* moved men and cargo from and to various islands, including Los Negros in the Emirau Islands, Hollandia in New Guinea, and Bougainville. Leaving Bougainville on December 15, 1944 it sailed to Huron Bay, New Guinea, and Manus in the Admiralty Islands. On December 27 it left Manus with Task Group 79.5 headed for the Philippines. Here it delivered troops and participated in the invasion landing at Luzon. Among the troops were the 754th Tank Battalion, 951st Anti-aircraft Automatic Weapons Battalion, the 37th Quartermaster Battalion and the 1117th Combat Engineer Battalion. During the invasion, they returned fire on enemy aircraft and provided a smoke screen for landing activities. On the 11th, another LST rammed her bow causing considerable damage to the ship. Other damage was caused by faulty equipment and the surf. Despite these problems *1029* proceeded to San Pedro Bay at Leyte. On January 23, 1945 it was back at Luzon unloading the 16th Cavalry Quartermaster Squadron and the 6th Engineer Signal battalion. On the move again, it dropped off and picked up troops in various locations including Admiralty Islands, Guadalcanal, and the Florida Islands,

On April 12, *1029* headed from Guam to Saipan, and on April 20 it headed for Okinawa, where Alton would earn his third battle star. The ship remained in and around the island for the next several weeks, moving troops and material. There were constant attacks. The LST made smoke constantly to cover operations. Calls to General Quarters were frequent. On June 1, Alton was placed on the binnacle "sick" list. The frequent movements continued as the battle raged. The tension impacted the men, and discipline was enforced in order to maintain efficient operations. On June 28, a sailor was found guilty by a deck court martial for culpably inefficiency in the performance of his duties. Following the end of the battle around June 30, other problems were dealt with. Men were found guilty of being AWOL and of trading rations for favors from prostitutes. On July 20 the LST Group executed its typhoon avoidance plan. On July23 a sailor was confined in irons for being drunk and for threatening a kill an officer and another sailor.

On August 15 word was received that President Truman had announced that the Japanese had surrendered unconditionally. The war in the Pacific was over. *LST 1029* now undertook occupation duties, moving troops and cargo to various locations in Japan, including Kagoshima, and Nagasaki. The ship arrived at Nagasaki on September 14, 1945, two months and one week after the B-29 *Bock Car* had dropped "Fat Man," the plutonium atomic bomb on the city.

Alton (Al) remained aboard *LSD 1029* until May 1, 1946 when he was transferred to the Receiving Station Galveston, TX. He was discharged June 1 from the Naval Hospital at Lido Beach, Long Island, NY.

John L. (Dude) Thomas of Hume entered the Navy on September 22, 1943. He was underage and his father Lawrence Thomas had to authorize his enlistment. Dude, as everyone called him, took his basic training at Sampson Naval Training Station, and then was assigned to Armed Guard School at Norfolk, VA. On December 25, 1943, Dude was assigned to the Armed Guard Center in Brooklyn, NY. He would officially be assigned to the Brooklyn Center for the balance of his service. He was seldom there. Dude served aboard merchant ships 25 of his 41 months in service.

The first was the *SS David G. Farragut,* a civilian merchant ship which transported supplies, ammunition, and troops to the war zones. Dude was an Armed Guard sailor who next served aboard the SS *Farragut* from January 27, 1944, until October 3, 1944. Armed Guards were responsible for protecting merchant ships, especially against submarines. Dude's specific duty was Pointer for a Gun Crew. As such he was responsible for the proper pointing (elevation and depressing) the gun and firing it. Where it would endanger the crew or the ship, he was responsible for assuring that the gun did not fire. Dude made three trips aboard the *Farragut*, all to Italy. As the NAO reported in April of 1944, on one of those trips the convoy that his ship was protecting, came under direct attack from enemy aircraft. These trips usually involved stop-offs in North Africa, particularly Oran, to deliver troops and/or supplies.

The NAO also reported that Dude had participated in the invasion of Southern France. His military records are silent on this, but he was aboard the *Farragut* on a trip to Italy during the Southern France campaign. Despite his records, it is likely that Dude did earn a battle star for that campaign.

His next assignment was aboard the tanker *SS Dilworth*. He served aboard the *Dilworth* from November 6, 1944 until May 17, 1945, and made one trip. That trip started in Baltimore, MD and ended in Leyte Gulf in the Philippines. In route it made stops at Biak in the Dutch East Indies, and Milne Bay, New Guinea. The *Dilworth* was delivering high octane gasoline. Crew members were at battle stations for the entire trip. Dude served aboard the *Dilworth* until May 17, 1945. It sailed from Lingayen Gulf in the Philippines on April 10, and arrived at Brisbane in Australia on April 30, 1945. His discharge record does not show that Dude earned the Asiatic Pacific Theater Medal during his service aboard the *Dilworth*. It appears he did earn the medal. In addition, an official document in the *Dilworth* file indicates that it earned eligibility for the Philippine Liberation Medal for its service during the period January 25, 1945, to April 13, 1945. Dude would also have earned that Medal since he was aboard the *Dilworth* during that period. That information is also not contained in his discharge record. Finally, it also appears that Dude should have received a battle star for his service aboard the *Dilworth* at Luzon (Lingayen Gulf). The ship was there during the qualifying time period for such a medal.

For his next voyage, Dude was transferred to the *SS Franklin K. Lane* by the Port Director at Guiuan in the Philippines. It appears that Dude was in the Philippines at the time this change was made. The explanation for the move was that the "men were put aboard (the *Franklin K. Lane*) by Port Director June 8, 1945 to build up total to required number." According to the *Lane's* sailing record, she arrived in Tacloban in the Philippines on June 5, 1945. Duke made one trip aboard the *Dilworth,* and he would make two aboard the *Lane*. The first was returning to San Pedro, CA, from the Philippines. The *Franklin K. Lane* then returned to the Philippines, leaving Long Beach, CA on August 18, 1945, and arriving at the Philippines on September 16, 1945. Thus, Dude was at sea when the war officially ended on September 8, 1945. The *Lane* sailed on to Shanghai in China before returning to Portland, OR. The trip to Shanghai may have made Dude eligible for the China Service Medal, although once again his discharge record is silent on this matter.

Dude would remain in the Navy until March 1, 1947. Part of that time was served in recruitment and training at Camp Perry in Williamsburg, VA, and part aboard the *USS Shannon* as a Gunners Mate.

Roy G. Tillinghast of Hume entered the US Army on August 3, 1942. Following basic training, and possibly technical training, Roy was likely assigned as a replacement to the 46th Engineer Construction Battalion. Specific information on Roy's early months of service were not available.

The 46th Engineer Battalion was redesignated as the 46th Engineer Service Regiment on March 18, 1943. It is likely that Roy joined this Army unit around that time (or shortly thereafter) when it participated in the New Guinea campaign. The 46th Engineer Service Regiment was redesignated as the 46th Engineer Construction Battalion on April 22, 1944.

The New Guinea campaign lasted from January 24, 1943, until December 31, 1944. The 46th moved from Oro Bay in New Guinea to Biak Island in June and July 1944. There it built runways that were key to the eventual outcome of the campaign to drive the Japanese out of New Guinea.

On October 13, Roy's regiment sailed to the Philippines. It arrived on October 20, 1944 and was part of the 4th assault wave at Leyte. Again, among other things such as roads and depots, it built key runways that were vital to the campaign. Moving to Luzon, it carried out similar activities. In Manila, it built a radio tower. During its construction efforts in the Philippines, the 46th was under repeated attacks. This was especially true during the construction of the Tacloban Airdrome at Leyte.

Efforts of the 46th did not go unnoticed. For building the Tacloban Airdrome it received a Commendation from Headquarters, 6th Army. The Commendation was for Heroism under constant air attack. It also received a Meritorious Service Commendation for superior performance of duty, achievement, and maintenance of a high standard of discipline, and outstanding devotion to duty during the period October 24, 1944 to March 15, 1945.

The 46th sailed for Japan on September 18, 1945. Roy was not with them. He returned to the US, and was discharged July 28, 1945. The reason for Roy's early return is not known. It may have been disease or injury, as Roy died June 21, 1947.

Hugh H. Van Buskirk of Allen (Hume post war) entered the service April 26, 1944 in Buffalo. He took basic training at Sampson Naval Training Station. Following this training and a home leave, he boarded the *USS Natoma Bay* (*CVE 62*) an Escort Carrier in San Diego on August 9, 1944. *Natoma Bay* was already a combat veteran when Hugh joined the ship, having participated in the Marshall Islands, Western New Guinea, and Marianas Operations. Ralph Kleinspehn of Fillmore also served on *Natoma Bay*.

By September 5, 1944 Hugh and the *Natoma Bay* were conducting training exercises in Hawaii. On September 15 the ship sailed for Manus Island to join the 3rd Fleet. On October 3, it sailed from Seeadler Harbor on Manus for the Philippine invasion. On October 18, it commenced operations at Leyte and Negros. Its planes bombed Japanese positions and conducted strafing runs against vehicles and small craft. During assault landings, the *Natona Bay* provided ground support, and launched spotting and air-cover strikes. As a result of this operation, the Japanese Southern Force was decimated. It retreated to the Mindanao Sea.

Nevertheless, the battle for the Philippines raged on. The powerful main (Central) Japanese Force still existed and it was, for a time, unchallenged due to a mis-judgement by Admiral Halsey. He believed the main Japanese force had been seriously mauled. It had not. Given his belief, Halsey set out to destroy the Northern Force and its all-important carriers. In fact, the carriers were virtually defenseless, as most of their plans had been destroyed. They retreated, but Halsey chose to chase them thus leaving the Japanese main force free to enter San Bernardina Strait unopposed to destroy the American landings. Admiral Sprague immediately requested all support possible and ordered attacks on all enemy ships without concentrating on any one vessel. The battle now pitted small escort carriers and their accompanying vessels against a large Japanese carrier support force. The American attack was ferocious. It was so furious that the Japanese Commander never understood the great advantage he had. The *Natoma Bay* followed orders and attacked as many ships as possible with six air strikes. On October 25, it sank a heavy cruiser, shot down one torpedo plane, scored hits on a battleship, three heavy cruisers, two light cruisers, and one destroyer. On the 26th, it continued to attack, sinking a light cruiser and her destroyer escort. *Natoma Bay* then resumed supporting American landing forces. On the 27th it shot down a Kawasaki Ki and a Mitsubishi G3M.

When the battle was over, the American Commander declared that the victory was due to superior seamanship, an effective smoke screen, great courage, and the definite partiality of Almighty God.

The *Natoma* went on to participate in the Luzon Operation. For efforts in the Philippines, Hugh and the *Natoma Bay* earned a US Presidential Unit Citation, a Philippine Presidential Unit Citation, and the Philippine Liberation Medal with two Bronze Stars.

The *Natoma Bay* next participated in the Iwo Jima Operation. Its planes conducted 123 sorties prior to the invasion, and on February 19 (D-Day) flew 36 sorties. These efforts included anti-submarine, anti-shipping, and air combat cover missions.

It was now on to Okinawa, where the *Natoma Bay* provided pre-invasion air cover. There the carrier's planes bombed and strafed strategic and tactical targets, flew observation and photo missions, dropped provisions and ammunition, and conducted combat air and anti-submarine missions. On June 7, at 6:35 a.m., two Japanese Zeros attacked the *Natoma Bay*. One was shot down, but the other, a *kamikaze*, crashed into the *Natoma Bay's* deck creating a 12 by 20 feet hole in the flight deck. This was one of the first uses of kamikazes (Japanese pilots flying suicide missions.) The carrier was forced to cancel its next scheduled strike mission; however, it soon resumed normal operations and carried out a planned 10:30 a.m. strike. The *Natoma Bay* returned to the States on June 20. After completing repairs to damages suffered in combat, the *Natoma Bay* returned to the Pacific to participate in the postwar "Magic Carpet" operation that transported US soldiers back to the homeland.

Hugh earned four battle stars during his service aboard the *Natoma Bay*.

He remained in the service until May 18, 1946, serving aboard the *USS Edsall* (DE 129) a Destroyer Escort from March 25, 1946 until May 17, 1946.

Harold Wesley Wass of Fillmore (known as Wesley) moved to the area in the early 1930's when his father became the Pastor of the Fillmore and Hume Methodist churches. He enlisted in the US Navy in Buffalo, attended basic training at Sampson, and by December 15, 1943 was aboard the *USS Fidelity*. He may have attended a technical training school just prior to boarding the *Fidelity*. At the time the *Fidelity* was a mine sweeper. Wesley would remain aboard the ship throughout his service, but on June 1, 1944, the *Fidelity* became *Patrol Craft (PC) 1600*, a submarine chaser.

Wesley served as a soundman (SOM), which was a particularly important job aboard a submarine chaser. He operated special sound detection equipment and interpreted the characteristics of echoes picked up when sound waves were reflected by an underwater object like a submarine. The same skills could also be used to identify echoes from mines.

Wesley's service aboard the *Fidelity* (but not PC 1600) was performed almost entirely at and near the naval base in Portland, Maine. However, less than a month after he boarded, the *Fidelity* moved to Boston, MA for a major overhaul that required about two weeks. At Portland, except for time that the *Fidelity* was in dry dock for repairs, it conducted almost daily patrols. These patrols included screening operations and sound radar searches. While enemy vessels were not encountered, officers and enlisted men were constantly challenged. There were frequent drills such as general quarters and abandon ship, along with physical exercises and gunnery practice. There was even a surprise inspection conducted by Fleet Officers.

Fidelity's personnel conducted training exercises for aspiring officers from Boudin College. *Fidelity* participated in the search for survivors of the *SS Empire Knight*, which sank after a collision. They also participated in the search for the missing fishing vessel, *Alicia.*, and for a lost plane. On May 13, *Fidelity* sailed for Hampton Bay, VA, arriving there on the 14th. While there Wesley received six days of furlough between May 24 and May 30. On June 10, after becoming the submarine chaser *PC 1600*, his ship sailed first to New Orleans, and then, through the Panama Canal to San Diego. It was about to became part of the shooting war.

On July 24, *PC 1600* sailed for Hawaii, arriving August 1st. While there it spent some time screening LST Flotilla 3. In September, it sailed to Eniwetok. On September 30 it went to general quarters due to an aircraft alert. This was the first of many such alerts over the next few months. It left Eniwetok on October 1 for Manus Island, part of the Admiralties Islands. On October 11, it sailed from Manus for the Philippines., to participate in its first war time operation, Leyte Gulf. For the next two weeks, it participated in that invasion. During that time, it provided smoke screens, conducted sound searches, and suffered through several air attacks.

On October 24, it departed Leyte for Hollandia in New Guinea. For the next two months, it visited New Britain, Manus, and New Guinea. It served as an escort, conducted several patrols, and provided screening for an LCI - LST group. On December 27, *PC 1600* departed Manus to participate in the Luzon invasion in the Philippines. It remained in the Philippines until February 16, 1945, when it sailed to Manus and then to Guadalcanal. From there it moved to the Florida Islands for repairs. Wesley and the ship would continue to move among the islands during the balance of the war, conducting screening operations and patrols. *PC 1600* was in Palau when the war ended. It remained in the Pacific for some time following the war. At the end of October 1945, it was at Guam. By February 1946 it was in San Francisco. On February 19, Wesley was ashore with a fellow seaman and was detained by civil authorities. The log for the 19th, reported no misconduct on his part. Further action was pending on his buddy. Harold was discharged March 10, 1946 at Lido Beach, NY.

Kenneth W. Wright of Houghton entered the service August 12, 1942. He served as a General Medical Office Company D, 113th Medical Battalion, 38th Infantry Division. He likely was in training from August 13, 1944 to December 31, 1944 at Fort Shelby, MS with the 38th. He departed for overseas on December 31 with the 38th arriving in Hawaii January 20, 1944. There the Division both received additional training and participated in the defense of Oahu. Ken and the 38th then proceeded to New Guinea where they served during the period July to November 1944. New Guinea had been captured by this point, but there were still many Japanese soldiers there who had simply been by-passed. These soldiers provided a great deal of realism to the so-called training received by the 38th.

The Division now headed to Leyte landing in December 1944. The 38th Infantry Division, 149th Infantry Regiment destroyed the organized resistance of Japanese troops attempting to capture three airstrips. The 38th was unstoppable as it secured air stripes and port facilities at Olongapo in the Southern Zambales Province. On January 30 it captured Grande Island in Subic Bay. It then destroyed a maze of enemy fortifications in Zig Zag pass. They then truly made good on MacArthur's promise to return when they, following the route of the Bataan Death March, recaptured the Bataan Peninsula. Elements of the 38th moved to Corregidor and cleared the remaining Japanese defenders. It was secured on February 21. In March dug-in Japanese defenders in the mountainous terrain between Fort Stotsenburg and Mount Pinatubo were routed and pushed aside. The two most famous names from the US losses in the Philippines in the early days of World War II had been redeemed and those famous locales were now under the control of the US Army. The 1st Battalion of the 151 Infantry Regiment captured Caraboa Island on March 27. The total freedom of the Philippines continued with Fort Drum on El Fraile Island returning to US control on April 13. Now elements of the 38[th.] Division, the 152nd Regiment, pushed north cutting off possible Japanese withdrawal routes.

They moved to an area east of Manila on May 1 and attached Japanese forces behind the Shimbu Line. By the end of June, it was essential over, although active combat operations continued until August 14 when President Truman announced Japan's acceptance of the Potsdam Declaration and unconditional surrender.

This ended 198 consecutive days of combat for the Division. The Division during this period had faced 80,000 Japanese soldiers, killed 26,469 and taken 1411 prisoners. The clean-up that followed would add a few more to these totals. These achievements were not without cost. Some 645 men of the 38th had been killed in action and another 2,814 had been wounded. Kenneth would have certainly been involved in treating many of the wounded.

The Commanding Officer of the 38th, William C. Chase, ordered that henceforth the Division was to be known as the "Avengers of Bataan."

James A. Young was the FCS Agriculture teacher at Fillmore Central in the early 1940's. He was a native of the nearby town of Angelica. One of his students and WW II veteran, Lyle Brown, remembers that Young drove a bunch of French students to Alfred University one day to see the French film, *The Baker's Wife*. Young was also a member of the FCS faculty basketball team. Three of the other team members, (William Appleford, Curtis Crandall, and Robert Boehmler) also served during the war. Lyle recalled that Young was big and strong, physical characteristics that would serve him well during his military career.

Young served with the 108th Infantry Regiment, 40th Infantry Division. He rose to the rank of Captain. After extensive training at Fort McClellan, Al., the Division was shipped to California in December 1941. They were scheduled to be sent to the Philippines to aid in its defense, but before that could happen, the Japanese had seized and occupied the islands. As a result, Jim Young, and others in the 40th Division, were shipped to Hawaii, where they remained until January of 1944, when they were shipped to Guadalcanal. In April 1944 they moved to the Bismarck Archipelago, where the Division earned its first battle star on New Britain. It would earn three more battle stars before the war ended. The NAO reported that while on New Britain, Young was awarded the Expert Infantryman Badge. The paper included the requirements for such an award: the physical stamina of a fast-cross country runner, the skill of a top-notch jungle fighter, crack marksmanship, and deftness with the bayonet. The NAO reported that one of Young's fellow officers visited his parents in late 1944. He assured them that James "was in excellent spirits, had never been sick, and had never missed a meal in three and a half years of service."

The next stop on the way home for the 108th was the Philippines. While not part of the initial landings on S-Day, January 1, 1945, the 108th was soon in the thick of the fight on Luzon (Lingayen Gulf). It engaged in brutal battles with the Japanese at Fort Stotsenburg, Clark Field, Hill 7 and Scuba Ridge. On March 8th, the 108th was sent to Leyte to clean out the remaining Japanese resistance. On May 10[th,] it joined the Battle of Mindanao, helping to clear the Sayre Highway and attacking a strong Japanese force at the Mangima River Canyon. After six weeks of fighting its way through jungle, heavy rains, knee-deep mud, and tall, razor-sharp grass, not to mention Japanese troops, the 108th rejoined the rest of the 40th Division at Panay.

On June 29, 1945, the Division was ordered to Korea to carry out garrison duties. It remained there until March 1946, when it was finally shipped home.

Volcano Islands - Iwo Jima - February 19 - March 26, 1945

"The raising of that flag on Suribachi means a Marine Corps for the next 500 years."
James Forrestal, Secretary of the Navy - February 23, 1945

"Among the men who fought on Iwo Jima, uncommon valor was a common virtue."
Fleet Admiral Chester W. Nimitz - March 16, 1945. A statement that says it all.

Robert L. Leet and Robert H. Speicher, Jr., "represented" the FCSD area at Iwo Jima.

The Battle of Iwo Jima has been called the greatest battle in the history of the US Marine Corps. US forces attacking Iwo Jima vastly outnumbered the Japanese defenders. Even so, it was the only battle in which the Marines suffered more casualties than the enemy, although the Japanese death total was three times the Marine total. The Japanese commander, General Kuribayashi, was a brilliant strategist and a practical man. He had learned from the mistakes of Japanese defenders on Saipan and elsewhere, and he avoided the same defensive tactics. He did not want to establish a beachhead defense, but his superiors ordered him to use this tactic. Kuribayashi knew such defenses were easily destroyed by fighter planes and naval gunfire. His defense, therefore, was minimal, enough to obey his orders. Kuribayashi real plan called for allowing the landings to occur unopposed until the beach was congested, and then to lay down heavy artillery and mortar fire. The beaches were also extensively mined.

Kuribayashi's defense system included snipers, pillboxes, camouflaged machine gun positions, hidden artillery, and mortar positions. Internal tunnels connecting defensive bunkers allowed for re-manning of bunkers overrun by the Marines, and then inflicting heavy casualties on Marines who thought the positions were secure. He also disavowed futile banzai charges until the very last battle. Kuribayashi was unable to finish tunnels connecting the northern and southern ends of the island in time for the battle.

Had he accomplished this, the battle would have been prolonged, and the death toll would have been higher, but the outcome would not have changed. This lack of connecting tunnels enabled the Marines to quickly capture the southern end of the island, which included Mount Suribachi. Thus, the famous flag-raising on February 23, even though the battle for Iwo Jima would last until March 26. The Marines had to adapt to these new tactics. Finding their guns virtually useless, they turned to flame throwers and grenades to seal the tunnels, and flush out the defenders.

Robert L. Leet of Fillmore entered the US Navy October 15, 1943, at Olean, NY. Robert's family lived off and on in the Fillmore area going all the way back to 1900. Robert took basic training at Sampson Naval Training Station. Later he likely attended a technical school to become a Hospital Apprentice (HA). Classes included dietetics, hygiene and sanitation, pharmacy, chemistry, nursing care and anatomy. The program lasted some 10 weeks and ran ten hours daily. This could have been at Bainbridge, MD, which had a major HA training program. It is likely that he then was assigned to a shore hospital for additional on-the-job training.

On December 23, 1944, Robert boarded the *USS Lowndes* (APA 154), an Amphibious Attack Transport ship in Hawaii. He would serve on the *Lowndes* as an HA. On January 27, the *Lowndes* headed to Saipan with troops and cargo. It then continued to Iwo Jima. It was carrying the 3rd Battalion, 23rd Marines, and Company C of the 133rd Naval Construction Battalion. Both units participated in the February 19 assault of Iwo Jima. Medical personal from the *Lowndes* went ashore to tend to and evacuate casualties. It is possible that Robert, given his job, was part of the shore groups. The *Lowndes* returned to Saipan on March 3, and prepared to participate in the final leg of the US island-hopping campaign. Once Okinawa was in US hands, only the Japanese homeland itself would remain.

On April 1, the *Lowndes* was off Hogushi Beach at Okinawa as the invasion began. She remained there, under constant air attack, until April 12 when she landed her troops and cargo. On April 18, she returned to Saipan. For the balance of the war, the *Lowndes* carried out training exercises at Saipan and the SW Pacific. On July 11, it sailed from Guam to San Francisco. Post war, the *Lowndes* performed occupation duties, carrying troops and cargo to the Philippines and Japan, and taking veterans home. During this period, while in San Francisco, Robert went through a Captain's Mast that ended in his reduction in grade from Seaman 1C to Seaman 2C. He, and several other men, had been AWOL for seven hours. On October 6, the *Lowndes* sailed from Saipan for the last time. Upon arriving in the US, Robert was transferred to the Seattle Receiving Station for reassignment. He was discharged January 18, 1946. after earning two battle stars for Iwo Jima and Okinawa.

Robert H. Speicher of Fillmore played a key role, and displayed extraordinary courage in addressing one of Kuribayashi's defenses, namely mines. For his actions, which occurred the same day as the flag raising on Suribachi, Bob Speicher was awarded the Bronze Star for heroism. His citation, presented in the name of the President of the United States, reads: "For heroic achievement in connection with operations against the enemy while serving with the shore party as demolitions sergeant on IWO JIMA, VOLCANO ISLANDS, on 23 February, 1945. When the Naval Construction Battalion equipment arrived on a congested beach, the area selected in which to store it required probing to assure the safety of the equipment from mines. His mine removal section was severely depleted by casualties, but Sergeant Speicher, unassisted and in a most expeditious manner, detected, removed, and disarmed the serial bombs and tape-measure mines restricting the use of the area, working all the while despite enemy artillery and mortar fire in the area. His courageous conduct was outstanding and in keeping with the highest traditions of the United States Naval Services."

Back in 1942 President Roosevelt had told those who considered the US a nation of weakling and playboys to tell that to, among others, the Marines. Nobody was volunteering to tell the Marines anything at this point, especially anybody in Japan. Bob Speicher on Iwo Jima despite being under intense fire from the enemy, had carried out his vital assignment virtually alone. He not only earned his second Bronze Star for Heroic Achievement he also earned his fourth Battle Star. (Since this was his second Bronze Star, he received a Gold Star.)

In his post-war life Bob worked on several construction projects. A life-long friend of the author, Jim Mowers, car-pooled to work with Bob during this period. Jim said that not once during the time they traveled to and from work together did Bob mention the war, much less his part in it.

Ryuku Islands - Okinawa – April 1, 1945

The island was "the most-ghastly corner of hell I had ever witnessed." "Every crater was half full of water, and many of them held a Marine corpse. The bodies lay pathetically just as they had been killed, half submerged in water, rusting weapons still in hand." "Men struggled and fought and bled in an environment so degrading I believed we had been flung into hell's own cesspool." Eugene B. Sledge, 1st Marine Division, from his book, *Battle of Okinawa, The Bloodiest Battle of the War. One of the most vivid and true description of the hell of war ever written.*

It was like old home week for FCSD area residents at Okinawa, except they were not there for a good time. A significant number served on Okinawa (or aboard ship at Okinawa) at some time during World War II.   They included Kenneth (Rod) Babbitt, John D. Ballard, Lionel R. Briggs, Robert Burns, Paul R. Fleming, John Russell Gillette, Jacob J. Hoffman, Frank Ward Lane, Dr. Robert H. Lyman, Robert F. Miller, Austin D. Morris, Alanson P. Papke, Gustave G. Prinsell, Howard Leo Ricketts, Allen Richard Smith, Clark Otis Smith, Alton A. Sylor, Alfred C. Wilday, Clair N. Williams, Frederick S. Winchip, and Leonard A. Wood.

The Battle for Okinawa has been called the "Typhoon of Steel." It was the largest amphibious assault in the Pacific during World War II. There were also more casualties at Okinawa than in any other Pacific battle. The US Navy suffered greater losses there than in any other battle in the Pacific. It lasted from April first until mid-June, 1945.

John Daniel Ballard of Centerville earned his fifth and final battle star at Okinawa. His family said that John did not talk much about Okinawa. He served there from July 1 to July 14, 1945, according to the family. During this battle, the 2nd Marine Division was designated as 10th Army Reserve and served as a divisionary force. In the middle of the month, the Division returned to Saipan.

Its orders now were to prepare for "Operation Downfall," the invasion of Japan. With the surrender of Japan, that invasion became unnecessary. The Division did move to Japan in September 1945 as part of the occupational forces, but it is not clear that John was part of that deployment. He was back in the states by October 1945. He was discharged November 1, 1945.

John was a proud Marine. He would never let anyone disrespect the Marine Corps. Lord help anyone who claimed that an Army man fought as well as a Marine. He found humor in such everyday events as the use of a helmet. He described its uses to his wife. First and primary, of course, was protection, and no Marine would be without it. But it could also be used for heating hot water and taking a bath. Many a meal was consumed from the helmet, even though it was used on occasion to dig the all-important foxhole.

John was also a robust man, and seldom had non-combat medical problems. His tonsils became infected at one point, and were removed. On another occasion, he contacted dengue fever. For a-while doctors thought he had elephantiasis. He faithfully took his atabrine tablets, and told his wife that, like everyone else, his skin turned yellow.

By the end of the war, he was ready to go home. Things were now wearing on him, and he became edgy. He also bored easily. He was busted from Sergeant to Private for insubordination. However, he was proud of those stripes and quickly earned them back. Anxious to get home, he and others had to wait their turn. Twice he and his unit were ordered to pack their sea bags and appear at the dock to board a homeward bound ship. Twice the ship never showed. The third time, they waited overnight, but still the ship had not appeared. John decided to visit the nearby town. While he was gone, the ship appeared. His unit and his sea bag were loaded aboard and the ship departed. John was forced to catch a later ship. He never did get his sea bag back. John died at the relatively young age of 52 during a routine operation. The doctors said his death was likely due to all the combat stress his body had endured. John never forgot that he was a Marine. As a young man, he had "U.S.M.C." tattooed on his arm. Once a Marine Always a Marine.

Lionel Roy Briggs of Hume, son of Roy and Lillian Briggs, joined the Navy on January 18, 1944. During the next two years, he would travel half way around the world, participate in some of the bloodiest battles in history, and visit several countries he probably had never heard of, or heard very little about, prior to joining the Navy. Lionel reported aboard the *USS Alaska* (CB 1), one of two new heavy cruisers, June 17, 1944. By February 1945, he was in the Pacific War Zone where the *Alaska*, now part of Task Force 58, the mightiest naval task force ever assembled, was providing anti-aircraft defense for the aircraft carriers *Enterprise* (CV 6) and *Saratoga* (CV 3) at Okinawa. On February 10, the *Alaska*, as part of the task force, participated in an unopposed air strike against Tokyo and its surrounding areas. It then participated for 19 days in the initial assaults on Iwo Jima. It returned to screen the carriers *Yorktown* and *Intrepid* during the Battle of Okinawa. Here it saw its first "combat" meaning it was also attacked. During the battle, it shot down its first two Japanese planes, two Yokosuka bombers. The first of these bombers had attempted to crash into the US carrier *Intrepid* (CV 11) aircraft carrier. Unfortunately, it also shot down a US 6F6 Hellcat. Thankfully the pilot survived.

The next day the aircraft carrier USS *Franklin* (CV 13) was badly damaged by bombs and a *kamikaze*, and the *Alaska* and other ships were ordered to escort her to Ulithi for repairs. During the trip, the *Alaska* fired on attacking planes and used its anti-air search radar to vector fighters that shot down a Japanese Kawasaki fighter. It then returned to Okinawa to continue its escort duties until it and *USS Guam* (CB 2) large cruiser were ordered to bombard the Japanese Island of Minami-Daito. By April 1 the *Alaska* was back at Okinawa to support the initial landings. While screening during the rest of the month, on April 11 the *Alaska* shot down one fighter plane, assisted with another, and likely got an Ohka piloted rocket bomb. It continued its marksmanship on April 16 when it shot down three more fighters and assisted with three others. In May, it returned to Ulithi for re-supply, but was back at Okinawa by the end of the month.

On June 9, *Alaska* and *Guam* bombarded the Japanese Island of Oki-Daito and then sailed to San Pedro Bay in Leyte Gulf for rest and maintenance. In mid-July, the two ships conducted a sweep into the East China and Yellow Seas, looking for Japanese shipping. They had limited success. *Alaska* also took part, in late July, in a major raid into the Yangtze River off Shanghai, again with limited success.

In late August and early September, the *Alaska* served as part of the 7th Fleet Occupational Force off Japan. With the war over it was sent to Inchon, Korea, to support Army operations, and then, from September 27 to November 13, to Tsingtao, China to support the 6th Marine Division. Ordered back to Korea, it participated in Operation Magic Carpet, the repatriation of US servicemen. Stopping first in San Francisco, it proceeded via the Panama Canal to Boston, arriving February 2, 1946, just a little more than two years since Lionel had joined the Navy.

Paul R. Fleming who lived in Belfast, but was the Fillmore barber for over 30 years, entered the service in July 1944. After basic training at Sampson Naval Training Station, Paul was assigned to the brand-new attack cargo ship *USS Tyrrell* (AKA 80). He boarded the ship December 4, 1944, the day it was christened.

After a brief shakedown cruise in the Virginia Capes, the *Tyrrell* headed to the Pacific on January 5, 1945, with a first stop at Pearl Harbor. During the next 12 months Paul, and the *Tyrell* made the rounds of the major Pacific battle zones. As the war neared its end, Paul and the *Tyrrell* participated in the deadliest battle of the Pacific, Okinawa. Its first stops, delivering supplies and troops, were Eniwetok and Ulithi. It then joined the Southern Task Force for the Okinawa invasion. During the initial landings on April 1, it was off Hogushi as its boats ferried supplies to the shore throughout the day. On April 2, it was attacked by a Japanese *kamikaze*. The plane dove on the Tyrell, trying to crash into the ship. It sheared off the main antenna, hit the lower yardarm support on the starboard side at the masthead, and side-swiped the starboard cargo boom at the number 5 hatch. It then crashed into the sea and exploded, showering the deck with pieces of wreckage.

From April 1 to April 9, the *Tyrrell* remained off Okinawa, debarking cargo, and fighting off Japanese planes. On the 4th, it resupplied the heavy cruiser *USS Minneapolis (CA 36)*, and took away the ship's empty casings. On the 5th, its gunners damaged a Japanese bomber attacking the ship. On the 9th, it finished unloading its cargo and headed back to San Francisco for new supplies. For the next three months, it made cargo runs between San Francisco and Pearl Harbor. On August 27th, it left San Francisco for the Marshall Islands. It was diverted in route, but on September 13th, while unloading cargo at Majuro, the men of the *Tyrrell* learned that the war was over.

Their work was not done, however. The *Tyrrell* immediately was assigned to supplying occupation forces in Japan. This primarily involved shuttles between the Philippines and various ports in Japan, including Wakayama, Nagoya, Kure (they returned to Seattle to pick-up the supplies for Kure), and Nagasaki. Members of the *Tyrell's crew* had a first-hand view of the devastation wrought by the atomic bomb at Nagasaki. On February 2, 1946, they headed back to Norfolk. Paul was transferred from the *Tyrrell* to the Norfolk Receiving Station on April 19, 1946. He finished his Naval career as a Coxswain (T), having been promoted November 1, 1945.

Paul had been a Boatswain's Mate during most of his time aboard the *Tyrrell*. As such he was involved in all activities relating to marlinspike, deck, and boat seamanship, as well as the maintenance of the ship's external structure and deck equipment. Boatswain's Mates also act as petty officers in charge of small craft and may perform duties as master-at-arms, serve in or take charge of gun crews and damage control parties.

Boatswain's Mates are responsible for the deck side watch while in port. They are close to the gangway, and monitor all comings and goings to and from the ship. At sea, on watch, they are within ear shot of the conning officer. They supervise all other watch standers on deck. They also make all announcements to the crew while at sea or in port.

Frank W. Lane of Houghton was one of Clark Smith's officers on Okinawa. (See below.) Frank had already spent 15 months in the New York Guard when he was appointed a Second Lieutenant in the Marine Corps with rank from May 5, 1944. He received his temporary appointment to First Lieutenant while undergoing Aviation Ground Officers training at Quantico, VA. While assigned to Cherry Point, NC, Frank was detached to St. Simons Island, GA for training at the Navy Radar (Fighter Direction) School. By June he was aboard the *USS Altamaha* (CVE 18) escort carrier on his way to Hawaii, where he was temporarily assigned as Fighter Director Officer with the Amphibious Forces Pacific Fleet. On

July 6 he was sent, by air, via Guam to Okinawa, arriving the same day. On Okinawa Frank served as a Fighter Control Officer with the Marine Air Warning Service, identifying targets for US fighters. Frank had some vivid memories of Okinawa. He told his son Frank that they were all sleeping on cots because there were snakes everywhere. Further, since there were Japanese on the island right up until the end of the war, many times during the night, the men would get up and go "Jap hunting" in the jungle. Like Clark Smith, Frank was asked to go on to China at the end of the war. He was even promised a promotion to Captain. Frank decided he had seen enough, and opted to return home.

Frank returned to the US in November of 1945, sailing aboard the *USS Shangrila* (CV 38) aircraft carrier. The name *Shangrila* originated as a mythical utopian place in James Hilton's novel, *Lost Horizon*." The name became more famous during WW II when President Roosevelt, asked by reporters where Jimmy Doolittle's planes which bombed Japan in 1942 had come from, replied, Shangrila. While it is not likely that Frank thought about it, it is ironic to think he was leaving a place Eugene Sledge was to call "Hell's Own Cesspool" on a ship named for an earthly mythical Paradise.

When he arrived at the bus station in Arcade, NY (30 miles from his home in Houghton) he called the family and asked them to pick him up. His wife Eileen was canning corn when he called. She was so anxious to see him that she left the stove on when they left the house. By the time they returned to the house, the corn had boiled dry, and the jars exploded as Frank and others entered the house. Frank's training and instincts took over and he knocked the entire family to the floor. His first night home from the war was spent cleaning dried corn and glass off the kitchen ceiling and walls.

Austin D. (Austy) Morris of Centerville arrived on Okinawa July 5, 1945, just five days late to qualify

Austy on his bulldozer on Okinawa. Lyle Brown Photo.

for the Okinawa battle star. Officially, the Okinawa Gunto Operation ended June 30, 1945. That did not mean the fighting in the area was totally over. The *USS Pennsylvania* was hit by a Japanese torpedo bomber in Okinawa's Bruckner Bay as late as August 12, 1945. Austy told his son Marty that he witnessed a *kamikaze* attack after arriving on Okinawa. While such attacks started in 1944, they reached their peak at Okinawa. Starting on April 6, they continued until mid-August. The last attack occurred August 15. The last ship sunk by a *kamikaze* at Okinawa, was the *USS Callahan* (DD 792) a destroyer on July 29. Estimates of ships lost vary, but it appears that the total was approximately 47. Others were damaged beyond repair. The reality was, the attacks had a minimal effect, since, by Okinawa, the US Navy was so big and powerful, it could absorb the losses.

Austy was a member of the FCS class of 1945. However, he and Fred Winchip left school in December of 1944 to join the Navy. (They both later received their diplomas.) After basic training at Sampson, Austy (and Fred) were assigned to the Naval Training School at Davisville, Rhode Island. They had been selected to become Seabees (from CB - construction battalion). The Seabees were a very select group. During World War II, some 325,000 men served in Navy Construction Battalions. They were, by and large, skilled craftsmen: plumbers, electricians, equipment operators, men with building trade skills. They built virtually anything, including advance bases, runways, and docks in war zones. The Seabees were right behind the Marines during invasions.

Of the 325,000 Seabees who served during the war, 55,000 participated in construction projects on Okinawa. There, they built ocean ports, bomber and fighter bases, roads, a seaplane base, Quonset villages, gasoline tank farms, storage dumps, hospitals, and ship repair facilities. By August 1945, there were sufficient facilities, supplies, and manpower available on Okinawa to mount an invasion of Japan.

It is entirely possible that both Austy and Fred would have been part of any invasion of the Japanese mainland.

On March 1, 1945, Austy arrived at Camps Parks, CA, assigned to the 86th Naval Construction Battalion. On March 16, he was transferred to the Naval Hospital in Shoemaker, CA, with appendicitis. By April 30, he was back with 86th. The 86th sailed for Okinawa on May 24, 1945. They clearly made stops in route, including for sure Hawaii, as they did not arrive at Okinawa until July 5, 1945. On July 8, the Battalion reported for duty.

The 86th would participate in several construction projects on Okinawa, but the biggest may have been the clean-up work following the devastation caused by Typhoon Louise in October. Austy, officially a Motor Machinist Mate, was operating a bull dozer near the beach at the time. His brother, Ensign Richard Morris, on his way to Japan to join his ship, the *USS Champlin* (CV 39) aircraft carrier, was on Okinawa when the typhoon struck. Even regular Japanese attacks continued after Austys arrival. He told son Marty that during one attack, he dived under a jeep, and cut his leg on a ration can.

In October 1945, the NAO published part of a letter Austy wrote his mother. He wrote that now that the war was over, a lot of ex-US POWs were coming to Okinawa. All the fresh food available was being given to these released men. The Seabees were back on C and K rations. He told his mother that she was not to have any Vienna Sausage or Spam around when he got home. He never wanted to see those two meats again.

On October 25, 1946, the 86th Naval Construction Battalion was deactivated. Austy was transferred to the 125th Construction Battalion on February 13, 1946. It was the first time, other than for the short period he was in the Naval Hospital in California, that Austy and Fred had been separated since they enlisted. Fred had been transferred to the 146th Naval Construction Battalion on the 13th. It is likely that, due to deactivation of the 86th, men were assigned to the 125th and the 146th alphabetically. Austy, being an M, ended up with the 125th and Fred, a W, went to the 146th.

Gustavo G. Prisnell of Houghton, aboard the *USS Planter* (ACM 2) mine planter, after participating in the invasion of Southern France, discussed below, arrived off the coast of Okinawa on August 4, 1945. Gustave was a Yeoman, First Class, and yeoman of the ship. The yeoman of the ship was really the ship's clerk. He was responsible for the ship's records, including all personnel records, officer and enlisted, as well as all ship communications. Many of the records were classified.

The *Planter* was on its way to Okinawa on April 12, 1945, when the crew heard on the radio of the passing of President Roosevelt. Gustave wrote in his dairy for that day, "Undoubtedly his passing, which is such a shock, will have an effect upon the history of the United States as well as the history of the world which cannot be appraised at present." He later added that, "to me it can probably be compared in many ways to the death of another great President of the U.S., Abraham Lincoln." The ship arrived at Pearl Harbor on April 17. From Pearl the *Planter* headed for Okinawa arriving on the Fourth of July. For a short period, she tendered YMS's (Auxiliary Motor Minesweepers). In August she headed for the Philippines.

On August 8, 1945, Yeoman Prinsell wrote, "yesterday became acquainted with the news about the atomic bomb." Later he added, "If this is true, (referring to the effects of the bomb) it should shorten the war so that it could end any time." And being prescient, Yeoman Prinsell added, "However, it is a threat to the continuance of civilization."

Yeoman Prinsell also recorded in his diary on October 10th and 12th, 1945, news of the worst typhoon in the history of Okinawa, noting that it destroyed "all Army construction put up there since the island was taken from the Japs."

Since there was no chaplain aboard the *Planter*, yeoman Prinsell volunteered to hold services for all ship personnel who wished to participate. A bulletin of the August 19, 1945 service survives. The Order of Worship that day was: Opening Hymn - No. 139; Hymn - No. 132; Hymn - No. 98; Doxology - No. 1; Prayer - Praise for good Providence - No. 30; Scripture - Titus 2; Duet; Sermon - The Christian and the World; Closing Hymn.

The *Planter* returned to Okinawa in late August and stayed until December. She then headed to Honshu, Japan where she provided mine tender service and Gustave earned his Asian Occupation Medal with a Japan Clasp. She returned to the US in April arriving in San Francisco on April 16.

Howie with friend on Okinawa. Lyle Brown Photo.

Howard L. Ricketts of Fillmore (Howie to everyone who knew him) joined the Navy six months after his high school graduation in June of 1944. Like most World War II servicemen and women, Howie spent almost the next year in training. And, like many others, he started at Sampson Naval Training Station. In a January 1, 1945, letter to fellow serviceman and back home friend, Lyle Brown, he stated that he was in Company 226, Unit D. At Sampson at the same time, were fellow FCSD men Roderick (Roddy) Babbitt (Unit D), and Austin Morris and Fred Winchip (Unit C).

The Navy decided that Howie should be a fire control operator. Following basic training he was sent to Lake Union, Seattle, WA for the initial phase of his specialized training. From there he was ordered to Fort Lauderdale, FL to study the use of radar in fire control. (Howie's job involved control in the firing of one or more guns aboard a naval ship.) Finally, on September 21, 1945, just as the war was ending, Howie was put on a ship headed for Okinawa. (Ironically, although he was in the Navy, he was shipped to Okinawa aboard the *J. Franklin Bell* (APA 16) attack transport ship, which at the time was an Army attack transport ship. Despite being Army, the *J. Franklin Bell* had a proud "Naval Battle History." It had participated in the Aleutians campaign, as well as the battles for Tarawa, Kwajalein, Saipan, Tinian, Leyte, and Okinawa.) On this trip, its mission was to deliver men and supplies to Eniwetok, Okinawa, and Leyte. Since Okinawa was the second stop, Howie did not debark until almost a month later, on October 18th. He would spend most of the next seven months at Camp Kubasaki on Okinawa, even receiving his promotion to Fire Control Operator Third Class there. However, despite his training, Howie was assigned to the Welfare and Recreation Unit on Okinawa. He had plenty of experience in this area, having been a star athletic at Fillmore Central and having served as athletic petty officer in charge of all sports activities for his company at Sampson.

Howie, however, also ran into a bit of good luck on Okinawa. Noticing a call for a 35-mm movie projector operator, he applied for and got the job. For the rest of his tour, he held that job in addition to his regular job, earning an extra $30.00 in pay a month. This enabled him to send home most of his regular pay. In another letter, Howie told Lyle Brown that he also repaired radios on the side. He described this activity in his letter as a "good racket." That "good racket" was likely also an aid in sending most of his regular pay home. After over seven months overseas, Howie was shipped to Lido Beach, Long Island, where he was discharged on July 22, 1946.

Allen Richard Smith of Houghton reported on board the *USS Minotaur* on February 26, 1945 for its second life as a repair ship. Allen originally enlisted June 23, 1942 and was commissioned June 27, 1944.

He attended the Naval Reserve Midshipman School at Plattsburg, NY for 16 weeks and the Amphibious Training Program at Little Creek, VA for six weeks. (Allen's discharge record indicates he trained at Camp Bradford, VA. However, while located at Little Creek, Camp Bedford was used for training Navy Seabees while Allen was at Little Creek.) The movie actor Douglas Fairbanks Jr was involved in the development of special amphibious warfare tactics.

Allen served as the communications officer aboard the *Minotaur* (ARL 15) landing craft repair ship and was responsible for all communications, including classified communications, to and from the ship. He was also responsible for the secret code books. He eventually also served as Navigator and Chief Censor. The *Minotaur* sailed for the Pacific April 6, 1945 via the Panama Canal, Hawaii, and the Marshall and Caroline Islands. It was carrying steel plates and marine engines. It arrived at Okinawa just in time to participate in the final stages of the most horrific battle of the Pacific War. It joined the battle on June 4, 1945. Its participation in the last two weeks of the battle earned it a Battle Star. While its primary function was repair, the *Minotaur* was armed and did fight. Located in Buckner Bay, the *Minotaur* experienced the terror of *kamikazes*. It and its men also rode out the famous typhoon that struck the area in late 1945. Allen told his family that it was the only time on board ship when he thought he was going to die.
He related other stories to his family. One involved a mess up during the ship's transit through the Panama Canal. He was instructed to pick up an updated code book as they exited the canal on the Pacific side. He only remembered this duty after a day's steaming in the Pacific. Realizing the seriousness of the situation, he reported to the ship Captain that the latest code books were still in Panama. Then he waited for the axe to fall. He expected the worst but after a long hard stare, the captain simply said, "Well Smith, I am glad you told me." The ship steamed back to Panama to get the very valuable code books.

Another story, one of those that is very funny after the fact, involved a kamikaze attack. Along with the rest of the fleet in Buckner Bay, the *Minotaur's* guns fired on the Japanese planes as they came within range. As one *kamikaze* dove on a ship near the *Minotaur*, its guns kept firing on the plane until it was level with the other US ship. The *Minotaur's* guns only stopped firing when they realized they were shooting up the funnel of their sister ship. Years later Al was relating this story in the Fillmore barbershop. One of the other men in the shop spoke up and said he remembered that incident. He had been on the other ship.

The *Minotaur* was named after the ancient Greek mythological beast of Crete that was half-man and half-bull. The ship was aptly named, since in a way, it too had two different sides. It had started life as an LST (landing ship tanks), and was converted to a repair ship. The redesign of the ship made it possible for the Minotaur to pull right up next to damaged ships for repairs. This enabled damaged ships to return quickly to battle, avoiding long trips to and from land-based repair facilities.

The *Minotaur* returned to the states in early 1946. Leaving Okinawa on December 12, 1945, it sailed first to Iwo Jima and then on to Orange, TX via the Panama Canal. From Orange it moved to New Orleans, docking there April 18, 1946. Allen left the ship there. He received one month and ten days of leave and was advised that effective the end of his leave, June 8,1946, he would be officially released from active duty. He remained in the Naval Reserve until October 15, 1954.

Neither Allen's nor the *Minotaur's* World War II credits include the Navy Occupation Medal, Asian Clasp. Since Allen and the *Minotaur* served several months post-war in the Pacific area, including in Japanese territories between September 2, 1945 and April 7, 1946, this appears to be an omission. Okinawa was clearly a Japanese territory at the start of World War II having been annexed in 1879. Iwo Jima was also a Japanese territory and the *Minotaur* served there post-war. Therefore, I have included the Navy Occupation Medal as one of Allen's awards.

Clark O. Smith of Rossburg, was assigned to Marine Air Warning Squadron (MAWS) 7 on Okinawa,

a radar unit. Prior to the invasion, his troop ship had been hit by a Kamikaze plane which took away part of the bridge above where he was sleeping. He never woke up and didn't know they had been hit until later.

Clark landed on day one (L Day) with the US First Marine Division. The date was April 1, 1945, and it was both Easter Sunday and April's Fool Day.

MAWS were new to the war. MAWS 1 was used for the first time in February of 1944 in the Marshall Islands. Many feel they reached their peak in performance at Okinawa where five stations encompassed the entire island. Everybody knew what they were doing, but not how it was done. Only the technicians like Clark knew that, and what they knew was top secret.

MAWS 7 was stationed at Hedo Saki, the very northern tip of the island. The primary role of the Squadrons was to provide early warning and intercept directions for day and night fighters. Initially, problems were encountered. As a communications trouble-shooter, Clark helped solve those problems, and the Air Warning Unit became highly effective and very successful. Marine Air Warning Squadron 7 (call sign Pineapple Base) assured its notch in history when it became the first radar station to pick up the Japanese peace envoy's planes on their way to Ie Shima Airport on Ie Shima Island right next to Okinawa. MAWS 7 guided the bombers to the airport. The envoys were switched from Japanese Betty Bombers (painted green with a white cross on its side for identification purposes) to a US C-54 at Ie Shima, and then they continued to Manila where the details of the surrender were worked out with General MacArthur's staff. The famous war correspondent Ernie Pyle had died on Ie Shima on April 18, 1945.

Along with the First Marine Division, Clark was sent to China after the war. Their primary function was to repatriate Japanese soldiers and civilians. Most Marines, however, were assigned to guard supply trains, bridges, and depots to keep food and coal moving to the cities. The civil war in China was in full swing, and the US would be unable to influence its outcome. *Picture - Clark received the China Service Medal (above) for his time there.*

Clair N. Williams of Centerville entered the military March 4, 1941. The NAO shows Clair assigned to Fort Tilden in March of 1941 through December. In fact, it appears the unit he was assigned to (initially identified as Battery D) was rotated among a number of bases. The History of Battery D shows multiple assignments, with changes involving units and even personnel at various times. The bottom line, however, appears to be the assignment of Battery D, a search light battery, to Fort Jackson, SC in August, 1943. There it was inactivated and its personnel were assigned to Army Ground Forces (AGF). There were no more items in the NAO regarding Clair until January 1945 when it reported that he wrote thanking the people of Centerville for the Christmas package's they sent him.

There was only one more item in the NAO. In November, 1945 it reported that Clair had just arrived back in Centerville from the Pacific and had received an honorable discharge. All of Clair's military records were destroyed in the St. Louis fire except for his final payroll record. That record indicates he arrived back in the United States November 2, 1945, and was discharged November 11 at Camp Atterbury, Indiana. It also indicates that his previous "place" had been APO 331. While the location of APO's appear to have changed during the war, there is information that indicates APO 331 was assigned to Okinawa at the end of the war.

Based on the above, especially assuming Clair did in fact serve with an Army division on Okinawa, this write-up is likely correct or very close to correct. Clair was likely assigned to an Army combat division at Fort Jackson, probably/possibly to a Field Artillery Battalion given his background of service in a Coastal Artillery battalion. Army forces on Okinawa were under the 10th Army. There were four Infantry Divisions, the 7th, 27th, 77th, and 96th. All had Field Artillery battalions. Of the four, it appears the most likely division to which Paul was assigned was the 96th. All four experienced extensive combat. The 96th participated in both the Philippines and Okinawa campaigns as did the other three divisions. The 77th also participated in the Marianas campaign, the 7th in the Aleutians and Marshall Islands and the 27th at Guam. The 96th arrived in Hawaii on July 23, 1944 and trained there from July to September 1944 before participating in the Leyte Gulf campaign. The 77th went overseas in 1942. The 7th was a California based unit that went overseas in January 1944. The 27th, while a NY unit, also went overseas in 1942. Realistically Clair could have been a replacement in any of these units, but the 96th still appears to be the most logical.

Clair returned to the states in November 1945. This was prior to the return of all four divisions. However, his early return was likely due to Clair's five years of service which was likely more than most of the men in all four divisions.

Frederic S. (Fred) Winchip of Fillmore was a member of the FCS Class of 1945. He enlisted in the Navy, along with classmate Austy Morris, in the fall of 1944. Fred entered the service (prior to graduation - he later earned a GED from FCS) in December of 1944, and took his basic training at Sampson Naval Training Station. He was assigned to the Seabees upon completing his basic training, was transferred to Davisville, Rhode Island, the major Seabee training facility, and assigned to the 86th Construction Battalion. The 86th records indicate that the Battalion was undergoing training at Davisville in January of 1945. (Seabee is a proper noun derived from the initials CB, which stands for construction battalion.) The NAO reported that Fred was a guest of the Rotary Club in March 1945. and that he was at a base with Austy Morris in April. Fred and Austy were together almost their entire time in the service.

The World War II Memorial indicates that Fred served with both the 86th Naval Communications Board and the 146th Naval Communication Board. No entities with those names have been located by the author. However, there were the 86th and 146th Naval Construction Battalions, both of which served on Okinawa. Fred served with both these organizations during his service.

The 86th Construction Battalion departed Camp Parks on May 24, 1945. It sailed from San Francisco for Okinawa that same day. (The normal complement for a Seabee Battalion was 32 officers, and 1073 men. The 86th had 25 officers and 1,070 men when it sailed.) It likely made stops in route, almost certainly in Hawaii, as the 86th records indicate it did not arrive at Okinawa until July 5, 1945. At Okinawa, it was assigned to the 8th Brigade, 37th Regiment. (A regiment consisted of more than one battalion, a brigade, more than one regiment.) Okinawa had the largest concentration of construction troops anywhere during the war, over 55,000.)

A Seabee Battalion was divided into four companies, plus a headquarters company. Each company could perform all Seabee functions, but generally concentrated on one function. At Okinawa, Seabees built ocean ports, a grid of roads, bomber and fighter bases, a seaplane base, a Quonset village, tank farms, storage dumps, hospitals, and ship repair facilities. They also provided maintenance for all types of facilities. In addition, smaller Seabee units (called Seabee Specials), performed such tasks as aiding in unloading ships, especially in combat zones, motor trucking, operating tire repair shops and dredges, and handling, assembling. launching and placing pontoon causeways.

Fred told his brother Joel that he drove heavy construction equipment on Okinawa. He also said that one of his jobs was to simply push excess equipment, some of it unused, over a cliff into the sea. This was likely a major task during Fred's tour, since he was there during two major storms, including Typhoon

Louise in October 1945. Louise leveled virtually everything built during the war, but since the war was over, only necessary facilities were rebuilt. It is likely that Fred helped push a lot of the destroyed facilities and equipment into the sea.

The NAO also reported on the typhoon, commenting that Seabees Austin Morris and Fred Winchip, both stationed on the island at that time, "lost everything they had as everything in the entire camp blew away." Fred's brother Joel told the author that just before the typhoon, Fred had left his watch on his footlocker in his tent. Afterwards, of course, everything was gone. But a few weeks later, Fred was walking in the surf and, lo and behold, there was his watch. Fred told Joel of the Seabees' reputation as scavengers, and of the extensive barter system in place. The Seabees would "acquire" items desired by other units, and then work out a quid pro quo. One item desired by all was beer. The Seabees had plenty of beer, but no way to cool it. So, a deal was hatched with the Air Corps. The Seabees would provide the beer, and the Air Corps the cooling system. The beer would be loaded on their planes and flown to altitudes where it cooled quickly.

The 86th Construction Battalion was inactivated on February 26, 1946. Fred was transferred to the 146th Naval Construction Battalion on February 12th. While he expected to be rotated home, Fred instead was assigned to the 96th Naval Construction battalion then stationed in Tsingtao, China. The 96th had been sent to Tsingtao to rebuild and repair a captured Japanese-built airfield, and the road leading to that field. While Fred likely arrived in Tsingtao in March or April 1946, the 96th arrived in November 1945.Since they first had to construct barracks for the Battalion, and then rebuild the road to the airfield, it is likely that Fred only worked on the airfield construction. It was a major project. Two 3,990-foot runways were repaired and extended to 5,000 and 6,000 feet respectively. In addition, 900-foot approach strips were built. The extension of the runways and approach strips required the removal of rock hills and the excavation of 350,000 cubic yards of weathered granite. A complete drainage system for the field was also installed.

In May 1945 the 96th completed its work in China. Word was received that month to deactivate the Battalion. The official deactivation occurred August 1, 1946. By that time Fred was at home. He had been discharged July 18, 1946 at Lido Beach, NY.

Leonard A. Wood of Hume entered the service on February 1, 1943. The NAO reported that he was initially assigned to a base in Missouri. It is possible that he was assigned to Fort Leonard Wood which was a premier Army basic training base at the time. Leonard next was ordered to Dyersburg, Tennessee which was an Army Air Force Base. It is not clear whether he was there for training or as base personnel. It likely was the latter as he was only there for about three months, possible in a holding position waiting for a training slot to be opened. By August 1943 the NAO reported that he was at Brookley Field, Mobile, Alabama. Several types of training were provided at Brookley including Air Depot personnel, logistics, mechanics, and other support personnel training. It is not known to which training unit he was assigned but it is possible that his training was general and that he worked in several different occupations during his service. The 1878th Engineer Aviation Battalion moved to Brookley Field, Alabama in November 1943. Since Leonard was already there at that time, he almost surely became a member of the battalion at Brookley.

By January 1944 the NAO reported that Leonard was "somewhere in the Pacific." That somewhere was Hawaii. By then he was assigned to the 1878th Engineer Aviation Battalion, possible as an Ambulance Driver. The NAO reported later that he had served an such a driver. The 1878th remained in Hawaii for several months preparing for the invasion of Saipan. US troops landed on Saipan on June 15, 1944 and by July 9th had control of the island. John Ballard of the FCSD area was one of the men who helped take the island.

The 1878th was on Saipan by July 25. Its job was to repair, extend and build runways for the airplane that would take the war to the Japanese homeland – the B - 29. While US planners originally aimed for having most of the runways ready by October 1944, Japanese resistance and horrendous weather interfered with those plans. However, the schedule was achieved somewhat when a temporary airstrip was made useable by late August. Five aviation engineer battalions, including the 1878th, labored around the clock for almost two months to extend the strip to 8500 feet and widen it by 200 feet. In addition to the rain, Leonard's unit, and the others, went without fresh food, and were delayed by bad roads running from the coral pits. Those roads eventually were impassable and engineers had to be taken from the runway construction in order to build a hard surface road to keep the trucks moving. The coral beneath the surface was so hard that blasting was constantly necessary. The effort made by the engineer battalions was rewarded when, on November 24, the first B-29's took off from Saipan for a bombing attack on Tokyo. Aboard one of those bombers was Robert Aldrich from the FCSD area. This effort was recognized when a Meritorious Service Unit Plaque was awarded to the 1878th for "superior performance of duty in the execution of an exceptionally difficult task on Saipan" from August 16, 1944 to March 26, 1945. (General Order Number 4, July 27, 1945.) It should be noted that Leonard is specifically mentioned in the General Order and that he was assigned to Headquarters and Service Company at the time. He was still assigned to the same unit when he received his Good Conduct Medal by General Order Number 3 on March 23, 1945. When he was among the men who received a Battle Star for the Okinawa campaign by General Order Number 5 on September 23, 1945 he was assigned to the Medical Detachment.

In January, 1945 Leonard received a letter from a friend at home giving him Robert Aldrich's address on Saipan. One day he boarded the local bus, a US military truck, to go looking for Bob. He sat down and turned to say hello to the man setting beside him. It was Bob. They had dinner together.

Much more needed to be done however. The war was not over. The 1878th now headed for Okinawa. It was there by May 5, 1945. The NAO reported that Leonard's unit was one of the first units ashore following the invasion force. It immediately began converting a newly captured airfield for use by US fighters and bombers. Leonard told the NAO that the work continued around the clock. He was on duty as an ambulance driver for the Medical Detachment as noted above. All the efforts were harassed by Japanese snipers and air raids. The airfield was made ready for US aircraft in a record ten days. The Okinawan airfields enabled US fighters to protect the bombers which were hammering Japan. It also provided crippled bombers a safe place for landing, without having to return to their much further away home bases.

While the war officially ended on September 8, 1945, duty for Leonard and the 1878th did not. The Battalion was sent to Korea arriving September 15, 1945. It was the first battalion of its kind sent to Korea and it was immediately ordered to Kimpo Airfield to repair and extend the existing runway. It also worked on taxiway, hardstand and building construction, including the control tower. Starting in November men of the 1878th began to be rotated home. By the 14th of December, 1945 the unit's strength had been reduced from 800 men early in November to about 90.

Leonard was one of the men who was rotated home during this period. He was discharged December 30, 1945. Leonard's Aunt Amanda was the mother of Medal of Honor winner Almond Fisher.

PART V - DELIVERING THE GOODS

"D Day would not have been possible without the Merchant Marine. It is not generally realized that the Merchant Marine has the largest ratio of casualties of any branch of the service, and many of the names on the list are not classified "wounded" or "missing. They were those of men whose grave was the sea." New York Times Editorial London, June 9, 1944

"It seems to me particularly appropriate that Victory Fleet Day this year should honor the men and management of the American Merchant Marine. The operators of this war have written one of its most brilliant chapters. They have delivered the goods when and where needed in every theater of operation and across every ocean in the biggest, the most difficult and dangerous transportation job ever undertaken." President Franklin D. Roosevelt September 9, 1944 statement.

The Merchant Marine did not have an historian during WW II, with the result that there are no "official" casualty figures. However, researchers agree that the Merchant Marine suffered the highest ratio of casualties with likely one out of every 34 Mariners dying in service during the war. The next highest ratio was the Marine Corps, where one out of every 48 died. In addition to Merchant Mariners, several US Navy personnel participated in the delivery of goods and material throughout the world. These men served as Armed Guards aboard merchant vessels.

The FCSD area provided at least two and possibly three Mariners during the war - Charles H. Ayer, Calvin F. Baker (May not have been from FCSD area.) and Howard E. Kopler. Men from the FCSD area who served as armed guards included Lloyd A. Cramer, Willis H. Hayes, Forrest L. Hodnett, and Robert E.W. Schultz.

Merchant Seamen

Carl Ayer. An item in the NAO in February 1944 reported a Carl Ayer home "on a furlough" visiting his parents, Mr. & Mrs. Chas. Ayer, and family. The NAO again reported him home on furlough in January 1945. No records have been identified which show a Carl Ayer living in the FSCD area during the World War II period. There was a Carl Ayer who lived in Buffalo at that time. A research of Merchant Marine files conducted at the request of the author, found no record associated with a Carl Ayer. The response did point out that that many positions aboard a merchant vessel did not require Merchant Marine credentials. However, it is likely that the NAO incorrectly reported his first name and that Carl Ayer was really Charles H. Ayer. (See Parts III and XIV.) (See Part XIV for more information on Carl J. Ayer.)

Charles H. Ayer, Jr. served two years in the Merchant Marines during the period 1941 to 1943. He then served honorably in the US Army. (See Parts III and XIV.)

Calvin F. Baker likely was trained by the US Maritime Service and then served aboard a US merchant ship. The NAO reported in February 1945 that Calvin had left for the west coast. It also mentioned that his address would be in care of Fleet Post Office. That appears to indicate that he would be serving overseas. No Calvin F. Baker living in the FCSD area has been identified, although he may have been in the area in the early 1940's. There was a Calvin F. Baker, who was born in Warsaw March 4, 1925. He was still living in Warsaw with his parents in 1940. He did serve in the Merchant Marines and is likely the Calvin referred to by the NAO.

The US Maritime Service trained men for the Merchant Marines and the US Army Transport Service to transport supplies and personnel to locations all over the world. The training included operation of anti-aircraft guns and canon, navigation, engine operation and maintenance and desk operations. Once trained these men served on merchant ships world-wide. While several training bases operated in California during the war, only the one at Avalon appears to have been in operation at the time Calvin departed for California. However, since Calvin was to have a Fleet Post Office address, it is possible that he was on his way to an assignment, rather than to training. Since there was also a Maritime training facility at Sheepshead Bay, NY it is possible that Calvin was trained there and was on his way to an assignment in California.

Howard Emerson Kopler of Hume was born October 17, 1923 in Fillmore. A member of the Fillmore

Central School Class of 1941, Howard joined the Merchant Marine in August 1943. He would spend most of the next two war years at sea or in ports around the world helping to deliver vital war supplies. The ports he visited were both dangerous and exciting, and undoubtedly intoxicating for a young man. The problem was, however, that the ships he sailed on were prime targets for enemy airplanes and submarines. That fact made the job a lot more dangerous and a lot less exciting. *Picture - Howard earned numerous Merchant Marine Medals, including the Victory Medal pictured left.*

Victory Medal
(World War II)

During the war, Howard was assigned to six different ships. First was the *SS Frontenac*. The *Frontenac* sailed on the Great Lakes. Howard served aboard as a maintenance man from August 8, 1943, until October 16, 1943. Except for an assignment for a short coastal trip late in the war, all the other ships Howard served on delivered war supplies to foreign ports. The first of these was the *Benjamin D. Wilson*, a freighter. Howard served aboard the *Wilson* from November 10, 1943, until May 20, 1944.

His next ship was the *Beaver Dam*, a tanker. Howard sailed on it from June 10, 1944 until August 20, 1944. He boarded the *Beaver Dam* in New York. It sailed to Liverpool, England (Convoy CU 028) on June 16, 1944. It was carrying 80 octane gas and pool white spirits, with Army supplies on the deck. The *Beaver Dam* arrived in Liverpool on June 27, 1944. The trip was uneventful, but escorts did drop death charges on both June 24 and June 26. This was a very tense time, with the D Day landings having occurred just two weeks previously. The *Beaver Dam* departed Liverpool July 1, 1944 (Convoy UC 028). Traveling alone part way, it arrived in Aruba on July 17, departed on the 17th, and arrived in New York on July 23, 1944. Two patrol planes were spotted, and the armed guards possibly sighted a submarine periscope, at which they fired. On July 26 the *Beaver Dam* again departed NY for Liverpool (Convoy CU 033), arriving August 5, 1944. It again was carrying gasoline and Army supplies. Patrol planes were spotted, but otherwise the trip was uneventful. The Beaver returned on August 9, arriving in New York August 20, 1944 (Convoy UC 033). It carried ballast in its tanks, and, interestingly, landing craft on its deck.

Howard then joined the crew of the *SS White River*, a tanker, serving aboard from September 6, 1944 until March 12, 1945. The *White River* sailed from New York on September 9, 1944, for Aruba, and then through the Panama Canal to the Pacific. It arrived at Ulithi on October 19, after a stop at Eniwetok. It then followed the same route back to Panama, where it took on more fuel oil and headed back to Eniwetok. It arrived in early January, unloaded its fuel, and headed for the US. However, its main generator and main turbine self-destructed in route, and it had to be towed to Portland, OR. Howard left the ship at Portland.

His last two ships were the *SS Deroche*, from April 18, 1945 to April 27, 1945, and the *SS Barren Hill*, from May 1, 1945 to October 29, 1945. Howard was aboard the *Deroche* for only one short coastal trip from San Francisco via San Pedro to Los Angeles. The *Deroche* was a tanker, and carried gasoline and crude oil.

On Howard's last wartime voyage, he went on a tour of the Pacific. Carrying aircraft and gasoline, the *Barren Hill* sailed from San Pedro, CA on May 4, 1945, arriving in Calcutta, India on June 19. From there it proceeded to Bahrein Island in the Persian Gulf (July 23) and then Port Darwin, Australia (August 12). Its next stop was Manus Island (August 20), after which it sailed to Subic Bay in the Philippines arriving August 27, 1945 with a cargo of diesel fuel.

Howard served in three major war zones: the Atlantic, the Pacific, and the Mediterranean Middle East. Once in San Cristobal in the Canal Zone, aboard the *White River,* Howard was recommended for punishment for failing to stand his watch. However, it turned out that, in accordance with instructions from the Chief Mate, liberty was authorized if you arranged for someone else to stand your security watch. Howard had made such arrangements and had received permission to go ashore. The situation became confused when it became necessary to "shift ship" meaning move to another location. Crew members were supposed to have been notified of this, but were not. The ship master later advised that Howard had not failed in his duties and all charges were dropped. Starting his career as an Ordinary Seaman, Howard rose to Quartermaster by the end of the war. Howard remained with the Merchant Marines following the war, and served on several other merchant ships.

Armed Guards

All the men on merchant vessels were not civilians. Aboard many ships were US Navy Armed Guards whose job was to provide defensive firepower to protect the merchant ships against enemy submarines, surface vessels and aircraft, either alone or in convoys. The FCSD area supplied at least four armed guards, Lloyd A. Carmer, Willis H. Hayes, Forrest L. Hodnett, and Robert E.W. Schultz.

Lloyd A. Carmer of Fillmore entered the service on November 27, 1943. After basic training at Sampson Naval Training Station, Lloyd attended the Navy armed guard school in Shelton (Norfolk), VA. The men selected for this duty had to be in good physical condition. They also had to be able to swim. At the school, Lloyd was exposed to several subjects, including seamanship, fighting fires, and aircraft identification. But the primary emphasis was gunnery, specifically anti-aircraft, and anti-submarine gunnery. The school was designed to expose the trainees, to the maximum extent possible, to the realities of combat. Near the Armed Guard School at Sheldon was the Dam Neck anti-aircraft firing range where the trainees were given actual firing experiences. Firing on ships was also employed to give more practical experience. Experienced armed guards were brought in as instructors, to explain the latest enemy tactics.

It took special men to be armed guards. It was not a preferred assignment, and many men dreaded it. There was constant danger from enemy submarines, surface ships and aircraft. Many, if not most times, especially early in the war, there were simply not enough escort vessels to provide adequate protection.

The normal complement of armed guards on a ship was 28 - one officer, three communications men, and 24 armed guards. Not all ships received the normal complement. They served on all types of merchant ships, including tankers, cargo ships and troop ships. They were "stationed" at three different centers, or duty stations. The centers would assign them to different ships. Duty stations also handled the men's records, mail, and pay accounts, and took care of their health and legal issues, furnished recreation, provided additional training, assured they had the proper clothing for warm and cold weather, and administered discipline. Lloyd was assigned to the Brooklyn Center, which assigned guards for Atlantic shipping.

Lloyd served on five merchant ships as an armed guard: the *SS Leslie M. Shaw* (freighter), *SS John W. Garrett* (troops and cargo), *SS Thomas W. Hyde* (troops and cargo), *SS Lone Jack* (tanker), and the *SS Palo Alto* (cargo). The *Hyde, Shaw* and *Garrett* were Liberty ships.

Lloyd's time aboard the *Leslie M. Shaw* was very short. He boarded the ship on March 8, 1944. On March 22, he was removed and transported to the US Marine Hospital in Baltimore for hospitalization. He left the hospital on April 4 and was assigned to the *John W. Garrett*.

All his trips except one, were to Europe. The NAO reported in November 1944 that he was home visiting his parents, and that he had just returned from overseas. He had been overseas since July 16. The NAO also reported that on previous trips he had been to both France and England. In June of 1945, the NAO reported that he had just returned from Europe. The convoy he was with had brought 5,000 men home from the war.

Lloyd's first trip to Europe aboard the *John W. Garrett* was clearly part of the build-up for the D Day invasion. It sailed from New York on May 5 to Liverpool, England (bound for Newcastle) as part of the 93 ship Convoy HX 290. Carrying grain, food, medicine, metal, machinery, and high explosives, it arrived May 19. The *Garrett* returned to New York on June 15 and arrived on July 2. Lloyd had spent D Day in England. His second trip aboard the *Garrett* took him even closer to the action. Departing NY on July 17, 1944, it arrived at Omaha Beach, France on August 15. The convoy contained 117 ships when it left New York, the largest of the war. More ships joined in route. The Armed Guards, including Lloyd, manned their battle stations at dawn and dusk. The cargo was listed as "Stores P.X." The Garrett remained at Omaha Beach for a month and a half, finally departing to New York on September 15, and arriving October 12. It is likely that the sheer number of ships that had to be unloaded contributed to the time spent at Omaha Beach.

Lloyd made one more trip aboard the *Garrett*. This time the ship delivered vehicles to another invasion site, Southern France. Departing NY on October 31, 1944, the *Garrett* arrived at Marseilles, France on November 23. As with Normandy, its arrival was just outside the dates required to qualify for a battle star. The *Garrett* spent almost two months at Marseilles, sailing for New York on January 4, 1945, and arriving January 23.

Lloyd's last trip to Europe began on March 14, 1945 when he was assigned to the troopship *SS Thomas W. Hyde*. The *Hyde* sailed from Hampton Roads, VA, on April 4 as part of Convoy UGS 85 carrying lubricants in drums. There were 51 ships in the convoy. The Armed Guard Report for the trip indicates that they dropped depth charges on positions marked by the escort blimp the day they sailed. This was part of a drill. No enemy ships were sighted during the entire trip. The war was still raging, but the Allies were pounding their way into and across Germany. Hitler had less than a month to live. The *Hyde* proceeded to Oran, and then to Marseilles, France, arriving on April 27. The *Hyde* now began a "tour" of the Mediterranean. It sailed to Port-de-Bouc, France to discharge cargo, and then returned to Marseilles on May 6. That same day it sailed to Oran with 999 German POWs and 52 American troops. It was then ordered back to Marseilles where all the German POWs and the Americans were put ashore. It then returned to Oran, arriving May 15 with 1,000 French troops. Ordered to Naples, it picked up more American troops and returned to Oran, arriving May 22. There it joined Convoy 91 and headed home. While Lloyd and the *Hyde* had been moving troops and POWs around the Mediterranean, the war had ended. Lloyd had been at sea on VE (Victory in Europe) day. The *Hyde* arrived in New York on June 7, 1945. Lloyd's assignment to the *Hyde* ended June 13.

On June 26 Lloyd was assigned to the *SS Lone Jack*, a tanker. On July 1, the *Lone Jack* sailed from Baltimore to Baytown, TX. It then traveled to Quincy, MA, arriving July 15. One day later it set sail for Philadelphia, and then continued to Port Arthur, TX. Taking on a cargo of gasoline, on July 28 it headed for Manila in the Philippines. The war ended while the *Lone Jack* was in route. It arrived there September 2, 1945. By late November it was on its way home, arriving at Colon, Panama on January 4, 1946, Baytown, TX on the 10th, Providence, R.I. on the 24th, and finally New York on January 25. It then proceeded to Baltimore, where a Navy Bureau of Ships message of February 12, 1946 announced that the *Lone Jack* had been disarmed, and all armed guard crew had been removed.

Lloyd spent almost 14 months at sea and overseas during his service. The ships Lloyd served on delivered supplies to three battle zones: Normandy, Marseilles, and the Philippines. Unfortunately, the ships arrived at each location just following the end of the time period necessary to qualify for battle stars.

Willis Harvey Hayes was originally from Hartford, CT, and served as the Agriculture Teacher at Fillmore in the late 1930's. He entered active service with the US Navy on February 3, 1943 and took his basic training at Dartmouth College. After Dartmouth, Willis moved on to Princeton where he participated in the two-month Navy V-12 program. This program combined college courses with military training. At Princeton, it, at least initially, focused on training officers for moderate sized Navy craft with emphasis on the new amphibious force. Willis then attended the Naval Training School in Boston for local defense training. The training focused on defensive measures designed to protect civilians from enemy attacks, including bomb shelters, air raid warning systems, patrols along the nation's borders, and distribution of information on emergency survival.

Willis was next assigned to the Armed Guard training school in Little Creek, Virginia. Armed Guards served aboard merchant ships transporting needed war materials and other goods to ports around the world. The training, especially for enlisted men, focused on anti-aircraft and anti-submarine activities. Willis was trained to command an armed guard unit. At the completion of his training at Little Creek, Willis was assigned to the Armed Guard Center in Brooklyn. Armed Guards units at the Brooklyn Center were assigned to merchant ships sailing the Atlantic Ocean and the Mediterranean Sea.

As a result of his trips to those areas, Willis earned the European, African Middle East Theater Medal. On one of his trips in late 1943, Willis was in London. There he accidently ran into Charles Hodnett. Charles had been one of his students when he was teaching at Fillmore.

Willis was discharged on November 16, 1945.

Forrest Luke Hodnett of Hume served two years in the US Navy as an Armed Guard. Forrest had already served three years (1933 to 1936) in the US Coast Guard before entering the Navy in 1943. Assigned as an armed guard on a merchant ship, it appears that his primary duty was as part of an anti-aircraft crew. He attended the anti-aircraft training school at the Great Lakes Naval Training Station shortly after entering the service. (As a Coast Guard veteran, it is unlikely that Forrest was put through any extensive basic training, although his records indicate he did complete the gas mask drill, and chamber instruction.) It is interesting to note, however, that while swimming was a particular requirement for armed guards, the Coast Guard had recommended that he not be considered for re-enlistment in 1936 because he could not swim. He attended the Armed Guard Training facility at Gulfport, MS following his training at Great Lakes.

After Gulfport, Forrest was assigned to the Armed Guard Center in New Orleans and to detached duty aboard the *SS Gasper De Portola* on October 6, 1943. The *Gasper De Portola* was a Liberty Ship that ran aground at Quito Sueno Bank on June 7, 1943. Quito Sueno is a sand bank belonging to Columbia, about 65 miles NNW of Providencia Island in the Caribbean. Declared a total loss, it was re-floated and "hulked." The ship was towed, first to Key West, Fl and then to Savannah, Ga. It is likely that Forrest joined the ship in Savannah on October 23 and remained aboard while the ship was towed to Baltimore. On October 23, 1943, according to a report of the Baltimore Port Director, Forrest was transferred from the *De Portola* to the *SS Theodore Parker*. He served on the *Parker* until June 29, 1944. The *Parker* made two crossings of the Atlantic while Forrest was aboard.

The first crossing was as part of Convoy HX 265 sailing from New York on November 6, 1942 with general cargo, and arriving at Hull, England on November 25. It sailed from Liverpool on December 31, 1943, as part of Convoy ON 217 to return to New York. The convoy encountered a violent storm on January 9, 1944, and the *Parker* had problems maintaining convoy speed. Gale winds increased, and the ship was pitched and rolled heavily. The main deck cracked from the hull to the forward end of number 3 hold and down the hull from the port side for about eight inches. Distress signals were issued, and orders were received to destroy all important papers. Three times "abandon ship" was ordered, but each time the violence of the sea made such an action impossible, although a few men did manage to get to another ship during the second attempt on January 10. Finally, a decision was made to stay with the ship as long as it stayed afloat. By January 11, the *Parker* was on its own, as both the rescue ship and the escort had disappeared during the storm. The crew fastened buckles and chains across the deck. The storm finally abated enough for the Parker to resume slow speed and head for the Azores. It was truly on its own for the next couple of days. The convoy was long gone, and heavy seas flooded the after-gun position, and the magazine. Although a tug and a trawler had been dispatched from the Azores, they never appeared, so the *Parker* had to make port on its own. Forrest received a payment of $1.75 for clothing lost during the storm. After repairs, the *Parker* returned to New York. On April 26, it sailed again as part of Convoy HX 229 to Sunderland in Scotland. It returned June 3, 1944 as part of Convoy ON 239. The round way trip was uneventful, except for the sighting of an enemy submarine on the way home. During his trips, Forrest served within the European Theater of war for more than the 30 days required to earn the European, African, Middle Eastern Theater Medal.

On July 1, 1944, Forrest was transferred to the Armed Guard Center in Brooklyn, NY, and on July 20, 1944, assigned to duty aboard the *SS Josiah B. Grinnell*. The *Grinnell* was in port the entire 10 days that Forrest was detached to the ship. On July 30, 1944, Forrest was admitted to St. Albans Hospital in New York for an unspecified treatment. He was released from the hospital on August 9 and reported back for duty. On August 19, 1944 he was detached to the *SS William Brewster*. He would serve on the *Brewster* until August 3, 1945, effectively, the end of the war.

The *Brewster* was used to transport primarily bauxite and general Army supplies between east coast cities (New York, Baltimore, Philadelphia and Mobile) and ports in the Caribbean. Forrest served as an armed guard on seven different voyages. The ports of call included cities in Venezuela, Trinidad, Cuba, Puerto Rico, and Dominican Republic. He also made a trip from Baltimore to Boston, and then on to Portland, ME. According to the armed guard reports, all the voyages were routine. On one trip from Port of Spain, Trinidad to Mobile, Al, there was what turned out to be a false submarine sighting. All men manned their battle stations, but no sub was found. Forrest was discharged from the Navy on October 8, 1945.

Robert E. W. Schultz of Fillmore entered the service in July of 1944. Robert went through basic training at Sampson Naval Station. He then was assigned to the Armed Guard training School at Norfolk. Upon completion of training Robert was transferred to the Armed Guard Center in Brooklyn. During his time at the Brooklyn Center, Robert would have been assigned to various merchant vessels transporting goods and war material to European locations. His discharge document indicates that he made at least one trip to the European Theater prior to the end of the war. Since it appears Robert may have been assigned to the Brooklyn Center for close to a year, he likely made several trips to the European Theater. In

December, 1945 following the end of the war in Europe, Robert was transferred to the *USS Bland* (APA-134).

The *Bland* was an attack transport ship used to transport troops to and from combat areas during the war in the Pacific Theater. As the war progressed, many armed guards were transferred to US warships as gunners. The *Bland's* muster records indicate Robert reported aboard the *Bland* on December 8, 1945 in Shoemaker, CA. Since the Pacific war officially ended a couple months earlier, Robert did not receive the Asiatic Pacific Theater Medal. Muster rolls also indicate that Robert left the ship on December 12, 1945 on 30 days emergency leave. He was officially transferred to the Navy Receiving Station at Sampson for assignment at the same time. He was discharged at Sampson, likely following his 30 days emergence leave, on January 24, 1946.

PART VI - FCSD WOMEN IN WORLD WAR II

"This is not the time for women to be patient. We are in a war and we need to fight it with all our ability and every weapon possible, Women pilots in this particular case, are a weapon waiting to be used." Eleanor Roosevelt - "My Day September 1, 1942" The Eleanor Roosevelt Papers. Digital Editions (2017)

FCSD Women in World War II

Women officially participating in war as combatants was still 70 some years away in 1940. Of course, their non-participation throughout history has always been fiction. Women, unofficially and now officially, have always participated in wars. During World War II they participated in all ways, including combat situations. The nurses on the beach at Salerno were just as much in combat as the men. Others were female spies and resistance fighters. And many of them were shooting back. Some probably even shot first.

While to my knowledge no FCSD area women served as spies or resistance fighters, they did serve in virtually every other way, including on the beach at Salerno. At least one woman from the area served in four of the five main branches of service during the war: the Army (WAC - Women's Army Corps, and US Army Nurses Corps), the Coast Guard (SPAR - Semper Paratus Always Ready [the Coast Guard Motto in Latin and English]), the Army Air Corps, (WASPS - Women Air Service Pilots), and in the Marines (Women Marines). It appears that the only services in which a FCSD area women did not serve were as a WAVE and a Navy Nurse. However, Mildred E. Schmidt, an Army Nurse, did serve aboard a hospital ship. A few of the WAC also served with the Woman's Auxiliary Army Corps (WAAF) prior to it being disbanded in favor of the WAC.

At least 15 women from the FCSD area served in the various military branches. They were Francis Janet Arthur (Edwards) , WAC; Generva Emelene Ballard, Army Nurses Corps; Alma Geraldine Farnsworth, Coast Guard SPARS; Mabel Elaine Fox (Edwards), Army Nurses Corps; Elin Griswold Harte (Raimondi), WASPS; Edith Rose Johannes, Army Nurses Corps; Genevieve D. (MI only) Kolakowska, WAC; Ada Ruth Mills, WAC; Roberta Pearl Molyneaux (Grange), WAC; Geraldine Faith Paine, US Marines; Elsie Jean Eldridge (Perry), WAC; Nancy Reid (McCreery), WAC; Mildred Elizabeth Schmidt, Army Nurses Corps; Hilda Louise Schmidt (Gibbons), Army Nurses Corps Cadet; and Avis Naze, (Wilmot), Army Nurses Corps Cadet.

During World War II, women helped keep the war machine's bureaucracy running, and running smoothly. They freed up men for combat and, in many situations, served on the front lines with them. Many of them died, although happily, none from the FCSD area. However, as detailed in Part II, Mabel Elaine Fox came close.

PART VII – SERVICE IN THE US

Not everyone in the military was sent overseas in World War II. In fact, most were not. There was simply too much which had to be carried out at home. This included training; and in World War II and ever since, the US military has had the finest trained men and women of any military service on the planet. It also included logistics of all sorts and the running of the mammoth administrative bureaucracy needed to keep the war machine functioning. Who did what was not left to the men and women who served. Those decisions were always made by someone "higher up," wherever higher up was. No one has ever answered that question, then or since. Men and women from the FCSD area performed many of these critical "home front" duties.

US Army

The following FCSD area residents served in the US Army in the American Theater of Operations during World War II: Charles G. Allen, William R. Appleford, Clair E. Arnold, Francis J. Arthur, Bernard P. Ayer, Ralph Black, Leonard Blakesley, Leland W. Bleistein, Wilfred C. Bleistein, Harold J. Briggs, Llewellyn R. Brueser, William C. Brueser, Ronald W. Carpenter, Victor J. Chizlette, Everett F. Clute, George A. Cole, Herbert T. Darling, Gerald G. Davis, Clarence E. Denning, Harold R. Denning, Harlan C. Evans, Jr., Harry W. Fairbank, James E. Fancher, Richard C. Farnsworth, David C. Fiegl, Albert E. Findlay, Harold F. Ford, Lynford S Fox, Clarence F. Gaus, Richard W. Hazlett, Frederich C. Hauser, Wendell A. Howden, Clarence A. Irish, Earl J.J. James, Francis I. James, Clifford C. Johannes, Richard S. Johannes, John V. Jones, John H. Keyes, Wells E. Knibloe, Genevieve Kolakowka, Joihn R. Krause, Alvin P. Miller, Ada R. Mills, Clyde F. Millspaugh, David W. Morgan, Avis A. Naze, Merton C. Pero, Elsie Jean Eldridge (Perry), David A. Pitt, Nancy Reid, David P. Richardson, Herschel C. Ries, Hilda L. Schmidt, Lawrence M. Smith, Sanford I. Smith, Norbert F. Sylor, Carl O. Turnstrom, Harold Van Name, Howard L. Voss, Llewelyn Washburn, Lyle A. Wilcox, Virgil E. Wilcox, and Norman L. Young.

William R. Appleford (Bill) of Fillmore was the Physical Education Director and Coach for male athletic teams at FCS when he was inducted into the military in June 1941. Bill was sent to Camp Croft, Spartanburg, South Carolina and assigned to the 8th Infantry Training Regiment, 26th Infantry Training Battalion. The NAO reported his address as Camp Croft through December of 1941. The next reference was in August 1942. He was in Mt. Morris, NY where he married Margaret Ruth Gormley. In October 1942, the NAO reported that he was one of 61 applicants accepted for the Adjutant General School in Miami., FL. It is likely that Bill was assigned to the huge Miami Beach Army Air Force Training Center. It contained an Officer's Candidate School. He may have been in either the 12-weeks or the 16-weeks program. It was expanded to 16 weeks in 1943, and it is not clear exactly when he entered. However, by June 1943, he had completed his training and, according to the NAO, was stationed at Jacksonville, FL. Most likely he was at Jacksonville Army Air Field, which was an anti-submarine base at the time. That month he was assigned to oversee the transfer of 100 soldiers from Jacksonville to Denver, Colorado, which at the least meant accompanying them to Denver. It is not clear if he was also being transferred. These transfers most likely were related to the July 7, 1943, designation of Lowry Army Air Field, near Denver, as the AAF Western Technical Training Command. Bill did manage to visit his wife in Mt. Morris during this period. In October 1943, he visited friends in Fillmore. Then, in November, he was discharged from the Army due to ill health. He had served two years and four months.

Clair Edward Arnold of Fillmore, **w**as tapped to be a basic training instructor. Clair was drafted in November 1943. He was sent to Camp Blanding, FL for his basic training. At the completion of his training Clair was made permanent staff at Blanding, and for the balance of the war was responsible for assuring that the men who trained there were ready for the ordeals they would face in combat.

The US has always prided itself on having the best trained military in the world. US Navy Captain Roman Kolakowski of Centerville wrote in his autobiography that he spent half of his time in the Navy in training. Ironically, during WW II, the men who scored highest in basic training were often tapped as instructors for the classes that followed them. While in training, Clair earned his sharp-shooter Badge.

Instructors like Clair had to possess other characteristics besides the knowledge, skill, and ability to teach the basics of fighting and surviving in combat. A key requirement was discipline. Lack of discipline was, as often as not, the path to disaster. Also required were patience and a sense of humor. Clair's sister Leora related a story told to her by Clair. During rifle training one day a young draftee approached Clair and asked if he pulled the trigger real-real slowly, would the bullet come out slower? Clair was able to deal with the question in a professional manner without even raising an eyebrow. That proved the Army had chosen correctly in making Clair an instructor. Many of us would have reacted differently to the question.

Clair's father Leo built the first Honor Roll Board in Fillmore. It was erected on the knoll across Emerald Street from the Fillmore Hotel in what is now Veteran's Park. Leo made slots on the board so that the names of new soldiers could be added in alphabetical order and moved around as necessary. The names were printed on small rectangular pieces of wood so they could be slid in and out of the slots.

Frances A. Arthur (Edwards) of Fillmore enlisted in the Women's Army Corps on July 21, 1943. She was the English teacher at FCS at the time of her enlistment. A many talented person, among other achievements, Frances served as Vice-President of the Student Council, President of the Library Club and was a prize-winning public speaker at her Seneca-Gorham-Potter Central High School. She also played basketball, was a member of the Glee Club, and was Salutatorian of her 1937 class.

Frances took her military basic training at Fort Oglethorpe in Georgia, and then spent several months at the Army Administration School in Richmond, KY. She remained in the service until January 31, 1946. Among others, she received the American Campaign Medal. There is no indication that she served outside of the US. She apparently worked in an administrative capacity at an Army base for the balance of her service following basic training. Besides the American Campaign Medal, she earned the WAC Service Ribbon, the Good Conduct Medal, and the World War II Victory Medal.

Bernard P. Ayer of Hume entered the service September 22, 1944. It is not clear where he took his basic training, but the NAO reported that he was stationed at Camp Robinson, Arkansas by November. At that time, Camp Robinson was an infantry training replacement center. Bernard was assigned to the 133rd Infantry Training Battalion. During training, it was determined that Bernard was deaf in one ear. (His daughter Judy said that the deafness was caused when he was hunting with his brothers. One of them fired a shotgun too close to him, and the sound punctured his eardrum.) He was honorably discharged from the service January 16, 1945, at Fort Dix, NJ.

Wilfred C. (Woody) Bleistein of Fillmore reported to the draft board in Belmont on June 3, 1942, with

Marlie Hodnett. He was immediately inducted, and then given a ten-day furlough. He went through his basic training at Camp Croft in South Carolina. Future Vice President Spiro Agnew went through training at Croft just before Woody, and New York Yankee broadcaster Mel Allen, just after. By September of 1942, he was stationed at Camp Kilmer, New Jersey (near New Brunswick). Kilmer had only been activated in June of 1942. (Woody may have been there by June.) The base was part of the Transportation Corps, and it was the largest processing center for troops heading overseas during the war. The NAO reported, in April of 1943, that Woody was assigned to do paper work at Kilmer, and that almost surely was related to the processing of troops heading for combat in the ETO (European Theater of Operations.) He remained at Kilmer until sometime in 1943 or 1944. *Picture – Woody with Sam Colombo on Prospect Street in Fillmore probably in June, 1945. Virginia Colombo peeking from behind. Colombo family photo.*

His next stop was Seattle, WA, although it is not clear when he arrived there. It is likely, however, that he was stationed at Fort Lawson, located in the Magnolia neighborhood of Seattle. Fort Lawton was the second largest processing center for troops and material heading for the Pacific. In June 1944, the NAO reported that he was in Seattle, but was being transferred to Camp Haan in California (near Riverside). Woody spent only a short time at Camp Haan, an anti-aircraft training center, and an Army Force Depot Center. He was likely assigned to the Depot Center. (WASP Elin Harte of Centerville, was also at Haan during this period, but she and Woody would not have known each other. They likely never met. Elin did not move to the FCSD area until after the war.)

From Haan, Woody moved to nearby Camp Roberts. Located in Monterey and San Luis Obispo Counties Roberts was both an Infantry Training and Field Artillery Training Replacement Center. Both training programs lasted 17 weeks. Roberts reached its peak population in June 1944 when 45,000 troops passed through the center. Woody may have been at Roberts by June. The NAO reported him still assigned to Roberts in September.

In January 1945, Woody was transferred to a new camp, Fort Knox, KY (south of Louisville), and to a new job. He entered the 17-weeks tank mechanic training program. As the NAO reported, the men were trained to repair both the big Sherman tanks and their little brothers. Other types of training were also provided. A write up on Fort Knox training (written years after the fact) mentions that the men were introduced to "Misery," "Agony," and "Heartbreak." Those words likely refer to a book written years later by Roger Cirillo. The book's title was *Misery, Agony and Heartbreak: The Ground War in Italy, January - June, 1944.* It is unlikely those words were used during Woody's training.

Woody was not destined to see overseas service. He was still at Fort Knox in July of 1945. That same month he was in Fillmore with his wife. He was discharged December 21, 1945.

Merton E. Byington of Centerville entered the service on April 21, 1941. It is not totally clear where he served throughout his service. He was at Camp Butner, NC. Butner started out as a training camp. Its primary mission was to train combat troops for deployment and redeployment. Artillery and engineering units were also trained at Butner. The Camp was capable of training up to 40,000 troops at a time. It also became a major assembly and staging point for overseas deployments. Among the many divisions that staged at Butner were the 35th, 78th, and 89th, Infantry Divisions. As the war progressed Butner became a major Prisoner of War camp, first for Italian POWs and later for Germans. It is possible that Merton was assigned to Butner for combat training and when he completed his training was assigned to the training staff. This was very common for men who received high scores during training.

In order to efficiently address the demands of World War II, the US Army and the War Department underwent a major change in 1942. The Army was divided into three major forces – Army Ground Forces (AGF), Army Service Forces (ASF), and Army Air Forces. The ASF was composed of seven technical services – Corps of Engineers, Signal Corps, Ordnance Department, Quartermaster Corps, Chemical Corps, Medical Corps and Transportation Corps. It was charged with assuring that the two other major commands received all the technical services they needed to successfully prosecute the war. ASF was divided into nine service commands. Camp Butner was part of the 4th Service Command with headquarters in Atlanta, Georgia.

It is possible that Merton was at Butner his entire period of service. He ended his career as a Technical Sergeant. Records show that he was transferred from Camp Butner to Fort Dix, New Jersey on July 3, 1945 and was discharged at Dix on July 16, 1945.

Victor J. Chizlette of Rossburg entered the Army on October 17, 1942. In December, the NAO reported that Victor had corresponded that "he was presently on his 18th day at Station Hospital, Ward 37, his illness due to an ulcerated stomach." Due to the ulcer, Victor received an honorable medical discharge in February 1943.

Vernon A. Closser II entered the US Army on November 6, 1942. He was 39 years old and had served during World War I with Company M, 74th Infantry Regiment, New York National Guard enlisting on November 11, 1919 as a Private. He was 16 at the time. During his World War II service Vernon was assigned to Second Service Command, Army Services Forces (ASF) Headquarters at Fort Jay, Governors Island, NY. There were nine ASF service command areas during the war. The Second Service Command was responsible for the provision of all services such as management of stations, supply, general services, personnel, administration, and technical supervision to military installations within its jurisdiction which included New York, New Jersey, and Delaware, plus, from time to time, Puerto Rico.

The exact services for which they had responsibility and Command authority depended on the classification of the installations. Since the Second Service Command's area of responsibility included Army Ground Forces it was primarily responsible for administration, housekeeping, and supply services. Vernon was assigned as a clerk. He served five months and was discharged March 25, 1943 at Albany, NY.

Colin C. Collver of Fillmore entered the service on December 20, 1944. The NAO reported that he took his basic training at Fort Dix, NJ. He then moved to Camp Blanding, FL. Blanding had been a combat infantry training center for most of the war, concentrating on training entire divisions. In 1943, its emphasis was switched to combat training for replacement personnel. Some 800,000 infantry combat personnel were trained there. A short time later a major portion of the base was converted to a POW camp. It eventually housed some 370.000 German POWs.

The NAO reported Colin home on leave in July 1945. He reported back to Camp Blanding. In August, the NAO reported Colin again home on leave. This time he reported back to Fort Meade in Maryland. It is not clear what he did at Meade, but by September the NSO reported him overseas.

The war was officially over by the time Colin reported overseas. He was assigned to a unit in Manila in the Philippines. Again, his specific duties are not known; but at that time, Army personnel were busy with occupation duties including transferring Japanese POWs back to Japan, and re- establishment of the

Philippine government. The NAO reported Colin still there in December 1945. On July 4, 1946, the United States recognized the independence of the Philippines from the United States.

Colin earned both the Asiatic Pacific Theater Medal and the World War II Victory Medal. He remained in the service until July 1951.

Herbert T. Darling of Short Tract entered the service December 12, 1941, five days after the attack on Pearl Harbor. The NAO reported him home on leave from training in Washington DC in August of 1942. It is likely that between December 1941 and August 1942, Herbert went through basic training and veterinarian technician training. After his furlough it appears that he was assigned to a Veterinary Detachment in North Charleston, SC. A July 1944 item in the NAO reported that he had been serving in the Veterinary Detachment of the Medical Corps in Charleston for the last two years.

In Washington, Herbert likely attended veterinary technician training at the Army Medical Center. This training was for a period of 12 weeks. The training focused on 1. Meat and dairy hygiene, 2. Animal management, and 3. Subjects such as forage and grain inspection and administration. Following the completion of his training, as reported in the NAO, he was ordered to the Veterinary Detachment of the US Medical Corps in Charleston, SC. At Charleston he would have been concerned with animal management.

Charleston was a key port for the shipment of animals overseas. Herbert would have been involved not only in the care and treatment of animals in Charleston, but also for their care and treatment when shipped to combat areas. In fact, his write-up at the World War II Monument in Washington, DC indicates that he earned the European, African, Middle East (EAME) Campaign Medal. He likely earned this decoration by participating in the shipment of horses, mules, dogs, and other animals to combat areas in Europe. He may also have served at European posts, although still officially assigned to Charleston. Detailed records of Herbert's service are not available, but his EAME Theater Medal is proof that he did spend time in Europe. In fact, one remaining record indicates that he returned from Europe for the last time on July 3, 1945. He was discharged December 15, 1945.

Clarence A. Denning of Fillmore entered the service November 14, 1942. It is not known where he took his basic training, nor is it known where he was stationed next. It is possible and probable that he participated in an advanced training program. In April 1944 he was assigned to Army Camp VanDorn near Centreville, Mississippi.

Camp Van Dorn was activated September 20, 1942 two months before Clarence entered the service. It provided combat training to two major infantry divisions, the 99th and 63rd Infantry Divisions, as well as several regiments, battalions, and non-divisional units. VanDorn was also the location of a major racial incident in 1943 that eventually resulted in claims of the murders of over a thousand members of the all Black 364th Infantry Regiment. While no evidence of mass murders has been authenticated, at least one member of the regiment was murdered by the Wilkinson County sheriff. Official reports of the incidents are still being challenged. The regiment was eventually shipped to Alaska to defend key installations in the Aleutians.

In September, 1944, according to the NAO, Clarence was promoted to Corporal. It is not known what duties Clarence performed at Van Dorn. However, based on information from his final pay record, it is possible and maybe likely that he was assigned to the Quartermaster Corps. The record says his Army component was OC. This was possibility a typo and may have meant to be QC. Another possibility is that Clarence was assigned to a Military Police unit and was guarding German POWs located at Van Dorn. In fact, the NAO, in a September 1944 issue mentioned that Clarence was at VanDorn which was "a Prisoner of War camp." The NAO did not publish any information regarding additional assignments. However, a Public Directory available on the Internet lists a Clarence A. Denning living with his wife Thelma Louise in Memphis, TN in 1945. It indicates that Clarence was a member of the US Army. Another 1951 Public Directory shows Clarence still living in Memphis with his wife Thelma. There was a Thelma Louise McDonald living in Memphis in 1940.

There were only a couple of Army installations located in Memphis at the time. One was Second Army Headquarters which was responsible for the combat training of Army Forces within its area. This included the massive maneuvers that were conducted in Tennessee during the war. The second installation was the Memphis General Services Depot. This appears to be a more likely assignment for Clarence. The depot was a Quartermaster unit facility but it also had a small POW population.

Clarence was promoted to Sergeant on January 3, 1946 and discharged January 31, 1946 at Fort Lewis, WA. It is not known whether he was sent to Fort Lewis specifically for his discharge or if he was in fact sent there or to another base in the area prior to his discharge. The latter seems unlikely. It is possible that his name was not removed from the Public Directory published in 1951 even though he was no longer in the area. The General Services Depot, with a name change, continued to operate until September 1997. Clarence died in Buffalo, NY November 10, 2005.

Elsie Jean Eldridge (Perry) of Granger, joined the Women's Auxiliary Army Corps (WAACs) on July  29, 1942, less than two weeks after her husband, Albert, enlisted. She was inducted at Ft. Niagara on October 1st and sent to the WAAC center in Des Moines, Iowa for basic training. The first WAAC trainee group had started July 20, 1942, at Des Moines, so the entire process was still new. During training, the enlisted personnel studied military customs and courtesies, organization of the Army, map reading, first aid, and supply. Trainees drilled, participated in ceremonies and parades, and stood guard duty. They awoke each morning to the boom of a canon and the sound of a bugle. They even had to perform KP. These women had a crowded daily schedule. Even though they were not officially in the Army, it was still "hurry up and wait." *Picture – Jean in training as a truck driver.*

Upon completion of basic training, they were assigned to unit training, usually at Des Moines. The assignments included training as clerks, typists, drivers, cooks, and unit Cadre. Jean told Nancy Gillette and Grace Niblo, who interviewed her for an article printed in the Winter 2001 issue of *The New Enterprise*, published by The History Club of Fillmore, that she was assigned to the Motor Corps. She said she "learned to repair engines and drive trucks. She was eventually able to drive a one and a half-ton truck."

Many WAACs were disappointed with their assignments. The women who joined the WACCs were, by and large, well educated. The officers' average age was 30, and 40 percent of them had college degrees. The average age of the enlisted personnel was 24, and 60 percent were high school graduates. Many of them had some college.

After completing Motor Corps school, Jean was chosen to take a test to qualify for radio training. She passed and was transferred to the Midland Radio and Television School, Kansas City, MO, for training in radio repair. (Apparently just prior to her moving to Kansas City, Jean's husband Albert, was able to obtain a ten-day pass, and they spent the ten days in Des Moines.) Jean told *The New Enterprise* that, at one point during her training, they gave her a sack of radio parts and a schematic drawing, and told her to make a radio. She did and it worked. While Jean was in Kansas City, Eleanor Roosevelt visited the training center on February 14, 1943. Mrs. Roosevelt had lunch with the trainees in the "consolidated mess." Jean was promoted to Corporal Technician 5th Grade at the completion of her training.

From Kansas City, Jean was sent to Ft. Oglethorpe in Georgia. (Several of the female volunteers from the FCSD area passed through Oglethorpe at one time or another, including Jenny Kolakowska and Frances J. Arthur.) Oglethorpe apparently, among other activities, served as a holding location until permanent assignments were finalized. By June 1943, Jean had been assigned to the Aberdeen Proving Ground in Aberdeen, MD. Jean told *The New Enterprise* that she worked in the Ballistics Research Laboratory at Aberdeen, wiring equipment. Aberdeen was, at this time, deeply involved in advancing and perfecting radar.

Jean had only been at Aberdeen a couple of months when legislation was passed establishing the Women's Army Corps. The WAACs were disbanded at this point and all WAACs received a "discharge." Jean was asked to enlist in the WAC, but chose instead to return to western, NY. *The New Enterprise* reported that Jean continued her service to America after her discharge. She went to work for the Bell Aircraft laboratory in Buffalo, working in the electronics lab in flight research.

Harlan C. Evans of Centerville entered the US Army on April 17, 1945. The war in Europe ended just two weeks later. It appears that he took his basic training at Camp Clairborne in Rapides Parish, Louisiana. Camp Clairborne was used for both basic training and artillery practice. Engineering and Special Service Forces were also trained at the camp. The war in the Pacific ended less than five months after Harlan entered the service.

It appears that Harlan remained at Clairborne for the entire period of his service. He was discharged in October 1945 after some seven months of service.

James E. Fancher entered the service on October 26, 1942. It appears that James spent his entire service as part of the Army Military Police in the United States. Only one item appeared in the NOA regarding his service. In September 1943 it was reported that he was home on furlough visiting his parents in Houghton. The NAO item also mentioned that he was a member of the Military Police.

Upon entry into service, James was likely immediately assigned to Army Service Forces (ASF). One of the commands of the ASF was the Provost Marshal General, which included the Military Police. James' picture (see Part XIV) shows the shoulder patch for the ASF and an MP whistle is attached to his shirt.

The duties of the Military Police were numerous. They included protecting military and industrial installations, guarding POW's, apprehending AWOL's, directing traffic, patrolling trains and major cities to assure proper conduct by off-duty soldiers and investigating complaints of alleged criminal acts performed by military personnel. It is not known in which of these activities James participated, but it is likely that it was more than one. It is also not known where James served.

James was discharged February 1, 1946 after some 39 months of service. He earned, at a minimum, the American Campaign Medal, and the World War II Victory Medal.

Richard C. (Dick) Farnsworth of Hume was inducted into the Army on August 13, 1941. He took his basic training as a Private with Battery A, 13th Battalion, at the Army Coastal Artillery Replacement Training center at Fort Eustis, Va. From Eustis, Richard was sent to Fort Levett, Maine, where he was assigned to Battery A of the 240th Coastal Battalion. The fort was located on Cushing Island in the middle of Casco Bay, and was part of the Portland, Maine coastal defense. By September 1942, Dick had been ordered to Fort Wetherill, Rhode Island, part of the defenses around Narragansett Bay guarding the approaches to Newport. A graduate of Houghton College, he had also been promoted to 2nd Lieutenant. He would be promoted to 1st Lieutenant by October 1943. Dick was now in charge of Battery E of the 243rd Coastal Battalion. He would officially be assigned to the 243rd for the balance of the war. A major priority at the beginning of the war, by 1943 it became apparent that the number of men needed for coastal defense activities had decreased dramatically. As a result, the Army transferred many men to other units.

Dick may or may not have been switched, but on December 15, 1943, he suffered a severely broken leg. He was moved to Lowell General Hospital at Fort Devens, MA, for treatment. He spent a good part of the remainder of the war in the hospital. The NAO published a letter from Dick in January 1944. In part he, "expressed his appreciation for receiving the Observer." He also wrote that, "he was recovering rather slowly, and was all rigged up with ropes, pulleys, and weights, and it would be another month before he would even get into a cast." He told the Observer that he was anxious to see his new daughter and he thanked the Junior Red Cross for the Christmas box he had received. In fact, Dick took over a year to recover. He was at Fort Devens, MA, initially, from December 15, 1943 until July 4, 1944. Then he returned to his unit in Rhode Island. However, by January 4, 1945, he was back in the hospital, and remained there until April 30. Dick was then granted terminal leave, and was discharged June 18, 1945.

Albert E. Findlay of Centerville entered the service on January 23, 1945. It is likely that he took his basic training at Fort Meade in Maryland, and then was made permanent party at Meade following completion of his training. The NAO reported that he was home on leave from Meade in June and then returned to Meade.

It is not known when or even if he served at a location other than Fort Meade. During this period (1945) Fort Meade was primarily a basic training and prisoner of war camp. Some 3,500,000 men and women were trained or passed through Meade during the war. The biggest number of personnel were there during the first part of 1945, with a peak of 70,000 being reached in March.

Besides basic training, a Cooks and Bakers School and training in all phases of the entertainment field were operated at Meade. The German and Italian POW camp was opened in September of 1943. The POW camp replaced an internment facility housing German, Japanese, and Italian immigrant residents arrested as potential fifth columnists, albeit without any evidence.

The Italian POWs were delighted when Italy surrendered to the Allies and then immediately switched sides. It became necessary to keep the German and Italian POWs apart to avoid conflict. The Italians all volunteered to serve. They were activated as Italian Service Companies with quartermaster duties at Meade.

German POWs were mostly from the Wehrmacht (German Army). Some ten percent of them turned out to be hard-core Nazis and had to be separated from the other Germans to avoid conflicts when most Germans agreed to a work program. This program was very successful. It was credited with creating a 35 percent increase in Maryland's tomato crop in 1945. At the end of the war, many of the German POWs wanted to stay in the US. US policy required all POWs to be returned to their home country.

All the activities mentioned above created the need for many guards to keep track of the participating POWs. It is possible that Albert served as a guard. He was discharged August 4, 1946.

Harold Frank Ford of Centerville entered the service on March 16, 1944. According to the NAO, he was sent to Fort Sill in Oklahoma for his basic training. It appears that he was at Fort Sill for about five months. Since Sill was also an Engineer Training Center, it is possible that, following basic training, he was assigned to the engineer training school. In September, he was transferred to Fort Leonard Wood. The NAO reported that he was home with his wife on furlough in September, and that he was returning to Fort Leonard Wood following his leave. At that time, Fort Wood was an engineer replacement training center. Ford spent three months at Fort Wood. Then, in November 1944, he was given an honorable discharge at Fort Dix, NJ. The NAO reported that he returned to Fillmore following his discharge. The paper did not indicate the reason for the early honorable discharge.

Vernon Gambrel of Fillmore entered the Army on March 30, 1945. No information on his service has been uncovered. However, since the war in Europe ended one month later, and the war in the Pacific five months later, it is likely that he was still in or just out of training when the war ended. Vernon did make the military his career, officially being discharged 20 years later, on March 31, 1965. It is not clear what Vernon was doing in Fillmore at the time of his entry into the military. He was born in Kentucky.

Clarence F. Gaus of Allen was Honorably Discharged from the US Army for "Below minimum physical standards for induction." This was after having already served almost two years. Clarence had bad feet, and presumably, at some point, someone decided that his problems disqualified him for service, even though he had already served 20 months. Clarence accepted his discharge at Fort Dix and went home. Prior to his discharge, however, Clarence had served as a light truck driver, although he was also qualified as a cannoneer (artillery gunner). It may be that while qualifying as a cannoneer or shortly thereafter, his foot problem was identified.

Following basic training and any technical training, Clarence was assigned to Station Complement 4416 at Camp Forest, TN, as a truck driver. Camp Forest, originally Camp Peay, initially served as an internment camp for German and Japanese-American internees. It later served as a POW camp for German and Italian soldiers. As a truck drive, Clarence could have had multiply responsibilities, including the transportation of POWs. He was discharged December 12, 1944.

Forrest L. Gilbert of Centerville entered the service on March 18, 1941. No records, except his Army enlistment records, pertaining to his service have been located. His name does appear on the Centerville Honor role of World War II soldiers. It is not known if he served overseas. He was discharged June 20, 1947 after 63 months of service. At a minimum he earned the American Defense Medal, the American Campaign Medal, and the World War II Victory Medal.

Frederic C. (Ted) Hauser joined the service on May 26, 1943. He entered active duty on June 9, 1943. Based on reports in the *Northern Allegany Observer* (NAO), Frederic apparently spent his entire military career at Camp Hulen located just west of Palacios, TX. In June 1943, NAO reported that Frederic had been called to service at a camp in Texas. An article in a March 1944 issue of the NAO, reported that his wife, Elsie, had moved their household goods to Houghton (probably to his parent's home), and joined her husband at a camp in the south. A June 1944 issue of the NAO reported that Ted was spending a two-weeks furlough with his parents, and then would return to Palacios. It is possible that Frederic attended basic training at another southern camp, and was later transferred to Hulen where he remained for the balance of the war.

The base was originally named Camp Palacios. Camp Hulen was initially a World War II antiaircraft training center. In January 1944 it was converted to a POW camp for Germans. Many of the prisoners were used as agricultural workers.

It is not known what Frederic's duty assignment was, but it may have changed during his service. Frederic at one time apparently was a Sergeant. For some reason he was reduced to private. Prior to his discharge he was promoted back to Corporal.

Frederic was discharged January 16, 1945.

Richard W. Hazlett of Houghton officially entered the service April 17, 1945 in Buffalo, but apparently did not leave for basic training until May. He was a student at Houghton College at the time. Before he entered active military service, the war in Europe was over. In October 1945 the NAO reported him home visiting his parents. By that time the war in the Pacific was over. Richard was discharged December 19, 1946 after some 20 months of service.

Wendell Allen Howden of Fillmore served in the US Army from October 25, 1945 until June 1, 1947. The NAO reported that he was accepted for service in November 1944, but did not enter officially until about a year later. Wendell graduated from FCS in June 1945. He was stationed at several bases during his two years of service. These included Fort Dix in New Jersey, Fort Knox in Kentucky, Fort Ord in California, and Fort Sill in Oklahoma.

Fort Dix, which was a major training and staging ground during the war, became a key demobilization center after the war. It is likely that Wendell was sent to Dix to assist in the demobilization process. From there he was ordered to Ft. Knox, KY. At that time, Knox was a major training center for armored personnel. Wendell's son Bruce said that his father was a cannoneer (artillery gunner) at one point, and it is likely that he received his training for that job at Fort Knox.

At the end of WW II, Fort Ord was a basic combat and advanced infantry training center. Wendell was there only a short time, probably for advanced training. From Fort Ord he was ordered to Fort Sill, where he worked as a classification specialist. He was assigned to Headquarters Battery, 18th Field Artillery Battalion. He rose to the rank of Technician 5th Grade, equivalent to the rank of Corporal, but without supervisory authority outside of his specialty. As a classification specialist, Wendel's duties could have included preparing correspondence, records, forms, and reports on personnel matters, including payrolls, special orders, court-martial proceedings, morning reports, sick reports, rosters, leaves, furloughs, and discharges.

Clarence L. Irish of Granger entered the service on October 3, 1942. It appears that he was assigned to Fort Riley, KS and remained there until late 1945. Clarence was assigned to Troop A, 2nd Training Regiment, a training unit. His specific occupation has not been identified. The NAO reported in March 1944 that he had injured his hand and was in the Fort Riley hospital. Clarence appears to have served the first 20 months of his military career with few if any problems. The last 17 months were not so good. During that time period he went AWOL four times. Each time he was captured and returned to Fort Riley. There is no solid evidence as to the cause for his behavior. One clue may be that at some point he courted and married a woman from Topeka, KS. In fact, his final pay record, the only document remaining from his personnel file which was destroyed in the St. Louis personnel records center fire, indicates that he was apprehended in Topeka after being AWOL from June 1 to June 13, 1944 and returned to Fort Riley. His second AWOL was for one day (August 13, 1944). He received the same sentence he received for both his first and third offenses, six months confinement at hard labor plus fines. It appears that he did not serve the entire six months for either the first, second or third AWOL, which occurred during the period February 6 to March 14, 1945.

In July 1945, the NAO reported Clarence home on leave with his wife. His final pay record shows that he was charged with being AWOL for the fourth time for the period July 26 to October 14, 1945. Apparently, his furlough was only through July 25. He may have been married during this furlough and decided to take his new bride to New York to meet his parents. The pay records indicate he was apprehended in Niagara Falls and returned to Fort Riley. As a result of this last AWOL, he was sentenced to five years at hard labor, plus fines, and confined at the US Disciplinary Barracks at Jefferson Barracks,

MO. He also received a Dishonorable Discharge effective November 12. 1945. However, the date of the discharge was suspended until his release from confinement. It is not known how long Clarence served in prison.

Earl J. James of Fillmore entered the US Army on June 5, 1944. He went through basic training and then was honorably discharged on September 22, 1944 after three months of service.

Francis L. James of Granger entered the service on April 1, 1943. He was immediately sent to Camp Mackall near Southern Pines, NC. It appears that he took his basic training there, and then was made permanent party. Mackall was a sub-camp of Fort Bragg and was a training facility for airborne troops. In fact, it was named after Private John Thomas Mackall of the 509th Parachute Infantry Regiment, who was killed in action during the invasion of North Africa. Mackall was also used as a camp for German prisoners of war. It is possible that Francis served as a guard after completing basic training. Francis served his entire time in service at Camp Mackall. In February 1944, he suffered a severe injury to his foot. He was honorably discharged on March 30, 1944, apparently due to the foot injury. He had served exactly one year.

Clifford C. Johannes of Houghton/Fillmore first entered the military on May 27, 1941. The NAO reported on his service monthly for the next six months. During that six-months period he was stationed at Fort Leonard Wood, MO. Per the NAO, he served initially with the 30th Battalion. This was likely an engineer battalion as in September NAO reported that he was now with the 369th Engineer Company. In December 1941 the NAO did not report any information on Clifford.

His last pay record provided additional information. However, some of it is confusing. The document indicates that Clifford was discharged November 26, 1942 for Convenience of the Government related to his importance to national health, safety, or interest. It further reports however, that Clifford was recalled to active service January 14, 1942. Finally, it reports that he was discharged at Fort Jay, NY on November 30, 1943. Based on the available information, it seems more likely that the first discharge occurred November 26, 1941. This would be consistent with the NAO not showing any service location for Clifford in December 1941. It would also be consistent with his being recalled to service on January 14, 1942, and then officially being discharged again November 30, 1943.

Virtually no information is available on Clifford's second term of service – January 14, 1942 to November 30, 1943. The final pay record does provide some clues. One is that he served with Company C, 713th Military Police Battalion. The second is that that he owed the laundry at Fort Mead $3.00. This would indicate that Clifford was at Fort Meade at some time, but may not have served there.

Fort Meade did serve as a recruit training center during the war. It also was used as a Prisoner of War Camp and as a detention center for Japanese, German and Italian immigrant residents of the United States arrested as fifth columnists. These activities certainly would have required a significant Military Police presence. However, no information has been located that shows the 713th Military Police Battalion (MPB) located at Fort Meade. Information does show the 400th MPB served there. The 713th did serve overseas during the war, including participating in the Utah Beach invasion force. Nothing has been located regarding its service in the ZI (Zone of Interior)

Richard S. Johannes of Allen entered the service August 23, 1944. Richard apparently was living in Fillmore at the time of his induction. The NAO in August, 1944 reporting his induction, indicated that he was from Fillmore. It is not known where Richard took his basic training, but likely at Fort Belvoir. His World War II Memorial page indicates that he served at the Army Services Forces Training Center at Fort Belvoir, VA during his service. Fort Belvoir was a major engineer training center during the war.

In April 1944 the Center added training for extended field service in various theaters. It also concentrated on training replacement engineers instead of units. In late 1945 it became a separation center. It is likely that Richard did well in his basic training classes and like many others who did so was assigned to the base as a trainer.

John V. Jones of Fillmore entered active military service on January 27, 1941. John had been a member of the New York National Guard prior to entering into full-time service. He was ordered to Fort Devens and assigned to Troop B, 101st Cavalry as a band member. It is possible that, as a member of the Guard, he was in Brooklyn when the 199th Army Band was initially organized and activated there. With that band, John was transferred to Fort Devens on February 4.

John served with the band for the entire war. On June 11, the band played its first event, a parade in Lowell, MA. It performed at several parades in states along the east coast. Throughout the war, it performed at all kinds of events. Among those were War Bond Drives, including the 3rd War Loan Rally at Fort Jay, NY, and others at Raleigh, NC, Bladensburg, NC, and Slocomb, AL. The band made regular appearances at Arms & Personnel events, and it even played at a ball game in Red Springs. NC.

In late 1942 or early 1943, John married Geraldine (Gerry) Damon. Gerry served as the Librarian at FCS for some 30 years.

While providing music for various events was the band's primary duty, members were not exempted entirely from standard Army activities. The band had to participate in long marches on almost a regular basis. In September of 1941, they participated in the Army maneuvers at Norman NC. John qualified as a Marksman with a 45-caliber pistol in May 1943.

In March 1943, the band was transferred to Fort Meade, MD. Returning by train to Fort Meade from a performance in West Virginia (where it was temporarily assigned to Elkins) in July 1944, the band was in a train wreck in Silver Spring, MD. No one was hurt, and band members were cited for assisting other passengers. The band was later transferred to Fort Bragg, NC. Its official name was also changed a couple of times. In June 1944, it officially became the 199th Army Ground Forces Band.

The band's last event was a concert for the Ozark Chamber of Commerce. On November 27, 1945, the band was inactivated. By that time, John had been discharged.

John H. Keyes of Wiscoy served with the US Army before and during World War I. While starting his service as an enlisted man, on April 12, 1915 he was discharged in order to accept a commission. He served the rest of the war as a Second Lieutenant. John was born in Canada in 1892 and emigrated to the US in 1909 according to the 1920 Federal Census. However, border crossing records indicate that a John H. Keyes arrived in the US from Canada in October 1910. This John listed his age as 14 (Born 1896.). Both John's were from Stratford making it likely that they were the same person. All other located records show John born in 1892. The 1925 Federal Census shows that John was naturalized as an American Citizen in 1917, which would have been during his World War I service.

The 1940 Federal Census recorded John as a "Caretaker" for the Buffalo City Recreation Agency, and living in Buffalo. His obituary indicates that prior to his service in Buffalo in WW II he was performing similar duties in Albany, NY. An October 1944 edition of the NAO indicates that John had a home in Wiscoy. Records at the World War II Memorial, provided by the Allegany County Veteran's Office, indicate that Lieutenant Colonel John H. Keyes served as Post Commander, 1202nd Army Service Unit Detachment in Buffalo during the war. The unit had responsibility for conducting physical examinations of men who volunteered or were drafted for service during World War II. His obituary states that he was the Commanding Officer of Armed Forces Mobile Induction Team, located in the Old Customs Building in Buffalo. Lieutenant Colonel John H. Keyes is buried in the East Koy Cemetery in Portage, NY, a short distance from Wiscoy.

Wells E Knibloe of Granger was a senior at the University of Buffalo when he entered the service on February 1, 1943. It is not clear where or if Wells took basic training, but by at least May 1943 he was technically assigned to the Staten Island Terminal at Stapelton. He then was reassigned to the Brooklyn Army Base. However, despite his official place of assignment, from at least May 1943 until April 1944, Wells was enrolled in a specialized engineering course at Fordham University. In April, 1944, he was transferred to the Ordnance Replacement Center at Aberdeen, MD.

Wells would remain at Aberdeen for the balance of the war. Initially he attended two schools, one for instrument repair and the other for fire control repairman. Wells was then made permanent party at Aberdeen and became an Antiaircraft Artillery Instructor, as well as a Fire Control Repairman. It is likely that Wells had excelled in his training since he was made an instructor.

Wells remained at Aberdeen until November 1945. He then was assigned to Atomic Bomb testing activities, and transferred to Long Beach, CA in December 1945. In March, 1946, he sailed to the Bikini Atoll in the Marshall Islands aboard the *USS Arkansas* (BB 33) battleship. An article in the NAO reported that, Wells was aboard the *USS Arkansas* at the Bikini Atoll in the Pacific on June 30, 1946 (Note: the testing took place from June 1 to July 15, 1946), where he witnessed the Bikini Island Atomic Bomb test. Wells reported that, complying with orders, observers turned their backs and covered their eyes just before the explosion. When they were allowed to look, they could see a small churning mass of smoke on the horizon. The expected column was not visible due to cloud cover. He did feel the heat of the explosion and compared it to the sun coming out from behind a cloud. The sound of the explosion took two minutes (119 seconds according to another observer) to reach them. Wells reported that he was able to see close-up what the bomb could do. However, due to security rules, he was not allowed to talk about results. On August 1, 1946, Wells sailed for the states aboard the *USS Chilton* (APA 38) attack transport, arriving in San Francisco in mid-August. He was discharged at Fort Meade in Maryland on August 19, 1946.

Genevieve Kolakowska of Centerville, joined the Women's Army Corps (WAC) in February of 1944;

and as the NAO put it, she was Centerville's only "Lady in Uniform" at the time. Having worked in a machine shop after graduating high school, Jenny was a "Rosie the Riveter" before there was a Rosie the Riveter. Jenny would always say that the Army did more for her than she did for the Army. Of course, Jenny was wrong about that. She did plenty for the Army. After completing her basic training at Fort Oglethorpe, Georgia (the closest big city was Chattanooga, TN), Jenny became part of the Cadre (permanent party) at Oglethorpe and was assigned to, as she put it, "training rookies." The Army, of course, would point out that, every one of those "rookies" freed up a male soldier for combat duty. Those "rookies," once their training was completed thanks to WACs like Jenny, among their many other duties, kept the bureaucracy of the Army functioning. While her primary duty at Oglethorpe was training other potential WACs, Jenny also served as mail clerk and as company clerk. Her training duties ran the gamut from close order drill to physical training to classroom instructions. The courses she taught included orientation to the Army and why we were fighting the war. Jenny told the author how, on off duty hours, she used to walk around the hills surrounding the camp. She said the area was covered with Civil War monuments, canons, and cannon balls. *Picture – Ginny at Fort Oglethorpe, Ga.* Family Photo.

In April 1944 Jenny was shipped to Washington and Lee University in Lexington, VA. There she underwent special services training. She was being groomed to develop, arrange for, and conduct USO-type shows and other forms of recreation for soldiers. From Lexington, she was shipped to Des Moines, Iowa, a staging area, where she was being readied for an overseas assignment. It was while at Des Moines that news came from home that necessitated her request for a hardship discharge. She was ordered to Fort Dix, NJ for her final discharge. Jenny never regretted enlisting, and only circumstances at home that required her presence caused her to end her military service. Jenny said the Army, "stiffened my backbone and brought out the best in me." Jenny was discharged in August 1945.

Alvin Paul (Dodd) Miller of Centerville was ordered to report to the Court House in Belmont at 7:30 AM on Monday, August 11, 1941 for induction into the US Army. Since the induction was to take place in Buffalo, Alvin was advised that, if it were more convenient, he could board the bus to Buffalo in Fillmore. The bus would be in Fillmore at 8:25 AM. A Mr. Chamberlain would be on board to make sure Alvin had all his necessary papers, and probably to make sure he was there. Welcome to the Army Mr. Miller.

Alvin, who went by Dodd, traveled from Buffalo to Fort Knox, KY for his basic training. Fort Knox was the home of the Armed Forces Replacement Training Center (AFRTC) for armored personnel. After completing basic training, men were trained in such armored disciplines as armor tactics, tank gunnery, communications, and maintenance.

The basic training was no picnic. Joseph J. Graham, who went through basic at Fort Knox at about the same time as Alvin, described the training as follows. There was a tough physical program which ended with a 25-mile forced march in full field pack (45-50 lbs.). The training included instructions in handling and firing rifles, pistols, carbines, tommy guns, and .30 and .50 caliber machine guns. The machine-gun training took place on the ground, as, at that time, there were not enough tanks available for such training. The men were also trained in keeping their equipment clean, orderly, and properly stored, either in foot or wall lockers. There were also classes in map reading, and in enemy aircraft and vehicle identification. Gas masks were issued and training took place in identifying and responding to gas attacks. Recruits were trained in driving the various vehicles of an armored organization.

Training also included how and when to wear uniforms, how to salute, and military courtesies. Cleanliness was stressed repeatedly. Those who did not maintain a high level of cleanliness received additional duties. At the end, Graham said, those who showed enough promise were made instructors. This is likely what happened to Alvin, as he spent a total of almost three years at Fort Knox. (Graham also stayed, but later went to Officers Candidate School, became an officer, and was sent to Europe.)

In May 1944, according to the NAO, Alvin was sent to Fredericksburg, VA. This likely was temporary duty, as the NAO reported in August of 1944 that he had been transferred to Fort Ord in California. The A.P. Hill Military reservation was in Fredericksburg. It had been a training site for armored divisions, including those under General Patton, early in the war. By 1944 it was a field training site for OCS candidates and enlisted personnel. However, no information exists that Alvin, while in Fredericksburg, was at A.P. Hill.

At that time, Fort Ord was a major center for training amphibious tractor operators for landing troops and equipment. The NAO did report that Alvin was trained as such. In fact, a proficiency record indicates that Alvin was authorized to drive the following military vehicles; halftrack car, cargo trucks (one-half to three-quarters tons), cargo trucks (one and a half to two and a half tons), a wheeled combat vehicle, and a landing vehicle tracked (LVT).

Fort Ord was a major training base for combat divisions early in the war. By late 1943, with most divisions now overseas, it became the biggest west coast replacement center for amphibious training. While Alvin was sent there for training, it is likely that he became a trainer himself, as he remained at Fort Ord for the balance of the war. He likely was assigned to the 18th Armored Group, an amphibious training unit. By 1944, the training at Fort Ord had evolved from the simple over-the-side Higgins boat approach to amphibious landings, to the sophisticated tracked vehicles and drop ramp landing craft approach. Alvin's proficiency record indicates that these more sophisticated craft were the vehicles he was authorized to operate. Alvin was discharged at Fort Ord on December 12, 1945

Ada Ruth Mills of Hume joined the Women's Auxiliary Army Corps (WAAC) on February 16, 1943.

Women's Army Corps Service Medal

Ada was an art and mechanical drawing teacher in Herkimer, NY, so her entrance into the active-duty service was delayed until the end of the school term. (During the remainder of the school term, she did serve in the reserves.) By the time she entered on active duty, the WAAC had become the Women's Army Corps (WAC). Ada, with a Fine Arts Degree from Alfred University, and advanced study at both the University of Buffalo and the Berkshire Summer School of Art, was advised to apply for Officers Candidate School, but she opted to remain in the enlisted ranks during most of her service. She was promoted to 2nd Lieutenant some eight months before her discharge on July 2, 1946.

Ada took her six weeks of basic training at Fort Oglethorpe, GA, and then spent six months at the Army Administrative School in Alpine, TX. In December, while at Alpine, she wrote the NAO to tell them how much she enjoyed the paper. She also mentioned that the area was experiencing its first rain since September. It was usually warm and dry. From Alpine she moved to Fort Bliss, TX, where she was assigned to the WAC Detachment 1852 Service Unit. Ada had been at Fort Bliss for only four months, when she was reassigned to Fort Belvoir, VA. Ada noted, on her Allegany County War Service form, that she was assigned to the Engineering Drafting School. The NAO reported that she took the engineer drafting course while there. The drafting school was part of the 12-week training for combat engineers. There was a WAC unit at Belvoir, the 50th Headquarters Company. The WACs at Belvoir performed communications, clerical and service duties.

Ada was at Belvoir for only three months, according to her War Service form, when she was reassigned again, this time to Fort Myers, VA. While stationed at Fort Myers, Ada worked at the Pentagon in the Operations Branch, Attorney General's Office (AGO), War Department General Staff Office. The Operations Office was responsible for what have been called the "central records of the War Department in the Adjutant General's Office (AGO)." These records constitute the most comprehensive body of important documentation of the activities of the War Department during the war. This included the War Department records classified as Top Secret, Secret, Confidential, and Restricted. Ada served at the War Department until the end of the war, rising to the rank of sergeant.

After the war, Ada attended the six weeks WAC Officer Candidate School in Des Moines, IA. She was commissioned a 2nd Lieutenant November 17, 1945. Ada was then transferred to the Convalescent Hospital at Fort Upton, Brookhaven, NY, where she served as Education Officer, reporting to the Officer in Charge of Occupational Therapy. That office was charged with serving combat veterans, most of whom were psycho-neurotics. These men suffered from distortion of social perspective, hostile attitudes, feelings of inadequacy, confusion, and occasionally, more serious emotional problems. Treatments included physical reconditioning, educational and shop classes, recreation, occupational therapy, and counseling.

While at Fort Upton, Ada purchased a lottery ticket for fifty cents from the Patchogue Veterans of Foreign Wars post. She won a brand new 1946 V-8 Ford Sedan. Ada was discharged July 2, 1946 and returned to teaching.

Clyde F. Millspaugh of Hume, according to an item in a February 1945 issue of the NAO, entered the service some time prior to February of 1945. At the time, he was assigned to Fort Sill in Oklahoma. Apparently, this was not correct. In February, he was in Fillmore visiting his mother and sister. He had been either assigned or detached to Detroit, Michigan to help make tires for the Army. The NAO, reported in November 1945 that he had been discharged and was again spending time with his relatives in Fillmore. He returned to his home in Los Angeles after his visit. He was discharged October 23, 1945.

However, Clyde's enlistment document shows he entered the service on June 25, 1945 at Fort Sheridan, IL That enlistment document appears to indicate that he had previously served as an enlisted man. Further, Veteran's Administration BIRLS records also show that he enlisted June 25, 1945. He may have previously volunteered to enlist, or did enlist at Fort Sill or was assigned to Fort Sill, but his enlistment must have been deferred and instead he was sent or detached to Detroit as part of the Army tire project.

Avis Naze (Wilmot) of Hume was originally from Ellendale, ND. She entered the University of Minnesota and the Army Cadet Nursing Corps in September of 1943. While she was at the University, she met her future husband, Stephen Edward (Ed) Wilmot, a member of the US Coast Guard (See Coast Guard below.) Avis was originally admitted to the US Public Health Service, Division of Nurse Education on September 27, 1943. She was then terminated, without default, on December 17, 1943. She was re-admitted to the US Cadet Nurse Corps on March 27, 1944. Her schedule provided she would enter her Senior Cadet period on July 4, 1946. By then the war was over, and Avis, like Cadet Hilda Schmidt, was no longer needed by the Army.

Merton C. Pero of Fillmore, brother of Deanne, had much the same experience as his brother. His enlistment documents show that he was also single with dependents (possibly his parents.) He joined the Army on August 3, 1942, and received an honorable discharge the following month. Merton had been a skilled mechanic and a carpenter prior to enlisting. No reason for his early honorable discharge has been identified.

Nancy H. Reid (McCreery) of Fillmore entered the Women's Army Corps (WAC) on July 1, 1943. Like Ada Mills (see above) she had been sworn into the Women's Army Auxiliary Corps (WAAC)) earlier, on April 26th. Since she was the homemaking teacher at FCS, she was allowed to complete the school year before entering full time service.

Nancy was initially assigned to Fort Drum (later Fort Devens) in Massachusetts for her basic training. By September she had been transferred to WAC Branch 7 at the Army Administration School in Alpine, TX for additional training. Upon completion of her technical training at Alpine, Nancy was assigned to Camp Pickett, VA. In February 1944, while stationed at Pickett, Nancy visited friends in Fillmore. Her travels were not over. She was next assigned to the Army recruiting station in Pittsburgh, where she performed administrative and secretarial duties. During her service, Nancy rose to the rank of Sergeant. She was discharged at Camp Pickett in 1946.

David P. Richardson was a native son of Fillmore, born there in 1906. In 1941 he was both running an  insurance business and "reading" for the law under the guidance of his father, a practicing attorney in Fillmore. Admitted to the bar in 1942, he immediately volunteered for the military, even though, at almost age 36, he was about to become exempt from military service. He entered as a private and his basic training was at Fort McClellan in Alabama. While there he wrote the NAO, saying in part, "The Army is really a much more strenuous life, at the outset, than I had expected to find it. But with the rest I have just had, together with time to think things over and plan a little, I expect to sail through the balance of this basic training without a hitch." (Dave came down with pneumonia while at McClellan and that is probably the "rest" he referred to in his letter.) Dave enclosed a clipping from the local (Anniston, AL) newspaper with his letter. The clipping reported that Company B boasted two experts with the rifle, one of whom was David P. Richardson, who had a score of 180. As a result, during the first full dress parade, Company B was presented with a white ribbon, reading "Highest Qualification - Rifle - 19th Battalion." The paper also reported that the men, when marching past the reviewing stand, displayed their pride in the best way they knew, by "strutting" to the beat of the band. *Picture – Dave,"Strutting". Family Photo.*

Dave's son Alan said that Dave was originally scheduled for training in an armored division in Texas. Instead, he entered Officer's Candidate School in Fort Washington, MD. Upon completion, he received his 2nd Lieutenant bars and was assigned to the Adjutant Generals Office in DC. His office was in one of the famous temporary Quonset huts erected on the mall during the war. The last of the huts were not removed until the late 1960's. Dave worked in the Casualty Office. Alan said that his primary responsibilities involved casualty notification and grave registration.

Harold E. Schmidt of Granger joined the Army in mid-1945. Despite this, his Army Enlistment Record indicates that he entered the service December 27, 1945. His Department of Veterans Affairs BIRLS death file indicates he served from December 27, 1945 until April 26, 1947.

The problem with these records is that the family has a letter from Harold written July 22, 1945, while he was in basic training at Fort Bragg, NC at the Field Artillery Replacement Training Center (FARTC). Given his discharge date, and that most men enlisted for two years plus six months past Victory Day, it is possible that Harold entered the service in April of 1945.

In his July 22nd letter, Harold told the family that he was training to be part of a Field Artillery unit. It is likely that he had already completed his basic training and now was moving on to more advanced specialized training. He mentioned that they were to be trained on how to use machine guns and rockets as well as grenades. This was in addition to learning the complexities of their main weapon, the 105 Howitzer, a two-ton behemoth. He also mentioned that they were facing 15 more weeks of training, which would mean that they would be in training until approximately mid-November.

Harold's letter home said that he was to be part of an instrument and survey battery. He was most likely training to be a Fire Control Instrument Operator. In a firing battery, the Operator would set up and operate fire control instruments such as aiming circles, range finders, steel tapes and chains. He would prepare firing charts for vertical and horizontal controls using protraction scale and straight edge showing battery positions, check points, base points, targets, elevations, front lines, minimum and maximum ranges, and zones of supported units. A survey course covered such topics as astronomic observations, grid systems and survey planning. The emphasis was on practical instruction in technique of survey.

Harold closed by saying that he may go on to even more advanced training or be sent overseas when he finished his current training. Since the war ended prior to the completion of his training at Fort Bragg, it is not clear where he was next assigned, although the family indicated that he did not go overseas.

Lawrence M. Smith of Wiscoy, while stationed in Upper Darby, PA, won a free telephone call to his wife at the Philadelphia Stage Door Canteen. The canteens were very popular with the G.I.s. The first one was started in New York City and was in the basement of the 4th Street Theater. Before the war was over, there were also canteens in Boston, Newark, Cleveland, San Francisco, Washington, D.C., and Los Angeles in the states, and overseas in London and Paris. The Philadelphia canteen was in the Academy of Music Building.

Lawrence entered the service in August 1944. He took his basic training at Camp Crowder in Missouri. By November he was stationed in Washington, DC according to the NAO, but by January 1945 he was at Upper Darby, PA. He won the call to his wife that month. His wife and two children joined him in Upper Darby for a time, but by June they were back at their home in Wiscoy. Lawrence was home that summer; and a birthday party, with 55 people in attendance, was held for him at the RG&E cabin in Wiscoy. This RG&E cabin was the scene of many events honoring local service men during the war.

Lawrence returned to Upper Darby after his furlough, but by August had been reassigned to Presque Isle, Maine. At that time, Presque Isle was a reentry point for G.I.s returning from overseas, who were scheduled for redeployment to the Pacific. After the dropping of the atomic bombs, redeployment activities were terminated. It was also a center for the care and treatment of casualties returning from Europe. On November 4, 1945, Lawrence received his discharge at Presque Isle.

Norbert F. Sylor of Granger was drafted March 20, 1945, three months before he was awarded his graduation diploma from FCS. Norb was sent to Fort Blanding, Florida for his basic training. At Blanding, he suffered a serious knee injury. On his way to the mess hall, he was walking on a wooden boardwalk when his foot slipped between two of the boards. His knee was severely damaged, and he spent almost three months in the hospital. After his release, he was transferred to a reconditioning service. Norb told the author that, he was loading logs one day when the knee went out again, and he was back in the hospital.

When he was released this time, in early November, the Army shipped him to Fort Bragg, NC. The war was over and many operations were being shut down. Norb was assigned to the security detail of a Field Artillery Battalion. He spent a lot of time driving around in a jeep, making sure the field artillery equipment and guns were adequately secured. He had been promoted to PFC and Squad Leader by this time, so he also spent time drilling and marching his squad.

As activities ground down at Bragg, Norb was shipped to Fort Bliss in Texas. He was now assigned to an antiaircraft unit. His job was to plot the accuracy of the antiaircraft gun trainees to determine their marksmanship. There were no high-tech computers available, so the work had to be done with paper and pencils.

In October 1946, Norb was transferred to Fort Dix, NJ for discharge. He had twelve days to get there. Hearing about free flights on military aircraft, Norb headed to nearby Briggs Air Force Base. There, after one night, he caught a hop on an A-25 bomber. He flew in the nose gunner seat to Shreveport, LA. After one-night there, he caught another A-25 to Lake Charles, LA. This time he flew in the bombardier position. In Lake Charles, he hooked up with a group flying a Beechcraft to Washington, DC. When they landed, he realized he had just enough time to catch the train north to Olean, NY, a few miles from home. There was only one taxi available at the airport, and an Army Major agreed to let him take the cab when he explained his connection problem. Norb said it took him almost as much time to travel the short distance from DC to Olean by train, as it had taken him to fly half way across the country. He was discharged at Fort Dix on October 28, 1946.

Lawrence Treusdell (Truesdell) of Fillmore entered the Army 2/1/1941. He had previously been a laborer with the Works Progress Administration. Lawrence was assigned to the 27th Infantry Division, 198th Infantry Regiment at Fort McClellan, AL. During basic training Lawrence was severely injured during the performance of his duties. He was honorably discharged May 19, 1941.

Lewis A. Wakefield of Houghton entered the service on July 2, 1942. Detailed information on Lewis' service has not been located. The Wakefield family moved quite frequently having lived in Hinsdale in 1910, Portville in 1920, Friendship in 1930 and Houghton in 1940. Lewis and his mother moved to Houghton in the early 30's. By 1940 Lewis was a chemistry major at Houghton College. He graduated from Houghton in 1942.

For his first nine months of service, he was an enlisted man. It is likely that most, if not all, of the nine months was spent in basic training and Officers Candidate School. On April 16, 1943 Lewis was discharged and then reentered the Army on April 17 as an officer. He would rise to the rank of Captain. He likely was immediately assigned to the Chemical Warfare Service (CWS). Lewis received a science degree from Houghton, and was a member of the Medic Club at the school.

The US was totally unprepared for a war that might involve chemical/biological (C/B) weapons with nations such as Germany, Italy, and Japan, all of whom had previously used C/B weapons during conflicts. (Germany used mustard gas against the Allies in World War I; Italy used mustard gas against Ethiopia during the second Italo-Abyssinian War and Japan used C/B weapons in China.) By 1942 the CWS had an appropriation of a billion dollars and employed 60,000 soldiers and civilians. President Roosevelt announced a "retaliation in kind" policy in June 1942, even though the US had hardly any chemical supplies and no biological supplies. By the end of the war, the US had more than 146,000 tons of chemical warfare agents available overseas for potential use. Conversely Germany had over a quarter million tons of chemical agents available for use. The decision by the various nations not to use C/B weapons in combat remains somewhat of a mystery. The Germans did use chemical agents such as Zyklon B in the unforgiveable murder of Jews, political prisoners, and others in extermination camps.

The Chemical Warfare Service prepared and deployed, but did not use, gas weapons throughout the war. Its main concern was the research, production, and neutralization of toxic agents. It also was involved in producing incendiaries for flame throwers, flame tanks and other weapons. CWS soldiers participated in smoke generation missions and with chemical mortar battalions. Decontamination units landed with invasion troops to clear the beachfronts if chemical weapons were used in any counterattack. The invasion troops themselves had gas masks, impregnated suits and information cards explaining the signs and symptoms of gas poisoning. As the slaughter in the Pacific continued in 1944, there was some public support for the US use of gas weapons against Japan. This intensified after the battle of Tarawa when the US suffered 3,400 casualties in three days. However, that support never exceeded 40 percent.

The CWS eventually had more than 400 companies and battalions. It is likely that Lewis was assigned to one of these units. According to his final pay record he did serve overseas. Lewis was discharged November 21, 1945.

Lyle A. Wilcox of Centerville entered the Army on December 3, 1940 in Olean. His twin brother Lowell entered a week later. It is likely that Lyle was mustered into the Army at Fort Devens in Massachusetts. The NAO reported him stationed there by at least April 1941, and he remained there until his honorable medical discharge in November 1941 due to ulcers. Lyle was with an anti-tank company in the 26th Infantry Regiment. His brother Lowell was also stationed at Devens during this period.

Virgil Eugene Wilcox of Centerville was 34 years old when he entered the service November 12, 1942. Initially stationed at Fort Hancock, NY, by November 1943, Virgil was stationed at Fort Wadsworth on Staten Island, New York City. Virgil remained at Wadsworth for the duration of the war. The NAO reported that Virgil managed to get a three-day pass for the Christmas season in 1943, and spent it at home with friends and family. The Army Coastal Artillery took over Wadsworth in 1941 and remained in operational control throughout the war. Wadsworth was part of the US coastal defense, but was primarily an anti-aircraft installation during World War II. The only real danger to the east coast came from submarines, and that threat was virtually non-existence by 1943. Neither surface ships nor aircraft ever proved any threat. The Coastal Artillery had several batteries. During one exercise, all the batteries were fired at once. It was the only time during the war that such an event occurred. In June 1944, Virgil was given the honor of unveiling the Centerville Roll of Honor. Virgil served with the Headquarters and Headquarters Battery. His primary military occupation was Field Lineman. He was also qualified as a gunner. Virgil was discharged on October 3, 1945 at Fort Jay.

Norman L. Young of Fillmore entered the service on March 1, 1943 at Buffalo. Norman spent most of the next 38 months in the Army Military Police, performing duties in various locations, including Virginia, Alabama, and two bases in Ohio. In between these assignments, he spent almost five months at locations in Washington, California, and Colorado being trained as a dental technician. These assignments do not include New Jersey, where he was discharged in 1946.

Norman was assigned to the famous Army base, Fort Myer, upon entering the service. At Myer, he was trained as an Army Military Policeman. He was then, apparently, assigned to the permanent military police unit at Myer. He would remain at Myer until August 1944. Fort Myer was, and is, one of the most prestigious Army bases in the world. It was and is the home of the 3rd US Infantry (The Old Guard), the oldest infantry unit in the Army. Elite ceremonial units, including the US Army Band (Pershing's Own), were and are stationed there. It is also the home of "Quarters One" the home of the Chief of Staff of the US Army. During World War II it was the home of General George C. Marshall. (Fort Myer has been greatly reduced in size since World War II. Much of the land has been turned over to Arlington National Cemetery.)

By 1941, due to significant problems in many locations, the Army recognized the need to upgrade the Military Police. On September 26, 1941, the Military Police Corps was officially organized under the Office of the Provost Marshal. A training school at the "South Port" location on Fort Myer was established. The initial classes were all officers. As the need for trained men ballooned, other locations (besides Ft. Myer) were quickly established. A major effort was made to identify men and women of the highest intelligence and integrity. This careful selection of personnel was followed by special training. Constant supervision was established.

Training was designed to include instruction in general military police duties, traffic control, military law, criminal investigations, countering fifth columnists, emergency plans, and POW alien enemies. It is not clear how many of these classes Norman really attended, nor whether they were all at Fort Myer. Due to the need, and the rapid increase in numbers, training classes were established at other facilities. However, all indications are that Norman was stationed at Myer during the first 18 months of his service. Part of this time likely included some training. He was assigned to the 703rd Military Police Battalion at Fort Myer.

WACs in training as MPs, as well as those that worked at the Pentagon, were billeted at South Port on Fort Myer. Ada Mills, of the FCSD area, was in the latter group, and her and Norman's time at South Port overlapped to a certain extent. Ada appears to have arrived at Fort Myer about May 1944, and Norman did not leave until August or early September. It is not known if they knew each other. Ada was older. (The current Fort Myer does not include the "South Port" area. That area has been taken over by Arlington National Cemetery. "South Port" was located along the southern end of the current cemetery. The Pentagon, where Ada worked, would have been very close.)

The NAO reported in September of 1944 that, following a furlough at home, Norman transferred to the medical corps at Fort Lewis, WA. Norman was there for no more than a month when he was transferred to the dental technician school at Letterman Army Hospital located at the Presidium in San Francisco. Sometime between October 1944 and January 1945, he was transferred to the dental technician school at Fitzsimmons Army Hospital in Aurora, CO. After some four months of medical and dental training, the Army, in its infinite wisdom, decided that Norman was more needed in the military police.

At this point, about January 1945, he was moved to Camp Siebert, AL for additional military police training. In reality, these moves were most likely related to the progress of the war and a review of future needs, based on changing priorities. By March, following a month of training at Camp Siebert, Norman was assigned to the huge German and Italian prisoner of war camp at Camp Perry, near Port Clinton, Ohio. This could have been recognition of the fact that the war in Europe was nearing an end and the United States would soon be repatriating POWs. In November 1945, Norman was moved to Cleveland, and was assigned to the Headquarters Service Unit. He performed passenger train guard duty until his discharge in April of 1946.

US Army Air Corps

The following FCSD area residents served in the US Army Air Corps in the American Theater of Operations during World War II: Charles G. Allen, Edwin D. Benjamin, Leland W. Bleistein, Robert G. Boehmler, Adelbert Bowen, Theos E. Cronk, Marvin H. Eyeler, Gerald B. Fish, Elin G. Harte, Richard R. Kirkpatick, John R. Krause, Elmer W. Mack, Silas R. Molyneaux, Deanne R. Pero, Albert R. Perry, John S. Raybuck, Nicholas W. Ringelberg, August Scherer, Jr., J. Whitney Shea, Robert Q. Smith, Francis Norman Stickle, Burt Swales, Alwin J. Ward, Elon C. Wiles, and William M. Yanda.

Charles G. Allen of Fillmore entered the service on March 25, 1943. His assignments during the next eight months are not clear but possibly included both basic training and likely some specialized training. Charles served as an aircraft welder during his service. On December 21, 1943 he sailed for Puerto Rico, arriving January 3, 1944. Giving the time involved it is possible his ship stopped at another port before arriving in Puerto Rico. He almost surely was assigned to Losey Army Airfield located near Juana Diaz on Puerto Rico's southern coast. He likely was assigned to the 417th Bomb Squadron, 25th Bomb Group. Losey was part of the Caribbean Defense Force and was used by both fighters and bombers.

The Army Air Corps departed Losey in April 1944 and the base was turned over to the Army. Charles sailed for home March 22, 1944 arriving March 31, 1944. The NAO reported him home on leave in April. Following his leave Charles reported to his new assignment, Alamogordo Air Field in Alamogordo, New Mexico. The 25th Bomb Group also was assigned to Alamogordo and it is likely he continued to work with that group. His actual assignment at the base was the 231st Army Air Force Base Unit. He would have continued to perform the same duties. The NAO reported Charles home on leave again in July 1945. Charles was discharged February 17, 1946.

Edwin D. Benjamin of Hume, a 1929 graduate of FCS, had ten years of experience as an engineer when he was commissioned as a 2nd Lieutenant in the Army Air Corps in September 1942. He would leave the service five years later as a Major. His first assignment was participating in the construction of a TNT plant in Williamsport, PA. He likely knew the man in charge of the construction, Colonel Kenneth D. Nichols. Nichols had managed the construction of the Rome Air Depot in New York at the same time Edwin was working for the U.S. Engineer Department in Albany, NY. Nichols left the Williamsport project in the fall of 1942 to become part of the Manhattan Project, the development of the atomic bomb.

Edwin spent only three months at Williamsport before being transferred to Herrington Air Field in Kansas. He was there to work on a major project. While there he was promoted to 1st Lieutenant and then Captain, eventually serving as Chief Engineer. The project included the construction of three giant runways, big enough to accommodate the B-29. It also required the construction of three hangers, a water storage and distribution system, roads, streets, walks, 100 buildings, electronic transmissions lines, and even a swimming pool. In effect, he participated in and oversaw the construction of a small town, one several times the size of Fillmore. He also found time while at Herrington, to marry Army Nurse Ruth Langdon. According to the Allegany County War Service Record he completed Edwin spent 34 months at Herrington. As the war ended, he was transferred to Chico Air Field in California for three months, and then in March 1946, he was sent to Guam as Commanding Officer of the 1899th Engineer Aviation Battalion. He later served 12 months as Post Engineer for all Army Air Force installations on Saipan and Tinian. Erwin returned to the states in May 1947, and was stationed at Fairfield-Suisun Air Base in California until his discharge in September.

Leland W. Bleistein of Fillmore enlisted in the Army Air Corps Reserve in the spring of 1944, according to the NAO. That was likely just before his 18-birthday on June 30, 1944. He may have been inspired to enlist by the D Day landings on June 6. Leland was called to active duty in December 1944, and inducted at Fort Dix in New Jersey.

By February 1945, the NAO reported that he was at Keesler Field in Mississippi, and would take Air Force examinations to determine his qualifications as a pre-aviation cadet. It is likely that he also took whatever basic training was still being provided. By 1945, the military had cut back on extensive basic training. Until mid-1944, Keesler had specialized in training B-24 maintenance men. It then switched, in July, 1944, to training B-24 co-pilots. In October, it added training for B-32 co-pilots. However, this training was terminated in January, probably just as Leland was arriving. The NAO reported that, by March, Leland had been transferred to an airfield in Kingman, AZ, for training as a ball turret gunner. Kingman specialized in flexible gunnery training for B-17s, although it appears that there was still some co-pilot training provided. Flexible gunnery introduced the men to all the gun positions on a B-17. Deflection shooting was emphasized. (Deflection shooting taught the gunners to shot in front of the attacking plane, thus accounting for the fact that both planes were moving. Shooting directly at the enemy plane would send the bullets to where the plane had been, not where it was going.) At some point, Leland was transferred to the flexible gunnery school at Williams Air Field in Mesa, AZ, near Phoenix.

He was stationed at Williams but was home on a 30-day furlough, when the war ended in the Pacific. On August 11, 1945, just prior to beginning his furlough, Leland reenlisted in the Air Corps for another year.

Robert G. Boehmler was the music teacher at Fillmore High when he was drafted in June 1942. He entered the service on January 4, 1943 at Fort Niagara, NY. He took his basic training at the Miami Beach Air Corps Training Center. The NAO reported in April 1943 that he had been assigned to Miami Beach. In an article for the Lyons Heritage Society, Patricia Gorthy wrote that he was assigned to the 378th Air Force Band and transferred to Atlantic City in 1943. The Atlantic City Air Base was organized in August 1943 and Robert was likely transferred there at that time.

It appears that he served at Atlantic City for the balance of his service. The NAO reported in May 1944 that he was visiting in Fillmore, was a guest of the Rotary Club and was still stationed at Atlantic City. Originally the base provided rest and recreation as well as reassignments for returning combat veterans. As a member of the band, Robert likely was part of the entertainment provided to the men. Patricia Gorthy, in articles she wrote, stated that he played with the band at various USO dances for the men six days a week. The band likely also performed other standard band duties such as participating in formations, parades saluting troops departing for other assignments and at special patriotic events. Gorthy indicated that he and the band performed at Cochran Field in Georgia and in San Antonio, Texas. Patricia stated that Robert played several different instruments. Originally trained on the clarinet and saxophone, he primarily played the saxophone in the band.

In mid-1944 the Atlantic City base was part of a general reorganization. It now performed three main functions – serving as a redistribution station, convalescent hospital, and overseas replacement depot.

In April 1945 Robert again visited Fillmore. As before he was a guest of the Fillmore Rotary Club, of which he was an Honorary Member. This time the club meeting was held at the Fillmore High School auditorium where there was a showing of the film "Diary of a Sergeant." Robert was discharged in 1946.

Adelbert C. Bowen of Fillmore entered the Army Air Corps on November 13, 1942. Apparently, he was assigned to Keesler Air Base for basic training and for additional training. The main technical training unit at Keesler at the time was the 56th Training Group. It trained men in airplane and engine mechanics, primarily for B-24's. Adelbert received an honorable discharge after only 10 months of service. No information for the reason for this discharge has been identified. However, it should be noticed that Adelbert died at the very young age of 41 in 1957. A headstone for his grave was provided by the military. Adelbert's Grandfather, Samuel Bowen, served with Company H, 136th NY Infantry during the Civil War.

Theos E. Cronk of Houghton entered the service in November of 1942 as an enlisted man and served as such until October 15, 1943. After basic training, there was a short assignment at Scott Field in Illinois. Scott Field was the premier Army communications training base. Its slogan was, "The best damned radio operators in the world." Theos also attended the Special Services School in Lexington, VA at some point, likely following his Officers Candidate Training (OCS) training. Theos entered 16 weeks of OCS training at Miami Beach, FL probably in June of 1943. On completion of his training, he was discharged as an enlisted man and reenlisted as a 2nd Lieutenant on October 16, 1943. Theos was then assigned to Headquarters, Army Air Force Central Training Command in St. Louis. He was there only a short time. It is likely this was due to the decision to eliminate the Central Training Command, and to distribute its responsibilities between the Eastern and Western Commands. Theos was then once again assigned to Scott Field in Illinois as Special Services Officer. This assignment may have been related to his background. Theos was a graduate of Westminster Choir College, and had worked for the college for six years as its Personnel Director and Concert Manager prior to entering the service. As Special Service Officer at Scott Field, his duties included: developing activities involved with morale, welfare, and recreation programs; developing and administering activities involving organized entertainment, social activities, varsity, intramural, and self-directed athletics; and developing off duty hobbies and diversions. He was promoted to Captain on February 19, 1946 a little more than a month before his discharge on April 5, 1946 after 41 months of service.

Marvin H. Eyler of Houghton entered the service on August 3, 1942 following his graduation from Houghton College. After passing his physical, he was ordered to Miami, FL for basic training. By November 1942, Marvin was at Lowry Field in Denver, CO in an aerial photography school. While at Lowry, Marvin applied for and was accepted for Officer Candidate School (OCS). He returned to Miami for OCS training.

OCS schools were famous for turning out "90-day wonders." The training was closer to four months when Marvin went through the program. It was later expanded to a full 16 weeks. Marvin also likely was among the first to experience a new OCS curriculum. The first 8 plus weeks of training dealt with the general duties of junior officers. The remaining four or so weeks focused on specialized areas. These areas included adjutant, personnel, training, supply, mess, intelligence, and guard company. Given Marvin's later assignments, he was likely in the training section. This was also consistent with his background. Marvin had been an exceptional athlete while at Houghton College.

Marvin's wife Catherine said that, following OCS training, he was stationed in Fresno, CA, probably at Hammer Field, for a short period of time. He then moved on, again for a relatively short period, to a base in Los Angeles. The NAO reported that Marvin and Catherine visited his parents in Houghton in September, 1943, and then returned to Los Angeles.

Marvin was next transferred to San Diego. Catherine remembers he was stationed at a base near a local airport. This could have been Lindberg Airport (named after Charles), which later became San Diego International Airport. He was the head of physical training, probably for air cadets going through pilot training. His wife Catherine said he was alerted for shipment to the Pacific Theater; but when the Japanese surrendered his orders were cancelled. He was instead, after two and a half years in San Diego, transferred back to Lowry Field in Colorado where he was discharged.

Marvin left active duty at the end of the war but remained in the reserves. He was recalled during the Korean War, but he received an assignment to Germany rather than Korea. Marvin served as Chief of Special Services for USAFE in Wiesbaden during this period. He eventually retired from the Air Force Reserve as a Lieutenant Colonel.

Gerald B. (Jerry) Fish of Hume entered the service in November 1943. During the next two years, like almost everyone else, he would undergo extensive training, at various locations, to prepare him for the rigors of combat. In Jerry's case, it would be for combat in the skies over enemy territory.

Jerry entered the service as an Air Cadet in the Army Reserve. By September of 1944, he was at Moody Air Field near Valdosta, GA. The NAO reported his rank as A-S. In November of 1944, he was transferred to Napier Field, AL and the NAO reported his rank as A-T.

It is likely that at the time Jerry was among the thousands of Air Cadets who were waiting for a spot in a training class to open before becoming a full-fledged Air Cadet. In the early part of the war, pilots were in demand, but there were not enough training slots for everyone. Therefore, a system was devised to assure that high quality candidates were not lost to the general draft. One part of this system was an exemption from the general draft from 1942 until 1944 for those accepted, but not inducted into the program. Another step was the reduction of the training program from nine to seven months. For those already in the service, a five-step process was instituted. The first step was called on-line training. This was essentially busy work in unskilled menial tasks for cadets as they waited for a class assignment. This is likely what Jerry was doing at Moody and Napier Fields, although both were pilot training facilities.

Jerry's cadet training likely began at the Aviation Cadet Training Center at Randolph Field, in San Antonio, TX, in January 1945. The NAO reported in February 1945 that he was at the Center studying maps and charts, aircraft identification, small arms, and other subjects, while being conditioned physically for the long training period ahead. That would have been part of his pre-flight training, which would have also included academics. In those courses, he would have studied the mechanics and physics of flight, aeronautics, deflection shooting, and thinking in three dimensions. He also would have spent three hours in a simulator. This training would have been based on a prior decision where he would have been processed and a decision made as to whether he would enter training as a navigator, bombardier, or pilot.

Following pre-flight, Jerry apparently was transferred back to Moody, as the NAO reported in April that he had been transferred from Moody to Perrin Field in Sherman, Texas. He was home on a 21-day furlough in June, and was a guest at the Rotary Club meeting on June 11, 1945. While Perrin was an advanced fighter pilot training base, it is unlikely that Jerry was transferred there for such training. In fact, on his "Allegany County War Service Record" he wrote that his last assignment was a B-29 Engineer school, which he did not complete. The war in Europe was already over at this point, and the war in the Pacific had less than two months to go. Perrin Field was shut down in October 1945, probably before his training could be completed. Jerry was discharged at Amarillo, TX on November 2, 1945.

WASPS. It was not until 1977 that "they" obtained veteran status, but during the war "they" were invaluable. "They" were women and they served in the Women's Air Service Pilots (WASPS) organization. While they were paid for their service, unlike males, they had to pay for their own training; and they were not eligible for veteran's benefits until 1977.

Elin Harte (Raimondi) of Centerville was a Woman's Air Service Pilots (WASP) member who moved to the FCSD area after World War II. The Raimondi's owned the farm on Route 3 in Centerville which was owned in 2012 by Ronald Frazier. Elin was one of the 38 women who made up WASP training class 43-3. She entered training in January 1943 and graduated July 3rd. While it was the third group to enter training, the first WASP training group had only started in November 1942.

To be a part of WASP training group 3, a woman had to be between the ages of 21 and 35, at least 5'2", have at least a high school diploma or equivalent, and have at least 75 hours of pilot training. Elin Griswold Harte Raimondi met all four qualification requirements. She was 25, 5'6", and a graduate of Julia Richmond High School in New York City, although she had attended schools in Pairs, London, and Monaco. She had more than enough flying hours, having used funds earned working for the Air Traffic Controllers and Columbia Studios in Los Angeles to take flying lessons.

Women accepted by the WASPs were clearly exceptional. Some 25,000 women applied. Only 1830 were accepted into training, and 1,074 completed training. The high rate of those completing compared to those entering training speaks to the quality of the women accepted.

They were also exceptional pilots. When word got around that the B-29 was a death trap, and male pilots showed concern about flying the plane, Colonel Paul W. Tibbets called on the WASPs to provide two women pilots to help train future male B-29 combat pilots. Dora Dougherty (Strother), who was a group 3 classmate of Elin, was one of the women chosen. The other was Dorothea "DiDi" Moorman. Clearly, part of Tibbets strategy was to challenge the male ego. But Tibbets was no fool. He was not going to put the most expensive and advanced super bomber in the world in the hands of somebody who could not fly it, and fly it safely. He knew the WASPs were great pilots, and he trusted them completely.

Fifinella (Fifi), a cartoon character created by Disney studios, was the WASP mascot during the war. Interestingly, the only B-29 still flying (2017) is named *Fifi*, although apparently there is no connection between the plane name and the WASPs.

Thirty-eight WASPS died during their service, including two from Elin's class, Mabel Rawlinson and Frances F. Grimes. Elin almost made it three. One day during a flight she ran out of gas and had to make an emergency crash landing. It turned out to be a lucky day, as her daughter Jean related. The Civil Air Patrol Pilot who came to rescue her, Adolfo (later Adolph, and still later Ted, for obvious reasons) Raimondi later became her husband.

Elin's class was known as "The Lost Platoon." They started their training at Howard Hughes Air Field in Houston and completed it at Avenger Field in Sweetwater, TX. Avenger Field is today the home of the WASPs Museum. They even had a poem about themselves. "We are The Lost Patrol. We could fly to the moon. We do inverted loops without parachutes. We peel off in a dive, some say that's suicide. Slap - happy though we seem, we've really on the beam."

Following her aircraft training at Avenger Field, Elin went through Officer's Training at Orlando, Florida. According to some, Orlando was the "glamour base of the world." Military personnel from many US allies were being trained there in various disciplines, many of which were top secret at the time. Elin also served at Love Field in Dallas, TX, probably as part of the WASP 5th Ferrying Group. Daughter Jean remembers her mother mentioning that, during part of her service, she delivered mail and passengers to various locations. This may have occurred while at Love. (Love Field is also known as the airport President John F. Kennedy landed at before he was assassinated.)

She was also assigned to Camp Davis Army Air Field in North Carolina. Her duties at Camp Davis involved towing targets for anti-aircraft gunners, including night target towing and flying radar deception missions and tracking missions. The night missions included training searchlight battalions to pick up enemy planes in the dark. Target towing was a dangerous occupation, because many times the trainee gunners shot up the tow-planes. Mabel Rawlinson, one of Elin's 43-3 classmates, was killed at Camp Davis on August 23, 1943, when the A-24 she was flying crashed. By early 1944, Elin was at Camp Haan, CA. Camp Haan, about 30 miles south of Los Angeles, was across the street from March Air Field. Her duties continued to be towing targets for anti-aircraft gunner trainees, but she also flew stimulated dog fight missions, probably for pilots being trained at March Field. (Daughter Jean said she also had a dog, named Skeets, hidden in her barracks.) In February Elin and several other WASPS were featured in an article about the WASPS carried in several newspapers. A picture of Elin in the cockpit of her plane accompanied the article, which was titled, "Target-Towing WASPS Doing Man-Sized Job." The article quoted one of Elin's fellow pilots. Summing up her job, Eloyne Nichols said, "When you're up there towing a target, the only thing you can think about is getting away as fast as you can."

During her service, Elin flew several types of aircraft, including the Fairchild PT-19 "Cornell" trainer, the Cessna UC-78 "Bamboo Bomber" trainer, the Douglas A-24 "Banshee", and the Curtiss A-25 "Shrike". The Bamboo Bomber, so called because it was made of wood, was used to move trainees from single- engine to multi-engine aircraft. The A-24 and A-25 were both combat aircraft. Both were virtually identical to their Navy counterparts. The A-24 was the Navy "Helldiver" dive bomber, and the A-25 was the famous SBD Dauntless dive bomber. At Camp Davis, both planes would have been used for towing targets and other support services.

On July 1, 2009, President Barack Obama signed Public Law 111-40, awarding the Congressional Gold Medal to the WASPS. Elin's daughter Jean attended the ceremony.

Richard R. Kirkpatrick of Allen entered the service July 25, 1944. It appears that he was immediately sent to Camp Fannin in Texas. Fannin was both an Army Infantry Replacement Training Center and a POW camp. Richard most likely took his basic training there. By December he was at Fort Riley in Kansas. Riley was primarily an Army base, but Richard was likely assigned to the 356th Air Base Unit at Marshal Air Field located on Fort Riley. Crews at Marshal flew air-ground support demonstrations and simulated strafing, bombing, and chemical warfare missions in conjunction with the infantry training at Riley. Richard was there only a short time before moving to Sheppard Air Base in Texas, again for a short period. At the time he was there, Sheppard was providing basic training in glider mechanics, technical and flying training for instructors, and B-29 flight engineer training. In February 1945, Richard was transferred from Sheppard to Keesler Field in Mississippi. There he was enrolled in a basic engine mechanic school. He received both instruction and actual experience in aircraft maintenance in a course that lasted about two and a half months. He remained at Keesler until the end of the war.

John R. Krause of Houghton was born in Olean but spent his youth on a farm near Houghton. He entered the service in November 1942. Following basic training he was assigned to the Army Air Force Technical School at Chanute Field in Illinois to study celestial navigation. He was then assigned to the Celestial Navigation Trainer Department at Alamogordo Air Base in New Mexico. During World War II, Alamogordo was used to train navigators for heavy bomber groups, initially B-17s and later B-24s. In 1945, it became a B-29 operational base.

The training was top notch. One of the men trained there was Jim Hussmann. On June 3, 1945, Hussmann was aboard the B-29 *The Spirit of F.D.R.* that was part of a massive attack against the city of Himez in Japan. As the *Spirit* made its bomb run, another B-29 suddenly appeared directly above them. The *Spirit* made a sharp turn to the right, while the other bomber swerved to the left. Unfortunately, the other plane, also on its bomb run, had its bomb bay doors open and its bombs ejected in the direction of the *Spirit*. A couple of its bombs tore thru the tail and fuselage of the *Spirit*. The pilot lost all control over the plane, but the co-pilot's controls continued to work. Other systems were also disrupted. Decisions had to be made. The crew voted to stay with the badly damaged plane as-long-as possible. Hussmann faced two major problems. He had to navigate the plane over 1,000 miles back to Tinian. He also had to constantly keep track of the plane's longitude and latitude positions, in order to radio such positions to rescue ships, if the crew was forced to bail out. And he had to do it by celestial navigation, since no other systems aboard the plane were working. Hussmann had only the sun and his sextant with which to work. His Alamogordo training paid off. The *Spirit* made it safely back to Tinian. It is not known whether John was involved in Hussmann's training at Alamogordo.

Elmer W. Mack of Fillmore entered the service February 1, 1943, at Buffalo. He was about to make a grand tour of the country. By April Elmer was at the Fort Logan clerical technical training facility in Colorado. From Logan, he was ordered to the Municipal Airport in Oakland, CA, where he performed clerical duties while awaiting entrance into an aircraft mechanics training school. By July he was in a specialized P-39 Airacobra training course at the Bell Aircraft facility in Niagara Falls, NY. Elmer returned to Oakland in September of 1943, but by April 1944 he was at Hamilton Field in Novato, CA. He remained at Hamilton for the balance of the war, rising to the rank of Sergeant. He apparently was assigned to the 46th Army Air Force Base unit at Hamilton Field. His profile at the WW II Memorial says he served with the 460th Air Base Unit. However, the 460th was located at Kingman Air Base in Arizona, and despite Elmer's wide array of travels, there is no evidence he served in Arizona. But then, who knows.

Among other awards Elmer earned the Combat Crew Wings. The Wings recognized training and qualifications required of a combat aircrew member. They were normally awarded to pilots, bombardiers, navigators, flight engineers, radiomen and gunners. Ground crew only received the Wings at the discretion of the commanding officer. Such awardees had to be essential to the concept, "Keep Them Flying." Among those eligible, at the commander's discretion, were aircraft maintenance supervisors. This award to Elmer showed the high regard in which he was held.

Silas R. Molyneaux was born in Houghton in 1918, a member of the remarkable Molyneaux family. (His brother Evan served as a doctor during the war, and his sister Roberta as a WAC with a detachment in England.) Silas enlisted in the Army Air Corps on December 8, 1941, although he did not enter the service as an aviation cadet until July 6, 1942. For the next year, Silas went through flight training earning his wings, and being promoted to Lieutenant. In November, Silas was in Houghton on leave.

Following his flight training, Silas was assigned to Shaw Air Field in South Carolina as an instructor. At the time, Shaw was an advanced (Phase III) training base. Cadets were trained in primarily the AT 6, a single engine aircraft, and the AT 10, a twin-engine plane. Silas remained at Shaw until early 1945. At that time, Shaw was transferred to another command (pilots were now trained on the P-47 Thunderbolt), and Silas was assigned to the Military Academy at West Point. He remained there for the balance of the war as both a Professor of History and an Instructor in Cadet Flight training.

Silas told the author that he remained in the service following the war. He served as a base commander in Japan during the Korean War, flying several combat missions. Later he was among the original corps of officers assigned to the new Air Force Academy in Colorado Springs, CO.

Deanne R. Pero of Fillmore was 19 when he enlisted in the Army Air Corps March 1, 1943. Deanne received his basic training at the Air Force Technical Training School in Miami Beach, Fl. The base was called "The Most Beautiful Boot Camp in America." The "King" of movie actors, Clark Gable, trained there. In fact, it is estimated that, one-fifth of all Army Air Corps enlisted personnel trained there. After completing basic training, Deanne was transferred to Coral Gables, FL for advanced training as an aircraft mechanic. Before his training could be completed, Deanne received an honorable discharge in July 1943. Since he was single, but with dependents, it is possible he was discharged to care for his dependents, or he may have been needed for a war-related crucial industry. (His dependents were likely his parents.)

Albert R. Perry of Hume, was a member of the NY State Police before entering the Army Air Corps July 17, 1942. For many years, he worked at Letchworth State Park, where he lived with his wife Jean. Jean also served during World War II, as did Albert's twin brother Adelbert. Albert was known throughout the FCSD area as "Trooper Perry." A corporal in the State Police, he became a private upon entering the service. He was inducted at Ft. Niagara, NY and then went to Keesler Field, MS for his basic training. During his time at Keesler Field, Albert became ill and spent time in the base hospital.

Upon completion of basic, he was assigned to Key Field, Meridian, MS. An interesting side note is that, George Ebenezer Meach, who like Albert was born in Hume Township, was shot to death in Meriden in 1873. Meach earned the Medal of Honor during the Civil War.

At Key Field, Albert was a Military Policeman assigned to the Provost Marshal Office. When Albert first arrived at Key, the mission was to train fighter pilots. Several groups were trained for air defense activities, including night fighting. The mission was then changed to train medium bomber groups, primarily B-25 groups. During this period the 86th Medium Bombardment Group became the host group at Key Field. When that group was deployed overseas in March of 1943, the base was redesignated to train aerial reconnaissance units. Albert, like his wife Elsie Jean Eldridge Perry, was discharged in March 1943 and returned to his home in Wiscoy, NY.

David A. Pitt of Houghton entered the US Army on June 25, 1941. On August 13, 1941, he enlisted in or transferred to the US Air Corps. His records indicate he served one month and 18 days in the Army before entering the Air Corps. He enlisted in the Air Corps at Fort Bragg, NC, and likely was in training at Fort Bragg before switching to the Air Corps.

David probably moved to Chanute Field in Illinois for his Air Corps basic training before being transferred to Bryan Field in Texas for more advanced training. Bryan was the home of the Army Air Force Instructors School, with an emphasis on instrument training.

David served as a Synthetic Trainer Instructor Operator during the rest of the war at Shaw Air Base in Sumter, SC. There he was assigned, most likely to the predecessor to the to the 139th Air Base Unit. The 139th was the Base Unit from March 31, 1945 to March 31, 1946.

Pilot training during the war consisted of three distinct stages for all candidates. They were primary, basic, and advanced. A fourth stage was specialized training, where pilot trainees focused on a particular type of aircraft. Shaw was part of the second stage, basic pilot training.

A part of this training used the Link Trainer, a non-flying simulated aircraft. David likely worked with the Link, Ant 18, the most advanced version. It could rotate through all three axes, simulate all flight instruments, and was able to model most flying conditions, including pre-stall buffet, overspeed of the retractable undercarriage, and spinning. A canopy could be used to simulate blind flying. This latter required expertise in instrument flying. At Bryan Field where David trained, instrument flying was a main feature of instructor training.

The Ant 18 used in the basic pilot training phase helped pilots learn to operate a plane of greater weight and complexity than the ones they had used in primary training, increase their knowledge of airmanship, become more proficient on instruments and in night flying, formation flying, and cross county flying.

David would have instructed the trainee pilots in the use of the Link trainer and likely evaluated their progress. He was discharged at Seymour Johnson Air Field, NC on November 24, 1945.

John S. Raybuck of Houghton entered the US Army Air Corps on December 2, 1942. He was initially stationed at Kearns Air Base in Utah. There he went through basic training, likely completing his training in January 1943. Since Kearns was initially a basic training center for air crews, it is possible that John originally trained to be part of a bomber crew. It is not clear where John was during his next year of service, but he was home in Houghton on leave in February 1944. The NAO reported in October 1944 that he was stationed at Briggs Field at Fort Bliss in El Paso, TX.

Briggs was also a bomber air crew training center at the time. Since it was 3rd phase training, that would account for the missing year. Briggs provided training for both B-17 and B-29 crews. Overall, it was aimed at effective unit operations. This included high altitude formation flying, long range navigation, and simulated combat missions. In April 1943 Briggs had switched to replacement training of personnel rather than group training. According to the World War II Memorial, John served as a dental laboratory technician. This was likely his final military occupation. Given the time period, it is possible that it was determined that fewer replacement personnel were now needed for air crews, so he was switched to a different military occupation. In fact, he may have received training as a dental technician at Beaumont Hospital, also located at Fort Bliss. The WW II Memorial indicates that he finished his service with the 110th Army Air Base Unit, which was assigned to Mitchell Field on Long Island. Mitchell was a staging area for crews being sent overseas, and a medical clearance was required before they departed. A dental check was part of the medical clearance. The NAO reported that John spent Christmas, 1945 with his family. This was probably leave granted just before discharge.

Nicholas W. Ringelberg of Granger entered the service on May 5, 1942. It appears that he was initially sent to Lincoln Air Base in Nebraska for airplane maintenance training and possibly basic training. He was then transferred to Chanute Air Base in Illinois for aircraft instrument training. Nicholas served on several bases in the United States during his service, including Camp Stewart in Georgia, where he earned his Good Conduct Medal in 1944 and Millville Air Base in New Jersey. Millville was a gunnery school for fighter pilots. At some point he apparently was also assigned to a base in Florida. At these bases Nicholas was assigned to service groups. His available records indicate he served with both the 27th Service Group in early to mid-1943 and the 30th Service Group by at least October, 1943. In May 1944 service groups were reorganized as Army Air Force Base Units (AAFBU). The 135th AAFBU took control at Millville in 1944, probably in May. Nicholas may have been assigned to Millville at that time. Nicholas worked as an Airplane Instrument Mechanic. His primary responsibility was testing and analyzing the functioning of aircraft instruments to reveal defective units.

Nicholas remained at Millville until he was transferred to Seymour Johnson Air Base in North Carolina where he was assigned to the 123rd Army Air Force Base Unit. He was discharged at Seymour Johnson Air Base on November 26, 1945.

John Gerald Whitney Shea of Houghton entered the US Army Air Corps on October 1, 1942. At the time John was an Associate Professor of Economics and Sociology at Houghton College. The NAO reported that he enlisted at an earlier date. October 1 is the date John was commissioned as a Second Lieutenant. Following his commissioning, he reported to Miami Beach, FL where he attended the Officers Training School. He then was sent to Bolling Field near Washington, DC where he spent three weeks at the cryptographic school. By late November of 1942, John was at Morrison Field in West Palm Beach, FL, assigned to the Code and Cypher Section.

It appears that John spent the next 17 months working for the 73rd Army Airways Communications Group (AACS). His duties were in cryptographic security. As such he was concerned with the provision of technically sound crypto-systems and proper use thereof. This included ensuring message confidentially and authenticity. He spent more than four and a half months in 1943 (May 13 to August 21) at various bases in the Caribbean, probably reviewing their communications systems for compliance with established standards and requirements. The 73rd had offices at bases in, among others, Panama, Mexico, and Puerto Rico.

John was then transferred to another occupation. Where he was physically located is not known. He spent his last 13 months in the service as a Historical Editor. An Historical Branch was established within the Military Intelligence Division (G2) of the General Staff in 1943. The purpose of the Branch was to assure that official and accurate records of all World War II activities were properly recorded and maintained for posterity. It is probable that John was assigned to this Branch.

John returned to Houghton College following his World War II service. In the 1950's he served on the Fillmore Central School Board of Education.

August Scherer, Jr. of Centerville, entered military service July 24, 1944. He had graduated from FCS in June. After basic training, he was sent to Fort Myer, Fl. (probably Buckingham Army Air Field) for training as an aerial gunner. Some 50,000 men were trained as aerial gunners at Buckingham during the war. He was home on leave in April of 1945 after completing his initial air gunnery training. He then made a stop-over in Lincoln, NB, where he was apparently assigned to an air crew, and sent to Davis-Monthan Air Field in Tucson, AZ for combat crew training. August was likely assigned to the 489th Bombardment Group (Very Heavy), a B-29 group training for the war in the Pacific. The 489th already had a distinguished combat record, having flown many missions as part of the 8th Air Force in Europe in B-24's. The group was an active participant in the D Day Invasion. It had been re-designated as a B-29 group and was in the final phase of training before being shipped out. August would have been a replacement gunner for one of the crews. The group was alerted in late summer that they were heading for the Pacific.

In August 1945, the NAO reported that August had qualified fully as an aerial gunner on a B-29 Superfortress combat team and "would soon be winging his way over Japan's diminishing empire to further devastate it by aerial bombardment." It further reported that he was a member of the fourth B-29 class to be graduated at Davis-Monthan and that he and his ten crewmates had achieved a high standard of training proficiency. They had been instructed by veteran fliers who had learned their lessons in enemy skies. Many of the "instructors" were likely veterans of the 489th who had seen combat in Europe. Part of their training had included long bombing missions flown under simulated combat conditions. This NAO article would have appeared just as the war was ending. Deployment to the Pacific was cancelled, and August's B-29 group was deactivated October 17, 1952.

Francis Norman Stickle of Centerville officially entered the service in August 1943. Francis, who went by his middle name Norman, was training to be a pilot prior to the war. On one of his last training flights, in May 1942, he circled over the family home in Higgins in a red monoplane. After finishing his training in August 1942, he moved to Lafayette, LA, to become an instructor of aviation cadets at the Lafayette School of Aeronautics under contract to the Army Air Corps. He was still at Lafayette when he was drafted in August 1943.

Once drafted, he was sent to Greenville, MS apparently for personal training on more advanced aircraft. At Lafayette, the primary trainer was the Fairchild PT-19, although some PT-17 Stearman's and P-40's Warhawks were assigned to the base. He was there for a short time. By March he was in Blytheville, AR. Blytheville had an advanced flying school where pilots were trained on multi-engine (two) aircraft. Again, it appears that he was in training at Blytheville and not an instructor. By June he was at Wilmington, DE, at Castle Air Base. There he was likely an instructor. At the time, June 1944, Castle was providing basic air training for pilots and crewmen. Castle was also training Women Air Service Pilots (WASPs).

Norman remained at Castle until early 1945, when he was transferred to Romulus Field in Michigan. At Romulus, he became a member of the 3rd Ferrying Group of the Air Transport Command (ATC). He had volunteered for the ATC in August 1943. The 3rd was ferrying planes from the famous Willow Run Factory in Michigan, as well as planes from the Curtis-Wright plant in Buffalo, to both stateside and overseas locations. It also transported personnel and cargo. In late 1945, just prior to his discharge, Norman was transferred to Nashville, TN.

Burt Swales of Fillmore entered the service in March 1943. Burt was President of his Senior Class at Houghton when he was called. Burt had registered for the Army Air Corps enlisted reserve on February 14, 1942, in Tioga County, PA. His father William was a minister in Lawrenceville, PA at the time. Burt was sent to Keesler Air Base in Biloxi, MS, for basic training. At the time of his entrance, basic training was going through a change. Its length was now six weeks. Those six weeks still covered the main courses (1. basic military conduct, drills decorum, 2. familiarization with weapons, 3. physical training, 4. gas mask training, 5. rifle range qualification with the 30-carbine rifle, 6. field training.) But there was also emphasis on determining for what type of occupational training the recruit was best suited. Especially in the Air Corps, basic training was now followed by some specialized technical training. In Burt's case, he either suffered some sort of physical disability during training or one was discovered. He was honorably discharged May 19, 1943.

Carl Oscar Turnstrom of Fillmore, enlisted in the Army Air Corps on August 4, 1942, one day later than Merton Pero of Fillmore. He was working at Oldenburg's Kendall Station in Fillmore at the time.

It is likely Merton and Carl were inducted at Ft. Niagara on the same day. Carl was a skilled mechanic. However, unlike Merton, Carl received his basic training at Atlantic City, NJ. The trainees there were housed in resort hotels, which had been stripped of the amenities provided to tourists. The room capacities were increased to the point where water pressure became a problem.

Basic training was still evolving at this time, and most men were merely processed, given superficial training, and then sent to technical schools, where it was hoped they would receive the real training they needed. While there was no standardization of basic training at the start of the war, a program developed in 1940 at Jefferson Barracks, MO, was utilized for a while, at least as a guide. It provided for training as follows: Military Courtesy - 6 hours; Articles of War - 4 hours; Personal Hygiene & First Aid - 12 hours; Wearing of Uniform - 8 hours; Alpha & Math Tests - 2 hours; School of the Soldier - 127 hours; Interior Guard Duty - 6 hours; Government Insurance - 3 hours; Miscellaneous (likely KP, etc.) - 24 hours. The core of the training was the "School of the Soldier."

From Atlantic City, Carl was shipped to Marianna Air Field, Marianna, FL. Marianna was opened in August of 1942, just as Carl was entering the service. A variety of training was being provided at Marianna, including the training of pilots, navigators, bombardiers, aircraft maintenance, and radio technicians.

At the completion of his training, Carl was assigned to the 791st Technical School Squadron, 75th Wing, at Seymour Johnson Air Field outside Goldsboro, NC. While Carl was there, Seymour was primarily a pre-technical school training base for bomber mechanics. Carl was permanent party at the base and worked in a number of capacities, but primarily in pre-flight testing of aircraft.

Unfortunately, Carl was an asthmatic, and by May of 1943 his condition was such that the Army decided to discharge him honorably for medical reasons.

Logistics. In July of 1942 the Army Air Transport Command (ATC) was created. Its origins were in the Air Corps Ferrying Command. The business of the ATC, spelled out in numerous orders, "was to provide long range air transport from the home front to the battle areas of the world, and to do this on predetermined and established schedules." The operation of this command posed a problem for long established Army policy, which gave theater commanders ultimate control over all operations in their area. At first, theater commanders were allowed some latitude with respect to schedules and disposition of materials. Eventually an order was issued which limited theater commanders to only altering orders for ATC operations that involved the security of those operations. No longer could the theater commanders alter ATC operations based on local emergencies.

Five routes were eventually established. The North Atlantic, South Atlantic, and Pacific routes were the first three. Later, mid-Atlantic and Canadian routes were created.

The ATC delivered high value cargo, important personnel, mail that included highly classified materials, and even troops all over the world during the war. On return trips to the states, ATC flights often carried wounded military personnel. The primary planes used by ATC were the C-47 (civilian DC- 3) and the C-54 (civilian DC-4). There were constant efforts to develop planes that gave more bang for the buck - bigger payloads and more economical, but none really worked out. The C-46 was one of the planes tried. It met both criteria, but proved to have too many problems even though over 350 C-46s were eventually put in service. Pilots referred to it as the "Flying Coffin." By default, the highly reliable C-47 became the workhorse. By the end of the war, the C-47 constituted over one-third of all of the planes used by the ATC. The second most used aircraft was the also reliable C-54.

Alwin Jay Ward of Fillmore, entered active military service on April 8, 1943. Nicknamed Banjo, he was stationed in the continental US throughout his war time service; but as a member of the Army Air Corps Air Courier Service, he traveled to war zones throughout the world. His job title was Flight Traffic Clerk and Courier, but his primary duty was the delivery of secret cryptographic materials. As a result, Alwin earned not only the American Campaign Medal, but also the European, African, Middle East and the Asiatic Pacific Campaign Medals.

Alwin was a 1938 graduate of FCS and a 1943 graduate of Cornell University. Like almost all recruits after 1942, Alwin spent most of his first year in the service being trained. In May 1943 he was at Greensboro, NC, probably in basic training. He took a pre-flight training course at Ellington Field in Texas, and advanced aerial navigation training at San Marcos, Texas. After San Marcos, he was assigned to a base in San Antonio, but a vision problem ended his flying ambitions. In June 1944, Alwin was transferred from San Antonio to Hamilton Field in California, but almost immediately was transferred to LaGuardia Field in New York. By July, he was at New Castle Air Base in Wilmington, DE. At LaGuardia and New Castle, he served with both the North Atlantic and Mid Atlantic Divisions of the Air Training Command (ATC). Near the end of his service, he was assigned to Ft. Totten on Long Island.

In addition to his regular courier duties, Alwin doubled as a hospital orderly on many return trips when the ATC planes became air ambulances transporting wounded G.I.s home. He told his son Jeff that many of the men suffered from gangrene. By the time of his discharge, Alwin had visited a good many of the most interesting and exotic locations on the earth, including the Azores, Lisbon, Casablanca, Marseille, Rome, Athens, Baghdad, Karachi, Calcutta, Istanbul, Paris, and Iceland. His travels also took him to England and Scotland. He was in Paris for "Liberation Day" and in London on V-E Day.

Many of his trips were extensive. His parents, pharmacist Lester Ward and wife Vesta, told the *Northern Allegany Observer* that he had informed them that on one trip he expected to be away for about 40 days. He also sent home items that he picked up on his trips. One time a copy of the overseas edition of *The New Yorker* magazine. The *Observer* also reported that Alwin flew some flights as a crew member of the new Douglas C-74 Globemaster. The first flight of the Globemaster occurred September 5, 1945, just days before the official end of World War II. Like many G.I.s, Elwin was not immediately discharged following the end of the war but served on active duty until February 13, 1946. He remained in the reserves until February 13, 1949.

Elon C. Wiles graduated from FCS in 1928. At the start of World War II, Elon was a practicing dentist in Fillmore. He enlisted in the Army Dental Corps on October 15, 1942, and was commissioned a First Lieutenant. Despite his commission, Elon's first assignment was to the Officer Candidate School in Miami Beach Florida. While attending the same school as other OCS candidates, Dental Officers' courses were separate. According to the NAO, by no later than December, Elon was at Kearns Field, just outside of Salt Lake City, Utah. Kearns was a new base, capable of supporting anywhere from 30,000 to 70,000 people. It was quickly the 3rd largest city in Utah. Kearns had the largest hospital in the state and the largest military dental installation in the country. It is not clear if Elon was there for additional training, or whether he was initially assigned there as permanent party. Whichever the case, by January 1, 1943, Elon was at Geiger Field outside Spokane, WA, where he would spend the rest of the war. While a member of the US Army Dental Corps, Elon spent his entire non-training military career at US Army airfields.

Geiger was a major training base for B-17 bombardment units. It was also used by the Air Technical Services Command as an aircraft maintenance and supply depot. After the war, the base was turned over to the city and became Spokane International Airport.

The US Dental Corps was part of the US Medical Corps, and as such, had no direct access to the Surgeon General. This chain of command arrangement did create some problems, although overall, the officers and men of both the Medical Corps and Dental Corps worked hard to avoid conflicts. One sore spot was promotions. While lower grades (Lieutenants and Captains) were not a problem, promotion to field grades (Major and above) were very slow in the Dental Corps. This problem is reflected in Elon's promotions. While he obtained the rank of Captain one year after entering the service, he was not promoted to Major until February 8, 1946, just months before his discharge. Although 21.6 percent of the non-dental medical staff reached the rank of Major, only 10.4 percent of the dental staff achieved such a ranking.

In the military, dentistry was practiced in large efficient clinics. (Initially there were only two types of clinics classified as DC-1 [25 chairs], and DC-2 [15 chairs]. Smaller clinics were added later.) It is likely that Elon worked in a DC-1 clinic at Geiger. The DC-1 clinics had the best equipment, including laboratories, x-ray equipment, prosthetics, and oral surgery. Each dentist had a standard chair unit, a cabinet, and an operating light. Assistants were usually Army enlisted personnel, who may or may not have had special training. Many times, these personnel had to perform other duties, although everyone worked to minimize this problem.

Military dentists treated thousands of men. While it is not known if Elon did so, military dentists many times treated men with severe facial injuries. Elon missed going overseas by the flip of a coin. It was either Elon or another dentist at Geiger. They decided to flip for it. Elon won, according to his daughter Nancy, who related the story to the author. (Nancy was a classmate of the author.) Elon's family spent the war with him in Spokane. Nancy, her brother Alan, and her mother, lived at Geiger during the war. Nancy remembers traveling by train to and from Geiger.

William M. Yanda was born in Centerville on January 12, 1923. He was inducted into the service on November 17, 1943, and entered active-duty December 20, 1943. It is unclear what he did initially, since the NAO reported in January of 1944 that he visited the area with Oprah Pratt of Buffalo. It is likely that the article was referring to an earlier visit, because by January 1944 Bill was almost certainly in basic training. It is not clear where he took his basic training. Nor is it certain where he trained next.

Bill was to spend almost half his military service in training. His brother Charles told the author that Bill was interested in becoming part of a plane crew. It appears that, following basic training, he was assigned to an airplane mechanic training school. That training lasted for five months, after which he received an additional month of training, apparently at the Willow Run B-24 Liberator plant near Ypsilanti, Michigan.

Either immediately after completing this training, or shortly thereafter, he likely was assigned to the Army Air Force Classification Center near Nashville, TN. The family knows that he was in Nashville for a time. The Nashville Center was opened in 1943. It was an induction center where cadets were brought for preliminary training, aptitude tests and physical examinations. (Given the function of this facility, it is unlikely that Bill was there prior to his aircraft mechanics training.) Cadets were classified according to the results of the classification process, their skills, and their talents. Then they were shipped to appropriate bases or schools, for further training as pilots, bombardiers, navigators, and gunners. In December 1944, the NAO reported Bill home on a seven-day furlough. He likely was home in late November, probably after completing the classification process. In March, 1945, the NAO reported that he had graduated from the Flexible Gunnery School at Tyndall Army Air Field in Panama City, Florida.

Bill's son Allen related that, while at Nashville, he had become friendly with a Chaplain, and it had an impact on his spiritual life. He started attended a church near Nashville, although not the church of his friend. There he met a young woman, Annie Sue Johnson, who later became his wife. Bill told Allen that he never lost his faith and never regretted embracing it.

Flexible Gunnery School was about three months in length. The most famous graduate of the school was Clark Gable, although a close second was Hank Greenberg of the Detroit Tigers. Requirements for attending the school were always strict, although there were constant adjustments. These changes recognized staffing needs for combat crews, as well as the psychological problems associated with the dangers of being an air gunner. The age limitation never reached a level that would have allowed Gable to enter, so clearly a waiver was provided. Nevertheless, Gable went through the entire course, and, according to all reports, worked hard to qualify. He graduated in 1943 and was always proud of being a qualified aerial gunner.

Bill's previous training as an airplane mechanic made him a prime candidate for the Flexible Gunnery School. In fact, at one time, the only men accepted into the program were those with specialized training such as airplane mechanics. Needs dictated a more liberal entrance policy. The training was intense, and the trainees had to be able to use both 30 and 50 caliber machine guns, and to fire them effectively from aircraft in flight. During training, they fired at cloth targets flown by other aircraft. They had to learn the blinker code system in case radio transmissions were not working. (Radio operators were another sought-after specialty group.) (Gable had trouble with the blinker codes, so he studied in bathrooms after lights out in order to keep up with his class.) Trainees also had to learn aircraft identification, both our planes and the enemy planes, for obvious reasons. Models of enemy aircraft were all over the training facility. Upon graduation, the men received Silver Wings and were now eligible to become part of a bomber crew. Unfortunately for Bill, according to his brother Charles, in the air he had problems with nose bleeds. Eventually this problem cost him his chance to join an active bomber group.

It appears that Bill ended his military career as permanent party at Tyndall Field, part of the 2135th Army Air Force Base Unit. As the war wound down, men were being moved into all kinds of jobs, and Bill ended up working for the base butcher. In fact, the wife of a high-ranking officer was delighted with the way Bill cut and prepared her meat purchases, and made her admiration clear to the butcher. This came up when the base was alerted that men were to be transferred to the Pacific to help end the war there. Bill returned from a leave home in June 1945 (reported by the NAO), and was told by the butcher to take another leave. That would avoid any possibility of his being shipped to the Pacific and keep the officer's wife happy. Thus, Bill remained on with the butcher.

The NAO reported Bill home on leave again in October and November 1945. When he left, he told the paper he was stopping off in Tennessee (likely to see Annie Sue), before returning to Florida. He was discharged on April 20, 1946, a relatively interesting date. Adolph Hitler was born on April 20. He wasn't around to celebrate his birthday in 1946, in part thanks to men like Bill and other FCSD area men and women.

US Navy

The following residents of the FCSD area served in the US Navy in the American Theater of Operations during World War II. Many of these men did serve "overseas" because they were stationed for various periods of time in Caribbean-area countries; however, such countries were considered part of the US Theater of Operations. Thus, these men did not receive credit for overseas service: Richard G. Allen, Robert M. Ashcraft, Gordon R. Barnett, Leslie R. Beach, Fred Beardsley, Larry H. Birch, Lyle C. Brown, Earl L. Herring, Kenneth E. Lindley, Gerald V. Luckey, Francis D. Morris, Richard E. Morris, Colin S. Nichols, Stephen J. Ortlip, Adelbert E. Perry, Ralph L. Phipps, John S. Rease, Warren S. Richardson,

Edwin J. Robinson, Vernon B. Slack, Clare J. Smith, Robert Q. Smith, Harry C. Stroud, Evar G. Swanson, Wesley Wass, Roy B. Weaver, Maurice R. Wiles, Ansel G. Young.

Robert M. (Bob) Ashcraft of Fillmore entered the Navy on August 23, 1944. After completing basic training at the Sampson Naval Training Center in November (his parents visited him at Sampson in September), Bob was assigned to the Naval Air Training Station in Atlantic Center, NJ. The station, which had only started operations in 1943, consisted of several adjacent locations, The NAO reported that Bob spent some time in at least three locations: Atlantic City, Woodbine, and Cape May. It appears that he spent most of his time prior to the end of the war at the Woodbine location. The NAO reported that Bob was home for Christmas in 1944. He also managed a ten-day furlough in March 1945.

The Atlantic City base had been established because, most of the time, there was good, or at least acceptable, flying weather. This was important in fulfilling the station's mission. Navy documents make clear that the main objective of every base unit was to prepare the air crews that trained there for combat. There were being trained to fly the Navy's elite aircraft. For fighter pilots, this included the F4F "Wildcat", the F6F "Hellcat" and the F4U "Corsair." Bomber crew training included the SB2C "Hell Diver" and the SBD "Dauntless." There was also training on TBF torpedo planes.

Woodbine, where Bob apparently spent much of his time between November 1944 and June 1945, was a satellite field. Due to a long runway, it was primarily used for aircraft carrier practice landings. There was also practice on day and night catapult launchings and arrested landings.

By the end of the war Bob had advanced to Seaman First Class. On February 10, 1946, he was promoted to Coxswain and he would serve as such until his discharge on June 23, 1946. During his last year in the Navy, Bob was assigned, according to the NAO, to a Naval unit in Philadelphia. It would appear he was transferred there sometime between April and September 1945. The transfer may have occurred closer to September, since the NAO reported that Bob had been at home with his parents that month.

Gordon R. Barnett of Houghton enlisted in the Naval Reserve Aviation Corps while a sophomore at Houghton College. By March 1943, according to the NAO, Gordon was attending Rensselaer Polytechnic Institute in Troy, NY, probably as part of the Navy's V-12 program. In April, he spent a short furlough at home. By May he was at Baylor University in Waco, Texas, most likely as part of the Navy's V-7 program. There, in addition to his classroom work, Gordon got in two months of practice flying. He then was ordered to Del Monte, CA for preflight training. He continued his training, this time primary flight training at the Naval Air Station in Hutchison, KS. It was then on to Barin Field in Alabama for fighter training. After completing his Barin training, he was sent to the home of Naval Aviation, Pensacola, FL, where he received his wings on October 31,1944.

Given leave, Gordon headed for Houghton, where, by chance he met his first wife Phyllis. As was common during the war, young people did not wait. On November 22, Gordon and Phyllis eloped.

He was then sent to Fort Lauderdale, FL, where he was trained to fly TBF Avenger Torpedo planes. In March 1945, while at home on leave, he was involved in a serious accident when his car collided with a snow plow. The war ended before Gordon could be sent into combat. However, he decided to stay in the Navy until retirement in 1963.

Gordon had many notable experiences while in the Navy. One that clearly stands out is when he was picked to be an extra in the John Wayne movie, *The Wings of Eagles*. During filming, he appeared in many scenes, but Gordon said that the final picture contained only one of these scenes.

Education: At the start of World War II, the United States needed everything all at once. Guns, bullets, and other materials were just part of the need. The US also needed men and women with specialized skills, from infantrymen to nuclear physicists. Maybe most of all, it needed leaders, lots of them, more than existed and more than the then current pipeline could provide in the immediate future. It needed them immediately, and it needed to be sure there would be a continuous supply.

The military had to plan and put in place programs to identify, train, and equip such leaders. One solution was to increase the numbers attending the service academies, and to educate them quicker, which would help with the continuous and long-term personnel problem. Another was to significantly increase the number of men selected for Officer's Candidate School (OCS). This would address the short-term need for leaders, and bring into being the phrase, "90-day wonders." A third solution was the V-12 program. It came into being in 1943 to meet the immediate and long-term need for commissioned officers to man ships, fly planes and command troops.

The V-12 program was a direct result of the decision to lower the draft age to 18 in 1942. This change created a massive shortage of college-educated officers, as well as a major economic impact on colleges, struggling with reduced enrollments. The V-12 program put many of these men back in college at the government's expense, thus alleviating the economic impact of the draft. It accepted students already enrolled in college reserve programs, enlisted men recommended by their commanding officers, and high school seniors who passed a nationwide qualifying exam.

The V-12 program was not a picnic for those accepted. It ran year around, with three trimesters of four months each. The men had to carry 17 credit hours each term, plus participate in nine and one-half hours of physical education each week.

At least the following FCSD area men participated in these efforts. Roy M. Weaver (FCS 1937) and Franklin G. Babbitt, cousins, were accepted into the US Naval Academy at Annapolis. Adair Wells Common (FCS 1935) of the 101st Airborne Infantry was accepted into OCS. Navy enlisted personnel Ralph Kleinspehn, Jr. (FCS Coach, Teacher/and Principal, 1948-1980), Lyle C. Brown (FCS 1943), Kenneth Eugene Lindley, and Clare James Smith (FCS 1942), and Richard Morris (FCS 1941) were accepted into the Navy V-12 program.

Lyle Clarence Brown of Rossburg, enlisted in the Navy at the age of 17, after graduating from FCS in 1943 and working on Les Rickett's Erie Railroad carpenter gang for two months. Upon completion of basic training at Sampson Naval Training Station in October, Lyle was sent to Texas A & M College for specialized training in radio. Upon completion of radio operator training in February 1944, Lyle entered the Navy V-12 Program at Louisiana Tech. He finished four trimesters at Tech in June 1945 and was ordered to the University of Oklahoma for NROTC training. By the time he finished at the University of Oklahoma and was commissioned as ensign in June 1946, the war was over. Lyle would remain on active duty until May 1947, during which time he served briefly at the Coronado Amphibious Base in California as the Athletic Officer before going aboard *LSM 463* of Service Squadron 3 for a year of duty in China and Korea as Communications and Commissary officer on that small amphibious ship. He would see combat at Inchon after he volunteered for the Korean War in 1950 and served on the ComServRon 3 staff as a cryptography officer aboard the *USS Piedmont* and the *USS Hector.* Lyle remained in the Naval Reserve until 1972 when he retired as a Commander with a specialty in Intelligence.

Many years later part of his Sampson boot camp diary, "A Young Sailor's Journal" was printed in the June 1999 newsletter of Sampson's WW II Navy Veterans. Excerpts from Lyle's "A Week on the Rifle Range of Unit E" (published in *Sampson* by Turner Publishing Company in 2000) will bring back "fond" memories to everyone who has had the honor and privilege of military basic training. The first thing you are told is, "Don't volunteer for anything." Some did not listen to this diamond of advice.

Lyle and several other men from his company 338, responded to a call for personnel experienced in handling rifles. Ten were selected to serve as range instructors. In one day, they learned the lingo of the range, mastered the firing positions, prone and sitting, and learned proper maintenance of the weapon. Then they were ready to instruct. This experience provided Lyle with the opportunity to learn some very important lessons about the military.

The first was that the firing range is a dangerous place. While no one was shot during Lyle's week as an instructor, there were some close calls. Weapons and careless people are not a good mix. Think before you act is a phrase too often ignored. One day a gunner's mate was demonstrating the operation of a .22 caliber pistol. He gave the loaded weapon to a boot instructor who proceeded to fire off several rounds. When asked if the weapon was empty, he turned the weapon 90 degrees to examine it and accidentally fired it. The bullet just missed the gunner's mate. Another time a weapon discharged as the bolt was moved forward. Maybe the worst thing for a country boy who had grown up hunting moving squirrels, rabbits, and woodchucks, was to watch men unable to hit a 6-inch by 12-inch stationary target 40 feet away, much less any part of the bull's eye.

Even more discouraging was the day some young officers showed up for practice. Not only did they not know how to load and fire the weapons, they exhibited a careless and joking attitude. They fired enough rounds to train a dozen companies, but seldom hit anything. Lyle felt they were treating the whole thing as a lark.

There was one more lesson of course. That was a reminder of why you are told not to volunteer. The range instructors were supposed to be exempt from certain other duties, such as guard duty and cleaning details. The company petty officer, of course, ignored the notes explaining the supposed exemptions, and he made them clean and guard with everyone else. The boot rifle instructors even went so far as to report this problem to the range petty officer, and were assured the matter would be addressed. It was not. During his week as a range instructor, Lyle also stood two four-hour night watches. Thanks for volunteering.

Lyle has no regrets about the week. He learned some valuable lessons, including lessons about leadership, or the lack thereof, and about exercising authority. He feels these lessons were useful when he became an officer himself, before the age of 20. He also feels they were helpful during his career as a university professor.

Earl Lewis Herring moved to the FCSD area in 1958 when he and his wife purchased a farm. Earl entered the Navy on March 22, 1944 in Buffalo as an Apprentice Seaman. His basic training was at the Sampson Naval Training Station. By June he had already risen to Seaman Second Class, and been assigned to the *USS Alaska* (CB 1). He reported aboard the *Alaska* on June 17, 1944 at the Philadelphia ship yards. Lionel Briggs of Hume reported aboard that same day. Unfortunately, four days later, June 21, Earl was transferred to the US Naval Hospital in Philadelphia. He was never able to return to duty. He was discharged from the Navy at the hospital on September 5, 1944.

Kenneth E. Lindley of Houghton entered the Navy on May 17, 1944. He received his basic training at the Naval Training Center in Farragut, ID. Kenneth was then accepted into the Navy V-12 program for electrical engineering at St. Thomas College, University of Minnesota, St. Paul, MN. He received further training at the University of Wisconsin at Madison. The war ended before Kenneth completed his V-12 studies. He was discharged June 30, 1946.

Gerald Voss Luckey of Granger entered the service February 23, 1944. A 1938 graduate of FCS, Gerald was working for the Curtiss Aircraft Plant in Buffalo when he was called. Gerald told the author that, due to his job at Curtis, he received two deferrals. When his draft number came up again, he rejected a third deferral.

After completing basic training, Gerald was sent to the Naval Air Technical Training Center in Norman, OK. During the next several months, Gerald was trained as an Aviation Ordnanceman. As such he was responsible for the maintenance of guns, bombs, torpedoes, rockets, and missiles aboard Navy combat aircraft. His duties included stowing, loading, and issuing of munitions and small arms.

The NAO, in a September, 1944 issue, reported that Gerald had been transferred to Alameda. CA. Specifically, he was assigned to the Naval Auxiliary Air Station at Santa Rosa, a part of the Alameda Air Station. Gerald served with Combat Air Service Unit (CASU) 36, which was permanently stationed at Santa Rosa during 1944 and 1945. From Gerald's arrival at Santa Rosa until the end of the war, several combat squadrons received advanced training at Santa Rosa. These included Naval squadrons VF 5 (fighters), VB 5 (bombers) and VT 5 (torpedoes), along with Marine combat units VMF 452 and 214 (fighters) from Combat Air Group (CAG) 5. The V designation stood for heavier than air aircraft.

(Upon completion of training, all the above units were assigned to the fast carrier, *USS Franklin* (CV 13). The *Franklin* was hit by two bombs during its air attacks on the Japanese mainland. Some 800 of its crew were killed. Due to heroic efforts of its remaining crew, the *Franklin* survived, and was the most heavily damaged carrier of WW II to do so. VF 5 flew the F4F Grumman Wildcats and later F6F Hellcats. VB 5 flew the Curtiss dive bomber SB2C. The two Marine units flew the F4U Corsair fighters. VMF 214 was the latest reincarnation of the famous Black Sheep Squadron of Gregory "Pappy" Boyington. It was now staffed with all new pilots.)

Following the departure of aircraft heading to the *Franklin,* squadrons from CAG 17 arrived. CAG 17 squadrons were flying the F6F Hellcat initially, but it was soon replaced by the new F8F Bearcat, although the F8F never saw combat in WW II. The base was training VBF 151 of CAG 11 at war's end.

There was a strip on the base the size of a deck on an aircraft carrier. Pilots practiced on the strip before moving to the carriers. Gerald said there were accidents. A lot of them occurred during air shows. One day a plane landed and when they opened the bomb bay door, a bomb fell out. The arming pin stayed in, so there was no danger.

Gerald told the author that, while they were busy, due to heavy fog in the area, their days started late. Gerald usually worked with torpedo bombers. But the men were called upon to perform many tasks that were not part of their regular duties. Gerald remembers going to the beach to load sand bags to be put around Quonset Huts for protection. He also worked with crews that protected and reclaimed downed aircraft in the nearby desert.

Gerald said he had a lucky career. Once he was due to be assigned to a ship heading for combat. For some reason the assignment did not go through. The ship was later torpedoed. While badly damaged, the ship survived and made it back to base. Gerald was discharged February 8, 1946, at Sampson.

Richard E. Morris of Centerville was inducted into the Navy on February 1, 1943, at Buffalo. He was assigned to Sampson Naval Training Station for basic training, and while at Sampson was selected for the Navy V-12 program. He was assigned to Middlebury College in Vermont, where he studied for eight months. His next assignment was Dartmouth College in Hanover, NH. After finishing at Dartmouth, he was sent to the Midshipman School at Asbury Park, NJ. On April 26. 1945, he became an Ensign in the

US Navy. Dick was now assigned for four months to Columbia University in New York City. He was then sent to the Advanced Fire Control School in San Diego. Upon completing his training in controlling the fire of guns on a US ship of war, he was assigned to the *USS Champlain* (DD 601), a destroyer.

The *Champlain*, was a battle-tested veteran of both the Atlantic and Pacific wars. She had earned six battle stars. In addition, she had been one of the ships assigned to protect President Roosevelt sailing to and from the Yalta Conference. Dick left San Francisco on September 1, 1945 to join the *Champlain* in Japan. His route took him through Okinawa, and he was there on October 9th, with his brother Austy, when the famous typhoon Louise hit the island. Dick may have made it to Japan to join the *Champlain,* but likely he joined it at Okinawa. The *Champlain* left Okinawa on October 31, 1945 transporting servicemen home. *Champlain* picked up more men at Saipan and Hawaii, and disembarked them at San Diego November 21 to 24. She then sailed to Charleston, SC. Shortly after arriving in Charleston, Dick made it back to Centerville; and on April 13, 1946, he married Suzanne Strahan in Fillmore. He was discharged November 19, 1946.

Stephen J. Orlip of Houghton entered the service in 1943 after graduating from Houghton College with a degree in Music. Stephen was assigned to the Navy School of Music in Washington, DC. It appears that he served as an instructor at the Navy school during the war. While in DC, Stephen was also able to earn his Masters of Music at Catholic University. Stephen primarily served as an instructor but he also composed music and performed as an organist and conductor.

The US Navy School of Music was originally located at the Washington Navy Yard. The school was operated by the US Navy Band. Members of the band served as instructors teaching classes as well as providing private lessons, while still performing with the band until the onset of World War II. With the advent of war performing all these duties became too much, and the band was separated from the school. The school was moved to the Anacostia Naval Receiving Station in DC.

As the war's end approached, the need for instructors at the School of Music decreased rapidly. The extra instructors were then sent to other Navy stations to complete their service. Stephen apparently was assigned to the Naval Station in Newport, RI, where he served until discharged in 1948. He then went to work for the Westside Presbyterian Church in Englewood, NJ.

Adelbert E. Perry entered the service on September 21, 1942. He was initially assigned to the Navy's Great Lakes Training Center in North Chicago, IL. The Center, despite being a thousand miles from the nearest ocean, was the premier Naval training center.

Upon completion of basic training, Adelbert was assigned to the Aviation Ordnance School at the Naval Air Station in Memphis, TN. Here over a period of fourteen weeks he received training on the maintenance of guns, bombs, installation, and related subjects. As in basic training Adelbert received high marks in each study area. He next attended a two-week course in Aviation Radar Operations, again receiving high grades. His next stop was the Navy Air Gunnery School in Hollywood, FL. Due to poor eyesight, Adelbert was unable to complete the training.

Adelbert was then assigned to Headquarters Squadron Fleet Air Wing 14 in San Diego, CA as an Aircraft Maintenance Man. The Wing flew Consolidated PBY Catalinas. PB stood for patrol bomber and Y for Consolidated, the company which built the plane. Fleet Air Wing 14 functioned as a patrol and reconnaissance organization on the west coast. Adelbert was discharged November 21, 1944.

John S. Rease of Wiscoy entered the US Navy on February 19, 1944. At the time of entry, John was already an accomplished carpenter. Following his basic training at Sampson Naval Training Station, where he was promoted to Carpenter's Mate 3rd Class (CM/3C) on March 26, John was transferred to the Radio Material School in Anacostia, VA for duty. Except for a short period, John would serve the rest of the war at the Radio Material School. There he engaged in the various duties of a carpenter's mate. Naval procedures provided that a carpenter's mate perform such duties as carpentry and joinery work, repairing and replacing deck planking and other wood work, and laying and repairing tiling.

The Radio Material School (RMS) was part of the Navy's National Research Laboratory. At that time, work at the Laboratory was centered on developing procedures for detecting and identifying enemy ships.

In July 1944, John was transferred to the Explosives Investigating Laboratory, Navy Powder Factory in Indian Head, MD. His records indicate that he was there to participate in a "Special Project." However, it appears that he was there to participate in a training course for PO (Petty Officer) 3c and PO2c.

John reported back to RMS in August. On February 20, 1945, he was transferred to the Bethesda Naval Hospital for treatment. The treatment was in fact, an operation, although his records do not state for what. He remained in the hospital until April 12, when he was given 14 days leave. He reported back to RMS on April 26. On October 1 John was promoted to CM2c. He received his discharge April 3, 1946 at Bainbridge, MD.

Logistics. It is impossible to fight and win a war without weapons, supplies, and other materiel. Most people realize that it is necessary to move troops, but often forget about everything the troops need to do their jobs. All that materiel, including tanks and planes, must also be moved. The logistics of WW II were staggering.

"Underway replenishment was the US Navy's secret weapon of World War II". Fleet Admiral Chester Nimitz

"Amateurs think about tactics, but professionals think about logistics." General Robert H. Barrow, USMC

"Because of my wartime experience, I am insistent on the point that logistics know-how must be maintained, that logistics is second to nothing in importance in warfare, that logistic training must be widespread and thorough, and that it is folly to waste time on mediocre talent." Vice Admiral Robert B. Carney, USN

These Officers made clear the importance of a part of warfare that most people do not know exists.

Warren Sherman Richardson of Fillmore, unlike his two brothers, Ransom and David, who also served during WW II, was not born in Fillmore. He was born in Rochester, but he did graduate from Fillmore Central with the Class of 1941. He was the class valedictorian. His family was from Allegany County. Warren's father was born in Angelica and his paternal grandfather represented the area in the US House of Representatives from 1879 until 1883. His grandfather also fought in the Civil War. His mother was from Fillmore.

Warren was a sophomore at the University of Rochester and a member of the US Naval Reserve when he entered active duty on December 5, 1942. After completing pilot training, Warren was assigned to Air Ferry Squadron 1, and later Air Ferry Squadron 4 of the Naval Air Transport Service. His job was to ferry various aircraft to locations where they were to be utilized. Since he was trained in seaplanes, Warren was specifically assigned to ferrying the flying boats, PBYs and PBMs.

The PBMs Mariners (PB for Patrol Boats and M for the manufacturer, Glenn Martin Aircraft Company) were built at the Martin plant near Baltimore, MD. The Consolidated PBYs Catalinas (PB for Patrol Boats, Y for the manufacturer, Consolidated Aircraft) were built at the Consolidated plant in San Diego.

The PBY was the most widely used aircraft of the war. It served in every branch of the service and even in the armed forces of other nations. In fact, some of the planes were built in Canada and Russia. It was used for anti-submarine activities, patrol bombing, convoy escorts, cargo transport, and search and rescue, especially air sea rescues. PBY Catalinas found the famous German battleship *Bismarck*, and they located the Japanese Fleet near Midway. The sinking of the *Bismarck* was a major victory for the British, and the Battle of Midway was the decisive turning point of the war in the Pacific.

Catalinas were slow and ungainly but exceptionally reliable. Warren remembers the difficulty of flying them. Pilots without the proper training found the planes almost impossible to manage. Warren and other pilots would be flown to the manufacturing plants (San Diego or Baltimore) in one of the planes permanently assigned to Ferry Squadron 4. They would then pick up the planes assigned to them and fly them to specified destinations. They then hitched a (free) ride on a commercial airline to return to their home base at Floyd Bennett Field on Long Island. Warren related how trips to San Diego took so long they had to stop overnight. They usually stopped at Eagle Mountain Lake, Texas. When Warren retired, he and his wife moved to Eagle Mountain Lake.

Air Ferry Squadron 4 was commissioned in November 1944. It started ferrying airplanes in December. According to the orders establishing the Squadron, its "Primary duty is ferrying of new large seaplanes and such other types of aircraft as may be directed by the CNO" (Chief of Naval Operations). From December 1944 until the end of August, 1945, the Squadron ferried 606 seaplanes: 420 PBM-5s and 186 PBY-6As. In that same time frame, it ferried 135 other types of aircraft. The peak months were March - 111, June - 122, and July -115. Another 81 were ferried in September 1945, following the end of the war.

A December report indicated the squadron had 22 flying officers. Assuming the staffing remained constant throughout the eight-months period, on average they were ferrying about 82 planes a month, or approximately 3 to 4 per pilot. Despite the busy schedule, the squadron did not have a single reportable accident. In fact, the only "mishap" contained in the War Diary Reports for the entire period is a forced landing at Tulare Lake, CA on January 23, 1945. A PBY lost one engine in flight.

Edwin J. Robinson of Hume entered the Navy in October of 1944. He took his basic training at Sampson Naval Base. For some unknown reason, he was discharged in February 1945 after completing his training.

Vernon B. Slack of Fillmore entered the Navy in July 1944. He took his basic training at Sampson Naval Training Station, and was then assigned to the Naval Torpedo Testing Range at Montauk, Long Island. The naval base was located on Gould Island, just off the coast near Montauk.

The Testing Range was used to determine whether a torpedo's propulsion systems functioned satisfactorily, and whether its guidance systems correctly controlled a torpedo's course. Torpedoes could be used over and over, as the "testing head" which replaced the war head contained water that would be blown out at the end of the run. The torpedo would then resurface and be retrieved. Only about seven percent of the torpedoes were never recovered.

Unfortunately, the tests could not determine if the torpedo would have exploded. The Mark 14 torpedo, used in submarines, often did not explode, immediately putting the submarine firing the torpedo at risk from the enemy.

By April 1945, Vernon was, according to the NAO, transferred to Hoboken, NJ. In less than a year in the Navy, he had risen from Apprentice Seaman to Seaman First Class. There were several Navy activities being carried out at Hoboken. During the war the shipyard there handled more than 8,000 ships and 34 million tons of cargo. It is possible Vernon was assigned to the yard in some capacity. However, this was a civilian activity. Given that Vernon was only there for approximately three months, it is possible that he was undergoing some sort of training. The Navy was using the Stevens Institute of Technology in Hoboken for some training. Or he may have been just passing through on his way to his next assignment. Since he was about to join the *USS Wicks*, which was in Hawaii, it may be that he was shipped to Hawaii from Hoboken. The NAO reported that he was home on leave during this time period.

On July 21, 1945, Vernon reported aboard the *USS Wickes* (DD 578*)*. Vernon would remain on the *Wickes* for the balance of the war. The *Wickes*, a destroyer, had an enviable war record. When Vernon joined her in Hawaii, she was at Hunters Point for an overhaul. The war ended before her overhaul was complete. That fall and winter, she conducted refresher-training exercises, but in December the ship was decommissioned. Vernon was assigned to the Naval base in San Diego. On May 29, 1946, he reported aboard the landing ship tank, *USS Esmeraldo* (LST 761). (The name was supposed to be *Esmeralda* after the Nevada County, but someone got it wrong.) The *Esmeraldo,* which had participated in the Iwo Jima invasion, was decommissioned on July 16, 1946. In October, Vernon was transferred again, this time to *USS Lyon County* (LST 904). *Lyon County* (named for Lyon Counties in five different states) was also a veteran of the Pacific war, having earned one battle star. It was decommissioned on November 11, 1946. Perhaps Vernon was part of a group assigned to move these now unneeded vessels to points where they could be decommissioned.

Clare James Smith of Hume, grew up on a farm near Fillmore and graduated from FCS in June 1942. He entered the Navy June 6, 1944. After spending a semester at the University of Michigan he was transferred to the University of Rochester (UR) under the Navy V-12 program. Clare was still at UR when the war ended. He was put on inactive duty, but was awarded a scholarship by UR to continue his education. He became a dentist and served with the U.S. Public Health Service during the Korean War.

Robert Q. Smith of Hume, an older brother of Clare (see above) graduated from FCS with the class of 1937. He then attended both Houghton College and Cornell University, graduating from Cornell, located in Ithaca, NY, in January 1942. While in college, Bob was also training to be a pilot; and he remained in Ithaca after graduation to complete his flight training, eventually qualify as a flight instructor. At that time, his long-term plan was to become a pilot for Pan American Airways. After qualifying, he served for the next year, in Ithaca, as a civilian instructor at the Navy Flight Training School. Then he was called into active service, and received his commission as an Ensign in late 1943. Bob was assigned to the Naval Air Station at Corpus Christie, TX but was shortly transferred to a plane ferrying unit in Dallas, TX. By March, 1944, he had been transferred again, this time to Floyd Bennett Field on Long Island, NY, where he remained for the balance of the war. That same month, on a ferrying trip to Pensacola, FL, he stayed overnight with fellow FCSer Ansel Young, who was also attached to the Naval Air Transport Service plane ferrying service. The next morning, another FCSer, Warren Richardson, arrived from Peru, IN to finish his flight training. Warren would eventually serve with ferrying unit VRF-4 at Floyd Bennett Field.

On December 1, 1943, Floyd Bennett became the heart and soul of a system that moved aircraft from the factory to battle. It was the busiest air station in the US during the war. Navy personnel picked up planes at factories, tested them for flight worthiness, fitted them out for service, got them commissioned in the Navy, and finally ferried them out to Navy and Marine combat units, usually on the west coast. After completing delivery, the ferry pilots returned to Floyd Bennett either on commercial flights, or by flying battle-worn planes. Sometimes, they flew planes produced at west coast factories. This system replaced previous systems which, given the number of aircraft being built, were simply too cumbersome.

Robert was assigned to Air Ferrying Squadron 1 (VRF-1), the largest naval aviation squadron ever assembled. During the war, VRF-1, VRF-4 (Warren Richardson squadron) and other units, ferried some

46,000 aircraft over 80 million miles. While all pilots were not qualified to fly all types of aircraft, some 29 different types of aircraft were ferried. Robert's son Craig said his father flew several types, including the famous F4F Wildcat, F6F Hellcat, and the F4U Corsair. The Hellcat became famous for outperforming the great Japanese fighter, the Mitsubishi Zero. Marine pilots provided close ground support to troops with the Corsair. The ability of the Corsair was demonstrated to the FCS area by Robert in March of 1945 (according to the NAO), on one of his trips to the west coast. Flying the F4U, he entertained the area with barrel rolls, loops, and a low-level buzz.

Robert was flying alone on the trip when he "buzzed" his home community. To qualify for solo flights, and thus be designated as a "single pilot," each pilot had to fly as least five cross-country trips as a "follow" pilot. There were two other designations, lead pilots and senior ferry pilots. The designations indicated increasing levels of experience. Once a pilot completed five transcontinental flights without an accident, he would be listed on the "Glory Board" in the Floyd Bennett ready room with a pair of gold wings. Twenty-five such flights were recognized by the squadron's insignia, a stork.

Weather was always a danger, but sometimes it brought unexpected dividends. In February 1945, the NAO reported that Robert had been grounded for eight days due to a storm, in New Orleans.

Harry L. Stroud, Jr. of Fillmore entered the service on July 6, 1942. Harry grew up in the nearby town of Pike and moved to Fillmore in the early 40's. He entered the service from Fillmore and took basic training in Newport, RI. At the time, such training lasted about six weeks or so, depending on the need of the fleet. Harry's training may have lasted slightly more than the six weeks, as he was assigned to the *USS Nightingale* on September 17, 1942, and ordered to report aboard October 9. Harry was designated a straggler on October 10, when he failed to report. He finally reported to the Norfolk Naval Receiving Station on October 22. On December 1st, he finally reported aboard the *Nightingale*.

On January 1, 1943 he was tried by a Summary Court Martial. He was convicted by his admission, and sentenced to 55 days confinement and a reduction in pay for the same period. Interestingly, on the same day, January 1,1943, he was promoted from Apprentice Seaman to Seaman 2nd Class. (Ascendent ranks in the World War II Navy were: Apprentice Seaman, 2nd class Seaman, Seaman 1st class and then to specialized 3rd class petty officer rate.)

On April 14, 1943, only 3 and a half months later, he was promoted to Seaman First Class. That same day he was transferred from the *Nightingale* to the New Orleans Receiving Station for further transfer to the *USS Capps.* On May 10 he was transferred from New Orleans to the Naval Receiving Station at Mobile, AL. On June 24, he was finally transferred to the *USS Capps.*

On August 25, 1943, Harry was declared a straggler and AWOL as of August 23, 1943. On August 31, his records were transferred to Charleston, SC for administrative purposes. On September 6, 1943, he surrendered at the District of Columbia Naval Yard having been AWOL for 15 days. He was also officially transferred from the *USS Capps* to DC. Then he was physically transferred to Naval Receiving Station at Pier 92, NY. On September 14, a court martial convicted him of being AWOL and sentenced him to loss of pay and ordered him to maintain a record satisfactory to his commander for six months or face a bad conduct discharge.

On October 30 he was transferred from Ship 2637 to AJRP 29 for duty. However, he again went AWOL on October 29, 1943, to November 1, 1943. A Captain's Mast on November 1st declared his probationary period terminated and ordered that Harry be discharged with a Bad Conduct Discharge. On November 30 he was discharged.

Roy Babbitt Weaver of Hume graduated from Fillmore Central in 1937 and Houghton College in 1941. After graduating from Houghton, Roy took a job with the US Civil Service. He worked as an instructor in radio at Scott Field in Illinois. In 1942 he accepted an appointment to the US Naval Academy. Roy was commissioned an Ensign upon his graduation from Annapolis on June 6, 1945. By August he was aboard the newly commissioned heavy cruiser *USS Los Angeles*. After a shakedown cruise, out of Guantanamo Bay, Cuba, the *Los Angeles* departed for Shanghai, China. For the next three-years it served with the US Seventh Fleet. Roy earned both the Atlantic and Pacific Theater Ribbons and the World War II Victory Medal. He remained in the Navy after the war. Roy marched with the Battalion of Midshipmen in the funeral procession for President Franklin D. Roosevelt in April, 1945.

Maurice Robinson Wiles of Fillmore, served in one of those vital US activities, keeping the mail rolling. And for once, that person higher up responsible for assignments seems to have used some good sense. Maurice had worked as a mailman prior to the war and thus was able to move from his civilian job to his military job with relative ease. While Maurice worked with the mail during his entire service, several men from the area were temporarily assigned to Post Office duty during their tours, including Marlie Hodnett, Bernard Mills and Beverly Luckey.

Maurice spent most of the war at the Naval Receiving Station in Galveston, Texas. Galveston was a place where sailors were stationed as they awaited operational assignments. There was also a shipyard nearby where naval vessels were built and repaired. These factors added to the volume of mail processed through the Center.

The Naval Base itself was on a small island near Galveston named Pelican's Spit. Twice daily Maurice, fully armed, would take the mail by boat to Galveston Island for delivery to the main Post Office. A jeep was assigned to him and he would use it to get from the dock to the Post Office. Maurice would then pick up Navy mail and return, first by jeep and then by boat, to the base. There were strict procedures for the entire process. The mailbags, anywhere from five to 20 bags, were tied together with a float tied to the top. His orders required him to stay with the bags on the deck of the ship. These requirements, once again, illustrate the importance the military placed on the mail.

One trip for the mail stood out in Maurice's mind. There was a hurricane in the area so when he arrived in Galveston, he found he was the only person on the street.

As previously mentioned, the mail was crucial for morale, both the morale of the men and women in service and their families at home. In an era when mail was virtually the only way of communicating with those in service, its importance cannot be overstated. Virtually every World War II movie contained a mail call scene or one where the soldiers are reading and discussing their mail.

Often it was not easy to locate someone overseas. They were on the move constantly. Maurice said his saddest moments in the service occurred when his office received back, from overseas, a large mail bag of letters sent from home to an overseas serviceman. There was nothing for Maurice to do except to return the letters to the senders. To this day, he still wonders why the serviceman did not get those letters, although deep down Maurice knows the answer. Mail was also lost when ships carrying it were sunk by enemy action.

Another major problem was mail being improperly addressed, especially when it violated national security rules. Those rules, designed to protect the men and women in service, prohibited specific addresses that included the name of a foreign country or the address of a steamship company in the case of the Merchant Marine. On the other hand, a loved one's letters could also help the military. The War Department recommended that, when writing to members of the armed forces, the folks at home should remind and encourage them to follow the advice of their medical officers. Maybe the very worst problem was when it was learned that the Germans were confiscating mail sent to prisoners of war if the mail bore patriotic slogans such as "Win the War", "For Defense", and "Buy Defense Bonds."

The volume of mail was enormous. Because of its impact on morale, mail had a high priority. But it was also heavy and took up valuable cargo space. For this reason, the use of V (for Victory) Mail was adopted. V mail was written on a special letter/envelope that was then microfilmed and sent overseas or home. It was then reproduced at about one-quarter its original size and delivered to the addressee. Despite V mail's value for reducing shipping space and tonnage, and major efforts to get families and soldiers to use it, regular mail remained popular. In 1944, for instance, the Navy reported that Navy personnel had received 38 million pieces of V Mail, but over 272 million pieces of regular mail.

The workload was so great that the military took to assigning returning overseas veterans to military post offices. Marlie Hodnett, for instance, after returning from his tours in Tunisia and Sicily, was assigned to the Army Post Office in New York City. Keeping the mail moving was a top military priority throughout the war. Bernard Mills also worked in the Post Office in between assignments.

Maurice Wiles was able to make an easy transfer from the military to civilian life. After the war, he returned to his US Postal Service job in Fillmore.

Ansel G. Young of Fillmore graduated from FCS in 1938 and the University of Pennsylvania in 1942 He enlisted in the Navy April 18, 1942 but did not enter active duty until September 15, 1942.

His first three months were spent at Chapel Hill, NC where he went through his pre-flight training. During this period, he was part of a drill squad that performed at an event in Washington, DC. His Mother attended the performance. After spending Thanksgiving at home, he moved to Dallas, TX for primary flight training. In a March 1943 letter to his parents, he informed them that instead of being sent to Corpus Christie, TX, his class was being sent to Pensacola, FL, the home of Naval air power, for basic flight training. In another letter home to his aunt in May of 1943, he mentioned that his training had specialized in patrol boat and two engine planes, landing in water, and gun training. His training group had set a record for the number of training hours flown. In June a letter mentioned that he had sat on a platform with Lowell Thomas during Thomas' radio broadcast from Pensacola. He had made Commander of his training squadron and was scheduled to graduate June 15, 1943. He remained at Pensacola following the completion of his training. The NAO reported in January 1944 that he had been home with his wife, probably for the holidays, before returning to Pensacola.

In February, 1944 he sent a card to the NAO indicating he had flown a PBY to Miami to participate in cross country navigation. In March he noted that it had been "Old Home Week" in Pensacola, as both Bob Smith and Warren Richardson had visited him. Bob had delivered a plane to Pensacola and stayed overnight. Warren had arrived to finish his flight training. In March he had flown a plane to DC where he visited his brother Norman who was stationed there. He was now an Instructor at Pensacola. In September, 1944 his parents visited him. He was promoted to Lieutenant in August 1944.

He apparently was transferred to Atlanta shortly after his parents visit as the NAO reported in February 1945 that he had been transferred to Atlanta for instrument training.

In March 1945 he was transferred to Alameda, CA. In Alameda he was assigned to VR -2, a newly commissioned transport squadron. VR – 2 flew the PB 24, a Consolidated built four-engine Coronado flying boat. In June he informed the NAO that he had just completed his first trans-Pacific flight from Alameda to Hawaii as part of the Naval Air Transport Service. He remained at Alameda performing transport services for the balance of his service. The transport service moved supplies, the mail, and personnel. He wrote the NAO in December 1945 that he had recognized a picture in the November 16 edition. It was of his squadrons operating area at Alameda. Ansel was discharged July 16, 1946. In 1986 Ansel purchased a World War II PBY and presented it to the Geneseo Warplane Museum in Geneseo, NY.

US Marine Corps

At least seven men and women from the FCSD area served in the Marine Corps during World War II. All of them served overseas. They were John D. Ballard, G. Alfred Bates, Frank W. Lane, Geraldine Faith Paine, James G. Ringelberg, Clark O. Smith, and Robert H. Speicher.

US Coast Guard

The following FCSD area residents served in the US Coast Guard in the American Theater of Operations during World War II: Alma Geraldine Farnsworth, Martin E. Ringelberg, and Stephen Edward Wilmot.

Alma Geraldine Farnsworth of Hume, enlisted in SPARS, the female arm of the Coast Guard, in June 1943. The Coast Guard was actively competing with the Navy for recruits at that time. Prior to mid-1943, the Navy had recruited for SPARS. The basic purpose of SPARS (Semper Parados - Always Ready) (Semper Parados is Always Ready in Latin), like most other military women's organizations, was to free up men for combat duty.

The first SPARS were Navy Waves, who were transferred to the Coast Guard. But Dorothy Stratton, who commanded SPARS throughout the war, wanted a special type of women. She set her sights high. Along with the usual requirements (age, nationality, marriage restrictions, and such things as no children under 18), recruits also had to pass a strict physical examination. Stratton wanted women with outstanding athletic fitness, who were excellent swimmers. She also wanted women to possess nautical knowledge, and to be part of the North-East abolitionist tradition. Black females were to be welcome in SPARS. Attracting recruits would be difficult. It was not just competition with the other service groups. Women could now earn high wages in industry jobs. Some might not accept the military life style, and many parents and boyfriends opposed their volunteering. Even recruiting limitations established by government agencies such as the War Manpower Commission, hindered enlistments. Some women did not think the effort was worth curtailing their social activities.

Nevertheless, Stratton and others plowed ahead. The Coast Guard had deduced that 1.13 Coast Guard people were needed to support each man at sea. They wanted women to be a major part of that support force, so they proposed an 81 percent increase in the size of SPARS. And despite the concerns, drawbacks and restrictions, tens of thousands of women applied during the period June 1943 to July 1944. A little less than 12,000 of these were found to meet the requirements. Only 62 percent of them were invited to enlist, and only three-fourths of those enlisted. On May 1, 1943, SPARS strength stood at 337 officers, and 2,838 enlisted. By D-Day, June 6, 1944, SPARS counted 771 officers and 7,600 enlisted.

SPARS training was originally conducted at Hunter College in New York City. Dorothy Stratton reasoned that a new, more attractive, location would enable her to compete with other services for the type of women the Coast Guard wanted and needed. As a result, Geraldine took basic training at the ritzy Biltmore Palm Beach Hotel in Palm Beach, FL. While it may not have seemed like an ideal locale for a military basic training site, it did achieve the results for which Stratton was looking. Some 7,000 SPARS would eventually receive their training in Palm Beach, compared to 1,900 at Hunter College, and another 1,900 at Manhattan Beach in New York near the end of the war.

The training Alma (who used her middle name Geraldine) faced was rigorous. It included military indoctrination (etiquette and customs), Coast Guard and Navy history, ships and aircraft, and military organization and regulations. Each day started with calisthenics. There were also classes in handling small boats and in marksmanship. For certain SPARS, there was advanced training in such areas as storekeeping and radio communications and repair. Geraldine may have been living in a ritzy hotel, but her days were not that glamorous. Mostly they were hard work.

At the completion of training, the SPARS were assigned to regular duties in the various Coast Guard District Offices. Initially they all replaced men in performing basic routine duties. Gradually this changed as women were giving more responsibility and authority. A few were even eventually sent overseas to Hawaii and Alaska, and a few took over LORAN (Long Range Aid to Navigation) monitoring stations. Most SPARS, however, performed crucial but routine duties as legal assistants, motion picture technicians, drafting, machine operators, tower watchers, chauffeurs, and delivery aids throughout the war. One publication lists 51 occupations performed by the SPARS.

Geraldine was assigned to the Coast Guard 4th Military District in Philadelphia, which was responsible for the Mid-Atlantic North region comprised of Pennsylvania, the southern part of New Jersey, and Delaware. She worked at the Benjamin Franklin Hotel in Philadelphia. Geraldine was a Store Keeper. As such, she was involved in the ordering, receiving, storing, and inventorying of supplies. She could have issued food, mechanical equipment, and other items. She could have also served as payroll clerk. Geraldine rose to the rank of Storekeeper 2C.

For Geraldine, working in Philadelphia carried a big bonus. It was fairly easy to visit her grandmother in Fillmore. The NAO reported that she made several trips to Fillmore during the war. When SPARS enlisted, they were required to sign up for the war's duration, plus six months.

Martin E. Ringelberg was born in Wisconsin in 1918, but was living in Granger by no later than 1920. On May 6, 1942 Martin entered the US Coast Guard. Martin served about 33 months as an electrician. He likely took six weeks of basic training at either St. Augustine, Fl or Cape May, NJ. He then, likely, was assigned to Cooks and Bakers School at Curtis Bay, MD for three months. It appears that it was determined that this was the wrong career field for Martin. Thus, Coast Guard forwarded him to the Franklin Institute in Boston for electrician's training. The training lasted four months. It was the most intense and difficult training ever provided enlisted personnel. The men selected for the training were considered among the top three to five percent of Navy wartime personnel, officers, and enlisted men.

The NAO reported in September 1943 that Martin was a visitor in the area. In July 1944 NAO reported Martin was being moved from Gulfport, MS to Morgan City, LA. So, it appears that, following completion of his electrician's training Martin was ordered to Gulfport. He likely was assigned to the Coast Guard Air Station in nearby Biloxi. The station was there to protect shipping in and out of the area. Several attacks were made by Coast Guard planes on German submarines, but the primary responsibility of the station was the rescue of crewmen from torpedoed merchant ships. The U-Boat menace in the area had virtually disappeared by the end of 1943. That is likely why Martin was reassigned to Morgan City in July 1944.

Electrician mates stood watch on generators, switchboards, control equipment; operated and performed organizational and intermediate maintenance on power and lighting circuits, electrical fixtures, motors, voltage and frequency regulators, controllers, distribution switchboards, and other electrical equipment; and tested for short circuits, ground and other casualties and rebuilt electrical equipment.

In Morgan City, Martin was likely assigned to the Naval Air Station where he would have performed the same activities for which he was responsible in Gulfport. In January 1945, the NAO reported that he was again visiting in the area. He may have been just on a furlough, or he may have been on pre-sea duty leave. His discharge record indicates that he served five months on either foreign or sea duty during the war. The document does not show any service at overseas locations, so it may be that his five months were all sea duty. Martin was discharged June 7, 1945.

Stephen Edward Wilmot of Fillmore (Ed to everyone who knew him) started his Coast Guard career on July 16, 1942. He took basic training at the Curtis Bay Training Center in Baltimore, MD. His first duty assignment was at the Wallops Beach, VA, life boat station., where his primary duty was beach patrol. He was also a yeoman striker at the Berkley Receiving Station in Norfolk. (A striker was a non-rated person working for promotion towards a specific rating. Ed was striking for yeoman 3rd class.) He also spent some time at the Receiving Station in Chincoteague, VA.

Ed's major assignment during his service was as an Aviation Radio Technician at the Coast Guard Air Station on Winter Island, Salem, MA. His job was to maintain and repair aviation radio equipment, other equipment using vacuum tubes, and other radio type parts. He was on flight status during his service at Winter Island. Crews there flew regular anti-submarine patrols in Vought OS 20 (Kingfisher) seaplanes. Winter Island was also the first official Air-Sea rescue station on the east coast. Apparently PBM Mariners were used for such missions. It is likely that Ed serviced the communications equipment on all the various planes at the base, as well as the shore-based equipment. He was well qualified.

In fact, his day-to-day activities were probably a piece of cake compared to his training. Ed attended the rigorous Naval Electronics Training Program. Getting in was hard enough. Staying in was next to impossible. There was an initial test that applicants needed to ace to even qualify to take the test to enter the program. That test, EDDY, named for William Eddy who developed it, was designed to measure not only the qualifications of the men for the job they were to perform, but to measure their character. The training was intense, and every effort was made to weed out those who, while technically qualified, may not have exhibited the determination to make it through the entire process. When it was determined that even these safeguards were not enough, a pre-radio course of 4 weeks was introduced to further weed out those who were not likely to be successful. Once this was accomplished, the men were put into the real training. Those that made it through were considered by many to be among the top 5 percent of the men who served in the Navy during the war. Presumably the same percentage applied to the Coast Guard.

Following the four weeks pre-radio school, men were sent to a three-months primary school. There were several such schools across the country, and Ed was sent to the one at Texas A & M University. Essentially these schools condensed 2 years of college electronics training into 3 months. The days, from Monday to Friday were 12 hours long, with 8 hours of lectures, and 4 hours of mandatory, and supervised study and homework. On Saturday, there was a test covering everything that had been taught during the week. Like everything else from entry into the program, it was either pass or leave. There were no second chances for anything. This had been true from the beginning. No one was given a second chance to pass the EDDY test.

Classes were very technical in nature. They included advanced DC and AC circuits theory, electrical motors and generators, vacuum tube characteristics, power supplies, transmission lines and antenna, amplifiers, oscillators, modulation techniques, filters and wave shaping, receiver circuits, transmission circuits, and basic electromagnetic propagation theory. Some math courses, namely trigonometry and basic calculus, were included. Each student built a super-heterodyne receiver. Fault finding was taught, using systemic signal tracing. All of this was carried out in a totally secure atmosphere. A secret classification was applied to the whole system due to the materials and sciences being discussed.

But the men were not finished. Those who made it through the primary school were now sent to the 5-months secondary school. Ed was sent to the Naval Air Technical Training Center on Ware Island near Corpus Christie, TX. At these advanced training sites, the curriculum was basically consistent, although the specific hardware studied varied a bit. At Ware Island, there was a concentration on electronic equipment in airplanes and submarines. Overall, there was some review of the previous material, but now there was a focus on high frequency, ultra-high frequency, receiver and transmitter principles, coaxial cable, wave guides, antenna arrays, beam forming, synchro's and plan position indicators, radio direction finding, pulse generation, wave shaping methods, basic radar theory, cavity magnetrons, radar jamming and counter measures, long range navigation, hyperbolic navigation technique, sonar theory, and underwater acoustics.

The basic reasoning behind the extensive training was that these men were likely to be in circumstances where no other help would be available. They would need to do everything on their own. They couldn't call in a factory representative for assistance. Ed was discharged October 31, 1945 in Brooklyn, NY.

PART VIII - THE BIGGEST IN HISTORY

Joe Buskin and John de Vries wrote a song in 1943 called, "They'll be a Hot time in the Town of Berlin," It was very clear about what the "Yanks" would do when they got there. It was performed by Bing Crosby with the Andrews Sisters, and also by Frank Sinatra. Unfortunately, the Yanks did not make it to Berlin in 1943.

The Ninth Air Force

Bernard Sweet of Centerville, and Douglas W. Pitt of Houghton flew with the Ninth.

Douglas Pitt of Houghton entered the service as an enlisted man on August 13, 1941. He took his initial training at Fort Bragg, NC. His brother David entered on the same day and was also at Fort Bragg. Both men later switched from Army Ground Forces to the Army Air Corps although David remained an enlisted man. Douglas became an Air Corps Aviation Cadet and took his training at Moody Field in Georgia. He completed his training in May 1943. He likely was then granted 30 days leave.

Douglas' home town newspaper reported that he returned home from overseas on December 6, 1944 after serving 16 months indicating that he arrived overseas in August 1943. His assignment to the 387th Bombardment Group, 588th Bomb Squadron likely occurred quickly. He probably entered combat, as part of the 8th Air Force, no later than September 1944 from Chipping Ongar Air Base, England. He and the group would remain there, even after the October 1943 transfer to the Ninth Air Force, until July 18, 1944. At the time a tour of duty required the completion of 50 combat missions. Initially the group flew tactical missions against air drones. During the 43-44 winter they attacked the deadly VI and V2 rocket sites. During one raid over France, Douglas was wounded, thus earning his Purple Heart.

Now came Big Week, 2/20-25/1944. The plan was simple – gain total control of the air. The Allied Air Forces attacked everywhere. The 387th hit airfields at Venlo and Leeuwarden. The German Air Force had to fight which is what the Allies wanted. Their intent was to make the Luftwaffe fight and then destroy it. They basically did just that. After Big Week it was never again able to combat allied Air Forces on a broad front. It was virtually a no show at Normandy. Douglas and the 387th attacked coastal batteries and bridges in the invasion buildup. On D-Day they pounded the east beaches of the Cherbourg Peninsula. After spending billions of Deutschemarks to build it, without air cover, Hitler's invincible wall around Europe disappeared in less than a day. On D-Day, Douglas and the 387th continued to attack. They pounded the areas around Normandy and then attacked the invasion coast itself. Throughout the month they continued to effectively support the ground forces invading Hitler's 1000-year Reich, which now had just a few months of its actual 12 years 4 months of life left. Hitler had miscalculated the life span of his Reich by over 987 years.

Post-invasion, Douglas and the 387th participated in the intense St. Lo missions and attacks on strong German forces at Brest. They continued to support ground troops by destroying railroad bridges, road junctions and fuel dumps. The 387th flew 396 combat missions during the war, about 30 with the Eighth.
.

During his 46 months of total service Douglas earned the American Defense Medal, American Theater Medal, the European African Middle East Theater Medal, the World War II Victory Medal, a Purple Heart, a Bronze Star, and the Air Medal with Seven Oak Leaf Clusters. He earned battle stars for each of the following campaigns: Air Offensive, Europe (7/9/42-6/5/44); Normandy (6/6/44-7/24/44); Northern France (7/25-9/14/44); and Rhineland (9/15/44-3/21/45). Douglas returned to the states in December 1944, and was discharged June 27, 1945 at Fort Dix, NJ.

Bernard Sweet of Centerville joined the Army reserves on May 15, 1942 at Buffalo. He entered full time active duty on October 27 and sailed for Europe March 23 1944. In the interim period, he went through the extensive and difficult training required of all who hoped to qualify as a fighter pilot in the Army Air Corps of World War II. This training included stops at Governor's Island, NY, Nashville, TN, Jackson, TN, Newport AR, Napier Field, AL, Dale Mabry Field, FL. Perry Field, FL, and Congaree Field, SC. He was commissioned as a Second Lieutenant on August 30, 1943, at Napier Field. He joined the 406th Fighter Group at Congaree Field, SC on 12/2/1943. When Bernard departed for overseas duties, he left behind his fiancé, Frances Westfall, of Caneadea.

Bernard, 2nd from right, receiving his Distinguished Flying Cross. Family Photo.

Bernard arrived in Liverpool, England on April 4, 1944, aboard the *H.M.T. Starling Castle*, a British transport ship. Between April 4 and March 25, 1945, when he was killed in action, Bernard participated in 84 combat missions, flying 161 sorties. Except for a brief return to the US between December 19, 1944 and February 10, 1945, Bernard was in constant combat. He continually exhibited outstanding skill, as both a pilot and as a leader. He rose from 2nd Lieutenant to Captain in less than two years and was flight commander with the 514th Fighter Squadron, 406th Fighter Group when he was killed.

The 514th flew the mighty P-47 Thunderbolt, one of the most durable, powerful, and destructive fighter-bombers of the era. Throughout the war, the 406th Fighter Group primarily flew tactical air missions in support of the Third Army and other combat units. This included close ground support, armed reconnaissance, bombing, and strafing missions. However, it also flew escort missions, such as the one on May 13, 1944, when it escorted 36 B-26 bombers to Abbeville, France. The 406th was originally stationed at Ashford in County Kent (Station 417) when it first arrived in England. It flew its first mission on May 9, a fighter Sweep over the NE coast of France, and attacked several locations. Following the May 13 mission, it flew its first dive-bombing mission, attacking a locomotive workshop at Cambrai, France, on May 19. Two days later it flew its first mission inside Germany, attacked rolling stock at Tirimont, Germany. Five locomotives, two trains and some sheds at the marshalling yards were destroyed.

On June 6, 1944, Bernard and the 406th provided air cover for the D Day landings. It is not known how many sorties Bernard flew that day. The 514th Squadron flew 4 missions on D Day. Each mission consisted of 16 P-47's. It is likely that Bernard participated in at least two of those missions. A history of the 514th indicates that the squadron provided air cover for 20 out of 24 hours during the invasion. The area they covered was code named "Utah." The 406th Fighter Group followed the same schedule over the Normandy beaches for the next several days. Following the D Day landing, the 514th attacked ground installations, defensive positions, bridges, communications centers, and rolling stock, concentrating on targets in the Cherbourg Peninsula area. The 514th squadron averaged two missions a day. On June 22 the 514th attacked gun emplacements at Alder-May, France. They encountered heavy flak and Bernard was hit over the target. He was forced to belly land which he accomplished successfully and returned to his base in another plane.

On July 4, 1944, Bernard's squadron celebrated by strafing an armored column, and disrupting communications centers. Later that month they destroyed a train load of tanks near Rouen and participated in the mass bombing of the area between St. Lo and Perrier.

In July, the 514th left England and took up residence at the Tour-en-Bessin Airfield in France. Bernard celebrated the move to France by shooting down an enemy aircraft on July 25. The mission that day featured mass bombing of an area between St. Lo and Perrier. A month later, the squadron moved to Cretteville, France. Their primary mission now became tactical support of the Third Army. At Cretteville they had to perform one of the least favorite duties of fighter pilots, dropping leaflets on German troops trapped on the Brest Peninsula, urging them to surrender. Shortly thereafter they moved to Loupeland, France (air strip A-36). Their missions were still of long duration, as Patton's Third Army was on the move. On September 1, 1944, returning from a support mission, they made an unscheduled stop and destroyed and damaged numerous planes at the Metz Airdrome.

On September 7, south of Loire, France, they destroyed a column of enemy vehicles and military transports, forcing the surrender of 20,000 troops. For this action, the group received a Presidential Unit Citation. They were looking forward to a sojourn in Paris, but had to skip it in order to keep up with Patton's Third Army. On September 24, they moved to Mourmelon le Grand Airfield.

Bad weather hindered flying for much of the rest of September, but in October, in only 19 flying days, they bombed rail yards and lines, tunnels, and bridges in the Metz area. This included a cluster bombing on October 9 in a wooded area around Metz that annihilated a heavy German troop concentration, resulting in 2,500 more prisoners. The US suffered no losses. On October 10, they strafed an airdrome at Biblis. Bernard was credited with damaging a HE-111. On October 20 they took out a train loaded with vehicles at Bad Kreuznach, Germany. On the 22nd, they provided equal treatment to a train loaded with half-tracks and trucks near Haguenau.

More bad weather limited flying in November. During 11 days of flying mostly close-support missions, they started using napalm. In December and January, the Group participated in the Battle of the Bulge. However, Bernard was home on leave during this period. The group moved three times while he was away.

On February 7, 1945, their third move, they settled at Asch, Belgium, and it was to this base that Bernard reported after returning from furlough. The group was transferred at this time to the 29th Air Tactical Command and were now supporting the XIII and XVIII Corps of the Ninth Army. During this period, they participated in 26 missions, all in preparation for the crossing of the Rhine. Many of these missions were to the Ruhr Valley. They attacked gun positions and cleared areas selected for parachute and glider landings as the Allies crossed the Rhine. The 514th Operations Report for early March indicates that it was "bombing and strafing enemy strong points of resistance. Motor transports, locomotives, armored cars, tanks, and gun positions were destroyed as the Jerries retreated toward the Rhine. In their haste, the Nazis were unable to evacuate their planes from an airdrome near Munster before the Squadron led by Capt. J.C. Bloom, attacked it and destroyed 20 aircraft on the ground and damaged 14. They also were reengaged by the German Luftwaffe."

Bernard never made it into Germany, on the ground. He spent plenty of time, however, in the skies over Germany. He was not a welcome visitor. He did not care. On March 25, 1945, only a month before the end of the war, the 514th Fighter Squadron flew three missions attacking the Bergen, Arnsberg, Korbecke and Hitdorf, Germany area. On the second mission of the day, 12 P-47's of the 514th (including Bernard) took off at 10:20 AM. They strafed 10 goods cars, bombed five large barracks, and attacked motor transports at four different locations before heading home. When coming in for a landing, Bernard crashed and was killed. The official report of the accident called it pilot error, although the family received a letter indicating that Bernard's plane had been shot up on the mission. A booklet was prepared at the end of the war by Bernard's unit, the 514 Fighter Squadron. It is dedicated to the 28 men of the unit who died during the war. Bernard's name is among the men honored. The booklet reports Bernard as killed in action.

Bernard Sweet crammed an enormous amount of combat into his 10 months in the European Theater of Operations. In those ten months, he flew 84 missions and 162 sorties. He also earned numerous combat medals including the European, African, Middle East Theater Medal, the Air Medal with 13 Oak Leaf Clusters (equivalent to 14 Air Medals), the Distinguished Flying Cross (the top flying medal and the 4th ranking medal overall), a Distinguished Unit badge, a Purple Heart, and two Battle Stars, according to a letter received by the family. Although not mentioned in the letter, he also earned the American Campaign Medal and the World War II Victory Medal. The Battle Stars were for the Normandy Invasion Campaign and the Rhineland Campaign. However, based on his unit's history, he also must have earned battle stars for the Air Offensive – Europe, Northern France, and Central Europe campaigns.

As mentioned above, at the end of the war, the 514th produced a booklet of its service. The booklet is dedicated to the 28 men of the 14th, including Bernard, who died during the war. The introduction reads, "This book is dedicated to these airman brave in battle who winged their way through God's firmament in great sacrifice and to those who, in faithful performance of their duties gave their lives. May their monumental deeds be preserved for posterity and be instrumental in bringing everlasting peace."

The Mighty Eighth (Air Offensive Europe)

"Hitler built a fortress around Europe, but he forgot to put a roof on it."
President Franklin D. Roosevelt – Roosevelts words make clear the type of war fought in Northern Europe during 1942 and 1943.

"It's the craziest sort of war. (Referring to the air war.) *In a few hours those men will be five miles over Germany on oxygen fighting for their lives. Tonight, some of them will be dancing at the Savoy in London, - - and some of them will still be in Germany."* Clark Gable dialogue from the movie "Command Decision." Screen play written by George Froeschel and William Laidlaw based on a play of same name written by William Wister Haines. Words that describe the strangeness of war being fought by air crews in the first couple of years.

In his book, "Fortress Without a Roof" Wilbur H. Morrison says that when Albert Spear (Hitler's Minister of Armaments) was interrogated after the war by officials of the U.S. Strategic Bombing Survey, he was emphatic in saying the bombing could have won the war without an invasion. He said that the war could have been won in 1943 if the vast but pointless area bombing had instead concentrated on centers of armaments. Easier said than done.

FCSD men of the Mighty Eighth included Alfred L. Colburn, Gerald B. Gayford, Bernard A. Mills, Charles M. Rice Jr., and David D. Wallace.

From the entry of the United States into World War II until June 6, 1944, the only major American force fighting in northern Europe, albeit in the skies above northern Europe, was the U.S. Army Air Corps, including the Eighth Air Force. The Eighth would eventually be the largest, strongest, and most destructive Air Force on the planet, and, to this day, the largest Air Force in the history of the world ever committed to battle.

Despite severe losses (The Eighth loss more men than the entire Marine Corps.), the Eighth Air Force took the war to Nazi occupied Europe; and before the war was over, it, along with other Allied Air Forces, had mostly leveled everything of any importance in the Third Reich. (The author visited Berlin several years after the war. The only remains of the Third Reich were Joseph Goebbels Propaganda Ministry and Hermann Goring's Luftwaffe headquarters.) The Allied air forces also defeated the German Luftwaffe on its home playing field and gained total control of the air over Europe. General Eisenhower told the Normandy invasion troops: "If you hear planes, you don't even need to look up. They will be ours." (That was not totally true, but was close enough.) The US Air Force flew 8,722 sorties on D-Day. Only four Luftwaffe squadrons engaged the invasion forces at Normandy. All three planes of one squadron were shot down. One pilot in another claimed a successful shot on an allied Victory ship. A third squadron shot down four British Lancaster's. The last squadron, consisting of two fighters, did strafe the landings at both Sword and Juno beaches on one pass.

The Mighty Eighth earned many distinctions during the war. One is really a badge of honor. In taking the fight to the Nazis, it had to fly missions deep into Europe. During the crucial years of 1942 and, especially, 1943, many of these missions were far beyond the range of fighter cover. Despite this, not once, not one single time, was a mission turned back due to enemy action. Except for missions aborted for weather and other non-combat reasons, the Mighty Eighth flew to and attacked its targets on every mission.

Great accomplishments are never free of cost. The Eighth's achievements were paid for with the lives of many men, including at least two from the FCSD area.

Gerald Burton "Buss" Gayford of Hume was born on December 7, 1914 (reverse the last two numbers and you have December 7, 1941). Buss worked for an electrical company in Buffalo in civilian life. His first love was baseball and he was a catcher on the Fillmore town baseball team. A redhead, he is remembered as a hard-working, fun-loving young man. (Buss was a third cousin of the author.)

On November 4, 1942, Buss was inducted into the military. He took basic training at Atlantic City, NJ, and technical training at Seymour Johnson Field, NC, and Mitchell Field, SD. Following completion of his technical training he was assigned to the 700th Bombardment Squadron, 445th Bombardment Group (Heavy). His next stop was England; and when he arrived there November 2, 1943 with the 445th, he had returned to the home land of his ancestors.

The 445th Bomb Group was stationed at Tibenham, England. Buss Gayford was an Assistant Engineer and waist gunner on the B-24, *Good Nuff*, commanded by Lieutenant Milton A. Patterson. Still fun-loving, his war time letters now hint at a much more serious side.

It did not take the 445th long to become a part of the war. On December 13,1943, the 445th flew its first bombing mission to Kiel, Germany. The *Good Nuff* did not participate in that mission. On December 16th, the 445th flew its second mission-- this time to Bremen. The *Good Nuff* successfully completed that mission.

On December 20, 1943, Buss' squadron was part of another mission to the German port city of Bremen. The mission was part of a series of attacks on Bremen, which was not only a key port city but also contained a large railroad marshaling yard and the largest submarine building works in Germany. This was a major strike with over 540 planes dispatched from several groups, including the 445th. More than 470 planes attacked the target. A total of 27 planes were lost and another 247 suffered battle damage. Over 300 men were killed, wounded, or missing in action. A Technical Sergeant Vosler won the Medal of Honor for his actions that day. The *Good Nuff* never returned from that mission. Thus, unhappily, it became the first plane lost in combat by the 445th Bomb Group.

Mission reports filed by other 445th air crews provide some clues to what happened to *Good Nuff*. In the battle formation that day, Lt. Patterson's plane was part of the high squadron led by Lieutenant Costain. Lt. Awalt, leader of the low squadron, reported that the high squadron seemed to be falling apart. It is not clear when in the mission he noted that fact. There are reports that two of the four planes in the high squadron aborted over the English Channel. Awalt may have been referring to those planes leaving the formation, although it is more likely he was referring to some later point in the mission during the battle. At least one of the aborted planes may have been (and likely was) replaced by a Lt. Raroha, who was flying spare that day. This is important because during debriefing, Roroha's crew reported a B-24 going down over the target. If Raroha did replace a plane in the high squadron, he would have been in the formation right next to Patterson's plane. Lt. Awalt also reported a plane leaving the formation at 11:27 A.M., about three minutes before the I. P. (Initial Point), the point where the planes turned to make their bomb run on the target.

The unsigned critique of the mission has Lt. Patterson's plane leaving the formation three minutes before the I. P. This information must have come from Awalt, although his crew's debriefing report does not mention Patterson. But subsequently Patterson must have rejoined the formation since the Air Commander's report of the mission specifically says that Patterson's plane was last seen over the target area, although "it was not clear it had bombed the target." This means Patterson's plane could have been, and likely was, the plane Roroha reported going down over the target area. (John Robinson, waist gunner with Lt. Wright's crew of the 701st squadron, in his book, *A Reason to Live*, wrote that he saw the only plane the 445th group lost that day going down over the target. Robinson also described the unbelievable horrors and difficulty of an air battle involving flak and enemy fighters in the freezing temperatures at 20,000 feet.) A 1949 letter from the Army to Buss' family also states that the plane was last seen going down over the target.

Given the available information, it appears that Patterson did pull out of the formation about three minutes before the I.P. The pull out may have been for mechanical reasons or due to enemy action. The Air Commander's report said fighters were seen, but did not attack. But some debriefing reports do mention fighter attacks. Further, a B-17 from the 381st Bomb Group was lost that day due to a collision with a German fighter. Whatever the reason, it appears that Patterson was able to regain control of his aircraft and continue with the mission, since two reports have placed him over the target area. Here the *Good Nuff* was hit by flak. The 1949 Department of Army letter states the plane "was hit by antiaircraft fire." The Air Commander reported heavy flak on the bomb run and over the target. Pictures exist of the air battle over Bremen that day and they show murderous flak. The pictures also show German fighters among the bombers. (These pictures do not identify the American groups being attacked.)

All the above tends to indicate that the *Good Nuff* went down over Bremen, but there is no other information. Neither the plane nor any of the crew, including Buss, was ever found. This lack of further information - prisoner of war records, German battle reports, etc. - leads one to believe that Lt. Patterson was once again able to gain control of his damaged plane and fly it out of the target area, almost certainly out over water, maybe around Bremen, but more likely over the North Sea. There it must have crashed, leaving no survivors. While there may be other scenarios based on the available reports, this seems the most likely. This scenario is a story of guts, determination, devotion to duty, and honor. The *Good Nuff* would have been entirely justified in turning back after its first problems at the I.P.

It is difficult to believe, despite the Air Commander's report, that the *Good Nuff* reached the target and did not drop its bombs. In every sense, these men had <u>fought</u> their way to the target. They did not do that to hold onto their bombs. The Air Commander's report is short and to the point. Less than two pages long, it covers everything from Assembly to Flak, to Fighters, to Return, to Lost Aircraft. The report is signed by the famous movie actor, then-Captain James Stewart.

Families of the lost airmen communicated with each other and with the government for some time after being advised of the loss of the aircraft. Their letters are full of hope, but so sad in retrospect. The families comforted each other with suggestions that the men had made it safely to earth and were hiding, or were with the French underground, or were prisoners. Buss' family tried to get information on what happened to him for years following the war. Unfortunately, even after the U.S. gained access to German records, no information on the *Good Nuff* or its crew ever turned up. It is an empty feeling to never know exactly what happened. Such a feeling never goes away; and in the back of one's mind, even years later, there is a want, a hope, a desire, that maybe, just maybe, the lost men will turn up. One feels that you dishonor the missing by giving up hope. The lack of finality stretches out the grief forever, and those closest to the lost ones take that grief with them to their graves.

The men of the *Good Nuff* were clearly heroes, although just as clearly, they did not see themselves as such. They had a job to do. They did it. They were up against a foe who pictured themselves as heroes and even more. They deemed themselves not mere mortals, but supermen, members of a master race. However, when they finally came up against average guys like the men of the *Good Nuff*, it was the so-called master race that blinked.

Like many 8th Air Force men before them and the many that would follow, with a damaged aircraft, and against what most people at the time considered the best air force in the world, the men of the *Good Nuff* completed their job. In the flak-filled and blood-drenched skies over Bremen on December 20, 1943, these men proved for all time that maybe they were not the best and certainly they didn't consider themselves supermen, but they didn't need to be. They were "Good Enough."

(Honored Men of the *Good Nuff*: Pilot - Lt. Milton Patterson; Co-Pilot - Lt. Marion Gore; Navigator -Lt. Robert Carlson; Bombardier - Lt. Eldon Smeltzer; Engineer & Top Turret Gunner - Sergeant James Maluda; Radio Operator - Technical Sergeant Loren Newell; Assistant Engineer and Waist Gunner - Staff Sergeant Gerald Gayford; Assistant Engineer and Waist Gunner - Staff Sergeant Kenneth Schyler; Assistant Gunner and Ball Turret Gunner - Staff Sergeant Lloyd Bush; Assistant ARM and Tail Turret Gunner - Staff Sergeant Frank Cassero. Also, aboard that day was a Lt. Christensen, who was a bombardier. No information has been found explaining his presence.)

Bernard A. Mills was a member of the Fillmore Central School Class of 1940, the last class to graduate

Bernie at Rougham Air Base, Bury St. Edmonds, England. NAO Photo.

in a peacetime year for the next five years. The United States would still be at peace when the Class of 1941 graduated, but it would be at war before the end of that year. Eleven of the 14 men, plus one female, from the Class of 1940, served in the military during the war. That constituted almost one-half of the entire graduating class of 26. After extensive stateside training, Bernard was shipped to England aboard the *SS Argentina*. They traveled with a convoy headed for Europe. The *Argentina* left the convoy as it approached England, heading for the port of Liverpool. However, they had to wait two days for a pilot to board the ship and take them through the fog and sunken ships to a dock. Bernard was then trucked to a replacement depot for assignment. While waiting for his assignment, like many

other soldiers, Bernard helped with the mail. Then Bernard became a member of the "Mighty Eighth", serving with the 94th Bomb Group (Heavy), 332nd Bomb Squadron, assigned to Group radar. The 94th was stationed at Rougham Air Base in Bury St. Edmonds, East Anglia. The night Bernard arrived, two B-17s crashed, killing nine men. Bernard was a radar/radio specialist. His job each day depended on to which of three eight-hour shifts he was assigned. The shift rotations generally lasted a week each. Personnel worked seven days a week, with an occasional three-day pass. While Bernard was extremely busy on mission days, he related that on non-mission days, he had nothing to do. There were very few days without a mission. Only weather kept the planes on the ground, although Bernard does remember a short lull during the 1944 Christmas season.

The midnight-to eight AM shift had to prepare the planes for the mission. Every mission day on that shift, around two AM, Bernard and the other radar experts received the day's mission orders. Those orders, extensive and detailed covering every aspect of the mission, also contained the frequencies likely to be used by the German anti-aircraft guns that day in the area of the mission. Jamming those frequencies was especially important as the bombers approached their targets. It was Bernard's job to set the two transmitters carried on each plane for jamming German frequencies. The 94th had three squadrons or usually a total of 48 planes whose transmitters had to be set before each mission. (Another squadron, the Mickey Squadron, was equipped with radar and did not require the transmitters.) Two technicians flew on each mission to identify and block frequencies discovered in flight that the transmitters were not set to block. Bernard said he and others were also responsible for loading the chaff, the tin foil used to confuse enemy radar. The chaff box was two feet high by two feet wide by two feet long. Each day, the bomb line had to be established. This was important in making sure US bombers did not bomb their own troops.

Bernard recalled that before one mission, a plane already warming up on its hard stand, contacted his unit and advised that the plane transmitters had not been set. Since it was believed that all the planes had already been serviced, the plane was assured that they were OK. The plane called again and was once again assured that the transmitters were okay. A third call then came in from the plane. This time it was the pilot. He told them that not only were the transmitters not set, they did not even have any transmitters on board. A quick check showed that the plane was new to the base and that the pilot was right. Transmitters were not aboard. Bernard was ordered to take two transmitters to the plane and install them. All of this was going on even as the bombers prepared to depart. Bernard boarded the plane and quickly installed the transmitters, including setting the correct frequencies.

As he prepared to depart the plane, it was getting ready to leave the hard stand and join the lineup for take-off. Bernard was anxious to leave, but a crew member advised him that the pilot wanted to see him. Bernard made his way to the cockpit, where the pilot lambasted him up one side and down the other. His words were choice. He was especially forceful in mentioning that without the preset transmitters he would have had to abort the mission. This really concerned the pilot as it was his first mission, and it was considered bad luck to have to abort the first mission.

Bernard, recognizing that the plane was seconds from departing, asked the pilot for permission to leave the plane through the rear door. The pilot told him to leave via the escape hatch. Bernard said that did not really appeal to him, since the engines were roaring and creating a massive back wind. The wind had already knocked his glasses off when he had entered the aircraft through the rear door. It would be even more dangerous so close to the engines. The pilot then gave Bernard an option. He could leave via the escape hatch or he could fly the mission with them. Bernard departed via the escape hatch, staying tight to the center of the aircraft as he made his way toward the tail and safety. Later he returned and found his glasses.

The day shift, 8:00 a.m. to 4:00 p.m., was primarily devoted to replacing and repairing obvious battle damage. Technical representatives from the various companies were also around during this shift, updating the men on new innovations to the jamming devices. One of the receivers, a 1000-cycle note (high pitched squeal) constantly had to be modified for a variety of problems. The same was true of a British navigation system (Gee) which constantly had to be adjusted. Humidity would cause it to break down.

The 4:00 p.m. to midnight shift was also concerned with aircraft readiness. Bernard's group would check with the pilots to identify any problems of which they were aware. Antennas frequently had to be replaced as well as nonworking transmitters.

Bernard's base was near Rougham Forest, thus the name. It was necessary to walk through part of the forest to get to the mess hall. The area had been heavily bombed by the Germans, and a large crater created by the bombing was difficult to see in the dark of the forest. Bernard related that one of the initiations for new men was to walk them along the edge of the crater on the way to a meal and then, at just the right moment, knock them into the crater.

By the end of the war, the 94th had flown 325 combat missions.

After VE Day, Bernard was transferred to the 486th Bomb Group (Heavy), 832nd Squadron at Sudbury. This group was scheduled to go to Okinawa. While waiting to be shipped, Bernard was assigned to the Army Post Office. His job was to reroute mail. He would look at the name on an incoming letter and then refer to a list containing the latest address of the individual. Then, he would readdress the letter. The war in the Pacific ended before the 486th could be transferred.

In late August, Bernard was finally shipped home, aboard the luxury liner, *Queen Elizabeth*. With almost 16,000 troops aboard, accommodations were anything but luxurious. Bernard reported that Jimmy Stewart and ex-New York State Governor Herbert Lehman were also aboard. Bernard was recalled during the Korean War.

Charles N. Rice, Jr of Fillmore entered the service on July 2, 1942. Charles was an armaments trouble-shooter for the 95th Bomb Group. It is not clear where Charles took basic and technical training, but the NAO reported that he was transferred to Ephrata Air Base, WA in November 1942. There the 95th underwent extensive training. It is likely that Charles received armaments and air gunnery training at Ephrata. Final training took place at Sioux Falls Air Base, SD. The air echelon then departed with their planes for England. The ground echelon, including Charles, after a short furlough in Fillmore per the NAO, moved to Camp Kilmer, NJ. They then sailed aboard the *Queen Elizabeth* for Scotland, arriving in early May.

In October 1943, Charles wrote the NAO stating, "I have recently received my first issue of The Observer. It was a day not to be forgotten. The one copy has been read by fellows from all over the country who are stationed near me. I read every line and believe me it was a thrill to read about the home town and local news. Even the want ads were very carefully read. You see we are very limited on reading material. There is a lot of morale boost in getting your home town paper. Sometimes I wonder if people realize that it is such things that give fellows more pleasure than a box of candy."

The 95th Bomb Group was initially stationed at RAF Framingham for a short period, but then was moved to RAF Horham, where it remained for the balance of the war. The 95th, the fifth oldest bomber group in England, established an enviable record. The Group flew its first mission May 13, 1943, attacking an airfield near Saint-Omer, France. It earned three Distinguished Unit Citations (DUC) that included one for participation in the famous double-strike mission on Regensburg and Schweinfurt. Instead of flying back to its base in England, the 95th continued to a base in Africa. Another DUC was presented for its complete annihilation of Munster, Germany.

This Group was then chosen to lead the first US air attack over Berlin. It received a third DUC for the success of that mission. The 95th participated in every "Big Week" mission. It flew its last mission April 20, 1945, a final birthday present for Adolph Hitler. Postwar it dropped food to the Dutch people, and transported liberated prisoners and displaced persons from Austria to France and England. It returned to the United States in June 1945. Charles sailed home on the *Queen Elizabeth*, the same ship on which he had sailed to war. After spending time at home in June and July, where he also spoke to the Rotary Club, per the NAO, he joined his group in Sioux Falls, SD, before being discharged in September. According to his entry at the World War II Memorial in Washington, DC, he served as an air gunnery instructor, and was a member of the 247th Army Air Force Base Unit. It is likely that these were all postwar assignments just before he was discharged. Charles received all three Presidential Unit Citations as well as the American Theater Medal, the European, African, Middle East, Theater Medal, the World War II Victory Medal and 6 Battle Stars: Air Offensive Europe, Normandy, Northern France, Ardennes-Alsace, Rhineland, and Central Europe.

The *Northern Allegany Observer* said it all. Its headline read "Former Fillmore Youth Lost Over the North Sea." That youth was David W. Wallace, son of William H. and Elizabeth Wallace. His father was then living in Warsaw and his mother in Syracuse. His sister, Flora Wallace (Washburn) (FCS Class of 1923) was still living in Fillmore.

David W. Wallace of Fillmore graduated from Warsaw High School in 1936. He joined the National Guard in January 1941 and reported for active duty on August 23, 1941. Initially he was sent to the Army's Camp Stewart in Georgia, but was soon transferred both to the Army Air Corps and Kessler Field, MS. David graduated at Kessler in March 1942. He then spent several months at Kessler as an instructor. In December 1942 he entered pre-flight training at Maxwell Field, AL, graduating in August 1943. David finished his training at March Field in California and was transferred overseas in January of 1944.

Units of the 453rd Bomb Group arrived at its home base, Old Buckenham, in East Anglia, England, in December 1943 and January 1944. David arrived in January. The group flew its first mission on February 5, 1944, when it bombed an airfield at Tours, France. David flew his first mission, the groups 12th, as co-pilot on March 3, 1944. The target was the railroad and railroad station at Oranienburg, Germany. Fifteen miles from the target, David's plane was forced to abort the mission. Electrical trouble caused its guns to freeze up. The Bombardier became sick and the malfunction caused the electrically-heated suits for the waist gunner and the top turret gunner to become inoperative. The top turret also became inoperative. David's plane was forced to jettison its bombs in the North Sea on the return. David's second mission was on March 5, two days later. This time the group attacked the airfield at Cazaux, but David's plane attacked the secondary target at Berger and successfully delivered its bombs on target. The plane's crew saw four Messerschmitt's 109s, during the mission, but only one made a pass through the group and it did not attack.

March 6, 1944 has often been called Black Monday, due to the heavy American bomber and fighter losses suffered that day, more than any other day of the war. That likely was due to the target. It was the first time American bombers had attacked targets in and around Berlin. Over 800 American bombers participated in the mission. The 453rd Bomb Group attacked the Genshagen Motor Manufacturing plant just outside of Berlin. The mission report states that there was moderate to intense flak at Brandenberg and Berlin, and that it was accurate and effective. The German fighters mostly went after planes unable to keep up with the bomber formations.

The 453rd flew its 14th mission on March 6. It was David's third, and last. His plane, piloted by Lieutenant Elmer Crockett, was hit by flak over Berlin and lost an engine. In his after-mission report, Crockett reported that they engaged in a running battle with German fighters all the way back across Europe. By the time they reached the French coast, they had lost another engine and the final two were damaged. Out over the North Sea, the last of their four engines quit. Crockett was able to glide the plane for a while, but then it became necessary for the crew to parachute. The plane was only five miles from the English coast near Yarmouth. Two minutes more and everyone could have parachuted onto English soil, instead of into the freezing and deadly North Sea. David Wallace was the next to last man out of the plane, followed only by the pilot.

Lieutenant Crockett wrote David's sister Flora, telling her that "two minutes more and we could have made it-- if that last engine had only held out a little longer. Although my boys knew they might never be picked up in time, before they jumped, they were betting on who would hit the water first… I was only in the water 10 minutes, but I was so numb I could not help myself when a British Navy launch saved me. An Englishman dived in the water to get me out. Another 30 seconds and I would not have got back here." Five of the nine men, including David, did not get back. The others were Robert A. Williams, the left waist gunner; Thail W. Wertz, the radio operator; Floyd B. Suter, the right waist gunner; and Floyd R. Rogers, the top turret gunner. Wertz's body washed ashore at Yarmouth a couple of days later. David's body was never recovered. All likely froze to death, although it is possible that one or more may have drowned. It is not known if Crockett survived the war. His plane was shot down on a later mission, however, he and all his crew parachuted to safety, just outside Paris. (The author knew David's sister Flora. Her daughters were his baby sitters for a while.)

In one of those strange twists of fate, by March 1944, the 453rd Group Operations Officer was the movie actor James Stewart. Stewart had been the Air Commander for a 445th Bomb Group mission only a few months earlier, when Gerald Gayford of Hume had been killed in an attack on Bremen, Germany. In another twist of fate, David's 733rd Squadron later set a record for the most consecutive missions flown (82) without a loss. The group flew B-24's Liberators.

(The 453rd arrived in England just in time to participate in one of the most important phases of the air war in Europe. During the last week of February 1944, from the 20th to the 25th, massive bomber raids were conducted on targets in Germany. The period is now famous as "Big Week." One of the imperatives driving this massive offensive was the imminent invasion of Europe. Before that occurred, it was important to render the German Air Force as impotent as possible. It was also important, however, to keep overall objectives in mind. General Carl A. Spatz, Eighth Air Force Commander, was constantly reminding everyone that the battle for Europe would not end on the beaches. A new directive to Allied Bomber Commands in early February summed it up. This directive called for "the progressive destruction and dislocation of German military, industrial, and economic systems, the disruption of vital elements of lines of communication, and the successful reduction of German air combat strength …" (Morrison). At various times during "Big Week," there were more than 2,000 American bombers in the skies above Germany. "Big Week" was expensive in terms of Allied lives and airplanes; but it broke the back of the German Air Force, which never again was able to challenge the Allied Air Forces everywhere over Europe. Now the German Air Force had to pick and choose targets and was essentially a no-show at Normandy. The 453rd Bomb Group participated in every "Big Week" mission. No information has been located that David flew any "Big Week" missions.)

A Memorial to David at the American Cemetery in Cambridge, England indicates that he received two Purple Hearts (Purple Heart with Oak Leaf Cluster). Purple Hearts were primarily awarded for wounds suffered in battle and for death in combat.

England

Many of the FCSD area men and women who served in continental Europe, North Africa and even the Middle East during World War II, reached those destinations through the British Isles. Most, not counting the men of the 8th and 9th Air Forces, primarily served in combat on the continent. Those who served in England included Robert G. Beardsley, Ralph E, Black, Elwin E. Butler, Alfred L. Colburn, Melville E. Lemonde, Roberta P. Molyneaux, Robert David Ostrum, Robert W. Stevens, and Robert B. Wolfer.

Robert G. Beardsley of Hume entered the US Navy on June 23, 1943. In the next two and a half years, he saw a great deal of the world. It is not clear what his initial assignment was after completing basic training, probably at Sampson Naval Station. However, the NAO reported in December of 1943, that he had been transferred to the Medical Corps, and that he would be stationed at a base hospital overseas.

The hospital turned out to be in England at Cardiff, Wales. There Robert served as an ambulance driver transporting wounded soldiers from ships, trains and probably airplanes to the Cardiff hospital. The wounded men were likely, initially, from the D Day invasion. Cardiff was a major shipping port. Some 75 percent of the supplies for American forces in Europe that came through England, were shipped out of Cardiff.

It is also likely that this assignment was a special or emergency assignment in anticipation of D Day. Such assignments were common in the Navy during World War II. This is further supported by the fact that, by August, Robert was home on a 27-day furlough. Following his leave, Robert reported to the Norfolk Navy yard for further assignment, which was not long in coming. On November 19. 1944, Robert boarded *LST 837* as a Seaman First Class. The 19th was the date of commissioning for the new ship, and Robert was transferred to the ship from the Naval Barracks in Pittsburgh. At some point between August and November, he had been transferred to Pittsburgh. Robert performed various functions during much of his time aboard *LST 837*. In April 1945, he was promoted to Coxswain.

LST 837 (Landing Ship Tank) headed for the Pacific, initially Hawaii. Robert now became one of several men from the FCSD area who served in three theaters during the war. *LST 837* was assigned to LST Flotilla 23, Group 68, Division 135. The *837* now began a tour of the Pacific. Its job was to transport men and material wherever they were needed. It carried everything from infantry regiments to bulldozers, trailers, dock mules, air compressors, tractors, and jeeps. It even carried passengers. And not only were these men and materials carried from island to island, many times the ship had to transport cargo and men from one part of an island to another. Add to this the need to change anchorage at many locations on numerous occasions, and you have a ship in constant motion. There was also the problem of being shot at. During its participation in the assault and occupation of Okinawa, the *837* survived several air attacks. Ironically, during an attack on April 25, it was determined that wounded crewmen had suffered from friendly fire.

When the war finally ended (on September 2, 1945, the *837* was at Saipan), the *837* was assigned occupation duties, which essentially were the same duties they had already been performing. These duties continued when the ship was ordered to China. Robert made it through the entire war safely. However, while on Guam after duty in China, he apparently was injured or took sick. He was transferred to the Naval Hospital on Guam on November 14, 1945. (The *837* returned to China.) After recovering, Robert was shipped home, and was discharged on February 1, 1946. In addition to his three theater medals (American Theater-Asian Pacific Theater-African European Middle East Theater) and the World War II Victory Medal, Robert earned a battle star for Okinawa, the Asian Occupation Medal, and the China Service Medal.

Ralph E. Black of Houghton entered the service February 5, 1942. The 1940's census shows Ralph living in Houghton, NY, but he apparently entered the service in Chattanooga, TN. He was born in Knoxville. His father was a Pastor and he had brothers and sisters born in both North and South Carolina. By the mid to late 1930s the family was living in Houghton.

Ralph's final pay voucher indicates his last place of service was APO 696. At that time the location of APO 696 was Bad Kissingen, Germany. The major unit there was Headquarters, 9th US Air Force. The 9th Headquarters had arrived at Bad Kissingen on June 6, 1945. Its primary duty was the administration of occupation forces in its area. However, his pay voucher also indicates that Ralph was part of the Army Services Forces, so he may have been assigned to a unit other than those discussed below.

The Ninth became operational in November 1942 in Cairo, Egypt (also APO 696 at the time) when the US Middle East Air Force was redesignated as the Ninth. The Middle East Air Force efforts were critical in support of British and US armies battling German General Edwin Rommel's forces. It is possible that Ralph joined the Ninth in Egypt. Assuming three months of basic training, and maybe some additional training, he easily could have arrived in Egypt in late 1942 with the Ninth. If he was with the Ninth from the beginning, he moved with it to Sunninghill Park, Berk, England in October, 1943. The mission of the new Ninth, under the command of General H. Bremerton, was to build a tactical air force to support the invasion of Hitler's Fortress Europe. By D-Day the Ninth was the largest Air Force ever assembled under one command with some 250,000 people and 3,500 airplanes assigned to 1,500 units. It consisted of fighter, bomber, troop carrier, air defense, engineer, and service units. Its people included pilots, navigators, gunners, engineers, clerks, mechanics, cooks, doctors, and truck drivers to name a few. It is not known to which unit Ralph was assigned nor what duties he performed, but it appears that he may have been assigned to Ninth Air Force Headquarters. At Bad Kissinger, the Ninth was primarily concerned with occupational duties.

On September 15, 1944 the Ninth headquarters moved to Chantilly, France. It would remain there until June 6, 1945 when it moved back to Bad Kissinger. The Ninth was deactivated December 2, 1945 at Bad Kissingen. The XII Tactical Air Command took control of the Bad Kissinger Air Field once the Ninth departed. It may have been that Ralph was assigned to or worked with the XII as part of a transition team. Ralph's pay voucher indicates he did not arrive back in the states until February 12, 1946. He was discharged March 7, 1946.

Clifford Blakeslee of Centerville entered the service on November 8, 1943. Since his records were destroyed in the St. Louis fire, very little is known about his service. His final pay records show that he did spend time overseas, likely with some time served in England. He arrived back in the United States on January 24, 1945 and was transferred on February 1, 1945 from Mitchell Field in New York to the KGH (Kennedy General Hospital) in Memphis, TN. This may indicate that he had been wounded. He was discharged on February 16, 1945. He served a total of some 16 months.

Elwin E. Butler of Centerville entered the service February 23, 1944. He took his basic training at Sampson Naval Training Station in New York. Elwin was assigned to Drew Unit 4. Drew units were organized to construct, repair, and operate captured ports. They were under the direction of the 25th Naval Construction Regiment. The mission of the 25th was to organize and train Naval construction units for movement of equipment and US troops over invasion beaches. They also participated in the unloading of supply ships. In this case, the units were vital clogs in the invasion of Hitler's Fortress Europe.

Drew 4, as well as Drew units 5 and 6 was formed from men from the 69th Construction Battalion, the 114th Construction Battalion and the 30th Special Battalion. It is not known if Elwin was first assigned to one of these organizations or was assigned directly to Drew 4 right out of basic training. The units were formed around April 4, 1944 which would have been around the time Elwin finished his basic training. Drew Unit 4 was assigned to the port of Malvern in Brest. The battle for Brest took place from August 7 through September 7, 1944. Following the battle, the Drew 4 unit quickly moved from England to France to repair and put back in operation the port of Malvern. However, the Germans had been so efficient in destroying the ports of Brest that, while repairs were undertaken, the damage was so great that the ports were only of limited use in the immediate future.

As a result, the Drew units were dissolved. Drew 4 was returned to England on *LCT 335*. It arrived at Southampton from Cherbourg on September 17, 1944. On September 30 it moved to Falmouth where it was broken up and the men assigned to different organizations.

Elwin was assigned to the US Naval Amphibious Base at Exeter. While the base had been one of the main shipping and storage locations, as well as the home of naval construction units during the build-up and initial days of the Normandy invasion, its role then changed a bit. The base was officially returned to the British, but the Navy's 1049th Construction Battalion continued to operate out of Exeter for the balance of the war. It is likely that Elwin was assigned to the 1049th, because he remained at Exeter until October 1945. The 1049th was a transportation unit that was involved in the movement of supplies. Elwin left Exeter October 20, 1945, aboard the *USS Champlain* (CV 39) for shipment to the US, probably Norfolk, VA. Elwin was discharged December 5, 1945, at Sampson Naval base.

Alfred L. Colburn of Fillmore entered the service on July 16, 1942. At that time, he was Principal of Cuba Central School, a school only about 20 miles from Fillmore. His basic training was at the Miami Beach Air Base, technical training at Fort Logan, Colorado, and administrative and personnel training at MacDill Field, Florida.

In April 1943 he was home on leave with his parents. By June the NAO reported that he had arrived safely in England, and was a member of the Eighth Air Force.

In August 1945 after returning home Alfred (Al) addressed the Fillmore Rotary Club. The NAO reported that he mentioned that he had been attached to the Eighth Air Force in England for several months and that he gave a comprehensive outline of his work which primarily involved planning bombing missions over France and Germany. Al served in England for 24 months all of it with the 8th Air Force. However, he may have been assigned to more than one 8th Air Force unit during that time.

His son Stephen advised that he was assigned to the 8th Air Force's 3rd Air Division. The 3rd Air Division was activated September 1943 shortly after Al arrived in England. At the time it consisted of three combat bombardment wings, the 4th, the 13th and the 45th each with seven or eight B-17 Flying Fortress Bomb Groups. It would add two more Bomb Wings and additional bomb groups prior to the end of the war. The 66th Fighter Wing was assigned to the Air Division in 1944. Its first Commander was the famous General Curtis LeMay who would gain even more fame post World War II as the Commander of the Strategic Air Command (SAC). The 3rd Air Division Headquarters operated out of Camp Blainey (Elveden Hall) in Suffolk. The closest 3rd Air Division base was Bury St. Edmunds, about 12 miles from Elveden Hall. Headquarters for the 4th Bomb Wing were located at Bury St. Edmunds (Rougham Airfield). Also stationed at Rougham was the 468th Bomb Group. It is possible that Al was initially stationed at Rougham assigned to either the 468th or the 4th Bomb Wing. It was more likely the 4th Bomb Wing as it, like Al, arrived in England in June 1943. At some point he was reassigned to 3rd Air Division Headquarters at Elveden Hall. At both locations he could have performed the mission planning duties he described to the Fillmore Rotary Club.

The planning for bombing missions that Al spoke about to the Fillmore Rotary Club took place at several different command levels. These included Eighth Air Force Headquarters, Air Divisions, Wings and Bomb Groups. The primary staff doing planning at each level were Operations personnel. Eighth Air Force Headquarters selected targets for missions from a prioritized list. The Eighth's Chief of Operations made target decision, force required and coordinated plans.

The Air Division then took over. They notified the Wings of the mission targets, the force to be used and the basic plan. The Division next undertook numerous specific activities including: studying the targets; establishing the mean point of impact (MPI), the intended center of all bombs dropped; identified the type and quantity of bombs to be use; assessed the force of aircraft needed; plotted routes and times; specified altitudes; and coordinated support by fighter command.

Wing operations staff now developed its plans. These especially included creating a coordinated plan for its bomb groups during all stages of the mission. Wing staff also acted as the controlling agency throughout the mission and coordinated changes and new information.

Wing personnel notified Operations staff at each group of the mission and the number of air crews the group would need to provide through a coded message. For each mission, security on combat bases was enhanced and personnel were restricted to the base. All appropriate personnel were notified. These particularly included the Base Commander, Air Executive, Intelligence, and others. Most important the men who would fly the mission were informed. The groups navigator and bombardier now became part of the planning staff.

Crew and aircraft status boards were updated. Crew and aircraft assignments were made. Intelligent staff plotted the MPI for the group. Material for the crews, including maps, photos and other target information was gathered. The group navigator plotted courses, distances, and times of assembly. The group bombardier computed bomb sight settings for the attack altitude. A detail time schedule was developed starting with waking the crews, breakfast, briefings, transport to planes, arrival at plane stations, starting engines, taxing to take off to first take off and air assembly. An hour was generally allotted from the time of the first take off until the group was assembled and ready to leave for the target. A detailed time schedule was also made for the flight to the Initial Point (IP), the point where the groups made the turn to fly directly to the target and arrival time on the target. These men were engaged in a deadly business. Everything that could be planned was planned. The lives of hundreds of men were at stake on every mission. While there were lots to do, it was done quickly and efficiently. This was not a day at the park.

In March 1945 Al was the guest of the Bournemouth, England Rotary Club. By that time there was not a lot of Germany left to blow up. The war ended a month later. Al returned to the States in July 1945 and was discharged September 4, 1945.

Lynford S. Fox of Houghton entered the service June 26, 1941. Lynford's personnel records were destroyed in the St. Louis file and very little other information has been identified. It is known that Lynford was assigned to Company F of the 7th Quartermaster Training Regiment at Camp Lee, VA during at least the period July through likely December 1941 and maybe longer. An article in the NAO in December 1942 reports him stationed at a camp in the south which could have been Camp Lee. That article also reported him home visiting his parents. It could be that this was a pre-overseas home leave.

No information is available regarding when he was moved overseas nor where he was stationed during that period of his service. It is assumed that he served with a Quartermaster unit. His final pay record indicates that he arrived back in the states, at Fort Dix, New Jersey on July 28, 1945 and was discharged July 31, 1945. He served a total of 50 months, with likely at least half of his service being in Europe.

Melville E. Lemonde of Centerville arrived in the United States from Canada April 23, 1923 when he was one month old. When he entered the service in April of 1943, he decided to fight with the armed forces of his native country. Thus, he joined the Royal Canadian Air Force (RCAF)

As reported by the NAO, Mel was initially assigned to a training base in Saskatchewan. By June of 1943, he was stationed in Alberta, training to be a pilot, according to the NAO. While there he suffered a severe injury to his foot and spent some time in the hospital. The NAO next reported that he had completed training at his camp in Valley Field, Quebec. He was now an Air Gunner. In April, he was home on leave visiting his wife Camilla (Paulsen). By May he was on his way overseas, just in time for the big show.

Mel was assigned to 218 Squadron, which was part of Royal Air Force (RAF) Bomber Command, Group 1. (Most RCAF personnel were assigned to Group 6, which was manned by Canadians. He was likely part of a replacement crew which ended up in the more English Group 1.) When Melville arrived in England, Group 1 was attacking V-Rocket sites, gun emplacements and railway centers. During June 1944, Group 1 dropped 15,062 tons of bombs, more tonnage than had been dropped during 1942 and 1943 combined.

At that time, 218 Squadron was stationed at RAF Woolfox Lodge in Rutland, and were flying a heavy bomber nicknamed "Short Stirling." In July, the Squadron was detached to RAF Methwold in Norfolk County. In August, it was officially moved to RAF Methwold. Also, in August, the Squadron started flying the heavy bomber Avro Lancaster, which they would use for the rest of the war.

As D-Day approached, 218 Squadron participated in "Operation Glimmer." The purpose of "Glimmer" was to fool the Germans into believing that the invasion would take place in the Pas de Calais area. It involved massive bombing attacks against the Nazi shore defenses near Pas de Calais. The goal was to keep German defense forces away from the real invasion sites. At this time, in a most unusual move, 218 Squadron was placed under operational control of a civilian physicist, Sebastian Pease of RAF Bomber Command's Operational Research Section. The purpose of this move was to assure that the deception was as authentic as possible. The operation was a complete success. German shore batteries opened fire on a "ghost" fleet created by 218 Squadron, and the elite 2nd and 116th Panzer Divisions remained in the Pas de Calais area for two weeks following the real invasion at Normandy. Hitler, totally convinced that the real invasion would occur at the Pas de Calais, refused to release the Panzer Divisions to Field Marshall Rommel.

In December 1944, Mel's Squadron moved to Cherbourg, where they remained until the end of the war. It was now primarily a transport unit, although apparently 18 Avro Lancaster's from the squadron did participate in the bombing of the marshalling yards at Bad Oldesloe on April 24, 1945. In May, 218 Squadron participated in the life-saving food drop to the Dutch at The Hague. Following Germany's surrender, the squadron's Lancaster's flew liberated POWs from the continent to England.

In July 1945, the NAO reported that Mel was home on leave. He and his wife Camilla visited relatives in Detroit. He was discharged on September 25, 1945.

On June 15, 1985, Father J. P. Lardie, Chaplain 419, 428 Squadron, at the dedication of the RCAF Memorial at Middleton, St. George, in part, said the following: "One day, when the history of the twentieth century is finally written, it will be recorded that when human society stood at the crossroads and civilization itself was under siege, the Royal Canadian Air Force was there to fill the breach and help give humanity the victory. And all those who had a part in it will have left to posterity a legacy of honour, of courage, and of valour that time can never despoil."

Lorenz H. Marsh of Fillmore entered the service on November 13, 1942. Very little information on his service has been located. The only file remaining appears to be his final pay record. That record shows that he did serve overseas, likely in Europe, as part of the American Ground Forces. He returned to the states on December 16, 1945 and was discharged as a Corporal at Fort Knox, KY on December 28, 1945. The pay record shows his home town as Fillmore. At a minimum, he likely earned the American Campaign Medal, the European, African, Middle East Theater Medal and the World War II Victory Medal in his almost 38 months of service.

Roberta P. Molyneaux of Houghton joined the WAAC on March 3, 1943. When the WAAC program ended and was replaced by the WAC, Roberta was discharged. She immediately enlisted in the WAC on

August 23, 1943. While still a member of the WAAC, she was stationed at Day
she likely underwent the six weeks of basic training that was common for WAAC's
at that time. Women were anxious to join the WAAC/WACs. Far more applied than
Only the most highly qualified were accepted. (Applications foundered at points due
segments of the society to denigrate the women who served.)

An article in the NAO in September 1945 indicates that Roberta had served two years
Assuming this is correct, Roberta must have arrived in England around July, August, or S
1943. In fact, a WAAC Detachment arrived in England led by Lt. Colonel Mary A. Hallaren in
These WACs were assigned to work with the 8th Air Force. A second contingent arrived in S
1943. It also was assigned to the 8th Air Force. However, a payroll document from Hondo AFB,
shows Roberta being paid for the month of April, 1944 at Hondo. Hondo was a training scho
navigators and Roberta clearly served there before going overseas.

Roberta's entry at the World War II Memorial says she served seven months overseas. An article in the
NAO in February 1945 indicates she had been overseas for seven months at that time. If that is correct,
she would have arrived in England in August 1944. A July 1944 directive spoke of using WACs in Field
and Service Forces, and Roberta's WW II Memorial entry indicates that she did serve with a service
command. However, her final pay record shows her returning from overseas on October 15, 1945.
Therefore, she clearly served more than seven months in England. If one assumes that the Hondo payroll
was her last at that station, she could have easily arrived in England by August 1944 or even a few months
earlier, making her overseas time at least 17 or 18 months. Roberta likely worked in administration.

The NAO also reported, in February, 1945 that Roberta served with a WAC Detachment at an Air Service
Depot under the command of General Morris Berman. That was likely Base Air Depot 1 at Buttonwood,
England. Air Depot 1 was the largest airfield in Europe, and was in range of Luftwaffe bombers. During
the war, it was attacked several times. Nevertheless, before the end of the war, the Depot repaired or
overhauled more than 30,000 aircraft engines, assembled, or modified 12,000 combat planes, and
handled 415,000 tons of supplies.

Roberta graduated from Houghton College in 1928 with a chemistry degree. She was a high school
teacher at the time of enlistment in the WAAC. It is not clear what her specific military occupation was
in the service. Given her background, there were many occupations that she could have handled.
Roberta's WW II Memorial entry indicates that the WAC unit to which she was assigned received a
Commendation from General Berman for its outstanding efficiency at an Air Force Command Depot in
England.

General Berman was not the only high-ranking official to recognize the importance of the WACs.
General Carl Spaatz, Commander of Strategic Air Forces in Europe, among other war time assignments,
stated: "The Women's Army Corps has been of inestimable value to our Air Forces operating against
Germany. Its members have worked devotedly, undertaking arduous tasks requiring exceptional
performances. Their success as a part of the team is a matter of pride to all of us."

The Supreme Allied Commander, General Dwight D. Eisenhower, said the following: "During the time
I have had WACs under my command, they have met every test and task assigned to them. I have seen
them work in Africa, Italy, England, here in France – at Army installations throughout the European
Theater. Their contributions and determinations are immeasurable. In three years, the WAC has built for
itself an impressive record of conduct and of service, and given the women-hood of America every right
to be proud of their accomplishments."

m was born in Hume in 1921. He enlisted in the service on March 15, 1943, at ___rk. Robert took his basic training at Camp Breckinridge, Kentucky. By April 1944, ___, and was about to take part in one of the most tragic events of World War II.

___peration Tiger" it was a massive rehearsal for the D Day Utah Beach landings by troops ___heduled to take part in the actual invasion. This rehearsal took place at Slapton Beach in ___land, an area that bore a resemblance to Utah Beach. Some 30,000 men were involved, and ___e as realistic as possible. Live ammunition was used. Live firing was supposed to cease just ___e men landed. Lyme Bay led to the beach, and the entrance to Lyme Bay was patrolled by the ___avy to guard against any possible U-boat attacks. The operation took place April 28, 1944. To ___t even more real, all the records of the 557th up to April 28, 1944 were part of the rehearsal.

___ much went right. German U-boats got into Lyme Bay and created havoc among the landing craft, ___lling almost 700 men. The live fire did not end as the men landed, so almost 300 men were killed by friendly fire. The official death toll was 946, more men than were killed on Utah Beach on June 6. Many more were injured. Of the 946 men killed, 38 were member of the 557th Quartermaster Railroad Company. All the records of the 557th were destroyed during the rehearsal.

Robert D. Ostrum was part of the 557th. It was scheduled to land on Utah Beach as part of the D-Day invasion force. He was aboard Navy *Landing Craft (LC) 507* at Devon. It was one of two LCs sunk by U-boats. Charles Ostrum informed the author that his brother Robert told him that, during the attack, he managed to get inside a gun turret, where he was protected by steel on three sides. His commander officer, within sight of Robert, waved for him to move, but he was having no part of that. He was, of course, eventually forced to abandon the sinking ship. Robert told brother Charles he was picked up by a British ship. Robert said they were then put ashore, where they simply wandered around town for a while. Disorganization reigned. It is likely that Robert was picked up by a British destroyer that put the men ashore at Weymouth, England. His LC was torpedoed about 2 a.m., and the men were picked up around 4 a.m. Sixty-nine men, out of a total strength of 166 in the 557th Quartermaster Railroad Company, were killed during the practice invasion.

The 557th was reassigned, and did not take part in the D Day landings. For the next several months it performed garrison duties at various locales, including Cornwall, England, Glamorgan, Wales, and Liverpool, England. Finally, on September 20, 1944 the 557th was ordered to Southampton, England where, on September 23, its men boarded an LCI for Utah Beach. They were four months late, but they had made it.

The 557th moved to Versailles, France, and then, on September 29, to a new station at Dol, Bretagne, France., where it was assigned to the 514th Quartermaster Battalion for administrative purposes. But its wanderings were not over. On November 18, 1944, the 557th moved to Fort des Flamands, Cherbourg, France, and on March 6, 1945, to Le Havre, France. Assigned to the 16th Major Port for administrative purposes, they worked at Depot Q-181. and remained at Le Havre for the rest of the war. At each location, the 557th personnel performed their regular duties. Robert was officially a Pioneer, or combat engineer. As such, he worked as a member of a crew in constructing and repairing roads and bridges. Robert was wounded in action on March 23, 1945. The 557th was located at Le Havre, France at that time. It is not clear how Robert was wounded as fighting in the area was essentially over. It is also not clear when Robert arrived in England. It was likely sometime in late 1943. In England his outfit trained for the D Day landing and then took part in the disastrous Operation Tiger. The 557th returned to the states on October 12, 1945. Robert was discharged December 10, 1945 at Camp Kilmer, NJ.

Robert W Stevens of Fillmore entered the service on October 3, 1942. Bob's son James remembers that his father was originally assigned, probably after basic training, to a bomb group and trained at both Walla Walla Army Air Base in Washington and Great Falls Army Air Base Montana. Both bases trained combat air crews. Due to back problems, he was removed from flight status. The NAO reported in November of 1943 that Bob was home on a ten-day leave. He returned to Salt Lake City following his leave. Bob was likely stationed at Camp Kearns, Utah, which conducted teletype training. According to information on Bob at the World War II Memorial, his military occupation was teletype operator.

In February 1944, the NAO reported that his parents had received notice that he had arrived safely in England. Son James believes that he was stationed at a location with Green in the name. The only US base meeting the "green" requirement was Deopham Green at Attleborough, England. It was the home of the 452nd Bomb Group. As a teletype operator (MOS Code 237), Bob would have operated a teletype, simplex or other kind of telegraphic typewriter for transmission and reception of communications. He would have kept a log in which a record of all messages received and transmitted was maintained. Also, he would have had to be able to operate equipment using perforated tape for transmission and reception, to operate teletype equipment at a minimum speed of 20 words per minute, and to be familiar with Army codes, the phonetic alphabet, Army wire and radio teletypewriter procedures, and Army methods of hand printing, as well as safeguarding cryptographic and transmission security.

The 452nd Bomb Group moved to England in December 1943 - January 1944, the same time that Bob arrived there. The group flew the famous B-17 and entered combat on February 5, 1944. As a heavy bombardment group, it participated in many of the key bombing raids of the war. The 452nd concentrated on key industrial targets such as the aircraft assembly plants at Regensburg and the ball bearing industry at Schweinfurt. It also carried out interdictory operations and helped prepare for the D-Day invasion by hitting airfields, V-weapon sites, bridges, and other objectives. On D-Day it attacked German coastal defenses. It also bombed enemy positions in support of specific ground actions, including the breakthrough at St Lo and the Brest offensive.

The group participated in all the major campaigns in Northern Europe. As a result of Bob's support of the activities of the group, he like the group, earned 7 battle stars, including Air Offensive Europe, Normandy, Northern France, Alsace-Ardennes, Northern France, Rhineland, and Central Europe.

Bob returned home aboard the *USS Lake Champlain* (CV 39), an *Essex* Class aircraft carrier. While the *Champlain* was completed too late to participate in the war, it did participate in "Magic Carpet" the return of servicemen to the US following the war. Bob boarded the *Champlain* in Southampton, England around October 19, 1945, and arrived in New York City on October 27. He was discharged November 1, 1945.

Richard A. Thayer of Fillmore entered the service on October 12, 1942. By October of 1943 he was stationed in Nashville, TN with the Medical Corps. It is not known in what capacity. In February 1944 the NAO reported that he was stationed somewhere in Texas and that he was shortly leaving for overseas. At that time his wife and likely daughter moved to Fillmore to stay with his parents. There were no more items reported in the NAO until October 1945. It is assumed that he served in the European theater of war. His military documents were destroyed in the St. Louis fire except for his final pay record. That record shows that he returned to the United States from overseas on October 25, 1945 and that he was discharged as a Private First Class on October 30, 1945. The NAO reported he had been honorably discharged on October 29 and that he, his wife and daughter were in Fillmore visiting his parents.

Fred (NMN) Williams of Fillmore entered the service on March 21, 1944. He was inducted at Fort Dix, NJ, and then immediately transferred to Fort Knox, KY and assigned to Company A, Army Replacement Training Center. It appears that he was primarily involved in armaments training. His military occupation was Light Tank Crewman. He was at Knox from March 30, 1944 until August 12, 1944. He was then transferred to Camp Gruber, OK when he joined the 1280th Engineer Combat Battalion. Arriving at Gruber on August 13, he remained there, except for a short furlough in Fillmore from October 30 to November 4, until the Battalion left for overseas shipment.

The battalion sailed from New York harbor on December 4, 1944 and arrived at Southampton, England on December 31. Fred spent virtually all the rest of his service in various hospitals. He was initially treated at the 186th General Hospital at Gruber. In England he was treated again for dermatology problems at both the 192nd General Hospital and Station Hospital 4150, where he was hospitalized from February 2, 1945 until March 13, 1945. Various treatments were unsuccessful and on April 14, 1945 he was shipped back to the United States, arriving April 29, 1945, and assigned to the hospital at Camp Miles Standish in Massachusetts. After a short period, there he was transferred to Walter Reed Hospital in Washington, DC where he was treated from May 3, 1945 until July 3, 1945 when he received an Honorable Medical discharge.

Scotland

As part of the famous FDR "Lend Lease" Agreement, the United States received permission to build four naval and air bases in Northern Ireland and Scotland. All the bases were located near the northern entrance to the Irish Sea. The primary, and almost sole purpose of the bases, initially, was to service ships, especially anti-submarine ships protecting sea lanes from the North Atlantic into the Irish Sea. Three of the bases were in Ireland. The fourth, in Scotland, was at Rosneath, located in the area of the Rosneath Peninsula, Argyll and Bute. Base headquarters were at Rosneath House. Nothing remains of the house and almost nothing of the base. Charles A. Cronk appears to be the only FCSD area soldier who was stationed in Scotland during the war, although others did pass through the country.

Charles A. "Pete" Cronk joined the US Navy on August 1, 1943. After completing basic training at Sampson Naval Training Station, and spending a furlough at home, Pete completed a six-weeks course in pharmacy at the School of Pharmacy at the Norfolk Naval Hospital. Pete was one of 24 honor students in his class of 600, and graduated with the seventh highest grade point average, 96.8 per cent. He then was assigned to the Sampson Naval Training Station Hospital.

In March 1944, the NAO reported that Pete's family had been advised that he was in Scotland. It is likely that Pete was assigned to the US naval base at Roseneath. Originally acquired by the US as part of Lend-Lease, following the completion of construction, the base had been used by the Royal Navy in support of Atlantic convoy vessels. In 1942, in preparation for the invasion of North Africa, the US again took control, and used the base to accommodate some 6,000 men preparing for Operation Torch. Following the Torch invasion of North Africa control of the base returned to the British, although certain areas did remain under US control. However, in August 1943, the US reacquired the entire base to prepare for the D-Day invasion. Pete was almost certainly assigned to Rosneath as part of those preparations.

Pete served as a Pharmacy Mate (Second Class) during the war. Pharmacy Mates worked under the direction of Medical Officers and performed general hospital duties, including administering medical assistance, treatment, and services to naval personnel. They served in shore hospitals and in sick bays aboard ship. Many received specialized training as did Pete, in pharmacy. As a pharmacy mate Pete was required to continue to attend regular classes in general medicine to maintain his skill and knowledge.

It appears that Pete remained at Rosneath until the end of the war. The base was decommissioned in June 1945 and Pete returned from overseas in July 1945. To celebrate his return, a dinner in Pete's honor was held in the Fillmore town park.

Azores

The Azores were and are a territory of the country of Portugal which was a neutral country during World War II. The Azores command a key geographical location in the Atlantic Ocean, and both Britain and the US wanted to reach agreement with Portugal for the use of the islands. In August 1943, Britain and Portugal reached an agreement whereby Britain was allowed to lease bases in accordance with a 14th Century treaty between the two countries. Prime Minister Winston Churchill was the moving force behind the surprise use of the centuries-old treaty. The result, however, was that England could now provide better air cover to convoys in the mid-Atlantic and more successfully hunt German U-Boats. In December 1943, Britain entered into an agreement whereby the US was allowed to use the British-leased bases for ferrying airplanes to Europe, and the US agreed to help England improve and expand the existing airfield at Lajes in the Azores. Eventually, the US was able to station combat aircraft in the Azores. These planes were used to assist the British in searching out and destroying German U-boats.

Colin S. Nichols of Fillmore entered the service on September 29, 1942. He took his basic training at the Naval Training Station at Newport, R.I., completing his training on November 14, 1942. Already an expert mechanic, he was transferred to Detachment 1, Headquarters Squadron (Hedron), Fleet Air Wing (FAW) 9 in Quonset Point, R.I. where he served until August 24, 1943. He would serve the rest of his time in the Navy with FAW 9, Detachment 1 as an Aviation Mechanist Mate (AAM). AAM's in World War II were aircraft engine mechanics that inspected, adjusted, tested, repaired, and overhauled aircraft engines and propellers.

From August 25, 1943 until November 20, 1944, Colin served with FAW 9-1 at the Naval Air Station in New York City. He was then transferred to Navy Station 815 in the Azores. While still assigned to FAW 9-1, it is likely that he worked with VP-114. It is not clear when he joined the squadron.

VB – 114 (V for heavier than air and B for bombing) was commissioned August 26, 1943 at Norfolk, VA. After a month plus of intensive training, the squadron moved to Naval Air Training Station at Oceana, VA. In December, it moved, initially, to Quonset Point, RI, and then to Floyd Bennett Field, Long Island. At Oceana, it focused on flight training, and at Quonset Point and Floyd Bennett on crew training. It then started training on anti-submarine warfare. This included the use of searchlights for locating submarines at night.

Even as the training progressed, parts of the squadron were being deplored. A detachment left for Casablanca in February 1944. Three crews were sent to French Morocco in March. Six more were assigned to Gibraltar in April. In June six aircraft trained in the use of searchlights were assigned to England to assist in the Normandy invasion. The remaining two aircraft of the squadron were assigned to Lajes in the Azores in late July. Two others, previously assigned to England, were also assigned to Lajes at this time. Another two arrived later.

Colin arrived in the Azores in December 1944. He served there for 10 months, half of the time with FAW–9-1, the other half with a Detachment of Hedron 11. FAW–9 was disestablished July 19, 1945. Colin returned to the states in September, 1945 and was discharged October 16, 1945.

VB–114 engaged in extensive anti-submarine patrols during its stay in the Azores. Some 50 combat flights a month were usually conducted, while using only six planes. The squadron flew PB4Y-1 aircraft. Maintenance schedules would have been tight. All these flights were over water, and many were likely at night. All 6 planes were equipped with searchlights.

217

Colin mentioned his service in the Azores to his sons Robert and William, although he provided no details. He did tell an abbreviated story of being on water, rice, and fish heads in a jail in Portugal. While AMM personnel did not normally fly combat missions, they likely did participate in many flights for many different reasons. Colin told his sons that they had to land in Portugal, with a full bomb load, due to an emergency, likely a mechanical problem. Combat aircraft would not have normally been allowed to land in a neutral county such as Portugal. The crew was likely jailed and detained there until their release was negotiated by the US State Department. Portugal carefully guarded its neutrality during the war, avoiding any action that would give Hitler or any other country an excuse to invade and seize the country. Colin was discharged on October 16, 1945 in Washington, DC.

Normandy (Normandy Campaign)

"Your task will not be an easy one. Your enemy is well trained, well equipped and battle hardened. He will fight savagely." General Dwight D. Eisenhower June 6, 1944. Ike's message to the men who would fight, and die, on D Day.

"I have returned many times to honor the valiant men who died ...every man who set foot on Omaha Beach was a hero. General Omar Bradley speaking after the war and paying tribute to the men who faced the absolute horror of Omaha Beach on D Day.

"They may walk with a little less spring in their step and their ranks are growing thinner, but let us never forget…… when they were young, these men saved the world." President William J. Clinton, Normandy, June 6, 1994 - 50th Anniversary of D-Day". Clinton honoring the men, both dead and alive, who faced the hell of the Normandy landings.

Invasion News Received with Far Deeper Concern than Pearl Harbor. It was noted that Fillmore, the Town of Hume, and our neighboring town citizens have too great a stake in the European invasion to pass it by as merely another phase of the war ... The 1940 census gave this township a population of 1,577, so roughly eight per cent of our total population is already engaged in this struggle for Freedom and Liberty. Northern Allegany Observer, June 1944

The following men from the FCSD area all earned a Normandy battle star. Phillip G. Ackerman, Edward M. Cole, Robert L. Cummings, Ronald G. Fridley, Evan W. Molyneaux, Donald C. Porter, Floyd K. Roberts, Herbert R. Rose, Edward F. Schramm, Robert W. Stevens, Bernard Sweet, Irwin K. Tuthill, Lowell J. Wilcox, Glenn C. Wilday, Oliver P. Wilday, and Robert Wolfer. To be eligible for this medal, one had to participate in the Normandy Campaign during the period, June 6, 1944 through July 24, 1944.

The following men participated in the D-Day invasion on June 6, 1944. Phillip G. Ackerman was a pilot in the lead squadron that dropped US airborne troops into occupied France, shortly after midnight on June 6th. Floyd K. Roberts, Lowell J. Wilcox, and Glenn C. Wilday all landed on Omaha Beach on D-Day. Glenn's brother Oliver P. Wilday, and Irwin K. Tuttle both landed on Utah Beach on June 6th. Douglas W. Pitt Edward F. Schramm and Bernard Sweet flew combat missions over France on June 6. Donald Carl Porter was aboard LST 338 off Omaha Beach with men and equipment aboard on June 6.

June 6, 1944 is considered by many historians to be the most important day of the 20th Century. It is one of the most important days in the history of the world. Had the invasion failed, the outcome of WW II could have been significantly different, and the world today would surely be very different. It did not fail. The Allies landed at five different locations along the coast of Normandy (Operation Overlord): the Canadians at Juno beach, the British at Sword and Gold beaches, and the US at Utah and Omaha (later dubbed "Bloody Omaha") beaches. In the movie *The Longest Day* Rod Steiger, portraying a US destroyer commander, spoke the following line: "We are on the verge of a day that will be remembered long after we are dead and buried." Whoever wrote that line surely knew of what he wrote.

Phillip George Ackerman of Fillmore, (FCS Class of 1938), was a C-47 pilot with the Ninth Air Force's 438th Troop Carrier Group, 87th Troop Carrier Squadron. His Group was selected by General Eisenhower to, in effect, lead the Allied invasion of Europe at Normandy. Their job was to drop paratroopers from the 101st Airborne Division and tow gliders behind the German lines prior to the Normandy landings. The mission which started at 23:48 hours on June 5 was led by the 87th Troop Carrier Squadron, Phil's

ike meeting with paratroopers from the 502nd Parachute Infantry Regiment, 101st Airborne Division. These men were dropped into France shortly after midnight on June 6, 1944 by the 438th Troop Carrier Group. Unmarked Post Card.

squadron. The drops occurred just after midnight on June 6. For its actions on June 5-6-7, 1944, the Group received a Presidential Distinguished Unit Citation for outstanding accomplishments against the enemy. Phil received his first Air Medal for his actions on June 6th. The award was for "outstanding gallantry," and further stated that "magnificent spirit and enthusiasm was displayed by Lt. Ackerman and combined with his flying skill, courage and devotion to duty, he remained at the controls of the ship without regard to personal safety against most severe enemy opposition, making the mission a complete success."

At this time, the 438th was stationed at RAF Greenham Common, Berkshire, England. General Eisenhower had visited the base prior to the start of the mission and talked with members of the 502nd Parachute Infantry Regiment. It was the men of that regiment that Phil's 87th Troop Carrier Squadron dropped northwest of Carentan, France a few hours later. Adair Wells Common of Fillmore had been a member of the 502nd in 1941, but had been transferred to the 513th Parachute Infantry Regiment when he became an officer. Adair had graduated from FCS in 1935 and likely knew Phillip.

The 438th Group was charged with carrying out numerous functions during the war, including flying supplies and reinforcements missions to combat zones, evacuating casualties, and hauling freight. Before the war was over, most of the Group, including Phillip, had participated in seven European Campaigns. Besides Normandy, they were part of the invasion of Southern France. Stationed at Canino, Italy, they again dropped paratroopers and towed gliders during the invasion. During their stay in Italy for the Southern France invasion, they also hauled freight, and participated in the Rome-Arno campaign. The Group also participated in the ill-fated Market Garden operation in Holland. They dropped paratroopers near Eindhover on September 17, 1944 without incurring a single loss. Led by Phil's 87th Squadron, the Group twice successfully flew supplies into Bastogne during the Battle of the Bulge. In February, the Group moved to Prosnes Air Field, France and operated from there and Amiens Gilsy for the rest of the war. During the Rhineland campaign, they dropped paratroopers across the Rhine. When the war was over, they evacuated Allies prisoners of war. Phillip received four more Air Medals prior to the end of the war. (Men who received more than one Air Medal received an Oak Leaf Cluster for each additional Air Medal to attach to the first Air Medal, rather than additional Air Medals.) The crossing of the Rhine was considered an invasion and all the participants received an invasion badge.

Donald C. Porter of Fillmore entered the service on February 15, 1944. Donald took his basic training at Sampson Naval Training Station. NY. He may have then participated in landing ship tank (LST) training at Camp Bradford, VA. It is not clear whether he attended LST training following basic training. He was assigned to Camp Bradford following the end of the war. It may have been both after basic and his war.

On May 5, 1944 Donald boarded *LST 338*. On June 5, 1944, *LST 338* sailed from Falmouth Bay, England, as part of Convoy B-3 of the D-Day invasion force (Operation Neptune.) The ship was carrying 21 officers and 292 enlisted men, along with their equipment. Also, aboard, beside the regular crew, were a Navy Medical Officer, 20 Navy Medical Corpsmen, an Army Medical Officer, and two Army medics to handle battle casualties. As the ship was being used as the Flagship for both the Group and the Division, the Commander of LST Group 36 and his staff were also onboard.

The Convoy moved slowly, too slowly as far as many of the men were concerned. After-action reports constantly comment that the slowness of the ship made it hard to maintain position within the convoy. The Commanding Officer of *LST 338* (D.A. Stratton) wrote that the convoy was routed too slowly: "Points were given not to be passed before a certain time and to meet these requirements we seldom got to two- thirds speed on our engines. For the most part it was one-third on one engine and then on the other. The sea and wind swept the tows faster than we could go. At times the tows were almost abeam. The ship in the meantime was rolling violently in the trough and the convoy was scattered, drifting from the bounds of the swept channel." The reason for slowness however, was due to the invasion plan. *LST 338* anchored off Easy Red Beach in the Omaha sector at 1145 on June 7. It did not unload until 0900 on June 8. The ship took seven battles casualties back to England.

On June 13, *LST 338* loaded a contingent of British officers and men, and delivered them to Gold beach on June 15. Returning to England, the *338* loaded another British contingent on June 16, and delivered them to Gold Beach on the 18th.

Donald had been in the Navy only four months, and had been an eyewitness and a participant in one of the most significant events in world history. *LST 338* however, had also participated in the landings at Gela in Sicily and Salerno in Italy. Commander Stratton wrote that, "As far as this ship is concerned, Neptune was a quiet operation compared to those at Gela and Salerno in which it took part."

Donald remained aboard *LST 338* until the end of the war in Europe. On July 17, 1945, he was transferred to Camp Bradford in Norfolk, VA. He then served aboard the *USS Marlboro*, (APB-38) a barracks ship, with the Atlantic Fleet. Donald was finally discharged on January 19, 1946.

"Omaha Beach will become, unquestionably, another glorious page in American History, but on the morning of June 6, 1944, it was a cold, wet, shell-splattered hell; and it will be forever etched in the memory of the men of the 58th (Armored Field Artillery Battalion) who participated in that landing. The beach and the defenses beyond the beach had been thoroughly bombed and shelled both by warships and guns on the landing craft. But as the small landing craft grounded and their ramps went down, a murderous crossfire from well-emplaced machine gun nests cut them down. Mortars and artillery fire crashed along the water's edge and men died in the water, and they died on the shore; and all that long day, Death walked the beach at Vierville-sur-Mer." From the "*Story of the 58th Armored Field Artillery Battalion*," National Archives. Written in 1945.

Floyd K. Roberts of Fillmore, (formerly of Bliss) was a member of the 58th Armored Field Artillery Battalion that landed on Omaha Beach on June 6, 1945 at H + 90 (0800). On D Day, June 6, 1944, H Hour was 0630 AM. Floyd had moved to Fillmore in the mid-1930's to work for farmer Edwin Minard. (He was engaged to Edwin's daughter Florine when he joined the military.) He entered the service February 7, 1941, and was assigned to the 1st Armored Tank Corps at Fort Knox, KY. Floyd was trained as a radio operator/repair man. He received further training at Fort Benning, GA, and in mid-1943 was ordered to the Personnel Replacement Depot at Greenville, PA. In June 1943 he boarded a ship for North Africa. Floyd joined the 58th Armored Field Artillery Battalion there.

The 58th was already a battle-seasoned outfit, having landed at Casablanca during the North Africa campaign. Floyd likely joined the 58th at El Alia, Tunisia, just prior to the Sicily invasion. For that invasion, the 58th was divided into two elements, the first of which landed July 14, 1943, two days after the initial invasion. It is not known to which element Floyd was assigned, but the first element began fighting on July 16 near Favara. It was in constant action and movement for the next several days, until it literally ran out of gas on July 21 near Corleone, a small village with no meaning then, but a name that became familiar to almost all Americans some 40 years later. A few days later, on July, 26, the 58th Battalion was reunited in the hills above Petralia. The battalion continued its assault across Sicily, attacking successfully Mistretta, where under constant fire, the first member of the battalion was KIA. A and B batteries, on August 7, participated in a successful amphibious assault at San Agata. On August 10, a second amphibious assault at Brolo was not as successful, and the battalion took heavy casualties Most of their equipment was destroyed and the men fought with the infantry for several days until additional equipment arrived. Brolo was taken, and on August 12 the war in Sicily was over for the 58th. The entire Sicilian campaign ended five days later.

The 58th Battalion now enjoyed several months of relief from combat, although not from training. Sailing from Palermo, Sicily, on November 18, the battalion arrived in Glasgow on December 9 and then traveled by train to Ivybridge, England. The history of the 58th describes its time in Ivybridge as the best period of its service, despite intensified training for the most important invasion in history. The 58th was scheduled to participate in its third amphibious landing, this time at Normandy, on deadly Omaha Beach.

Elements of the battalion landed periodically through the long June 6 day on the western end of Omaha beach at Vierville-sur-Mer, with the first element landing at 0630, H Hour. By 1830 the entire battalion was ashore. The *Story of the 58th* described the situation. "Personnel were scattered up and down more than a mile of beach, wet, shivering, and slightly bewildered. The beach was littered with wreckage and the still, twisted forms of men who had gone as far into France as they were going to go." But the 58th regrouped, and during the first hectic hours of the landing, provided the only effective artillery support on their stretch of beach. The *Story of the 58th* also reported that, "for the first few days our FO's (Forward Observers) and liaisons provided the only communication for elements of the Infantry and Rangers." Giving his Army occupation, it is possible that Floyd was part of that communication system.

The 58th now joined the push off the beach and across Europe. This unit continued to be independent, and was assigned as necessary to infantry and armored units. It pushed through France, Belgium, Luxembourg and then into Germany. The next few months saw constant advances, severe conflict, and furious battles. The 58th suffered many fatalities, especially in its officer corps. At one point, its units were virtually without leadership. Clearly the officers of the 58th led from the front. In December, the advance slowed and then stopped due to the surprise German winter offensive. On December 16, the battalion was ordered to Wiltz, Luxembourg. That same night German parachutists dropped near the battalion and had to be rounded up. The next two days the 58th was under constant air attacks. Their route led them through Bastogne. It became obvious that something big was going on and just after leaving Bastogne, a decision was made to dig in and fight. The German advance was powerful and swift. The 58th was ordered back to Bastogne, but it was too late. By December 22 the Battalion was surrounded, and its equipment nearly destroyed. Its personnel were ordered to destroy their remaining equipment and then to break into small groups and walk out of their encircled position. A heavy snowstorm was both an aid and a deterrent. It was during this withdrawal, on December 22, that Floyd was killed in action. He would never know, but he and his battalion had participated in one of the most famous battles in American history, a battle that would eventually be won by the US Army. Although a list of those lost has never been compiled, Floyd will forever be one of the "Battling Bastards of Bastogne."

Floyd's body was recovered and he is buried at the Luxembourg American Cemetery. Floyd's brothers believed that Floyd may have been one of the GIs murdered by 1st SS Panzer Division (part of the Waffen SS) troops under the command of Standartenfuhrer (Colonel) Joachim Pieper during the Battle of the Bulge. News from Europe reported that many of the murdered victims were American artillery observers. Floyd was an observer with the 58th Armored Artillery Battalion. It was later learned that the murdered artillery observers were members of the 285th Field Artillery Observation Battalion. While these murders were the most famous, known as the Malmedy murders, they constituted only 84 of the 362 American POWs murdered by their captors.

(Members of the Panzer Division, including Colonel Pieper and his boss General (Oberst-Gruppenfuhrer) Sepp Dietrich, were later tried for the murders by the US Military Tribunal at Dachau. While most were convicted and sentenced to death or life in prison, including Pieper and Dietrich, all were released after serving much lesser periods. These commutations were due to evidence of pre-trial mistreatment of the prisoners in obtaining confessions, among other actions. Pieper was murdered in 1976 while living in France by either Communists or more likely members of the former French resistance. John Beardsley of Fillmore served at Dachau during the trials.)

Edward F. Schramm of Centerville entered the service on February 1, 1943. Edward was one of those

men who lived in the FCSD area (Centerville) but did not attend FCS. It is not clear where Edward received basic training or gunnery training. His eventual group, the 390th Bomb Group, was activated at Blythe, CA in March 1943, and trained at both Geiger Field, Spokane, WA, and Grenier Field, Manchester, NH. It shipped overseas in July 1943 from Presque Isle, Maine, and was assigned to Station 153 at Framlingham, England. Edward likely did not arrive overseas as a replacement until April or May 1944. He was assigned to the 390th Bomb Group, 571st Bomb Squadron, as a left waist gunner. He participated in the D-Day invasion on June 6, 1944. It appears it was his first combat mission. That day the 390th mission was to support

Ed Schramm - top row, 2nd from right. Gilbert Crew, Framlingham, England. National Archives Photo.

the 3rd British Infantry Division. The 3rd Division's objective was to capture a strategic point that lay astride the Orne River and the Caen Canal. It was also a road hub that allowed units holding the area to rapidly shift forces to support key objectives. Unfortunately, the 3rd was unable to achieve its objective that day, even with the assistance of the 390th. Bombing took place at Caen some 15 minutes before the Normandy landings. In July, the 390th attacked enemy artillery during the breakthrough at St. Lo.

Edward participated in at least 33 missions. He flew 17 missions with Lieutenant Quniter O. Gilbert's crew, (# 79) most likely in the B-17, "Joker." He flew 15 more missions with Crew # 64 and one mission with the 96th Bomb group. Twenty of his missions with the 390th were over Germany, another seven over France. He participated in two missions over Poland, and one each to Holland, Belgium, and Romania. The mission with the 96th Bomb Group was to Szolnok, Hungary. As an indication of the level of effort being exerted on the Germans, Edward flew all 33 of his missions during the period June 6 to October 2, 1944. The October 2 mission was to Kassel, Germany. While it was Edward's 33rd mission, it was the 198th mission flown by the 390th Bomb Group. Edward participated in several key missions. On June 12, his group attacked V-2 bunkers at St. Omer, France. The bunkers were enormous. In addition to reception, storage and preparing the V-2 rockets for launch, there was also on-site preparation of the liquid oxygen that powered the rockets and two pads for launching. On July 19 the group attacked

Schweinfurt, a center for producing antifriction ball- bearings. On July 21, it went to Regensburg and attacked a Messerschmitt BF 109 factory and an oil refinery. These last two cities would later be the focus of a famous, but unsuccessful, double strike mission. There were numerous missions to both locations, both before and after the July 19 and July 21 strikes. Edward earned the American Campaign Medal, the European African Middle East Theater Medal, the World War II Victory Medal and three battle stars: Normandy, Rhineland, and Central Europe. He also earned at least one Air Medal.

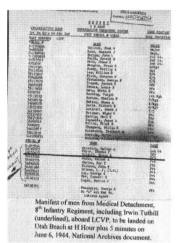

Manifest of men from Medical Detachment, 8th Infantry Regiment, including Irwin Tuthill (underlined), aboard LCVP, to be landed on Utah Beach at H Hour plus 5 minutes on June 6, 1944. National Archives document.

Irwin K. Tuthill of Fillmore landed on Utah Beach on D Day, June 6, 1944, with the first wave (Victor Sector) at H + 5 minutes. (H Hour was 0630 AM.) Irwin was aboard an LCVP (Landing Craft, Vehicle, Personnel) with members of the 8th Infantry, 3rd Battalion Headquarters Company. (See copy of manifest with Irwin's name.) Counting Irwin, there were 37 men aboard the LCVP. Before the day was over, Irwin, part of the Medical Detachment, 8th Infantry Regiment, 4th Infantry Division, had earned a Bronze Star for Valor and the Medical Combat Medal.

His Bronze Star citation reads in part, "…for heroic achievement in connection with military operations against an enemy of the United States near St. Mere du Mont, France, 6 June 1944. Technician Third Grade Tuthill was serving as a surgical technician on the night of D-Day, following the initial landings on Normandy. Many glider troops had crashed among the hedgerows in forced landings close behind the lines. The enemy had good observation on their positions and immediately launched a concentration of fire on the area. Many casualties resulted. Technician Third Grade Tuthill, disregarding the hazards of the concentrated enemy fire, advanced to the shelled area and administered excellent first aid to the casualties. His untiring efforts surely saved the lives of many men. Technician Third Medical Grade Tuthill's courage and devotion to duty reflect credit upon himself and the military service. By Command of Major General Hayes."

Irwin served with the Medical Detachment all the way to Germany. More of his service is discussed later in the book.

Irwin K. Tuttle graduated from FCS in 1937. Oliver Paul Wilday, discussed below, graduated from FCS in 1932. Like Irwin, Oliver served with the 4th Infantry Division, 8th Infantry Regiment, and landed with the first wave on Utah Beach on June 6, 1944. It is not known if Irwin and Oliver knew each other.

Lowell J. Wilcox of Centerville entered the service with his twin brother Lyle on December 10, 1940. Both men earned the American Defense Medal as a result of serving prior to December 7, 1941. By April 1941 Lowell was at Fort Devens, MA with the 26th Infantry Regiment of the 1st Infantry Division, the "Big Red One." It is likely that Lowell was assigned to the 26th immediately after enlisting and then participated in the October/November, 1941 maneuvers in North Carolina. The division arrived back at its home base, Fort Devens, on December 6, 1941. On December 7, the Japanese attacked Pearl Harbor.

Events then moved rapidly for Lowell and the 1st Infantry Division. By February 1942 they were at Camp Blanding, FL for additional training. In May, they were at Fort Benning, GA. During this period, the NAO reported that Lowell wrote his sister Anna, saying he was at a southern Army camp, but was leaving soon for a new company as a mechanic. Lowell was a PFC, and served as the regimental carpenter and an acting squad leader at the time. By June the division was at Indiantown Gap Military Reserve readying for deployment overseas. The NAO reported him home in July, and in September noted he had arrived in England.

The 1st Infantry Division sailed for England from the Port of New York on August 1, arriving at Beaminster in Southwest England on August 7. The division then prepared for the North Africa invasion. On October 22, it sailed for North Africa. On November 5, 1942, Lowell and the division made the first of three amphibious landings they would make during the war. They landed at Oran in Algeria. For the next two-months the division battled Vichy French, Italian, and German forces in both Algeria and Tunisia. They were in combat in Tunisia during the period January 21 to May 9, 1943. The division participated in battles at Maktar, Tebourba, Medjes El Bab, Kasserine Pass, and Gafsa. It led assaults at El Guettar, Beja, and Mateur. While in North Africa, Lowell was wounded by shrapnel in his back.

With North Africa secure, Lowell's division prepared for the invasion of Sicily. On July 10, it earned a second arrowhead badge with the amphibious landing at Gela in Sicily. Facing the elite Herman Goering Tank Division, the 26th blasted its way through 100 tanks and slugged its way through central Sicily, and then to the Straits of Messina. (Marlie Hodnett served in the 1st Infantry Division, 16th Infantry Regiment and several other men from the FCSD area were also in Sicily with Lowell.)

Part of a V letter Lowell sent to his parents from Sicily was published in the NAO in September 1943. "It read, "I have moved a little way since I last wrote you. We are now on the island of Sicily. I guess we are on our way home via Berlin. Ha. Ha. We landed here on the 10th of July. I am fine and going strong. I have a bad cold but ought to get over it soon as it is so hot and dry here. They raise a lot of almonds and walnuts here on the island. They are a little green but do not taste bad. The island is practically all mountains. They raise a lot of grain here also. This last birthday (July 18, Author's Note) is one I will never forget as I was dodging shells that day. We are starting to get mail now and I am expecting my pen and pencil set soon. Tell Anna to have my Fillmore paper sent on as she does not need permission from the captain now."

The 1st Division now headed back to England to prepare for the most important invasion in the history of warfare. On June 6, 1944, the division landed at bloody Omaha Beach at 0930, earning its third arrowhead amphibious invasion badge. It was part of the 18th Regimental Combat Team and landed on the section of Omaha Beach designated as "Easy Red." By the evening of June 6, American, British, and Canadian forces had blasted their way through Hitler's Atlantic Wall. His Fortress Europa, which FDR had already pointed out, did not have a roof, also now had a gigantic hole in its wall. The Nazi's had spent years and billions of Reichsmarks, building the wall. Now, in less than a day, the less than supermen of the free world had blasted a gaping hole in the wall of that fortress, and thousands of troops and tons of materiel flowed through it. The "Big Red One" with Lowell's 26th Infantry Division were among the leaders of that breakout. Lowell received a Bronze Star for "meritorious achievement in connection with military operations against the enemy in the European Theater of Operations from 6 June 1944 to 6 December 1944."

Following basic training, Lowell principal duty was as a Rifleman for some 15 months. He then became an Armorer/Artificer for the next two and a half years. Lowell was serving in that military specialty during the 1st Division's invasions of Oran, Sicily, and Normandy. During the last 10 months of his service (roughly November, December 1944 thru September 1945), he served as a Supply Sergeant for the 26th Infantry Canon Company.

It is possible that Lowell was carrying a paperback book when he landed on Omaha Beach. Early in the war, a mostly unorganized effort had been made to gather books for servicemen. Later, more organized, 1,227 different titles, known as the Armed Service Editions, were collected, and distributed all over the world. Certain titles were reserved for D-Day. They included, *The Adventure of Tom Sawyer, The Adventure of Huckleberry Finn, McSorley's Wonderful Saloon,* and *A Tree Grows in Brooklyn.*

Glenn C. Wilday of Centerville wrote his mother upon hearing of the death of President Roosevelt. She had part of the letter published in the NAO. It said: "He has been our Commander-in-Chief throughout the war and has always been a friend of the doughboy. He has always upheld the things he and we are fighting for. We will carry on, never ceasing, to win this war and to win the peace. By the help of God, victory will be won and justice will be done. Our nation, nor any nation, will never forget the great fight he has carried on and won." (NAO 4/1945)

Glenn knew of what he wrote. He had entered the service on December 12, 1942. He was in the 2nd wave in the Normandy invasion at Omaha Beach on D-Day. (The entire 116th Infantry Regiment landed within the first hour of the invasion at Omaha Beach.)

When General Omar Bradley, after the war, spoke of the "hero's" who set foot on Omaha Beach, he was talking about men like Glenn C. Wilday. When President Clinton, in 1994 at Normandy, spoke of the men who saved the world in 1944, he was speaking of men like Glenn C. Wilday.

Glenn was a Radio Operator with the 116th Infantry Regiment, 29th Infantry Division. Fighting ashore at

Wrecked Landing Craft Assault (LCA), Omaha Beach, June 6, 1944. This LCA landed troops from the 116th Infantry Regiment on D Day. War Department, Historical Department Photo.

Normandy was just the first step. Glenn and the Division blasted their way across France and into Germany. Along the way, they participated in four separate European campaigns starting with Normandy, and including Northern France, Rhineland, and Central Europe.

Following a titanic struggle to secure and get inland off Omaha Beach, in heavy fighting, Glenn's regiment captured the French town of St. Lo on July 18. They then joined the battle for Vire, which was captured on August 7th. From August 25 to September 18, 1944, they took part in the assault on Brest. Then they began a drive to the Roer River, fighting their way through town after town, including Sierdort, Setterich, Durbosler, and Bettendorf in Germany. They destroyed Julich Sportplatz and Hasenfeld Gut. At the Roer, they set up defensive positions that were held from December 18, 1944, until February 23, 1945. Crossing the Roer on February 23 they captured Julich, Broich, Immerath, Titz; and on March 1, they took Monchenglad Bach. By April 16, they were helping to mop up the fighting in the Ruhr Valley area.

Glenn's son Dana said that his father talked very little about the war. He did tell Dana that the 29th was within striking distance of Berlin when they were stopped. Dana also said his father commented that he spent the entire war within sight of the German lines, but never fired his weapon. (General Eisenhower made the decision to let the Russians take Berlin due to intelligence that reported the Germans were regrouping in the area of Berchtesgaden. He wanted to get troops into that area to make sure no regrouping would occur. The reports proved to be false, but his decision was necessary given the intelligence available at the time.)

Oliver P. Wilday of Centerville entered the service on October 6, 1943. He took basic training at Camp Blanding, FL. Oliver wrote Mrs. Frances Little of Rochester on February 2, 1944, that the training lasted

17 weeks. He was then in his 13th week. Camp Blanding was very level, and was nothing but sand and Pine trees. He was assigned to Company B, 231st Infantry Training Battalion. Oliver was working hard, and putting in tough days. The Army was a rough life. He informed her he was about to leave for two weeks of bivouac training. He was hoping the war would end soon so that "Doug" would not have to go. (Doug was apparently a relative of Frances.) Oliver also mentioned that rumors were flying about where they were going, but he did not believe any of them. Frances had written him on October 7, sending an article commenting on the waste of war.

The NAO reported in April, 1944 that Oliver was home on leave and attended church in Higgins. It later reported that he arrived in England on May 18, 1944, but a subsequent article reported he arrived in England on May 13, 1944. There is some question as to when Oliver was assigned to and joined the 8th Infantry Regiment, 4th Infantry Division. An article in the NAO in August of 1944 stated that he wrote his last letter home on June 9, and was sent to France soon after writing the letter.

However, the family believes that Oliver was part of the invasion force that landed on Utah Beach on D Day (June 6) with the rest of the 8th Infantry Regiment. The 1st and 2nd Battalions of the 8th Infantry Regiment were the first allied units to hit the beaches. The Division had sailed to France aboard the *USS Barnett*, and started boarding the landing crafts at 2:20 AM. Although many men were sea sick, the landings started at H Hour, 6:30 AM, on June 6, and continued throughout the morning. The division blew through Utah Beach and then relieved the 82nd Airborne at Sainte Mere Eglise. It then cleared the Cotentin Peninsula and participated in the battle to capture Cherbourg. During the battle for Cherbourg, Oliver was killed in action. The NAO, in an article reporting Oliver's death, stated that his training included both artillery maintenance and combat training.

After exiting the beach, the 4th Infantry Division continued to advance slowly but surely. Operations Reports show that, on June 9, progress was continuous but slow. On the following day it faced stiff resistance, but continued to advance, and reached its objective for the 10th prior to darkness. June 11 was spent consolidating its position, although it received heavy artillery fire during the day. Oliver's regiment again held its position on the 12th, but called in artillery fire and then attacked late in the day. It partially succeeded in seizing and holding part of Montebourg. June 13 was pretty much a repeat of the June 12. The 8th Regiment held their positions but were unable to move the Germans out of Montebourg despite two attempts. This temporary stalemate continued through the 19th. On the 20th a coordinated attack took them beyond Montebourg and toward Valognes. It was during this attack, near the city of Ruffosses, that Oliver was killed in action.

Oliver is buried at the Normandy American Cemetery and Memorial in Colleville-sur-Mer, Normandie, France.

Southern France

The invasion of Southern France (Operation Dragoon) was one of the most successful amphibious invasions in history. Initially planned for earlier in the war, it was delayed after problems with the Anzio, Italy invasion. However, following the Normandy landings it was revived, despite the opposition of British Prime Minister Churchill. The French Resistance played a major role, supplying vital information and sabotaging German operations, especially communications. The success of this operation became even more vital once the German's destroyed the port of Cherbourg and a violent storm did great damage to the artificial port created at Normandy. The ports of Marseilles and Toulon, captured during the Southern France invasion, enabled needed supplies to keep moving. This southern supply line was providing one-third of the Allies' supplies by the end of the war.

Several men from the FCSD area participated in the invasion of Southern France, including Almond E. Fisher, Carroll S. Phipps, Gustave George Prinsell, Melvin L. Slocum, Gerald F. Thomas, John "Dude" Thomas, Roland J. Thomas, and Glenn F. Williams

Gustave G. Prinsell of Houghton entered the service in October, 1942. He took his basic training at Newport, RI. He received further training at both Boston and Washington, DC. He boarded the mine layer *USS Planter* (ACM) in April, 1944.

On May 13, 1944 the *Planter* sailed for the Mediterranean as part of Service Squadron Five, Atlantic Fleet. After stops in the Azores, Bizerte, Tunisia and Naples, Italy she headed for France as part of the Operation Dragoon invasion force. The *Planter* supported minesweeping and buoy-laying operations during the Southern France invasion. Ironically this was the exact opposite of what the *Planter* had been built to do. This ship had been built by the Army as a mine "planter" or layer. From August 15 until the middle of November 1944 the *Planter* also served as the flagship for the commander of Squadron 105, Atlantic Fleet. On September 1, at Toulon, the *Planter* rescued 31 men from YMS - 21 (Auxiliary Motor Minesweeper), which had struck a German mine in Toulon Harbor. The *Planter* ended its support of the Southern France invasion on November 12 and returned to the US.

As discussed in Part IV, the *Planter* sailed for the Pacific on April 6, 1945. By August 4 she was anchored off Okinawa providing tender services to YMS's. *Planter* was later involved in occupation duties, including sweeping mines in the Japanese Inland Sea while operating out of Hiroshima. She sailed for home on February 25, 1946. Back in civilian life, Seaman Prinsell, became Doctor Prinsell. (see Okinawa section for more on Gustave.)

Gerald F. (Gatie) Thomas of Hume participated in three amphibious invasions during his military service. Gatie entered the service February 17, 1941. He took basic training at Fort Benning, GA, and then received advanced mechanics training at Ft. Knox, KY, where he graduated from the automobile mechanic school. Assigned to the 2nd Armored Division, during 1941 Gatie participated with the division in the Tennessee, Carolina, and Louisiana maneuvers. It was during this period the Division earned its nickname, "Hell on Wheels." It also gained a reputation for spit and polish. By January, 1942, according to the NAO, Gatie was stationed back at Fort Benning, and came home on leave. He brought young Janet Gayford a fancy pillow from his base. That summer the 2nd again participated in the Carolina maneuvers and then was assigned to the overseas staging area at Fort Bragg, NC. The 2nd Division had become the most maneuvered armored division in the Army, and it was about to face combat for the first time. They were moved to Norfolk, VA where they participated in amphibious exercises on the beaches of the Chesapeake Bay. They then waterproofed and loaded their equipment. Part of the division sailed from Norfolk, and part from New York. Both were headed directly to the beaches of North Africa.

On invasion day, November 8, 1942, the 2nd Armored Division landed at three different points in French Morocco. Gatie, assigned to the 66th Armored Regiment, landed at Port Lyautey, some 80 miles north of Casablanca. The Port Lyautey force was up against Vichy French forces. Opposition was initially light, but stronger forces quickly appeared. These forces were defeated, and the American took command of the area. Throughout the winter, they bivouacked in the "Cork Forest" near Rabat, simultaneously guarding the French Morocco-Spanish Morocco border and participating in more intensive training.

In April, they moved to near Oran, Algeria, where they rehearsed amphibious landings, among other  activities. Gatie was about to participate in his second invasion. His 66th Armored Regiment became part of Combat Command (CC) B, which also included the 1st Infantry Division. On July 2, 1943, Gatie was visited by his brother Roland. A picture of the reunion appeared in the NAO, with the brothers giving each other a big kiss *(see photo left)*. They had not seen each other in over two years. When writing home about the reunion, Roland mentioned that Gatie was out repairing some anti-aircraft guns when he arrived. While trained as an automobile mechanic, it appears that Gatie worked on more than just automobiles. Roland also participated in the Sicily invasion.

On July 10 and 11, 1943, the 2nd Armored Division landed at Gela, Sicily. Marlie Hodnett of Fillmore, and the 1st Infantry Division, beat Gatie ashore that day, but probably not by much. (It is not certain when Gatie went ashore, as, due to heavy surf, part of the armored division did not land until July 11th. Marlie Hodnett was one of the first men ashore at Gela. Marlie and Gatie, life-long friends in Fillmore, did not know at the time that they were both part of the same invasion force.)

Landing forces now began a mad dash for Palermo, literally blasting everything out of their way. On the way to Palermo, Combat Command "B." moved through Campobello, Partinico, Terrasini, and Cinisi. The advance was so rapid that south of Partinico, German engineers installing demolitions and mines had to depart so quickly, they ran over their own mines activating explosions. An Italian artillery battalion and infantry regiment in the same area were so surprised by the advance that they had to surrender without a fight. Palermo fell quickly. The division now engaged in more training, and in administering the captured area.

A short time before the 2nd Division moved to England, to prepare for the Normandy invasion, Gatie became ill, or suffered a non-combat injury. The NAO reported in October of 1943 that in a letter home, he mentioned being in a North Africa hospital. Gatie had been in the hospital for a couple of months. On August 8, thirteen men from the 66th Armored Regiment were killed by an ammunition dump explosion in Sicily. It is possible that Gatie was injured during that explosion, which was why he was in the hospital in North Africa. In his letter, Gatie also mentioned that he had been transferred to a different company. Parts of another letter from Gatie appeared in an August 1944 edition of the NAO. Gatie wrote that he was now in Corsica, and he expected to be there the rest of the war. He was somewhat mistaken.

The different company to which Gatie had been transferred was likely the 2670th Medical Motor Ambulance Company. It was disbanded in Oran in June of 1944, and a new company, the 599th Medical Motor Ambulance Company, was activated to replace it. Gatie's service record shows that he ended the war as part of the 599th. During its initial phase of operations, the 599th, working out of Oran, was responsible for loading and unloading Army and Navy hospital ships, and Army hospital trains. It also assisted with some British hospital ships and with some air evacuations. In June 1944, the unit was moved to Corsica. (The 599th consisted of three platoons. It is not clear to which platoon Gatie was assigned, but it was likely the 2nd Platoon that arrived on Corsica on July 6, 1944. The 1st Platoon did not arrive until August 1, and giving that Gatie's letter was published in the NAO in August, and it said he was now stationed on Corsica, it is likely that it was written in July. The third platoon had been on Corsica for a long time.) During its stay on Corsica, the 2nd Platoon supported the transport of patients to and from station hospitals at Clavi and Ajaccio. During its short time on Corsica, the 2nd Platoon transported 1,224 patients.

On August 17, 1944, Gatie's company gathered at Ajaccio to prepare for what would be Gatie's third invasion, Southern France. They were now part of the Seventh Army. The company landed in France at Riviera Beach near Cavalaire on D Day plus 4 (August 19). It was attached to the 1st Air Borne Task Force on the east flank of the beach head. From this point through the end of the war, the company, and the individual platoons, would constantly be assigned and reassigned as they served temporarily with different medical battalions, and other units. For nine straight days following their landing, the 599th evacuated men night and day from battalion aid stations at the front lines. About 3,870 patients were transported, and the company traveled some 112,000 miles.

Gatie's company moved to Dijon in mid-October and continued evacuations. In late November, the 2nd Platoon evacuated the entire 51st Evacuation Hospital from the Seventh Army area. By the end of the year, the 2nd was at St. Die. During this mid-October to end of year period, the company evacuated more than 18,000 casualties and traveled almost 270,000 miles. While the Allies advanced across Europe, the 599th moved right along with them, as reflected by their various locations: March 15, Sarre-Union, France; March 27, Neustadt, Germany; April 3, Walldurn, Germany; April 23, Welzheim, Germany; May 17, Kaufbeuren, Germany; June 16, Hessental, Germany; and June 20, Heppenheim, Germany. In preparing material for the 599th unit history, 1st Lt. Bruce Y. Brett answered the unknown question for Part F (3) of a questionnaire with the words, "Unconditional Surrender of Germany." The 599th had completed its mission. So had Gatie. He was discharged July 11, 1945, after 53 months of service. It is assumed that Gatie primarily worked on keeping the ambulances running properly, and various reports indicate that this could be a problem due to the hard use to which the vehicles were subjected and the fact that replacement parts were sometimes difficult to obtain. There are also indications that, on occasion, mechanics were used as drivers, as well as bearers for the wounded.

Glenn F. Williams of Centerville entered the service on February 2, 1942. It was the start of an almost two-year odyssey at military bases throughout the US. His first stop was basic training at Fort McClellan in Alabama. He was then stationed for several months at the Fort Rodman Coast Defense Facility near New Bedford, MA. According to the NAO and his separation papers, he then made stops at Framingham, MA., Fort Devens, MA, and Machias, Me. By January 1944, he was at Fort Meade in Maryland for a few weeks prior to being shipped overseas. On January 21, 1944, Glenn departed the states for the Mediterranean Theater of Operations, arriving February 1, 1944 at Anzio Beach in Italy. Here he joined Company I, 30th Infantry Regiment, 3rd Infantry Division, which had landed on Anzio on January 22. From his arrival until the end of the war, Glenn would be in almost constant combat.

Glenn suffered the first of four wounds at Anzio, likely on February 29, when three German Divisions attacked the beachhead. That day the division suffered 900 casualties, the most suffered by a single division in any one day during the war. Glenn wrote home in May reporting he had recovered from a wound suffered in February and that he was back at duty. (Glenn's discharge record does not list this wound. See paragraph on awards below.) In late May, the 3rd Division led the Fifth's Army thrust out of Anzio where it had been bottled up for four months.

Shortly after this, the NAO received a press release directly from Headquarters, Fifth Army in Italy. The release mentioned Glenn by name. In part, it read, "PFC Williams and others infantrymen of the squad of Staff Sergeant Russell Dunham had a "field day" capturing Germans in the Fifth's Army great offensive in Italy. Part of the 3rd "Rock of the Marne" Division, the squad had participated in the taking of Valmontone and was hiking down Highway 6 toward Rome when another small town came into sight. In the ensuring efforts to take the town, many Germans were taken captive. Upon returning to the town one soldier was kissed by an Italian woman who appreciated the liberation of the village."

American Troops entered Rome on June 4, 1944. Shortly afterwards, the 3rd Division was pulled from the line for some rest and to prepare for the invasion of Southern France. Glenn was about to earn his Arrowhead Assault Badge.

The 3rd landed at St. Tropez, France on August 15. Five days later, on August 20, probably as the Division was advancing up the Rhone Valley, Glenn suffered his second wound. Interestingly, his separation document does not mention the Purple Heart for his first wound, but does mention his second Purple Heart, the August 20 wound, and adds, "with Oak Leaf Cluster." The addition means he had already earned one Purple Heart. The Oak Leaf Cluster cannot be referring to his 3rd or 4th Purple Hearts, since the award document (for the second Purple Heart) is dated September 5, 1944, and the discharge document does acknowledge that he was wounded again on November 21, 1944. There is no Purple Heart Award citation in his discharge document for his November 21 wound. The NAO reported that the November 21 wound was his fourth wound. His third would have occurred between 8/15/1944 and 11/21/1944 as the Division advanced up the Rhone Valley and through the Vosges Mountains. It must have been a minor wound, by Glenn's standards, as he apparently did not mention it in any detail in his letters home.

This last wound on November 21 was likely near Strasburg, France, and was just before the 3rd Division reached the Rhine River on November 27. Glenn would be in a French hospital for most of the next two months, part of that time with a leg infection most likely related to his wound. During this period the 3rd Division took up defensive positions for the winter, and it helped repel the German winter offensive. By late January 1945, the Division and Glenn, were moving forward once again. On the 23rd, they helped clear the Colmar Pocket. a semi-circular bridgehead near Colmar in Alsace, France. The Germans considered Alsace their own territory, and they fought fiercely to protect it, to no avail

On March 15, the 3rd Division struck the Siegfried Line, the German answer to the French Maginot Line, south of Zweibrucken, Germany; but the Siegfried Line did not stop them. On March 26, they crossed the Rhine River, and Glenn F. Williams earned a Silver Star. His citation reads:

"Glenn F. Williams, 32 212 296, Staff Sergeant, Infantry, Company I, 30th Infantry Regiment. For gallantry in action. When his platoon was left without any officers during fighting for Lampertheim, Germany, the morning of 26 March 1945, Staff Sergeant Williams, platoon sergeant, assumed command. Taking a BAR from one of his men he advanced 100 yards to get into firing position, 75 yards from an enemy machine gun supported by riflemen which was harassing his platoon. There he laid the BAR fire on the German emplacement and killed three enemy manning the weapon. With the machine gun silenced, Staff Sergeant Williams led his platoon in an assault on the supporting riflemen which resulted in the cracking of the hostile positions and the capture of 30 enemy. Residence: Centerville, New York."

During April 17 to 20, the regiment helped capture Nuremberg, home of the Nazi Party. The fighting was fierce, and they had to take the city block by block. With Nuremberg in their bag, they now blasted their way through Augsburg and Munich. They were nearing Salzburg when the war ended. The 3rd Division picked up one more prize in its advance, although Glenn was not involved. Elements of the 7th Infantry Regiment, 3rd Infantry Division, captured Hitler's retreat at Berchtesgaden.

Glenn was finally rotated home in October 1945, arriving in New York aboard the *Queen Elizabeth*. He made it to Centerville just in time to surprise his niece, Darlene Williams, and help eat her birthday cake.

Glenn was discharged October 4, 1945. He had served overseas for almost 21 months. During that time period he had earned four Purple Hearts (of which apparently only two were recorded in his records), a Silver Star, an Invasion Arrowhead badge (Southern France Invasion), a Distinguished Unit Badge (with other members of his unit, for the battle of Besancon, France. Besancon is the home of the Citadel, an architectural masterpiece. It was captured by the Germans in 1940 and retaken by the 3rd Division on September 8, 1944), a Presidential Unit Citation for action in the Colmar Pocket - see below), the European African Middle Eastern Theater Medal, five battle stars (Naples Foggia, Rome Arno, Southern France, Rhineland, Central Europe) and the Good Conduct Medal. He was also awarded the Combat Infantry Badge, the award most coveted by "grunts". In 1947 Congress awarded a Bronze Star to every man who had earned a CBI. It is likely Glenn never even knew of this award. (While his military record does not so indicate, it is likely that Glenn was also entitled to two other battle stars, one for the Anzio Campaign, and the other for the Ardennes-Alsace Campaign. The 30th Infantry Regiment earned both battle stars, and Glenn was with the Regiment during the eligibility time period for the awards. These would give him a total of seven battle stars.) He also earned the American Theater Campaign Medal since he served more than one year in the states during the war. That award is also not included on his discharge record. It is important to note that these awards may have been included in his official military file, but that is no longer available.

In addition to the above, he also was entitled to wear a Croix De Guerre with Palm, awarded to his unit by the French government. The French award recognized the unit's fight against the German's 14th Army at the Colmar pass during the period January 20 to February 9, 1945. This vicious three-week battle, fought in temperatures reaching minus four degrees, was a desperate attempt by the Germans to stop the Allies' thrust into the German homeland. It failed. Further, the French government also awarded the 3rd Division the French Fourragere in 1945, making Glenn eligible to wear that award. The Fourragere is awarded for special meritorious conduct in action. It is only awarded to a unit which has twice received the Croix de Guerre. Even then it is not automatic. It is only done by a specific decree of the French Government. The 3rd Division was originally awarded the Croix de Guerre for action during World War I. It received its second Croix de Guerre for it actions at the Colmar Pocket during World War II. In 1945, the French Government, by decree, awarded the Fourragere.)

Audie Murphy, often cited as America's most decorated World War II soldier and recipient of the Medal of Honor, also served with the 3rd Infantry Division during World War II. The Italy, France, and Germany sections of the movie *To Hell and Back* which depicts Murphy's World War II service, is, to a great extent, a depiction of the World War II service of Glenn Williams.

The Medal of Honor

Almond E. Fisher of Hume entered the service in December, 1937. Almond was born in the Town of

Hume in 1912, the son of John A. Fisher and Amanda E. Wood. His Dad's family had lived in Hume Township from at least 1865 and his mother's since at least the 1880s. He was likely named for his paternal great grandfather.

Almond served honorably during his first six years, quickly rising to the rank of Master Sergeant. According to a War Department Press Release, he worked in administration during this part of his service. He applied for and was accepted into officer's candidate school in early 1943. On July 23, 1943, he was commissioned a 2nd Lieutenant and would serve as an officer until discharged on September 11, 1945.

It is not clear when he was assigned to Company E, 157th Infantry Regiment, 45th Infantry Division. The 45th was ordered to active service on September 16, 1940, at Fort Sill, OK, and departed for overseas service on June 3, 1943. It served in Oran, participated in the Sicily invasion and campaign, and then participated in the invasion at Salerno and the Italian campaign. It moved to a rest area near Naples in January 1944. In Naples, the Regiment was refitted and trained for an assault landing at Anzio. The 157th landed at Anzio after the initial landings and thus did not receive assault credit for that invasion. The regiment entered the line on January 30 and February 1. On February 7, it was hit hard by a German night attack. The Germans smashed through L Company and by the next morning were behind the American lines. The 157th, especially the third battalion, fought back and the line was reestablished. However, the following day the Germans launched a tank-supported attack. E Company was destroyed. Tanks drove right up to fox holes and then fired into the holes. Only three men from the company survived. The entire 2nd Battalion, which landed with 713 men and 38 officers, had only 162 men and 15 officers still on their feet at the end. But the regiment fought back, including hand-to-hand combat, and called in artillery fire on their own positions. The Germans were forced back to their original line.

The NAO reported in June of 1945 that Almond had returned to the United Stated (probably in May) after 17 months overseas. That indicates that he arrived overseas around January or February 1944. He almost surely was assigned to Company E, 157th Infantry following the battle at Anzio Beach and the devastation of Company E. From then until the breakout for Rome on May 23, 1944, Anzio was quietly deadly. The regiment was in the forefront of the breakout, and the fighting was ferocious. Company B, trapped in a ditch, was virtually wiped out by German tanks. Once again, on May 27, 1944, Company E was decimated by a German counter attack that drove them into a mine field. On May 29, the regiment was relieved. Even then when stragglers sought shelter under a large ledge, it was toppled by artillery fire with many casualties.

From June 4 to August 15, the regiment rested and prepared for the Southern France invasion. Here they fared better. Landing in France on the 15th, the regiment suffered only seven wounded while capturing 350 Germans. The race for Germany and Berlin was now on. Almond's regiment pushed the Germans up the Rhone Valley toward their own border. It encountered stiff resistance from time to time, but nevertheless advanced rapidly. On August 29, it was removed from the line for a rest. On September 11, it returned to the line and attacked the Belfort Gap. Two days later Almond Fisher led his platoon on a pre-dawn attack near Grammont. France and became the Regiment's third Medal of Honor winner.

"Almond E. Fisher" "For Conspicuous gallantry and intrepidity at the risk of his life above and beyond the call of duty on the night on 12/13 September, 1944, near Grammont, France. In the darkness of early morning, 2nd Lt. Fisher was leading a platoon of Company E, 157th Infantry, in single column to the attack of a strongly defended hill position. At 2:30 A.M., the forward elements were brought under enemy machine gun fire from less than 20 yards. Working his way alone to within 20 feet of the gun emplacement, he opened fire with his carbine and killed the entire gun crew. A few minutes after the advance was resumed, heavy machinegun fire was encountered from the left flank. Again, crawling forward alone under withering fire, he blasted the gun and crew from their positions with hand grenades. After a halt to replenish ammunition, the advance was again resumed and continued for 1 hour before being stopped by intense machinegun and rifle fire. Through the courageous and skillful leadership of 2nd Lt. Fisher, the pocket of determined enemy resistance was rapidly obliterated. Spotting an emplaced machine pistol a short time after, with 1 of his men he moved forward and destroyed the position. As the advance continued the fire fight became more intense. When a bypassed German climbed from his foxhole and attempted to tear an M1 rifle from the hands of 1 of his men, 2nd Lt. Fisher whirled and killed the enemy with a burst from his carbine. About 30 minutes later the platoon came under the heavy fire of machineguns from across an open field. 2nd Lt. Fisher, disregarding the terrific fire, moved across the field with no cover or concealment to within range, knocked the gun from the position and killed or wounded the crew. Still under heavy fire he returned to his platoon and continued the advance. Once again heavy fire was encountered from a machinegun directly in front. Calling for hand grenades, he found only two remaining in the entire platoon. Pulling the pins and carrying a grenade in each hand, he crawled toward the gun emplacement, moving across an area devoid of cover and under intense fire to within 15 yards when he threw the grenades, demolished the gun, and killed the gun crew. With ammunition low and daybreak near, he ordered his men to dig in and hold the ground already won. Under constant fire from the front and from both flanks, he moved among them directing the preparations for the defense. Shortly after the ammunition supply was replenished, the Germans launched a last determined effort against the depleted group. Attacked by superior numbers from the front, right, and left flank, and even from the rear, the platoon, in bitter hand-to-hand engagements drove back the enemy at every point. Wounded in both feet by close-range machine pistol fire early in the battle, 2nd Lt. Fisher refused medical attention. Unable to walk, he crawled from man to man encouraging them and checking each position. Only after the fighting had subsided did 2nd Lt. Fisher crawl 300 yards to the aid station from which he was evacuated. His extraordinary heroism, magnificent valor, and aggressive determination in the face of pointblank enemy fire is an inspiration to his organization and reflects the highest traditions of the U.S. Armed Forces."

Once recovered from his wounds, Almond returned to combat with his regiment.

France

They are French
The proud reaction of citizens of Paris, when they realized the first allied soldiers liberating Paris were French. From the movie, *Is Paris Burning*. Elements of the 2nd French Armored Division under the command of General Philippe Leclerc entered Paris on the night of August 24, 1944. General Eisenhower ordered that the first troops into Paris during the liberation be Free French troops. However, during the battle for Paris, the first combat troops to enter Paris on the night of August 24 may have been led by a Frenchmen, Captain Raymond Dronne, but the unit itself was primarily Spanish.

Paris must not fall into enemy hands except as a field of ruins.
Message from Hitler to General Dietrich von Cholitz, Hitler's military commander of the Paris region. Von Cholitz had been a true believer until meeting with Hitler to receive his appointment to Paris. When he met him, he realized Hitler was insane and that the war was lost. This knowledge guided his future decisions, especially his decision not to destroy Paris.

Among the many FCSD area veterans who served in France were Paul A. Abbott, David N. Ayer, Ivan R. Ayer, William C. Brueser, Everett M. Clark, Robert L. Cummings, Stewart E. Folts, Edith R. Johannes, Evan W. Molyneaux, Lester E. Noble, Charles R. Ostrum, Charles F. Porter, Ransom L. Richardson Jr., Llewellyn M. Washburn, Albert Williams, and Robert Wolfer.

David N. Ayer of Fillmore entered the Army Air Corps on March 1, 1943. Following basic training, David attended flexible gunnery school at Tyndall Air Base in Florida. Both Clark Gable and David's brother Ivan also attended the flexible gunnery school. By January 1944, David was at Barksdale Air Base in Louisiana where he went through air crew combat training. He then moved on to Chennault Air Base in Lake Charles, LA, to complete his training. At Lake Charles he was assigned to his brother Ivan's squadron. Ivan was an instructor at Chennault. In May Dave was at Hunter Air Field, Savannah, GA for B-26 Medium Bomber crew training.

By the end of May, David was in Toome, Ireland, at the 3rd Combat Crew Replacement Center, likely attached to the 4th Training Group, a crew replacement training group for gunners. David was then assigned to the 386th Bomb Group, 552nd Bomb Squadron. The 386th had arrived in England back in May 1943. The 386th was likely stationed at RAF Boxted when David arrived. The group had arrived there June 10, 1943, and would remain there until September 24. He was assigned to the John Armstrong crew. *(Dave is third from right in the photo.) The 386th flew the Marin B-26 Marauder. National Archives Photo.*

The NAO reported in August 1944, that David had recently became a member of the Caterpillar Club having bailed out of an airplane. The records for the 552nd Squadron do not show any missions where Dave bailed out. According to apparently incomplete records, his first mission was August 28. Clearly, he had flown missions prior to that date since the NAO had reported in August that he had already joined the Caterpillar Club. (The Caterpillar Club is likely the only prestigious club in the world composed of people who were not asked nor did they volunteer to join. You become a member automatically when you are forced to bail out of an injured aircraft and parachute safely to earth.)

The bail-out likely occurred July 11, 1944. His pilot, Captain John Armstrong put information on the internet that discussed that mission. They were flying in a plane named 'Phew," which was the nickname of the crew chief's brother who had been a member of a bomber crew and who died when his plane was shot down. Armstrong indicated the "Phew" was also shot down and they had to bail out. They had attacked a fuel storage facility in Flers, France.

Records do show that David flew, counting the July 11 mission, twenty missions with the Armstrong crew. He few an additional eight missions with other crews. It is likely that he participated in several other missions. The NAO reported he flew a total of 46 missions as a radio operator and top turret gunner. The 386th Bomb Group moved to Beaumont-sur-Oise Airfield in France on October 2, 1944. it is possible that David flew additional missions in both July and August of 1944 that for some reasons do not appear in the 552nd records. Those missions would make up the difference between the 46 missions reported in the NAO, and the 28 missions identified by the author. David was awarded the Air Medal with an Oak Leaf Cluster which indicates multiple missions.

The NAO also reported that David returned to the states in March 1945. His last mission was apparently February 28, 1945. He was then assigned to Scott Field in Illinois as an instructor. The NAO reported, in September, that David had received his discharge.

David's known Combat Missions: 7/11/44, Flers, Fr, Fuel Storage Tanks - 8/28/44, Fort Delargne, Fr, gun positions - 9/6/44, Brest, Fr, Gun Positions -9/6/44 - Brest, FR, Gun Positions (2nd mission same day - 9/10/44, Fraye, Fr, target unknown - 9/11/44, Metz, Fr, Gun Positions, - 9/19/44, Duren, Ger, Marshalling Yards - 9/23/44, Velong, Holland, Marshalling Yards - 9/30/44, Arnhem, Holland, Bridges and Roads - 10/7/44, Hengelo, Holland, Marshalling Yards - 11/19/44, Merode, Ger, Strong points before a village - 11/29/44, Pier, Ger, Strong points defending an area being attacked by Allied forces - 12/2/44, Saarlautern, Ger, defended area - 12/12/44, Schoneseiffen, Ger, defended area - 12/18/44, Blumenthal, Ger, defended area - 12/23/44 - Arweiler, Ger, RR Bridge - 12/25/44, Kenchinger, Ger, Railroad Bridge - 12/26/44, Ahrweiler, Ger, Railroad Bridge - 1/1/45, Kanz Karthus, Ger, Railroad Bridge - 1/29/45, Neuwied, Ger, Highway Bridge - 2/1/45, Bendorf, Ger, Railroad Bridge - 2/6/45, Rheinbach, Ger, Ammunition Dump – 2/9/45, Nierson, Ger, Road Junction - 2/8/45, Grevenbroich, Ger, unknown - 2/14/45, Kevelaer, Ger. Defended Bridge - 2/22/45, St. Wendel, Ger, Railroad Bridge - 2/26/45, Grazweiler, Ger, Defended Village - 2/28/45, Viersengar, Ger, Defended Village. Many of these raids were clearly in support of advancing ground forces.

Ivan R. Ayer of Fillmore entered the service on July 2,1942 but did not report for active duty until July 16, 1942. Following basic training, Ivan was assigned for five weeks of training at the Air Gunnery School at Tyndall Field in Florida. Following completion of training, Ivan was apparently assigned to Tyndall as permanent staff. He was still there in November 1943 when his brother Dave was assigned to Tyndall for air gunnery training. By March 1944, the NAO reported that he was at Lake Charles, LA, and had been there for several months. He was home on leave in February 1944; and upon returning to Lake Charles learned that his brother Dave had been assigned to his squadron. Ivan was a flight instructor at Lake Charles. He remained at Lake Charles until sailing for England on November 21, 1944, arriving there on the 28th. Likely achieving a goal to participate in the shooting war, Ivan was assigned to the 394th Bomb Group, 587th Bomb Squadron. He probably joined the 587th in December 1944 at Cambrai/Niergnies, France. The 394th had been at Cambrai since October 12, 1944. The 587th Bomb Squadron flew the Martin B-26 Marauder.

Ivan Ayer (right) with his brother Dave at Lake Charles Air Base, LA, March 1944. Ivan was a flight instructor and Dave was a trainee assigned to his squadron.

The 587th Bomb Squadron records are not available at the National Archives, so the missions flown by Ivan cannot be determined at this time. However, his discharge document indicates that he received the Air Medal with three Oak Leaf Clusters. By the time Ivan arrived overseas, the award criteria for an Air Medal varied by command. Basic requirements provided for an air medal for each naval vessel or three enemy aircraft destroyed, or for 25 operations flights with exposure to enemy fire, or 100 operational flights. In Europe, later in the war, during the time Ivan was there, it was awarded to bomber crews for five flights. Assuming this was the criteria used during Ivan's tour, it means he flew at least 20 combat missions.

By the time Ivan arrived, the 587th was engaged primarily in supporting ground troops advancing across France and Germany. Ivan's group moved to Venlo, Holland on May 7, 1945, and Kitzingen, Germany, on September 28, 1945. Ivan earned battle stars for the Ardennes-Alsace, Central Europe and Rhineland campaigns.

Everett M. Clark of Centerville entered the US Army December 2, 1942. After basic training, he was assigned to the 14th Armored Division, 48th Tank Battalion. Everett was with the Division, stationed at Camp Chaffee in Arkansas, and participated in major maneuvers in Tennessee from November 17, 1943, until January 10, 1944. After the exercise, the Division was ordered to Camp Campbell in Kentucky. In September, it was alerted for overseas duty and sailed for Europe October 14, 1944. It landed in Marseille October 29th, and elements of the Division were in combat within two weeks. The entire Division was in combat by November 20th. Between November 20th and the end of April, 1945, the Division would spend 133 days in combat., most of that time as part of the 7th Army. It blasted its way through the Voges Mountains and across the Lauter River into Germany. Then it pushed its way through the heavily defended portion of the west wall of Germany. It was poised to break into the German rear when it was ordered to stop. The last of two major German offensives of the war was underway. The German offensive was to last from December 31, 1944 to January 25, 1945, and the 14th Armored Division was needed to defend against the attack. The Battle of the Bulge, lasting from December 16, 1944 to January 25, 1945, was also underway during this period.

Operation Nordwind, planned by Hitler, had one objective. Hitler had ordered his Army to break through the US 7th Army and the French 1st Army in the upper Voges Mountains, and to destroy the armies. The offensive had no other goal. It was not after territory, resources, or anything else. Its objective was to kill Allied soldiers.

Everette's division withdrew to a position south of the Lauter River and there waged a battle of historic proportions. In his memoirs, German Colonel Hans von Luck, wrote that, "This was one of the most-costly battles that was ever waged on the western front." (Von Luck had fought with Rommel in North Africa, and had led the only armored counter attack at Normandy.) The attack was halted by the 14th at Hatten - Rittershoffen, two small towns on the Alsace Plains. The fighting was furious and fierce. It was said that success was measured by the number of buildings a side controlled. The Division was isolated, re-supply was difficult and evacuation of wounded soldiers was dangerous. Nevertheless, it held. The 7th Army and VI Corps were given time to prepare defensive positions. The 14th was finally able to withdraw. The German attack had failed.

Everett M. Clark was "wrecker chief for the 58th Battalion." His job was to assure the rapid repair of damaged tanks on the spot, or to see that the tanks were taken to the rear and repaired. His unit and other wrecker units made major contributions to the victory. The 48th Tank Battalion reported that at one time during the battle, its tank companies were reduced to squad size. Division after action reports stated that 150 tanks were damaged and repaired on the spot during the battle. General Devers, commander of 6th Army Group, called this battle one of the greatest defensive battles of the war.

With the battle won, the 14th rested a bit and then resumed its way through Germany. The same day the Marines landed on Okinawa (Sunday, April 1, 1945), the 14th captured Germensheim and moved across the Rhine near Worms. The 14th was now to earn a nickname, "Liberators." As it pushed the German defenders aside, it also liberated concentration and prisoner of war camps. By the end of the war, it had been credited with liberating 200,000 Allied soldiers, as well as thousands of concentration camp prisoners.

For its incredible stand at Hatten-Rittershoffen, the 14th was nominated for four Presidential Unit Citations and was awarded two.

At war's end, Everett was near Munich, Germany. In June, while on his way to headquarters with his driver to pick-up mail, his jeep was side-swiped by a truck. Everett was banged up with cuts to his hands, and a gash to his head that required seven stitches. He had to spend the night in the hospital. This was Everett's second trip to the hospital during his service. The other time had been in September of 1943 before shipping overseas. Everett survived some of the fiercest fighting of the war without a scratch. He fared less well in non-combat situations.

Robert L. (Bob) Cummings of Houghton, a member of the 5th Engineer Special Brigade, said he "won" a trip onto Omaha Beach on D-Day plus one. His unit was scheduled to land on D-Day, but it was split into two groups. His group landed at noon on June 7th. The 5th Engineer Special Brigade had been formed in Swansea, Wales out of Headquarters and Headquarters Company, 1119th Engineer Combat Group, on November 12, 1943. Its purpose was to support the landing and subsequent supply operations at Omaha Beach. Bob told the Fillmore History Club, for an article they did on him, that his first job at Omaha, was policing the beach. That meant loading dead soldiers onto trucks and taking them to a nearby cemetery. He also unloaded supplies and moved them to the front a few miles inland. He said his original invasion assignment had been as part of a bazooka team. The primary duties of the Special Engineer Brigades were to get ashore, remove heavy obstacles and build roads to assist troops and equipment in landing and getting off exposed beaches. In fact, initially they were called Engineer Amphibian Brigades.

A Monument to the 5th Engineer Special Brigade, and the men it lost in battle, sits today above Omaha Beach. It is a massive structure built upon another massive structure, a German bunker.

The 5th Engineer Special Brigade remained on Omaha Beach until November 19, 1944. It was then transferred to the Seine section of Paris, where the Brigade supervised construction activities. Just as Germany was surrendering, Bob's Brigade had begun studying Japanese planes and uniforms for a potential move to the Pacific. The Brigade returned to the states on July 11, 1945. However, Bob's platoon had been ordered to Berlin to clear out an old Buzz Bomb plant, and to work with supplies for the occupation Army. He finally sailed for home on Christmas morning, 1945

Stewart E. Folts of Fillmore entered the Army Air Corps in March of 1943, four months before his

graduation from Houghton College. He spent the next five months, according to an article in the 1945 WW II Special Edition put out by the Fillmore History Club, studying math at Syracuse University. During his time at Syracuse, he also played in the band. (After his service, he served for 30 years as the music teacher at FCS.) His training continued at Stuttgart Air Field in Arkansas, where he was commissioned as a 2nd Lieutenant in August. Then he moved on to Sedalia Field, Warrensburg, MO, where he joined the Army Air Transport Command. It appears that he was at Sedalia only a short period before being shipped overseas. A story he told son Dwight likely occurred at Stuttgart. During his long- distance multi-engine training with another pilot, one of the engines failed. Stewart tried everything he had learned and practiced to keep the plane in the air. Eventually he had to land in a farm field. This was the first of two crash landings he endured. Both Stewart and the other pilot trainee were uninjured. When he returned to his home base, his instructor put him right back in the air, and shut down an engine. He successfully restarted the engine.

Just prior to shipping overseas, Stewart was given ten-days leave. He immediately sent a telegram to his future wife. It read, "Have ten-day pass, let's get married." The family still has the telegram. *Picture – Stew in training. Family Photo.*

He likely arrived at his new assignment with the IX Troop Carrier Command in September 1944. Stewart told the History Club that he was assigned to the 62nd Troop Carrier Service. This was likely the 62nd Troop Carrier Squadron, part of the 314th Operations Group, 52nd Troop Carrier Wing, IX Troop Carrier Command. As such, he may have participated with the 62nd in the ill-fated Market Garden operation. The 62nd dropped paratroopers into Holland in September and carried supplies and munitions to the troops after the drop. At the time, the 314th was flying out of RAF (Royal Air Force) base Saltby in England. They continued to operate out of Saltby until late February of 1945, and their major activity continued to be the dropping of supplies and ammunition to ground troops.

Son Dwight related that his dad's second crash landing occurred while landing after a mission over France. For several missions in a row, the seventh plane in the landing formation crashed. At the time, Stewart was co-pilot to the "hot-shot" squadron leader. Believing the crashes were the result of pilot errors, the "hot shot" put his plane in the seventh landing spot. He crashed also, although both he and Stewart were uninjured. It turned out the problem was turbulence created by the first six planes landing.

By March 4, 1945, Dwight's squadron was at Poix-en-Picardie Field in France. It would spend the rest of the war at Poix. One of its first assignments there was dropping paratroopers across the Rhine River near Wesel, Germany on March 24 as part of Operation Varsity. The mission was dangerous enough to begin with, but a British newspaper announced the plans a day before the actual crossing, thus enabling the Germans to be even more prepared. The troop-carrying C-47's led the attack, followed by B-24 bombers that, on this mission, were dropping supplies rather than bombs. The combat crews on the 24's said the flak surpassed anything they had seen on a bombing mission. It was the largest single day airborne assault in history. A total of 17,132 men and 7,000,000 pounds of supplies and equipment were delivered by air. The air armada was so huge that it took three hours and 12 minutes to pass a single point. Postwar German military experts called it "Practically a mass crossing of the river by air." General Eisenhower said, "The March 24 operation sealed the fate of Germany."

The 62nd then continued to fly missions bringing supplies and equipment to combat troops. It also airlifted wounded American and Allied soldiers to hospitals. This function continued even after the end of hostilities, as did the evacuation of prisoners of war (POWs) from German POW camps. Stewart told the History Club that he primarily evacuated French POWs back to France. The group also was flying regular military and other personnel to various locations, as well as transporting freight at this time.

Stewart told his son Dwight that he was in the air over France when they heard about V-J Day. They landed and spent three days celebrating in Marseilles. Since everyone else was also partying, it is likely they were not missed.

During the summer of 1945, Stewart took advantage of his situation to spend two months at the Shrivenham American University near London. His group, the 314th Operations Group moved from Poix to Villa Coublay Airfield in France on October 25, 1945, and it returned to the states to Bolling Field outside Washington, DC, on Febraruy15, 1946. Stewart was discharged on June 29, 1946 at Fort Dix, NJ, as a First Lieutenant. He earned battle stars for his participation in the Rhineland and Central Europe campaigns.

Charles E. Hodnett of Hume entered the service November 7, 1941. His brother Russell also served. He was assigned to Fort Lee, VA. Only the month before Fort Lee had been designated as the basic training base for quartermaster officers and men. In January the NAO reported that he was visited by his parents and wife and in February noted that he had been promoted to Private First Class. It appears that Charles was at Fort Lee for about four to five months. In May 1942 the NAO reported that he and his wife were home visiting his parents and that he was stationed at Fort Hamilton, NY. He was now a Sergeant. Fort Hamilton served primarily as a mobilization center during the early years of the war. Its responsibility was to prepare men for and arrange for their deployment to war zones. During the war Fort Hamilton (named for Alexander Hamilton) processed some three million troops on their war to the European war zones.

On July 31, 1942 the US officially established a separate Transportation Corps. It acquired most of his units from the Quartermaster and Engineer services. It appears likely that Charles had been assigned to the Transportation Service since his arrival at Fort Hamilton. Charles worked in administration and likely helped in the arrangements for boarding and shipment of troops being deployed to the European Theater. The NAO reported in November 1944 that he was with the Transportation Corps. He remained at Fort Hamilton until at least June of 1943. The NAO reported that he was there when his son Nicholas was born in December 1942, and that he was in the Fort Hamilton Hospital in June 1943. He was shipped overseas sometime during the next three months as the NAO reported in November 1943 that he was in England and that he ran into his former agriculture teacher at Fillmore High, Willis Hayes (see Part V) in London. (As with many veterans, Charles' military personnel file was destroyed in a fire. No other documents regarding his service have been located except a final pay voucher which contains no information regarding his units of service or assignments. Therefore, his service activities have been deduced from the little information available and some personal remembrances of people who knew him.)

No more entries regarding Charles appear in the NAO until August of 1944. During that time period December 1943 to August 1944 massive preparations were being made for the Normandy invasion.

Charles likely still assigned to administrative activities, would have been deeply involved in such preparations. Based on later information it appears that he may have been part of the Military Railway Service, one of the major components of the Transportation Corps. In June the invasion began. The NAO reported Charles in France in August 1944. There is no information on when he first arrived. A November 1944 NAO entry reported that he was still in France, was assigned to the Transportation Corps and had, with his detachment, helped establish a railway traffic office at a French rail center. Charles mentioned in his letter, reported by the NAO, that his unit was right behind Patton's army.

Under the Transportation Corps there were three Military Railroad Services. The 2nd Military Railroad Service was assigned to Europe. Under each Service there were Railway Grand Divisions. The Grand Divisions were composed of Railway Operating Battalions along with a Railroad Shop Battalion. Each Division was responsible for some 250 to 450 miles of track. Each Division and operating battalion were sponsored by a major US Railroad Company such as the New York Central Railroad. Each sponsor provided key personnel and training for Army personnel. These battalions had the responsibility of repairing damaged railroad lines, stations and equipment and then operating the railroads themselves. The task was huge. In a way they had to keep up with the advancing armies, but also the advancing armies depended on them to keep the supplies and troops coming to enable them to advance. The railroads, once made operational took the supplies as far as possible, and then the Transportation Corps truck units, such as the famous "Red Ball Express, would deliver them to the forward troops. When necessary, they brought in their own rolling stock (trains.) They incorporated local civilian personnel into their operations and once the war was over turned the railroads over to the local personnel.

In December 1944 Charles sent a letter home written on paper which had "Made in Germany" on the reverse, giving the family a clue perhaps to his location. In February he wrote thanking the Junior Red Cross and Rotary for Christmas gifts. A letter in May 1945 announced that he had been awarded two Bronze Stars. These may have been and likely were battle stars. He was again stationed in France.

He also sent his mother birthday greetings. He said he was still with the Transportation Corps and serving the Third Army (Patton's Army).

In June he met up with his brother Russell who was stationed near Munich, Germany. Charles was at Everu? (Possibly Evry France) France. They took in the movie "Keys to the Kingdom" and then took the train to Paris. Charles was still working in an office of the transportation system.

Charles rode back to the states in the nose of a B-17 via the South American route. He arrived September 17, 1945 and was discharged September 30, 1945 at Fort Dix, NJ.

Edith R. Johannes of Houghton was living in a French chateau in Etretat, France, on January 1, 1945. She was supposed to be treating wounded soldiers, but still, the 201st General Hospital unit, of which she was a part, did not have a hospital. Instead, along with the rest of her unit, Edith was sweeping stairs, tending fires, and trying to make the chateau more livable. The 201st had arrived in England on November 4, 1944. It was stationed at Oulton, which was a staging area for shipment to the continent, before moving to France on December 26, 1944.

On January 7, 1945, the unit was moved to Rouen. Living with nurses from eight other general hospitals, the 201st nurses continued their cleaning routines, but now added daily road hikes to their schedule, at least for a while. When scattered cases of the measles broke out, they were pretty much confined to their rooms in the attic of their quarters. They were finally shipped to Verdun. This trip took four days and three nights on a crowded train, but at last they were at their hospital site. They all agreed it was a trip that they never wanted to take again.

Their hospital at Verdun was not ready for use, but at least the personnel were there. Supplies eventually arrived and so did patients: 144 of them on January 26, 1944. The engineers were still installing plumbing and lighting, while making other repairs. The work of the engineers lasted from January to April. On January 16, the 201st had 300 beds for patients. By March 15, it was a 1000-bed hospital. The hospital and the nurses continued to serve patients even as the ceilings were fixed over them, floors under them, and walls around them. In April 1,300 patients were admitted.

Constant innovation was necessary. The operating room was moved three times before work on the building was completed. In one of its incarnations, the operating room was located in a tent with tank treads for a floor. The scrub sink was built in the manner of a trough, with rubber tubing sending water by siphon suction from a bottle when released by a foot pedal. Captain Clara A. Traver reported that this arrangement was cherished by all of the nurses. Other innovations included using bomb racks wired together for patient stands. The center shelf was used for the patient's belongings, and a side rail was used for towels and washcloths.

It was putting together a hospital on the run. SOPS (Standard Operating Procedures) were developed and distributed to all personnel. These procedures covered everything from thermometer trays, hypodermic trays, recording and maintenance of narcotic records, uniform set-up of the medicine cabinet and linen rooms to catheterization procedures. Nurses were also urged to spend any extra time they had training ward men and medical and surgical technicians in nursing procedures and ward administration. Later, when a German POW stockade was added to the hospital compound and the prisoners were put to work in the hospital, it was necessary to develop, write up, and train the prisoners on ward cleaning and kitchen duties. These procedures were written in both English and German to make sure there was no confusion regarding who was responsible for what.

All the extra work involved in training paid off. The organization and training of a penicillin team of enlisted men proved to be of immeasurable help.

Managing the nursing staff was not easy. They were constant disruptions. Nurses who had left England with the advance party, and had been on temporary duty with two other general hospitals, didn't return to the 201st until January 24. (The Advance Party included 12 nurses. It was sent to Cherbourg for training on European Theater of Operations (ETO) methods.) While the engineers were completing the hospital, only two wards were functioning. Two surgical teams with one nurse each were detailed to other hospitals (39th and 101st Evacuation Hospitals). Eventually the original assignment of 83 nurses was reduced to 74. Five nurses were permanently reassigned, two returned to the states due to illness, and another was transferred to the Public Health Section of 12th Army Group.

As time passed, living conditions also improved. Nurses were quartered in a French three-story barracks-like home. Groups of six nurses each shared a four-room apartment consisting of three bedrooms and an outer room with a titled floor and a sink. The outer room served as a group "kitchen-sitting room." One apartment was set aside as a Day Room. This apartment was painted, the chairs were upholstered and curtains were installed. It had a table and even a piano. Another apartment was turned into a shower room, greatly appreciated by all. The nurses even had a French housekeeper who took care of the nurse's laundry. On May 5, the Officers Club opened.

The six-month report for the period ending June 30, 1945, shows that as of June 14, the 201st had admitted 4,033 patients. Of these 3,311 were US military. The others were POWS, allied soldiers, and civilians. More than 30 percent of the patients were battle casualties. Over 50 percent were ill with various diseases, with trench foot and infectious hepatitis being the big two. In April, 240 American returned POWs had been admitted. They were all suffering from starvation, with some having lost as much as 75 pounds.

The report indicates that 73 of the patients were returned to duty, with 83 percent of the them being returned to full combat duty.

All was not work. Eventually many nurses received passes to Paris. Five managed to wrangle seven-day leaves to the Riviera. On V-E Day, they all marched in the victory parade in Verdun.

Edith entered the service on August 30, 1944. She was ordered to Atlantic City, NJ, for basic training. Nurses received limited training. By 1944, each nurse was trained for a total of about 144 hours. The training consisted of basic military matters, administration, organization, sanitation, ward and clinic training, military courtesy, care, clothing, and equipment, dismounted drill and physical training. The NAO reported in November, 1944 that her address had been changed to US Army APO, New York City.

Evan W. Molyneaux (M.D.) of Houghton entered the service as a Major in August 1942. He served the next 18 months at various locations within the US. In February or March 1944, Evan moved overseas. The 45th Field Hospital with which Evan served as a doctor, arrived at Cardiff, Wales on March 10, 1944. Personnel were billeted at Upton upon Severn. On June 8, 1944, the 45th landed on Utah Beach in France.

Evan later described for his family his initial experience after landing. He wrote, "We spent two miserable nights trying to sleep in jeeps and ten-ton trucks. Then we got on board like a bunch of cows with twelve ten-ton trucks, thirty-six ambulances, and a few half-tracks. The ship was called LST (landing ship tank). (Authors Note: The 45th history indicates that the unit traveled from England to France aboard the US Merchant Marine freighter *William N. Pendleton*.) Well, we got organized and placed guards all over the ship to keep order and to keep men from smoking while sitting on piles of five-gallon gas tanks. That was some job and if I had not already lost all my hair, I would have lost it all at this time. We saw a chance to get close to shore and we started to head in. We moved into shore and shortly let down the whole front of the ship, making a ramp to drive on. There was a tremendous roar and everyone gunned their motors in order to take off. I was in the second ambulance in the right lane. I watched the 2nd ambulance on the left veer off to the left and disappear under water. I opened the door of the ambulance and said "no thanks, I'll walk." I made my way ashore and there found that the engineers had cleared a path for walkers like me. Most of the medical I did was to access the extent of the injury and to send them to the right place. I gave a lot of morphine to dying boys and they were grateful. I want to mention one of the saddest things I saw at Normandy. We climbed onto a big field and between hedgerows and there in the fields as far as the eye could see were rows and rows of the dead from D Day. Here and there were miles of burial crews collecting belongings from each body."

In the first month following the June 8 landing, the 1st, 2nd, and 3rd platoons of the 45th Field Hospital served in several locations in France. These included the 2nd platoon near Audouville la Hubert and then near Fauville, only one mile from the famous Sainte-Mere-Eglise. By June 17, the 2nd platoon was at Beuzeville au Plain. By June 21, the 1st platoon was in Cherbourg. Information is not available as to where Evan was at this time, but he had earned his first battle star. (Normandy Campaign). By July the platoon was at Orglandes.

The movement of the Allies out of Normandy, along with the clearance of the Germans from France and Belgium is known as the Northern France Campaign. By late September, the 45th had joined this campaign. It was now operating in Bastogne, Belgium primarily as a semi-evacuation hospital. In October, it was attacked by German artillery but continued to operate in the area for the next several months as the battles raged to drive the Germans out and then to defend against the surprise German winter offensive. Evan had earned his second battle star.

By January 1, 1945, the 45th Field Hospital was in bivouac at Fallais, Belguim. By January 17 they were at Malmedy, site of one of the most dreadful slaughters of the war. On December 12, 1944, at Malmedy, members of Kampfgruppe Peiper, an element of the German 1st Panzer Division Leibstandarte SS Adolph Hitler commanded by General Joachim Peiper, cold-bloodily murdered 84 American prisoners of war. At that time, the 45th was supporting the American units recapturing St. Vith, as part of the Battle of the Bulge. Evan had earned his third battle star. (Ardennes Alsace Campaign – Battle of the Bulge)

On March 8, the 45th moved to Euskirchen, Germany. During this time, the 45th supported troops that captured the Ludendorff Bridge that crossed the Rhine at Remagen. The battle of Remagen occurred during the period March 7 to 25, 1945. German attempts to blow the bridge had been only partially successful. Early capture of the bridge reduced the life span of the Third Reich by at least two weeks. During the advance to the Rhine, the 45th and Evan had earned their fourth battle star. The 45th Field Hospital semi-annual report for the period January 1 to June 30, 1945, stated that its personnel were especially proud of being the most forward hospital supporting the troops who captured the Ludendorff Bridge and won the battle of Remagen. (Rhineland Campaign) They were also proud of being the most forward hospital at the time the American and Russian troops came together.

The 45th now supported troops smashing their way through Germany. On March 11, 1945, the field hospital moved to Bad Neunahr while still receiving casualties from Remagen. It then moved to Ahrweiler, Germany and on March 26 to Nieder Bieber. Tents were set up to provide medical services. In Nieder Bieber the 45th Field Hospital served the 2nd Infantry Division. Then it moved to Montabaur, where they supported troops from V Corps and functioned as an evacuation hospital. On April 2, the field hospital's personnel were in Wolfhagen, again in tents. Subsequently, they worked out of a captured German hospital in Montabaur. On April 14, now in Naumburg, they used an existing building. Then on April 20 it was on to Weiden, where they worked out of a large hotel.

During this period, the 45th served 2,490 patients. Over 1,100 of these had to be hospitalized. Some 340 major operations were performed, many in tents and others in various captured and converted buildings. Under these less than perfect conditions with patients who were suffering severe combat wounds, only 26 died. The semi-annual report notes the versatility of a field hospital. Sometimes it received only non-transportable casualties. On other occasions, due to the troop's rapid advances, it received all types. In those situations, the field hospital retained the seriously wounded and evacuated the others. Evan had earned his fifth battle star. (Central Europe Campaign)

The 45th Field Hospital ended the war in Weiden. For a short period, it acted as a holding unit for air evacuations. Then, the hospital moved to Pilsen in the Czech Republic, where it performed occupation duties. This involved acting primarily as a holding unit for air evacuation of wounded men. Evan was discharged in March 1946.

Lester E. Noble of Granger was chosen in 1942 as the FCS Junior Class Standard Bearer by Principal Andrew Haynes. This honor recognized a junior who was outstanding in citizenship, character, and scholarship. Lester was always very proud of that award. Following graduation in 1943, Lester attended Cornell University for one semester before enlisting in the service on March 20, 1944. It was clear that, even while at Cornell, his mind was not far from the war. In a letter to his parents (published in the NAO) he wrote. "This, then, is what we are fighting for --- a land of human kindness and good will, a place where all men are equal, a place where all men can worship as he wishes, and where he can join in with others to help benefit himself and all mankind. We are fighting to set free all those under tyrant's rule and to again have peace and quiet over the entire world. We are fighting for our families and our country and for ourselves. We are fighting for life itself."

Lester received his basic training and infantry training at Camp Wheeler, Macon, GA. After a ten day leave at home, Lester was assigned to Fort Jackson, Columbia, SC. He may have joined Company K, 347th Infantry Regiment, 87th Infantry Division at Fort Jackson. The NAO reported that he was shipped overseas in October 1944. The 87th moved overseas October 17, 1944. It arrived in England on November 12th.

It moved to La Havre, France in November, 1944. Some units debarked La Havre and others at Rouen. It reassembled near Saint Seans and was assigned to the Third Army. It then moved through Mars La Tours to the vicinity of Meta, France where it replaced the 2nd Infantry Regiment, 5th Infantry Division. By the 10th of December it was replacing other units and engaging in combat. The 347th relieved the 328th Infantry during the night of December 12-13 and took up positions in the Weisviller area. They were now engaged in the Saar battle, part of the Rhineland Campaign. On December 14, at 7:00 AM, the 347th made its first attack. While the initial resistance they faced was light, by afternoon they were counterattacked, but held. They had achieved their objectives for the day and they had held. They attacked again on the 15th. Again, they were counterattacked and again they held. While the battle was primarily in the area between Saargumeines and Bitchie, France, by the end of the day on the 15th elements of the regiment had entered Germany.

On December 16th Lester was killed in battle. The 347th Historical Report for December 16 says: "The 345th and 347th Infantry attacked at 0700. Both regiments encountered heavy resistance from the vicinity of Mittselheim and the Baumbusch Woods. Counterattacks on both fronts were repulsed. All troops were subjected to intense artillery fire." Other reports indicate that on the 16th, Lester's 3rd Battalion captured the town of Obergailbach. Obergailbach is in France, but on the Germany border opposite the German town of Niedergailbach.

Lester had served a little less than nine months. He had turned 19 years old on December 10th. He had earned the American Campaign Medal, the European African Middle East Theater Medal, the World War II Victory Medal, a Purple Heart, likely a Good Conduct Medal, the Combat Infantry Badge, and the 1947 Congressionally awarded Bronze Star. He had also earned one battle star for the Rhineland Campaign.

Charles F. Porter of Hume initially entered the service on December18, 1940. It is not clear where he took any basic training, but by April 1941 the NAO reported him at Fort Totten, L.I. and by May he was at Fort Devens, MA assigned to Company M, 26th Infantry Regiment. It appears that he was serving as an Infantryman. He remained with the 26th until October 1941. On October 11, 1941 he received an Honorable Medical discharge. The reason cited was sun stoke. His medical file listed his home town as Fillmore. For this service Charles earned the American Defense Medal.

There is evidence that Charles reenlisted or at least was recalled by the military. With his records destroyed in the infamous St. Louis fire, little concrete information has been located. The only document located to date is a medical report originally prepared in 1944. The Service Number on the report is Charles's number, the same one that appeared on his 1941 medical report which has also been located. A service number is assigned only once. The 1944 report indicates that Charles had been wounded in action in France. He was wounded in both the arm and the thigh by artillery shell fragments. The report calls them penetrating wounds and indicates that he suffered the wounds in battle.

Charles was initially treated at the 3rd Station Hospital, which records show was in France at the time. He was then moved to 2nd General Hospital which had only recently arrived in France and was located at Lison, a small town in the Calvados section of Normandy. It had only opened for patients a few days before Charles arrived there. In total he spent 51 days in the two hospitals. The exact July date of Charles' wound is not known. The 3rd Station Hospital where Charles was first treated arrived in France on June 30, 1944.

The 2nd General Hospital where he received his final treatments arrived in France August 15, 1944.

Picture – US Medical Center, Unit History book.

No information has been located which identifies when Charles reentered the service nor the unit to which he was assigned. It is possible that he was assigned to his original unit, the 26th Infantry Regiment

Partial view of the new setup of the **2d General Hospital** at Lison, France, the organization's new station from 15 August 1944 to 16 November 1944. In the foreground runs a section of the "Red Ball Express" highway.

of the 1st Infantry Division. The 26th landed on Omaha Beach on D Day. There is also a possibility that he was assigned to the 175th Infantry Regiment of the 29th Infantry Division. The 175th landed on Omaha Beach on July 8, 1944 and helped liberate Lison on June 9, 1944.

Charles R. Ostrum was born in Hume July 2, 1920. He enlisted in the Army on July 19, 1942. After basic training at Fort Bragg, Charles joined the 7th Field Artillery Observations Battalion. The Battalion became famous as "Patton's Forward Observers." His outfit landed on Utah Beach after spending four days at sea in rough weather, unable to get ashore. They then began a whirlwind dash across Europe. At one point they traveled 600 miles in 30 days while following armored units. The 7th was a small outfit that had a major impact. Its job was to identify, as closely as possible, the location (coordinates) of enemy artillery. Once established, coordinates were provided to US artillery units that would pound German artillery impeding the US advance. Charles said the job also included a lot of record keeping. On many occasions they were enlisted to help with other duties. He said he spent short periods acting as a driver for troops.

Charley in combat gear in France. Nunda, NY Historical Society

Charles explained that there were numerous methods they could use to carry out their job. The most sophisticated was to plant seven microphones. When the German artillery fired, the 7th could plot its location based on when the sound of the artillery was picked up by each microphone. Another method was to dig two fox holes some distance apart. Men in the fox holes would then pinpoint the artillery flashes and establish a triangle between the two fox holes and the artillery flashes. Charles said they could also use the old "hold up your fist to the flashes, and then plot an angle" technique. Once observers had the needed information, Charles said, they could broadcast the locations in the clear. Even if the Germans picked up the transmission, all they would hear would be a bunch of numbers. They could not know the locations without access to the charts identifying the meaning of each number.

Charles' unit was on call constantly to assist any outfit taking artillery fire. For instance, one time a small artillery outfit was taken fire near the Saar River in Austria. Charles was sent there with two other men. He started looking for shell fragments so he could determine the size of the artillery being fired. While searching, he was only half paying attention to the sound of the incoming fire. Suddenly he realized that a shell was going to land just a bit behind him. It was too late to take cover, and the concussion of the shell knocked him out. He was helped up by a buddy. Nevertheless, while he did not hurt and could not find any blood on himself, he thought for a second, that he had crossed over to the promised land. Charles quickly realized he was OK and decided he needed to get out of there. He tried to run, but his legs were not working too well. Anyway, after going a short distance, he realized he still had a job to do. He then returned to look for shell fragments and to plot the coordinates of the enemy artillery.

Charles also earned a Bronze Star. His citation reads: "BRONZE STAR. Technician Fifth grade (then Private First Class) Charles R. Ostrum, 42021094, FA, Field Artillery Observation Battalion, for meritorious service in connection with military operations against the enemy in Germany between 25 January 1945 and 30 January 1945, Technician Ostrum, while serving as a member of a shell reporting team, displayed courage and technical skill during coordinated armored and infantry operations in the Saar Moselle Triangle near Besche and Wies. When heavy enemy artillery fire pounded forward infantry elements, he advanced fearlessly through the shelling, calculating the direction of the hostile gun placements, and assisted materially in locating them. Technician Ostrum's actions led to the neutralization of the positions and contributed greatly to the success of the attack. Entered military service from New York."

Charles also experienced some amusing moments. One involved bivouac duty, locating billets for officers and men in German occupied territory. After moving Germans out, they discovered a wine cellar. The cellar had a lot of wine stored openly, but the good wine was concealed in holes in the walls. The commanding officer ordered the wine moved to the officers' trailer. The enterprising enlisted men quickly decided to move the lesser wine to the officer's quarters, and the good wine to their own. Charles managed to get a few bottles of the good wine himself. The switch was discovered, too late to do any good, but the officers got even. At dinner that night, a sign informed the men that anyone caught with wine in their trucks would be subject to court martial. The men solved that problem by drinking as much of the wine as possible before moving out.

Another time, a German civilian reported his watch had been stolen. The officer in charge lined all the men up outside their billet and proceeded to read the riot act. All the time he was chewing them out, behind him, but visible to the men facing him, a truck pulled up. Two G.I.'s got out, went into a house, picked up someone's piano, loaded it on the truck, and drove away. The officer never had a clue.

At war's end, Charles returned home on the Liberty troopship *SS Joseph Leidy*. The trip back was much nicer than the trip over. Charles said that when going over, he had been aboard the British ship *HMS Arawa*. The *Awara* was an old and slow ship. While it started out one night in the middle of the convoy, in the morning it was at the outer edge. The *Awara* was then attacked by a German U-boat that had managed to evade the destroyer escorts. Charles was on deck and could see the torpedo fired by the sub heading directly for the *Awara*. But then a courageous destroyer commander steered his ship directly into the path of the torpedo. Charles said that the destroyer survived, although many men were killed and it had to be towed to England. The death toll would have been much higher had the torpedo hit the *Awara*.

Charles believes the destroyer was the *USS Thatcher*. However, the then current *USS Thatcher* (DD 514) destroyer was in the Pacific at that time. It may, however, have been another ship once named *USS Thatcher*. The original *Thatcher* had been one of the 50 destroyers transferred to England under the Lend Lease agreement. It was then one of six ships provided to the Canadian Navy. The Canadians renamed it the *HMCS Niagara*, and it was assigned to convoy duty during at least part of 1944. It also saw duty as a torpedo training ship in 1944. The 7th Observation Battalion returned to Camp Kilmer, NJ, where Charles was discharged in October 1945.

Ranson L. Richardson, Jr of Fillmore entered the service on August 12, 1943. He took his basic training and then training for the medical corps at Camp Grant, Illinois from September of 1943 until February of 1944. He then sailed to Wales on March 5, 1944, moving to England almost immediately. Within weeks, according to the NAO, he was transferred from the medical corps to an infantry outfit. The NAO reported that he continued to do clerical work after his transfer.

The infantry unit to which he was transferred was likely the Provost Marshal Branch of the First Army Group, located in London. His time with the First Army Group was limited. On July 14, 1944 the First Army Group became the 12th US Army Group. It officially became operational on August 1, 1944. Obviously, operations continued uninterrupted during the designation change from First Army Group to 12th Army Group. The 12th continued to be located in London. The various units of the 12th moved to France over the next several months The Twelfth Headquarters moved several times prior to the end of the war. It was located near Verdun and Wiesbaden when the war ended. The Twelfth Army Group was commanded by Lieutenant General, later General, Omar Bradley. Bradley would remain in command until the end of the war.

The Provost Marshal Branch moved to the continent sometime during the latter half of 1944. The NAO reported in January 1945 that Ransom had written a letter informing them he was now in France. He also thanked the NOA for sending him copies of the newspaper. He remarked that it contained "the names of persons and places familiar to him "since life began"." The Provost Branch was charged with planning all matters pertaining to military discipline, law and order, road traffic control, and criminal investigations related to operations Rankin (contingency plans for invasion of Europe) and Overload (D Day Invasion). It also was responsible for planning matters related to military police basics and training and supply for military police units. It was not responsible for the day-to-day activities nor oversight of the Military Police.

The 12th Army Group was inactivated on August 1, 1945. Around that time Ransom was transferred to the Army Information Education Staff School of the Army Services Forces where he served as an instructor. Ransom returned to the United States on November 4, 1945, arriving in the US on the 19th. He was discharged November 24, 1945.

Llewellyn M. Washburn of Hume, according to the NAO, expected to leave for military service in May or June of 1942. He entered the service almost two years later, on March 24, 1944. LLewellyn was ordered to Camp Blanding, FL, which was both a basic training camp and a replacement training center at that time. There was also anti-aircraft training at Blanding, and it is likely, giving his future assignment, that Llewellyn participated in such training. In October, he was transferred to Fort Meade, MD, probably to prepare for overseas service. Llewellyn arrived in England on October 12, 1944.

It is likely that he received his assignment to the 893rd Anti-Aircraft Automatic Weapons Battalion in England. Records show that the 893rd did receive replacements in late October. At that time its assignment was harbor defense at Marseilles, France. This included defense of the Southern France invasion landing beaches at Cavalier, St. Raphael and Frejus. The Battalion had been part of the Southern France invasion force and had been at Marseilles since the invasion. The 893rd had previously served as the 2nd Battalion of the 62nd Coast Artillery Regiment and had participated in the North African and Sicily invasions. The 62nd was inactivated at Palermo, Sicily on November 10, 1943. Llewellyn arrived too late to receive credit for the invasion.

The 893rd remained in Marseilles for several months. By April 1945 it was in Nancy, France. It was now tasked with defended Rhine River bridges in the Tour, Metz, and Nancy areas. In late April, as the war ended, the 893rd was moved to Germany with its headquarters at Sandhofen. This assignment included defending bridges near Mannheim, Frankenthal and Ludwigshafen. Following the war, it remained in Germany for many months, performing occupation duties from May 20 to October 31, 1945. Llewellyn was discharged on May 24, 1946.

Albert Williams of Fillmore entered the service on February 2, 1942. The NAO reported that he took his basic training at a camp in Alabama. The newspaper did not report again on Albert until September 1944 when it reported him in France. A US Headstone Application document filed by his wife indicates that he served with the 45th Infantry Division, 179th Infantry Regiment, Canon Company. There is no indication as to when or where he joined the 179th. It is possible and perhaps likely that he was assigned to the regiment following basic training. The 179th was training at Camp Barkeley in Texas at that time. On May 1, 1943 it was at Camp Pickett, VA staging for overseas. The regiment sailed June 8, 1943 for the battlefields of the Mediterranean. It landed at Mers el Kabir, Algeria on June 22. During its stay in North Africa, the division underwent additional training at Arzew, French Morocco.

On July 5, 1943, aboard the *USS Leonard Wood*, the regiment sortied with Task Force 65 for Sicily. It, and presumably Albert, earned their first Amphibious Assault Badge July 10, when they stormed ashore at Woods Hole, a few miles west of Scoglitti. (Part of the invasion at Gela.) The 179th, and the rest of the 45th Division, now slugged their way across Sicily. On July 23-26 they forced a strong German contingent out of the Motta Hill area. By July 31 they had reached Cefulu on the north shore and now headed east toward Messina. On August 17, Messina fell and organized resistance on Sicily ended. Albert had earned battle star number one.

The division now regrouped and organized for its next assault. On September 8, 1943, the country of Italy surrendered to the Allies. Most Italian forces immediately switched sides and joined the Allies. However, Italy was defended by German forces and the surrender had little effect on the war. The 45th was aboard an invasion ship on September 8. On September 10 it landed on Blue Beach at Salerno and became part of the bloody and seemingly never-ending battle for Italy. It was a war of defend and attack. Both sides fought furiously over every inch of ground. Progress was slow both due to the strength of the German Army and Italy's rivers and mountains. In early November the 45th reached the Volturno River and captured the city of Venafro. Progress now slowed even more. The division, like other American as well as British units inched forward to the Gustav Line where it stalled. The 45th, after finally reaching the Monte Cassino area in early January, was removed from the line to a rest area.

To break the stalemate a second landing was conducted at Anzio. The 179th was part of the assault forces and earned its third Amphibious Assault Badge, the second being for Salerno. The 45th and the allies faced heavy German resistance at Anzio. Even getting off the beach was a problem. The Germans counterattacked several times. On February 18 the 179th absorbed a massive attack. The months of March, April and May were more of the same with little forward progress. The fighting was ugly and mostly resembled the trench warfare of World War I. Finally, in late May under new leadership, V Corps, which included the 5th Division broke out of the impasse and the rush to Rome was on. The left half of the breakout was led by the 45th. The Germans were pushed aside, their defenses shattered. On June 4, the 45th crossed the Tiber River. Men of the 45th were the first to reach the Vatican.

Following a rest period, the 45th now earned its fourth assault badge during the Allies landings in Southern France. It landed at St. Maxime. The Germans, still reeling from the Normandy invasion, offered light resistance. An overall withdrawal was underway to reform and regroup. The 45th continued its advance taking the strongly held city of Epinaland crossing the Moselle River of September 30. Albert wrote home in February reporting that "the weather was pretty good there and the people were treating them very decently. Almost every time they stopped, people would pass around a basket of tomatoes or some fruit. However, they had a very embarrassing habit of grabbing soldiers and kissing them on the cheeks." The NAO added that Albert had said that, "some old boy with about a week's growth of beard" had convinced him to keep his distance from overly ardent-looking admirers. The paper reported in December that Albert was still in France.

Following the Moselle crossing the division was given a 30-day rest. It then resumed its march into Germany. After crossing the Zintel River, it pushed through the Maginot line. Now came the German winter offensive. From early January until the middle of February the 45th defended against the "Nordwind" attack near the Moder River. It then was given a short rest which included additional training. The final push was on. It smashed through the Siegfried line on March 27, took the battered city of Homburg on March 21. It crossed the Rhine on March 26. The city of Aschaffenburg was captured on April 3 and Nuremburg on the 20th. It crossed the Danube on April 27 and liberated the concentration camp at Dachau on April 29. Its war ended with the capture of Munich on April 30 and May 1. It was in Munich when the war ended.

The division was shipped home in September 1945. It then was sent to Camp Bowie in Texas where it was deactivated December 7, 1945. Albert was discharged December 3, 1945.

Battle of the Bulge (Ardennes Campaign)

The Battered Bastards of Bastogne. Name given to American troops at Battle of the Bulge.

"The poor bastards. They've got us surrounded". Stephen Ambrose attributes the quote to an Army Medic explaining to an injured soldier why he couldn't be evacuated. Battle of the Bulge – 1944.

"They've got us surrounded again, the poor bastards". A similar quote attributed to Colonel Creighton S. Abrams. Battle of the Bulge, 1944. Abrams served as Army Chief of Staff from 1972 tom1974.

"Nuts!" General Anthony C. McAuliffe's response at the Battle of the Bulge to the demand by German forces that McAuliffe surrender his troops. His remark was not sanitized.

A German Officer to an American Officer after General McAuliffe's famous response. *"I speak English fluently and I know what the word nuts means, but I don't understand it in this context."* The American Officer's response. "It means Go to Hell! Do you understand that?" From memory, not necessarily an exact quote. The author read this in the *"Humor in the Uniform"* section of an issue of *"Readers Digest"*, he believes, sometime during the late 1950's.

At least six men from the FCSD area participated in the Battle of the Bulge: Gordon W. Barnett, Adair Wells Common, Kermit A. Davis, Lester E. Noble, Floyd K. Roberts and Harold E. Thayer. Five of the six were killed in action.

The Bulge was one of Hitler's last desperate attempts to turn the tides of war and almost worked. The "Nordwind" offensive was the other, which supported the Bulge operation. The plan basically called for splitting the Allied Forces and then surrounding and destroying four individual armies. Hitler wanted to recapture the port of Antwerp, cutting off a major supply port for the Allies. Fighting took place over a wide area, but the failure to capture Bastogne helped doom it to failure. The seven main roads in the area all went through Bastogne which was protected primarily by the 101st Airborne. The 101st suffered 342 killed, 1,691 wounded, and 516 missing during the battle. The other major American force there, the 10th Armored Division, suffered 55 casualties. Despite the situation, not a single member of the 101st Airborne ever agreed they needed to be rescued. Willie and Joe spoke for them.

Glenn W. Barnett completed his freshman year at Houghton College in the spring of 1941. For financial reasons, he then went to work for the Curtiss-Wright Defense plant in Buffalo. Glenn also continued his college education at night at Canisius College, taking radio training as a repairman, completing the course in June, 1943. During this period, he also enlisted as an Army reservist in the Signal Corps.

On July 15, 1943, Glenn was inducted into the Army at Camp Upton, Long Island. He remembered receiving the usual accoutrements of military service: uniform, dog tags, boots, mess kit, soft cap, and shots, lots of them. He also remembered the hurry-up and wait of military life; double time everywhere, only to wait in line forever. His basic training was at General Tombs Army Camp in Toccoa, GA, at the foot of the Currahee Mountains. He became a member of A Company, 2nd Platoon, 38th Signal Construction Battalion. Glenn's basic training was like that of most other G.I.s: a butch haircut, jogging and hiking, learning to fire a rifle (in his case a Garand rifle), long parade formations, K.P. in the mess hall, guard duty through the night, cleaning the barracks every Friday night, and, of course, weekly inspections. At the end, he advanced from Private to PFC.

When giving a choice of assignments, Glenn smartly chose the Motor Pool. That made him exempt from K.P. and guard duty. He was assigned to drive a 1st Lieutenant with whom he did not see eye to eye on all occasions. In November 1943 Glenn participated on the Blue Team in "Winter Maneuvers." His job was to travel many miles inspecting telephone lines. Like everybody else he endured weeks of outside living, with no fires, no hot food, and no bath from Monday to Friday. The battalion traveled to New Mexico in February 1944 for further training, living in tents in the desert and building superfine copper-wire telephone lines. One more stop was made at Camp Crowder in Northwest Missouri, where the battalion received training on using a machine gun. Glenn's comment was that he "finally passed."

On April 7, 1944, Glenn sailed for Europe aboard the luxury line *Ile de France*, along with 3,000 other GIs. They slept on canvas bunks five deep in stifling heat. The food was miserable. They arrived in Scotland on April 13 and were immediately transported by train to southern England. While they did get some time in London, (where Glenn saw Buckingham Palace, Big Ben, and Parliament), their main job now was preparing for the invasion. On June 5, 1944, Glenn was on guard duty and heard the roar of the Allied air forces as they headed for France in the early hours of June 6.

The 38th Battalion landed on Utah Beach in Normandy on June 22. Upon landing, Glenn picked up his jeep and drove through Ste-Mere-Eglise (where American paratroopers, dropped off course on June 6, were slaughtered as they floated helplessly to earth) to his Battalion's bivouac site. Battalion personnel dug fox holes, put straw in them, and put pup tents over the top. The holes provided partial protection from German bombs, but some men from Company B were killed by such bombs, and others lost their lives to land mines.

The main job for the 38th Battalion was to maintain communications by field wire between its headquarters and Corps. Members of this battalion were usually 20 to 30 miles behind the front lines, but hardly safe. Glenn remembers hearing the V-2 bombs on their way to England. He listened carefully in case the hum stopped, at which point it was important to find cover. Glenn did get to see the sights of Paris once it was liberated. His battalion was stationed near the grounds of the Versailles Palace. On one of those chance encounters, Glenn ran into a neighbor from home, Reverend Reisdorf, in Paris.

Next stop for the 38th was Maastricht in Southern Holland. Billeted in an abandoned schoolhouse, Glenn spent several nights hiding in straw stacks and looking for German paratroopers who had been dropped behind the Allied lines. He never sighted one. However, when the Germans counterattacked in the winter of 1944, the 38th was caught up in the Battle of the Bulge. Glenn narrowly escaped death or capture when he drove his jeep into a wooded area one night, only to find himself surrounded by Germans. He turned around and escaped. During this period, Glenn was trouble-shooting. This involved finding and repairing cut telephone wires at night. (Despite carrying out this and other assignments, Glenn's primary responsibility continued to be driver for the Company Commander.)

In January and February 1945, Glenn was temporarily detailed to the British Army in northwest Germany. He particularly enjoyed the British custom of tea and crumpets in the afternoon, no matter where they were. On the other hand, they were constantly on guard, as this was a period when the Germans were filtering through the allied lines in captured uniforms. Passwords changed every day to help address this threat.

By April, Glenn was back with the 38th and in May learned he had been promoted to T-5, Corporal Technician. The battalion was ordered to southern France - Marseilles - the very area that several FCSD area men had helped liberate in September 1944. There the 38th Battalion members were advised that they were on their way to the Pacific, where the war was still going on. They traveled aboard the troopship *General Butner* through the Strait of Gibraltar, across the Atlantic, through the Panama Canal and into the Pacific. It was now September. The war in the Pacific was over and they would not be needed. Glenn's war was over. He was discharged January 10, 1946.

Of the six FCSD area men who are known to have participated in the Battle of the Bulge, Gordon Barnett is the only one who survived.

Adair Wells Common was a 1935 graduate of Fillmore Central. He entered the service February 20, 1936 as a private and rose to the rank First Sergeant. After attending Officer's Candidate Training school at Fort Benning, GA, he was commissioned a Second Lieutenant on March 24, 1943

Adair initially served with the 502nd Parachute Battalion. After becoming an officer, he served with the 513th Parachute Regiment, 101st Airborne Division. In January, 1944, he was promoted to First Lieutenant at Fort McCall, NC. The 513th moved to England in August 1944. His regiment was stationed at Tidworth Barracks, Windmill Mill, England. In October 1944, it moved to Andover, England. On December 24, 1944, it moved to a tent area at Mourmelon le Grand, France.

December 16, 1944, the official starting date for the Ardennes Alsace Campaign (Battle of the Bulge), marked the beginning of Hitler's last desperate attempt to save his Reich. The 513th was charged with defended the line along the Meuse River in the vicinity of Stenay-Verdun against further German penetration in the Ardennes. It was there to relieve the 11th Armored Division in the vicinity of Flamierge and Flohament. During the period December 27 to 31, the 513th conducted patrols and attempted to pick up enemy parachute drops. There was light strafing and bombing of towns, railroads, and bridges along the Meuse River. On January 1, 1945, the regiment moved further to the front lines west of Bastogne. It was during this move that Adair was killed in action. Thanks to men like Adair, the German's never captured Bastogne. This winter offensive was both a scare to the Allies, and a complete failure for the Germans. Hitler's Thousand Year Reich had only four months of its mere "12 years, 4 months" life left. Hitler had the same amount of time left to live.

At the time of his death, Adair was 27 years old and left a wife and a daughter. His body was returned to the states in November 1945 and he was buried in Fillmore's Pine Grove Cemetery. Six of his high school classmates acted as Pall Bearers.

Kermit A. Davis of Centerville was 33 years old when he entered the Army at Buffalo in April of 1943.

He was sent to Fort Leonard Wood in Missouri, where he was assigned to the 275th Engineer Combat Battalion. During his first 13 weeks he went through the standard basic training for a combat engineer unit with drills, hikes, and orientation sessions, but also map reading, scouting, laying mine fields, and actual job practice where the men became specialists in a particular activity. These specialties included maintaining water supplies, handling explosives, and operating power equipment such as power launches, and bulldozers. Subsequent events made it clear that Kermit specialized in handling explosives.

Purple Heart Medal

The 275th was assigned to the 75th Infantry Division, and following the initial training period, it, participated in the Louisiana-Texas fall maneuvers of 1943. On April 7, 1944, the division, was ordered to Camp Breckinridge, Kentucky. By November 7, 1944, it was at Camp Shanks in New York, staging for movement overseas. Kermit's division sailed for England on November 14, arriving on November 22. He spent the next month in Pembrokeshire, England, before being shipped to France, where they arrived on December 13, 1944. By December 18, Kermit and his division were in the Netherlands; and by the 21st they were in Belgium. The 75th Infantry Division was committed to battle on December 25.

On December 28, 1944, Kermit was wounded in action in an area between the towns of Heyd and La Forge, in the Liege area of Belgium. The Daily Journal for the 275th Combat Engineers, for the time period 1300 to 1700 on December 28th, states: "Co. C reported 3 E.M. (enlisted men) killed and one man wounded by German M.G. (machine gun) fire in laying mine fields in 290 sector." While the report does not provide names, the man wounded was Kermit. The battalion reported no other men killed or wounded during the balance of the month. Other reports indicate that Kermit died December 31, 1944. Kermit had been overseas only two and a half months, and in combat only three days, when he was wounded.

Kermit earned the Purple Heart, among other medals, for his World War II service.

Harold E. Thayer of Fillmore entered the US Army on June 3, 1942. It is not clear if Harold went to a basic training camp initially, or whether he was immediately assigned to Camp Pine (Fort Drum), NY, for training with the 4th Armored Division. By at least November of 1942, Harold was at Fort Knox, KY being trained as a tank mechanic. The NAO reported that following the Fort Knox training he reported back to Camp Pine. In between he spent a short leave with his parents in January 1943.

By July 1943, Harold was at Fort Riley in Kansas. There he became part of the 9th Armored Division, which had been activated July 15, 1942 at Riley, and had been training there for the past year. That training included some time in the Mojave Desert, near Needles, CA in June 1943. Harold joined the group in time to participate in the fifth Louisiana maneuvers beginning in late October 1943. The Division was stationed at Camp Polk. Harold and his wife visited his family in February 1944. He returned to Louisiana, and she stayed in Buffalo. They visited the family again in July. This was Harold's pre-overseas shipment leave. In August, the 9th Armored Division staged for overseas at Kilmer, NJ. They arrived in England August 26, and were stationed at Tidworth Barracks near Amesbury, England.

The Division landed at Normandy at October 9, 1944. It entered Luxembourg on October 20, and was there when the German offensive known as the Battle of the Bulge began on December 16. For 6-days the Division stopped attack after attack. It was outnumbered 5-1 by the Germans. The Division's infantry companies were surrounded most of the time. Everybody in the Division, including clerks, cooks, mechanics, and drivers, manned the line. Harold was one of those men, and on December 18 he was killed in battle. For its heroic actions during this battle, the Division earned a Presidential Unit Citation. Harold is buried at the Ardennes American Cemetery in Neupre, Belgium.

Germany

"Do not say that it had to do with their leaders. They are a people (Germans) *whose fate it is always to choose a man whom they force to lead them in a direction they do not want to go."*
An elderly French man speaking to Gertrude Stein during the war. Book - *1941*

"Sure, we want to go home...The shortest way home is through Berlin and Tokyo. And when we get to Berlin, I am personally going to shoot that paper hanging son-of-bitch Hitler. Just like I'd shoot a snake." General George S. Patton June 5, 1944

There would be no World War I type Armistice this time. The end goal was defeat of Germany and unconditional surrender. The FCSD area was well represented as the Allies ground troops fought their way into Germany. A few FCSD area men had already been there, or at least in the skies above Germany. Gerald Gayford, and David Wallace had been there with the Mighty Eighth and had not returned. Royal Strait and Lowell Mix, with the 15th Air Force, had been there several times, and made it back safely each time. David Ayer had been there with the 397th Bomb Group. Bernard Sweet and his P-47 had been there on strafing mission's numerous times. Now came Ralph L. Alderman, Edward J. Amore, Ivan R. Ayer, Glenn W. Barnett, Richard G. Beach, John W. Beardsley, Jr., William C. Brueser, Frank R. Butterfield, Burdette H. Byron, Everett M. Clark, Everett F. Clute, Robert D. Colburn, Edward M. Cole, William C. Crandall, Robert M. Dinkel, Leon P. Ellis, Maxwell L. Fancher, Donald W. Finnemore, Steward E. Folts, Ronald G. Fridley, Charles E. Hodnett, Russell C. Hodnett, Wesley E. Hopkins, Alfred H. Kingsley, Earle C. Knorr, Frank J. Kopler, Irving C. Letson, Beverly A. Luckey, Burton A. Markham, Donald D. Marriott, Hubert H. McMaster, Arthur C. Miller, David W. Morgan, Lewis J. Morgan, Charles R. Ostrum, Carroll S. Phipps, Lloyd L. Prentice, Milton C. Rathbun, George A. Rennicks, Gerald W. Rennicks, Floyd K. Roberts, Herbert L. Rose, Sanford I. Smith, Robert W. Stevens, Gerald R. Thomas, Roland J. Thomas, George W. Tisdale, Irwin K. Tuthill, Anthony R. Vasile, Gerald J. Voss, Donald L. Whalen, Lowell J. Wilcox, Glenn C. Wilday and Robert B. Wolfer.

Ralph L. Alderman of Fillmore (originally Rushford) entered the service on January 11, 1943. His twin brother Robert entered the service the same day. The NAO reported that he was assigned to Fort Bragg. Based upon his Separation Qualification Record, it appears his basic training was as a combat engineer. However, the Record also shows that he spent the rest of his service, 34 months, as a musician. Ralph's daughter, Lola (Hardy), said her father played clarinet and the drums, and read and arranged music. He was assigned to the 82nd Airborne Division Band.

Ralph originally trained as a combat engineer (officially Military Occupation Code (MOS)729 - Pioneer). The Army described pioneers as crews of troops specially trained in constructing and repairing roads and bridges, removing natural and man-made obstacles to facilitate movement of friendly forces, executing demolitions, and creating man-made obstacles to prevent or slow the advance of enemy forces.

Ralph told his daughter Lola that even though he was assigned to the 82nd Airborne Infantry Band, he had to select another area of training. Lola said Ralph selected parachute training as one earned more money as a parachutist. Lola said he completed glider as well as parachute training. She also said that Ralph participated in the Tennessee maneuvers before going overseas. *Family Photo – Ralph on patrol in Berlin in 1945 performing occupation duties possibly wearing his Orange Lanyard on the wrong shoulder.*

It appears that Ralph was assigned to bands in a several different units during his service. This is based on shoulder and hat patches that appear in his war time photos. These units included the 17th Airborne Infantry Division, the 82nd Airborne Infantry Division and the 504th Airborne Infantry Regiment. All of these units had bands, but it is not known whether the bands went overseas at the same time as their division or regiment. The list does not include training units. Both the 82nd Airborne Division and the 504th Airborne Infantry Regiment were overseas before Ralph completed his training. However, the 17th Airborne Division did not go overseas until August 1944. The 17th and Ralph both participated in Tennessee Maneuvers during the period February 6, 1944 to March 24, 1944. Ralph may have been assigned or attached to the 17th at that time. The 17th did train at Fort Bragg during the period that Ralph was there, but was transferred to Camp Forrest at the completion of the maneuvers. It appears that Ralph remained at Fort Bragg.

The 17th Airborne sailed for Europe August 20, 1944 from Boston aboard the *USS Wakefield*. It arrived in the United Kingdom on August 26, 1945. It appears the Ralph sailed to Europe from New York City on August 17, 1944 likely aboard the *Ile de France*. He arrived in England August 25, 1944.

By the time Ralph arrived in England, the 82nd had already participated in combat in Sicily, Italy, and Normandy. The 504th Parachute Infantry Regiment, a unit of the 82nd, did not participate in the Normandy invasion although they had been part of the original invasion forces. The Regiment had returned to England early due to excessive combat and to prepare for the Normandy invasion. It arrived in Liverpool on April 22. One report says they were greeted by the 82nd Airborne Division Band playing "We're all Americans and Proud to Be." This may have been the 504th Infantry Regiment Band. Another document says the 82nd Airborne Division band was organized March 1, 1945 at Suippes, France. The document also says that personnel for the Band were transferred from other units including the 82nd Airborne Artillery Band and the 504th Parachute Infantry Band

Given the above, it is possible that Ralph was assigned to the 504th Airborne Infantry Band. This is supported by a 504th patch that appears on Ralph's cap in a war time photo. As part of the 504th Band Ralph would have participated in ceremonies involving the arrival and departure of 82nd Airborne Division troops, as well as possibly dances and other official ceremonies and parades.

The unit Citation and Campaign Participation Credit Register indicates that the 82nd Band earned four campaign (battle) stars. Ralph likely earned three of those stars – Ardennes-Alsace, Rhineland, and Central Europe. Ralph was with the 504th Band and the 82nd band during the eligibility time period for these awards. His daughter says that there are three small bronze stars among his medals. Like the Band, Ralph would also have earned two foreign decorations. Those were from the government of the Netherlands for the 504th and 82nd achievements during the failed Market Garden operation. It should be noted that while the overall operation failed, the 82nd and 504 achieved their objectives. The Netherlands awards were the Military Order of William "Militaire Wilems Orde" and the wearing of the Orange Lanyard.

The reorganized 82nd arrived in Suippes, France on March 1, 1945. The Band, or parts thereof, were assigned to the following locations over the next several months – Weiden, Germany, Hohenzethen, Germany, Bleckede, Germany, Lundquist, Germany, Sisone, France, Epinal, France, and Berlin, Germany. During this period the Band followed its normal training schedule as well morning marching with instruments. It also was called on to perform certain occupation duties. Those occupation activities primarily involved guard and patrol duties.

Ralph remained on duty in Germany until December 1945 when he and his unit returned to the states. Ralph was discharged January 5, 1946 at Fort Dix, NJ.

Edward J. Amore of Fillmore entered the service on June 10, 1941. By serving between June 10 and December 7, 1941, Edward earned the American Defense Medal. He was originally assigned to Fort Niagara which served as a reception center for recruits from 1941 to 1943. According to the NAO, he was stationed at Fort Niagara during June and July 1941. In August the NAO reported he was assigned to Troop A at the Cavalry Replacement Training Center (CRTC) in Fort Riley, Kansas. A CRTC unit consisted of a Headquarters Regiment and four training regiments. Each regiment consisted of two squadrons and each squadron consisted of an A and B Troop. The purpose of the CRTC was to provide men, as replacements, who could operate efficiently in garrison and field positions. Initially training was provided for both horse and mechanized cavalry units. By 1942 the training was virtually all for mechanized units. Further the goal of the training evolved into providing tactical units individuals who fit into a given spot in the organization.

The first training period ran from March 24, 1941 until June 14, 1941. While the NAO has Edward still at Fort Niagara in July, it is likely that he had already moved to Fort Riley by late June. Fort Niagara was an induction center and Edward would not have remained there for an extensive period. Therefore, it is likely that he was assigned to the 13-week training program which began about July 1 and ended September 27. The NAO reported that Edward remained at the Center until January, 1942. The history of the Center states that some specially qualified men who completed training were not sent on to regiments, but instead were retained at Fort Riley as specialists and non-commissioned officers to train incoming troops. That may have happened to Edward or he may have remained at Fort Niagara for two months waiting for a training slot to open at Riley. He could then have been part of the third training class at Riley.

The NAO reported him home in January visiting his sister (Mrs. Margaret Ricketts with whom he was living at the time of his enlistment. Edward had been living in the Fillmore area since at least 1935). He likely reported to Fork Polk, Louisiana following his furlough. The NAO reported him stationed at Fort Polk in November 1943. At that time, he was again visiting his sister, this time with his wife and child. (His wife, Elizabeth Gleason of Caneadea, was born Elizabeth Meach. She was a descendant of the family of Civil War soldier and Medal of Honor winner George Meach. Elizabeth's grandfather George A. Meach was possibly named after the Civil War George who never had any children.) Given that the NAO reported his wife visited him at Fort Polk in April 1944, it is possible that the November visit was for the purpose of settling his family in Fillmore or Caneadea, likely in anticipation of a future overseas assignment.

At Fort Polk Edward was promoted to the rank of Master Sergeant. Given his rank, he likely was serving as an instructor, or possibly as top sergeant in a training unit. Fort Polk was a training center for armored units during Edward's service there. It was also the home for the Louisiana maneuvers and starting in 1943 a German POW camp.

Edward almost surely was assigned to one of the armored units being trained at Fort Polk, and joined the shooting war in Europe with that unit sometime after April 1944 following his wife's visit. A prime candidate would appear to be the 8th Armored Regiment which was training at Folk Polk at the time, and whose history is consistent with Edward's history from that point on. No evidence has yet been identified that proves he served with the 8th Armored. The 8th proved to be a formable unit and was a main cog in the Allies effort to destroy Nazi Germany. It also proved adept in carrying out key occupation duties following the war.

In November 1945, the NAO reported Edward home from service in Germany with his discharge. He was discharged October 19,1945 having returned from Europe on October 13 according to his final pay record. Edward earned, among others, the American Defense Medal, the American Campaign Medal, the

European African Middle East Campaign Medal, and the Word War II Victory Medal. He likely also earned some battle stars, the Good Conduct Medal and possible the Combat Infantry Badge. Many members of the 8th Armored did in fact earn that prestigious award.

Richard "Dick" G. Beach of Houghton was drafted into the US Army on July 22, 1943. He was 19 years old. For the next year Dick participated in basic and combat training.

On August 17, 1944 he sailed from New York Harbor aboard the *Ile De France* (Ralph Alderman sailed on the same ship) for Edinburgh, Scotland, arriving that same month. From there he was transported immediately by train to Portsmouth, England. The next day, now early September, he was on his way to Europe to join the 79th Infantry Division, His unit was Company L, 3rd Battalion, 315 Infantry Regiment. Landing at Omaha Beach, he joined the Division outside the French village of St. Lo. The 79th Division had been given the important job of seizing Cherbourg. It was recognized that the Cherbourg's ports would be needed for handling the vast tonnage of supplies that would be required for the Allied advance into France and Germany.

Dick was immediately thrust into action as the 79th concentrated on forcing the Germans from the Joinville area of France. The Germans fought furiously and there was heavy combat, but the 79th Division was able to clear the area. The 315th Regiment seized Neufchateau on September 13, 1944. The division resumed its offensive and by September 20 had reached the Meurthe River near Luneville. On September 21 the 315th lost and then recovered part of Lunesville during intense fighting, but on October 5 it was temporarily isolated in fighting at the main road junction. By October 9 the 79th Division had captured the road junction. On October 13 it captured Embermenil and then engaged in a furious battle for the high ground east of the city until October 22. Dick's son Bradley said that during this battle, on October 27, he was badly wounded by gunfire. The 315th operations report indicates that it was in the vicinity of Bayonne during this period.

Despite the seriousness of his wounds, thanks to excellent surgical treatment, Dick was able to rejoin the 315th near Rittenshoffen in early January, 1945. By this time, Dick was a proven combat veteran. He moved with his regiment to the southern portion of the Rhine River, which was being held by Task Force Linden (42nd Infantry Division). Elements of the Task Force had been surrounded so Dick and the division battled through the German lines at Stattmattten to relieve them. The division crossed the Rhine on March 29, 1945. It then relieved the 35th Infantry Division west of Gelsenkirchen and attacked across the Emser and Rhine-Herne canals on April 7. It reached the Ruhr on April 9, establishing a beachhead at Kettwig on April. 11,1945. It was relieved the following day, and Dick's combat was finally over.

Dick remained in Germany after it's surrender, becoming part of the Occupation Army. His primary duty was driving a gasoline truck between German cities. He returned to the states in the summer of 1946. Dick earned the Purple Heart and a Bronze Star, among several other medals, including five battle stars. He also earned the Combat Infantry Badge and probably the Good Conduct Medal. As a result of earning the Combat Infantry Badge (CIB), he also earned a Bronze Star. This award was established by Congress in 1947 for all men who had earned the CIB.

William C. Brueser of Centerville entered the service on July 24, 1944. It is not certain where he took his basic training, but he likely trained at Fort Leonard Wood, MO. The regiment to which he was eventually assigned, 274th Infantry Regiment, 70th Infantry Division, was transferred from Camp Adair, OR, to Fort Wood in July 1944. In November 1944 the Division moved to Myles Standish, MA to stage for shipment to Europe.

Due to the critical situation in Europe at that time the 274th Infantry Regiment, identified as Task Force Herren was shipped to Marseilles ahead of the rest of the Division. This Task force arrived in Marseille during the period December 10 to 15, 1945. By December 28, the Task Force assumed defensive positions on the west Bank of the Rhine near Bischwiller. William was assigned to Company A, part of the first battalion. By early January, the German winter offensive was finished. In fact, the 3rd Battalion of the 274th helped plug the gaps, especially the 3rd Battalion at Rothback, France, that doomed the advance. The Allies now resumed their own offensive, the final push into the heartland of Nazi Germany. The life span of the Third Reich was now down to some four months. The 274th would play a role in its final demise. Its first key objectives were an important highway intersection and rail line at Phillipsburg, France. The Germans were desperate to keep control of the village and thus the transportation nodes. They fought desperately to hold them, and almost succeeded. But the 274th prevailed.

Next came Wingen, France. The job of taking this village was given to the 2nd Battalion. The men of the battalion became veterans overnight by defeating some of the best the Germans had to offer. They took the village, destroyed two highly rated German battalions, liberated over 250 American prisoners from a third German Battalion and earned themselves a Presidential Unit Citation.

Next came the advance into Germany. The Seventh Army was ordered to clear the Saar Basin and capture German strongholds in the area. One of those was Saarbrucken. They also had to cross the Siegfried Line. The attack began on March 15. The 274th was ordered to cross the Saar River at one of its most heavily defended points. This was accomplished the night of March 19-20. By afternoon of March 20, Saarbrucken belonged to the Allies and the Third Reich was another step closer to death.

Saarbrucken was the last major conflict for the 274th. After hostilities ended, it was assigned to occupation duties in Germany from May 20 until September 18, 1945. It returned to the US October 10, 1945.

On April 17, 1945, General Order Number 14 awarded William the Combat Infantryman Badge (CIB). He also earned the 1947 Congressional awarded Bronze Star as a result of earning the CIB.

Frank Rozell Butterfield of Fillmore entered the service on January 6, 1941. In February he wrote his grandparents in Fillmore that he was with the coast artillery at Fort Hancock, NJ. He was enjoying Army life and had gained ten pounds. In May he was transferred to the Army cooking school at Fort Slocum, NY where he spent some four months learning the ropes of preparing Army cuisine. In September 1941 he returned to Fort Hancock. While at Hancock he likely served with the 245th Coastal Artillery Battalion. It appears he remained at Hancock until February or March of 1944 when he was transferred to Fort Chaffee, Arkansas. He was still at Hancock in December 1943 when he wrote the NAO thanking the Junior Red Cross and his friends in Fillmore for Christmas packages.

On December 1, 1944 he sailed from New York City for England likely aboard the *Marine Panther,* arriving December 12 at Southampton. It is also likely that he sailed with the 663rd Field Artillery Battalion, the unit he would serve with over the next several months. He and the regiment spent the next couple of months in England preparing for combat. In March they arrived at Camp Twenty Grand near DuClair, France. The 335th was initially assigned to the VIII Corps, 416th Field Artillery Group, 3rd US Army on March 1. Frank spent his entire service as an Army cook.

On March 8 they were reassigned to 402nd Field Artillery Group also part of VIII Corps, and still assigned to 3rd Army. They would remain assigned to VIII Corps for the rest of their service in Europe. Entering combat almost immediately, the Battalion crossed France in days and blasted their way into Germany along with General Patton's Third Army. Their only two stops in France were Soissons and Longway.

By the end of the month, they had roared through four German cities, Pronsfel, Flerigen, Saffig and Waldesch. During the drive, the 663rd expended 1,782 rounds of artillery fire. The unit was equipped with 8-inch howitzers. Most of their rounds were used for harassment and interdiction with the next highest target being enemy artillery batteries.

April was more of the same as they raced through Lohrheim, Iba, Herrenbrestungen, Freidreroda, Nauendorf, Sundremda, Vartchesfend, Grafendorf, Kauschwitz, Moschwita and Friesen. Their major targets remained harassment and interdictions, but the total rounds fired fell to only 376.On April 22 the unit was transferred to the 1st Army from the 3rd. They were also called upon to perform additional duties, including clearing areas of enemy personnel, policing towns, and guarding hospitals. Qualified personnel were also called upon to perform motor and material maintenance. The NAO reported in April that a message from Frank indicated that his unit was "in mortal combat with the Nazis." His April letter likely referred to the unit's March activities.

On May 2nd they were reassigned again, this time to the 18th Field Artillery Group. The unit moved only twice more before the end of the war on May 8. They went to Friesen and then Mitteltrohad. Only 105 rounds of ammunition were expended during the eight combat days in May.

In September he returned to the states arriving on September 10, 1945. Frank earned two battle stars during his service in Europe. He was discharged November 10, 1945.

Burdette Henry Byron of Allen entered the service on June 10, 1941. His personnel file was destroyed in the St. Louis fire so limited information is available about his service. His write-up at the World War II Memorial in Washington, DC does provide some information. Burdette saw quite a bit of combat during the war serving in all three European combat areas – North Africa, Italy, and Northern Europe, likely including both France and Germany. He participated in four major campaigns, Tunisia, Rome Arno, Rhineland, and Central Europe. He served with Combat engineer units as a tractor mechanic and was likely used as a combat infantryman in at least North Africa. Since he participated in the Tunisian campaign, he likely was in North Africa by November 17, 1942. However, he could have arrived a few months later, but no later than May 1943 and still participated in the campaign.

The NAO reported that he sent relatives an Easter greeting from North Africa in March 1944. Shortly after that, he must have moved to Italy with his unit as his WW II write-up at the Memorial shows that he received a battle star for the Rome-Arno Campaign. Following the Rome-Arno, it is likely that he moved to first England and then France. He may also have been transferred to a different engineer unit at this time or it is possible his entire unit was transferred. He now participated in his final campaign, the Central Europe campaign which took the American Army into Germany, the heart of the Third Reich. By the time this campaign ended, the Third Reich no longer existed.

An August 6, 1945 Journal entry of the 237th Engineer Combat Battalion, issued in Mourmelon, France, indicates that Burdette had transferred to the 237th on July 30 and was assigned to Company A. The information on the unit from which he was transferred is not available. A later entry dated September 4 has the unit in Juvincourt, France. Burdette likely returned to the states in late September and was discharged October 3, 1945. The NAO reported him home visiting family in October.

Everett F. Clute of Wiscoy entered the service July 16, 1942 in Buffalo. Everett spent a month in basic training before being assigned to a unit. He then served as a truck driver light for a month. It is not known where Everett was assigned during these two months. Everett's Qualification Separation Record indicates that he served the remainder of his service as a Dispatcher Clerk. As such he worked in a motor pool. His responsibilities included keeping records of gasoline and oil used, and repairs made to all vehicles.

For one year he served as the chief dispatcher. In this position he supervised 12 enlisted men and 40 civilians. The duties of these men included maintaining records and doing general paper work. He was responsible for sending vehicles to the garage for repairs and making out disability reports on vehicles being repaired. Other duties were requisitioning new parts and performing duties necessary to the operation of a motor pool. Again, it is not known where Everett was assigned during most of his time as a Dispatcher Clerk.

It is known that on February 7, 1945 he sailed from the United States to India. Upon arrival he was assigned to the 1959th Quartermaster Truck Company (305th Service Group) in Ondal, India. He remained at Ondal for the balance of his service. The 1959th was responsible for transporting bombs, other ordnance, commissary, and other supplies to various units in their service area. These areas included distribution points at Bushkarp, Ninja, Pandaveshwar, and Nadhigans. This was a major undertaking, especially when it is understood that it took place over a broad area that lacked modern highways even by the standard of the day. In some cases, there were not even paved roads. Under these conditions the drivers put up large numbers, with many driving over 1,000 miles a month. Some far exceeded that figure. In April one driver made 14 trips driving 2,350 miles. In May 1945 the top driver made 21 trips traveling 1,497 miles.

The 1959th remained in Nodal until the end of 1945. The report of activities for the after-war months indicate that many efforts were made to help the men fill up the time. Some received furloughs back to the states. Others received passes to major India cities. Recreation activities were stepped up. A softball league continued but other activities were added. Basketball and volleyball courts were constructed. Even educational classes were made available and many men participated. It is important to remember that many of these men left the final years of high school to enter the service. This gave them an opportunity to catch up a bit. The 1959th was inactivated January 19, 1946. Everett sailed for home January 9, 1946 arriving February 4, 1946. He was discharged February 12 at Fort Dix, NJ.

Robert D. Colburn of Hume was drafted into the Army twice. The first time, the Army subsequently notified him that a mistake had occurred and to ignore the call. On December 11, 1942, he was drafted for the second time. This time there was no mistake. Robert was sent to Camp Chaffee, AR, for basic training. He also became a member of the 14th Armored Division, which had been activated at Camp Chaffee on November 15th of that year. For the next 21 months Robert went through extensive training with the 14th Division at Chaffee, and Camp Campbell, KY, and he participated in extensive maneuvers in Tennessee in the fall of 1943.

On October 14, 1944, Robert and the 14th Armored Division sailed for Marseilles, France aboard the *Santa Rosa*. They arrived on October 28th. After a brief training period, the Division was committed to battle on November 20, 1944. Robert spent some 29 days in combat before being severely wounded.

Robert was assigned to the 25th Recon Platoon of the 25th Tank Battalion. Such platoons were the eyes and ears of the Battalion. Their primary responsibility was to gather information that would answer key questions: Where is the enemy? Where is there resistance? What is the terrain? Is it passable? Recon platoons also performed other duties such as manning observations posts and acting as guards. In emergencies, they were also used as front-line troops. Recon Platoons did enjoy one amenity. Due to their jobs, they were assigned jeeps. Robert immediately named his jeep "Hume" after his home town. Further he told his son David, that while the jeeps were unarmed, they had managed to jerry-rig a 50-caliber machine gun to "Hume."

The first combat task of the 14th was to participate in the drive through the Vosges Mountains. This was a daunting task, as detailed elsewhere in this book. It was something that had not been done by a modern army, and many believed it could not be done. But the 14th along with other divisions smashed their way through the mountains, and onto the Alsatian Plain. The 14th advanced from Maguenau, captured the key city of Wissemberg, and crossed into Germany. The Siegfried Line, which was the German equivalent of the French Maginot Line, was no obstacle to the 14th. Robert's unit was assigned to Combat Command A (CCA) which had been given the mission of attacking the Surbourg-Wissembourg axis, seizing Wissembourg, and crossing the Lauter River. Ready to advance further into Germany, the 14th had to stop and fight back against the winter counter offensive led by German General Gerd Von Rundstedt. The 14th was diverted to help repel the attack; and it battled elite Nazi troops in the Bitcue salient, stopping the Nazi attempt to overrun Alsace, and retake Strasburg. American General Jacob L. Devers called this action, "the greatest defensive battle of the war."

As the 14th advanced through the Vosges and onto the Alsace Plains, fighting was vicious. By the end of the war, the 14th had suffered 555 men KIA, 221 MIA, 206 captured, and 2,030, including Robert, WIA. He was wounded on December 18, 1944. The History of the 14th Armored Division notes for December 16, "The 25th (Tank Battalion) re-attacked through Schweighofen and fought its way into Kapsweyer. Capt. Warren E. Benoit's A-68 cleared and out-posted the town. C-25 (Company C, 25th Tank Battalion) deployed along a ridge to fire directly at the pillboxes. The assault guns and the 501st Field went into position. Capt. Thomas Tweedle and Lieut. John Larsen set up a FO (forward observation) post in a church steeple; the enemy knocked the steeple down; they were not wounded. The 25th Recon Platoon formed the CP (Command Post) guard. Artillery fell in town all night." On December 18 the history notes, "The 25th Tank Battalion, meanwhile, was under continual enemy fire in the vicinity of Kapsweyer; Col. Watson, Lieut. Kirby and men of the Recon Platoon were caught in the open by one barrage, and Lieut. Kirby and Sgt Robert Colburn were severely wounded. Besides the artillery, the town was under direct fire, every vehicle that moved drew fire and the buildings were being cut to pieces. Robert told his son Loren, that he and the others had dived into two shell holes. Incoming artillery exploded between the two holes, causing his wounds.

Robert's wounds ended his war. He was hit by shrapnel in his back, and his left ankle was almost ripped off. In fact, Army doctors at one point suggested to Robert that part of his leg be removed. Instead, after numerous treatments, his leg was fused, and he was able to walk satisfactorily for the rest of his life. Healing took a long time. After treatment in Europe, he was shipped home aboard the hospital ship *Algonquin*. He received treatment at Halloran Hospital on Long Island and at Northington General Hospital in Tuscaloosa, AL. Due to his prolonged treatment, Robert was not discharged until April 4, 1947. Among the many medals he had earned were the prestigious Combat Infantry Badge (CBI), and the Purple Heart. He also earned the 1947 Congressionally awarded Bronze Star since he had earned the CBI. This award recognized that men with the CBI, deserved additional honor for their service.

Edward M. Cole entered the service on October 16, 1942. Edward was from Nunda but by 1940 was living in Fillmore with his sister Marie Bleistein and Mother Leah. It is not clear where Edward served during his first eight to nine months. At least part of that time was basic training and some was likely also specialty training. A June 1944 item in the Nunda News reported that Edward was in England. A November 1945 article in the *Nunda News* reported that he went overseas 26 months ago. That would have put him in England around September of 1943. Other information puts him in England in the fall of 1943. The November article also indicated that he served with an anti-aircraft unit while in England. These reports indicate that Edward arrived in England before the 4th Infantry Division arrived in January 1944.

In August 1945 Edward sent his Aunt Mrs. Chester Bugman, a booklet about the *Famous 4th* (4th Infantry Division.) He indicated that he had served with the 4th for most of the war. The anti-aircraft unit which was attached to the 4th Infantry Division for most of the war was the 377th Anti-Aircraft Automatic

Weapons Battalion (AAA AW BN). However, it is more likely that by the time he was with the 4th he was assigned to the Military Police Platoon. A June report in the NAO indicated he was stationed in England and had just been made orderly of the guard. Another article in the NAO published in June of 1945 indicated that he was doing special police work in Germany. The above indicates that Edward could have been assigned to an anti-aircraft unit when he arrived in England, but later was transferred to the Miliary Police Platoon of the 4th Infantry Division after it arrived in January 1944. Therefore, he could have served with the 377th. Anti-aircraft during his initial period in England, but the subsequent articles in the NAO tend to indicate he was with a Military Police unit for most of his tour in Europe.

The 377th arrived in England in the fall of 1943. It defended a B-17 bomber base while in England and trained for the Normandy invasion. The 377th was attached to the 4th for the invasion. It would remain with the 4th through March 1945. The 8th Infantry Regiment of the 4th Infantry Division was the first surface borne unit (as opposed to airborne units) to land on Utah Beach on June 6, 1944. The 377th landed a few days later. The 4th Division was attached to Patton's Third Army.

The Military Police Platoon attached to the 4th Infantry Division landed on Utah Beach over the period June 6 to June 9, 1944. It is not known which day Edward landed. They were immediately put to work. Their first job was traffic control getting men and machines off the beach. These initial duties continued until the capture of Cherbourg. Another major duty related to the invasion was the handling of refugees from the battle. This involved the housing, feeding and rehabilitation of the refugees. The unit was also charged with handling almost 10,000 POWs. Other duties included operating road blocks to stop other traffic from interfering with the off-the beach traffic, operating road patrols, providing private escort service as required, enforcing traffic regulations and other priorities. These duties continued throughout the war. Others were eventually added including responsibilities for POWs and other prisoners, tracking enemy agents and AWOL servicemen and straggler control and guard duty. Still more were added when they served as part of the occupation forces, including evacuating refugees and thief of government property. Edward's unit was in the thick of the war. An indication of this is that, while it was a small unit compared to others, the platoon's September Report announced that 11 men had earned the Bronze Star for action against the enemy.

Of special note is the Ardennes Alsace (Battle of the Bulge) battle star earned by the 4th Division. That combat star was awarded only to the Headquarters and Headquarters Company, the Band, the Military Police, Division Artillery and Headquarters and Headquarters Battery.

According to the NAO Edward returned to the states and was discharged in November 1945. (He reenlisted in December and made the military a career.) The 4th ID (Infantry Division) returned to the states in July 1945. Edward's Military Police Platoon apparently remained in Germany possibly carrying out the special police work referred to in the June 1945 NAO article. As reported by the NAO, it appears that Edward returned to the states in November 1945. Among other medals, Edward's occupation duties would have earned him an Occupation Medal with a Germany Clasp.

The famous author Ernest Hemenway attached himself to the 4th. A not very favorable article about Hemenway's time with the 4th was written by Charles Whiting and printed on the Warfare History Network. He was apparently not well received as the men saw him more as promoting himself rather than reporting the war. The author J.D. Salinger who wrote the classic *Catcher in the Rye* served with the 4th throughout the entire war. He was assigned to counter-intelligence with the 12th Infantry Regiment. He participated in the D Day landing, the Battle of the Bulge and Battle of Hurtgen Forest. It is unlikely that Edward met either man. Hemenway attached himself to the 22nd Infantry Regiment and Salinger was part of another infantry regiment. Further, Salinger was not really known at the time although he wrote several short stories during his service. His classic book was not published until 1945 and 1946.

Robert M. Dinkel of Fillmore entered the military on August 3, 1943. He was assigned to Camp Picket,  VA for training in the Medical Corps. The training emphasized training in actual situations including medical and evacuation problems on battlefields. By October 1942 he was at Fort Bragg, NC where he went through additional training with the 66th General Hospital. The NAO reported him home on leave in June of 1943. This was apparently a pre-overseas leave as when he returned to Fort Bragg, his unit shipped out. Bob however, along with 25 other men, was assigned to Camp Ellis, Il as a trainer. He was assigned to the 341st Station Hospital at Fort Ellis. While at Ellis, he went through numerous tests and at one point it was feared he had a brain tumor. It was finally determined that he had a serious left eye problem. Once treated, he was declared fit for overseas service. He shipped out May 10, 1944 arriving at Exeter, Devon, England May 20, 1944. He was assigned to the 61st Field Hospital. The 61st remained in England for the next several months performing several types of service. Their equipment was late in arriving hampering the ability of the hospital to begin functioning as a unit. At times, the men of the unit were assigned to other units. In September 1944 the 61st moved to Cornwall, England where it functioned as a station hospital. *National Archives Photo – Bob is not in the photo but he did work with x-ray machines like the one in the photo.*

The historical records for the 61st are only available through September 1944. It appears that it moved to France sometime early in 1945, where initially it was located near Le Mans, France. The NAO reported in March 1945 that Bob was stationed in France as medical technician in a field hospital. He had been promoted to Corporal. As a medical technician Bob performed various duties in care of sick, injured and wounded soldiers. He provided emergency treatment to causalities and prepared them for evacuation; cleaned and bandaged injuries and wounds, applied arm and leg splints, administered hypodermics and sterilized instruments and equipment. He also performed various administration duties such as taking temperatures, operating the electrocardiograph machine, and determining blood types. Bob also served as an x-ray technician (see picture of machine) which required him to be capable of operating an x-ray machine, including positioning the patient, determining the proper voltage and amperage and length of exposure. He had to be capable of developing the film and making minor repairs to x-ray machines such as replacing fuses, switches, circuit breakers, wires, and x-ray tubes.

In May 1945, Bob was awarded his good Conduct Medal by General Order 3. By May the 61st had moved to Reims, France. The General Order indicates that Bob was assigned to the 2nd Hospitalization Unit.

In September, 1945, as reported in the NAO, Bob used some leave to visit his dad's sister in Switzerland. Bob informed the NAO that he was away from his unit for four weeks although he only spent seven days with his aunt. It took him over a week of travel to get to Switzerland and over a week to get back to his unit. The paper reported that the 61st moved from Germany back to France in September. However, other documents indicate that at least some elements of the unit performed occupation duties in Germany until late December. Bob and the 61st earned battle stars for the Central Europe and Rhineland campaigns. He and the unit also earned the Germany Occupation Medal for service during the periods May 20 to July 5. Bob sailed for the US December 22, 1945 arriving January 1, 1946. He was discharged January 2, 1946.

Leon R. Ellis of Hume entered the service March 31, 1944. He took basic training at Fort Dix NJ. The NAO reported in August that he had spent two weeks at home with his parents. In November, the paper reported that he had been transferred to Camp Bowie, in Texas.

At Bowie, Leon joined the 13th Armored Division, which has been transferred to Bowie from Camp Peale California in December 1943. He was assigned to the 46th Tank Battalion. In January, the Division sailed for Europe, landing at Le Havre, France, on January 29, 1945.

A March 1945 edition of the NAO reported that Leon had arrived safely in France. In a letter to his parents, Leon said that he and others "slept in a straw barn, and were very comfortable." The barn he slept in was near the small French village of Beaunay in Normandy. The 13th Division and Leon, spent the next six weeks in that area, preparing for battle. They moved out on March 15, expecting to help force the collapse of the Ruhr Pocket and to cut a path to the Inn River. Instead, they were assigned policing tasks, including assisting with handling displaced persons. On April 6, the 13th Division became part of Patton's famous Third Army but were moved to Beise Forth, Germany to assist with the military government in that area. Very shortly however, the Division again was reassigned, this time to the 1st Army, and moved to cover the southern boundary of the Ruhr Pocket. On April 10, it entered battle, coming under fire at Diessem, and suffering several casualties. Leon's Task Force and the entire 13th Armored Division now proved their mettle. They blasted their way through one German town after another. They crossed the Regen and Danube Rivers, and they secured the area around Dunzling. On April 28 they crossed the Isar River. They then smashed their way into Brannau in Austria. To make sure everyone knew who was in charge, they established their Command Post in the house where Hitler was born. Leon was in Brannau when the war ended. The 13th Armored Division remained in Germany until June 25. It sailed for home on July 14, 1945.

Maxwell L. (Max) Fancher of Houghton was 16 years old when the Japanese attacked Pearl Harbor. Two years and one day later, he was inducted into the United States Army. After completing basic and technical training, Max was assigned to the 411th Infantry Regiment, 103rd Infantry Division (known as the "Cactus Division"). Max was a radio operator with an anti-tank company. Such companies were generally composed of a headquarters unit and three anti-tank squads. One squad was armed with 57mm anti-tank guns, another with 12.26-inch bazookas, and the third was trained to remove and plant mines. Max likely joined the 103rd at Camp Howze, Gainesville, TX, where it was undergoing final preparations for combat.

On September 11, 1944, the 103rd participated in its final "Pass and Review" at Howze and headed for Camp Shanks in New York, where it would be processed for overseas service. The Division sailed on October 6, and arrived at Marseilles, France, on October 20, 1944. By November 1, it was on its way to Dijon, to join elements of the 7th Army. Its first combat was on November 16. The Division was part of the 7th Army winter drive through the Vosges Mountain. Such a drive had never been accomplished, and most believed it could not be done. But previous attempts had not included the American Army. The 103rd took the high ground near St. Die, France, and then, on November 22 took St. Die. St. Die was the home of cartographers who had first given the name "America" to the North American continent. The Germans, following Hitler's scorched earth policy, had burnt the cartographers' building to the ground. Other cities soon fell - Maisonsgoutte, Eichfoffen, Epfig, Ebesheim, Selestat. The 103rd crossed the Zintel River at Griesback on December 10th and in a brutal battle, took Climbach.

At Wissenborough, the 411th Infantry Regiment, became the first 7th Army Infantry unit to enter Germany. Its push was then interrupted by the 1944-45 German winter offensive. The Division had to pull back to the Moder River and to cover two fronts during the German offensive. (To counter Germans wearing American uniforms, the men came up with questions that were put to everyone. What is a juicy fruit? Where do you put the quarterbacks? What is a Baby Ruth? If you gave the wrong answer, you likely were shot. (In January, the Division's Commander, General Haffner, had to leave due to health problems. He was replaced by one of the most articulate generals in the Army, Brigadier General Antony

C. McAuliffe. (When told that he was surrounded and had no chance at Bastogne, McAuliffe had responded "Nuts" to the Germans demanding his surrender.)

As the German offensive was repulsed, the 103rd regained the offensive and started its final push. It crossed the German border March 18 near Mittenwald and started capturing German cities and German soldiers. In one instance, after clearing the town of Buchlo, the 411th headed into Landsberg. They took 200 Germans prisoners after a brief firefight with an ambush party outside the city. They were then clearing snipers when a Hungarian officer announced that his commander wanted to surrender. Since the men were busy, a small squad was sent to accept the surrender. When they arrived at the garrison, the squad found a battalion of 918 men, dressed in spotless uniforms standing at attention, with their arms piled in a huge stack at the other end of the parade ground.

At Landsberg, the Division also found six German concentration camps. These camps were full of the bodies of Jews, Poles, Russians, French and un-Nazified Germans. The 411th forced German civilians to pick up and provide a decent burial for the dead and dying. As they did so, the grand excuse was heard over and over. The civilians had no idea that such things were going on, despite the stench that covered the area. The place was filthy, especially the hospital. The 411th made German prisoners scrub the place clean.

Landsberg was famous for something else. It was the birth place of the "New Order." Adolph Hitler had written "Mein Kampf" in Landsberg prison. Many American soldiers visited Hitler's cell, which was now, or had been a sort of shrine. In late April, the Division captured Mittenwald near Innsbruck, in southern Germany. As the war ended the 103rd was at Brenner, and was guarding the Brenner Pass.

The Division had enjoyed some diversions during its drive across Europe. At one point, its troops were entertained by a USO show. The star of the show was Marlene Dietrich. At the show's conclusion, Marlene brought a huge roar from the men, when she raised her skirt, and showed them a long glamorous leg with the Division's Cactus Patch on her garter.

On May 9, 1945, one day following the official surrender, the Division participated in a victory parade in Innsbruck.

Donald F. Finnemore of Fillmore entered the service on April Fool's Day, 1943. He was assigned to Fort Leonard Wood in Missouri for basic training. Donald would remain at Fort Wood until February/March of 1944 when he apparently was enrolled in a 20-week college training program. It is not clear whether this took place in California or Iowa. In any event at the end of his training, he was transferred to Camp Butner in North Carolina. It is likely that Donald was first assigned to 355th Infantry Regiment, 89th Infantry Division at Butner. He was assigned to Company E, 2nd Battalion. In December, the Division was shipped to New York City; and on January 10, 1945, it sailed aboard the *USS Uruguay* for Le Havre, France. Arriving on January 21, the Division moved to Camp Lucky Strike where it was reorganized for combat operations.

In early March, the Division moved into the line near Speicher, Germany. The first assignment was to secure the north and west banks of the Moselle River. It crossed the Moselle March 17. The advance was now continuous. On March 24, it crossed the Rhine between Kestert and Kaub. On March 26, the 355th Regiment again crossed the Rhine River near St. Goar. and moved forward to screen the Division's front. On April 4, men of the 3rd Battalion of the 355th were among the first American soldiers to enter Orhdurf Concentration Camp. The entire 355th would be there for at least a short time. (See section below on concentration camps.) On April 6, the Division attacked Eisenach, capturing the town. They now moved into the Nazi Redoubt in Thuringia, capturing the key town of Friedrichroda on April 8. Still the advance continued, moving eastward toward the Mulde River, and capturing Zwickau on the 17th. On April 23, the advance was halted. The Germans were about finished. Between the 17th and the end of the war, the Division saw only limited action, primarily conducting patrols and general security. They did keep three towns (Lossnitz, Ave, and Stolberg) under constant pressure, but mounted no serious attacks.

Following the German surrender on May 8, the Division was alerted on May 17 that it would either be shipped to the Pacific, or would conduct occupation duties in Germany. Instead, on June 5, the Division was assigned to process men returning to the States. They were stationed at Camp Old Gold near Le Havre. On December 16, the Division was shipped home. However, Donald remained in Europe until March 26, 1946, when he was finally shipped home, arriving in the states on April 1, 1946, three years to the day after entering the service. He was discharged at Fort Dix, NJ on April 5, 1946.

The NAO reported in June of 1945, that Donald had earned a Purple Heart. Clearly, he could have been wounded during any of the April battles. However, his discharge record does not show the award of a Purple Heart. The record does indicate that Donald earned the very prestigious Combat Infantryman Badge (CIB). As a result of this award, Donald also earned the Bronze Star awarded in 1947 by Congress to men who had earned the CIB. This award probably means that Donald was an infantryman during most of his service. His discharge record shows his military occupation as Supply Clerk. It is possible, and likely, that he served as a supply clerk only at the end of the war, since the discharge record usually shows only the last occupation held.

Donald's family has an unsigned document which purports to list the medals Donald earned. While most of the medals cited are listed on his discharge record, three others, not including the Purple Heart, are not listed. One of these other three is the American Defense Ribbon. This was awarded only to veterans who served prior to December 7, 1941. It is likely that this is an error, and the medal that should have been listed was the American Campaign Medal, which Donald did earn. The document also indicates that he earned an arrowhead. This is likely incorrect as arrowheads were awarded only to men involved in amphibious assault landings, combat parachute jumps, helicopter assault landings, or combat glider landings. The 89th Infantry Division, and thus the 355th Infantry Regiment, did not participate in any types of landings during the war. Finally, the document also indicates that Donald earned a Silver Star. No other evidence of this award has been located. It is entirely possible that Donald earned all the awards, and the official documentation has been lost, destroyed, or not located.

Along with other soldiers, Donald received a letter thanking him for his service. It reads, "To you who answered the call of your country and served in its Armed Forces to bring about the total defeat of the enemy, I extend the heartfelt thanks of a grateful Nation. As one of the Nation's finest, you undertook the most severe task one can be called upon to perform. Because you demonstrated the fortitude, resourcefulness, and calm judgment necessary to carry out the task, we now look to you for leadership and example in further exalting our country in peace." **The White House Harry S. Truman**

Ronald Gleave Fridley of Granger officially entered the service on January 6, 1942. Ronald was quickly put to work. Following a two- months training period at the combat engineering school in Fort Belvoir, VA., Ronald departed for Alaska on March 10, 1942. In Alaska, he became part of an ambitious and crucial project to connect the American Territory of Alaska, by road, to the United States. In less than one year, some 10,000 American and Canadian soldiers and civilians constructed the key Alaskan-Canadian Highway. Built through a wilderness, the men, including Ronald, faced extreme temperatures, clouds of mosquitoes and flies, ice, snow, and muskeg (swampy ground). When finished, the road extended 1,543 miles, contained more than 200 bridges, and 8,000 culverts. The official dedication occurred November 20, 1942 in fifteen-degree below zero weather.

Ronald returned to the US by ship, sailing from Alaska on April 15, 1943. The NAO reported him home in April, having just returned from the Yukon District in Alaska. It is not clear where Ronald spent the next 7 months, but on November 16, 1943, he sailed for Europe. It is assumed that Ronald was sent to Europe as a replacement for a combat engineer battalion. He likely was assigned to the 234th Combat Engineers shortly after arriving in England. By the time Ronald arrived, the 234th was in training at the Assault Training Center at Ilfrancombe, England, where they remained until April, 1944.

On June 6, 1944, the 234th was aboard landing crafts in the English Channel. Most of the battalion landed on Omaha Beach on June 8. Some landed on June 26, and the balance landed on June 29. The primary mission, immediately after landing, was the maintenance of the road being used as the main supply line from Formigny to La Mine. During the next several months, the battalion was busy with its main tasks, graveling bivouac areas, patrolling, building, and maintaining roads, laying, and removing mines and booby traps, building dumps for supplies, setting up water points and gravel pits, building culverts, and most important, building bridges. At the end of August, the 234th built a floating Bailey Bridge across the Seine at Meulan in 10 hours. The battalion now passed quickly through Belgium and into Holland. On September 29, 1944, Company B was attached to the 113th Cavalry as infantry, and it participated in the attack on, and capture of, Nieuwstadt. For this action while a member of an infantry regiment, Ronald should have won the Combat Infantry Badge (CBI). However, there were three requirements for earning this coveted medal. 1. A soldier had to be an infantryman. 2. A soldier had to be assigned to an infantry unit. 3. A soldier had to engage the enemy in ground combat. Clearly Ronald met the two most important requirement. He was not, however, officially an infantryman. Therefore, apparently, he was not eligible for the CBI.

During October, the 234th built a barrier line of anti-tank mines from Limbricht to the Meuse River west of Born. By mid-October, Company B was at Hoensbroek. On November 21, the 234th moved into Germany at Alsdorf. There the troops took up a castle as their residence. They spent Christmas destroying roadblocks with explosives near Eschwizer, and on December 27 destroying German pillboxes. General E. N. Harmen praised all the engineer units who assisted in this effort. The 234th commendation reads, "Confronted with the worst conditions in the form of enemy mines, poor terrain conditions and heavy rains, our division engineers received unhesitatingly the complete support of your group. This assistance contributed greatly to the success of the division in reaching all its objectives." The 234th celebrated New Year 1945 by blowing up more pillboxes forming a segment of the Siegfried line. This time they used an average of 400 pounds of TNT per pillbox. When questioned why they used so much per pillbox they responded that they not only wanted to blow up the pillboxes, they wanted to warn the Germans not to come back. The Germans got the message. The 234th spent January at Eschweiler, Germany, performing regular duties.

In February, the 234th was with the armies smashing their way to the Rhine. They cleared routes of mines, wrecked vehicles, and tanks. They also filled shell craters, removed road blocks, dug in radar equipment and performed road maintenance. When volunteers were needed to drive assault "alligators" (big blue tank like vehicles) filled with troops across the Rhine, many men from the 234th volunteered, including Ronald although the crossings were extremely dangerous. The Germans had flooded the river, and while the assault force had waited for the water to subside, it was still swift and strong. Further, they were under machine gun and mortar fire all the way across. The German commander, Field Marshal Van Rundstedt, had wanted to pull back to a better defensive position instead of trying to guard the west bank of the Rhine, but Hitler had ordered him to stay and fight. His forces were cut to pieces by the advancing Americans. Ronald earned a Bronze Medal for his actions that day. The citation reads, "Ronald G. Fridley …., is awarded the Bronze Star Medal for heroic achievement in Germany, on 23 February 1945, in connection with military operations against the enemy. Private First-Class Fridley, an Alligator Driver for his company, distinguished himself by ferrying assault troops through known enemy mine fields and across the swollen river. Private First - Class Fridley also supplied the troops with food and ammunition, evacuated casualties, and prisoners on the return trips. The outstanding courage and devotion to duty displayed by Private First- Class Fridley reflect great credit upon himself and the Military Service. Entered Military Service from New York." For this action, Ronald also received the prestigious Bronze Arrowhead denoting an amphibious assault landing.

In March, the 234th built 8 miles of road to support more troops crossing the Rhine. A Treadway bridge was built by Company B at Mehrum, with help from the 989th Treadway Bridge Company, in 29 hours. It only took 15 hours, but 9 hours were lost to accidents and 6 hours lost due to enemy action. In April, after the war in Germany ended, the 234th erected the FDR Bridge at Breiten Hagen. The 234th and Ronald served on occupation duty in Germany from May 2 to July 4, 1945. Ronald sailed for home on October 2, 1945, arriving October 12. He was discharged October 18.

(There is some confusion regarding Ronald's period of service. While his discharge record shows that he entered the service on January 6, 1942, and was discharged October 18, 1945, for a total service of some 46.5 months, the record also shows that he served some 15.5 months in the continental US and almost 36 months overseas, for a total service of 51.5 months. The record also indicates that he received the American Defense Service Medal which was awarded only to individuals who served prior to December 7, 1941. He did receive the medal. Finally, the record indicates he lost 193 days of service for some reason. This likely means that he entered the service in 1941, likely in June, but lost time changed the official entry date to January 1942. Time lost usually related to a soldier being away without leave, but it could have been for other reasons as well. Ultimately, if a soldier served his full time and received his honorable discharge, time lost was meaningless, except maybe for pay. Other men from the FCSD area also "lost" time.)

FDR reviewing American troops in Rabat, French Morocco 1/21/1943. FDR is in a jeep customized for him by men of the 89th Ordnance Heavy Maintenance Company under the command of Captain Russ Hodnett. National Archives Photo.

Russell C. Hodnett of Hume was a 1939 graduate of FCS. He enlisted in the service on January 7, 1941 as a private. Having served prior to December 7, 1941, Russell was another from the FCSD area who earned the American Defense Medal. His first stop, after enlisting at Fort Niagara, NY, was the Quartermaster Corps at Camp Normoyle.

Picture – FDR reviewing American troops in Rabat, French Morrocco1/21/1943. FDR is in a jeep customized for him by men of the 89th Ordnance Heavy Maintenance Company under the command of Captain Russ Hodnett of Hume. National Archive Photo.

In a letter to his parents, published in the *Northern Allegany Observer*, Russell wrote, in part: "During the last few months, everybody's attention has been centered around the lives of the new soldiers of our country. Some have been sent here and others have been sent there --- you never know where you are going. I, among others, came from Ft. Niagara to the Quartermaster's camp named Camp Normoyle in Texas. "Camp Normoyle… is not like the other camps because of several reasons, namely, it is a motor transport depot. The plan of the camp is to receive by train all the trucks and cars, light and small. The cars are checked and OKed here and then sent on to other camps as orders come in for them." In most respects, the camp was the same as other camps. Russell also wrote: "I forgot to mention one thing we do every week and this continues the entire year. We have a very rigid inspection every Saturday morning and then everybody drills and marches the rest of the forenoon," And he mentioned that "The meals here are very good and consist of everything we would find on the ordinary family's table. We have a good variety and plenty of everything." In letters home, few FCSD area men complained about the meals.

After Camp Normoyle, Russell worked as an auto mechanic and rose to the rank of Corporal with the 55th Ordinance Depot Company in San Antonio, TX. After Pearl Harbor, he entered Officers Training School at Fort Lee, VA, and graduated as a Second Lieutenant. Over a year of training followed, at such places as Ft. Warren, WY. He also spent time at Ft. Custer, MI, as an instructor. From there he was assigned to Company B of the 67th Ordnance Maintenance Company at Fort Moultrie, SC. Promoted to 1st Lieutenant, he was ordered to Ft. Bragg, NC. By January 1, 1943 he was in Casablanca in North Africa. It was in North Africa that he earned his first battle star for his participation in the Tunisian Campaign.

Immediately assigned to the 7th Army, 89th Ordnance Heavy Maintenance Company, he was initially stationed in a cork forest near Rabat in French Morocco. By August, he was a Captain and serving as Company Commander of the 89th. Their job was to service everything from tanks and artillery to small arms. At about the same time as his promotion to Company Commander, he sent home a piece of a shot-down German plane. A couple of months earlier he had written his parents that the grasshoppers were so thick that drivers had to stop and clean them off their radiators. Later he wrote his parents about the cold winter weather, even though he was in a desert.

In mid-1944 Russell wrote the NAO. In part, he said, "I'm ready, and have been for a long time to push on, but then an ordnance outfit has to work where it is needed. All would have liked to have gone to Italy, but we have agreed to meet the other boys in Berlin," He finished by adding, "All in all we're doing OK, but "brother," we would like to finish this mess and come on back home." It would be over a year before he was able "to come back home." By June of 1944 he was in Italy. He managed to send home another souvenir, this time a captured German rifle. The rifle was displayed in the Fillmore Central School Library for a while.

In Italy, his Ordnance Company moved rapidly up the Italian boot, from Salerno to Naples through Rome and all the way up to the Brenner Pass, almost into Austria, as the Germans were pushed out. At the Brenner Pass they were ordered back to Naples. Russell and his Ordnance Company were about to join another Army in a different area, and they were going to be a part of finally cleaning up the mess.

Italy had not been all work. He had visited the ruins of Pompeii and seen Mt. Vesuvius, with smoke still pouring from it.

At Naples, his Company and equipment, including 40 special shop trucks and vans packed with spare parts, several jeeps, and four 6x6 troop trucks were loaded aboard a ship. They sailed to Marseilles in France, recently captured in the invasion of Southern France. From there they headed to Paris. There Russell and his Company became part of the 3rd Army under General George Patton. Russell was familiar with Patton. Patton and staff officers sent by him had visited Russell's company several times. Patton was always asking for something to be made for him, or for something to be modified. One time he asked that a cane that could be used as a seat be made. Another time, he wanted a tank turret modified so that he could get in and out easier when he used the tank as an "observation site." Still another time he had Russell's company make ashtrays out of German airplane propeller hubs. Patton gave the ashtrays to visiting big wigs from Washington.

Patton was not the only dignitary Russell assisted. At the end of the Casablanca Conference, President Roosevelt decided to review the troops. Traveling in a Daimler automobile from Casablanca on January

21, 1943, Roosevelt switched to a jeep at Rabat. Russell had arranged for that jeep to be modified. The back seat was removed and the front seat was higher and provided more leg room. It also swiveled. A handle-bar for the President to hang onto was installed. He also provided his personal driver, Oran Lass, for the President. Roosevelt reviewed troops from the 2nd Armored Division, and the 3rd and 9th Infantry Divisions, before returning to Casablanca.

Russell's personal jeep was named "88 Bait." The name had been earned. On a scouting trip for a location for his company, a German 88, out of sight in an open field that was reported to be clear of the enemy, opened fire on his jeep. The shell passed over the jeep, but missed it and everyone in it. Russell said it did cause them to get the hell out of there in a hurry. Russell and 88 Bait did a lot of traveling together. Part of the job of servicing the trucks, jeeps, and armaments was to visit the various armored divisions to inspect artillery guns for wear and tear. It was important to be proactive and identify weapons that needed to be replaced before they broke down in combat situations.

In November of 1944, Russell volunteered to pick up a pilot's jacket for a friend of the pilot. Russell was wearing the jacket due to heavy rain. They were on a main road in France when another jeep, filled with Free French soldiers, pulled out in front of them. Russell's driver swerved to the left to avoid impact, but was forced off the road into a deep rut that had been dug for water drainage. The jeep hit a tree and Russell was thrown through the windshield. He woke up behind a wood stove in a Frenchman's kitchen. His men put him on the kitchen table and proceeded to pick glass out of his face. They then took him to a Field Hospital where he spent the next few days. The Doctors believed that the pilot jacket he had volunteered to pick up and was wearing, probably saved his life. Finally, he was able to make his own arrangements to return to his company. Years after the war ended, Russell was having trouble breathing. Doctors determined that his breathing problems were caused by a smashed septum, which required surgery. The sternum has been smashed in the jeep accident back in 1944, but never diagnosed.

Russell wrote another letter home during the 1944-45 winter. In it he provided some candid comments. He wrote, that the newspapers he was receiving appeared to indicate that there seemed to be a "marked movement on the people's part, from war work back to peace time jobs." He stated that "the war was far from finished and there was plenty of need as far as the servicemen were concerned." Russell knew of what he spoke. He had now been in the service for almost five years, and actively at war for almost three of those.

Russell became part of the dash across Europe with the 3rd Army. From Paris, they headed east to Alsace Lorraine and to Strasburg. This was during and after the Battle of the Bulge. Russell said that sometimes they had to move backward before continuing east. They crossed the Siegfried Line and the Rhine River into Austria. During the crossing of the Rhine, Russell said he lost some company records and reports, and he almost had a heart attack until they were found. American troops were now just north of the Brenner Pass, only a little way from where they had been about a year before. There were at that location when the Germans started surrendering. The war in Europe was coming to an end.

It was at this time that Russell received his Bronze Star Medal for Meritorious Service. The citation reads: "Russell C. Hodnett, 01 573 285, Captain, Ordnance Department, 89th Ordnance Heavy Maintenance Company (Field Artillery), for meritorious service in direct support of combat operations from 26 November 1944 to 8 May 1945, in France and Germany. Captain Hodnett exhibited exceptional ability in training and supervising his company in direct, ordnance, maintenance support of combat units. Through his consistent, diligent efforts, he developed a highly efficiency company that contributed greatly to the successful action of the Field Artillery units it supported. Entered military service from Fillmore, New York."

At war's end, Russell did not go home right away. While his company was broken up and other men were shipped home, he was made commander of the 489th Ordnance Evacuation Company at Nuremburg, Germany. Their task was to gather up leftover or abandoned military equipment. This included some big items, such as tanks, trucks and artillery. The American G.I.s were ready to go home, and they were not too concerned about things they could not carry. When in late summer he was finally shipped home, Russell said he expected he would be heading to Japan. Instead, as he put it, "the 'Big Bomb' closed all activity down so I was discharged to go home." Following his active service discharge, Russell was promoted to the rank of Major and stayed in the reserves for another year.

Wesley E. Hopkins of Fillmore entered the service October 18, 1943. He had graduated with the Class of 1943 from Fillmore Central in June. While his records do not contain any specific information, he likely took his three months of basic training at Fort Benning, GA and six to seven months of advanced combat training at the Infantry Replacement Training Center at Camp Livingston, LA. Wesley served as a rifleman during his service.

Wesley likely sailed for the European Theater of Operations (ETO) on September 18, 1944 aboard the *RMS Arundel Castle*. He arrived September 25, 1944. Wesley was assigned to the 26th Infantry Regiment, 1st Infantry Division probably shortly after his arrival in the ETO. He likely joined the 26th sometime in early October. The men of the 1st Division were among the first wave of men to land on deadly Omaha Beach on D Day. It then smashed its way across France and was knocking on the door of Aachen, Germany by the end of September.

It is likely that Wesley was present when the Division battled through the Siegfried Line and participated in the battle for Aachen which was captured October 21, 1944. In November the Regiment attacked east of Aachen through the Hurtgen Forest to the Ruhr. In early December they were pulled out of the line for refitting and rest. It was then the Hitler's counterattack began. The 1st held the critical shoulder of the "Bulge" at Bullingen, destroying scores of German tanks. The 1st Division fought continuously from December 17 to mid-January to help end Hitler's last gasp. The Allies then returned to the offensive. On January 15, 1945 it attacked and blew through again the vaunted Siegfried Line. For a period, it occupied the Remagen bridgehead as American G.I.s poured across the Rhine and into the German heartland. On February 22 Wesley was injured in the line of duty. He was cutting wood, probably for a fire, and hit his right foot with the tip of the axe. He suffered lacerations and an oblique fracture of the first metatarsal bone. As a result, he spent several weeks in various hospitals. (A discharge document prepared at Fort Dix says he was in the hospital for two months, but documents in his file indicate he may have been returned to duty at the end of March. This suggests he was out of action for a little over one month.) Wesley was treated by at least three different hospitals – the 102nd Evacuation Hospital, the 12th Field Hospital, and the 108th General Hospital.

With Germany open the Division was redirected to the area of Siegen. On April 8 it crossed the Weser River into Czechoslovakia. Wesley likely rejoined his unit in Czechoslovakia and may have participated in battles at Kynsperk nad Ohri, Prameny, and Mnichov.

Following the war, the 26th performed occupation duties in Germany from May 2 to October 31, 1945. At some point following the end of the war, Wesley participated in the Army Education Program at Shrivenham American University in Shrivenham, England. According to the Shrivenham Defense Academy, the purpose of the university was to provide a transition for US troops between Army life and subsequent attendance at a university back in the states. Wesley took 40 hours of psychology, 40 hours of economics and 40 hours of business law during his nine weeks at the school.

The 3rd Battalion of the 26th Infantry Regiment was selected to provide guard service for the Nuremberg trials. This included guarded the war criminals in the prison, and guarding the buildings and grounds where the trials were taking place. K Company was assigned the duty of guarding prisoners during the actual trials. It is not known if Wesley was assigned to the 3rd Battalion.

Since Wesley did not rotate back to the states until March 7, 1946, it is possible that he participated in both occupation duties and the war crimes trial, as well as attending Shrivenham American University.

Wesley earned three battle stars during the war. In 1956 Wesley and his wife Edna spent three months in England.

Alfred H. Kingsley of Granger enlisted in the Canadian Army on December 21, 1941. On his volunteer enlistment document, he stated his reason for joining was, "a spirit of adventure." Alfred went through his initial training at Camp Borden in Ontario, Canada. On March 12, 1942, he was shipped to England, where, over the next 21 months, he was subjected to a much longer, more intense, and more diversified period of training. Initially, Alfred was assigned to a Canadian Artillery Reinforcement Unit (CARU). He then was assigned to a Canadian Radio Location Unit for training, while remaining permanently attached to a light artillery unit. His assignments to various units, both permanently and for training purposes, would continue for the next year and a half, although most would be related to anti-aircraft activities. During this time, on October 10, 1942, he was admitted to Kearney Court Hospital for treatment of injuries. He remained in the hospital until October 19, 1942. He also took more training, qualifying as a Fire Control Operator. His rank during this period was "Gunner."

He was back in the hospital on November 22, 1943, with another injury. He remained until December 7, 1943. For a short period, he was assigned to the Canadian Signals Reinforcement Unit. Then in April, he was assigned to the 22nd Technical Training Group and was enrolled in a Royal Air Force meteorological course (a Royal Canadian Electrical and Mechanical Engineers Course) in Kilburn. Apparently, during this period, he met and became engaged to the daughter of the woman whose home he was staying in while in training. Her name may have been Maida Vale. After completing the training, for a short period he was assigned to the Winnipeg Grenadiers. On September 1, 1944, he was "awarded" seven-days barracks confinement for causing a disturbance in a public place. On September 7, he landed in France assigned to the Canadian Infantry Corps. On September 19, he was a private assigned to the First Canadian Scottish Infantry Regiment.

Alfred was now part of the push into Germany. He was involved in seven distinct actions. His first action called for clearing enemy forces from the coastal areas in the north of France. The job was given to the First Canadian Army, which included the First Canadian Scottish Regiment. Albert, and the regiment helped clear the Calais area during the period September 17 to 22. With it and the other port areas (Dieppe, Dunkirk, Boulogne) open, vital supplies could now move through these ports. The Germans, however, still controlled the Schedt River, connecting Antwerp to the North Sea. To open the important port of Antwerp, they had to be driven out. The First Canadian Army was again given the job. On October 9 and 10, Albert, and the Canadian Scottish Regiment, helped clear the Breskens Pocket. They did the same for the Leopold Canal area on October 11 to 16. Both these actions involved heavy fighting. The overall effort was called The Battle of the Schedt.

They now turned their attention to Germany. The first battle on German soil would be the Battle of the Rhineland from February 8 to March 10, 1945. It was part of what was called the Rhineland Campaign. Allied forces were commanded by Canadian General Crerar. This was the largest military force ever under Canadian command. Albert participated in two violent actions during the period February 8 to February 21, 1945. The first was the Battle of Waal Flats, and the second was Moland Wood. These were followed by the Rhine action from March 25 to April 1 and the Emmerich-Hochelten action from March 28 to April 1.

The Germans were now fighting on their homeland for their homeland, and they fought viciously. During the advance, the Canadians faced not only small arms fire, but also blasts from machine guns, bazookas, and artillery. One report mentioned that the Germans appeared to have an unlimited supply of ammunition. Despite that, there was eventually hand-to hand-fighting. On March 28, the Allies approached Emmerich. Here, fighting started at 0715 in the morning and lasted until 2300. They were numerous encounters during which there were casualties, including men killed in action (KIA). One of the KIA was Albert. It is not clear in which encounter he was killed. At the end, the objective (a factory area) was achieved.

Albert's service record indicates he earned a battle star for France and one for Germany. It appears he should have also earned one for Belgium, since he was involved in the fighting to clear the Germans out of Antwerp, That action however, may be considered part of a larger battle for which he did receive credit.

A final irony here is that, on June 9, 1917, during World War I, near Vimy, France, a Canadian soldier named Alfred Kingsley was also killed. It is not known if the World War I Alfred was related to the World War II Alfred. Alfred's Granger family was from Canada.

Earle C. Knorr of Allen entered the service on July 24, 1944. It appears that he was assigned to Fort Benning, GA, probably for both basic training and infantry combat training. Fort Benning was, at that time, a replacement training center for combat infantry. Apparently, he arrived overseas in January or February, 1945. The NAO reported in a February 1945 edition that he had been home visiting relatives.

Assigned to Company K, 39th Infantry Regiment, 9th Infantry Division, Earle was just in time to join the Division as it roared across Germany. Colonel Flint, the Regimental Commander, told the men that "The enemy who sees our Regiment coming, if they live through the battle, will know to run the next time they see us coming." The Division now helped secure the Ludendorff Bridge at Remagen, the famous bridge that provided a major opening for the US Army on its way into the heart of the 3rd Reich. By March 11, all combat teams of the 9th Infantry Division, including the 39th Infantry Regiment, had crossed the Rhine. Earle was among them. Earle had written his parents (who passed the information onto the NAO) that he had been in Aachen, where he did not see a single standing building that wasn't damaged by bombs and shells. Earle also reported seeing the same in Cologne and other German cities. He told them that he would not have missed the trip for anything.

After crossing the Ludendorf Bridge, the Division conquered all the area between the Rhine and Wied Rivers. The heart of Germany was now open to the Allies. Division troops then worked on shrinking the Ruhr Pocket. During this effort, they freed some 900 slave laborers from five different countries with the capture of Sinu on the Dill River. In late April, the Division relieved the 3rd Armored Division near Dessau, and held that area until V-E Day. Following the war, the Division was assigned to occupational duties in Ingolstadt, Germany.

On May 1, 1945 Earle officially received the Combat Infantryman's Badge. (G.O. 7, May 7, 1945.)

Frank J. Kopler of Hume entered the service on April 15, 1942 in Richmond VA as an enlisted man. The NAO reported in April that he was assigned to Fort Warren in Wyoming where he apparently was permanent staff. That same month he was promoted to Corporal. By September he was a First Sergeant.

During Frank's time at Warren, it was a training center for the Quartermaster Corps. In December 1942 the NAO reported Frank was transferred to Fort Meade, MD.

Meade was also a training center but for Frank, it appears it was just a temporary assignment. The NAO reported Frank home visiting his mother in January 1943, and then he reported to Fort Belvoir, VA to the Officer's Candidate School. On March 31, 1943 Frank, after having been discharged from the Army as an enlisted man, was sworn in as a Second Lieutenant. The NAO in April 1943 again has him stationed at Fort Meade. In May however, Frank was assigned to an engineering unit as an Intelligence Officer at Fort Shelby. Frank remained at Shelby for several months likely as permanent party. At some point he was transferred to Camp Polk, LA where he served with the 183rd Engineer Combat Battalion until February 1944 when he was transferred to Fort McCain, MS and assigned to the 1256th Engineer Combat Battalion. He reported for duty on February 26, 1944. In May his brother Howard, who was serving with the Merchant Marines, visited him at Camp McCain. The 1256th was a new unit and it started it's training on February 28. Frank served as the Intelligence Officer. In August 1944 Frank was made Commander of Company C. On August 20, 1944 he was promoted to Captain. On September 18 he also assumed the duties of Summary Court Officer. That same month the Battalion was transferred to Camp Polk, LA for additional training.

On October 13 the Battalion moved to Camp Kilmer, NJ to stage for overseas shipment. On October 21 the unit sailed from New York aboard the QSMV *Domion Monarch* arriving in Plymouth, England on November 2. They encamped at Tiverton initially before moving to their permanent camp at Ivybridge, Devonshire, England. For the next three months the Battalion and its men were engaged in various training activities at Ivybridge and other locations. On December 4 Frank was released from Company C and assigned to Headquarters, again as the Intelligence officer.

On March 2, 1945 they moved to Southampton where they boarded LST's. By March 6 they were Camp Lucky Strike in France. In March they moved to Germany. Their first permanent camp was at Amern. During the next several months they carried out numerous assignments, from the serious to the mundane. Two of the major assignments were building a wooden bridge over the Lippe River near Wesel and another over the Wesel River at Bad Oeyahausen. They also maintained and operated three water plants at Rheydt, Wegberg, and Munchen Gladbach. These duties assisted the infantry and armored units as they destroyed the German Army. They also removed rubble and road blocks, including, as necessary, corner buildings which blocked the advance of large armored vehicles causing traffic jams at various locations. These types of duties continued even after the war ended as part of the Battalion's occupation duties. In November the Battalion was shipped home aboard the *USS General J.C. Breckenridge* (AP 176) troop transport. They docked at Boston on November 26 and moved to Camp Myles Standish on the 27th Frank was discharged December 4, 1945. Among his medals were two battle stars as well as an Occupation Medal, Germany Clasp.

Irving C. Letson of Wiscoy entered the service on October 27, 1943. He was assigned to Camp Campbell in Kentucky and became part of the Service Company, 23rd Tank Battalion, 12th Armored Division. The 12th would remain at Campbell until mid-1944, when it was moved to Camp Barkeley outside of Abilene, TX, to complete its training. It then headed to the European Theater of Operations (ETO). The NAO reported in late October that Irving had arrived safely in England. The Division, with Irving, had sailed for Liverpool on October 2nd. It arrived at La Havre, France, on November 11th but remained in France only a little longer than it had stayed in England.

The 12th Armored Division moved against the Maginot Line on December 7th, 1944 and on December 21st it seized Utweiler, Germany.

Two things were now about to happen to the Division. It was about to engage in one of the most violent battles in the Division's history, and it was about to start a drive which would earn its nickname. The Division attacked the Rhine bridgehead at Herrlisheim. The Germans had established this bridgehead as part of "Operation Nordwind", their last major disparate attempt to turn the tides of war. On January 8-10, and 16-17, 1945, the battles were fought, but neither side gained ground. Post-battle analyst determined that the American commanders had used poor tactics that along with the treacherous terrain had resulted in the stalemate. The Germans were likewise unable to advance. The 36th Infantry Division relieved the 12th after this horrific encounter.

Success of the division in its drive across Europe was in no small part due to the outstanding support provided by the 23rd Tank Battalion. Irving was an important cog in the battalion. He drove ammunition and fuel trucks that replenished the tanks and kept them moving. By General Order 74 dated 20 July 1945, Irving (along with others) was awarded a Certificate of Merit in recognition of his service. The Award reads: "...a Certificate of Merit to (Irving Letson) of Service Company, 23rd Tank Battalion for meritorious, and often times, outstanding performance of military duty from 17 March to 6 May 1945 in Western and Central Germany. (Irving), driving fuel and ammunition trucks, displayed untiring efforts during the offensive through Western and Central Germany. Without rest or food, and often times subject to enemy fire, (he) worked day and night to keep the combat elements of the battalion supplied."

The 12th rested for a short period, before resuming its attack. In a blazing offensive, by February it had sealed the Colmar Pocket, ending German resistance in the Vosges Mountains. Again, it rested for a short period, but resumed its attack on March 18th, driving to the Rhine, and taking the cities of Speyer, Ludwigshafenfell, and Germersheim by March 24, thus clearing the Saar Palatinate. The 12th men crossed the Rhine at Worms on March 28, captured Wurzburg, and aided in capturing Schweinfurt. Next the Division headed for Munich but diverted to take the bridge at Dillingen before the Germans could destroy it. Then US troops poured across this bridge into southern Germany.

Now spearheading the 7th Army drive, the 12th Division secured Landsberg and helped liberate the Kaufering Concentration Camp. By May 3rd, it had crossed into Austria. There the 12th Division was once again relieved by the 36th Infantry Division. The 12th was nicknamed the "Hellcat Division" after its ferocious drive across southern Germany.

This drive was to assure that the Germans could not establish a National Redoubt in the mountains around Berchtesgarden. Rumors, primarily based on propaganda put out by Goebbels, had it that the German government and Army would withdraw to this area to reconstitute their armies. The rumors indicated that efforts had been underway for some time to make the area impregnable. While little of this was true, Eisenhower, decided he could not take a chance. Thus, he left Berlin to the Russians while the US overran southern Germany. Interestingly, Patton had consistently advocated a narrower approach that called for smashing our way directly into Berlin.

Irving sailed home from Marseille, France, with the rest of the 12th Armored Division on November 22, 1945. The division had spent 102 days in combat.

Beverly A. Luckey (Bev) of Hume arrived in France February 24, 1945. In the next three-plus months he would participate in two major European campaigns, while earning two battle stars, the Combat Infantryman's Badge, and a bronze star. Serving with the 94th Infantry Division, 301st Infantry Regiment, Bev ended up performing, with his unit, military government duties in Krefeld and Dusseldorf, Germany and in Czechoslovakia. Oh yes, he also earned a Silver Star.

The 94th was already engaged in its third European campaign when Bev joined them at the end of February 1945. The Division was in the process of clearing out the left bank of, and establishing a bridgehead over, the Saar. This action is considered one of the four major accomplishments of the 94th. (The first involved bottling up of Nazi holdout garrisons at Lorient and St. Nazaire, which occurred before Bev's arrived.) By early March, they had crossed the Saar and attacked the Siegfried Line. Breaching the Siegfried Line was the third major accomplishment. Then came the fourth, the thrust to the Rhine.

The 94th was picked to spearhead the 3rd and 7th Armies' drive to the Rhine. This included the bloody battle to take the key industrial city of Ludwisshaven. After taking Ludwieshaven, the 94th received a short rest and was then sent to the Krefeld area to contain the western side of the Ruhr pocket. While it was in this position, the war ended. The 94th was initially ordered to occupy the Ruhr. On April 18, 1945, the Division took up military government duties. Bev was assigned to assist in taking care of displaced persons.

Bev's regiment, the 301st Infantry Regiment, played a major role as the 94th Division smashed its way into Germany. During the period February 19 to March 24, the 94th moved 123 miles, took more than 17,000 prisoners, broke the Siegfried Line by establishing a bridgehead over the Saar River, and then battled 85 miles to the Rhine River. The 301st headed north across the ridgeline between Borg and Munzingen during this drive. It swept through minefields, which according to the "Story of the 94th Infantry," were as thick as a GI loaf of bread. Against heavy mortar and artillery attacks, it took the towns of Munzingen and Keblingen. The entire division was up against the elite German 11th Panzer Division, which it severely damaged and then swept past.

On March 20th, the 94th headed for the Saar. A squad of the 301st knocked out six German 88's (anti-aircraft and anti-tank guns) and their crews in a stretch of 200 yards. Then the 94th took the towns of Kollesleuken and Frendenburg. A task force, which included the 301st, virtually erased the town of Orscholz. On that day, the entire division gained 4,000 yards on a 5,000-yard front. By the time the division reached the Saar, the 301st had aided in the capture of 8 cities.

Despite the success, Patton demanded more. Improvising, the 301st and 302nd Infantry Regiments now paddled across the Saar against a 7-mph current. They established a beachhead at Serrig and Taben. Before bridges could be built, these regiments were supplied by Piper Cub airplanes. The fighting in Serrig was house-to-house, with many German pillboxes camouflaged in houses. With forces spread out, the 301st was ordered to take up positions along the Hocherberg Ridge to protect troops advancing from Taben. They held these positions for two days without support. By March 13, the 94th was zeroing in on the Rhine, with the 301st and 302nd Regiments spearheading the drive. On March 24, they captured the town of Ludwigshafen, one of Germany's leading chemical-producing centers.

During the drive to the Rhine, Beverly earned his Silver Star. The 94th Infantry Division General Order 263 dated 10/16/1945 describes Bev's actions. (The order is missing from files. According to a summary, Bev destroyed two German machine gun nests. This likely occurred in Serrig, where such nests were camouflaged in houses; but it could have happened earlier. For instance, the "Story of the 94th" indicates that a squad of the 301st knocked out six German 88's. However, the 88s were antiaircraft guns, not machine guns. Thus, based on his Silver Star summary, the battle in Serrig appears the most likely action in which he earned his Silver Star.)

With the war now over, the 94th now took up Military Government duties. Bev specifically dealt with dislocated persons. Often this included Germans who had fled their homes as the Allies advanced. A 94th Division Report of Operations for the period May 8 to September 30, 1945, states that the attitude of the

German people was docile, amenable, and solicitous. There was evidence of an underground resistance movement, but it never became a major threat. Military Intelligence was very aggressive in dealing with those who attempted to implement resistance activities. Interviews with German civilians showed that they now wanted all Nazis swiftly removed from all positions of importance and thought. On the Czechoslovakian border, where Bev also worked, the major issue was again the return of German civilians and POWs. Underground resistance here was virtually non-existent, as the Czechs had been very thorough in their liquidation of Nazis and their collaborators.

Beverly finally sailed for home on January 22, 1946, arriving on February 1. Proving the bureaucracy does not move slowly all the time, Beverly received his discharge February 2, 1946. Beverly spent eleven months overseas during his 16 months of service. His son Gary told the author that his dad spoke to him only once about the war. They were watching a documentary on Nazi concentration camps. Bev told Gary he had seen such camps, and that it was an awful experience. The author personally knew Bev Luckey. He remembers him as a big, quiet, gentle man who almost always had a smile on his face.

Burton H. Markham of Fillmore had one of the shortest, but most complete combat experiences of the war. Burt lived in Fillmore only for a short time during the mid-40s, mostly after the war. He was married to Melrose Marriott of Hume, whom he had met while they were students at Cornell University. Entering the service on September 21, 1944, he was sent to Fort McClellan, AL, for his basic training. On February 19, 1945, only five months after entering the service, he sailed for Scotland aboard the Royal Mail Ship (RMS) *Queen Mary*, arriving February 24. On March 1, he left Scotland, crossed England, and arrived in France. He was now part of the 5th Infantry Division assigned to George Patton's Third Army.

Six days later, March 7, 1945, Burt entered the shooting war. It was his first and his last day of combat. He was both wounded and captured at Bitburg, Germany on that day. (Bitburg became famous and controversial years later when President Ronald Reagan decided to visit its cemetery. The cemetery contained the remains of members of the Waffen SS, the military arm of the SS that was the Nazi elite guard. The Nuremburg War Crimes Tribunal had designated the SS as a criminal organization. One of the crimes of the Waffen SS was the murder of POWs.) Burton said that after being captured, POWs were forced to march almost 140 miles to Limberg, Germany, where he was imprisoned in Stalag 12A. A couple of weeks later, noticing confusion among the guards, Burton managed to escape. He was quickly recaptured however, and was held by a German military unit for an additional four days before being liberated by American troops. At some point during his POW period, Burton witnessed an attack by American fighter planes on an American POW train. The POWs were able to stop the attack by ripping off their shirts and forming the letters P, O, W, on the ground. During his captivity, Burton lost 25 pounds in 24 days. He was transferred to the American hospital in Verdun, France, to recover. On May 8, 1945, he was in Paris for VE day. He was then sent to Camp Lucky Strike to be processed and shipped home. He arrived back in the States on June 5. After an extended home leave, Burton reported to Lake Placid, NY, for reassignment. He was discharged March 29, 1946.

Donald D. Marriott of Hume entered the service on March 25, 1944. He took his basic training at Fort Dix, NJ. He may have attended a short course on cooking at Dix, but likely at another location. By July he was stationed at an army base near Texarkana, TX. The NAO reported in September, 1944 that he was returning to Texarkana, TX with his wife after spending a few days of his furlough with his parents. In December the NAO again reported him home with his parents for a few days. He returned to Texarkana. It appears that the only Army base near Texarkana was the Red River Army Depot. It was initially established as an ammunition storage facility. It was later designated as a general storage supply site. Repair of tanks was also added. Donald would have been one of the cooks at the facility.

Donald worked as a cook (Military Occupational Specialty (060)) during World War II. As such he prepared food for the personnel of a military organization, using a daily menu as a guide. Documents depicting Donald's first two years of post-World War II service shows that post-war he served as a Tech Instructor, MOS 659. As such, he taught in cook and baker schools, gave lectures on mess management, preparing and cooking of foods, and sanitation.

Marjory Marriott, a niece of Donald, advised that Donald served as a cook in Germany during the war. This could only have occurred during 1945. Since the NAO reported in December 1944, that he was home for a few days, he could have only left for overseas in late December or January 1945. No information regarding the unit in which Donald served and where the unit was located have been identified. Since Donald served in Germany during the war, it is likely that he earned either the Rhineland Campaign or the Central Europe Campaign battle star. He also earned the American Campaign Medal, the European African Middle East Campaign Medal, and the World War II Victory Medal.

Donald returned to the states likely in December 1945 or January 1946. He was discharged January 13, 1946 and immediately reenlisted January 14, 1946. Donald eventually made a career of the military.

Hubert H. McMaster of Hume entered the service on January 18, 1943. The NAO reported in February of 1944 that he was stationed with a headquarters battalion at Keesler Field, LA. It also stated that he had qualified for aviation cadet training and would be moving to a new location. Since Keesler was, among other things, an Air Force basic training center, it is possible that Hubert received his basic training there. Basic training at Keesler lasted only four weeks. Trainees were then usually transferred to other training opportunities, including aviation cadet training, at Keesler or some other location. In many cases potential aviation cadet trainees were assigned to other activities while they waited for a cadet training slot to become available. That may be what happened to Hubert.

In early 1944 many of the aviation cadet training classes were being cut back or terminated. The need for pilots and co-pilots was much less than it has been in the early years of the war. In fact, it may have been that Hubert was transferred out of the cadet aviation program when he was relocated to another base.

A 1945 entry in the NAO reported that Hubert has been in the service for three years and had served part of that time in Brazil. Given his later military history, it is possible that he was transferred to Brazil when he relocated from Keesler. There were both Army and Army Air Corps personnel stationed in Brazil where US bases, primarily at Belam, Natal, and Recife, were refueling stops on the southern air route to Europe and points east. Combat air crews which guarded the air and sea routes to Europe were also located at these bases. David M. Babbitt of Hume was stationed at Natal during this period. Hubert may have been assigned to headquarters staff at one of these bases

Hubert's military career then took a dramatic turn. At some point he was transferred from the Army Air Corps to Army Ground Forces. Again, this was a period when, due to the progress of the war, men were no longer needed in some specialized units, but still needed in Army ground combat units. This was especially true for units such as Coast Artillery units since the danger of air attacks on the US had decreased dramatically. Hubert's unit may have been affected by these changes or he may simply have volunteered for another assignment. In any event he was relocated from Brazil and transferred to the European Theater of Operations. The exact date of his arrival in Europe in not known, but Hubert's entry at the World War II Memorial indicates that he earned both the Rhineland and Central Europe campaign battle stars. His daughter Maureen provided information that Hubert served with the 104th Infantry Division in Europe. To earn the Rhineland Battle Star, he would have had to be with the 104th sometime during the period September 25, 1944 to March 25, 1945. If he had been with the unit prior to September 25, he would have also earned the Northern France Battle Star.

The 104th was part of the push out of France and into Germany. A major portion of its combat activities took place in Germany. In November it participated in the battle of the Hurtgen Forest. During its push it cleared the German forces from several areas and towns. In November it helped clear Germany forces from the area west of the Roer area. During the surprise German winter offensive, it successfully defended its sector which covered the area near Duren and Merkel from December 15, 1944 to February 22, 1945. It then returned to the offensive blasting its way through and capturing town after town, including Huchem-Stammein, Birkes Perf and North Duren. It entered Koln on March 5. On March 22 it attacked just east of the famous Remagen Bridge. It then helped clear the remaining German troops in the Ruhr Pocket. It captured Paderborn on April 1 and on April 11 helped liberate the concentration camp at Nordhausen. From April 15 to 19 it engaged in a brutal battle to capture the town of Halle. On April 26 it contacted Russian forces at Pretzach. The war in Europe ended six days later. The 104th suffered battle casualties of 4,961 with 1,119 killed in action.

Hubert's 2nd Battalion participated in all these actions. In October it engaged in heavy fighting to secure the area astride the Belgium-Dutch border. In Holland it secured the town of Etten and forced the Germans to retreat as the Regiment advanced. On November 1 and 2 the regiment was ordered to capture the south bank of the river. The 2nd Battalion blasted the defenders as the 415th Infantry Regiment crossed the river. The 414th Regiment was then ordered to join the 1st Army as it attacked Aachen, Germany. More German towns fell as it advanced – Eschweiler, Stolberg, Volkenraat, Tuck. On November 25 at Weisweiler, the Battalion suffered heavy casualties as it took the town in close house to house fighting. On November 27 it aided in taking Frenz against heavy machine gun, mortar and artillery fire. On December 2 it took Enden. On December 7 it faced fierce resistance from tanks, mortars, and machine guns. Enden was reduced to rubble. The offensive was now halted as the winter closed in. Defensive positions were established against the surprise German winter offensive. The 2nd Battalion was in reserve in the south sector of the Roer River line near Birgel, 2000 yards behind the 1st and 3rd battalions. They remained in this position until mid- February 1945.

To celebrate 1945, every cannon fired one round of high explosives at 0001 January 1. At 0600 every weapon in the division gave the enemy across the Roer River a deadly greeting. There was no response. During the lull some men received coveted passes to Paris. The biggest problems were German night fighters and the noise from German artillery.

In late December the offensive advance was resumed. Hitler's 1000 Year Reich now had a little over four months left of its disgusting 12 plus years of existence. Hitler had miscalculated the life expectancy of his Reich by only 987 years. The 2nd Battalion crossed the Roer and moved to Langelwehe. It moved into Merzenich on February 25 now riding on supporting tanks. More German towns fell to the Regiment as they moved to capture the key city of Cologne. The fighting was heavy and furious. A major problem was German civilians trying to get out of the way. The men made every effort to avoid shooting them. By March 7 they were in Cologne. A small celebration took place on March 15 at the Cologne Sports Palace. The advance then resumed.

Two changes now occurred. Hubert's Regiment, the 414th was detached from the 104th and assigned to 3rd Armored Division. Hubert 2nd Battalion was further detached and assigned to Combat Command B. Along with the 2nd Battalion, 33rd Armored Regiment it now constituted Task Force Lovelady. The Task Force crossed the famous bridge at Remagen on March 25. They now attacked the defense fortress of the Ruhr River, the heart of German war production. Again, riding on tanks and again roaring through small towns the Task Force engaged in a bitter day-long battle on March 26 to capture a bridge. They then took

Marburg in a pitched battle which lasted four hours, Three-thousand Germans soldiers were captured. They now headed north to capture Paderborn, the back seat of the Ruhr Valley. A vicious battle took place at Wexen. To avoid delay, a decision was essentially made to simply by-pass Wexen and leave the defenders hanging. On April 1 it faced formidable defenses manned by fanatical SS troops around Paderborn but were able to blast through. The city itself was lightly defended. By noon it belonged to US troops. The capture completed the surrounding of German troops in the Ruhr.

On April 4 the Task Force left Paderborn. Company F was ordered to take North Hagen. It roared through town after town tossing the German defenders aside. On April 6, Companies F and E captured the town of Manrode. On April 11, the second battalion with Company F on the left flank attacked Nordhausen. Hubert and the battalion were now about to see what General Eisenhower meant when he ordered troops to visit the concentration camp at Ohrdurf. The 414th History reports that the men were disgusted and felt there was no punishment too severe for the Germans. A member of the medical staff is quoted in the *Timberwolf Tracks,* the story of the 104th Infantry Division. Sergeant Ragene Farris said, "Men lay as they had starved, discolored, and lying in indescribable filth." To help clean up this horror men from the town were forced to help carry the living to treatments and to dig holes and bury the dead. No one believed their claims that they had not known what was going on at the camp. The 104th Infantry Division is recognized as a Liberating Unit by the Holocaust Museum.

Many of the prisoners had been forced to work at nearby underground facilities that were producing V1 and V2 rockets. The 2nd Battalion was ordered to establish road blocks at intersections near the entrances to the underground factories.

The 2nd Battalion returned to the 414th Regiment for the attack on Halle, a university town on April 13. By April 16 Halle surrendered even though the regiment still had to clear out fanatical SS troops and die-hard Hitler youths.

The division was rotated back to the states on July 3, 1945. It was shipped to San Luis Obispo CA. At some point it was notified that plans called for a move to the Pacific to become part of the Japan invasion force. The dropping of the atomic bombs ended the need for any more troops in the Pacific theater although the division was not deactivated until December 20, 1945. It may have been that consideration was being given to using the 104th as occupation troops. The NAO reported in October 1945, that Hubert had been home on a 45-day leave. He then returned to California where he was discharged December 12, 1945.

Arthur C. Miller of Centerville entered the service in January 1941. He took his basic training at Fort Dix in New Jersey. The NAO reported in April 1941 that he had gained 13 pounds since entering the service in January. By June of 1941, Arthur was at Camp Pine, NY. He remained there until October 1943 when he was transferred to Camp Ellis, Il. While his duty assignment at Camp Pine is not clear, he was performing at a high level. Arthur was promoted on a regular basis, achieving a rank of Corporal by September 1942 and Sergeant by December. He also was awarded a Good Conduct Medal in January 1943. He was in a technical career field.

At Camp Ellis, Arthur became part of the 371st Special Service Regiment, which in February 1944 was redesignated as the 371st Engineer Combat Battalion. From October 1943 through May 1944, the battalion prepared for the duties to be performed in Europe, including building of fixed and floating bridges across the Illinois River. On May 25, they sailed to Liverpool, England, aboard the US Army transport *SS Brazil*. On June 5, Arthur and other members of his battalion watched airborne troops head for France from their camp at Druids Lodge, England. They also continued to prepare for combat duties by learning how to build Bailey bridges and Nissen huts; and constructed a depot for incoming troops.

The 371st arrived in Europe on September 7 at Utah Beach. They then walked 8 miles through rain and mud to set up their camp.

For the next nine months, Arthur and other members of his battalion were constantly at work. They were always close to, and sometimes in front of, the infantry. They built, repaired, and maintained roads and railroad bridges; and they constructed hospitals, including the 130th General Hospital at Ciney, Belgium, and converted a facility near Verdun into St. Nicholas Hospital. They even repaired and operated a sawmill for a short time. They prepared for demolition work but also guarded highway and railroad bridges over the Meuse River between Sedan, France and Namur, Belgium. During this time, they were constantly strafed and bombed by German planes. Prior to building one bridge, they had to clear a mine area. When the Battle of the Bulge ended, they repaired roads and even took prisoners from time to time.

During the Battle of the Bulge, Company A of the 371st, in which it is believed Arthur served, discovered the bodies of 159 men from one of the most infamous acts of the war, the murder of unarmed American POWs at Malmedy, and other nearby locations. General Patton was furious and called upon his men to take no prisoners. Some complied.

In late April and early May, the 371st participated in one of the war's great accomplishments. Colonel George F. Griffith of Headquarters, Advanced Section Engineer Group "A" summed it up when he wrote to all the men involved. He said, "By coordinated and cooperative effort, by team work of the highest order, you have accomplished the impossible task of building a railroad bridge, 2815 feet in length, 36 feet above the water, over the Rhine River, in exactly 6 days,16 hours, 20 minutes. This feat has upset the carefully calculated plans of the Corps of Engineers. Each and all of you together have exceeded the most optimistic estimates as to the time required to accomplish your mission. The long-standing tradition of the Corps of Engineers, that 'the impossible just takes a little longer' has been broken…" This was the first railroad bridge across the Rhine, and it was named the Peace Bridge, as it was completed on VE Day. This "temporary bridge" was used for seven years. For its work on the bridge, the 371st received a Meritorious Unit Commendation. General Patton sent his 3rd Army across the bridge.

Arthur and the 371st remained in Europe until November 4, 1945, when they sailed home aboard the *USS General Breckinridge*. Arthur was discharged on November 8, 1945.

David W. Morgan of Centerville entered the service February 2, 1942 at Fort Niagara, NY. By July 1942 he was likely at Camp Forest, TN, as part of the 305th Engineer Combat Battalion. The Battalion was part of the 80th Infantry Division. During the next year, the Battalion underwent extensive training to prepare it for both its job, and the horrors of war. The job, among others, was to build roads and road blocks, construct bridges such as pontoon and Bailey bridges, repair bridges, if necessary, but also blow them up. These Army engineers learned to clear and set mine fields, camouflage all kinds of items, carry out reconnaissance, and even stand guard duty where necessary. On one exercise, they constructed an 80-foot fire control tower for weapons. They also learned to handle weapons. Serving as an Engineer Combat Battalion meant they were with or very close behind the combat infantry units. In some situations, they were in front.

Their training included the use of weapons and exposure to the hazards of the battlefield. One exercise involved traversing an active mine field at night. Another required them to crawl under live machinegun fire. They learned well, but nevertheless many of them died in combat. In July, shortly before departing Camp Forest, David's battalion was visited by President Roosevelt. In August, it was moved to Camp Phillips in Salina, KS, where training included being conditioned to desert life, one of the few things David and others were not called upon to face in Europe.

The 80th Infantry Division, which included the 305th, sailed for England on July 1, 1944. They were stationed at Colborne Park, England, for the balance of July. On August 5 and 6, they landed on Utah Beach in France. Once there, the engineers did not waste any time.

David was trained as a truck driver, but was likely called upon to perform other duties as well. Trucks not only carried troops, they also hauled or pulled heavy equipment, supplies, and critical materiel needed for construction and repair projects. Engineers were incredibly busy. They literally tore through France and Germany. This is reflected in their August itinerary – August 7 St. Jores, August 8, Aurenches, August 9 Montsurs, August 11 Conlie, August 13 St, Mans, August 15 Jublains, August 17 Montrae, August 18 Almenches, August 26 Almeneches, August 28 Villesneaux, August 30 Challons, September 1 Laheycourt. They also participated in the three-day battle of Argantan, when the 80th helped close the Falaise - Argantan Gap. The rest of the war was more of the same.

In October, the 305th Battalion disarmed an incredible 4,779 mines, while laying 1,771 of their own. And this was just one facet of their job. On October 10, the Division hosted a visit from Generals Marshall (Army Chief of Staff), and Patton. In November, they built a bridge over the Seille and Gneid Rivers. During this period, they also had to deal with Germans pretending to be French citizens, and fake German deserters. Even the French presented problems. Many were sympathetic to the Germans and were outright hostile. Some were caught booby-trapping American vehicles, something that David would have had to be prepared to address. An example of the engineers' dangerous work was removal of four 250-pound bombs from a road culvert.

In December and January, 1945 with the rest of the 80th Division, David and his battalion faced the German winter offensive. Just in December, they stopped four German advances in Luxembourg. With the winter offensive behind them, they continued their march to and through Germany. By the end of March, they were across the Rhine. In April, they plowed through Germany territory that included cities like Neukirchen, Oberzwehrn, Gotha, Dictendorf, Weimer, Gera, Kandler, Scheszlitz, Nurnberg, and Regensburg. In May, they moved on into Austria as part of the occupation forces. The 305th Battalion performed occupation duties for the balance of 1945. It returned to the US in January 1946, and David was discharged on January 8, 1946.

Lewis John Morgan of Centerville (brother of David Morgan, see above) entered the service March 7, 1942. Lewis spent the next two and a half years preparing for the rigors of combat. It is possible that he became part of the 44th Infantry Division at Camp Claiborne, LA, but for sure was with the Division while it was at Fort Lewis, WA. The Division was part of the defense of the west coast at that time. In early 1944 (February, March, April), it participated in the Louisiana maneuvers, and then moved to Camp Philips in Kansas for further training. During the period August 24 to 27, it moved to Camp Miles Standish, MA. On September 5, 1944, the Division with Lewis, sailed for France.

Lewis and the 44th landed in Cherbourg, France on September 15, 1944. They entered combat on October 18 at Foret de Parroy, just east of Lunesville, France. Over the next two months, they pummeled their way across France. On October 25 and 26 they stopped a massive German counterattack and then continued their advance across France. They were part of the allied advance through the Vosges Mountains, something that had not been done in centuries, and many believed couldn't be done. On November 17, they captured the French city of Auvicourt.

That same day, Lewis was wounded in action. It was a serious wound for which he received the Purple Heart. His son Roy related that his dad never allowed his children to see the wound. He said he never saw his dad without a shirt. Lewis was moved to the 9th Evacuation Hospital for treatment. His days with the 44th were over. General Order 24, issued by Headquarters, 324 Infantry Regiment on December 9,

1944, awarding Lewis the prestigious Combat Infantry Badge, indicating that he was a former member of the 44th. The Journal of the 324th indicates that on the morning of the 17th, the men were in position and moving forward for the attack. At 0300 (3:00 AM,), a message was sent saying that they had not heard from Lewis's 1st Battalion. At 0705 a Lt. Askins was sent out to try and locate the 1st. At 0750, the Battalion is reported as definitely being on a hill that was the point of attack. A report at 1145 from Graves Registration indicates that they had picked up American bodies, but still had to police the Germans. The 3rd Battalion had been chewed up badly. The Air Force had been called in and P-47s were attacking Avricourt. At 1430 another report said that the 1st and 2nd Battalions had hooked up and were attacking. A report at 1515 indicated the 1st Battalion was pinned down by mortar fire. At 1545 it was reported that the 1st Battalion has been badly hit. (It is possible that it was during this period that Lewis was wounded, likely by mortar fire.) At 1605 an outgoing message indicated that the 1st and 2nd Battalions needed food, ammunition, and ambulances. By 1730 the 1st Battalion was on the high ground north of Deutsch Avricourt. At 2330 a report of the effective strength of the 324th Regiment showed 1175 men. Sixty-five had been KIA, and 200 wounded, one of them being Lewis, but Avricourt no longer belonged to the Third Reich.

Upon his release from the hospital, Lewis was transferred to the 89th Infantry Division, with which he spent the remainder of the war. The 89th arrived in France on January 24, 1945. By March 5 it was in Luxemburg. And on March 12 it entered combat. The Commanding General of the 89th wrote a message for the men assuring them that they were ready for combat. The message ended with the order, "Kill Germans and Go Forward." Between March 12 and May 8, the 89th spent 57 days in combat. On March 13, it started its drive into Germany. On the 18th it crossed the Mosel River near Reil under enemy fire. Lewis was assigned to Company I of the 354th Regiment, the second unit to cross that river. On March 25, the 89th crossed the Rhine River between the towns of Kestert and Kaub. Hitler's dream of a thousand-year Reich was just about over, after a mere 12 years, four months eight days. The Division now blasted its way through Thuringia. The first city to fall was Eisenach, despite a stiff defense put up by SS troops. The cities of Arnstadt, Blakenheim, and Zwickau were next, with Zwickau being captured on April 17, ending the 89th advance.

The 355th Infantry Regiment of the 89th Infantry Division made history during its drive across Germany, when it freed the concentration camp at Ohrdruf. It was the first of such camps to be liberated.

The Division now was assigned to occupation duties, which included guarding displaced persons at Ohrdruf and Gotha, radar laboratories at Geogenthal, and railroad bridges at Mechterstadt. It also patrolled the Autobahn. It is not known to which specific duties Lewis was assigned.

Following these duties, the 89th was ordered back to France to Camp Lucky Strike and other such camps where they processed men being shipped home. While the Army tried to build up the assignment, the men knew it was a matter of first come, first home. The 89th had to wait until December to be shipped home, arriving back in the states on December 24. Lewis was discharged five days later. Ironically, Lewis was not a late comer, but he still had to wait. His original unit, the 44th Infantry Division was shipped home July 15, aboard the Queen Elizabeth, the same ship on which they had arrived in Europe.

Lewis' records do not indicate he earned the Army Occupation Medal, Germany Clasp. However, since the 89th was assigned such duties for at least 30 days, Lewis is entitled to that medal.

Lloyd L. Prentice of Hume entered the service on August 14, 1939. It is not clear where he was initially assigned, but given his later history, it is likely that he was ordered to Fort Belvoir, VA. for basic training as a combat engineer. In 1939, that training lasted some four months. Likely following a furlough, Lloyd was assigned to an engineer unit in Panama. The NAO, in a May 1943 issue, reported that he had served two years in Panama before heading to Iceland. That service almost surely was with the 11th Engineer Combat Battalion.

Lloyd's Panama battalion's primary assignment was to train with the Canal's Zone defense forces, and, as possible, to help with construction projects. This was all about to change. With Europe officially at war, the US Military began a process of preparing its forces, including its defenses. This included what was called the Strategic Triangle: Hawaii, Alaska and Panama. With Congress finally passing some appropriations, moves were made to upgrade defenses in the Canal Zone. These moves included case mating guns, building additional bomb-proof storage for ammunition, constructing access roads, and improving the Rio Hata airfield. Efforts were further increased when it became apparent, that Japan also posed a threat, and the US was almost surely going to need a two-ocean Navy. This led to efforts to make anti-aircraft batteries more mobile, to build joint command posts, to speed up construction even more on Rio Hato, to build a new dock that could handle increased needs for equipment and supplies, and to build new roads.

It is not known which of these projects Lloyd worked on, but he likely worked on several. At that time, enlistments were for two years, so when his enlistment was up in August 1940, Lloyd likely was transferred back to the states, probably back to Fort Belvoir, given his later assignments, and where he likely reupped for more years in the service. On August 1st, the 56th Engineer Company was established at Fort Belvoir. Lloyd was likely assigned to the company when he arrived back in the states. In November 1941, the 1st Platoon of the 56th Engineer Company, including Lloyd, was transferred to the 467th Engineer Company (Mobile Shop), likely as the 2nd Platoon. By December, the 467th was transferred to the 475th Maintenance Company. On April 20, 1942, the company was ordered to Iceland where it would serve until November 1943. In Iceland, its personnel were primarily involved in the development of airfields.

Leaving Iceland on November 30, 1943, Lloyd's company moved to Scotland and then England, arriving in December. A May 1944 edition of the NAO reported that Lloyd was now in England. On July 4, 1944 the Company landed on Omaha Beach in France. The Company's operations took Lloyd through France (including a trip through Paris), Belgium and Germany. In some 12 and a half months, it had 15 official bases. Their last was Nuremburg, the official home of the Third Reich. By the time Lloyd arrived there on July 12, 1945, the Third Reich no longer existed. The Company primarily performed maintenance work for Army Ground Forces as well as Air Corps and Naval Construction units. It repaired equipment and ordnance. Lloyd, and the company earned five battle stars during their trip: Normandy, Ardennes Alsace, Northern France, Rhineland, and Central Europe. They ended their European trip by performing occupational duties in Germany from May 2 to October 15, 1945.

George A. Rennicks moved to the Hume area in the 1930's when his mother Mary married widower Charles Mix. George's brother Gerald and new step-brother Lowell Mix, also served in the military during the war. George entered the service February 11, 1938 in Niagara Falls, NY. By 1940 he was at the Plattsburgh Barracks in Clinton, NY with Company C, 28th Infantry Division. His job was listed as soldier. By January 17, 1941, according to General Order No. 3, dated that day, he was with Company E of the 28th Division stationed at Fort Jackson, SC. That day he was transferred to the 11th Training Battalion as Cadre. In February of 1943, the NAO reported that he had been promoted to Staff Sergeant and was now serving at Camp Butner, NC. The NAO again reported in June of 1943 that he was still at Butner. In August of 1943 NAO reported that he and his wife were spending a 10-day furlough in Rochester, NY visited his parents. Following his furlough, he was to return to Butner, but was soon to be transferred to Fort Bragg. No information has been located that indicates that he was in fact transferred to Fort Bragg. It is likely that during this two-year period, he continued as a trainer of men being prepared for combat.

In November, or possible October of 1944, his parents visited him, maybe at Fort Bragg. He was preparing to be shipped overseas. Precise information on the unit in which George served while overseas has not been located. However, his final pay record (his other files were destroyed in the St. Louis fire), in a section labeled Army component, indicates that he was RA (Regular Army) with 22-C (possibly 22nd Infantry Regiment, Company C.) The following information assumed he did serve overseas with the 22nd as a replacement.

The 22nd Infantry Regiment arrived in England on January 29, 1944. It began training immediately for the Normandy invasion. On D-Day, the 22nd landed on Utah Beach. Over the next year it established an enviable war record earning combat honors for Normandy (including an invasion Arrowhead), Northern France, Rhineland, Ardennes-Alsace, and Central Europe. Assuming George did join the unit as a replacement, he would have participated in the Rhineland and Central Europe campaigns and possibly the finish of the Ardennes-Alsace campaign (Battle of the Bulge.)

In addition to the invasion at Utah Beach, the Regiment participated in the Cherbourg Peninsula battles, and the Cobra Operation. The 3rd Battalion broke through the Siegfried Line on September 14, but due to bad roads and especially bad weather which limited air and artillery support, it was not able to exploit the break through. It moved to Belgium on December 28 and again entered Germany on February 7, 1945. It is likely that George joined the 22nd in January assuming he did serve with the 22nd. The Regiment performed mop-up duties and occupational duties until July 12, 1945. Returning to the United States to Camp Butner, it began preparing for the invasion of Japan. The war in the Pacific ended before the 22nd was needed and it remained at Camp Butner until it was deactivated March 5, 1946.

According to his final pay records, George was transferred to Camp Gordon Johnson, Florida on October 20, 1945 and discharged on October 22. It is likely he was discharged earlier than other men of the 22nd due to his length of service. By the time of his discharge George had served some 93 months, including some 8 to 10 months overseas. He had earned numerous medals including American Defense Medal, an Occupation Medal with a Germany clasp and at least two and possible 3 battles stars.

Gerald W. Rennicks of Hume and brother of George, was still a student at FCS when he entered the service on June 25, 1940. It is not clear where Gerald served his first year or so, but it is likely that he was at Fort Niagara, as the 28th Infantry Regiment was stationed there at the time. The Rennicks family had lived in Niagara County in 1930. For sure, by no later than March of 1943, Gerald was with the 28th at Fort Leonard Wood in Missouri. At that time his unit was shipping out, but Gerald was being left behind to undergo an operation. The 28th was ordered to Camp Young in California for further transport to the Pacific Theater of Operations. In May, however, the Regiment's orders were changed and the regiment was sent to Camp Forest, TN to train for the European Theater. Sent to Camp Kilmer in November, the 28th sailed for Europe in December 1943. In November 1944, the NAO reported that Gerald had been overseas since December 1943. It is likely that he rejoined his regiment at Camp Forest and shipped out with them.

The 28th Regiment 's first stop was Northern Ireland when its troops were based at Enniskillen, County Fermanagn. There they underwent extensive training in everything from all types of weapons, to scouting, patrolling, night operations, small unit tactics, and elemental amphibious landings. In March, General Eisenhower visited the regiment. On July 1, the regiment, now part of the 8th Infantry Division, sailed for France, landing on Utah Beach on July 4, 1944. On July 7th, they entered combat. Not wasting time, they established a critical bridgehead over the Ay River, enabling attacks into Brittany and Northern France. By the end of the month, the 28th Regiment had already earned a Presidential Citation. In fact, the Citation was earned by the First Battalion. Company A, Gerald's Company, was part of the First Battalion. Advancing into Brittany it participated in the murderous battle of Brest. During this battle, on

August 29th, Gerald was captured. The NAO reported in September 1944, that his mother had received a telegram informing her of his capture. Despite this telegram, there appears to be no official records of his capture. This may be because it was later reported that he reported back to his outfit in late September after being a POW for 21 days. The regiment's Journal reported on September 19th that "3 enlisted men returned today." The Journal also indicated that the "Crozon Peninsula has fallen, fighting has ended." The NAO reported in November that he had been freed by his own unit.

The regiment now moved into Luxembourg near Province, commanding an area along the Our River. Continually moving, in mid-November, the regiment was near Aachen, Germany. It now participated in the brutal battle of the Hurtgen Forest. It was the worst fighting of the war for the regiment, and its troops not only had to face German infantry and artillery, but also, they suffered bitter cold and snow. Company I of the 28th Regiment earned a Presidential Citation for its performance at this time. On January 7, 1945, Headquarters, 28th Infantry Regiment issued General Order #5, announcing that Gerald had earned the Combat Infantryman Badge, the Holy Grail for infantrymen during the war. In February, they conducted an assault across the Roer River, now swollen and flooded with melting snow. In late February they captured the German town of Stockheim. As that engagement was winding down, the 1st Battalion was giving the mission of clearing the town. The regiment's history reports that the Battalion was successful and suffered few casualties. However, Gerald was one of them. The NAO reported in March 1945 that Gerald had been wounded and had been operated on four times in an Army hospital near Paris. It is not clear when Gerald was released from the hospital and returned to the US. He was discharged September 8, 1945. Gerald earned at least eight medals and four battle stars during his service.

Herbert L. Rose of Hume entered the service on April 14, 1942. Herbert was assigned to basic training  at Fort Monmouth, NJ. Only 10 weeks later he was on a ship heading for Iceland. Despite the short distance, it took the vessel 12 days to get there, arriving on July 12. This was a critical time in Iceland. The US was in the process of establishing a sufficient present in the country to assure it did not fall under the control of Germany and to secure the northern sea and air routes to Europe. Massive construction was underway to build runways, ports, troop facilities, and communication systems. The latter was what Herbert was there for. While assigned to Reykjavik, Herb would see a lot of the country as communications such as control cables, submarine cables, open cables, buried cables, and various systems were installed. Herb's basic assignment was to drive a jeep providing transportation primarily for officers. He told the Fillmore History Club that his battalion was involved in the construction of its own Quonset huts, probably near Hafnar Jordur. *Picture – Herb in combat gear.*

Herb spent 13 months in Iceland. Then, instead of heading home, his battalion, the 26th Signal Construction Battalion, bordered a ship and headed to England. Arriving at Kittering on August 17, 1943, they went right to work. The work here was about the same as in Iceland.

Communication systems were being installed at many of the air bases that were being built. The 26th worked on six bases. These bases were to be vital to the ability of the Allies to take the war to the Nazi's in northern Europe prior to the invasion on June 6, 1944. Over 13, 540 yards of underground cables were installed. The Battalion also serviced Royal Air Force bases, as well as Naval Depots.

On July 10, 1944, the 26th landed on Utah Beach. The battalion would be directly involved in the drive across Europe. Its personnel installed a major telephone line from Cherbourg across France and Belgium and into Germany. They were also directly involved in the Battle of the Bulge. As the German counteroffensive in the winter of 1944-1945 emerged, members of Herb's unit became infantrymen and were ordered into the lines to help stop Hitler's last gasp.

Even after the war ended, Herb and the 26th continued with vital work. The Battalion spent three months in Berlin and were instrumental in the installation of the communication systems for the Potsdam conference, the last of the Big Three (USA President Harry Truman, British Prime Ministers Winston Churchill and Clement Atlee, and Russian Premier Joseph Stalin) meetings. This meeting dealt with the most serious issues facing the post-war world, including the German economy, punishment of war criminals, land boundaries, and reparations. The Allied Control Council for Post War Administration of Germany was established, and Japan was notified once again that the Allies would only accept unconditional surrender.

Herb had a stroke of luck when he found a German camera. It turned out the PX sold film that worked in the camera, and Herb was able to take many pictures during his tour.

Herb's duty to his country was now over. The Army said he could go home. Traveling on a "local" which stopped in practically all the towns (both small and large) across Europe, he boarded a Liberty Ship in southern France on October 13, 1945. Herb arrived back in the states on October 23, 1945, and was discharged October 28, 1945.

Sanford I. Smith of Houghton entered the service at Buffalo on June 3, 1941. He was assigned to training at Fort Knox, KY. In July the NAO reported that he was assigned to Company B, 3rd Battalion, Armed Forces Replacement Training Center (AFRTC) at Fort Knox. NAO reported in November and December, 1941 that Sandford was now assigned to The Band, 31st Armored Regiment, 5th Armored Division at Fort Knox. The 31st Armored Regiment and the Band were activated at Fort Knox on October 1, 1941. Also activated on October 1, 1941 at Fort Knox was the 81st Armored Regiment, 5th Armored Division. The 81st also had a Band.

On January 1, 1942 the 31st Armored Regiment (and presumably the 31st Band) was inactivated at Fort Knox. No further information regarding this 31st Armored Regiment Band at Fort Knox has been located. It is possible that members of the band may have been transferred to the 81st Armored Regiment Band at Fort Knox or disbanded, or the 31st Armored Regiment Band became the 81st Armored Regiment Band. Another 31st Armored Regiment with a Band was activated on March 2, 1942 at Camp Polk, LA. On August 5, 1943 all the second 31st Armored Regiments units were redesignated as other entities except for the Band, which was disbanded. No relationship between the Camp Polk 31st Armored Regiment and Band and the Folk Knox 31st Armored Regiment and Band has been identified.

The Fort Knox 81st Armored Regiment moved to Camp Cooke, CA on February 16, 1942, the first of several moves over the next year. On March 24, 1943 it arrived at Camp Pine, NY where on June 24, 1943 most of its units were redesignated. The rest of its units including the Band were disbanded.

On September 20, 1943 the 5th Armored Division Band was activated at Camp Pine, NY. According to General Order 5, 5th Armored Division 1943, the original personnel for the band were obtained from several sources, including the 81st Armored Regimental Band, 5th Armored Division. It is assumed that this included Sandford I. Smith, although no documents have been located which confirm he was a member of the 81st Armored Regiment Band and was transferred to the 5th Division Band.

The 5th Armored Division Band has a robust history. It sailed to England on February 11, 1944 aboard the *Edmund B. Alexander* arriving on February 23rd. During the next five months it was located at several different camps while carrying out its assigned duties. On July 24, 1944 it landed on Omaha Beach. The Band's constant movement would continue as it moved through several locations in France, Belgium, Luxembourg, and Germany. It arrived in Zweifall, Germany on December 11, 1944. During its travel the

Band encountered numerous obstacles from the weather including heavy snow, poor and congested roads, and even enemy action. On August 12, 1944 at Sees, France a band member had to serve as an out-post guard and was wounded by an explosion in his section. At another location it assisted with some POWs. Nevertheless, it continued to carry out its primary responsible as a morale and service unit. It performed at various ceremonies, including awards ceremonies, parades, social and official gatherings. During its time in Europe the Band was awarded five battle stars including Normandy, Northern France Ardennes-Alsace, Rhineland, and Central Europe.

Sandford's final pay record indicates he returned to the states on October 7, 1945 and was discharged October 9 at Fort Dix, NJ.

(The above narrative assumes that Sandford did in fact serve with the 5th Armored Division Band. The sequence of units clearly indicates that it is highly possible he was assigned to the 5th. Like many men, Sandford's military files were destroyed in a fire in St. Louis, MO. No documents listing the members of the 5th Armored Division Band have been located. Likewise searches of 5th Armored Division documents such as awards documents have not found his name listed. This is not unusual since small units like Bands did not have historians assigned, nor did they issue orders making awards. No members of his family have been located.)

Leon H. Swartout entered the service September 24, 1943 at Binghamton, NY. He was a student at Houghton College at the time. It is not clear that he had any basic training. He more likely was immediately assigned to Beaumont General Hospital in El Paso, Texas to be trained as a Surgical Technician. Leon did have some background in the medical field.

Surgical Technicians were a critical field in the military. As the war progressed more and more technicians were needed. Technicians performed such functions as sterilizing instruments, caring for operating room patients, suturing, and draping. Part of their training involved the procedures and processes of the operating room. In many cases they also served as Combat Medics. As part of a combat battalion, it is possible that Leon performed both operating room and medic duties, although it does not appear his unit saw any combat. However, since he earned the Rhineland Battle Star, he may have served in a combat capacity with another unit. (See Below.)

Leon sailed for Europe on February 27, 1945. He was assigned to the 665th Field Artillery Battalion. The 665th had trained at Camp Chaffee, AR. The Battalion and Leon sailed aboard the *SS Sea Owl* troop transport. They arrived in La Havre, France on March 11, 1945. They were transferred to US Camp Lucky Strike on March 17. The 665th was then attached as a unit to the 426th Field Artillery Group for administrative purposes. It is possible that at some point during this period Leon was detailed to the 426th Group. Leon's discharge paper show that he earned a battle star for the Rhineland Campaign. The 665th Field Artillery Battalion did not earn the Rhineland Medal. However, the 426th Group did earn the medal, and assuming that Leon was detailed to the group during the last part of March, he too would have earned the medal. Leon's records indicate that he ending the war with the 665th so his detail to the 426th would have been short. In fact, it likely only lasted during the period the 665th was attached for administrative purposes to the 426th. That attachment lasted from March 17 to April 2, 1945. The war was rapidly coming to an end, with less than a month of combat left. The final campaign of the war, the Central Europe Campaign was in full progress, but the 665th was not a participant. Instead, like many other units its duties were aimed at post war issues.

From Camp Lucky Strike the 665th was moved by truck convoy to Trier, Germany, arriving April 13. The various batteries of the battalion were assigned to different locations, including Battery B to Saarbrucken to take charge of a displaced persons camp. A Battery was sent to Kirchburg, Germany also to take charge of a displaced persons camp. Other batteries moved to Torcheinbollen and Bad Krueznach to perform similar duties. Headquarters and the Service battery moved to Baumholder. The entire battalion eventually reunited at Baumholder. That included the Medical Detachment which likely moved with the headquarters section although some medical personnel may have been assigned to different batteries. During the period starting officially May 2, the battalion performed occupation duties. This duty officially ended July 4, 1945, although the 665th departed Baumholder in late June.

The Battalion moved back to Camp Lucky Strike from where they sailed for home on July 1, 1945 aboard the *SS Sea Pike* hospital ship. They arrived back in the states July 10, 1945. Among his other medals, Leon also earned the Army Occupation Medal, Germany Clasp.

Roland J. Thomas of Hume was in Munich, Germany when the war ended. In a sense, he was at the place where, had things turned out different, the whole war could have been avoided. It was in Munich where the Nazi's first tried to start a movement to seize control of the German government. The major event was the famous "Beer Hall Putsch" in 1923. During a march, some Nazis were shot. Unfortunately, Hitler escaped with a shoulder injury. His remaining followers in Munich did not escape when Roland and the 42nd Infantry Division arrived in 1945.

Roland was inducted into the service March 4, 1941. He was assigned to Fort Totten, NY, and would be stationed there for the next 14 months as part of Battery D, 62nd Coast Artillery. He was trained as an anti-aircraft artillery gun crewman. In January 1942 he was sick in the base hospital with an infection in his arm and hand, but he was home on leave in both February and June. On August 29, along with the rest of the 62nd, he sailed for England. They spent about a month in England and Scotland, and then on November 11, 1942 they landed at Oran in Algeria. For the next three months, their mission in Oran was to provide anti-aircraft protection for that city and seaports under US control. During this period, they defended against two major air raids. The outfit then moved to Chatezudun du Rhumen, where its personnel provided protection for US fighter and bomber bases. Here they fought off three air raids in six weeks. In one raid, they destroyed an entire formation of planes. In the other two raids, they were credited with 6 enemy planes destroyed and "2 probable's" (likely shot down). Battery D's next move was to Perryville, Tunisia, where its gunners defended the staging area for the Sicily invasion near Lake Bizerte. They were credited with another plane destroyed at this location.

It was during the end of his stay at Lake Bizerte that Roland learned that his brother Gatie was in the area. His commanding officer gave him permission to leave the base camp, and to use a jeep. When he arrived where Gatie was stationed, he was told Gatie was out repairing some anti-aircraft guns. He visited several gun emplacements before locating his brother. There a fellow soldier captured the famous kiss of the brothers (See piece on Gatie – Southern France). Roland wrote home, "Oh boy did it seem good to see him once more. He looks better than he did before he went into the Army. Hadn't seen him for nearly two years."

The 62nd landed at Licata, Sicily on July 23, 1943. Their first job was defending Porto Empedocle at Gela where they were credited with another enemy plane shot down. Then they joined the drive to Palermo. Before the fighting on Sicily ended, the 62nd defended against several more air raids, and its gunners were credited with nine more planes destroyed and three more "probable's." On November 11, 1943 the 62nd Coast Artillery was inactivated, and its components were split up. Roland remained with Company D which was part of the first battalion. It was re-designated the 62nd Anti-Aircraft (AAA) Battalion, and on July 7, 1944, moved to Italy. There it participated in the wind-up of the Rome-Arno Campaign, which was Roland's fourth campaign, and fourth battle star of the war. The NAO published part of a letter from Roland in August, 1944. He said that he had been in Italy for some time and that he even spent a week at a rest camp. He mentioned he had been awarded some medals, but like many servicemen from the

FCSD area, specifically mentioned only one, the Good Conduct Medal. This was Roland's second Good Conduct Medal, as the General Order (G.O.) # 2 published 2/25/1944 mentions that he was awarded a Clasp (actually, a loop) to the Good Conduct Medal. A Loop award indicated a second award for the Good Conduct medal. Good Conduct Medals were usually awarded only once. The Good Conduct Medal was not just for behaving oneself. As G.O. 2 said, it "demonstrated fidelity through faithful and exact performance of duty, efficiency through capacity to produce desired results, and for behavior…" (A letter published in part in the NAO in November, 1943 mentioned that Roland had now been in two invasions (obviously French Morocco and Sicily). Southern France would be his third. That letter also mentioned that he saw Donald Smith of Fillmore frequently as they had been in the same outfit since they entered the service. Don was part of the Headquarters Battery.

Roland and the 62nd AAA Gun Battalion now headed for the invasion of Southern France. Arriving in August 1944, the Battalion was initially assigned to the defense of Marseilles. In October, Roland was one of four men from Company D who were assigned to temporary duty with the 1st Airborne Task Force. It is not clear when Roland returned to the 62nd, but by November, the Battalion was at Hagenau, France. The Battalion's history indicates that Company D was within range of enemy small arms fire, but suffered no casualties.

By November 19 they were at Le Rouiles, France. Advancing rapidly, the 62nd reached Strasburg by November 29. Its gunners put up constant fire at both enemy rail and road junctions as well as aircraft that dared to attack. By December 22nd they were at Hunspach. On the 23rd, Company D was attached to the 36th Infantry Division for operational purposes. They became a part of Task Force Linden. By the 27 they were moved to VI Corps, and on the 29 to the 91st AAA Group. In a letter home, part of which was published in the NAO in January, 1945 Roland informed his parents that he had been slightly wounded, although it had been a close call. Since the wound put him in the hospital, it was likely more serious than he indicated. But he wrote that he was now back with his outfit and that France was the best country he had been in since he arrived overseas.

Roland's days with the 62nd were about over. A 62nd report dated January 17, 1945 announced that he had been transferred to the 42nd Infantry Division (the Rainbow Division). For the rest of the war, Roland was an infantryman with the 242nd Infantry Regiment. The 42nd had arrived in Marseilles on December 8, 1944. Elements of the Division repulsed German attacks during "Operation Nordwind.," in January 1945. The entire Division entered combat in mid-February near Hagenau. (Roland had already been there.) They then attacked through the Hardt Forest, breaking through the Siegfried Line in mid-March, then cleared the towns of Dahn and Busenberg. They captured Wertheim au Main April 1 and Wurzburg on the 6th. In hand-to-hand fighting they captured Schweinfurt by April 12. Furth, near Nuremburg, was taken on the 19th, after four days of fanatical resistant by the local Nazis. On April 25, they captured Donaworth on Danube and on the 29th helped liberate 30,000 inmates at the Dachau concentration camp. By April 30, they were in Munich. Elements also moved across the Austrian border into Salzburg. German soldiers had grown to fear the 42nd. They called them Roosevelt's SS for their fierce fighting. On July 5, 1945, after 53 months of service, including 33 months of service overseas, three invasions, and seven campaigns with a battle star for each, Roland Thomas was discharged.

George W. Tisdale of Centerville enlisted in the Army on December 16, 1943, after turning 18 just five months earlier. In June 1944, he was transferred from Fort Hood TX, to Camp Bowie, TX. Fort Hood was the home base for the training of Tank Destroyer Battalions, and George's outfit, the 822nd Tank Destroyer Battalion underwent extensive training there. Camp Bowie was the largest Army training base in Texas. The motto of Tank Destroyers Battalions was "SEEK STRIKE DESTROY".

Tank destroyer battalions were formed to counter massed formations of enemy armored units. These units were to act as independent battalions attached to either a division or corps. In practice, they were generally used in support of infantry units. There were two types of tank destroyer battalions. By the time George arrived in Europe, the first type featured towed 3-inch guns. Such battalions were made up of three companies, each with 12 guns. The second type tank destroyer battalion was self-propelled like a tank but without heavy armor. George's battalion, the 822nd, entered combat with towed guns. By March 1945 they were equipped with M 18 tanks, called Hellcats. The M 18 was the fastest tracked armored fighting vehicle in the war. Its top speed was 60 miles per hour, and it operated with a 76-mm canon. A Hellcat could ford six feet of water, climb low walls and ram through structures. Its armor however, was light; and it needed to use its speed in battle to maintain the upper hand.

George and the 822nd Tank Destroyer Battalion arrived at La Havre, France on January 23, 1945. It entered combat with the 63rd Infantry Division on February 7, 1945. The 822nd apparently was not officially attached to the 63rd until March 21. It remained with the 63rd until May 28, 1945.

On February 7, the 822nd entered the fight near Sarreque Mines. Initially it provided armor protection as the 63rd conducted local raids and patrols in the area. Both units smashed across the Saar River around February 27 and broke through the Siegfried Line at Saarbrucken on March 15. The 822nd crossed the Rhine on March 27 and participated in the capture of Heidelburg on April 1. In April, the Battalion was switched from towed to self -propelled, although it had had some M 18 tanks by late March. The 822nd, with the 62nd Infantry Division, now rolled through Germany. Both were involved in heavy fighting at Adelsheim, Mockmulk and Bad Wampfen. Nevertheless, they powered through, participated in the capture of Lampoldshausen and helped clear the Hardthauser Woods. By April 27 they reached Munsterhausen, and here they took up occupation duties.

Anthony R. (Tony) Vasile of Fillmore entered the Army on April 25, 1941. Being in the service prior to December 7, 1941, Tony was another FCSD area resident who earned the American Defense Medal. It is not clear where Tony took his basic training. It is likely that he was assigned to Fort Ethan Allen in Vermont within months after entering the service, and he may have taken his initial training there. At Ethan Allen, he became a member of the 771st Tank Destroyer Battalion. The Battalion was activated there on December 15, 1941. (Many of the men assigned to the Battalion came from the 186th and 187th Field Artillery Battalions, which were stationed at Ethan Allen. Tony may have been with one of these battalions.) The 771st was originally armed with the M10 3-inch gun motor carriage (GMC). Later, the battalion was equipped with the more powerful M36 90mm GMC, the most powerful anti-tank weapon used in the war.

For 20 months after activation, the Battalion engaged in numerous training activities at various locations throughout the states. This included maneuvers at Fort Devens, MA, in September 1941, maneuvers at Fort Bragg, NC, in October, November and December of 1941, and training at Fort Edwards in Massachusetts in March 1942. By June 1942 they were at Camp Hill in New York., They spent six months at Fort Hood in Texas. Here they rolled out of slit trenches and crawled through barbed wire entanglements, while live machine gun fire blazed two feet above their heads. Back in Vermont in late January 1943, they continued training until April when they were shipped to Kingston, NY. The 771st proudly declared that they were the toughest of the tough. Their combat training started where everyone else's left off. Finally, in October 1943, they were notified they were heading overseas. They were moved to Camp Shanks, NY for shipment. They sailed from New York on October 21, aboard the *RMMV Capetown Castle*, a converted British passenger liner, that arrived at Liverpool, England November 3rd. By January 1944, they were in Glamorganshire, Wales. Expecting to be assigned to the invasion force, they were disappointed to learn that they were to be involved in more training. This time, however, they were the trainers. For four months, they drilled all the Tank Destroyer troops in the ETO. Finally, in May, they were moved to Devonshire, England, and were prepared for movement to the continent of Europe. On June 19, 1944, Tony and other deserving men of the 771st, were awarded the Good Conduct Medal. On September 15, 1944, Tony, who was assigned to Company B, and the rest of the Battalion, landed on Omaha Beach.

The battalion's stay in France was short. In fact, short stays were the norm, as the battalion helped the Allies punch their way across France, Belgium, and Holland as they pushed into the heart of the Nazi Empire, Germany. They arrived in Tongres, Belgium on October 24, 1944. Passing quickly through Holland, they first entered combat on November 3, in Germany. The battalion were attached to the 102nd Infantry Division primarily; but it would support several other units including the 11th US Cavalry Group, the 5th Armored Division, and the 83rd Infantry Division. The battalion participated in both the Rhineland and Central Europe Campaigns, earning a battle star for each. During six months of combat, the Division was never out of light artillery range of enemy gunners. From November 3 until December 31, 1944, all its combat was between the Wurm and Roer Rivers, from Geilenkirchen to Flosdorf. Tony's primary assignment was supply. In battle, things break down, and there is a constant need for replacement materiel. A history of the 771st speaks specifically to this issue, and to the performance of the men responsible for keeping the battalion supplied. At times the supply lines stretched for 200 miles. Despite that distance, Tony and the other men in supply made sure the battalion always had the necessary equipment and parts, as well as gasoline, oil, and food.

In 1945, the 771st joined the push into central Germany. The Battalion's Journal lists 22 "headquarter sites" for the period January 1 to May 14, 1945. The last one was Calbe at Milde, Sachsen, Germany, which is where the battalion celebrated the end of the war. It is also where the men of the 771st undertook their next assignment, occupation duties. They were involved with such duties in several locations until the middle of September. In route to one assignment, Teugh, Bavaria, they passed through Nuremberg, the site of the famous Nuremberg Nazi rallies of 1933 to 1938. Tony was too late to see the famous huge Nazi swastika about the grandstands. The US Army blew it up on April 24,1945. On September 22, the 771st was transferred to Marne, France, and then to Camp Philip Morris, Gainneville, France for processing for the trip home. Tony and the rest of the 771st, sailed home on November 9 aboard the *USS Edmund B. Alexandrer.* Ironically the *Alexander* was a German passenger ship that was seized by the United States when it entered WW I. Its original name was SS *Amerika*. She had also been used to transport men home after World War I. On April 14, 1912, the *Amerika* has sent a wireless message about icebergs in the North Atlantic. Less than three hours later, at the location the *Amerika* had warned about, the *Titanic* struck an iceberg, and sank.

Tony was discharged at Fort Dix in New Jersey on December 2, 1945.

Gerald J. (Jerry) Voss entered the service on December 9, 1942. After finishing basic training at Camp Eustice, VA, he was transferred to Fort Edwards, MA, where he likely became a member of the 449th Anti- Aircraft Automatic Weapons Battalion. At Edwards, the 449th was engaged in combat training. Then, along with other members of the 449th, Jerry was sent to Fort Dix, NJ, to prepare for overseas shipment. In early November 1943, the Battalion moved to Camp Shank, the last stop before boarding a British ship and heading for England. On December 17, they arrived in Liverpool and were immediately loaded on a train and moved to Scotland. While the stay in Scotland was short, the men appeared to enjoy it. A stanza, of a poem entitled, "The Epic of the 449th", written by Technical Sergeant John T. Spain. Sergeant Spain's poem *is from the 449th Unit History booklet in the National Archives.*

In Scotland we met people who
Spoke a language no one knew.
We learned of "round-abouts" and "Pubs"

The Scots were far from being snobs.

After a short stay, they headed back to England and were assigned to air bases to protect against attacks of German aircraft. Spain's poem had a stanza for this part of their stay in England:

At nite the German planes came down
To strafe and bomb some near-by town.
The guns around would spit their fire
and down would come some Jerry flier.

The battalion also endured combat and amphibious training. But the sojourn in England was about over. On May 10, the Battalion was assigned to the 3rd Army. On May 30, General Order 6, awarded Gerald the Good Conduct Medal. On June 14, 8 days after the invasion at Normandy, the 449th landed on Omaha Beach. The 449th was now ready to join the Allies as they smashed their way across Europe and into the Fatherland of the Third Reich. Throughout their operations the primary responsibility of the 449th was to protect Field Artillery Battalions. Gerald's Battery C primarily protected the 50th Field Artillery Battalion. They participated in battles at Verdun, Reims, Metz, and Saarlautern; and the fighting continued at the Siegfried Line, the crossing of the Rhine, the taking of Frankfort au Main, and the cleaning up of the Ruhr Pocket. They were the first anti-aircraft unit to cross the Rhine, and they fought in four countries: France, Luxembourg, Germany, and Czechoslovakia.

We went through Verdun Reims and Metz
They're places that one ne'er forgets
The people lined the road in lines
To offer us their flowers and wines
Through Luxembourg, the Siegfried Line
We soon were standing near the Rhine
The Jerry planes were overhead
Our guns gave them a blast of lead.

When the battle was done, Sergeant Spain's poem captured the end, and saluted his buddies who would not return home.

At 0001 on the 9th of May,   That day we thought of all our men
The Nazis had no more to say,   For whom this war had been the end.
For they were beaten bitter then.   We'd like to shake their hands and say,
And far from being "Super-Men".   "It's you who made the Nazis pay".

Gerald and the 449th collected five battle stars (Normandy, Northern France, Ardennes-Alsace, Central Europe, and Rhineland) as they blasted their way across Europe. They also helped blast the Luftwaffe out of the European skies. The Luftwaffe had helped take the German Army everywhere it went in World War II. With its demise, the only place the German Army went was back to Germany. The 449th performed occupational duties in Germany from May 2 to July 5, 1945, before heading for the states.

Donald L. Whalen of Fillmore first entered the service, the US Navy, in February 1943. The NAO reported that his parents went to Olean to see him off to his training at the Great Lakes Naval Training Station. There is no more information on his naval career. He was only 17, but must have had his parent's approval since they saw him off.

In July 1944, Don enrolled in the Army. This time he stayed. He took his basic training at Fort Dix, in New Jersey, and then transferred, in August or September, 1944, to Fort Belvoir. At the time, Belvoir was an engineer replacement training center. There is also an indication that he spent a short period at a base in Texas in December 1945 or January 1946. By February 1945, he was on his way to Europe. His first stop was England, and then, again according to the NAO, to Holland. If he did serve in Holland, it was not with the 292nd Combat Engineer Battalion, his future unit, which was attached to the Ninth Army. The 292nd arrived in England on November 11, 1944. By December 15 it was in France and on December 23, it entered Germany. In early February it prepared to cross the Roer River. The crossing, code named Operation Grenade, was supposed to occur on February 9. However, the Germans destroyed the up-river dams resulting in a flooding of the Roer. It was two weeks before the river receded enough for the 9th Army to cross. The 292nd Combat Engineers had to build bridges for troops and vehicles to cross the Roer while under constant attack from German artillery and troops. German General Gerd von Runsted had supported the flooding with the idea that while the flooded waters were receding, he could withdraw his armies across the Rhine and re-establish his defenses. Hitler refused his request to withdraw. As a result, once the Allies crossed the Roer on February 23 von Runsted's Army was essentially destroyed. Some 90,000 men were lost, with 50,000 being captured. The Allies suffered 23,000 casualties. The 292nd was in Merkstein, Germany on February 28, 1945. It spent the month of March in Hula, Germany where it continued to carry out regular combat engineer activities.

In April the battalion was part of the mad dash across Germany. On April 1st it was in the vicinity of Hiddingsel. By the 6th it was at Belke; by the 13 it was in the vicinity of Nordgoltern and by the 17, at Octerburg. It ended the month and the war at Arandsee.

At some point during the March-April time frame, Don joined the 292nd Engineer Combat Battalion as a truck driver. The 292nd was part of the 1149th Combat Group, that was with the 9th US Army. Don was with it as the 9th spearheaded a drive to the Elbe River in Germany. The NAO published a release from the War Department which stated, "The 292nd Engineer Combat Battalion, commanded by LT. Colonel George M. Reves, veteran engineer battalion of the Roer River crossing, is one of the units which smashed into the heart of Germany to the Elbe River with the Ninth Army spearhead." Among the members of the battalion according to the War Department release was Donald L. Whalen, Fillmore.

The crossing of the Elbe on April 25, 1945 and the meeting of Soviet and American soldiers at Torgau, Germany is celebrated to this day. While not an official holiday, Elbe Day has continued to be celebrated in various ways in various countries.

In August, 1945 the NAO reported that Don's Dad Leo received a letter from Captain George J. Leskowitz of the 292nd. The letter (NAO did not report the date of the letter.) was a commendation for the work that Don had performed as a driver of Army vehicles for the 292nd. The captain said that Don had proven to be one of the unit's most capable drivers. It is interesting to note that truck drivers were essential to the war effort, both in the states and worldwide. As pointed out earlier, Russian Chairman Stalin had, in a slightly different context, opined that American trucks were one of the ten most important weapons of the war.

The 292nd remained in Germany performing occupation duties from May 2 to July 5, 1945. Don remained in Europe until the end of the year. His Allegany County War Service Record indicates he arrived back in the states January 2, 1946 aboard the Victory type *Sheephead Bay* troop ship. Don was married February 9, 1946 and remained in the service until 1948. During that period, it appears he was stationed in Yuma, Arizona.

Concentration Camps

"You ask. What is our policy? I will say; "It is to wage war, by sea, land and air… against a monstrous tyranny, never surpassed in the dark lamentable catalogue of humane crime."
British Prime Minister, Sir Winston Churchill. From a passage in a speech in the House of Commons, 1940.

If you do not believe you will surely end up in Dachau. It is said that German parents used the above to frighten their children into believing, presumably in Hitler. It is also said that the Germans did not know what was happening in the concentration camps.

"We are told the American soldier does not know what he is fighting for. Now, at least, he will know what he is fighting against." General Eisenhower, after visiting the German concentration camp at Ohrdruf. Afterwards Ike ordered all nearby soldiers not on the front lines to visit Ohrdruf. April 12, 1945.

Herr Yanning: *Those people, those millions of people. You must believe me. I never knew it would come to that.*
Judge Haywood: *Herr Yanning, it came to that the first time you sentenced a man to death you knew to be innocent.*
Dialogue of Burt Lancaster as Nazi Judge Ernst Yanning and Spencer Tracy as Chief American Judge Dan Haywood in the movie *Judgement at Nurnberg* about the complicity in and legal justifications provided by German judges in defense of the Holocaust. There could be no better answer to such a sick question. Written by Abby Mann.

The catalogue of human crime would be immense if anyone could ever write it all down. But there is no doubt that the biggest chapter in the catalogue would be the Nazi Holocaust. One begs for words to describe how any people, civilized or not, could devise and execute a plan designed to systematically exterminate an entire population of human beings, and nearly succeed.

At least eleven men from the FCSD area saw first-hand the results of this unsurpassable legacy of hate and horror - John W. Beardsley, Jr. (Stationed at Dachau); William C. Crandall (90th Infantry Division-Flossenburg), Maxwell L. Fancher (103rd Infantry Division-Kaufering sub-camps); Donald W. Finnemore (89th Infantry Division-Ohrdurf/Buchenwald); Hubert F. McMaster (104th Infantry Division-Dore /Mittebau); Lewis John Morgan (89th Infantry Division-Ohrdurf); Carroll S. Phipps (45th Infantry Division-Dachau); Roland J. Thomas (42nd Infantry Division-Dachau); Irwin K. Tuthill (4th Infantry Division-Fischbachau), Lowell J Wilcox (1st Infantry Division -Zwodau & Falkenau an der Eger/Flossenburg) and Robert Wolfer (551st AAA AW Battalion-Dachau). All these men, except Robert Wolfer, were with units which were designated by the Holocaust Museum in Washington, DC as Liberating Units. Robert's unit arrived at Dachau after the liberation, but they did see the horrors of the camp. John W. Beardsley was likely not with his unit when the Dachau liberation occurred. He was wounded March 18, 1945 and may not have been with his unit when it participated in the liberation of Flossenburg sub-camps. However, he did serve at Dachau during the trials of Nazi murderers. The Holocaust Museum and the US Army have recognized 36 divisions as Liberating units. Ten men from the FCSD served in nine of the 36 divisions. In addition, Horace H. Thayer, not listed above, served with the 9th Armored Division. He was KIA before the 9th helped liberate Swodacs and Fenauan der Eger, subcamps of Flossenburg, May 8, 1945. Horace was killed December 18, 1944 during the Battle of the Bulge.

John, third from left, with buddies in Germany.

John W. Beardsley, Jr. of Hume entered the service on March 21, 1944. He was initially stationed at Camp Wheeler, GA (1st Platoon, Company B, 8th Battalion) where he likely took his basic training. He was then transferred to Fort Benning Ga. Fort Benning is famous as the Army's infantry training center. By 1944, it was training replacements for infantry regiments. Given that John's wife Blanche indicated he served as a rifleman, John almost surely received his infantry combat training at Benning. John was next transferred to

Camp Shelby, MS. It appears that he received his final infantry combat training at Shelby as part of the 65th Infantry Division, assigned to the 260th Infantry Regiment. The NAO reported in November of 1944 that John had been transferred from Fort Benning to Camp Shelby. In February 1945, the NAO reported that his family had been notified that he was now in France. He had been shipped overseas with the 65th on January 10, 1945, arriving at La Havre, France on January 21, 1945. Elements of the Division entered combat on March 5, taking over a defensive sector on the Saar River. The Division crossed the Saar on March 17-18, attacking Saarlautern. John was wounded in action on the 17th, while breaching the Siegfried Line. Blanche said that he was in a building that was hit by a German shell. The blast blew him through a wall of the building. The NAO reported, on April 4, that John was serving with the Third Army when wounded. The 65th was with the Third Army on March 17. The NAO later reported that he was in a hospital in France. His discharge document shows that he was treated by the 32nd Evacuation Hospital. General Order No. 71, issued March 18, 1945 while he was at the 32nd, awarded him his Purple Heart. *Photo – Family photo. John – third from left.*

John served as a Rifleman for six months and a Scout for 12 months during his service. He likely was a Scout for battalion intelligence reconnaissance during his combat service. As such he observed enemy positions and fire from advanced observation posts and relayed the information to the battalion command post. He was likely performing such duties when he was wounded as the regiment attacked across the Saar River at Dillingen on March 17.

It is not certain how long John was in the hospital. His wife said he was released May 11. When he was released, he probably did not return to the 65th. (The 65th Infantry Division was in Linz, Austria when the war ended; and it was involved in occupation duties until rotated home and deactivated in August, 1945. Its history says that many of its members were assigned to other units after the war ended, and it is also possible that John was transferred during this period.)

John was assigned, maybe immediately, but maybe a little later, to the 47th Infantry Regiment, 9th Infantry Division upon his release from the hospital. The 47th Infantry was assigned to occupation duties until late 1946. Generally, this meant organizing, occupying, and governing a specified area (one or more Landkreis' or districts), while demobilizing its own personnel and units, A multitude of activities fell under those general headings, including maintaining contact with Soviet forces, using troops in case of armed resistance, stopping riots and insurrections, fighting fires, and maintaining law and order. The Division was also responsible for taking action to protect against and address health hazards. They also had to maintain good relations with the civil populations and guard key installations which could represent a threat to peaceful order. It also was responsible for apprehending wanted individuals (war criminals) and controlling movement in its area. It is not clear where the 47th was initially assigned to perform these duties, but it may have been the Dachau Landkreis, home of the notorious concentration camp Dachau. (Unfortunately, there is a gap in the history of the 47th for the period May 1945 to December, 1945. It is likely that following the end of the war, record keeping became a little lax or possibly the reports were lost. The historical reports continued in January 1946.

The NAO reported in December that John was stationed at Dachau. He wrote wishing all the people in Fillmore a Merry Christmas and a Happy New Year. It is possible that John and his unit were assigned to Dachau as part of the War Crimes Trials taking place there. These trials were held to prosecute all war criminals caught in the US zone of occupation in Germany. The trials were held in the infamous Dachau Concentration Camp and were conducted entirely by American military personnel. The proceedings lasted from November 1945 until August 1948, although John was rotated home in 1946, and discharged in May of that year. Of the 1,672 criminals tried at the trials, 1,416 were convicted. Of those convicted, 297 received the death penalty, and 279 received life sentences.

The persons tried included members of the SS who had been imprisoned at the camp after the war. Some of the most infamous of the prisoners were members of the Waffen SS tried for executing (murdering) 84 American POW's at Malmedy (the Malmedy Massacre) during the Battle of the Bulge. Seventy-three members of the Waffen SS involved with Malmedy murders were convicted and executed. John may have served as a guard or in some other capacity during the trials.

The 1st Battalion of the 9th Infantry Division, John's battalion, was assigned to Landkreis Memmingen on March 5, 1946. It remained there for the balance of John's service, although its areas of responsibility continually increased. On March 10th it was assigned two more Landkreis' and the day John sailed for home, May 10, 1946, it gained five more. John arrived back in the states May 18, 1946 and was discharged May 26, 1946 at Fort Dix, NJ.

(John's original unit, the 65th Infantry Division, is a designated Liberator Unit. It liberated a Flossenburg concentration sub camp in Bavaria April 20-21, 1945. John, due to his combat wound, was not with the 65th at the time. It is possible, and maybe likely, that John's last division (the 9th Infantry Division) carried out only occupation duties as described above while at Dachau.)

William C. Crandall of Houghton entered the service on December 5, 1942. William was a transportation dispatcher with the 357th Infantry Regiment, 90th Infantry Division. The 90th landed in England on April 4, 1944, and conducted training exercises there until June 4, 1944. On June 6th, elements of the 90th landed on Utah Beach. The rest of the Division entered combat on June 10.

The 90th wasted no time once it got ashore. By August 12, it had crossed the Saar River near LeMans, and help close the Falaise Gap. On August 19, it united with the 1st Polish Armored Division in Cambois. The 90th continued to slug its way across France, reaching Verdun on September 6 and participating in the siege of Metz from September 14 to November 19. During this period, it captured Maizieres-le-Metz on October 30 and crossed the Moselle River on November 9. On December 4 it crossed the Saar. Here it was stopped under orders from Ike, due to the German winter counter offensive. During the period December 6 to 18, it withdrew to the west bank of the Saar and took up defensive positions. It remained on the defense until January 5, 1945. Then the 90th resumed its march through the Nazi defenses, crossing the Our River near Oberhausen on January 29 and smashing through the Siegfried Line during February. In March, it crossed the Rhine, Main and Werra Rivers before reaching the Czechoslovakia border on April 18. Then it moved into the Sudetes Mountain Range in route to Prague, and in the process, it freed the remaining prisoners at the Flossenburg Concentration Camp.

Flossenburg was owned and operated by the Schutzstaffel (SS) Economic Administrative Office. It was a slave labor camp. The prisoners were forced to mine granite used in construction. They were starved and murdered at the whim of the guards. Polish and Russian prisoners were prime targets. It is estimated that some 96,000 people were imprisoned there. Only 30,000 survived. However, the most famous prisoner may have been the head of Abwehr (German Intelligence), Admiral William Canaris. He had participated in the plot that led to the unsuccessful attempt to kill Hitler on July 20, 1944. In early April, as the war was coming to an end, he was summarily executed at Flossenburg.

Another prisoner was Marian P. Opala, who had been born in Lodz, Poland. Opala served in many capacities throughout the war, but primarily with the Polish underground. He was captured during the Warsaw Uprising and imprisoned at Flossenburg. Freed by the 90th Division, Opala came to the US, and spent his life upholding the principals of law and justice that had been so brutalized by the Nazi. He served 32 years on the Oklahoma Supreme Court, becoming Chief Justice in 1991.

Donald K. Finnemore of Fillmore was at Buchenwald and Ohrdruf, two of the more notorious concentration camps. Buchenwald's sole reason for existence was to kill innocent people. Ilse Koch, wife of camp commander Karl Koch, committed some of the most sadistic acts of inhumanity ever at Buchenwald. These acts included having the skin of murdered prisoners made into lampshades. One of Buchenwald's sub-camps was the work camp Ohrdruf. Work camp is something of a misnomer. It did work people, to death. If they did not die, they were sent back to Buchenwald where they were murdered. Systemic murders also occurred at Ohrdruf, especially at the end as American troops approached.

Robert H. Abzug in his book, *"Inside the Vicious Heart: Americans and the Liberation of Nazi Concentration Camps,"* quoted Rabbi Murray Kohn. Kohn, who was an inmate at Ohrdruf, in a speech years later, commented, "The last days of Ohrdruf were a slaughterhouse. Nazi guards executed with hand guns, emptying their bullets into whoever they encountered." Abzug wrote "A pile of dead prisoners, all in striped uniforms. The corpses were fleshless and at the back of each skull, a bullet hole."

Ohrdruf was liberated April 4, 1945 by elements of the 4th Armored Division and patrols of the 355th Infantry Division. By April 6th, Donald W. Finnemore's outfit, the 355th Infantry Division, had taken

over the camp. (Charles T. Payne, brother of President Barack Obama's maternal grandmother, was also with the 355th, and took part in the liberation.) General's Eisenhower, Bradley and Patton visited the camp, the first such camp liberated in Germany.

April 12, 1945 - General Eisenhower (third from left) at the Ohrdruf concentration camp. He is viewing the charred remains of innocent people, including children, murdered by the Nazis. Following this visit Ike ordered that all men in the area, not on the front lines, visit the camp. He stated that he had heard many times that the American soldier did not know what he was fighting for. By visiting the camp Ike said, they would at least know what they were fighting against. Holocaust Memorial Museum photo.

Irwin K. Tuthill of Fillmore, who earned a Bronze Star for heroism on D-Day (see Normandy section), saw the results of the Nazi extermination policy at a concentration camp in Germany. On May 1, 1945, he wrote his father, "The papers and movies did not exaggerate the camps any. We saw the bodies piled like cord-wood, except that they were reduced by starvation to skeletons. We met some internees on the road, and the way they grabbed for food was pitiful." Tuthill was likely speaking of the concentration camp at Fischbachau since his outfit, the 4th Infantry Division, was at Miesbach, Bavaria by May 2, 1945. Fischbachau, a sub-camp of Dachau, was only 9 miles from Miesbach.

Irwin in his battle gear.
NAO Photo.

Robert Wolfer of Centerville entered the service on February 2, 1943. By May 15, 1943 he was at Fort Edwards, MD, with the 551st Anti-Aircraft Artillery Automated Weapons (AAA AA) Battalion, Battery B. His basic training may have been at Fort Edwards. The 551st had originally been organized in 1940 as a Coastal Artillery Battalion, but was re-designated in May 1943, as an anti-aircraft artillery battalion. Its home base was Camp Edwards, MA. Over the next few months, this battalion engaged in extensive training. From September 1943 through January 1944, the battalion participated in three separate maneuvers, two in Tennessee (Fall 1943 & Winter 1943 &1944) and one in South Carolina (Winter 1943). In February 1944, the battalion was at Camp Butner, NC. Robert was awarded his Good Conduct

Medal there according to General Order 3 dated February 18, 1944. During this period, the 551st was still officially stationed at Fort Edwards.

The battalion departed Fort Edwards for overseas in late March. However, it did not arrive in England until July 2, 1944. After a brief stay in Upton Louvil Wittshire it was transferred on July 21 (arriving on the 26) to Barnes-Sur-Mer, France. It officially entered combat on August 9, 1944, supporting the 10th and 11th Regiments at Barnesville-sur-Mer, against the German 11th Panzer Grandier Division. At via Sceaux they were attacked by Focke Wulf 190 fighters. A Battery shot one down. As the war progressed, encounters with the German Luftwaffe decreased dramatically. The Luftwaffe had literally been destroyed. Many US anti-aircraft battalions were deactivated and the men transferred to other units. The 551st was maintained as a AAA AW battalion.

Robert's battalion now became part of the dash across France and into the German homeland. Primary assignments of the 551st were defending bridges, airfields, other installations, and infantry regiments as they literally blasted their way across Europe. This included numerous locations, Bad Kreuznach, Frankfurt au Main and Regensburg. There was constant movement. The 551st, like all AAA AA units, was a mobile unit. It likely was a truck-towed unit; and Robert, as a truck driver, likely towed the unit's armament. The 551st was armed with 40 mm Bofors Canons and 50 Caliber machine guns.

In May, at war's end, the battalion was in Regensburg, a city that had been a prime target for American bombers during the height of the war. By the end of the month, it was at Dachau. Robert and the rest of the 551st now saw what General Eisenhower had spoken of when he said that visiting the concentration camps would show the American soldier what he was fighting against.

The 551st was later assigned to occupation duties. This included such tasks as moving rations from Wirzburg, Germany to Kinz, Austria, and transporting Italian displaced persons from Mittenwald, Germany to Bolzano, Italy. In July, Robert's Battery B, helped move Polish displaced persons to camps throughout XX Corps area. Robert was likely transferred back to the states in early August. He was discharged August 18, 1945.

Another local man, **Gerald A. Rennicks** of Hume also served with a liberator unit. However, he was seriously wounded on February 25, 1945. His wounds required four operations and it is likely that he was not with his unit, the 28th Infantry regiment, 8th Infantry Division, when it liberated the Wobbelin concentration camp on May 2, 1945.

PART IX - CIVILIANS AT WAR

"There is one front and one battle where everyone in the United States - every man, woman, and child - is in action, and will be privileged to remain in action throughout the war. That front is right here at home, in our daily lives, and in our daily tasks."   President Franklin D. Roosevelt April 28, 1942

Supporting the Troops

The most famous home front story of the war was likely that of "Rosie the Riveter." Rosie, of course, was really about the enormous role women assumed in society during the war. The women of the FCSD area did their share in this regard. For instance, Miss Martha Jerman, a waitress at the Fillmore Hotel, went to work for the General Motors Corporation in Buffalo. Jean Eldridge Perry, employed in her home before the war, first served with the Women's Auxiliary Army Corps, then went to work for Bell Aircraft in Buffalo, working in the electronics lab on flight research. Miss Marion Thomas of Fillmore went to work for the Buffalo Arms Corporation. Miss Katherine Benjamin, who had worked for the Rochester Gas & Electric office in Fillmore, moved to Buffalo to work in the office of a defense industry company. Eva Schneider did the same, and in 1944 was one of the workers at the Curtiss plant in Buffalo to receive an award as a 100 percent production worker.

But there were numerous new roles played by all citizens on the home front, which both aided in the war effort and directly supported the men and women in the service.

One of the first things accomplished in the FCSD area was the establishment of aircraft warning posts.

At first, these posts were manned by American Legion members and other male civilians as part of Civilian Defense efforts. By late 1942, women were being invited to "man" the posts. (I can remember being with my mother at a post, and I remember we saw and reported at least one airplane. Author.) For more than a year most of these posts were manned 24 hours a day. By late 1943, however, the War Department advised that manning the posts at intervals rather than continuously would be sufficient. Originally there were three warning stations in the area - one at A.B. Spencer's on the Hume-Pike Road Rose Hill, headed up by George Stekl; another at English Hill headed by Frank Gayford, and a third at Fink Hollow run by Clyde Walker. Eventually a post was also established just off Emerald Street in Fillmore, above a barn owned by, eventually, George and Isabel Hall. Photo - *Observation Tower – Rose Hill.*

Air War Wardens were also recruited. Fillmore resident Bob Gleason remembered the street assignments in Fillmore: Prospect - L.S. Gleason, Hovey Gelser; Lowell - Leo Arnold; Emerald - Alvin Bleistein, Harvey Howden; Minard - John McCarns; North Genesee - Claude Sandford, Charles Bliss, Robert Butler; South Genesee - Everie McCrea, Charles McElheny; Main - Lores Towner, Sam Colombo; East Main - Carl Oldenburg; West Main - C.J. Winchip, Gilbert Bloomster, A.F. Haynes; Torpy - Albert McCarthy. Each street warden had an armband with the word "Warden" in capital letters. Polly Cockle Miller remembers that her brother-in-law, Robert Bennett, patrolled in Hume. The Boy Scouts, using their bicycles, served as messengers for the wardens.

There were also practice blackouts. Blackouts were signaled by the local fire siren. Those who "forgot" to comply would receive a visit from a warden. A steady blast of the siren was adopted in 1943 as the new "all clear" signal. In early 1944 the War Department and the office of Civilian Defense ended practice air raid alerts and blackouts.

Early in the war, the FCSD area was canvassed to determine how many evacuees might be accommodated, if an evacuation became necessary. There was a feeling that Buffalo, Rochester and especially New York City were vulnerable to German attacks. Ruby Williams canvassed Centerville and Ida Hatch canvassed Higgins. Others did the same for the other communities in the area. Ruby's daughter, Darlene Williams Mowers, remembers that her mother, and the other canvassers received a free edition of the NAO for their efforts.

The FCSD area also did its share in War Bond Drives. L. S. Gleason, Chairman of the drives, reported in the NAO that the Fillmore/Houghton June, 1942 quota of $11,000 had been met. Quotas were met throughout the war. In 1943 Lyle Bliss built and erected a Red Cross "thermometer" on Main Street in Fillmore. It kept rising to show how much had been raised toward the then current goal of $900; $1,000 was raised. In 1944 purchases began to lag a little and extra efforts were made by local businessmen to assure that quotas were met. Bruce Sweet, owner of the Fillmore Opera House, let everyone who bought War Bonds at the Opera House in free to showings of *Swing Shift Maisie* and *Hoosier Holiday*. Purchases jumped sharply when word spread of Japanese atrocities in the Philippines, especially the Bataan Death March.

The area also fully participated in the other drives that took place during the war. These included waste paper, which usually was collected by Boy Scout Troop 47. Waste paper included newspapers, magazines cardboard boxes, and even wrapping paper. Wrapping paper became even less available in 1944. Shoppers were urged to keep and reuse shopping bags with handles. Ironically, on the other hand, people were urged to destroy paper wrappings from overseas as it might contain eggs of harmful insects.

The Girls Scouts conducted a Hosiery Salvage Campaign to collect old silk and nylon stockings. Those were used for making powder bags for military use.

Polly Cockle Miller (whose brother Allen and husband Alvin served during the war) remembers Bill Sandford, whose dad owned the grocery store in Hume, sponsoring a tin can drive. To encourage donations, Bill offered prizes. First prize was a $50 War Bond won by Elmer Van Dusen. Second prize was a Kodak flash camera that Polly won. She kept the camera for many years but in 2012 donated it to the Hume Museum.

The Boy Scouts, as has been noted, participated in numerous war-related activities. In 1944 the local troop secured the largest number of pledges for the purchase of War Bonds in Allegany County. For this the Troop was awarded a captured Italian Flag. The flag had been captured at Caltanisetta in Sicily in a battle that broke the communications lines of the Axis forces and helped lead to victory in Sicily for the Allies. Clint Rauhe was serving as Scout Master at the time.

Rubber, especially old tires, a vital wartime commodity, was usually collected by local service stations such as Carl Oldenburg's Kendall Station. Rubber was so precious that citizens were encouraged to turn in their old rubber bands. Jack Allen, who soon would be chasing German submarines in the Atlantic, helped run Oldenburg's for a while in 1944, when Carl had to have an operation. Jack was working with Carl Oscar Turnstrom, who had already completed his military service.

Metals of all kinds were collected, including scrap metal, copper, brass, lead, and zinc. A special effort was made to collect old license plates. This did not include 1942 plates. Citizens were told those plates, along with dog tags and peddler's licenses, would have to last for the duration of the war. The NAO in 1942 carried this message: "A small magnet is a help in picking up pins and needles from the floor, from the dust pan and from the sweeper bag. They need to be saved now."

Mildred Kopler, owner of the "Fashion Shoppe," collected discarded clothing. Goodwill Industries arranged for the shipping of such clothing to people of unoccupied countries in Europe, where it was disparately needed. Two of Mildred's sons served during the war: Frank in the Army, and Howard in the Merchant Marine.

Even waste fats were reused. Towner's Store paid four cents a pound for waste fats delivered to it in tin cans, no glass containers. It was then passed on to the factories. Ida Webster Curran advised that she used fat from pork for cooking and that it made wonderful piecrusts.

Blood drives were common and important. The American Red Cross would bring their mobile units to the towns to collect blood. The drives were sponsored by such groups as the American Legion and its Auxiliary, and the Rotary Club. The NOA reported there were many repeat donors at the January 1943 drive, including "most of the boys from the RG&E" as well as Dr. John Marvin, Raymond Kopler, Winifred Vedder, Gladys Botsford, Claude Sandford, Mildred Whalen, Lois Curry, Elizabeth Winchip, Eva VanBurskirk, and Mr. & Mrs. Ellsworth Smith. (Winifred's son Grant was killed in action when his submarine was sunk.). In April 1943, the Pasteur Pre-Medic Club of Houghton College held a blood drive in which over 150 people participated.

Fillmore Librarian Mrs. Forest Lahr led a Victory Book Drive to collect books for soldiers. Local school students also helped with this effort. Mrs. Lahr reported that 302 books were collected against a quota of 161.

Schools in the area took part in developing and teaching vital skills that were needed by the military and at home. Fillmore Central School developed and provided an elementary electricity program taught by Roger Mills. Carl Oldenburg taught a War Production Board class on machinery - repairing it and keeping it in working order. Houghton College had a course for the initial training of prospective naval officers. Houghton resident and Aviation Cadet Gordon Barnett was one of the participants in this program. Houghton also was approved by both the Army and the Navy for providing education to enlisted Reserve personnel. By mid-1943, Houghton had students in the Army Reserve, Marine Corps Reserve, Army Air Corps Reserve, the Navy V-1, V-5 and V-7 programs, and the Army Medical Services. Dr. Robert R. Luckey, Instructor of Mathematics, was liaison officer for the Reserve programs. The college, in cooperation with the government, also offered evening classes in drafting, electricity, and radio.

The Hume Methodist Church, the Wiscoy school, and the Short Tract Town Hall hosted Civilian Defense Toxic Clinics

There were ration books for everything, from coffee and sugar and meat to gasoline. (In 1943 and 1944,  civilians received only 67 percent of the entire meat production in the country.) The famous newsman, Edward R. Morrow, explained food rationing by commenting that, "Rationing means that everyone has bread before anyone has cake."

Ida Webster Curran remembers that the ration stamps were highly valued. Everyone was careful to make the stamps last the required time. For some products, however, this was very difficult. Boots and shoes either did not last or were outgrown. Ida remembers going to the ration board for extra stamps to address such problems.

Getting a new telephone installed was virtually impossible. The military needed the materials used to install phones. Priorities were established for long distance phone calls. The number of new cars available was limited and you needed a Federal Stamp to use your car. Even bicycles were rationed, although the use of bicycles was encouraged to save gasoline. Hollis G. Young, a local official of the Rochester Gas & Electric, was named Allegany County War Transportation Administrator. He called for Car Sharing Clubs, reminding people that "We are not taking away or hindering transportation - that's already been done by the enemy. We are trying to keep it going..." It was estimated that 90 percent of the family budget was under rigid controls.

There were numerous efforts, beside blood drives, undertaken in cooperation with, or akin to, services provided by the Red Cross. Local groups were designated the Junior Red Cross and performed many valuable services throughout the war years. One, which soldiers always commented on in their letters home, was the preparation and sending out of Christmas packages. Women in the FCSD area, usually as part of a local club or church activity, also prepared surgical dressings. Ida Webster Curran helped make bandages as part of a Wesleyan Church activity. Houghton College students also assisted on many occasions. The dressings were usually prepared at the Fillmore Hospital. Many other groups participated. This was a vital war service. The Red Cross provided some 5,000,000 dressings in 1943 and was asked for 6,000,000 in 1944, which it met, with the help of women and students in the FCSD area.

The Red Cross was very popular. Soldiers wrote home praising their work and urging those at home to support the Red Cross. John Ballard of Centerville, who participated in several Pacific Islands invasions, wrote in early 1944 urging everyone to donate to the Red Cross. Arnold Eldridge of Fillmore did the same. Arnold had a real reason. His furlough money was stolen. The Red Cross arranged a loan so he could continue with his leave.

The American Legion Post and its Auxiliary were local leaders in the Christmas package effort that continued throughout the war, and even beyond the war. An article in a November 1945 edition of the NAO reminded readers of the collection of Christmas gifts for the wounded, disabled or sick servicemen and women at home or abroad. Donors were advised to keep the cost of the gifts under $3.00. Suggestions included playing cards, billfolds, new books, and leather cigarette cases. Foodstuffs and sharp objects (razor blades, knives, etc.) were not allowed.

The *Northern Allegany Observer* did its part. Letters home from soldiers constantly mentioned how much they enjoyed the newspaper. The *Observer* did its best to make sure they all got a copy.

Everything was not all safe at home. Many civilians faced danger in their jobs. Raymond Yager, a popular local figure, was almost killed when a US warplane crashed through the roof of the Curtiss-Wright plant in Buffalo where he worked. Ray was seriously injured and burned. Fifteen other men were killed. Theodore "Dutch" Parker was also injured in a serious accident at a war plant in Buffalo. Many locals worked there in the defense plants. Some moved to Buffalo, and others formed car pools and commuted.

Ida Webster Curran remembers the RG&E power plants in Wiscoy and Mills Mills operating constantly to produce electric power. To protect against any sabotage attempts, special doors with secure locks were installed at the plants.

In a way, the war was brought even closer when, in May, 1943, a prisoner of war camp was established at the lower falls in Letchworth State Park, ten miles from Fillmore. Some 200 German prisoners were held there and were put to work on local farms (usually harvesting crops and picking corn) and in local canneries. The prisoners were paid prevailing wages for their work. They also created some excitement when three of them escaped in early August. They were caught when Forrest Redanz noticed them sleeping in his wheat field. Forrest called Deputy Sheriff George Stekl who organized a "posse" of local FCSD men, consisting of William Stekl, Ray Kopler, Charles McElheney, Voney Wilson, Bernard Ayer, and Leland Lafferty. The men, armed with their own guns, quickly surrounded, and captured the escapees. Deputy Stekl returned them to prison authorities on Saturday afternoon. They had been free for a little over two days. The newspapers facetiously referred to them as "Supermen," but one does have to wonder. They had no idea where they were going, since they did not know where they were. Apparently, their plan was to follow the river, maybe with the idea of heading north into Canada for some reason. The Canadians were on our side. It is unlikely that they knew that the Genesee is one of only three rivers in the Northern Hemisphere that flows north rather than south. If Canada was their goal, even "Supermen" would have had to notice that, by following the river against its flow to go north, the sun was coming up in the west. Reality most likely was that they were three terrified young men (their ages were 23, 22, and 18) who had spent half of their lives listening to the ravings of a mad man.

The author remembers being told how he could help the war effort. Walking down the street, he could: "Step on the cracks, break Hitler's back."

Carrying On

In December 1940, the NAO published portions of a letter that Patricia Morris, who was born in England, had received from her mother. Her Mother wrote of the horror of the London bombings, and of life in the air raid shelters. Patricia's three sons all served during the war, but they all served in the Pacific theater.

Things had changed, and they would never be exactly the way they had been ever again. Yet, in many respects, life did go on as before. There were a great many clubs in the FCSD area, and they continued to meet and engage in their normal activities. In 1944 these activities included: The Rotary Club held its annual Community Father and Son Banquet on March 20; The Granger Grange held a dance on March 3. The cost was 50 cents for men and 20 cents for women; The Garden Club, under President Vesta Ward, celebrated Arbor Day on May 3. Members worked on their park project adding more polyanthus roses and evergreens. They also landscaped around the Honor Roll. The Short Tract Home Bureau had a meeting at which Mrs. Lawrence Gaus gave a lesson on sharpening scissors and knives. The Wide-Awake Library Club continued its activities. In October, it held its fall meeting at the home of Mrs. O.J. Smith. The library had been established in 1899 and has been in constant operation ever since. The Librarian at the time was Mrs. George Smith. (Mrs. George Smith also helped complete the Allegany County War Service Record for many of the returning veterans. Those records have been very useful to the author in writing this book.) The Thimble Club held a tureen dinner at the Wiscoy church parlor on October 11. There were numerous clubs in the area besides those mentioned. They included the Kard Club, the Grandmother's Club, and the Community Club.

In July 1941, Daniel E. Roach of Dan's Bar was granted a liquor license. A goodly number of the men in the area breathed a lot easier that night.

The churches in the area remained active with many pre-war type activities. St. Patrick's Church in Fillmore had its annual St. Patrick's Day party on March 17th. And, of course, its card parties continued. In October, an announcement was made of the dates of the next ten parties, beginning October 17, 1944. The Hume Methodist Church held a church supper on June 2, 1944. In October 1944 the Hume Baptist Sunday School held a Halloween party, as did the Wesleyan Methodist Church.

The schools continue to function almost normally, although at Fillmore Central, the number of males in the upper classes were cut at least in half, as the boys left to join the service. The class of 1944 had six males in a class of 21, and three of those were in the military before the end of the year. This contrasts with the class of 1941, which had 15 males out of a class of 34. Of those males, at least six served in the military. Hilda Schmidt, also Class of 1941, after college, became a Cadet trainee in the Army Nurses Corps; and Robert Boehmler, the Class of 1941 Advisor, served in the Army. Even with so many men in the service the sports programs (baseball, basketball, and soccer) continued. Intramural competition between the Greens and the Whites (the school colors) also continued. In 1943, Howie Ricketts (who would soon be in the Navy), was captain of the intra-class "Green" basketball team, came up with a new idea. He decided the "Green" team would shoot one handed, copying the way the women in the school shot. The Junior Class held its annual prom in 1943. Music was supplied by the "Checkerboard Boys." The "Know Your School Day" at Fillmore Central was held as usual on May 12, 1944.

In September 1944, Johnnie Bleistein enrolled at Fillmore Central. School. Officials in Mt Morris had felt that it might be better if John continued his education at some other facility.

The Houghton College A Cappella Choir presented a special Easter concert on April 9, 1944. The Choir had just returned from a tour of Michigan and Ohio. Members of the Hume Baptist Church and Sunday School spent Easter, 1944, caroling at the home of shut-ins. Margaret Hamilton, a senior at Houghton (who would become an instructor at the college after she graduated), conducted organ recitals regularly at the Fillmore Methodist Church. Houghton College, looking to the future, accepted a $75,000 donation to build a new dormitory.

The Fillmore Opera House may have been even busier than normal. An ad in the NAO announced movies for the first week of October, 1943. From September 30 to October 2 there was *Stormy Weather,* with Lena Horne and Bill Robinson, and *Jitterbugs,* with Laurel and Hardy; on October 3and 4, *Edge of Darkness,* with Errol Flynn and Ann Sheridan, and *The Man from Music Mountain,* with Roy Rogers. For years, there was at least one western each week at the Opera House. On October 5 and 6, there was a special showing of *Mission to Moscow*, with Walter Houston. The ad informed everyone that the following weekend, October 7-8-9, *Heaven Can Wait,* and *Stranger in Town* would be shown. That same month, the Farm Bureau reminded everyone that "Fall plowing time is here."

Even the Boy Scouts continued regular activities. In April 1944, they held a pancake supper at the RG&E cabin in Wiscoy to raise funds. In July, twelve members of the Troop participated in a week of camping at Thunder Rock Scout Camp in Allegany State Park. They included Bill Eagan, Harry Hatch (brother of Silver Star earner Paul Hatch), Merle Lapp, Gordon McElheney, Lowell Preston, Bev Howden, Bob Sandford, Paul Ricketts, Bill Young, Charles Miller, Russ Smith, and Robert MacEwan.

Polly Cockle Miller remembers the World War II July 4th celebrations. She said it was a highlight of the year for everyone. People got a chance to see each other and to have a good time. In July 1945, the NAO reported that "July 4th saw a good many people enjoying old friends and visiting with acquaintances as they did on no other day of the year. Some people even extended the celebration for two or three days longer." The *Observer* noted that year that "… uppermost in the hearts of every war-touched family is the sincere trust that those youngsters will be back for the big celebration after the war." When those words were written, the war in Europe was over. Six weeks later the B- 29 bomber *Enola Gay* visited Hiroshima, and the war in the Pacific came to an end shortly thereafter.

PART X - ASIA AND THE MIDDLE EAST

FCSD area veterans also served at locales in the Middle East and on the Asian mainland. They included Lionel R. Briggs, Ralph L. Common, Ralph H. Cox, Thurlow H. Gleason, Valgeane C. Luckey, Raymond H. Sandford, and Clark O. Smith in China; Vernon A. Closser, III, Thurlow H. Gleason, Meridith W. Kellogg, Raymond H. Sandford, Percy, J. Van Name, and Burdette F. Wilday in India; Roy M. Noble in Ceylon; and Roy M. Noble and William A. Sandford in Iran.

China

Ralph H. Cox arrived in Fillmore in 1969. He and his wife Rose established a NAPA Auto Parts store in a building that had been a store during World War II. Ralph enlisted in the Navy on May 12, 1945. He was 17-years old. He entered basic training at Sampson Naval Training Station on June 4, 1945. After completing basic, he was shipped to Camp Shoemaker in California. From there he was shipped to the Treasure Island Naval Base where he boarded the merchant ship *SS Fair Isle* for transport to Okinawa. There he was assigned to the destroyer tender *USS Dixie* (AD 14). Soon, however, the *Dixie* sailed to Shanghai. Ralph apparently arrived at Okinawa just as Hurricane Louise struck. Like other ships, the *Fair Isle* troopship rode out the typhoon at sea, and then anchored in Bruckner Bay. It was then that Ralph boarded the *Dixie*. When Ralph boarded the *Dixie*, she was serving as the Flag Ship for the US 7th Fleet while also servicing ships in Okinawa.

The *Dixie* sailed from Okinawa to Shanghai in late October, and for a while serviced ships there. It anchored back in Seattle on December 17, 1945. When the *Dixie* returned to the states, Ralph was assigned to the *USS Orvetta* (IX 157). His new home was a merchant ship converted for naval service into a barracks ship. She was on occupation duty in China. Ralph would live aboard the *Orvetta* and work at the Naval Operating Base in Shanghai for the balance of his time in China, except from January 25, 1946, to February 20, 1946 (per Naval Muster Rolls), when he received treatment aboard the hospital ship, *USS Repose* (AH 16).

Ralph was discharged from the Navy on August 7, 1946. As a result of his service in China, Ralph was eligible for both the China Service Medal and the Navy Occupation Service Medal, Asian Clasp, among others. The eligibility period for those two medals is September 15, 1945, through May 12, 1946.

Valgeane C. Lucky of Hume entered the service December 3, 1942. After basic training at Jefferson Barracks in Missouri, he attended mechanics school at the Stockton Ordnance Depot in in Stockton, CA.

By April 1943, he was stationed at Pinedale Camp in Fresno, CA. When he arrived, Pinedale was being used to train Army Air Corps signal technicians. Prior to providing signal technician training, however, Pinedale was involved in one of the most infamous acts in US history. It had been an assembly area for the internment of loyal Japanese Americans citizens. Parents of one of the authors best friends were ordered to Pinedale for further assignment to a permanent internment camp. Built on a former lumber yard, during the period May 7 through July 23, 1942, Pinedale Camp processed 4,823 Japanese American citizens for internment.

In July 1944 Pinedale became the home of the 840th Air Force Specialized Depot. Valgeane however, was soon assigned to the 1377th Signal Company Wing, which was activated on September 30, 1944. The Wing immediately began extensive training for an overseas assignment. The NOA reported Valgeane home on leave in October. His training continued when he returned to Pinedale. In February 1945, trainees were issued new clothing; new sights were installed on their carbines; and their helmets were repaired, and if necessary, received a new coat of paint. On February 18, Valgeane and others in his signal company moved to Camp Anza, an overseas staging area in Arlington, CA. They received a final round of vaccinations that including a plague shot. On February 26, they embarked for their new assignment aboard the *USS Admiral Benson* (AP 120) troop transport. On board, many members of Valgeane's unit performed duties as auxiliary gun crews. When they boarded the *Benson*, their commanding officer had warned them that, "We are not going to war, we are at war."

Valgeane and the rest of the 1377th were on their way to the Peishiyi Air Field near Chonging, China. Despite being an Air Corps unit going to an Air Corps base, they traveled by ship and truck all the way and did not arrive at Peishiyi until June 13, 1945. During their trip, the war in Europe ended.

Valgeane's unit first landed in Australia, and then at Calcutta, India, on March 27th. They remained at Calcutta until May 6, when they departed for China in a truck convoy. It took them more than six weeks to make the trip. They passed through Siliguri, Chabua, and Ledo in India, before entering China on May 22nd. Then they made their way through Kunming before finally arriving at Peishiyi. It is likely that Valgeane expertise as a mechanic was useful during the trip, because reports note numerous problems with the trucks. They were to remain at Peishiyi for the balance of the war and beyond. The airfield was a Command-and-Control base for the 68th Composite Wing (23rd Fighter Squadron and 308th Bomb Group). There were also C-47 Skytrain transport aircraft at the location. These planes carried troops and supplies to the area, and flew wounded soldiers to the rear. When the war ended, Peishiyi Field became Headquarters, China Air Service Command. Its mission was to supply equipment and logistical support to American and Chinese forces.

In November 1945 the NAO reported that Valgeane was still in China, and expected to be there until the start of 1946.

Raymond H. (Ray) Sandford of Fillmore was an airplane wing repairman at the Curtiss-Wright plant in Buffalo before entering the service in August 1942. The Army Air Corps made quick use of his skills, putting him to work as an airplane sheet metal worker in the China-Burma-India Theater of war. Ray was part of the famed "Over the Hump" operations.

The "Hump" was the eastern end of the Himalayan Mountains. When the Japanese seized and cut off the Burma Road, it was necessary to supply by air our allies, the Chinese Nationals under Chiang Kai-Shek, as well as US air bases in China. This delivery service operated daily from May 1942 until August 1945. Ray arrived in India December 1, 1942, and was an integral part of the operation until the end of the war. Over 680,000 gross tons of cargo were flown over the "Hump" into China. Once the route became operational, every drop of fuel, every weapon, every round of ammunition and 100 percent of all supplies used by Americans were flown in "over the hump." The route was extremely dangerous. There were high mountains, especially the "Hump" and deep gorges; violent turbulence shook the planes. Winds reached 125 to 200 miles per hour, and there was constant icing. Initially, experienced personnel were not available. Planes were often overloaded, and centers of gravity rules ignored. Ray's service as a sheet metal worker would have been important in keeping the airplanes airworthy while flying this route. The planes were serviced in the open, with tarps covering the engines. Many times, the work was done during violent storms. A total of 373 aircraft were lost and 1,313 crewmen killed during the operation. One of the pilots flying the "Hump" was the famous cowboy movie star, Gene Autry.

This "Hump" airlift operation was the second largest airlift in history, exceeded only by the Berlin airlift after the war.

Ray worked both ends of the route. He started out in India. In January of 1943, the NAO reported that Ray had written to say that he was stationed somewhere in India. He said their camp was fine. It was winter there, but the temperature reached 100 degrees in the daytime, and dropped to 50 degrees at night. The land was level and dusty, and their trees looked like thorn bushes. He commented that, "The natives riding their camels were quite a sight to watch."

By April 1943, Ray had been transferred to China. He wrote a letter home, part of which was published in the NAO. He said, "I am now located in the land of rice, tea, and honey. We are in a swell camp up in the mountains; it is such a beautiful place. I like it much better than India. We made the trip from India to China by plane; the weather was beautiful and it was a very nice trip, especially over the mountains. The peaks were all snow covered, and at about 18,000 feet, it was quite cold. The valleys below were green and crisscrossed with rivers and lakes. I snapped a picture from the plane, but I do not know how it will turn out. I may not get it developed for some time; such work is at a premium over here. A roll of film costs somewhere around 85 Chinese dollars. A Chinese dollar is worth about 5 cents in American money. Yesterday I took a walk over to the foot of the mountains and there I saw an old mill, run by water power, where they hulled rice. It looked to be about 500 years old, but it did work. I got some rice before it was hulled; am sending you some. I also saw what you might call a tile plant - at least that is what they made there; that is far as the resemblance went. They molded the tile and brick by hand and then burned them in a hole in the ground, and are they hard. They sure have good clay to work with." He then added, maybe to let his family have a better feeling for where he was, that "We spent Christmas day some place in India, playing volleyball and baseball with a bunch of Indians. We sure had a lot of fun, and was it hot!"

Ray was part of the India-China Wing which later became the India-China Division. At the personal direction of President Roosevelt, the India-China Wing was awarded a Presidential Unit Citation, the first such citation presented to a non-combat organization. Ray was present in India and China during the India-Burma Campaign, and the China Defensive Campaign, thus earning a battle star for each campaign. It is likely that initially he was assigned to the 1st Ferrying Group, which consisted of the 3rd, 6th and 13th Ferrying Squadrons. Ferring groups transporting only supplies. Transport squadrons transported troops.

It is likely that Ray was stationed at Chabua, Mohanban, or Sookerating field in India. According to his entry at the WW II Memorial, Ray's last assignment was with the 565th Army Air Force Base Unit.

India

Vernon A. Closser III entered the service on March 19, 1943. His first assignment was basic training at the Army Training Center in Miami, FL. He would spend most of the next seven months in training at various locations throughout the US. Such periods of training at different locations were not unusual in World War II. Vernon spent time at both Lowry Field, Colorado and Kirkland Field, Albuquerque, N.M. He was trained as a Bomb Sight Mechanic. In December 1943 and January 1944, he was stationed at bases in Utah where he primarily served with the 6th and 7th Bomb Maintenance Squadrons. The 6th Bomb Maintenance Squadron apparently was assigned to 677th Bomb Squadron prior to shipping overseas.

On February 26, 1944 Vernon was shipped to the Asiatic Pacific Theater of War, arriving in India on April 1, 1944. He was still officially assigned to the 6th Maintenance Squadron which was servicing the planes of the 677th Bomb Squadron. The 677th arrived in India in mid-April, 1944. It flew most of its missions from Dudhkundi Field (near Jhargram, India), although it was also assigned to Charra Field (near Purulia) for a short period. The Squadron, part of the 444th Bomb Group, flew B-29's, which indicates that Vernon primarily worked on the famous Norden Bomb Sight. (Despite its renown and the efforts to protect its technology, the Norden bomb sight may not have been the best bomb sight available during World War II and its secrets were known to the Axis powers.) The squadron's first mission on

June 5, 1944 was against railroad yards in Bangkok, Thailand. The next day Allied forces landed on the beaches of Normandy. On July 16, 1944, the 677th participated in the first US attack on Japan since the 1942 attack by the Jimmy Doolittle group. The squadron attacked the iron and steel works at Yawata. On August 20 it again attacked Yawata and this time was awarded a Distinguished Unit Citation.

Men of the 6th Bomb Maintenance Squadron would have also shared this award. However, Vernon's discharge document does not give him credit. Since he was apparently assigned to the squadron at that time, it appears he should have been credited. The 677th received two other Distinguished Unit Citations during its service. Vernon's discharge record only notes that he received one of the other two. Again, since he was with the maintenance unit at the time of the missions which earned these awards, it appears he should have been credited with all three, not just one. The other two were for a series of attacks on oil storage facilities at Oshima, an aircraft plant at Kobe and the incendiary bombing raid on Nagoya during the period May 10 to 14, 1945, and for an attack against light metal industries in Osaka on July 24, 1945.

The 677th continued to fly combat missions out of India until mid-1944 when it moved to West Field on Tinian. In a way, at West Field, Vernon reconnected with the greatest secret of the war. He had previously served at Kirkland Airfield in Albuquerque, N.M. It was from Kirkland that a C-54 took off with the plutonium core for the *Fat Man* atomic bomb aboard. It landed on Tinian on July 28, 1945. And now Vernon was on Tinian. Also there, was the 509th Composite Group which on August 9, 1945 would drop the *Fat Man* bomb on the Japanese city of Nagasaki, destroying the city.

The 677th returned to the United States in September, 1945. Vernon, returned October 27, 1945, arriving in the states on November 10, 1945. The ground crew traveled by ship, while the air crews flew their planes home. Vernon was discharged November 24, 1945.

Thurlow H. Gleason of Hume entered the service on June 17, 1938. When he was officially discharged on October 2, 1945, he immediately re-enlisted and would not finally leave the service until July 31, 1959. Thurlow, also known as Thurlo, was trained as a S-1 bombsight and C-1 automatic pilot repairman. These systems were primarily used on B-24s during the war. Joining the service represented a significant change in career plans. Following high school, Thurio had attended the New York School of Agriculture. Post-war Thurlo served with the Strategic Air Command, worked with the B-47, and received training on both A-12D and F-1 auto-pilot systems. The A-12D system was used on the B-47.

Thurlo spent most of World War II in domestic assignments. Prior to 1945, only one item on Thurlo appeared in the NAO. That was in December of 1942 when an item mentioned that Thurlo was home on leave visiting his mother. In January 1945 another item appeared, reporting that he had arrived safely "somewhere in India." By that time Thurlo had risen to the rank of Master Sergeant.

The only major air command operating in India in 1944 was the 10th Air Force. While there were many bomb groups assigned to the 10th, there was only one B-24 bomb group which may have been using the S-1 bombsight on which Thurio had been trained. It is unlikely he was assigned to that group as in May 1945, the NAO reported that he had been transferred to China. The one bomb group transferred to China at that time from the 10th Air Force was the 341st Bomb Group and it flew B-25s. The 341st was assigned to the 14th Air Force in 1944. It is likely that Thurlo was assigned to the 341st as a replacement in January 1945 and served with that group in China. He most likely served with the 11th Bomb Squadron, but maybe the 490th. Thurlo's personnel records at the Military Personnel Records Center in St. Louis were destroyed by a fire, as were the records of almost all World War II Army and Army Air Corps personnel. As a result, it is difficult to positively identify his actual service assignments.

B-25 groups were used primarily for interdiction, close air support and battlefield isolation missions in India, Burma, and China. The B-25 gained fame as the plane used by the Doolittle Raiders on the surprise raid of Japan in 1942.

The 11th Bomb Squadron after successfully serving in the Pacific in the early part of the war was dismantled, with planes and equipment assigned to one command and the men rotated back to the states for reassignment. On September 15, 1942, a reorganized 11th was assigned to the 341st. The 341st operated as two separate groups. The headquarters, 22nd and 491st squadrons operated as one group flying missions against Japanese forces in Burma. The other two squadrons the 490th and 11th formed the second "group". The 11th received its operational orders from the China Air Task Force which later became the 14th Air Force. Operating out of several different airfields, both the 11th and 490th squadrons attacked enemy troop concentrations, storage areas, sea sweeps and inland shipping in China. The 11th remained in China until the end of the war. It then flew to India, left its aircraft in Karachi, and sailed home. Thurlo was discharged October 2, 1945 … and then immediately reenlisted. The 11th was inactivated November 2, 1945.

The 11th Bomb Squadron earned the following battle stars for 1945 campaigns: Western Pacific, India - Burma, China Offensive, China Defensive, and Air Offensive, Japan. It also earned a Distinguished Unit Citation for an outstanding Air Force Unit.

Meredith W. Kellogg of Houghton entered the service July 16, 1942. On December 7, 1941, he was in his Houghton College dorm room (the attic of the Alex Steese House) listening to the radio when he learned that the Japanese had bombed Pearl Harbor. Meredith was initially sent to Camp Gruber, OK, where he became part of the 88th Infantry Division. He remained at Camp Gruber until the spring of 1943, rising rapidly from PFC to Tech 4. Meredith then agreed to a reduction in rank back to private in order to attend the Army Specialized Training Program (ASTP) at St. Norbert College in West DePere, WI. When the ASTP was cancelled in 1944, Meredith was assigned to communications training at Camp Crowder, MO. After nine months of training, he was advised that he would be assigned to a detachment at the SHEAF Headquarters of General Eisenhower. Just before departing, however, he was ordered to replace a sick soldier who had been ordered to India. In short order, he was on a troop train to Long Beach, CA, and then aboard a ship heading for India via Melbourne, Australia. Forty-two days later, after crossing the equator twice, he and 3,500 other G.I.s arrived in India.

Meredith was assigned (likely) to Headquarters, 236th Signal Service Battalion in Dikom. The 236th had arrived in Dikom September 1, 1943. The battalion provided communications services for a cluster of C-46 and C-47 bases that were flying supplies for Chaing Kai Shek's troops "over the hump" (eastern end of the Himalayan Mountains) to Kunming, China. Meredith remained in Dikom for six months following VJ Day when he was finally shipped home aboard the *USS General C.C. Ballou* (AP 157) transport ship. He was likely aboard the *Ballou* when it arrived in San Francisco on March 8, 1946. He was discharged March 16, 1946 at Camp Atterbury, IN.

Percy S. Van Name of Fillmore entered the service on June 5. 1944. Percy was a Trackman with the Pennsylvania Railroad and a member of Fillmore's baseball team before entering the service. Based on an article in the NAO, his first months in the military were quite different from those experienced by most recruits. He was sent to Camp Pine, (now Fort Drum) NY, for basic training. While there, he also performed guard duty at the German/Italian prisoner of war camp on Camp Pine. In addition, his wife Madeline and daughter Donna stayed in a cabin at Black River, about a mile from his barracks. The NAO reported that Percy got to see them a little every day.

From Pine Camp, Percy was ordered to Fort Dix, NJ, another basic training camp at that time. However, it is possible that Percy continued to perform Military Police duties at Dix. The NAO reported in November 1944 that Percy had been transferred to Fort Riley in Kansas. In February, the NAO reported that he had been ordered to a camp in Maryland. On June 1, 1945, Percy and over 3,000 other men, sailed from San Pedro, CA aboard the *General H. B. Freeman*, (AP 143) for Calcutta, India. Percy was now part of the key India - Burma - China supply operation. The India operations were responsible for supplying American forces in China and Burma, and for supplying the Chinese Nationals forces. The *General Freeman* arrived in Calcutta on August 9, 1945, the same day the second atomic bomb was dropped on Nagasaki.

In India, Percy was a Quay foreman with a Port Battalion, part of the Army Transportation Corps. A Quay was a stretch of paved bank or a solid artificial landing place beside navigable water that was used for loading and unloading ships. As foreman, Percy was involved in the construction, maintenance, and repair of the quays, as well as overseeing the loading and unloading of cargo ships. Percy remained at Calcutta until April 1, 1946, when he sailed home aboard the *USS General Harvey*. He arrived in the US on May 15, 1946, and was discharged at Fort Dix, NJ on May 31, 1946.

Burdette F. Wilday of Hume entered the service October 3, 1942 at Buffalo. He had graduated from FCS in 1938. The NAO reported that he was initially assigned to the Atlantic City Army Air Corps basic training site. The Air Corps had only started training at Atlantic City June 29, 1942. By June 1943, the training had been moved to Greensboro, NC. Trainees at Atlantic City lived in luxury hotels; but, especially during Burdette's time there, winter temperatures were not that pleasant. At other times, winds caused dust storms. Nevertheless, it is likely that Burdette went through the standard basic training of the time. That would have included lectures, viewing films, taking tests, and receiving a general orientation. Trainees would have also been welcomed by their commander. A standing order at Atlantic City provided, "All recruits are entitled to a well-presented inspirational talk by their squadron commanding officer. This should be given on the first or second day after arrival, in the form of a welcome, and should include an explanation of the training about to be received." Other activities included issuance of uniforms, shots, blood typing, drilling and activities that turned them into soldiers. One of the more important activities was classification whose results separated the men into three groups: those going directly to their jobs, those identified for technical training, and all others. Burdette was assigned to the further training group.

His initial technical training took place in Richmond, VA. By April he was being trained as a radio mechanic in Chicago. He graduated from that training in June 1943. The NAO reported that he was then assigned to a Fighter Control Squadron at Bradley Field in Winter Locks, CT. Fighter Control Squadron 94 was at Bradley and it is likely that this was the squadron to which he was assigned. The NAO has him still at Bradley in February1944, but in August reported that his family had been notified that he was in India.

Ceylon

"I want to tell you, from the Russian point of view, what the President and the United States have done to win the war. The most important thing in this war are machines. The United States has proven it can turn out 10,000 airplanes a month. Russia can turn out, at most, 3,000 airplanes a month. The United States is a country of machines. Without the use of those machine, through Lend-Lease, we would lose this war." USSR Premier Marshal Joseph Stalin - Teheran, Iran, Big Three Conference November, 1943

Roy M. Noble of Granger entered the Army in July 1942. He was sent to Fort Bragg, NC for three months of basic training. From Bragg, Roy was ordered to Fort Jackson, SC as part of the Quartermaster Corps. Roy was originally sent to Ceylon but quickly was sent on to Iran. On June 26, 1943, he arrived in Iran with the 3467th Medium Ordnance Company. He was now part of the Persian Gulf Command. The company was stationed at Andimeskh. His job was to help reassemble trucks built in the US, and ship those trucks to the USSR.

Forty-five percent of American trucks sent to the USSR during World War II, reached there through the Persian corridor. The trucks were built in the US, and then partially disassembled. They were shipped to Iran, where they were reassembled. Fully 88 percent of the trucks were reassembled in American operated plants at Andimeshk and Khorramshahr during the period March 1942 through April 1945. Under the lend-lease program, almost 410,000 trucks were sent to the Soviet Union. These trucks represented two years and seven months of the pre-war truck production capacity of the entire USSR. However, the total represented only seven and one-half months of production of trucks in the United States during 1943. The men at Andimeshk and Khorramshahr also reassembled trucks sent to Iran for the British Army, the United Kingdom Commercial Corporation, the US Army, and the Iranian government.

According to his profile at the WW II Memorial, Roy was a tool clerk with the Ordnance Company. He returned to the states in April 1945, arriving at Fillmore on April 23 for a 30-day furlough, In May he returned to Fort Dix, NJ, where he was re-assigned. He was ordered to a camp in Texas for six months prior to his discharge in November, 1945. Roy's brother Lester was killed in action in France on December 16, 1944.

Iran

William A. (Bill) Sandford of Hume entered the service in early 1945. He received training in the Quartermaster's Corps at Camp Lee, Virginia. While at Camp Lee, Bill was one of 250 men selected to march in a ceremony honoring General Edmund B. Gregory, the 31st Quartermaster General of the US Army. The war ended while Bill was at Camp Lee. Bill, however, would not be discharged until July 1946.

He was instead sent to Fort Belvoir, Virginia. Fort Belvoir was a Combat Engineer Training Center. Bill received additional training relating to the engineers while there. Following a 15-day leave, Bill was ordered to Fort Jackson, SC to serve as a supply clerk with the Engineer Corps. Fort Jackson actually served as a replacement depot.

In October 1945, Bill was shipped to Iran. According to the NAO, he called his family and told them he was taking a sea voyage to Persia. What Bill was doing was heading to Iran to help shut down the Iranian portion of the "Persian Corridor." The "Corridor" was one of five routes which had been opened to deliver supplies to Russia. From 1941 through 1945 more than 3,900,000 long tons of supplies had been shipped to Russia through Persian ports. A war time agreement had allowed the US, Russia, and Britain into the country for the purpose of shipping supplies to Russia. This was pre-major oil production in Iran, and the country had benefited greatly as a result of the construction of roads and docks. The treaty expired in January of 1946 and the Allies had to depart the country by no later than six months following the expiration of the treaty. The Americans and Britain left, but the Russians stayed.

Bill had sailed to Iran aboard the *General J.H. McRae*, a transport ship nicknamed "The Mac." The log of "The Mac" states that the ship had sailed from Staten Island on October 27, 1945 with 2,200 "kaki clad brethren" aboard. It arrived at its destination on Iran's Shaat-el-Arab River on November 19, 1945. Bill sailed home aboard the *USS Rensselaer* (A Victory troop ship that was faster and had greater range than the earlier and more famous Liberty ships), arriving in the US on July 3, 1946. While waiting to be discharged at Ft. Dix, NJ, Bill was assigned to (where else) the Post Office. Bill was one of several men from the FCSD area who spent some time working in an Army Post Office after completing various assignments. Others included Bernard Mills and Marlie Hodnett.

PART XI - IT ENDS

Germany - Peace

"The mission of this Allied Force was fulfilled at 2:41 local time, May 7, 1945."
Message sent by British Sergeant Susan Hibbert announcing the signing by German General Gustav Johl of the terms of unconditional surrender, and the official end of World War II in Europe. Up to that point only a few people in General Eisenhower's headquarters in Reims, France knew of the official surrender. Johl, in a brief statement, said he hoped the victors would treat the German people and Armed Forces with generosity. No one even answered.

"Just a few minutes ago, Germany surrendered all its land, sea and air forces. It has been thoroughly whupped. May 7, 1945, Reims, France. "Supreme Allied Commander Dwight D. Eisenhower, in a radio broadcast, a few minutes after the formal surrender." Whupped was right.

It was over in Europe. Hitler, a coward to the end, committed suicide in his bunker in Berlin. No one, especially another "Hitler," would ever be able to claim, as Hitler had after World War I, that Germany had lost due to weak politicians; that the German Army and people had been stabbed in the back; that the military had been sold out by its leaders. (The new German Chancellor after World War I, Friedrich Eber, on December 10, 1918 at a parade in Berlin welcoming soldiers home said, "your sacrifice and deeds are without equal! No enemy has conquered you!") (Marshal Ferdinand Foch, leader of the allied armies, presumably said after signing the Versailles Peace treaty, "This is not Peace, it is an armistice for 20 years.")

This time there was no doubt. Germany and the German Army (and soon the Empire of Japan) had been beaten on the field of battle, or better put had been destroyed. Ike said it all, "It has been thoroughly whupped." Despite the seemingly unending conflicts which have occurred since the end of World War II, there has been no World War III. While determining the total people who died as a result of "war" is not easy, available data indicates that the total number of people killed in all post WW II conflicts are not close to the death toll of the Second World War. This is remarkable when one considers that the total population on the planet is some three to four times greater than the planets population during World War II.

It seems to me that this point should be considered by historians when debating the controversial decision to demand unconditional surrender from the Germans and Japanese at the end of World War II.

Jack Edward Allen of Hume enlisted in the Navy in 1944 at the age of seventeen. After basic and gunners mate schools at Sampson Naval Training Station, he was assigned to the destroyer escort *USS Muir*. In mid-November the *Muir* served as a school ship. It then sailed for Europe where it performed convoy escort duty. During this period the *Muir* earned a battle star. The *Muir* then became part of Task Force 22.13, a "Killer Group" whose primary duty was to hunt and destroy enemy submarines in the Atlantic. Toward the end of the war, the *Muir* was transferred to Task Group 63, whose job was to halt last-ditch efforts by German subs trying to interfere with shipping in the North Atlantic. Jack's duties aboard ship involved taking care of the guns and depth charges.

The *Muir* was unable to stop and celebrate the end of the war in Europe. It had to help round up German submarines still roaming around the North Atlantic and to make sure they did not do something foolish. In fact, the *Muir* accepted the surrender of *U Boat 858* on May 8, the very day President Truman announced Victory in Europe. It turned this boat over to a couple of other destroyers and continued to patrol. On May 17, over a week following the end of the war in Europe, the *Muir,* and the *USS Sutton*, accepted the surrender of *U Boat 234* and escorted it to Portsmouth, NH.

U 234 was no ordinary U boat, and it was not on an ordinary mission. It was a type XB, the largest class of U boat ever built. The 234 has often been called Hitler's last U boat. In addition to high-ranking personnel, aboard was 240 tons of cargo. The cargo included 560 kilograms of uranium oxide. The presence of this uranium oxide was kept secret until the end of the Cold War, some 50 years later. It was estimated that the oxide would yield 7.7 pounds of Uranium 235, about 20 percent of the amount needed for an atomic bomb. Other cargo included technical drawings, one crated Me 262 jet aircraft, and a Henschel HS 293 glide bomb. The HS 293 was a radio-controlled anti-ship guided missile, with a rocket engine underneath the 500- pound bomb. (Henschel was the name of a German owner of many factories that manufactured aircraft parts, including parts for the V 1 and V 2 rocket bombs.)

The personnel aboard were no less impressive. They included General Ulrich Kessler of the Luftwaffe, who was to take over duties as Luftwaffe liaison in Tokyo; Kai Nieschling, a Naval Fleet Judge Advocate, who was to rid the German diplomatic corps of the remnants of the famous Richard Sorge spy ring; Dr. Heinz Schlicke, a specialist in radar, infra-red, and countermeasures, and Director of the German Naval Test Fields in Kiel; and, August Bringewalde, who was in charge of Me 262 productions at Messerschmitt. The United States later recruited Schlicke as part of "Operation Paper Clip" an effort to make sure German scientists did not end up working for Soviet Russia or a divided Germany.

Two Japanese Naval officers were also aboard. They were Lt. Commander Hideo Tomonaga, a Naval architect and submarine designer, and Lt. Commander Sheji Benzo, an aircraft specialist and formal Naval Attache. The two Japanese officers requested permission to commit Hara Kari. Permission was granted and the two men took luminal, rather than using the traditional method. They were buried at sea.

News of the capture of this submarine brought multitudes of reporters to Portsmouth. However, when the cargo manifest was released, it listed the cargo as aircraft drawings, arms, medical supplies, instruments, lead, mercury, caffeine, steel, brass, and optical glass.

There was still a war on and the *Muir* now underwent preparations for operations in the Pacific. While doing so, some preliminary pre-flight training for pilots was conducted aboard the destroyer. Carrier pilots were still needed, and anyone could apply. Those who made it through the pre-flight training were sent to the carriers for further training, including take offs and landings. After a brief period, the *Muir* was on its way to the Pacific. It had just passed through the Panama Canal when the war in the Pacific ended. Jack's war was over, but he would stay in the Navy until October 1947. Jack said he spent almost his entire three years in the service at sea.

Japan - Peace

"The thoughts and hopes of all America--- indeed of all the civilized world --- are centered tonight on that battleship Missouri. There on that small piece of American soil anchored in Tokyo harbor, the Japanese have just officially laid down their arms. They have signed terms of unconditional surrender."　　　　　President Harry S. Truman

"It looks like the war is over, but if any enemy planes appear shoot them down in friendly fashion." Message sent by Admiral Bull Halsey to his pilots upon receiving word that the war was over. That same day, five enemy planes were shot down by US Aircraft Carrier pilots. NY Times, August 15, 1945. Admiral Nimitz signed the instrument of surrender aboard the USS Missouri on September 2, 1945 on behalf of the United States.

Author aboard USS Missouri
at spot where Japanese signed
terms of unconditional surrender.
Authors Photo.

Tokyo Harbor was host to a lot of people that day, September 2, 1945 (local time), including at least the following men from the FCSD area - Arnold H. Eldridge, Richard Fuller, Walter D. Makowski, Lawrence W. "Hank" Miller, Robert F. Miller, Francis David Morris, and Leroy Thayer. It is likely that all of these men would have participated in any invasion of Japan.

Picture – Bob Colombo aboard the USS Missouri at the location where the unconditional surrender documents were signed. Personal photo.

Lawrence W. (Hank) Miller of Fillmore wrote his parents from Tokyo Harbor after visiting Tokyo and Yokohama. He said, in part, "I couldn't half explain how bad the place really is, but it has been blown to bits. It is nine miles between the two cities and everything in that entire nine miles is a flat mess. The downtown section of Tokyo seems fair, but shows plenty of shaking. Today was the first day the Navy has been allowed in Tokyo. Twelve of us went today. We took along a lunch, and you should have seen those people look at us when we were eating. I believe they are about starved. They all looked, waved, and saluted us most everywhere we went. We took along some extra cigarettes and sold them for 30 yen a pack, which is equal to $2 in our money. They want everything we have. All in all, it is a dirty hole, no sanitation of any kind or anything else. I can really see where the US has a mess on their hands now." Hank also mentioned that Leroy Thayer, who graduated from FCS the year after Hank, was also in Tokyo Bay.

It took Hank a little less than two years to get to Tokyo. He entered the service on September 18, 1943. His ship the *USS Matar* entered Tokyo Harbor September 7, 1945. The *Matar* was a Crater Class cargo ship, and Hank went aboard on May 17, 1943, the day the ship was commissioned in Jacksonville, FL.

After a shakedown cruise, and loading cargo in Davisville, RI, and Bayonne, NY, the *Matar* sailed for the Pacific on June 15, 1944. By July 25, it was at Pearl Harbor. It next sailed, via Marshall and Admiralty Islands for Palau as part of Task Force 31. During part of this time, it served as the flagship for Task Group 31.4. *Matar* arrived at the Kossol Passage off the Palau Islands on September 20 and on October 17 at Anguar Island, also part of Palau. It then stopped at Peleliu. At all these stops, it discharged cargo. At Peleliu, it picked up Marines. Some of these were debarked at the Russell Islands on November 7. Others were debarked at Guadalcanal on November 9. It now headed for San Francisco via Hawaii, arriving December 11, 1944. In San Francisco, the *Matar* was modified for duty as a stores ship, and loaded with medical supplies and ships stores. During this break, the NAO reported that Hank managed to spend a week at home.

By January 8, 1945, the *Matar* was back at sea on its way to Eniwetok. It was now assigned to Service Squadron 10. It first steamed to Saipan; and during February, March, and April, it dispensed medical and general stores from there. On May 15, it arrived at the Keramo Retto in the Ryukyu Islands and discharged cargo. By the 29th it had anchored off Okinawa, where it issued day provisions and medical stores, but also provided smoke cover during Japanese air attacks. On June 27 it sailed for Pearl Harbor via Ulithi to replenish.

The *Matar* departed for Eniwetok August 7, arriving August 14. It was then ordered to Tokyo Harbor, where it performed occupation duties until November 5, when it sailed for home, arriving back in San Francisco on December 1, 1945.

Hank served as a Boatswain's Mate (BM). His duties included training and supervising personnel in all activities relating to marlinspike, deck, and boat seamanship. The BM also oversaw the maintenance of the ship's external structure and deck equipment. At times, the BM could act as petty officer in charge of small craft and perform duties as master-at-arms, serve in or take care of gun crews and damage control parties.

Robert Franklin (Bob) Miller of Houghton moved to the area in 1963 when he accepted a position at Houghton College. He also served as an ordained minister for several churches in the area for many years. Bob was originally from the neighboring town of Rushford.

Bob entered the Navy on October 25, 1943 in Toledo, Ohio. He took basic training at the Greats Lakes Naval Training Station in Illinois. After basic, Bob spent some time at the University of Minnesota. He was then assigned to the brand-new light cruiser, *USS Springfield* (CL-66), which he boarded on September 9, 1944. The *Springfield* was designed to provide ant-aircraft protection for the fast carriers. She was also capable of providing shore bombardment support.

Bob was an electrician's mate. Petty officers with this specialty were responsible for operation and repair of the ship's electrical power plant and electrical equipment. They also maintained and repaired power and lighting circuits, distribution switchboards, generators, motors, and other electrical equipment. Bob specifically worked on the ship's electric generators.

After shakedown cruises, the *Springfield* headed for Norfolk, VA. On January 23, it joined Task Group 21.5 escorting the *USS Quincy*, with President Franklin D. Roosevelt aboard, to the Yalta Conference. Reaching the Azores on January 28, the *Springfield* left the convoy, and headed for the Panama Canal and the war in the Pacific. After stops at Pearl Harbor, Eniwetok, and Ulithi Atoll, it joined Task Force 58 on March 15, 1945. The *Springfield* was about to join the shooting war. On March 18 and 19, it took part in raids on two Japanese home islands: Kyushu and Honshu. It then participated in the bombardments leading up to the invasion of Okinawa, directly bombarding Minami Daito Shima on March 27 and 28. While its primary job remained the protection of the carriers, it supported assault forces landing on Okinawa on April 1. She was credited with shooting down at least three Kamikazes. After getting one on April 17, through good seamanship, she avoiding being hit by another suicide plane. On May 10 and 11, she turned her guns once again on Minami Daito Shima. On May 13 and 14, she sailed with the Task Force to strike air bases on Kyushu.

At the end of May, *Springfield* anchored in San Pedro Bay at Leyte for maintenance and upkeep. She remained for a month. In July, she took up fleet protection duties, as Task Force 38 (now the 5th Fleet because Admiral Halsey had relieved Admiral Spruance) pounded Japan. The task force continued to pound targets until August 13. On August 15, combat ended.

On August 30, *Springfield* covered the entrance of the 3rd Fleet Task Force 31 into Tokyo Bay. She entered the Bay herself on September 3. The *Springfield* was there on September 2, when the Japanese signed the documents of unconditional surrender. She remained in the far east until January 1946, carrying out occupation duties. *Springfield* arrived back at San Pedro, CA on January 25, eventually docking at the Navy Yard at Mare Island.

The B - 29

The name in Japanese is *B Niju Ku*. Laura Hillenbrand tells us that in her magnificent book, *Unbroken*, the story of the incredible World War II survival of the great mile runner Louis Zamperini, first from the sea and then from the horrors of Japanese prisoner of war camps. Hillenbrand ably describes the impact of the *B Niju Ku*. Put simply, everyone who saw it in the skies over Japan, the Japanese as well as the POW's, knew the US had won the war and the Japanese had lost. It was just a matter of time. One of those prisoners who likely saw the B-29 in the skies above Japan was Charles H. Conklin. He was not from the FCSD area, but was from the neighboring school district of Friendship. Conklin was captured in April 1942 in the Philippines. He survived the Bataan Death March and was a POW until September 2, 1945, first in the Philippines and later at a camp near Osaka, Japan.

The major destruction caused by the B-29 occurred after General Curtis LeMay was made Commander of the XXI US Air Force. LeMay switched tactics form daylight high altitude precision bombing to night time incendiary bombing. The first such attack, on Tokyo March 10, 1945, was deemed highly successful. The fire caused by the incendiaries destroyed some 16 percent of Tokyo. The latest estimate is that 105,000 people (including hordes of children, women and animals perished. Most of the city, built with wood, became a giant fireball. A million people were left homeless. One justification for this attack on helpless civilians was that Japan had moved some industry into individual homes to escape complete destruction of its industries. Another was the desire to avoid an invasion of Japan which many estimated could cost millions in American lives. LeMay himself admitted that if the US loss the war, he and others would clearly be tried as war criminals. More humans were killed during this raid than during any similar time period in the history of the world. Sixty-six Japanese cities were similarly attacked prior to the end of the war. Despite these attacks however, and the glowing reports that followed, the war waged on for six more months. The March 10th attack was conducted by 325 bombers and thousands of incendiaries were dropped. In August two airplanes each dropped one bomb. Japan surrendered six days after the dropping of the second bomb.

Robert Aldrich of the FCSD area participated in the bombing campaign against Japan.

Robert G. Aldrich of Hume entered the service on January 4, 1943. On November 24, 1944, he left Saipan aboard a B-29 (A-47), on what may have been his first mission, bound for Tokyo. It was the first bombing raid on Tokyo since Doolittle's Raiders in 1942. Bob's raid would not be as easy as the Doolittle Raiders that caught the Japanese totally by surprise. B-29 mission reports at the National Archives do not identify the crew members aboard each plane. In most cases, but not all, they do identify the aircraft commander, and the number of the plane he was flying. The 497th Bomb Group Association, on its web site, lists the crew for each aircraft commander. Robert G. Aldrich is listed as a member of the Lampley crew, 871st Bomb Squadron. Lampley was flying A-47 (named *"Sweat" er Out*) with a very attractive woman in a very tight sweater painted on the plane on the November 24 Tokyo mission. Ironically, the web site lists the *Dixie Darlin* (B-29, A-45) as Lampley's plane. Crews did not fly the same plane on every mission. In fact, Lampley flew A-44, *Ponderous Peg*, on at least 16 missions., the most for any single aircraft. (The A-45 was apparently lost on the December 18, 1944 mission to Nogoya. Bob was aboard the *Ponderous Peg* on that mission.) In a June, 1945 edition of the NAO, a letter from Bob was quoted. In it, he said he had completed 25 missions, and had five to go. The letter was probably written in early May, and mission reports do show more missions for the Lampley crew in late May and three in June. The author identified 24 missions flown by the Lampley crew. As indicated above, some mission reports failed to identify the aircraft commander, so that could account for the missing missions. Bob

Lampley Crew, Bob Aldrich bottom row, 2nd from right.
497th Bomb Group B-29 Memorial Photo

also may have flown some missions with other crews. The NAO reported in July that Bob had completed 30 missions.

Due to the altitude at which the B-29 could fly and bomb (over 31,000 feet), fighters did not accompany the bombers on many raids, including the November 24 raid on Tokyo. However, many of the missions were incendiary raids flown at lower altitudes. Based on mission reports, it appears fighters would have been useful on the November 24 mission. Bob's group, the 497th Bomb Group (Very Heavy), counted 59 fighter attacks. The mission report credit's the A-47s top turret gunner with damaging or destroying a Tojo (a Wakajima KI-44 single engine fighter used mostly in defense of the Japanese home land) that day. It is likely that Bob was the gunner. During the mission, flak ranged from moderate to heavy. The bombing results were only poor to fair, according to strike photos. Bombing would improve. On another mission to Tokyo in which the Lampley crew participated, the strike photos showed 15.45 percent of Tokyo destroyed. Picture – Langley crew - *Bob Aldrich – second from right, first row – National Archives photo.*

Bob served as the Central Fire Control gunner. The B-29 guns were operated off a remote-control turret system; a new innovation. In that system, a single gunner could operate two or more turret guns. The guns were aimed electronically from five sighting stations. Bob was situated in the upper sighting station in the central fuselage. He managed the distribution of turrets among the other gunners during combat. Bob also was responsible for the upper rear and forward gun turrets.

Mission reports at the Archives show that the Lampley crew flew the following combat missions. (The mission numbers are 497th Bomb Group missions. The 497th flew 85 combat missions during the war, plus 20 missions dropping supplies to ex-prisoners of war. Bob was already home when the POW missions were flown. An interesting side note is that Laura Hillenbrand in her book "Unbroken" about Louis Zamperini said that so many supplies were dropped, that ex-POWs took to putting up signs telling the planes they didn't need more.) 11/24/1944, Mission 7 - Tokyo, Musashino aircraft plant; 12/8/44, Mission 11 - Iwo Jima; 12/18/44, Mission 13 - Nagoya, Mitsubisha plant; 1/23/1945, Mission 21, Nogoya, Mitsubishi aircraft plant, aborted, engine #4 malfunctioned; 1/27/1945, Mission 22 - Tokyo, bombed secondary target, harbor facilities; 2/4/45, Mission 23 - Kobe, urban area, aborted; 2/15/45, Mission 25 - Samoan Islands, any industrial city; 2/9/45, Mission 29, Tokyo - urban area; 3/12/45, Mission 30 - Nagoya, urban area; 3/13/45, Mission 31 - Osaka, urban area; 3/14/45, Mission 32 - Nagoya, urban area; 3/17/45, Mission 33 - Kobe urban area (bombed shipyards and steel mills); 3/21/45 Mission 34 - Nogoya, Mitsubishi Aircraft plant; 3/31/45, Mission 36 - Kyushu, Tachiarai machine works; 4/2/45, Mission 37 - Tokyo, Musashino Aircraft engine factory; 4/12/45, Mission 40, Tokyo, Musashino aircraft engine plant; 4/21/45, Mission 45 - Kyushu, USA Airfield; 4/27/45, Mission 49 - Miyazaki Air Field; 5/1/45, Mission 52 - Hiro Naval aircraft factory; 5/14/45, Mission 55 - Nogoya, urban area; 5/19/45, Mission 57 - Hamamatsu, city center; 6/1/45, Mission 61 - Osaka , urban area; 6/5/45, Kobe, urban area; 6/15/45, Mission 65 - Osaka, urban area.

Bob's aircraft was the target of flak on every mission but one, and on most missions, it was attacked by fighters. The largest number of fighters counted on a mission was 70, on Mission 55 (the Group's 55th mission, not Bob's.) Nevertheless, fighters tended to be leery of the B-29. The most reported attacks were 554 on Mission 22. While fighters appeared on virtually every mission, on several occasions they did not attack. Bob's plane suffered battle damage several times. On Mission 62, flak caused structural damage to the wing tip, and two engines were damaged. On Mission 29, flak hit the #2 engine cowling, causing two big holes; and on Mission 52 flak damaged the aircraft stabilizer. The NAO reported that Bob's plane was hit by anti-aircraft fire more than 60 times.

The crew also had to deal constantly with malfunctioning aircraft systems on most missions. On Mission 11, the 1st and 4th engine cylinder head's temperatures were out, the fuel pressure in engine #1 was low and engine #3 consumed too much oil. On Mission 30, the trailing antenna would not extend (this occurred on other missions), and there was an electrical malfunction in a compass. Also, the missions were long. They were not a trip to the grocery store. For mission 61 to Osaka, the Lampley crew took off at 6:58 PM on May 31, and did not land until 6:32 AM the next morning, June 1st. They had spent over 11 hours in the air. Many missions were even longer.

After every mission, crews were debriefed and asked for comments and suggestions. The one topic that always came up was the food. Most of the comments were not good. The crews also did not like taking off after dark, and always felt the missions should be flown at higher altitudes.

Flying a combat bombing mission was not a job for amateurs. The care and detail that went into each mission was amazing, but still things went wrong. It would take pages to cover it all. A few examples may suffice. Everything was timed: wake-up, breakfast, briefings, arrival at planes, arrival at stations aboard planes, starting engines, order of take-off, take off, points along the way, and arrival at the target. Every plane had to report at least 20 different items just for the bombing run, including wind direction and velocity, drift, heading, length of bombing run, and how long it was in minutes to the time of the bomb drop. For aerial combat, reporting the number of fighters and the number of attacks made was just a start. The tactics used were most important. From what angles and altitudes did the Japanese attack? At what speeds? Alone or in combinations? At what distance did they start firing? An awful lot to think about when somebody is shooting 50 caliber bullets at you.

Bob was stationed at Isley Field on Saipan for some time. It was one of those airfields taken by men like John Ballard and Bob Speicher. One of Bob's letters told of life on the field for him and others. Most evenings they would watch a movie at an open-air theater, even if they had already seen it. If it rained, they just huddled closer together. Things usually ran smoothly, except when there were Japanese air raids, which occurred quite frequently. This often required some quick digging in the coral rock, often with bare hands. Goats were all over the place when he first arrived, even at the movies. But later, these animals seem to resent the presence of the humans and even stopped attending the movies. Like everyone else, Bob mentioned the mail and how important it was to the men.

Among other awards. Bob earned the Distinguished Flying Cross. This medal, authorized in 1926 by Congress, was awarded to anyone who "distinguished himself by heroism or extraordinary achievement in aerial flight." The first recipient of the award was Charles A. Lindbergh.

The Enola Gay

"The bomb will never go off, and I speak as an expert on explosives."
Admiral William D. Leahy - Advising President Truman on the atomic bomb project in 1945

"A bright light filled the plane. The first shock wave hit us. We were eleven and a half miles slant range from the atomic explosion, but the whole plane crackled and crinkled from the blast. We turned back to look at Hiroshima. The city was hidden by that awful cloud…… mushrooming, terrible and incredibly tall." Colonel Paul W. Tibbets, Pilot of the Enola Gay

The bomb had gone off. The B-29's and the men who manned them devastated Japan. When the B-29 *Enola Gay*, flown by Colonel Paul W. Tibbets, Jr., dropped the atomic bomb on Hiroshima on August 6, 1945, it signaled that the total annihilation of Japan was now possible. The B-29 *Bock's Car*, flown by Charles "Chuck" Sweeney, confirmed this when it destroyed Nagasaki August 9, 1945. (The primary target had been Kokura; but due to poor visibility there, the bomb was dropped on Nagasaki.) The effectiveness of strategic bombing, still raging to this day regarding the European war, would not be an issue as far as Japan was concerned. There was now no question that an enemy's ability to wage war could be destroyed by air power. Now the problem was, so could everything and everybody else.

Was this right? Is it right? There are probably two answers. One, with respect to WW II, is clearly yes. There is no reasonable doubt that the Hiroshima and Nagasaki bombings, as horrible as they were, saved more lives than they took, by a wide margin. There is not a realistic estimate that does not predict more Americans dying in an invasion of Japan than the number of lives taken by the two bombs. And one can be assured, the Japanese death toll in an American invasion would have been far greater than the American death toll. That leaves the arguments that Japan would have surrendered if this or if that. Some claim that the entry of the Russians into the war was the real catalyst for the Japanese decision to surrender, and therefore the bombs were not necessary. Recent scholarship discredits this idea. The Japanese leadership did not believe the Russians had the necessary naval capability to effectively wage war against Japan. Another argument is that the Japanese were concerned about a looming food crisis that could or would lead to riots, and that drove them to surrender. Giving the influence of the Emperor over the Japanese people at that time, that seems unlikely. With respect to today and the future, the use of nuclear weapons is clearly problematic and most likely unsupportable.

Worse, in my opinion, are those who were not there or even alive, but argue that the bombs shouldn't have been used. I have never heard any argument made by someone who was scheduled to invade Japan, nor by the men who invaded the Pacific islands, against the use of the bombs. Maybe Jacob Beser, Electronics Officer aboard the *Enola Gay* to track electronic signals that might prematurely detonate the bomb, summarized the situation as the men saw it. When interviewed years later he commented that, if there had never been a Pearl Harbor, there would have been no Hiroshima. (Beser was one of three non-crew members aboard the *Enola Gay*, who knew they were carrying an atomic bomb. The other two were aboard to arm the bomb in flight. Beser also had some rather colorful words for those who argue the bomb was used on an Asian race but not on a European one. Beser, a Jew, made it clear that the only reason that was true was because the bomb was simply not ready for use before Germany surrendered. In words leaving no doubt about meaning, he asserted that we were planning to use it on the Nazis and that those bastards certainly deserved it. Tibbets probably summarized it best. In an interview taped for an exhibition of the *Enola Gay* at the Smithsonian Institution in Washington, D.C. he said, "We just wanted to end the war and go home." Tibbets got the job of commanding the 509th Composite Group because, according to the movie *Above and Beyond*, he was "the man least likely to make a mistake."

The Invasion That Never Happened

Estimates varied regarding the number of expected US and Japanese casualties as a result of Operation Downfall, the military plan for invading Japan. Furthermore, these estimates kept changing as situations changed. A major unknown factor was the resistance of the Japanese civilian population. Other factors were known, especially the casualties from the invasions of Japanese strongholds on Iwo Jima and Okinawa. One projection was 200,000 dead for the US. Another was as high as 500,000, and some estimates saw US casualties in the 1,000,000 range. Some 500,000 additional Purple Hearts produced just for casualties of the invasion became surplus. (These medals have been used for more recent wars.) The number of extra Purple Hearts produced is an indication of the number of casualties the military thought might occur. For the Japanese, the estimates are always at least double the US dead. A few people saw five to ten million Japanese fatalities. The estimating did not end with the war. The new estimates are used to prove that the atomic bombs were or were not necessary. While postwar estimates and arguments to support not using the bombs may be legitimate, estimates by people who did not have to risk their lives in what would have been a blood bath, no matter the final estimate, are too self-serving for me.

No matter how one counts, the numbers are spine chilling. It did not happen, of course. Whatever one thinks, the bombings of Hiroshima and Nagasaki finally convinced the Japanese warlords to surrender.

It is likely that numerous FCSD area men would have participated in any invasion of Japan. Men like Arnold Eldridge, Lowell B. Fancher, Richard H. Fuller, Jacob Hoffman, and August Scherer, Jr. knew they were to be part of any invasion force. They were not unhappy that it never occurred. Other men from the area who almost surely would have participated in the invasion include Richard H. Fuller, Walter D. Makowski, Lawrence W. Miller, Robert F. Miller, Gerald R. Rennicks, Leroy W. Thayer, and Everett E. Voss. Richard Miller spoke for all of them when he remarked, "I am very thankful to be alive." NAO.

Jacob J. Hoffman of Fillmore entered the service on the 3rd anniversary of the attack on Pearl Harbor, December 7, 1944. He took basic training at Camp Blanding in Florida and was assigned as a rifleman to Company C, 17th Infantry Regiment, 7th Infantry Division. After completion of training, Jacob was sent, along with other replacements to Portland, OR, where they embarked for Okinawa. They stopped in Hawaii for a couple of weeks for additional training and for necessary gear. They were being prepared for the invasion of Japan. In August, they finally arrived on Okinawa, where they were to stage for the invasion. However, the bombing of Hiroshima and Nagasaki negated the need for an invasion.

The plan for the invasion of Japan was code named "Operation Downfall." It was divided into two parts. Part one, which would take place first, was code named, "Operation Olympic." It called for an initial landing on Kyushu, the farthest main island in the south. As the Japanese reacted to this initial invasion, the second part of "Downfall" would take place in the north. That invasion was codenamed "Coronet" and it called for two landings to the east and west of Tokyo. Jacob, with the 7th Infantry Division, XXIV Corps, under the command of General Courtney H. Hodges, was to land on Kujikurihara Beach east of Tokyo. While Jacob was a replacement, the XXIV Corps was composed of veteran combat units from the European campaign. Thankfully all of this proved unnecessary. Instead, Jacob's unit was sent to Inchon, Korea as part of the Korean Occupation forces.

Jacob decided to reenlist in December of 1945 as a Military Policemen. A year later, learning that he was being reassigned to Alaska, and having just been married, Jacob decided to end his military career.

Admiral Yamamoto's presumed concern following the attack on Pearl Harbor, that the attack had "awakened a sleeping giant and filled it with a terrible resolve" had proved true and was now history.

Occupation Duties

When the war ended, everyone did not just pack their gear and go home. There were occupation duties, and some of those duties fell on men and women from the FCSD area. Those involved in such duties included Charles H. Ayer, Jr, Allen W. Cockle, Kenneth (Rod) Babbitt, John W. Collopy, Larry H. Birch, Ralph H. Cox, Harold N. Emmons, Richard H. Fuller, Norman A. Gaus, Beverly A. Luckey, Dr. Robert H. Lyman, Francis D. Morris, Everett C. Voss, and many others.

Charles H. Ayer Jr of Wiscoy entered the US Army on July 27, 1944. He had already served two years with the Merchant Marine. His discharge document indicates that he served seven and a half months in the US before shipping overseas on March 14, 1945. During that period, he likely went through basic training and possibly some technical training although his papers do not show that he attended any service schools. Charles served as a general clerk which could mean he did receive some technical training before being sent overseas. A general clerk performed a variety of clerical tasks. These duties included compiling and filing reports and statistics, tabulating, and posting data in record books, performing general bookkeeping, processing, and handling military orders and using various office machines.

A February 1945 edition of the NAO reported that Charles was home for a few days, likely in January, visiting his mother in Wiscoy. This was almost surely a pre-overseas leave. He arrived in France on March 27, 1945. However, his obituary in the December 4, 1997 edition of the East Aurora, NY Advertiser indicates he served in Italy. Based on information provided in his discharge document, it is likely that he served with either the II Army Corps or the 15th Army Group or both in Italy. Charles received credit for participation in the Central Europe Campaign and both the II Army Corps and the 15th Army Group did participate in that campaign. Charles would have participated in the end of the campaign.

Both these units also became part of the occupation forces assigned to Austria following the end of the war. Charles discharge shows that he served with Headquarters Company, US Forces Austria. Both the II Corps Headquarters Company and the 65th Army Group were assigned to US Forces Austria. The Headquarters Company would have reported directly to General Mark Clark, Commanding General of US Forces Austria. Those US forces were charged with establishing a free and independent Austria with a sound economy capable of insuring an adequate standard of living. While it was not directly charged with denazification of the country, that clearly had to be an indirect goal of its duties.

Austria was treated separately from Germany post-war and escaped to a certain extent the stigmatism attached to the Nazi movement. Post war Austria's leaders tried to create the false belief that it had been the first victim of the Nazi Anschuss (annexation by force) of captured countries. The Allies decided to recognize this interpretation. The truth was that Austria was more a partner than a conquered country. Thousands of Austrians fought for the Nazi cause.

Charles was discharged from the service on August 22, 1946 in Vienna. It appears that he remained in Austria or Europe for some time before returning to the United States.

Kenneth Roderick (Rod) Babbitt of Fillmore was a member of the Fillmore Central School Class of 1945. However, he entered the service January 10, 1945. After basic training at Sampson Naval Training Station, he attended radar technical school in Virginia Beach. The NAO reported in March that he had been home on a seven-day furlough, probably just after finishing at Sampson and being assigned to radar school. Following radar training, he reported aboard the *USS Oracle* (AM 103), a minesweeper, on June 7, 1945. The *Oracle* had an impressive war record. It started the war in the Aleutians, performing towing, escort, patrol, salvage, and survey operations. It then participated in the invasions of the Marshall Islands, Saipan, Tinian, and Okinawa. On May 14, 1945, it sailed from Guam to Pearl Harbor and then on to the US for an overhaul in Seattle, WA. Rod would have boarded the *Oracle* at Pearl Harbor, just in time to return to the US. On August 29, it left Seattle for Pearl Harbor. It reported to Sasebo, Japan, on November 5. Next it participated in minesweeping in the Formosa Straits until December 23, when it docked in Shanghai, China. The *Oracle* then headed for home, with a stop off in Sasebo, Japan. Rod was transferred to the *USS Adams* on January 13, 1946, in Sasebo.

The *USS Adams* (DM 27) also swept mines. It was part of the 5th Fleet and carried out minesweeping operations until April 1946, when it returned to the US. The NAO reported, in November 1945, that Rod served as a radar technician. Radar operators during the war were required to stand radar watch for long periods. They used and regulated the radar equipment, converted relative bearings to true bearings, and read ranges. They also read and plotted polar coordinates.

Rod told his wife Virginia (Ginny) that he was amazed at all the little Japanese boats that collected garbage dumped from the American ships. It is possible that he observed these events while standing watch. It is also an indication of the desperation of the Japanese people following the total devastation of their country. Rod was discharged from active duty on August 10, 1946.

Larry H. Birch of Houghton was born in Chicago, but spent much of his youth with his missionary parents in Sierra Leone in West Africa. He attended both the Houghton Academy and Houghton College. Larry entered the service June 5, 1944. It is likely that he attended basic training at Sampson Naval Training Station. He then almost assuredly attended the Naval Training School in Chicago where he was trained as a radar, sonar, and radio repairman. The men in this program were among the top 3 to 5 percent of Navy wartime personnel. The program by 1944 lasted some 28 weeks. It was broken into a four-weeks pre-radio section, a 12 weeks primary section and a 12 weeks advanced section. Coupled with approximately 11 weeks of basic training, Larry would have completed his training around April 1945. His obituary indicates that he served on 11 ships. One of the last, if not the last, was the *USS Cossatot (AO 77)* tanker. Muster records indicate that he boarded the *Cossatot* on September 13, 1945. It appears, based on the ship's history, that he joined the crew on Okinawa. The ship was on its way to Japan to perform occupation duties. The *Cossatot* was a tanker that fueled other ships. Its previous duties had included fueling convoy escort vessels in the Atlantic, as well as fueling operations off both Iwo Jima and Okinawa. At Okinawa, it had managed to destroy a kamikaze plane attempting to dive into the ship. It later served as part of the mighty Task Force 38 during the final strikes against the Japanese homeland. Stationed at Sasebo, its duty in Japan was to fuel the ships of the occupation force. On November 12, 1945, the *Cassatot* sailed from Yokosukato to San Francisco, arriving November 26. Larry was discharged in June of 1946.

Allen W. (Sonny) Cockle of Hume entered the service on March 21, 1945. It appears he entered the service at or took his basic training or both at Fort Dix, NJ. In May 1945, during basic training, he qualified with the M1 rifle. It is not clear where Sonny served during the next 6 to7 months.

On October 13, 1945, he sailed for Japan. Arriving on October 25, he was assigned to Company C, 62nd Signal Company as a replacement. The 62nd possessed an admirable war record, having already served in the European Theater in Italy. It was assigned to Occupation Duty in Japan. Sonny likely joined the 62nd as a replacement in Kure, Honshu. In Kure, the 62nd occupied a stone barracks once used by the Japanese Navy. Sonny, according to his Military Occupation Specialist code, was a linesman. His sister Polly said he told her he also served as a Radio Operator. It was not unusual for men to perform multiple duties. Company C was a construction unit for his Battalion.

In December, 13 men were placed on temporary duty with the 30th Signal Company. It is not known if Sonny was one of the men. In January, the history of the 62nd, indicates that all the men and officers were assigned to the 58th Signal Battalion. The Battalion moved to Otaru and then Sapporo in January, 1946. On March 28, the unit moved to Koriyama, Honshu to continue its occupation duties. They were about 3 miles outside the city at the former Kanaya Naval Air Base. Most of the buildings were wood, and the base itself had been mostly destroyed by American bombers. The camp was named "Camp Jones" after the first 62nd soldier killed in combat when the Battalion was in Italy.

The battalion engaged in extensive training in addition to regular duties. Company C's training occurred in mid-June, 1946, and included installing cables, removing old "bad" Japanese cables, and training in all aspects of a field operation company. It was not all work. The Army also provided a range of off-duty activities. There were frequent USO shows as well a softball league and dances at the "Baxter Club."

Sonny sailed home on October 6, 1946, arriving October 21. He likely sailed from Sendi. A few months later, the remaining men of the 62nd sailed home from Sendi. For his service in Japan, among other medals, Sonny earned the Army Occupation Medal, Japan Clasp.

John W. Collopy entered the service January 26, 1945. He moved to the FCSD area after the war, and died in Fillmore. John likely completed basic training and possible military police training before being assigned to the 209th Military Police Company. Camp Gordon near Augusta, GA had a school for training military policemen during the war.

The 209th Military Police Company was established at Fort Lewis, WA, on January 25, 1941. It arrived in New Caledonia, a French Island in the SW Pacific, about 700 miles from Australia, on March 21, 1943. New Caledonia's Capital, Noumea, served as headquarters for both the US Army and Navy during the war. It is likely that John joined the 205th in New Caledonia.

On June 1, 1945, the 205th moved to Cebu City in the Philippines. Cebu City had been the location of a vicious battle during the period March 26 to April 8, 1945. The Leyte Campaign was still raging when the 209th arrived. Hostilities would not officially end until July 1, 1945. John earned a battle star for his participation in the Leyte campaign. The 205th engaged in normal military police duties during its time in the Philippines. These included traffic control, town patrols, operating the base stockade and guarding the 59th Station Hospital. The 205th was also charged with protecting the port area against unauthorized personnel.

Troops in the Philippines enjoyed many amenities, including good food, swimming, dances, parties with locals, and various sports. The USO also arranged for shows. John told his son that he boxed as a middleweight in USO shows.

In January 1946, the Company moved to Japan to participate in occupation duties. They performed duties in the Yamate section of Yokohoma. They conducted patrols, investigated accidents, guarded Red Cross women's billets, and maintained a criminal investigation section. In addition, they investigated "black market" operations, guarded war crimes POWS and escorted VIP visitors. In May 1946, that included escorting General Eisenhower. The 209th remained in Japan until November of 1946. John was discharged December 9, 1946.

Richard Harlow Fuller of Houghton entered the Navy on June 8, 1945. After basic training, at Sampson Naval Training Station and likely some technical training, Richard was shipped to California and then to Saipan where he joined the crew of the repair ship *USS Luzon.* on September 20, 1945, according to the *Luzon's* muster records. Other records indicate the *Luzon* was in Saipan until October 1, when it sailed via Iwo Jima, to Wakanoura Wan on Honshu, arriving October 8. The *Luzon* would spend the next several months providing fleet and repair services supporting occupational forces and activities in various Japanese ports, including Wakayama and Nagoya. In early 1946 it sailed for the US, arriving at Orange, Texas on February 9, 1946. It then went on to New York. Richard was transferred to the Lido Beach, NY, naval station for discharge on July 10, 1946. He was discharged July 17th.

Richard served as a skilled optical specialist (Optician's Assistant) aboard the *Luzon.* His official rating was Special Artificer (O). Men in this rating were trained to repair various optical instruments, including telescopes, compasses, and obviously, in Richard's case, optical equipment. Richard told members of The History Club that he also worked with a repair crew during his time aboard the *Luzon.* The History Club reported that Richard said, "that, if the bombing of Hiroshima and Nagasaki had not occurred, (his) boot camp class would have been fleet reserves for the invasion of Japan." He added, "I am very thankful to be alive."

Norman A. Gaus of Allen was inducted into the service on April 17, 1945. He was assigned to Fort  Knox, KY, to train as a medium tank crewman. The NAO reported him home on leave in August and September 1945, most likely the same leave reported twice. The September news item also mentioned that he would be returning to Fort Meade in Maryland after his leave. His time at Meade was very short as he sailed for overseas on October 5, 1945. By the end of October, he was in Japan as part of the 44th Tank Battalion. The 44th had been overseas for some time and had earned many honors as a combat unit in New Guinea, and especially in the Philippines. It had arrived in Japan on September 15, 1945, just eight days following the official surrender of Japan.

Norm in Japan where he served with occupation forces.
Gaus Family Photo

Norman spent almost a year in Japan, primarily in the Tokyo area performing occupation duties. Norman was a tank crewman, but the principal duty assigned to the 44th was guard duty. They mainly guarded the 71st Quartermaster Depot, the 73rd Ordnance Base Depot, and the Tsurami River Engineer Equipment Depot, as well as various assignments guarding ships, freight yards and similar locations. Norman may also have either guarded a Japanese prison camp, or at least was near one based on the picture shown here. The guard demands were enormous and forced the battalion to ignore its on-going tank training to maintain combat efficiency. Most of the time, it could only put a platoon of tanks on the road. This was important as the battalion was also expected to be prepared for any foreseeable crisis. In January, they participated in a practice alert.

Occupation duties were not without danger. In December one of the men on guard was killed by a freight train. There were also outbreaks at some posts, with pilfering a major problem. Guards were frequently forced to fire on Japanese who refused to halt when challenged. Maintaining order became even more difficult when the men were ordered to unload their carbines and carry their ammunition in their cartridge belts.

Despite the demand of their duties, the men in Norman's tank battalion managed to celebrate, somewhat traditionally, both Thanksgiving and Christmas. There was constant turnover of personnel as men were rotated back to the states. In March, pressure was reduced as the battalion was relieved of responsibility for 25 guard posts. The battalion was inactivated on April 30, 1946. Most of the men were transferred to the 95th Light Tank Company. It is not clear where Norman was assigned, although it appears his records continued to carry him as a member of the 44th. Norman was rotated home on September 4, 1946, arriving on September 19. He was discharged at Fort Dix, NJ, on November 1, 1946.

Norman earned the Asiatic Pacific Theater Medal, the Army of Occupation Medal with Japan Clasp, and the World War II Victory Medal.

Robert Henry Lyman of Fillmore. entered the service on July 21, 1942. At the time, he was one of two doctors in Fillmore. Both his father and his grandfather had practiced medicine in the village. Grandfather Henry Lyman had treated many of the men from the area who served during the Civil War. Robert served in many of the same war zones where men from the FCS area served, but no information has been found which indicates he treated any of those men. He did treat the author. A boyish prank resulted in the tip of one of the authors fingers being almost entirely chopped off. Doctor Lyman sewed the tip back to the rest of the finger. He also closed a nasty wound caused by an ax.

Robert served as Chief of Surgery for four different entities during the war, two in the US and two overseas. He initially was assigned to Camp Holabird in Baltimore, MD. Holabird was a signal depot during most of his service there. He also served at the Edgewood Arsenal in Aberdeen MD. Edgewood is more famous as the Aberdeen Proving Ground today. During Doctor Lyman's service there, it was primarily concerned with readying soldiers for gas warfare. Men were instructed in using and trusting their gas masks.

In October 1944, Robert sailed aboard the *Queen Mary* for England, and the European Theater of War. He landed in Glasgow, Scotland, but by November he was in Lison, Normandy, France, with the 195th General Hospital. A January 12, 1945, report signed by Dr. Lyman, outlined the activities of his Surgical Service for the month of December, 1944. It stated, "During this period the Surgical Service received a total of 1,157 admissions, which aggregated 30,520 patient days, performed 56 major operations, 401 minor operations, applied 294 plaster casts, and performed 191 diagnostic procedures (non-routine X-ray and laboratory procedures). Three deaths occurred during the month, all POWs, two of which were completely autopsied." At the end of his report he noted, "The quality of the professional work accomplished has been excellent." In February,1945, the 195th moved to Mourmelon-le-Grand, France. At this time, it was also designated as a Station Hospital for the 101st Airborne Infantry Division. More than likely many of the 101st men treated were wounded during the Battle of the Bulge.

His report for March, 1945, dated 7 April, reflects the flexibility required of a hospital in a combat zone. The first paragraph of his report says it all: "During the month of March, the professional activities of the 195th Gen Hosp have been varied, the organization having served as a General Hospital, a Station Hospital for the 101st Division, an Evacuation Hospital for Com Z transportable patients, and as a 24 hour or less transient hospital in the evacuation chain. Such multiplicity of function imposed severe demands upon our personnel and called for reorganization of Admissions and Dispositions. It added materially to the administrative duties of the Medical Officers and limited the definitive therapy carried out."

Two months after he signed the March report, the war in Europe was over. Dr. Lyman already had an envious war record. By this point he had earned the American Campaign Medal, the European African Middle East Theater Medal, two battle stars for the Ardennes-Alsace and Rhineland campaigns, and shared a 195th General Hospital Unit Citation.

But Dr. Lyman's war was only half over. On July 7, 1945, he sailed from Marseilles, France, aboard the *USS General H.W. Butner* (AP 113) transport for Okinawa, arriving September 1, 1945. For the next two months, he served with the 35th Station Hospital, assigned to the Tenth Army on Okinawa. In November, the 35th and Dr. Lyman were shipped to Japan, arriving November 15. By November 19, they were at their permanent assignment in Nagoya. The 35th, and Dr. Lyman, now became part of the US 6th Army Occupation Forces in Japan. The 35th would serve in Nagoya until March 31, 1946. Dr. Lyman would leave a month earlier, sailing home aboard the *USS Hermitage* (AP 54) troopship and arriving in Seattle on February 14, 1946. He was also now entitled to wear, along with the rest of his hardware, the Asiatic Pacific Theater Medal, US Army of Occupation Medal with the Japan Clasp, as well as the World War II Victory Medal. Doctor Lyman had entered the service as a Captain. He departed as a Lieutenant Colonel.

Francis David Morris of Centerville boarded the USS *San Marcos* (LSD 25) in Philadelphia on April 14, 1945. The *San Marcos* was a dock landing ship. David went aboard the ship on the day it was commissioned. The *San Marcos* sailed May 19 for Pearl Harbor via the Panama Canal, with landing boats aboard. The *San Marcus* was now at war. From Pearl, she headed to Guam, where she picked up some dredging equipment. Her next stop was Okinawa, where she docked August 12, 1945. That same day Japanese bombers dropped torpedoes that severely damaged the mighty *USS Pennsylvania,* berthed in Buckner Bay, not far from the *San Marcos.* Dave saw the *Pennsylvania* get hit. He had graduated from

FCS in 1944, five years after Erwin Howden who was on the *Pennsylvania*. It is possible they knew each other.

From Okinawa, Dave and the *San Marcos* headed to Naha, where she repaired some LCT's (Landing Craft Tanks), and then proceeded to Saipan, where she picked up some LCM's (mechanized landing craft) and LCVP's (Higgins type landing craft for personnel) for use by occupation forces at Tokyo Bay. For the rest of its stay in the Pacific, the *San Marcos* was engaged in occupation duties. Francis arrived in Tokyo with the *USS San Marcos* September 4, 1945, two days late for the official surrender ceremony. *San Marcos* immediately commenced operation and maintenance of the port services. In December, she was assigned to cargo operations, ferrying boats from Aomori to Yokohama.

Dave told the NAO that during his time in the Pacific, after leaving Pearl Harbor, he made visits to the Marshall Islands, the Caroline Islands, Guam, Saipan, Mariana Islands, Iwo Jima, Okinawa, and Japan.

Francis, who was called David or Dave, entered the Navy November 3, 1944. After basic training at Sampson Naval Training Station, he attended the Pre-Commissioning School at Newport, R.I. The school was designed to bring men who were being assigned to the same ship together for training before they boarded the ship. The theory was that these crew members, already knowing each other, would reduce the time needed to make the ship combat ready. In March 1945, the NAO reported that Dave had transferred to an amphibious unit, probably meaning the *San Marcos*.

In January 1946, the *San Marcos* was assigned to Task Force 1 for Operations Crossroads, the atomic tests at Bikini Atoll. Dave was one of at least three FCSD men who, to some extent, were involved with the Bikini Atomic bomb testing.

In February, they were at Kwajalein and assigned to help prepare the test site. However, on March 8, according to the *USS San Marcos* sailing report of March 11, 1946, Dave was transferred to the USS PC 574 a submarine chaser for duty. PC 574 reported that he was transferred to Navy Receiving Station 128 on April 3, to be forwarded to the United States on emergency leave. It is not known what the emergency was, but Dave was assigned to the *USS Douglas H. Fox* (DD 779) destroyer upon his return to duty. He remained with the *Fox,* which was engaged in various training and escort duties in the Caribbean, until he was discharged on July 7, 1946.

 **Herschel Claude Ries** of Houghton entered the US Army on June 22, 1943, in Wellsville, NY. He was a student at Houghton College at the time. It is not known where he took his basic training. Following basic it appears that he was assigned to a training class at the University of Nebraska in Lincoln, almost surely as part of the Army Specialized Training Program (ASTP). The NAO reported in January, 1944 that he was reporting back to Lincoln, Nebraska after visiting his parents in Houghton. His Dad was a Professor at the College. *ASTP training book photo.* Herschel is in 3rd row from bottom, 2nd from right.

Herschel was assigned to Company C, 1st Platoon at the University of Nebraska Lincoln. Given his later assignment, he likely was in signal service training. According to the book, "US Army in World War II: The Technical Services -The Signal Corps: The Outcome (Mid 1943 through 1945), by George Raynor Thompson and Dixie R. Harris, the US Signal Corps was the least prepared of all the technical services for the war. Herschel was in training at Lincoln for approximately one year. The NAO reported in

December 1944 that he attended church in Houghton. This likely was just a holiday pass, or maybe leave in between assignments.

Following his leave, he may have been assigned to Fort Monmouth, NJ. However, it is not known to which unit he was assigned, if any. He may instead have been shipped overseas as a replacement. On March 20, 1944, the 3163rd Signal Service Company was officially organized at Camp Edison on Fort Monmouth. The one remaining report for the Company at the National Archives says that the men assigned to the 3163rd were transfers from other units. Herschel's entry at the World War II Memorial indicates he served with the 3163rd Signal Company. It is probable that many of the men were from the 501st Signal Company. In fact, it is possible the 3163rd replaced the 501st. No information on the 501st was located at the Archives. But both the 501st and the 3163rd were organized at Fort Monmouth on the same day and both received the same battle credits. Additionally, both received credit for occupation duties in Germany during the period May 2, 1945 to July 4, 1945. It appears likely that one or more other units were involved. The 3163rd received credit for the Rhineland campaign. The period of eligibility for such credit ended March 20, 1945. It is impossible that the 3163rd or the 501st could have arrived in Europe in time to earn credit for that campaign. Therefore, it is more likely that the 3163rd absorbed a unit that had earned the Rhineland credit. It may have absorbed one or more other units as well. A veteran named Nicholas H. Hemmer Jr. was interviewed for the Oral History Program of the New York State Military Museum. He recounted that he had served with the 3163rd Signal Company in France, Belgium, Germany, and Austria and had earned battle stars for the Ardennes-Alsace, Rhineland, and Central Europe campaigns. In this case it appears that he was transferred to the 3163rd since he received credit for campaigns not credited to the 3163rd. His occupation award however, likely was earned during his duty with the 3163rd. This indicates that the 3163rd performed occupation duties in Germany and Austria or maybe just Austria. Such duties in Austria did earn the men an Army Occupation Medal, with a Germany clasp.

Herschel may also have been a member of another unit, absorbed by the 3163rd since he could have and likely did arrive in Europe as early as January 1945, well before the 3163rd. A sentence in the Thompson - Harris book, referred to above, indicates that the 3163rd arrived in Europe during the last months of the war. The book states that the 3163rd professed a AN/TRC-6 radio relay that could and did carry very heavy traffic during the last months of the war. It was the prototype for microwave pulse-modulated communications systems of the future.

The Signal Corps managed communications and information systems for the command and control of combined armed forces activities. Hershel served as a Radio Repairman for frequency mod equipment. Interestingly, after the war he served as Chief Engineer for radio station ELWA in Liberia for 20 years. The NAO reported in September 1945 that Hershel was home on leave, and was stationed at Monmouth, NJ. He was home again in October with a lady friend from Philadelphia and again for Christmas in December, 1945. This tends to indicate that any overseas tour would have lasted no more than seven or eight months. While it is questionable that he earned the Rhineland Battle star, unless he did arrive overseas in January 1945, assuming he was overseas with the 3163rd, he certainly earned the Central Europe battle star and the Army Occupational Medal, Germany Clasp. Herschel was discharged February 24, 1946.

Everett E. Voss of Granger entered the service on January 11, 1943. He took basic training at Camp Blanding in Florida, but his training was interrupted by a hernia. According to the NAO, Everett was home on leave, in June, 1943, and he was still stationed at Fort Blanding. This probably was after six months in the hospital recovering from the hernia operation. Following his leave, he likely returned to Blanding to finish basic training. At Blanding, he was assigned to Company L of the 475th Quartermaster Truck Regiment.

Everett, better known as Jack, served primarily as a truck driver during his service, He told his wife Anne that he also was assigned as a driver for a General at one point. His primary duties, aside from driving the General, would have been transporting supplies, materiel, and troops. He was also expected to perform maintenance and upkeep. Anne said Everett mentioned that he delivered a lot of supplies unloaded from ships. He likely was involved in moving supplies and materials to ships while stationed in San Francisco and Boston, and moving supplies and materials from ships in Japan.

In January 1944, the NAO reported that Everett was stationed at San Francisco, but was home on leave. In April, the NAO reported him at the Bay Shore Staging Area in San Francisco. He likely was permanent party at Bay Shore, involved in moving supplies and personnel to the Pacific battlegrounds. However, it is also possible that he was staging for an overseas assignment. Whatever, for some reason this assignment was changed. In June, again per the NAO, he was ordered to Boston. Since the invasion at Normandy had just occurred, it is again possible that he was in the process of being shipped to Europe. More likely, he was participating in the massive shipment of supplies and materiel to Europe in support of the invasion. At this time, he was assigned to the 3791st Quartermaster Truck Company. In November, he was home on leave.

The NAO also reported him home on furlough in February 1945. By March 1945, Everett was on the move again, He was in Texas at Camp Howze with Company D, ITB, 13 Regiment, Platoon 3. At Howze, Everett was assigned to an Infantry Training Battalion. In May, he was at Camp Meade, MD with Company C, 30th Battalion, 8th Replacement Regiment. Assigned to a replacement regiment at Meade, he likely was there awaiting a new assignment. In July, he was at Camp Adair, OR with Company B, 6 Battalion, 2 Regiment, Army Ground Forces. Camp Adair was being used as a POW camp for German and Italians at this time. It is possible that this was a permanent assignment, but Everett was only there for a short time. He sailed for the Philippines from San Francisco on July 31, 1945. He arrived at Luzon on August 24, 1945.

In October 1945, the NAO reported that he was now at Lingayen Gulf (Luzon), in the Philippines. He

Bomb Plot – Mission 62, 497th Bomb Group, June 5, 1945, Kobe, Japan Bob Aldrich's plane, A-44 (See Arrow) led the attack. National Archive Photo.

was assigned to the 90th Field Artillery Battalion. The 90th shipped out of Luzon for Japan in late August 1945. Everett's Battalion was originally scheduled to be part of the Japanese invasion force; but once the war ended it was assigned to occupation duties. The 90th was equipped with 155 mm howitzers that were towed by a truck. Everett could have been assigned to tow artillery had the war not ended. The 90th landed on the main island of Honshu, Japan and was stationed at Camp Ireland. For a short time in December, it was moved to Kobe, Japan as a security guard force. In one of those ironies of war, on March 28, 1945, Robert Aldrich of Fillmore had been in a B-29 that bombed Kobe while attempting to destroy the very facilities Everett was now protecting. See photo. The blue arrow is pointing to Bob's B-29 which is visible in a larger picture. Everett earned the Asiatic Pacific Theater Medal and the Army Occupation Medal with Japan Clasp for his efforts in the Pacific. The 90th was deactivated at Camp Ireland in early 1946. Everett sailed from Japan on January 27, 1946, arriving back in the states on February 7. He was discharged February 16, 1946, at Fort Dix, NJ.

PART XII - ENJOYING THE FRUITS

When World War II was over, and sometimes before, like others in Europe and the Pacific, many FCSD area men and women took advantage of opportunities to visit cities, towns, and other places they had heard or read about in their history books. Some took advantage of opportunities to see what they had been helping to achieve over the past four years.

Viewing the Destruction, Visiting Relatives, Recreation, Education

One of the men was **Bernard Mills** of the 94th Bomb Group. In a letter published in the NAO, Bernard wrote, "Yesterday I went flying over Belgium, France, and Germany. They have been taking the ground crews over the cities that we have been bombing for the past few years. They do not have any trouble finding enough fellows to go. I have been trying for a few days to go and I finally made it. It is about a nine-hour trip and it's pretty tiresome but I really enjoyed it. We went in some of the Forts here on the base. Some of the bigger towns we saw were Brussels, Liege, Aachen, Essen, Munster, Hanover, Brunswick, Kassel, Frankfurt, Luxembourg, Rheims, Paris, and Calais." What was not in the part of his letter printed in the NAO, was that what he really saw was what was left of the towns that the Eighth Air Force had visited during the war, especially those in Germany. Bernard later wrote that the devastation was nearly complete. Factories, bridges, and homes were all in ruins. He also mentioned that he saw the outline of trenches from World War I. The Air Force called such flights "Trolley Missions."

Other men opted for more recreational activities. Wilbur Histed managed to arrange for nine days on Lake Geneva while he was stationed in Germany. **Frank J. Kopler** and several of his friends spent a few weeks on the Riviera. **Alwin J. Ward** wrote his parents about four wonderful days he spent in Rome. He wrote, "I visited St. Paul's, St. Peter's, and St. Cecelia's churches. I went to the Pantheon, the Catacombs, and the Colosseum. I saw the tomb of Shelley, Greek Temples, one called Vesta (Author - his mother's name). I have been to the opera, and Saturday night saw Rigoletto. Today I visited Vatican City, Vatican Museum, and the Sistine Chapel and went to an audience with the Pope. St. Peter's Church is the most beautiful man- made thing I have ever seen."

Kent Weaver really took advantage of his situation. In August 1945 he spent a couple of weeks at a rest camp at the town of Alassio on the Italian Rivera, and a few days in Genoa. In September and October, he attended college in Florence, Italy. In November, he spent five days sightseeing in Rome.

Robert M. Dinkel took a trip to the land of his Father's birth, Switzerland, to visit his dad's sister. It took him almost four weeks, most of it traveling. He did manage to spend seven days with his aunt.

David M. Babbitt managed to visit the famous carnival city, Rio de Janeiro, before he departed Brazil

Lawrence "Hank" Miller, like Bernard Mills, took some time to view the results of the war. He visited Yokohama and Tokyo. In a letter home, in part he wrote: "I could not have explained how bad the place really is, but it has been blown to bits. The residential part was hit the worst and a few factories. It is nine miles between the two cities and everything in that entire nine miles is a flat mess."

Glenn F. **Williams** took a few days off to visit Rome, as his division blasted their way up the Italian boot. He wrote home that it was a beautiful city, and he had visited St. Peter's Cathedral. Glenn later used a 60-hours pass to visit Paris.

There were likely many more who took advantage of their situations to visit historical and other locations, but no information has been located regarding such visits.

PART XIII - THE FINAL COUNT

At War's End

Fifteen men from the FCSD area were killed in combat during World War II. Another died of an illness. This was a small part of the estimated 50 to 80 million that died worldwide (some estimate the death toll as 85 million or higher), but 15 was a big number for a small area. There were, however, others from the area who were never quite able to put their lives back together, to leave the horror they had witnessed behind them. One of these, years later, apparently committed suicide, quite possible due to the horrors he saw in liberated concentration camps. Others, physically, were also unable to escape the impact of the war.

Even the estimated 70 to 80 million dead were equal to over 50 percent of the US population at that time. While the United States did not suffer a 50-percent killed rate, the percentage of US citizens negatively impacted by the war was probably higher than 50 percent. The 80 million dead were only a start. One must also consider the numbers wounded, those maimed for life, both physically and mentally, the untold millions displaced, and the millions more whose lives were disrupted and would never be the same. In Asia and Europe, the percentage of persons negatively impacted was almost surely higher than the US percentage.

Not counting Antarctica, only the continent of South America escaped with minimal disruption. Australia was significantly impacted. While the continent of Africa overall escaped damage, North Africa took a beating. North America escaped physical destruction, but both Canada and the United States suffered major casualties and long-term disruptions to millions of lives. Many Asian countries, including China suffered greatly. Japan was practically destroyed. The countries of Europe were mauled, and Germany, deservedly, was leveled. Large areas in Russia were devastated and millions, the most of any country, were killed.

The Count Goes On

The toll of World War II did not end when the fighting ended. It continued for many years. Reports on the after effects of the atomic bombs have focused primarily on the Japanese people. Clearly those most affected for years afterwards were Japanese. But they were not the only ones, as the examples below indicate.

While serving in Kobe in October and November 1945, **Lowell Fancher**, along with other men in the Kobe area, were trucked by the Army to Hiroshima and Nagasaki for a first- hand view of the destructive power of the atomic bomb. Shortly after, but too late for Lowell, the military stopped such sightseeing trips due to the exposure to leftover radiation from the bombs. Years later the Veteran's Administration admitted that this exposure resulted in major health issues, including cancer, for Lowell.

John Ballard picked up a case of malaria during his service. The disease caused an enlarged liver. As mentioned earlier, John died at only 52 years of age after an emergency gall bladder operation.

Medals

Please note that the page number for a page listing a medal earned by a combatant is listed only once for each medal. Many pages may list more than one medal and many combatants may have earned more than one of the medals listed on a single page.

As mentioned earlier, determining medals earned was not easy since many of the documents needed were not available or had been destroyed in the St Louis fire which burned most of the World War II Army and Army Air Corps personnel files. Therefore, the medals listed for each veteran are those that the author believes, based on the information available and his understanding of the requirements, the veterans earned. It appears that, except for five medals, at least one of all the other medals issued during the war, was awarded to an FCSD area participant. The five medals not awarded to any FCSD area veteran were the Navy Cross, the Distinguished Service Medal, the Distinguished Service Cross, the Navy Distinguished Service Medal, and the Legion of Merit. On the other hand, at least one FCSD area veteran earned an award issued by the government of France, Belgium, Netherlands, or the Philippines.

Except in rare circumstances all World War II participants who served any amount of time honorably earned the **World War II Victory Medal.** Most also earned the **American Campaign Medal**, the **European, African, Middle East Theater Medal** or the **Asiatic Pacific Theater Medal**. Many of the veterans earned both the American Campaign Medal and one of the other theater medals. At least six veterans earned all three medals, Robert G. Beardsley, Lloyd A. Carmer, Robert H. Lyman, Gustave G. Prinsell, Robert E.W. Schultz, and Howard J. Wilcox.

Most of the veterans also earned the **Good Conduct Medal**. However, the Good Conduct Medal is only listed in Part XIV for veterans where actual information was available to indicate that the Medal was awarded. Available records show 68 men earned the medal. The actual count was likely more than three times that number. Three men from the area earned the **Prisoner of War (POW) Medal**, Gene D. Burgess, Burton H. Markham (24 days) and Gerald W. Rennick (21 days). It is not clear that Rennick ever officially received his POW Medal as he was freed by advancing American troops some 21 days after he was captured. The same may be true for Markham who was also a POW for a short period before being liberated by American troops. Their POW status was reported in the NAO during the war. Howard Kopler earned three **Merchant Marine Theater Medals (Pacific, Atlantic and Mediterranean)** as well as the **Merchant Marine World War II Victory Medal**.

In addition to the above, US decorations earned by FCSD area World War II servicemen and women included at least the following: (Note: KIA by name - Killed in Action; LOD by name - killed in Line of Duty; Number beside name - number of Purple Heart awarded or number of Oak Leaf Clusters by name or number of additional same medal earned; number of Battle Stars by name - total number earned.)

Medal of Honor - Almond E. Fisher. (See Medal, Part VIII, Medal of Honor)

Silver Star - Grover A. Bates, Paul S. Hatch (KIA), Allen L. Isham (KIA), Beverley A. Luckey, Glenn F. Williams. (See Medal, Part IV, Pacific Islands – Bougainville, Paul Hatch)

Soldiers Medal - Lowell E. Mix. (See Medal, Part III, 15th Air Force, Lowell Mix)

Distinguished Flying Cross - Robert G. Aldrich, Lowell E. Mix, Bernard Sweet.

Bronze Star – Richard G. Beach (Merit), Lloyd D. Clark (Heroism), Ronald G. Fridley (Heroism), Donald R. Haskins (Merit), Charles E. Hodnett (2 - Merit), Russell C. Hodnett (Merit), Allen L. Isham, (Heroism), Evan W. Molyneaux (Merit), Charles R. Ostrum (Merit), Carroll S. Phipps (Merit), Douglas W. Pitt (Merit), Robert H. Speicher Jr (2 - One Merit, One Heroism), Harold E. Thayer (Heroism), Irwin K. Tuthill (Heroism), Lowell J. Wilcox (Merit). A "V" devise worn with the medal is for Valor in combat. Oak Leaf Clusters denote additional awards for Army and Army Air Corps recipients. A 5/16-inch star indicates additional awards for Navy, Marine and Coast Guard recipients. (See Medal, Part III, 15th Air Force, Donald R. Haskins)

Purple Heart - Mark L Armstrong, John D. Ballard, Richard G. Beach, John W. Beardsley, Warren H. Bennett, Franklin L. Brown, Gene David Burgess, Robert D. Colburn, Adair W. Common (KIA), Kermit A. Davis (KIA), Albert E. Ferrin (LOD), Almond E. Fisher, Gerald B. Gayford (KIA), Paul S. Hatch (KIA), Marlie J. Hodnett (3), Allen L. Isham (KIA), Alfred H. Kingsley (KIA), Burton H. Markham, Lewis J. Morgan, Lester E. Noble (KIA), Robert D. Ostrum, Raymond I. Peck, Douglas W. Pitt, Gerald W. Rennick, Floyd K. Roberts (KIA), Melvin L. Slocum, William J. Stickle (LOD), Bernard Sweet (KIA), Harold E. Thayer (KIA), Roland J. Thomas, Grant A. Vedder (KIA), David D. Wallace (KIA), Lowell J. Wilcox, Oliver P. Wilday (KIA), Glenn F. Williams (4), Frank W. Wolfe Jr. (See Medal, Part VIII, Battle of the Bulge, Kermit A. Davis)

Air Medal – Philip G. Ackerman (4 Oak Leaf Clusters), Robert G. Aldrich, David N. Ayer (with Oak Leaf Cluster), Ivan R. Ayer (3 Oak Leaf Clusters), Gerald B. Gayford, Lowell E. Mix, Douglas F. Morris, Douglas W. Pitt, Edward F. Schramm, Royal S. Strait (2 Oak Leaf Clusters), Bernard Sweet, Warren M. Woosley. (Those for whom no Oak Leaf Cluster is mentioned probably earned one or more, but information confirming such awards was not located.)

China Service Medal – Kenneth R. Babbitt, Robert G. Beardsley, Warren E. Beardsley Jr., Lyle C. Brown, Ralph H. Cox, Ralph Kleinspehn, Robert S. Preston, Clark O. Smith, Federic S. Winship. (See Medal, Part IV, Okinawa, Clark O Smith)

American Defense Medal - 55 FCSD area veterans earned the American Defense Medal. (See Medal, Part I, Pearl Harbor, all awardees listed)

Occupation Medal – Army/Army Air Corps – Germany Clasp (Germany, Austria, Italy): Ivan A. Ayer, Glenn W. Barnett, Richard S. Beach, John W. Beardsley Jr, Everett M. Clark, Robert L. Cummings, Donald W. Finnemore, Ronald G. Fridley, Earle C. Knorr, Beverley A. Luckey, Arthur C. Miller, Lewis J. Morgan, Charles R. Ostrum, Carroll S. Phipps, Lloyd L. Prentice, Millton C. Rathbun, Herbert L. Rose, Gerald F. Thomas, George A. Tisdale, Anthony R. Vasile, Gerald J. Voss, Llwellyn M. Washburn, Donald L. Whalen, Albert Williams, Robert B. Wolfer. Japan Clasp (Japan, Korea): Clifford H. Beardsley, Allen W. Cockle, John C. Collopy, Arnold H. Eldridge, Horace N. Emmons, Lowell B. Fancher, Norman N. Gaus, William C. Gelser, Jacob J. Hoffman, Robert H. Lyman, Leonard A. Wood.

Navy/Marine Corps/Coast Guard Occupational Medal – Asia Clasp (Japan, Korea): Kenneth R.

Babbitt, John D. Ballard, Robert G. Beardsley, Warren E. Beardsley Jr, Lyle C. Brown, Ralph H. Cox, Eugene, R. Eldridge, Paul R. Fleming, Richard H. Fuller, Manfred C. Griggs, Robert L. Leet, Walter D. Makowski, Lawrence W. Miller, Robert F. Miller, Francis D. Morris, Alanson C. Papke, Robert S. Preston, Gastave G. Prinsell, Donald L. Slack, Allen R. Smith, Laurence A. Sweet, Alton A. Sylor, Leroy W. Thayer, Harold W. Wass, George R. Wells, Alfred C. Wilday, Richard J. Wilson.

Combat Infantry Badge (CIB) & 1947 Bronze Star – Richard G. Beach, John W. Beardsley Jr, Warren

H. Bennett, William C. Brueser, Gene David Burgess, Robert D. Colburn, Adair W. Common, Almond E. Fisher, Marlie J. Hodnett, Allen L. Isham, Earle C. Knorr, Beverley A. Luckey, Hubert F. McMaster, Burton H. Markham, Lewis J. Morgan, Lester E. Noble, Raymond I. Peck, Gerald W.

U.S. Army Combat Infantryman Badge

Rennicks, Roland J. Thomas (with Clasp), Kent M. Weaver, Lowell J. Wilcox, Oliver P. Wilday, Glenn F. Williams. This is probably not everyone who earned the CIB. At least 23 men (listed above) and 10 to 15 other men, served in combat infantry regiments. Information to determine if all these men earned the CIB is just not available. Given the prestige of this award, there has been no speculation about who may have earned it. Those listed above as having earned the award served in infantry regiments and records show they earned the award and/or were wounded or killed in action.

Invasion Assault Arrowhead Device – John Ballard (Tarawa) (Saipan), Gene David Burgess (Oran,

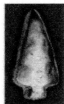

Algeria), Edward M. Cole (Normandy, Omaha Beach), William C. Crandall (Normandy, Utah Beach), Lowell B. Fancher (Palawan, Philippines), Ronald G. Fridley (Normandy, Omaha Beach), Mabel E. Fox (Salerno, Italy), John R. Gillette (Luzon, Philippines), Marlie J. Hodnett (Gela, Sicily), Allen Isham (Salerno, Italy), Milton C. Rathbun (Salerno, Italy) (Anzio, Italy) (Saint Maxine, Southern France), Floyd D. Roberts (Normandy, Omaha Beach), Robert H. Speicher (Iwo Jima), Gerald F. Thomas (Casablanca, Morocco) (Gela, Sicily), Roy G. Tillinghast (Leyte, Philippines), Irwin K. Tuttle (Normandy, Utah

Beach), Lowell J. Wilcox (Oran, Algeria) (Gela, Sicily) (Normandy, Omaha Beach), Glenn C. Wilday (Normandy, Omaha Beach), Oliver P. Wilday (Normandy, Utah Beach),

Battle Stars – FCSD area veterans earned at least 452 Battle Stars (also called Campaign Stars). Two

men, (Donald R. Haskins and Robert L. Van Name) each earned ten stars; Seven men (Phillip G. Ackerman, Everett R. Eldridge, John R. Gillette, Milton C. Rathbun, Roland J. Thomas, Lowell J. Wilcox, Albert Williams) each earned seven stars. Six men (Vernon A. Closser III, Charles M. Rice, Donald

Bronze and silver 3/16 inch stars

L. Slack, Robert W. Stevens, Royal S. Strait, Gerald F. Thomas) each earned six stars. Seventeen men (John D. Ballard, Warren H. Bennett, Edward M. Cole, Russell C. Hodnett, Walter D. Makowski, Evan W. Molyneaux, Charles R. Ostrum, Lloyd L. Prentice, Ransom L. Richardson Jr., Floyd K. Roberts, Herbert L. Rose, Bernard Sweet, Irwin K. Tuthill, Gerald J. Voss, Glenn F. Williams, Robert B. Wolfer, Warren M. Woolsey) each earned five stars. Three women from the area, all Nurses, also earned Battle Stars. Generva E. Ballard earned three, Mabel E. Fox earned three and Edith Johannes earned one. Many other men earned one to four stars which are listed in their summary section under Part XIV.

For the initial battle star, a small bronze star was awarded. If five stars were earned a Silver Star was awarded to represent the five bronze stars. Most veterans preferred to wear the five bronze stars (or more) rather than the single Silver Star. It looked more impressive. The Bronze battle star was smaller than the regular Bronze Medal which was awarded for both valor and meritorious service.

Women's Army Corps Service Medal – Frances J. Arthur, Genevieve Kolakowski, Ada R. Mills, Roberta P. Molyneaux (Grange), Elsie Jean Eldridge (Perry), Nancy H. Reid (McCreery). (See Medal, Part VII, US Army, Ada Mills)

Women's Airforce Service Pilots Gold Medal – Elin G. Harte.

WASP
Congressional Gold Medal

Honorable Service Lapel Button ((Ruptured Duck) – The button had several purposes, but primarily it was designed to be worn on the left lapel of civilian clothing to identify veterans who served honorably and were discharged prior to the end of the war. There was also a cloth lozenge that could be sewn onto the right breast of the uniform that enabled men to wear their uniforms for up to 30 days after they were discharged, even after the war ended. This was necessary due to the shortage of civilian clothing. The button was commonly called "Ruptured Duck" by veterans. This was because the Eagle faced to the right, which was the direction doctors instructed inductees to face during an examination for ruptures. Most early releases were due to injury or medical issues. For a few individuals, fitness was an issue. Age may also have been an issue. Regarding FCSD area veterans, the strangest situation was Clarence F. Gaus. Clarence was accepted for service, served one-and-a-half years and then was told by the Army that he couldn't performed his duties due to bad feet, and shouldn't have been accepted for service. Clarence had performed all his duties satisfactorily during the entire year and a half.

FCSD area veterans who likely received the Honorable Service Lapel Button included: William A. Appleford, Adelbert C. Bowen, Victor J. Chizlette, Vernon A. Closser II, Everett F. Clute, Harold F. Ford, Clarence F. Gaus, Elin G. Harte, Earl L. Herring, Earl J.J. James, Deane D. Pero, Merton C. Pero, Adelbert E. Perry, Albert R. Perry, Burt Swales, Lawrence L. Truesdell, Carl O. Turnstrom, Lyle A. Wilcox.

FOREIGN DECORATIONS

Many FCSD veterans also earned foreign decorations, both individually or as part of a unit. A few received special recognition. It is possible that others received the same decorations as those mentioned below, or other similar decorations, but documents available to the author did not mention the awards.

The **Philippine Liberation Medal** was awarded to at least 30 FCSD area veterans who served in units or on Navy vessels during the liberation of the Philippines. It is likely that many more also received the medal, but the discharge documents documenting the award were either destroyed in the St. Louis fire or were not available to the author by offices having the information. The area men known to be authorized to wear the medal were Mark L. Armstrong, Clifford H. Beardsley, Orson D. Beardsley, Warren E. Beardsley Jr, Lionel R. Briggs, Glenn E. Burgess Jr, John W. Collopy, John Curtis Crandall Jr, Arnold H. Eldridge, Horace E. Emmons, Lowell O. Fancher, Lowell B. Fox, Lynford S. Fox, Manfred C. Griggs, John R. Gillette, William C. Gelser, Erwin C. Howden, Walter D. Makowski, Robert F. Miller, Douglas F. Morris, Alanson C. Papke, Robert S. Preston, Alton A. Sylor, John L. Thomas, Roy G. Tillinghast, Hugh H. Van Burskirk, Mark K. Washburn, Harold W. Wass, Frank W. Wolfe Jr, and James A. Young.

At least seven FCSD area men were authorized to wear the **French Croix de Guerre**, including at least two **with Palm**. Palm indicates an additional award. The medal was awarded both to individuals and to units. The men were Warren H. Bennett, Lloyd D. Clark, Almond E. Fisher with Palm, Floyd K. Roberts, Glenn C. Wilday, Glenn F. Williams with Palm, and William C. Crandall.

Richard G. Beach and Leon R. Ellis were authorized to wear the **French Fourragere**.

Gerald F. Thomas was authorized to wear the **Belgium Fourragere**.

Lowell J. Wilcox was recognized in the **Order of the Day of the Army of Belgium.**

Lowell J. Wilcox was authorized to wear the **French Fourragere aux coueurs du ruban de la Medaille Militaire**, one of the rarest unit awards in the French military. Lowell's unit, the 26th Infantry Regiment, was recognized due to its participation at Normandy.

Ralph L. Alderman was authorized to wear the **Netherlands Orange Lanyard** when a Royal Decree issued by the government of the Netherlands awarded his unit, the 82nd Airborne Division, the **Military Order of William**, that country's oldest and most prestigious military award, for the 82nd participation in the Market Garden operations. A Ministerial Decree then authorized the wearing of the **Orange Lanyard**. The 82nd Airborne Division is the only US unit ever authorized to wear the Orange Lanyard.

Many men and women earned Letters of Commendations as well as shared in Unit Commendations. These commendations are discussed in the section of the book dealing with the veteran's service.

PART XIV - WHO THEY WERE

The Men and Women Who Served

Following is an alphabetical listing of men and women from the FCSD area who served in World War II and lived and/or worked in the FCSD area sometime during their lives. The information for each veteran is outlined below. The initials INA stand for Information Not Available. The initials NA stand for Not Applicable. Not all information is available for every veteran, and some information is only partially available. Most of these names were obtained from the Northern Allegany Observer (NAO). A few, especially those who moved to the area following the war, are from a work produced by the local History Club. Others were obtained from several individual sources such as relatives, draft records and census information.

Last Name, First Name, Middle Name/Initial , Prefix/Suffix - Military: Military Branch - Date Inducted-Enlisted/Where/Entry Rank - Principal Military Unit/Ship - Military Occupation/Highest Rank - Stateside Assignments and Dates or Months - Dates or Months Overseas/Total Time Overseas - Areas Served Overseas – Campaigns (Army, Army Air Force), Operations/Engagements (Navy, Marine Corps, Coast Guard), War Zones (Merchant Marines) - Killed in Action (KIA)/ When /Where/How - Wounded in Action (WIA)/ When/Where/How - Prisoner of War (POW)/ When/ Where Captured/ Where Imprisoned/When Released - Other war time Injuries or Illnesses/ What/When/Where - Discharge Date/Where - Medals and Awards (Where there is a year after a Medal, it means that the medal was awarded post war by an act of government, US or other.) - Other Relevant Information as Appropriate.

Civilian: Date of Birth/Where Born - Full names of parents (Mothers Maiden)/birth year/birthplaces - Names/birth year of Siblings - Full names/birth years/ birthplaces of maternal grandparents (Maiden Name of grandmother) - Full names/birth years/birthplaces of paternal grandparents (Maiden Name of Grandmother) - Education - Pre-war civilian occupation/employer - Post-war civilian occupation/employer - Full name/birth date/birth year of spouse (s)/Date(s) of Marriage(s) - Names/birth year of children - Date of Death - Where Buried - Proof of Residency - Personal Sources - Other, if Appropriate. (Some birth years obtained from census data may be off one year. All siblings and children may not be listed.)

Abbott, Paul James Military: US Army - 9/4/1941 (Served in the reserves starting in 1930) - 4168 AAF Base Unit (last unit), Lubbock, TX - Adjutant/Captain - Washington, DC, Mitchel Field, NY, France, Oklahoma, Texas/12 months - 42 months - Iceland, England – Normandy, Rhineland, Northern France - NA- NA - NA – Planters Wart, Right Foot, 1943. Removed. 16 days in hospital. - 2/28/1946 - American Defense Medal, American Campaign Medal, African Middle East European Theater Medal, 3 Battle Stars, World War II Victory Medal. Stayed in reserves post war. Rose to rank of Major. Civilian: 5/16/1905, Camden, NJ - Charles F. Abbott (1876 NY) & Lydia R. Weinnard (1884 NY) - Dorothea (1907 NY) - INA - James M. Abbott (1850 NY) & Sarah Ellen Hosey (1851 PA) – Southside High School, Elmira, NY, Syracuse University - Agricultural Teacher, Fillmore Central, Castile High School - Farm Representative, Active & reserve duty, USAF – 1. Ethel Sautermann 2. Hilda Anna Zylstra – Jane E. - 10/10/1982, Lafargeville, NY - Grove Cemetery, Jefferson County, NY - NAO, May, 1945 Fillmore - None.

Ackerman, Phillip George Military: US Army Air Corps 7/2/1942/Buffalo/Private - 438th Troop Carrier Group, 87th Troop Carrier Squadron - Pilot/First Lieutenant - Mitchell Field, NY, Blytheville, OK, Bennettville, NC/ 23 months) - 2/1/44 - 8/4/45 (18 Months) - England, Italy, France, Germany - Rome-Arno, Normandy, Southern France, Central Europe, Ardennes, Northern France, Rhineland - NA - NA - NA - NA - 10/11/1945, Ft. Dix, NJ - American Campaign Medal, Distinguished Unit Citation, European, African Middle East Theater Medal, World War II Victory Medal, Air Medal with 4 Oak Leaf Clusters, 7 Battle Stars - First Air Medal - D-Day Invasion. Civilian: 3/7/1920 NY - Glen F. Ackerman (1889 NY) & Fanny M.? (1894 NY) - Beatrice M. (1916 NY), Dorothea V. (1918 NY) Marie J. (1923 NY) - INA - INA - Fillmore Central, Class of 1938, Cornell University - Board of Education, Fillmore -Custodian/Student - INA - Audrey? - INA - 7/6/1997/Locust Grove, GA - INA - 1940 Federal Census - Allegany County War Service Record. Photo – NAO.

Alderman, Ralph Lincoln Military: US Army January11,1943/Pennsylvania/Private - 82nd Airborne Division Band - Clarinetist, Drummer, read, arranged music/PFC - Fort Bragg, NC, Others/19 months - 17 months - England, France, Holland, Germany - Ardennes-Alsace, Rhineland, Central Europe - NA - NA - NA - NA - 1/5/1946/Fort Dix, NJ - American Campaign Medal, European, African Middle East European Theater Medal, Good Conduct Medal, Army Airborne Glider Badge, World War II Victory Medal, 3 Battle Stars, Netherlands Military of William, Wearing of the Netherlands Orange Lanyard. Twin brother Robert also served. Civilian: 2/12/1923 NY - Arthur H. Alderman (1886 NY) & Grace Miller Dilcher(1891 NY) - Harvey (1921 NY), Robert (1923 NY), Donald (1926 NY) Leora (Dilcher Anderson -Half-sister) (1913 NY) - David Miller (1860 NY) & Barbara Harter (1861 NY) - A. Harvey Alderman (1822 NY) & Harriet T. Penfield (1843 MA) - Rushford Central School, Class of 1942 - Truck Driver, Repairman, Homestead, PA - Automobile Garage, Fillmore, LPN - Eva Smith (M 7/3/1948) - Lola (Hardy) - 12/30/2003 Fillmore, NY - White Cemetery, Rushford, NY – SSDI, Fillmore - Daughter Laura (Lola). Photo- Family.

Aldrich (born Burdick), Robert George (Bob) Military: US Army Air Corps - 1/04/1943/FT. Niagara/Private - 20th Air Force/497th Bomb Group/871st Bomb Squadron - Central Fire Control Gunner/Technical Sergeant - Maxwell Field, AL, Nashville, TN, Jefferson Barracks, MO, Sioux Falls, SD, Lowery Field, CO, Salinas, KS/22 months - 9 months - Isley Field, Saipan - 30 combat mission/Air Offensive, Japan, Eastern Mandates, Western Pacific - NA - NA - NA - NA - July, 1945 - American Campaign Medal, Distinguished Flying Cross, Air Medal with 3 Oak Clusters, Asiatic Pacific Theater Medal, WW II Victory Medal, 3 Battle Stars. Participated in first B-29 raid over Tokyo since Doolittle. Civilian: 12/17/1919 Warsaw, NY - Charles Burdick (184 NY) & Florence Aldrich (1886 PA) (Adopted Parents - Uncle, Landis D. Aldrich (1869 PA) & Maud E. Satchwell (1872 NY)) Landen Burdick (1908 NY), Frederick Burdick (1910 NY) - George D. Aldrich (1851 PA) & Agatha? (1852 PA) - INA - Fillmore Central, Class of 1938, University of Rochester - Farm Hand - Editor, Northern Allegany Observer - 1. Evelyn Ross 2. Sandra M. Carter - Steven, Marc - 11/4/1972 - Pine Grove Cemetery, Fillmore, NY - 1930 Federal Census Hume - None. Photo – NAO.

Allen, Charles Gustave Military: US Army - 1/5/1942/Ft. Niagara, NY/Private – likely 417th Bomb Squadron, 231st Army Air Force Base Unit - Aircraft Welder/PFC – Basic Training, Tech Training, Alamogordo, NM/3.5 months - 31.5 months - Puerto Rico - NA - NA - NA - NA - NA - 2/17/1946, Fort Dix, NJ - American Campaign Medal, Good Conduct Medal, WW II Victory Medal. Brother Jack Also served during the war. Civilian: 6/18/1924 NY - Charles H. Allen (1895 NY) & Emma H. Schlicht (1897 NY) -Clara M. (1922 NY), Jack E. (1926 NY) Emma L. (1928 NY) - Gustave Schlicht (1869 Germany) & Alveira Bronki (1867 Germany) - Charles J. Allen (1874 NY) & Isabelle M. Beaton (1875 Canada) - Buffalo School System, FCS - INA - INA – Esther Lee Mousseau (M 7/1/1950) - Curtis Brian – 8/26/1991, Buffalo - INA - 1940 Federal Census Hume - None.

Allen, Jack Edward Military: US Navy - 8/1944/Apprentice Seaman – *USS Muir (DE 770)* - Gun Handler/Gunners Mate 3rd. Class - Sampson Naval Training Center/4 months, Gunners Mate School, Sampson, NY - 1/45-10/47 at sea - Atlantic Ocean, Anti-Submarine - INA - NA - NA - NA - NA - 10/20/1947 - Navy Good Conduct Medal, American Campaign Medal, European African Middle East Theater Medal, Battle Star, WW II Victory Medal. Brother Charles also served during the war. Civilian: 12/19/1926 NY - Charles H. Allen (1895 NY) & Emma H. Schlicht (1897 NY) -Clara M.(1922 NY), Charles G. (1924 NY), Emma L.(1928 NY) - Gustave Schlicht (1869 Germany) & Alveira Bronki (1867 Germany) – Charles J. Allen (1874 NY) & Isabelle M. Beaton (1875 Canada) – Buffalo School System, Fillmore Central School - Oldenburg's Service Station, Lake Ontario Ordnance, Bell Aircraft - Hinde & Dauche Paper Co., G.M. Chevrolet, Rochester Gas & Electric Fillmore 35 years - Sally Ann Sink, married 5/26/1951 (Higgins) - Joseph, Nancy, Jeffrey, Connie, Marilyn - NA - NA - 1940 Federal Census Hume - Veteran Jack E. Allen. Photo- NAO.

Allen, Richard Leigh (Dick) Military: US Navy Air - 1/4/1943NY, NY/Aviation Cadet - VPB-1 - Naval Aviator/Ensign - Pensacola, FL, Quonset Point, RI, Elizabeth City, NC/maybe 17 months - maybe 17 months - NAS, Baltra Island, Galapagos, NAS, Canal Zone - None - NA - NA - NA – NA - October 29, 1945/NY, NY - American Campaign Medal, Asiatic Pacific Theater Medal, WW II Victory Medal. Civilian: 3/22/1922. PA - Ray L. Allen (1892 KS) & Alice H. Marshall (1894 PA) - Florence E. (1916 PA), Robert R. (1918 NJ), C. Eugene (1919 NJ), Edgar M. (1921 KS), Margaret R. (1924 PA) - William C. Marshall (1858 PA) & Sarah E. (Beck?) (1858 PA) - Joseph H. Allen (1865 PA) & Irene B. Harris (1867 PA) - Summerville High School, NJ, Alfred Agricultural and Tech School - RG&E, Fillmore, General Electric, Schenectady, NY – Marketing Engineer, NY Telephone Co. – 1. Helene Miller, 2. Shirley Paddock - David P., Jane P. - 11/26/2013, East Aurora, NY - Oakwood Cemetery, East Aurora - NAO, September, 1944 - None.

Amore, Edward Joseph Military: US Army - 6/10/1941/Ft. Niagara. NY/Private - INA - INA/SSgt - FT. Riley, KS, Camp Polk, LA/maybe 33 months – maybe 18 months (arrived back in US on 10/12/1945 - Germany - Central Europe - NA - NA - NA - NA - 10/19/1945, Fort Dix, NJ - American Defense Medal, American Campaign Medal, European African Middle East Theater Medal, likely one and possibly two battle stars, WW II Victory Medal. Civilian: 6/15/1913 NY - Joseph D. Amore (1877 Italy) & Christina Marsella (1875 Italy) - Philip R. (1900), Joseph (1902), Christina Margaret (1904,) Leo P. (1907), Anthony P. (1908), George A. ((1909), Anna R. (1911), Patrick R. (1912) - INA - INA - Eighth Grade, Cattaraugus County Public Schools - Laborer, Public Works Administration - Molder, Clerk, Meat Cutter, Olean, NY - 1. Lois P. Aldrich, (M7/31/1937) 2. Elizabeth F. Gleason - Linda, Sandra Kay (Conner), Eva M.- 4/1971/ INA - 1935, Short Tract per 1940 Census, 1940 Federal Census Fillmore, NAO November, 1941 Fillmore, Final Pay Record has Hume as Home Address - Nephew Calvin Ricketts. His parents came to the US in 1890.

Anderson, Leonard Warren Not FCSD. Parents lived in Centerville in 1940. Served with the Signal Corps, US Army, in Europe. Earned a Battle Star for the Northern France campaign. Brother Philip also served during the war.

Anderson, Philip Fourier Not FCSD. Parents lived in Centerville in 1940. Served as a Chaplin for the 457th Bomb Group. Brother Leonard also served during the war.

Appleford, William Raymond (Bill) Military: US Army Air Corps 6/17/1941/Buffalo/Private - INA - Adjutant /Lieutenant - Camp Croft, SC, Miami Beach, FL, St. Petersburg, FL, Denver, CO/28 months - NA - NA - NA - NA - NA - Serious Illness - 10/1943 - American Campaign Medal, WW II Victory Medal. Civilian: 9/13/1915 NY - Thomas William Appleford (1892 NY) & Olive Mae Miller (1893 NY) - Ruth (1914) - Maybe David & Kristan - INA - INA - Physical Education Director, Fillmore Central School - Athletic Director, Leroy Public Schools, Veterans Administration, Batavia - Margaret Ruth Gormley (M 8/1942 Mt. Morris) - INA - 2/11/1991 Charlotte, NC - Cremated - 1940 Federal Census Fillmore, NAO December, 1941 Fillmore – None. Photo – NAO.

Armstrong, Mark Lynhurst Military: US Navy - 6/8/1942/AS - *USS Palmer* - Assistant First Lieutenant/ Lieutenant (JG) - INA/16 months - 26 months - Hawaii, Kwajalein, Majuro, Saipan, Guam, Philippines, Manus, - Occupation of Kwajalein, capture & occupation of Saipan, Leyte Landings, Lingayen Gulf Landings - NA - WIA 1/7/1945 - NA - NA - 11/25/1945 - American Campaign Medal, Asiatic Pacific Theater, World War II Victory Medal, Purple Heart, Philippine Liberation Medal, 4 Battle Stars. Civilian: 12/18/1920 NY - Chauncey I Armstrong (1896 NY) & Ruth E.? (1898 NY) - Doris R. (1923 PA) - Alexander Armstrong (1837 NY) & Emma C.? ((1851 NY) - INA - Houghton, Class of 1942 - College Student – College Professor, Iowa - Bertha Reynolds (Born 1920/Married 1945) – John, Barbara, Karen - 7/11/1995, Johnson Co., Iowa - INA - 1940 Federal Census Houghton – None.

Arnold, Clair Edward Military: US Army -11/17/1943 Buffalo/Private – 205th Infantry Battalion, 63rd Infantry Training Regiment - Basic Training Instructor/Staff Sergeant - Camp Blanding, FL, FT. McClellan, AL/3 years - NA - NA - NA - NA - NA - NA - INA - American Campaign Medal, WW II Victory Medal. Civilian: 9/11/1925 NY - Leo Gilbert Arnold (1901 NY) & Olive Newell (1895 NY) - Laverne F. (1927 NY), Leora G. (1929) - Edward Newell (1858 PA) & Ana Stephens (1866 NY) - Floyd I. Arnold (1877 NY) & Iza Wakefield (1873 NY) - Fillmore Central, Class of 1943 - Student, Undertaker Training - Undertaker, Fillmore - Louise Tunningley (M 5/24/1945 Nunda, NY) - Sharon (1948), Claire (1950), Dana (1953), Laura (1962), Mark (1963) - September 3, 1970 Warsaw, NY Hospital - Pine Grove Cemetery, Fillmore - 1940 Federal Census Fillmore - Sister Leora Jean Arnold. Photo – Family.

Arthur (Edwards), Frances Janet Military: Women's Army Corps (WAC) - 9/1943/Private - INA - INA/Sergeant - Ft. Oglethorpe, GA, Richmond, KY/16 months - NA – NA - American Campaign - NA - NA - NA - NA - 1/31/1946 - American Campaign Medal, Good Conduct Medal, WAC Army Service Medal, WW II Victory Medal. Civilian: 6/24/1921, Stanley, NY - James Arthur (1884 Scotland) & Ida C.? (1887 NY) - William D. (1918), James Jr. (1920 NY)- INA - INA - INA - English Teacher, Fillmore Central - INA - INA - INA - INA - INA - NAO, November, 1943 Fillmore - Women's Military Service Memorial. Photo – NAO- School Yearbook.

Ashcraft, Robert Melvin (Bob) Military: US Navy - 8/23/1944/Apprentice Seaman - Naval Air Station Base Unit - INA/Coxswain - Sampson Naval Station, Naval Air Station, Atlantic City, Atlantic City Satellite Air Naval Base, Woodbine, NJ, Atlantic City Naval Base, Cape May, NJ, Philadelphia/22 months - NA - NA - NA - NA - NA - NA - NA - 6/23/1946, Lido Beach, NY - American Campaign Medal, World War II Victory Medal. Civilian: 6/2/1922 Newark, Ohio - Virgil Ashcraft (1897 Ohio) & Margaret? (1897 Kentucky) - Virginia (1917 Ohio), Clinton (1918 Ohio) - INA - INA - Fillmore Central, Class of 1941 - INA - INA - Roberta Holland - INA - 12/12/2008 Fillmore - Pine Grove Cemetery, Fillmore, NY - 1940 Federal Census Hume – None. Photo NAO.

Ayer, Bernard Purdy Military: US Army: 9/12/1944/Buffalo/Private - 133rd Infantry Training Battalion - Infantryman/Private - Camp Robinson, AR/4 months - NA - NA - NA - NA - NA - NA - 1/16/1945, Ft Dix, NJ - WW II Victory Medal. Brothers David & Ivan also served during the war. Civilian: 1926 NY – Roy J. Ayers (1887 NY) & Bertha Purdy (1887 Michigan) - Maynard (1907), Doris (1909), Iris (1910), Roderick (1912), Oliver (1914), Ivan (1921), David (1925) - Elbert A. Purdy (1857 NY) & Elizabeth M.? (1859 Ohio) - Joseph W. Ayer (1838 NY) & Sarah E. Vreeland (1843 NY)- Fillmore Central - Carpenter - Pump Mechanic/Welder, Ashland Oil - Katherine Humphrey - Judy, Patricia (Smith) - March 3, 1983, Buffalo - Elm Lawn Cemetery, Tonawanda, NY - 1930 Federal Census Hume - Daughter, Judith Ayer. Photo – School Yearbook.

Ayer, Carl J. (MI only) Jr. Military: US Army. The NAO reported in March 1944 that a Carl Ayer of the Merchant Marines was home on leave visiting his parents, Mr. and Mrs. Charles Ayer and family. It again reported Carl Ayer of the Merchant Marine home on furlough in January 1945. No Carl Ayer has been located in any FCSD area census. The 1920 census for Buffalo does contain a Carl Ayer with a father named Carl. It is possible that a Carl Ayer, Senior and his wife were living in Fillmore by 1944, but that their son was not and had never lived there. The National Maritime Service was unable to locate any information on a Carl Ayer. It is possible that Carl did work aboard a merchant ship but did not have a record of service because he had never been issued a Merchant Marine Document or a Certificate of Identification. Many positions aboard merchant vessels did not require such credentials. However, Carl J. Ayer Jr. of Buffalo, son of Carl A. Ayer did serve with the US Army during World War II. He entered on June 2, 1942 and was discharged December 15, 1945.

A Charles Ayer of Buffalo, who apparently had a second home in Wiscoy, did not have a son named Carl. He did have a son named Charles whose middle name was Herbert. Charles Herbert did serve in the Merchant Marine, but by January of 1945 he was in the US Army. It may be that Carl Ayer was a relative of the Ayer family of Wiscoy and was merely visiting in the area. It is also possible that NAO was referring to Charles Herbert Ayer Jr. (See Below.)

Ayer, Charles Herbert Jr. Military: US Army - 7/27/1944/Buffalo/Private – Headquarters Company, US Forces Austria - General Clerk/Technician 5 - INA/8 months 2 weeks - 16 months 1 week - France, Italy, Austria - Central Europe - NA - NA - NA - NA - 8/22/1946 - American Campaign Medal, Good Conduct Medal, European African Middle East Campaign Medal, One Battle Star, Army Occupation Medal, Germany Clasp, Combat Infantry Badge, 1947 Bronze Star, World War II Victory Medal. Charles also served two years in the Merchant Marines during the war, probably from 1941 to 1943. Civilian: 4/29/1925, Buffalo - Charles H. Ayer (1904 NY) & Ruby E. Williams (1909 NY) - Edith (1928 NY), Doris (1919 Y), Donald - Lawrence W. Williams (1882 NY) & Jennie Alvord (1884 NY) - Herbert Ayer (1872 Maine) & Christina? (1880 Canada) – Lancaster, NY School System - Student - Salesman, Prudential Life Insurance - Karoline S. Steininger - Clarke C., Clyde C. - 11/28/1997, East Aurora, NY - Griffin Mills Cemetery, Griffin Mills, NY - NAO, February, 1945 - Robert L. Goller, East Aurora, NY Town Historian.

Ayer. David Norbert (Dave) Military: US Army Air Corps - 3/1/1943/Ft. Niagara/Private - 9th Air Force, 386th Bomb Group (Medium), 552nd Bomb Squadron - Top Turret Gunner, Radio/Staff Sergeant - Tyndall Field, FL, Barksdale Field, LA, Lake Charles, LA, Hunter Field, GA/19 months - 12 months - England, France, - Normandy Campaign, Northern France, Rhineland, Ardennes-Alsace - NA - NA - NA - NA - 9/1945 - American Campaign Medal, Presidential Unit Citation, Air Medal with Oak Leaf Cluster, European, African, Middle East Theater Medal, WW II Victory Medal, 4 battle stars. Brothers Bernard & Ivan also served during the war. Completed 46 missions. Member of Caterpillar Club. Civilian: 1924 NY - Roy J. Ayers (1887 NY) & Bertha T. Purdy (1887 Michigan) - Maynard (1907), Doris (1909), Iris (1910), Roderick (1912), Oliver (1914), Ivan (1921), Bernard (1926) - Elbert A. Purdy (1857 NY) & Elizabeth M.? (1859 Ohio) - Joseph W. Ayer (1838 NY) & Sarah E. Vreeland (1843 NY) - Fillmore Central, Class of 1942, Bryant & Stratton Business School, Buffalo - Farmer - Construction - Dorothy? - Kenneth - 1/12/2012/Merchantville, VA - Tonawanda Creek - 1930 Federal Census Hume - Son Kenneth Ayer, Mike Smith, B26.Com Internet Site, Trevor Allen, B-26 Com Internet site. Photo – National Archives.

Ayer, Ivan Roy Military: US Army Air Corps - 7/2/1942/Buffalo/Private - 9th Air Force, 394th Bomb Group, 587th Bomb Squadron - Flight Instructor, Flexible Gunner/Sergeant - Tyndall Field, Fl, McDill Field, Fl, Lake Charles, La, Hunter Field, GA/29 months - 11 months - England, France, Germany, Belgium, Holland - Ardennes-Alsace, Rhineland, Central Europe - NA - NA - NA - NA - 10/26/1945, Fort Dix, NJ - American Campaign Medal, European, Middle East Theater Medal, WW II Victory Medal, Good Conduct Medal, Air Medal with 3 Oak Leaf Clusters, 3 battle stars, likely Army Occupation Medal, Germany Clasp. Brothers Bernard & David also served during the war. Civilian: 9/21/1920 NY - Roy J. Ayer (1887 NY) & Bertha T. Purdy (1887 Michigan) - Maynard (1907), Doris (1909), Iris (1910), Roderick (1912), Oliver (1914), David (1924), Bernard (1926) - Elbert A. Purdy (1857 NY) & Elizabeth M.? (1859 Ohio) - Joseph W. Ayer (1838 NY) & Sarah E. Vreeland (1843 NY) - Fillmore Central, Class of 1938, Bryant & Stratton Business School, Buffalo - INA - Contract Analyst, General RR Signal - Genevieve - Susan - 3/26/2008, Rochester - Chili, NY - 1930 Federal Census Hume - Daughter Susan Ayer (Niggli), Mike Smith, B26.Com Internet Site, Trevor Allen, B26, Com Internet site. Photo – NAO.

Babbitt, David Meager (Dave) Military: US Army Air Corps - 9/2/1941/Buffalo/Private - 4th Operational Training Unit, 568th AAF Base Unit - AP Maintenance Technician/Master Sergeant - Ft. Niagara, NY, Jefferson Barracks, MO, Chanute Field, IL, Brownville, TX, Greenwood, MS/21 months - 29 months - Brazil - NA - NA - NA - NA - NA - 10/28/1945/Rome, NY - American Defense Medal, American Campaign Medal, Good Conduct Medal, Brazilian Air Crew Member Badge, 4 Overseas Bars, WW II Victory Medal. Civilian: 10/25/1926 - Grover Clair Babbitt, (1886 NY) & Emma V. Meager (1893 NY) - John S. (1919), Elsie J. (1922), Grover Clair. Jr. (1924), Edward E. (1926), Edward (1926), Florence (1929), Larry? - INA - Benjamin Franklin Babbitt (1854 NY) & Mary Fairolia Stephens (1858 NY) - Rushford High School, Class of 1940 - Farmer - Farmer, TV Repairs & Sales, Fillmore, Photographer - 1. Geraldine Penman, 2. Elsie Irene Kingsley (M 8/13/1960 Fillmore) - Donna L. (1947), Robert W. (1949) - 10/21/1999, Opelika, AL - Podonque Memorial, Rushford - 1930 Federal Census Rushford, SSDI, Houghton, NY - Wife Elsie I. Kingsley Babbitt, Family History from Virginia Aspell Babbitt. Photo – NAO.

Babbitt, Franklin Goodspeed Not FCSD. Military: Not US Naval Academy (1942 - 1945) Civilian: 1/9/1923 (NY) - Shirley D. Babbitt (1888 NY) & Grace Goodspeed (? NY) - Shirley, Jr. (1924), James (1925) - Benjamin Franklin Babbitt (1854 NY) & Mary Fairolia Stephens (1858 NY) - INA - US Naval Academy - INA - INA - Norma Weaver (NY) - NA - INA - INA - INA - Family History from Virginia Aspell Babbitt. (Probably not FCSD.)

Babbitt, Grover Clair Jr. Not FCSD. Military: US Navy Civilian: 9/10/1924 - Grover Clair Babbitt (1886 NY) & Emma V. Meager (1893 NY) - John S. (1919), David M. (1920), Elsie J. (1922), Edward E. (1926), Florence (1929) - Benjamin Franklin Babbitt (1854 NY) & Mary Fairolia (1858 NY) - INA - INA - INA - INA - Betty Haynes - Richard, Sandra, Grover Kenneth, Herbert Alan - 6/1/1998 South Dayton, Cattaraugus County - Rushford Cemetery - INA - Virginia Aspell Babbitt. (Probably not FCSD.)

Babbitt, James Charlton Not FCSD. Military: US Navy Civilian: 1925 (NY) - Shirley Dare Babbitt (1888 NY) & Grace Goodspeed (? NY) - Franklin (1923), Shirley, Jr. (1924) - Benjamin Franklin Babbitt (1854 NY) & Mary Fairolia Stephens (1858 NY) - INA - INA - INA - INA - Jean Miller (? PA) - James Jr., Bonnie, Robert - INA - INA - INA - Family History from Virginia Aspell Babbitt (Probably not FCSD.)

Babbitt, John Shirley Not FCSD. Military: US Army – Worked on a hospital ship. Civilian 1919 (NY) - Grover Clair Babbitt, (1886 NY) & Emma V. Meager (1893 NY) - David M. (1920), Elsie J. (1922), Grover Clair. Jr. (1924), Edward E. (1926), Florence (1929) - Benjamin Franklin Babbitt (1854 NY) & Mary Fairolia Stephens (1858 NY) - INA - INA - Shipping/Receiving Clerk - INA - Muriel Nolan - John, JR., Stephen, Susan - INA - INA - NAO February, 1941 - Family History from Virginia Aspell Babbitt. (Probably not FCSD.)

Babbitt, Kenneth Roderick (Rod) Military: US Navy - 1/101945/Buffalo, NY/AS - *USS Oracle (AM 103)/USS Adams DM 27)* - Radar Man Third Class - Sampson Naval Base, NY, Flight  Service School (Radar), VA. Beach, VA, Manchester, WA/11 months - 8 months - Hawaii, Japan, Taiwan, China- NA - NA - NA - NA - NA - August 10, 1945, Lido Beach, LI, NY - American Campaign Medal, Asiatic Pacific Theater Medal, WW II Victory Medal, Navy Occupation Medal - Asian Clasp, China Service Medal. Rod served during the Korean War from October 10, 1950 until August 6, 1951, aboard the USS Ault (DD -698) His father served on the USS St. Louis during World War I. Civilian: 9/9/1927 NY - Kenneth Kennedy* Babbitt (1896 NY) & Clarice I. Herman (1905 NY) - None - Joseph Herman 1868 NY?) & Isabelle? (1878 NY) - Benjamin Franklin Babbitt (1854 NY) & Mary Fairolia Stephens (1858 NY) - Fillmore Central, Class of 1945 - Student - US Postal Service - Virginia Aspell (Married 6/28/1952) - Gary Lynn (1957 NY) Gail Susan (1967 NY) - 1/17/1994 Fillmore - Podonque Cemetery, Rushford - 1930 Federal Census, Houghton, SSDI Fillmore - Wife Virginia Aspell Babbitt *(His father's original middle name was Comfort, but he disliked it. Changed it to Kennedy). Photo- Yearbook.

Babbitt, Shirley Dare Jr. Not FCSD. Military: US Army Civilian: 1924 NY - Shirley Dare Babbitt (1888 NY) & Grace Goodspeed (? NY) - Benjamin Franklin Babbitt & Mary Fairolia Stephens - INA - Rushford Central, Class of 1942 - INA - INA - NA - NA - INA - INA - INA - Family History from Virginia Aspell Babbitt. (Probably not FCSD.)

Babcock, Elmer Arthur Military: US Army 10/3/1942/Private - INA -?/TSGT - INA/7 months - 31 months - Australia, Philippines, New Guinea - INA - NA - NA - NA - NA - 10/27/1945, Fort Dix, NJ - Asiatic Pacific Theater Medal, Battle Stars, WW II Victory Medal. Civilian: 9/9/1907 PA - Maurice C. Babcock (1885 PA) & Calla T. Beeson (1887 WI) - Margaret L. (1910 PA), Helen (1911 PA), Maurice

(1912 PA), Alpha (1915 PA), Catherine (1917WI) - Calvin Benson (1861 WI) & Darah Page? (1865 Eng) - John R. Babcock (1860 PA) & De Etta H.? (1854 PA) - one-year high school - Truck Driver/Farm Mechanic - INA - Janette Howard - Etta Myers - Stepson Clyde Cromwell, Stepdaughters Etta Myers, and Ruth Gladhill - 9/26/1978 Nunda - Hunts Hollow Cemetery, Portage - NAO 12/1943 – None.

Baker, Calvin Floyd Military: The NAO reported in February of 1945 that Calvin was with the US Maritime Service and he was leaving for the west coast. His future address was to be in care of the Fleet Post Office. No other information has been located. The Maritime Service was first established under the Coast Guard. It trained men for maritime service. The Service taught navigation, engine operation and maintenance, and deck operations aboard training vessels that operated in hazardous waters subject to mines and attacks by German and Japanese submarines. The men were trained for the US Merchant Marine and US Army Transport Service. While no Calvin Baker from the FCSD area has been identified, there was a Calvin Baker from Warsaw who did serve with the Merchant Marines. Civilian: 3/5/1925/Warsaw, NY - Floyd B. Baker (1894 KS) & Florence A. Botts (1899 NY) - Bernice I. (1921 NY), Gerald R. (1921 NY), Shirley R. (1929 NY), Myron W. (NY), Walter Cass (NY) - William Calkins (1862 NY) & Myrtle E. Kelly (1871 NY) – Cornelius Baker (1854 NY & Ada E. Morgan (1864 NY) - Warsaw NY School System (8th Grade) - Warsaw Button Company - INA - Joyce A. Clark - Dale, Jerry Wayne - 8/6/1947, Perry, NY - Glenwood Cemetery, Perry – 1925, 1930, 1940 Federal Censuses, Warsaw. None.

Ballard, Generva Emelene Military: US Army Nurses Corps - 10/28/1942/Rushford/Lieutenant - 23rd

General Hospital - Nurse/Captain - Fort George Meade, MD, Camp Patrick Henry, VA, Hampton, Roads, VA/12 months - 28 months - French Morocco, Tunisia, Italy, France - Naples-Foggia, Rome-Arno, Rhineland - NA - NA - NA - NA - 2/6/1946, Ft. Dix, NJ - Meritorious Unit Citation (8/1/43 – 7/31/45), European, African, Middle Eastern Campaign Medal with 3 Battle Stars, American Campaign Medal, World War II Victory Medal, Service Lapel Button.. Civilian: 9/26/1912 NY - Frederick C. Ballard (1876 NY) & Jeanie D. Olthof (1889 NY) - Federica (1911 NY) - Abraham Lincoln Olthof (1865 NY) & Anna M. Dunlap (1836 NY) - Miles P. Ballard (1830 NY) & Fidelia M. Bingham (1836 NY) - Rushford Central, Houghton College - Nurse, Houghton Infirmary & Fillmore Hospital - Nurse - 1. John Theodore Hollenbach, 2. John Cosgrove - None - 6/24/1987, Warsaw, NY - Warsaw Cemetery - NAO, September, 1943, Fillmore – Rushford NY, Library. Photo – Rushford, NY Library.

Ballard, John Daniel Military: US Marine Corps - 11/3/1942/Private - 6th Marines, 2nd Marine Division

- Light Machinegun Crewman. Rifleman, Mortar Crewman/Sergeant - Parris Island, NC, Camp Lejeune, NC, San Diego, CA 3 months - 33 months - British Samoa, Guadalcanal, Tarawa, Saipan, Tinian, Okinawa - Capture and Defense of Guadalcanal, Tarawa, Capture and Occupation of Saipan, Tinian, Okinawa Gunto - NA - Wounded by shrapnel, temporarily blinded, Saipan - NA - Tonsils removed, Dengue Fever - 11/1/1945, Marine Corps Base, San Diego, CA - Presidential Unit Citation for Tarawa, Purple Heart, Occupation Medal, Asian Clasp, Asiatic Pacific Theater Medal, WW II Victory Medal, 5 Battle Stars. Civilian: 8/27/1925 (NY) - Lloyd E. Ballard (1906 NY) & Ellen Laura Ford (1907 NY) - Elbert L. (1927), Evelyn M. (1928), Laura J. (1930), Leona M. (1931), Elizabeth R. (1933), Virginia M. (1936), Frank W. (1937), Mary O. (1939), Fred R. (1941), Mable G. (1942), Joan E. (1944), Lloyd R. (1945), Ellen J. (1948) - INA - Elbert F. Ballard (1866 VT) & Carrie B. Whitcomb (1875 NY) - Fillmore Central School - Student, Comstock Canning Co. - Foreman, NYS Highway Department, School Custodian - INA - Laurel Louise Uphill - Elaine Carrie, Paul James, John Daniel, Jr., Barry Erwin - 9/12/1977 - Potterville, NY Cemetery - 1930, 1940 Federal Census Centerville - Sister Virginia M. Ballard (White), Wife? History of his service, Military documents provided by son Paul. Photo – NAO.

Barnett, Glenn Wilford Military: US Army - 7/15/1943/Private - 38th Construction Battalion - Driver for Company Commander &Communications Technician/Corporal - Camp Upton, L.I., Tombs Army Camp, GA, FT. Bliss, TX, Camp Crowder, MO/17 months - (4/44-9/45) 18 months - England, France, Holland, Germany - Normandy, Ardennes-Alsace (Battle of the Bulge), Rhineland, Northern France, Central Europe - NA - NA - NA - NA - 1/10/1946 – American Campaign Medal, European Middle East African Theater Medal, Normandy Campaign Participation Bronze Star, 5 Battle Stars, Army Occupation Medal Germany, World War II Victory Medal. Civilian: 4/4/1922 Massillon, Ohio - Clarence Henry Barnett & Lucy Minerva Miller - Gordon, Lucille, Allan (1937) - James Patton Miller (1860 TN) & Candy Plemons (1867 NC) -Henry Richard Barnett (1859 NY) & Della Ann Bateman (1857 NY) - Melton Bell High School, KS (1940), Houghton College (1941), Canisius College (1942), Houghton College - Riveter, Curtiss-Wright Defense Plant, Buffalo - Minister – Janice M. Gracely (M 1947) - Marilyn Ann - 1/31/2010, Florida - Mount Pleasant Cemetery, Houghton - NAO, 7/1943 - Brother Allen Barnett. Photo -NAO.

Barnett, Gordon Richard Military: US Navy Air - 1/29/1943 - Pilot, Torpedo Plane/Commander - Troy, NY RPI, Del Monte, CA, Waco, TX, Naval Air Station, Hutchison, KS, Barin Field, AL, Pensacola, FL, Fort Lauderdale, FL/INA (thru 9/2/1945, end of WW II) - NA (did not serve overseas during WW II) - NA - NA - NA - NA - NA - NA - Remained in service after war. Retired 10/31/1963 - American Campaign Medal, World War II Victory Medal. Civilian: 11/29/1923 - Clarence Barnett & Lucy Minerva Miller - Glenn,, Lucille, Allan (1937) - James Patton Miller (1860 TN) & Candy Plemons (1867 NC) -Henry Richard Barnett (1859 NY) & Della Ann Bateman (1857 NY) - Melton Bel High School, KS (1940), Houghton College, RPI, Troy, NY, Pepperdine University, CA - Student, Houghton College - Career, US Navy - Phyllis (11/22/1944, Divorced 1971), Elida (May 2, 1978) - Karen, (1943), Dennis (1946), David, Douglas Whitney (1948), Darla Joyce (1951) - 1/28/2014 - Ashes spread in Spain - NAO, March, 1945, Family moved to Houghton in March of 1940 per brother Allan - Brother Allan Barnett, Veteran Gordon Barnett (Gordon's book - "The Serendipities of a Mother's Prayers"). Photo – NAO.

Barney, George NAO reported in the December 1945 edition of the NAO, page 154, that Seaman 2nd Class George Barney, son of Frances Barney was visiting at home. No additional information on his service has been located. (Northern Allegany County Observes 1945 book. Prepared by The History Club.)

Barrett, John Emerson A October 1942 edition of the NAO, page 138, shows a John Barrett of Fillmore being called for induction on October 3. No additional information on his service has been located. (Northern Allegany County Observes 1945 book. Prepared by The History Club.)

Bates, Grover Alfred Military: US Marine Corps: 9/30/1942/Private - 2nd Marine Division, Tenth Marines - Artillery Forward Observer/1st LT - Parris Island, SC, Quantico, VA/ 23months - 19 months - Tarawa, Saipan, Tinian, Okinawa - NA - NA - NA - NA – 4/9/1946 - American Campaign Medal, Asiatic Pacific Theater Medal, Silver Star, 4 Battle Stars, World War II Victory Medal. Civilian: 6/4/1913/Elmira, NY - Grover Thomas Bates (1885 NY) & Meda B. Seaman (1885 NY) - Edwin S. (1917 NY), Jean 1929 NY) - Benjamin Seamon (1858 NY) & Ruth C. Bastian (sp) (1855 NY) - Thomas Bates (1854 NY) & Mary A. McGeniers (1855 NY) – Elmira High School/FCS (1932 Training Class), State Normal School, Geneseo, NY (1935), Buffalo State Teachers College, Class of 1940, M.S. Cornell University - Machine Operator, Aviation Corp. – School Principal - Evelyn Persons - Alan, Nelson, Ades - 4/30/1999, Broward, FL - Woodlawn Cemetery, Elmira, NY - NAO, December, 1942. Grover remained in the Marine Reserves after the war and rose to the rank of Colonel. Photo – National Archives.

Beach, Leslie Robert Military: US Navy - 9/1/1944/Buffalo/AS - Supplementary Radio Station, Hawaii

- Radioman 3Class/Seaman First Class - Samson Naval Base, Bainbridge, MD, Washington, DC/Approximately 9 months - Approximately 14 months - Hawaii - NA - NA - NA - NA – NA - 7/5/1946, Shoemaker, CA. - American Campaign Medal, Asiatic Pacific Theater Medal, World War II Victory Medal, Navy Unit Commendation. Brother Richard also served during the war. Civilian: 8/28/1926 Crystal Valley, MI - Harry R. Beach (1874 Iowa) & Eva May Wightman (1883 Iowa) - Gerald (1918 MI), Norman (1922 MI), Richard (1915 MI) - Elias Edwin Wightman (1837 NY) & Mary H. Granger (1845 Ohio) - Josiah H. Beach & Abbie T.? (1844 MI) - Houghton College, (BA), Wayne State University (MA), University Michigan (PHD) - Student - Psychology/General Motors Institute, Whitworth College, WA, Bowling Green University, OH - Carla? - Randy, Lisa, Michael - 9/7/2008 Holland, MI - Restlawn Memorial Gardens, Holland - 1940 Federal Census Houghton, Holland Sentinel, 9/7/2008, Holland, MI. Leslie attended a meeting of the Fillmore Rotary Club at which Staff Sergeant Alfred L. Colburn, home from Europe, was the main speaker, in August of 1945. Photo- NAO.

Beach, Richard Gordon Military: US Army - 7/23/1943/Private - 79th Infantry Division, 315th Infantry

Regiment, Company L, Third Battalion - Rifleman/Tech 5 - INA - INA - England, France, Germany - Normandy, Ardennes-Alsace, Northern France, Rhineland, Central Europe - NA - WIA, 10/27/44, France - NA - NA - 3/16/1946 - American Campaign Medal, Purple Heart, Bronze Star, Combat Infantry Badge, European, African Middle East Theater Medal, World War II Victory Medal, 5 Battle Stars, Distinguished Unit Award, French Fourragere, Army Occupation Medal, Germany Clasp. - Civilian: 9/4/1924 Michigan - Harry R. Beach (1874 Iowa) & Eva May Wightman (1883 Iowa) - Gerald (1918), Norman (1922), Leslie 1926 MI) - Elias Edwin Wightman (1837 NY) & Mary H. Granger (1845 Ohio) - Josiah H. Beach & Abbie T.? (1844 MI) - Student - NA - INA - Lucille? - Bradley, Sharon L. - 1/26/2010 Rochester, NY - Mt. Pleasant Cemetery, Houghton, NY - 1940 Federal Census Houghton - Son Bradley Beach. Photo – Yearbook.

Bean, Frank Harlan Not FCSD. Military: US Army Civilian: 9/6/1921 (NY) - Frank M Bean (1886 NY) & Lena J.? (1889 NY) - Donald F. (1910), Alton C. (1913), Clifford (1915), Mamie (1917) - INA - INA - INA - INA - Foreman, Construction - INA - INA - 9/22/2001 Castile - La Grange Cemetery- INA – None.

Beardsley, Clifford Harlen Military: US Army - 2/3/1943/Buffalo/Private - Hd. & Service Company, 27th Engineer Construction Battalion - Power Shovel Operator/Technician, 3rd Grade - ?, Fort Knox, KY/18.5 months - 16.5 months - New Guinea, Philippines, Japan - New Guinea , Southern Philippines, Luzon - NA - NA - NA - NA - 1/14/1946/Fort Knox, KY - American Campaign Medal, Asiatic Pacific Theater Medal, Good Conduct Medal, Philippine Liberation Medal with Battle Star (Philippine Government), 3 US Battle Stars, Philippine Presidential Citation, Army Occupation Medal, Japan Clasp. Father Willis served during World War I with 3 different Army regiments. He was overseas from 9/8/1918 until 6/21/1919. His great grandfather Willis W. Beardsley, served with Company D, 4th NY Heavy Artillery during the Civil War. Civilian: 10/17/1923, Pike, NY - Willis E. Beardsley (1894 NY) & Ethel Fayhe (1906 NY) - Bonalyn B. (1925 NY), Harold W. (1927 NY), Monica F. (1928 NY) - William Faye (Northern Ireland) & Benita? (NY) - Reuben Beardsley (1862 NY) & Flora (likely Baker) (1870 NY) - Pike High School - Machine Operator - Appliance Technician, RG&E, Fillmore - Dorothy Schlicht - David, Christian, Craig - 5/3/2007, Bolivar (Wellsville Hospital) - Alger Cemetery, Hume - May 5, 2007 Bolivar, NY. Obituary, Daughter Christian Beardsley Evans.

Beardsley, Fred Lewis Military: US Navy - 2/29/44/AS/Dunkirk, NY - USA Navy Base 3505 (Biak Island, NG), US Navy Base (Manila, Philippines) - Construction/Seaman 1C - Great Lakes. IL, US Naval Construction Training Center, Williamsburg, VA/5 months 2 weeks - 15 months - New Guinea,

Philippines – Western New Guinea Operation, Luzon Operation - NA - NA - NA - NA - 11/19/1945, Sampson, NY - Asiatic Pacific Theater Medal, World War II Victory Medal - 2 battle stars. Civilian: 3/22/1912, NY - Frank Beardsley (1885 NY & Lois Clark (1886 NY) - Myrtle M. 1908 NY, Violet M. 1910 NY - Fred G. Clark (1862 NY & Julia E.? (1864 NY) - Arcade Public School, NY - Farm Laborer, American Brass Company - INA - Ruth E. Davis - E. Arlene, Jeannette, Joyce - 9/28/1963 - Bates Cemetery, Centerville, NY – Post War Centerville, Buried Centerville.

Beardsley, John Walter Jr. Military: US Army - 3/21/1944/Private – 265th Infantry Regiment, 65th Infantry Division, 47th Infantry Regiment, 9th Infantry Division - Scout/PFC - Camp Wheeler, GA, Ft. Benning, GA, Camp Shelby, NC/10 months - 17 months - France, Germany - Rhineland - NA - WIA 3/17/1945 - NA - NA - 5/22/1946 – American Campaign Medal, Purple Heart, European, African, Middle East Theater Medal, one battle star, Combat Infantry Badge, Distinguished Unit Citation (3/18-19, 1945, Action in Germany), World War II Victory Medal, Army Occupation Medal, German Clasp - Stationed at Dachau in 1945. Civilian: 9/29/1920 - John H. Beardsley (1881 NY) & Maude Sumeriski (1882 NY) - Bryon (1910 NY), George (1912 NY), Florence (1914 NY), Jean (1916 NY), Wilma (1917 NY), Gerald (1926 NY - Benjamin Sumeriski & Alice King - Alfonso W. Beardsley (1848 NY) & Hannah Moore (1840 NY) - Fillmore Central School, Pike Seminary - Farm Hand, RG&E - Farmer - Blanche Alice William (M10/10/1943) - John, Cathy, Beverly, Susan, Patricia - 4/15/1974, Fillmore - Alger Cemetery, Hume - 1930,1940 Federal Census Hume - Wife Blanche Williams Beardsley, Son John. Photo- Family, NAO.

Beardslee (Beardsley), Orson Donald Military: US Army - 3/7/1942/Ft. Niagara, NY/Private - Battery  C, 165th Field Artillery Battalion - Gun Crewman, Cannoneer/Sergeant - Fort Lewis, WA, , Seattle, WA Debarkation Port, Fort Lawton, WA, Camp Gruber, OK, Fort Hood, TX (2 days), Fort Bragg, Camp Shelby, MS, Ft. Knox, KY NC/18 months - 28 months - Aleutian Islands (Dutch Harbor, Attu) , Philippines (Luzon, Miami) - Aleutian, Southern Philippines - NA - NA - NA - NA - 12/28/1945, Ft. Knox, KY - American Campaign Medal, Asiatic Pacific Campaign Medal, Good Conduct Medal, World War II Victory Medal, Philippine Liberation Medal, 2 Battle Stars. Civilian: 9/6/1919, Hume, NY - Albert Beardslee (1885 NY) & Elizabeth Baldwin (1895 NY) - Gladys (1913 NY), Ernestine (1923 NY), Albert Jr. (1925 NY) - INA – Moses Beardslee ((1860 NY) & Nancy? (1862 NY) - Fillmore Central - Farmer - Farmer - INA - Linda (Christ) - NA - NA - 1930 Federal Census Hume - Daughter Linda. Photo – NAO.

Beardsley, Robert George (Bob) Military: US Navy - 6/28/1943/Olean - Naval Medical Corps/*LST 837*  - Ambulance Drive, Coxswain/S1C - Sampson Naval Station, Norfolk Naval Base. Pittsburgh Naval Barracks, New Orleans Naval Facility/ 13 months - 19 months - Cardiff, Wales, Hawaii, Eniwetok, Ulithi, Okinawa, Manus, Russell Islands, Tulagi, Noumea, China - Okinawa - NA - NA - NA - 11/1945 (Sick or Injured) - 2/1/1946 - American Campaign Medal, European African Middle Eastern Theater, Asiatic Pacific Theater Medal, WW II Victory Medal, Navy Occupation Medal, Asian Clasp, China Service Medal, One Battle Star. Civilian: 1926 (NY) - Orson Beardsley (1901 NY) & Helen Lowry (1903 NY) - Mary Jean (1930) - INA - George Beardsley (1861 NY) & Mary? (1866 NY) - Fillmore Central - INA - INA - Helen? - INA - INA - June 25, 1987, Martin County, FL - INA - 1920, 1930 Federal Census Hume – None. Photo – NAO.

Beardsley, Warren Elmer Jr. (Mike) Military: US Navy 11/17/1943/Buffalo/AS - *USS Currituck (AV 7)* - Machinist Mate/S2c - Sampson Naval Base/7 months - 21 plus months - Pacific Fleet - Luzon Operation, Leyte Operation - NA - NA - NA - NA - INA - American Campaign Medal, Asiatic Pacific

Theater Medal, China Service Medal, Navy Occupation Medal, Asian Clasp, World War II Victory Medal, Philippine Liberation Medal, 2 Battle Stars. Civilian: 6/12/1924 - Warren Elmer Beardsley (1903 NY) & Ella J. Cromwell (1902 NY) - John (1921), Gordon C. (1927), Betty A. (1929), Harlan (1931), Marjorie H. (1935) – Elmer G. Beardsley (1860 NY) & Cora C. ? (1876 NY) - INA - INA - INA - 1. Winifred Williams 2. Maxine Bailey - INA - Barbara, Joanne, Danell - 3/13/2009 - Oakland Hill Cemetery, Portage - 1940 Federal Census Hume – None.

Benjamin, Edwin Delos (Ed) Military: US Army Air Corps -9/26/1942/Lieutenant - Corps of Engineers
 - Engineer/Major (Post War) - PA Ordnance Works, Williamsport, Herrington Air Field, KS, Chico Air Field, CA/43 months (9/42-3/46) - NA (Post War 3/46-5/47) - NA (Guam, Saipan, Tinian) - NA - NA - NA - NA - NA - 8/5/1947 - American Campaign Medal, World War II Victory Medal - Wife Ruth E. Langdon was an Army Nurse who served at West Point, Camp Kilmer, NJ and Saipan from June, 1942 to February,1946. Civilian: 5/17/1910 - Frederick Houghton Benjamin (1868 NY) & Anna Van Dyke (1874 NY) - None - INA - INA - Fillmore Central, Class of 1929, Houghton College, Rensselaer Polytechnic Institute, Troy, NY - US Geological Survey, US Department of Agriculture, US Engineer Department - INA - Ruth E. Langdon (Mar. 2/10/1945) - INA - 1920, 1930 Fed Cen Hume - Allegany County War Service Record. Photo – NAO.

Benjamin, George Lee Not FCSD. Military: US Navy - 9/10/1941/Olean/AS - *USS Denebola, USS Markas, USS New Mexico, USS Sloat* - Coxswain, Bosum Mate/SIC - Portland, ME, USS Denebola/Est. 24 months – Estimated 31 months (These estimates are for his entire service which ran from September 1941 to April 1946.) - Hawaii, Aleutians, Majuro, Eniwetok, Marshall Islands, Ulithi, Caroline Islands, Saipan, Guam, Iwo Jimi, Shanghai - NA - NA - NA - NA - April, 1946 – American Campaign Medal, Asiatic Pacific Theater Medal, World War II Victory Medal. Family lived in area, especially Belfast, in early 1900's. Moved to Bradford, PA area. Likely returned to area in early 1940's. The NAO reported that George was "home" for a few days in April,1942. He was killed in an automobile accident during another leave in April 1946. He is buried in White Cemetery in Rushford.

Benn, Richard Charles (Doc) Not FCSD. Military: US Army - 2/4/1943/Private - Third Army, Light Tank Division. Richard also served with the New York National guard, 27th Recon. Company. Civilian: 1924 - Charles L. Benn (1903 NY) & Gladys B.? (1898 NY) - None -? & Mary M.? (1886 England) - INA - INA - INA - INA - INA - INA -INA - INA - INA – None. His parents lived in Fillmore for many years. His Dad worked at the Fillmore Market Basket and part-time at the Fillmore Hotel.

Bennett, Warren Harding Military: US Army - 9/17/1942/Buffalo/Private - Battery ?, 532 Anti-
 Aircraft Artillery Automatic Weapons Battalion/Company E, 473 Infantry Regiment, 92 Infantry Division, Co. l, 349th Infantry Regiment, *8th Infantry Division - Rifleman/PFC - New York City/6 months - 31 months - North Africa, Italy - Tunisia, Naples-Foggia, Rome-Arno, North Apennines, Po Valley - NA - WIA 4/15/1945(Back Wound) - NA - NA - 9/26/1945, Ft. Dix, NJ - Purple Heart, Good Conduct Medal, European, African, Middle Eastern Theater Medal, World War II Victory Medal, Combat Infantry Badge, Bronze Star (1947), 5 Battle Stars, French Croix de Guerre. Civilian: 3/16/1921 (NY) - George H. Bennett (1871 NY) & Neva Buchholz (1888 NY) - Robert (1913 NY), Clifford (1915 NY), Newton (1917 NY), Charles (1918 NY), Edna (1924 NY), Helen (1927 NY), Harold (1929 NY), Lucille (NY) - Charles Buchholz (1857 Germany) & Celestia.? (1867 NY) - Horace Bennett (1849 NY) & Emma? (1852 NY) - Fillmore Central - Farm hand - INA - Marie Clark (M 6/14/1947) - Walter (NY 1949), Karen (Truax) (NY 1950), Victoria (Decker) (NY 1952), Frank (NY 1953), Arthur Clark

(NY 1956) - 7/9/1986, Watkins Glen, NY - Montour Falls Cemetery - 1930 Federal Census Hume - Son Walter L. Bennett, Daughter Victoria (Decker). Photo – NAO.

Bentley, Royden Fuller Military US Army - Enlisted 5/25/1943, entered 6/8/1943/Buffalo/Private - 20th

Base Post Office - ?/PFC, Tec 5 - INA/6 months - 24 months - North Africa, Italy, France, Belgium - Rome Arno Campaign, Rhineland Campaign - NA - NA - Sick in 182nd Station Hospital, Naples at least 7/13-7/18 - NA - 11/18/1945 - European, African, Middle East Theater Medal, Two Battle Star, WW II Victory Medal. Paternal Grandmother Victoria A. Randall Bentley member of Sons of the American Revolution. (Descendant of Captain Elishama Tozer who served with the Seth Warner Regiment of the State Militia, better known as the "Green Mountain Boys." Civilian: 5/7/1906, Fillmore, NY - Frederick F. Bentley (1879 NY) & Elmina L. Fuller (1881 NY) - Martha V. (1905 NY), Marian D. (1908 NY), Doris L. (1913 NY), Merlin C. (1918 NY) - Fred Fuller (1851 NY) & Martha E.? (1851 NY) - Ira Bentley (1853 NY) & Victoria A. Randall (1854 NY) - FCS, Class of 1921 - US Post Office - US Post Office, Railroad Service - Gertrude Roche - None - 8/13/1957, Heart Attack, New York City, but lived in Buffalo- Elm Lawn Cemetery, Tonawanda, NY - 1910, 1920 Federal Census Granger. Photo – NAO.

Birch, Larry Harmon Not FCSD. Military: US Navy - 6/5/1944/Apprentice Seaman - *USS Cossatot*, 10 others - Electronics Technician Mate/Seaman 1Class -Probably Sampson Naval Base, Chicago Naval Training School /18 months - 6 months - Okinawa. Japan - None - NA - NA - NA - NA - June, 1946. Civilian: 10/11/1924, Chicago, IL - Frank R. Birch & Zola Kinnison - Marilyn, Marion - INA - INA - Houghton Academy, Houghton College, University of Michigan - Student - Medical Physician, Cardiologist - Robert Chess, 1946 - Richard Craig, Robert Allen, Gregory Lynn, Stephen - 5/7/2009, Jacksonville, FL - Jacksonville National Cemetery - NAO, June, 1944.

Black, Ralph Evert Military: US Army - 2/5/1942, Entered 6/3/1942/Private – Army Service Forces, Ninth Air Force - INA/ SSgt - Possible Bolling Field, DC/5.5 months - 44.5 months - Egypt, England, France, Germany - Egypt-Libya, Air Offensive Europe, Tunisia, Sicily, Naples-Foggia, Normandy, Northern France, Rhineland, Ardennes-Alsace, Central Europe - NA- NA - NA - NA - 3/7/1946, Camp Atterbury, IN – American Campaign Medal, European African Middle East Theater Medal, WW II Victory Medal, US Army Occupation Medal, Germany Clasp, 10 Battle Stars. Civilian: 7/11/1919, Knoxville, Tennessee - Ernest W. Black (1891 SC) & Margaret Marie Caston (1892 SC) -Watson C. (1913 SC), Melvin (1916 NC), Bedford W. (1918 NC). Clara A. (1922 NC), Martha E. (1923 NC) - Wilbur Fisk Carson (1861 SC) & Mary Christine Thomas (1861 SC) - Frank Black (1856 SC) & Mattie C. Likely Culp (1868 SC) - Houghton College - College Student - INA - INA - INA - 2/15/1989 - INA - 1940 Federal Census Houghton.

Blakeslee, Clifford (NMN) Military: US Army - 10/18/1943/Buffalo/Private - INA - INA - INA - Total Service 16 months - England - INA - NA - NA - NA - NA - 2/16/1945 - American Campaign Medal, WW II Victory Medal Others? Father Orley Blakeslee registered for WW I. Brother Leonard also served during the war. Civilian: 6/3/1925, Centerville, NY - Orley L. Blakeslee (1892 PA) & Lelah Dexter (1893 PA) – Lawrence (1912 NY), Lucille (1913 NY), Raymond (1916 NY), Leonard (1920 NY), Robert (1922 NY), June E. (1932 NY), Orley (1934 NY) - John W. Dexter (1867 PA) & Lena? (1881 NY) - Elmer M. Blakeslee (1859 PA) & Doreleska Stoker (1862 PA) - Grammer School - Farm Hand for Father - Town of Boston Highway Department – 1. Evelyn I. Ludlow (M 7/14/1945, Hamburg, NY), 2. Angeline Miliotto - Clifford R, Lonnie - 2/5/2002, Eden, NY - Evergreen Cemetery, Eden, NY - Centerville WW II Honor Roll, NAO, 1943.

Blakeslee, Leonard Orley Military: US Army - 2/13/1943/Buffalo/Private - 218th Quartermaster Salvage and Repair Company - Salvage Handler/Technician 4th Grade - INA/25 months - 2 months - Naples, Italy, (Mediterranean Theater of Operations, Peninsula Base Section) - NA - NA - NA - NA - 2/19/1946, Fort Dix, NJ - American Campaign Medal. Good Conduct Medal, European African Middle East Theater Medal, World War II Victory Medal. Honorable Service Button. Leonard served with the NY National Guard in Company C, 65 Regiment, from 5/13/1941 to 9/4/1941. Father Orley Blakeslee registered for WW I. Brother Clifford also served during the war. Civilian: 5/29/1920, Buffalo, NY - Orley L. Blakeslee (1892 PA) & Lelah Dexter (1893 PA) - Lawrence (1912 NY), Lucille (1913 NY), Raymond (1916 NY), Robert (1922 NY), Clifford (1925 NY), June E (1932 NY), Orley (1934 NY) – John W. Dexter (1867 PA) & Lena? (1881 NY) - Elmer M. Beardsley (1859 PA) & Doreleska Stoker (1862 PA) - Grammar School - Chemical Industry/Chemical Mixer – Airco Co, Arcade, NY - Jean L. Brown (2/21/1947, Hamburg, NY) - Daniel, Susan, Connie, Rose, Julie - 5/26/ 1991, Farmerville Station - White Cemetery, Rushford, NY - Centerville WW II Honor Roll.

Bleistein, Leland Warren Military: US Army Air Corps - INA (Reenlisted 8/11/1945)/Private - INA - Ball Turret Gunner /PFC - Ft. Dix, NJ, Keesler Field, MS, Williams Field, Kingman, AZ/? - NA - NA - NA - NA - NA - NA - NA - INA - American Campaign Medal, World War II Victory Medal. Leland enlisted in Company I, 21 Regiment, NY National Guard on 8/16/1943. Civilian: 6/30/1926, Perry, NY - Leonard Bleistein (1897 NY) & Viola E. Tucker (1900 NY) - John (1928 NY) - John D.W. Tucker (1874 NY) & Minnie M. ? (1881 NY) - Peter Bleistein (1857 NY) & Frances A. (Likely Clark) (1861 NY) - FCS - Sheet Metal Worker - INA - Jeanine Sprowl- INA - 3/1/1995 Clifton Springs, NY - INA - 1930 Federal Census Hume - Brother John Bleistein.

Bleistein, Wilfred Carl (Woody) Military: US Army - 6/3/1942/Buffalo/Private - INA - Clerk/Sherman  Tank Mechanic/ Corporal T5 - Camp Croft, SC, Camp Kilmer, NJ, Seattle, Camp Haan, CA, Camp Roberts, CA, Ft. Knox, KY/6/42- 12/1945 - NA - NA - NA - NA - NA - NA - NA - 12/21/1945 - American Campaign Medal, World War II Victory Medal. Civilian: 6/2/1913, NY - Clayton Bleistein (1879 NY) & Edith H. Wilklow (1885 NY) - Alvin (1910 NY), Harold (1912 NY), Frances (1917 NY) - George Wilklow (1853 NY) & Dedamona Laselle (1851 NY) - Peter Bleistein (1857 NY) & Frances A. Clark (1861 NY) - FCS, Class of 1933 - Motor Vehicle Repair - INA - INA - INA - 8/4/1973, Joplin, MO - Ozark Memorial Park Cemetery, Joplin - 1920 Federal Census Hume, 1930, 1940 Federal Census Fillmore - None. Wilfred was a direct descendant of William Brewster of Plymouth Colony who came to the United States aboard the Mayflower. Photo – NAO.

Bloomster, James Gilbert (Gil) Military: US Army - 3/8/43/Fort Niagara/Private - 491st Port Battalion  - Office Clerk/ Corporal, Tech 5 - Ft. Niagara, Indiantown Gap, PA, San Francisco/4 months - 28 months overseas - Oro Bay, New Guinea/8/43-8/45 - New Guinea Campaign - NA - NA - NA - NA -11/8/1945 Ft. Dix, NJ - One Battle Star, Asiatic Pacific Theater Medal, World War II Victory Medal. - Brother Raymond E. also served. Civilian: 10/1/1909, PA - James H. Bloomster (1881 PA) & Nellie Marie Shelander (1886 PA) - Evelyn M. (1905 PA), Edna L. (1907 PA), Erma S. (1911 PA), Raymond P. (1915 PA) - Frank A. Shelander (1861 Sweden) & Amanda L. Horknett (1862 Sweden) - John Bloomster (1851 Sweden) & Hannah likely Olson (1853 Sweden) - McKean Co., PA Public Schools, Smethport High School, PA, Class of 1928, Bryant & Stratton Business Institute (Advanced Accounting) - Manager, Fillmore Market Basket - President, State Bank of Fillmore, President, Allegany County Bankers Association - Onalee M. Yeager (M 4/1/1934 East Bloomfield, NY) - Melanie - 2/1/1985, Bradenton, FL - Pine Grove Cemetery, Fillmore, NY - 1940 Federal Census Fillmore - Daughter Melanie Bloomster Samsel. Photo – NAO Family.

 **Bloomster, Raymond Edward (Red)** Military: US Army Air Corps - 9/3/1942/Buffalo/Private - 48th Air Base Squadron - Field Supply Clerk/Corporal – Fort Niagara, NY, INA/22 months - 18 months - France Field, Panama - None - NA - NA - NA -NA - 1/28/1946 - American Campaign Medal, WW II Victory Medal. Brother James Gilbert also served. Civilian: 5/30/1915, Crosby, PA - James H. Bloomster (1881 PA) & Nellie Marie Shelander (1886 PA) - Evelyn M. (1905 PA), Edna L. (1907 PA), James Gilbert (1909 PA), Erma S. (1911 PA) - Likely Frank A. Shelander (1861 Sweden) & Amanda L. Hoknett (1862 Sweden) - John Bloomster (1851 Sweden) & Hannah likely Olson (1853 Sweden) - Fillmore Central, Class of 1935 - Manager, Market Basket Stores Kane, PA, Andover & Fillmore, NY - Market Basket Company, RG &E, Fillmore - Mildred Maxine Burgess (M 6/15/1946 Houghton, NY) - None - 1/26/1995 Kane, PA - Mt. Pleasant Cemetery, Houghton, NY - FCS Graduate, 1935 - Nephew Jason Burgess. Photo – NAO.

 **Boehmler, Robert Graf** Military: US Army Air Corps - 6/3/1942/Private - 378th Army Air Force Band - Technical Sergeant - FT. Niagara, Miami Beach, FL, Atlantic City, NJ/approximately three years - NA - NA - NA - NA - NA - NA - NA- - INA - American Campaign Medal, World War II Victory Medal. Civilian: 2/2/1915 - Albert A. Boehmler (1877 NY) & Sarah E. Graf (1882 NY) - None – Henry Graf (1836 Germany) & Sarah ? (1846 Germany) – Fritz Boehmler (1833 Germany) & Elizabeth (probably) Pflug (1838 NY) - Lyons NY School, Ithaca College, Class of 1938 - Music Instructor, Fillmore Central – Music teacher, Palmyra Macedon School District, NY - NA - NA - 9/21/1998 Lyons, NY – Wayne Rural Cemetery - NAO, 1/1943 – Patricia Gorthy, Lyon's NY Heritage Society. Photo – Lyons, NY Heritage Society.

Bowen, Adelbert Charles Military: US Army Air Corps – 11/13/1942/Buffalo/Private - 56th Training Group - Trainee, likely Aircraft and Engine Mechanic/Private - Keesler Air Base, Biloxi, MS/10 months - NA - NA - NA - NA – NA - NA - NA - 9/9/1943 - American Campaign Medal, World War II Victory Medal. Civilian: 6/25/1916/NY - Allie C. Bowen (1893 NY) & Gertrude Trost (1896 NY) - Lillian T. (1918 NY) - Charles Trost (1858 Germany) & Phoeba? (1861 NY) – Samuel A. Bowen (1842 NY & Marian Akins (1845 NY) – Probably Belfast Central – Laborer on railroad - INA - NA - NA - 12/20/1957/Fillmore - Pine Grove Cemetery, Fillmore - 1940 Federal Census, Fillmore - Grandfather Samuel A. Bowen served with Co. A, 136th NY Infantry during the Civil War.

Briggs, Harold Clifford Military: US Army - Harold was called for a physical in October 1942. No further information concerning his military service has been located. It is likely that Harold did not serve. He was born in 1899. Civilian: 6/27/1899, Hume, NY - Stephen R. Briggs (1857 NY) & Eliza Grace Finnemore (1861 Canada) - Marvin (1887), Roy A. (1896 NY) - David G. Finnemore (1826 Eng) & Harriett Glidden (1831 Eng) - Charin Briggs (1820 NY) & Phebe Ann Dunbar (1827 NY) - FCS - Trackman, Penn RR - INA - INA - INA - INA - INA - 1930 Federal Census – None.

 **Briggs, Lionel Roy** Military: US Navy - 1/18/1944/Apprentice Seaman - *USS Alaska* - ?/Seaman 2 Class - Sampson Naval Base, NY, Newport News, RI, Brooklyn Naval Yard, NY, Philadelphia/5 months - 22 months - Philippines, Okinawa, Iwo Jima, Tokyo, Japanese Islands Minamidaito Okidaito, Korea, China - Iwo Jima, Okinawa Gunto - NA - NA - NA - NA - 5/1/1946/Lido Beach, NY - Philippine Liberation Medal, American Campaign Medal, Asiatic Pacific Theater Medal, 2 Battle Stars, World War II Victory Medal - Was aboard the *Alaska* when it was Commissioned, *Alaska* crossed the 180 meridian 2/1/1945 with permission of the Golden Dragon. Civilian: 11/14/1925/ Wiscoy, NY - Roy A. Briggs (1896 NY) & Lillian Belle? (1898 NY) - None - INA - INA - Fillmore Central (2 years high school) - Perry Knitting Mill - INA – 1. Bonnie Nevinger, 2. Gloria Perry - INA - 10/8/2001 Portageville - East Koy Cemetery - 1930 Federal Census Hume - None. Photo – NAO.

Brown, Franklin L Military: US Army - 9/4/1942, Buffalo, Private - Airborne Unit, Coast Artillery Battalion, Ant-Aircraft Automatic Weapons Battery - INA/Staff Sergeant - INA - Total service 33 months 2 weeks - Italy - INA - NA - 4/18/1944 (head wound caused by artillery shell fragments/compound fracture of first metatarsal bone) - NA - NA - 6/30/1945, Fort Dix, NJ - European African Middle East Theater Middle, American Campaign Medal, Purple Heart, Battle Star, World War II Victory Medal. Civilian: 7/6/1911 NY - Leo H. Brown (1887 NY) & Alice A. Hay (1887 NY) - Herbert (1915 NY), Anna (1913 NY), Alice (1924 NY) - Francis L Hay (3/1854 NY) & Luna Andress (Andrews) (5/1859 NY) - Franklin Brown (1835 NY) & Caroline N. Berry (1842 NY) - High School, Perry, NY, 2-years college - Farm Hand - INA - Mildred - INA - 4/14/1988, Wellsville, NY - Alger Cemetery, Hume, NY - Lived in Fillmore/Hume after war. – None.

Brown, Lyle Clarence Military: US Navy - 8/7/1943/Olean, NY/Apprentice Seaman - Navy V-12 Program/Ensign - Sampson Naval Base, NY, Texas A & M College, Louisiana Tech, La, University of Oklahoma, Amphib Base, CA/36 months - *USS LSM 463*, Service Squadron 3 (8/1946-5/1947), Pacific - NA - NA - NA - NA - NA - May, 1947 - American Campaign Medal, World War II Victory Medal, Navy Occupation Service Medal, China Service Medal. Lyle returned to the Navy in 1950 and participated in the Korean War, including the Inchon Landing, serving on ComServ Ron 3 staff aboard the *USS Piedmont* and the *USS Hector*. Leroy Thayer of Fillmore had served aboard the *Piedmont* during WW II. He served a total of 29 years on active and reserve duty. He retired as a Commander, Intelligence in 1972. Civilian: 8/26/1926 (Hume, NY) - Forrest J. Brown (1898 NY) & Laura Hoagland (1904 NY) - Ruth E. (1928 NY), Francis (1933 NY), Robert (1941 NY), James (1947 NY) - Clarence Hoagland (NY & Harriet Holly (NY) - John Brown (NY) & Emma Powell (NY) - Fillmore Central, Class of 1943, Louisiana Polytechnic Institute, University of Oklahoma (BA 1948) (MA 1952), Texas A&M College, University of Texas (PhD 1984) - Carpenter Gang, Erie Railroad - Political Science Professor (Mexico City College, Texas College of Arts & Industry, Wayland Baptist College, Baylor University) - Sylvia Sills (May 28, 1949, Crowville, LA) - Paul Roland (1959 TX), Gloria Ann (1957 Mexico), Alita Kaye (1950 TX) - NA - NA - 1930 Federal Census Hume, Allegany County War Service Record - Veteran Lyle C. Brown. Photo – Veteran.

Brueser, Llewellyn Rudolph (Jack) Military: US Army - Llewellyn served in the military after the end of World War II. The NAO reported that he had been called for induction in November of 1945. The Army enlistment records show his enlistment date as May 24, 1946 with a discharge date of 6/22/1947. The Wyoming County Veteran's Agency indicated that he was awarded the Word War II Victory Medal. Since eligibility for this medal ended 12/31/1945, it is likely that he was inducted in 1945, but did not report for duty until May of 1946. His brother William served during the war. Civilian: 9/8/1827 - Chester J. Brueser (1899 NY) & Laurel Histed (1896 NY) - June B. (Dumbleton) (1922 NY), William C. (1924 NY) - William R. Histed (1871 NY) & Sarah J. Grant (1873 NY) - Herman W. Brueser (1869 Ger) & Anna J. (maybe Robinson) (1875 NY) - FCS - Student - Maintenance Worker, Fisher-Price Toys - Phyllis Roblee - Gary, Jacquelin (Dimon), Cheryl (Anderson) - 3/1/1987, Mercy Hospital, Buffalo - Sandusky Cemetery - 1930 Federal Census Centerville – None.

Brueser, William Chester (Bill) Military: US Army - 7/24/1944/Buffalo/Private - 70th Infantry Division, 274th Infantry Regiment, 1st Battalion, Company A - Infantryman/PFC - INA - INA - France, Germany - Ardennes Alsace, Rhineland, Central Europe - NA - NA - NA - NA - INA - Combat Infantry Badge (Bronze Star 1947), European, African, Middle East Campaign Medal, World War II Victory Medal, 3 Battle Stars. Civilian: 5/22/1924, Centerville, NY - Chester J. Brueser (1899 NY) & Laurel Histed (1896 NY) - June B. (Dumbleton) (1922 NY), Llewellyn (1927 NY), Lois (NY) - William R. Histed (1871 NY) & Sarah J. Grant (1873 NY) - Herman W. Brueser (1869 Ger) & Anna J. (maybe Robinson) (1875 NY) – One-year high school, FCS - Farm Hand - INA – Charlotte Powell – Leith G. -

5/18/1963 Centerville, died from self-inflicted wounds -22 caliber rifle) - Bates Cemetery, Centerville - 1930 Federal Census Centerville – None.

Bucheister, William (NMN) Jr (Bill) Military: US Navy - 7/8/1943/AS/Buffalo - Navy Blimp Fleet Airship Wing (HEDRON) 4 Maceio, Brazil - INA/Seaman First Class – Sampson Naval Station, NY/13 months - 16 months - Maceio, Aratu & Fernando de Noronha, Brazil - None - NA - NA - NA - NA - 12/17/1945 - American Campaign Medal, WW II Victory Medal. William also served with the US Marine Corps from 1950 to 1952. Civilian: 2/25/1926 Olean, NY - William John Bucheister (1899 NY) & Linda M. Stevens (1897 NY) - None - William J. Stevens (1862 NY) & Mabel E. Bennett (1874 NY) - John Bucheister (1847 Germany) & Caroline (Carrie) likely Achilles) (1857 NY) - INA -Farm Hand - INA - INA (1945) - INA - 8/18/1989, Milton, LA - INA - 1930 Federal Census Houghton – None.

Burgess, Gene David (Dave) Military: US Army - 7/2/1942/Buffalo/Private - 1st Infantry Division, 6th  Armored Infantry Regiment, 1st Battalion, Company B - Infantryman/PFC - Ft. Bragg, NC, Walter Reed Hospital, Washington, DC/21 months - Ft. Bragg, NC, England, Scotland, Ireland, Algeria, Tunisia, Italy, Czechoslovakia - Algeria French Morocco Campaign, Tunisia Campaign - NA - WIA, 12/6, 1942, near Medjez, Tunisia - POW, Tunisia (captured by Germans), Italy (Caserta POW Hospital), Germany (Stalag 344, Lamsdorf, Silesia, Czechoslovakia (later Poland)) - INA - 11/2/1945, Walter Reed Army Hospital, Washington, DC - American Campaign Medal, European African Middle Eastern Theater Medal, Lapel Button, 2 Battle Stars, Combat Infantryman's Badge, Bronze Star (1947), Invasion Arrowhead (Oran, North Africa), Purple Heart, WW II Victory Medal, POW Medal (1985). Brother Glenn E. Jr. also served during the war. - Civilian: 11/22/1920 NY - Glenn E. Burgess (1889 NY) & Mildred P. Leet (1897 NY) - Glenda (1915 NY), Mildred M. (1916 NY), Glenn C. Jr. (1919 NY), R. Jack (1935 NY) - Frank Leet (1873 NY) & Madge Swethland (1878 NY) - Emeroy D. Burgess (1854 NY) & Emma B. Palmer (1862 Iowa) - Fillmore Central - INA - House Hershey Corporation, Buffalo - Myrtle Adams (Married 11/22/1945) - Nancy Jo (1946) - 1/31/1955, Fillmore, NY - Mt. Pleasant Cemetery, Houghton, NY - 1940 Federal Census Houghton - Daughter Nancy Jo Burgess (Gartenman). Photo – Family.

Burgess, Glenn Ellery Jr. (Bud) Military: US Army - 7/24/1944/Buffalo/Private - 737th Railroad  Operating Battalion - Station Agent/Telegraph Operator/Technician 4th Class - Fort Warren, WY, Camp Robinson, AR/7 months - 10 months - Philippines, Korea - Luzon Campaign - NA - NA - NA - Injured eardrum in a fall - December, 1945 - Asiatic Pacific Theater Medal, World War II Victory Medal, Philippine Presidential Unit Citation, one battle star. Civilian: 3/24/1919 NY - Glenn E. Burgess (1888 NY) & Mildred P. Leet (1897 NY) - Glenda (1915 NY), Mildred M. (1917 NY), Gene David (1921 NY) , Robert Jack (1936 NY) - Frank Leet (1873 NY) & Madge (Maggie) Swethland (1878 NY) - Emory D. Burgess (1854 NY) & Emma B. Palmer (1862 Iowa) - FCS - Manager NEC - INA - Virginia Eldridge - Judith, Glenn E. III, Robert J. - 9/6/1990 - Alger Cemetery, Hume - 1940 Census Fillmore – None. Photo – NAO.

Burlingame, Clarence Elmer Not FCSD. Military: US Army Air Corps - 10/3/1942/Private - INA - Navigator, B-24 Liberator/Lieutenant - INA - INA - Europe - INA - NA -NA - NA - NA - INA - INA. Civilian: 3/11/1923 Hinsdale, NY - Floyd J. Burlingame (1893 NY) & Florence E. Hamilton (1894 NY) - Lucy E. (1915), Ruth L. (1919) - INA - INA - Houghton College, Alfred University (BA & MA), Columbia University (Professional Degree) - INA - Director of Guidance/ Chautauqua Central School - Helen Ananenko (M-8/20/1949) - INA - 2/21/2007 Mayville, NY - INA - Mayville Lions Club, Veterans of Foreign Wars, Chautauqua County Guidance Association - INA - None.

Burns, Robert S. (Bobby) The NAO reported in June 1945 that Robert Burns of Fairport, NY had been seriously wounded on Okinawa on May 13. Robert called Bobby had lived with the Kenneth Ellwood family for some time and was remembered by many of the local FCSD area residents. NAO also reported that he was in a hospital on Guam. Bobby was originally from Fairport, NY. (From Northern Allegany County Observer 1945 book prepared by The History Club.)

Butler, Barton Burdette Military: US Army - 10/15/1940, Olean/Private - 11th Coast Artillery/INA Field Artillery - INA - Fort H.G. Wright, Fishers Island, NY/approx. 48 months - approx. 10 months - Philippines - Philippine campaign? - NA - NA - NA - Broken Ankle, Hospital, Portsmouth, NH - 12/20/1945 - American Defense Medal, American Campaign Medal, Asiatic Pacific Theater Medal, WW II Victory Medal, ? battle stars. Brother Elwin also served. Civilian: 1/29/1920 Centerville, NY - Julius E. Butler (1879 NY) & Minnie Belle Westfall (1884 NY) - Arvilla (1906 NY), Erma (1908 NY), Elwin Ellsworth (1912 NY), Pauline (1915 NY), Marjorie B. (1923 NY), Elna (1929 NY), Velma (1929 NY), E, Almond (NY) - Austin Westfall (1849 NY) & Mary Frost (1852 NY) - Marcus C. Butler (1849 NY) & Emma Statira Ballard (1846 NY) - FCS, 8th grade - Farm Laborer - Inspector, Eastman Kodak - Margaret Milroy - Donald Eugene, Stephen Carl, Kathryn (Fretz), Ruth (Rock) - 12/22/2017, Telford, PA - Fairview Cemetery, Macungie, PA - 1920, 1930, 1940 Federal Census Centerville - Rushford, NY Library.

Butler, Elwin Elsworth Military: US Navy - 2/23/1944/Belmont/AS – Drew Four Unit, D2/US Naval Amphibious Base, Exeter, England – Seaman Construction, Cargo Mover/Seaman 1Class - Sampson Naval Base /6 months - 16 months – England, France – None - NA - NA - NA - NA - 12/5/1945 - European African Middle East Theater Medal, WW II Victory Medal. Brother Burdette also served. Civilian: 9/19/1912 NY - Julius E. Butler (1879 NY) & Minnie Belle Westfall (1884 NY) - Arvilla (1906 NY), Erma (1908 NY), Pauline (1915 NY), Barton Burdette (1920 NY), Marjorie B. (1923 NY), Elna (1929 NY), Velma (1929 NY) - Austin Westfall (1849 NY) & Mary Frost (1852 NY) - Marcus C. Butler (1849 NY) & Emma Statira Ballard (1846 NY) - FCS, Grammar School – Dairy Farmer/Lumber Mill - INA - INA - INA - 10/9/1985, Centerville - White Cemetery, Rushford, NY – 1920, 1930 Federal Census Centerville – Rushford, NY Library.

Butler, Leonard According to the March 1945 NAO page 39, Leonard Butler of Fillmore entered the service on March 20, 1945. However, he is listed on the World War II Honor Roll for Centerville. He has not appeared in any federal census as living in either Fillmore or Centerville. The World War II Army Enlistment Records for the period 1938 to 1946 list a Leonard F. Butler of Buffalo as having enlisted in the Army on October 10, 1941 but does list any Leonard Butler for either Fillmore or Centerville. No military records for a Leonard Butler from either Fillmore or Centerville have been located. (Northern Allegany County Observer 1945 book. Prepared by The History Club.)

Butterfield, Frank Rozell Military: US Army - 1/6/1941/Buffalo/Private - 245th Coastal Artillery, Battery A, 663rd Field Artillery Battalion - Cook/Sergeant (Tech 4) - Fort Hancock, NJ, Fort Jay, NY, Fort Slocum, NY, others/49 months - 9 months - England, France, Germany - Rhineland, Central Europe - NA - NA - NA - NA - 11/10/1945, Camp Atterbury, Ind. – American Defense Medal. American Campaign Medal, European, African, Middle East Theater Medal, Good Conduct Medal, two battle stars, World War II Victory Medal. Frank was the Great Grandson of Civil War soldier Rozelle Butterfield (Co. C, 104th NY Infantry). Civilian: 7/22/1919 Centerville, NY - Clifford Rozell Butterfield (1899 NY) & Grace M. Sink (1897 NY) - Juanita (1921 NY) - Steven Butterfield (1869 NY) & Daisy Clara. Gillett (1878 NY) - Frank Sink (1869 PA) & Edith M. Bilton (1874 NY) - FCS, Dayton NY School Systems - Student - Psych Tech, Porterville State Hospital - Estella

D. Fiegl - INA - 1/ 4/1994 Fresno, CA - INA - 1900/1920, 1930 Federal Census Hume - None. Photo – NAO.

Byington, Merton Earnest Military: US Army -4/21/1941/Buffalo/Private - INA - INA/Tec 5 - Camp Butner, NC/Total Service time 51 months - INA - INA - INA - NA - NA - NA - NA - 7/16/1945 - American Defense Medal, American Campaign Medal, World War II Victory Medal. Brother Roy also served during the war. Grandfather Roswell N. Byington served with Company E, 5th NY Cavalry during the Civil War. Civilian: 3/7/1917 NY - Friend R. Byington (1873 NY) & Lillian M. Flint (1885 NY) - Raymond H. (1908), Leon F. (1913), Ruth (1914), Roy N. (1915), Pearl E. (1919), Carrie M. (1920), Haylord H. (1924), Glenn N. (1928) - Smith Flint (1846 NY) & INA - Roswell N. Byington (1840 NY) & Clara Freeman (1848 NY) (2nd wife) - FCS (Grammar School) Franklinville School system (two years high school) - Truck Driver - Driver, Evans, Oil - Betsy Grice McCluer - INA - 5/25/1998, Getzville, NY - Rt. 3 Cemetery, Centerville, NY - 1920 Federal Census Centerville, 1925 NYS Census Centerville - None.

Byington, Roy Norton Military: US Army- 1/12/1943/Buffalo/Private – Special Services - INA/S/Sgt - INA/15 months - 21 months - New Guinea, Philippines - INA - NA - NA - NA - NA - 1/13/1946, Camp Atterbury, IN - American Campaign Medal, Asiatic Pacific Theater Medal, WW II Victory Medal. Brother Merton also served during the war. Grandfather Roswell N. Byington served with Company E, 5th NY Cavalry during the Civil War. Civilian: 10/13/1915 NY - Friend R. Byington (1873 NY) & Lillie M. Flint (1885 NY) - Raymond H. (1908), Leon F. (1913), Ruth (1914), Merton E. (1917), Pearl E. (1919), Carrie M. (1920), Haylord H. (1924), Glenn N. (1928) - Smith Flint (1846 NY) & ? - Roswell N. Byington (1840 NY) & Clara Freeman (1848 NY) (2nd wife) - FCS - INA - Truck Driver/Farmer - Jean Goreski - Roy, Brian -10/17/1999 Centerville - Rt. 3 Cemetery, Centerville - 1920 Federal Census Centerville, 1925 NYS Census Centerville - None.

Byron, Burdette Henry Military: US Army - 6/10/1941/Buffalo/Private - ?, 237th Engineer Construction Battalion - Tractor Mechanic/Truck Driver Light, Technician 5th Grade (Corporal) – INA, Fort Dix, NJ/18.3 months – 39 months - North Africa, Italy, France, England, Germany - Central Europe, Rhineland, Rome-Arno, Tunisia - NA - NA - NA - NA - 10/3/1945 - American Defense Medal, European African Middle East Theater Medal, World War II Victory Medal, 4 Battle Stars, Good Conduct Medal. Civilian: 10/23/1917, Hornell, NY - Arthur E. Bryan (1891 NY) & Myrtle M. Lelear (1982 NY) - Doris (1916 NY), Deo (1920 NY), Iona (1922 NY) - Henry F. Lelear (1861 NY) & Mirander Robinson (1868 NY) - Luis J. Bryon (1859 NY) & Nettie L. Vincent (1863 NY) - Belfast & Fillmore Central School systems – Farm Hand (Employer – Leon Short Belmont) - INA - Alda Gelser (11/16/1946) - INA - 9/17/2000, Mount Morris, NY - INA - 1920 Federal Census, 1930 Federal Census Angelica, 1940 Federal Census Belfast. (Note; Despite the 1930 Census, he is listed in a 1933-34 Class picture in Fillmore. His Army papers indicate Fillmore in 1934 was last school attended.)

Carmer, Lloyd Albert Military: US Navy - 11/27/1943/Buffalo/Apprentice Seaman - *USS Leslie M. Shaw, Lone Jack, Palo Alto, John W. Garrett, Thomas W. Hyde* - Armed Guard/Seaman 1st Class - Sampson Naval Base, Baltimore Ship Yard, Norfolk Naval Yard, Brooklyn Naval Yard, Staten Island/INA - 13.5 months - England, France, Philippines, Panama - None - NA - NA - NA - Sick, Baltimore Hospital 3/22 to 4/3/44 - INA/Lido Beach, Long Island - American Campaign Medal, European African Middle East Theater Medal, Asiatic Pacific Theater Medal, World War II Victory Medal. Civilian: 7/21/1925 NY - Albert A. Carmer (1899 PA) & Gladys (Likely Byron) 1902 NY - Pearl E. (1922) Dorothy W. (1924), Betty S. (1928), Ella M. (1929) - Likely Arthur Byron (1892 PA) & Myrtle L. (maybe Lelear) (1892 NY) - Luman Carmer ((1863 PA) & Fannie (likely Galpin) (1879 NY) - INA - INA - INA - Carol M. ? (M8/26/1951) - Cathy (Crandall) - 6/21/1983 Fillmore - Short Tract Cemetery- SSDI – None. Photo – NAO.

Carpenter, Ronald Willis Military: US Army - 3/12/1941, Syracuse/Recall to Service 1/19/1942 Fort Niagara/Pvt - Company D, 366th Medical Battalion - Surgical Technician/Tec 4 - Camp Lee, VA/15 months 2 weeks - 30 months 2 weeks - Italy, France, Germany - Rome Arno, Rhineland - NA - NA- NA - NA - 11/17/1945, Fort Dix, NJ – American Defense Medal, American Campaign Medal, Good Conduct Medal, European, African Middle East Theater Medal, World War II Victory Medal, 2 Battle Stars. Civilian: 11/20/1908, Marilla, Erie Co, NY - Charles L. Carpenter (1867 NY) & Frances A. Kerns (1874 NY) - Francis E. (1911 NY), Fred C. (1903 NY), Lewis B. (1907 NY) - Fred J. Kerns (1846 NY) & Martha A. Bennett (1849 NY) - Lewis Carpenter (1830 NY) & Emily L. (maybe Lathrop) (1843 NY) - Collins NY & Gainesville, NY school systems – Salesperson, Weed & Co. - INA - Emma J. Winspear (M 8/11/1956, Middleburgh, NY) - David Carl, Joann - 12/18/1990, Batavia, NY - Grand View Cemetery, Batavia – 1935 Rural Allegany per 1940 Federal Census, NAO, April, 1941, (formerly of Fillmore) - None.

Cartwright, Truman (NMN) Not FCSD. From Dalton. Military: US Navy Civilian: 5/30/1927 Portage, NY - Devillo Cartwright (1879 NY & Laura ? (1889 NY) - Adaline (1925) - Half Sibs: Martin (1903), Frances E. (1904), John (1907), Harry (1908) - INA - INA - INA – Farm Hand - INA - Evelyn Wyatt (1931) (M4/8/1950) - INA - 10/9/2003 Olean, NY - Union Cemetery, Dalton, NY. NAO 1944, p 40.

Chamberlain, Wilbur Page. Not FCSD. From Caneadea. Military: US Army Air Corps Civilian: 2/7/1923 NY - Hugh D. Chamberlain 1891 (NY) & Winifred E. ? (1895 Idaho) - Hugh D. (1927) - INA - INA - INA - INA - INA - INA - INA - 8/8/1998 - Riverside Cemetery, Belfast. Mentioned NAO several times.

Chizlette (Chizlett), Victor James (Vic) Military: US Army - 10/3/1942/Private - INA - INA/Private – INA/5-months total service - NA - NA - NA - NA - NA - Ulcers - 2/1943 - American Campaign Medal, World War II Victory Medal. Civilian: 7/2/1904, Wiscoy, NY - Richard James Chizlette (1872 NY) & Rosa May Van Middleworth (1878 NY) - Walter (1902 NY) - Victor Van Middleworth (1852 NY) & Frances A. (possibly Herrick) (1849 NY) - Frederick Walker (1847 NY) & Lucy (First name was likely Mary A., the same as her Mother) Chizlette (1854 NY) - FCS (one-year high school) - Construction & Maintenance – Guard, Warsaw Mallory Timers Plant - Hattie A. Goodnenow - INA - 10/17/1986/Warsaw/NY - Warsaw Cemetery - 1940 Federal Census Hume.

Clark, Everett Monroe Military: US Army - 12/7/1942 Buffalo/Private - 14th Armored Division, 48th Tank Battalion - Chief, Wrecker Repair Company/Tech-4 - Camp Chaffee, AR, Camp Campbell, KY/23 months - 17 months - France, Germany - Ardennes-Alsace, Central Europe, Rhineland - NA - NA - NA - in hospital, September, 1943, June, 1945 - 2/27/1946 Ft Dix, NJ - 3 Battle Stars, Battalion Commendation, American Campaign Medal, European African Middle Eastern Theater Medal, Good Conduct Medal, Army Occupation Medal Germany, World War II Victory Medal. June injuries, suffered in a jeep on his way to pick up mail, when side swiped by a truck, caused a gash to his head requiring seven stitches. His brother Lloyd also served during the war. Everett's great grandfather Andrew Clark and great-great grandfather George Clark (father & son) both served in the Civil War with the 104th NY Infantry. Civilian: 9/15/1922 Centerville, NY - Nathaniel David Clark (1885 NY) & (Ida) Pauline A. Redman (1897 NY) - Lloyd (1921 NY), Margaret (1924 NY), Mildred (1926 NY) - Everett Redman (1872 NY) & Nora ViolaWilcox (18720MD) - Addison N. Clark (1850 NY) & Caroline (Carrie) Hope (1852 NY) - Fillmore Central - Truck Driver, Al Randall, Franklinville, NY - INA - Jeanette Grace H? - INA - 6/27/1992 -Rushford - 1930 Census Hume - Allegany County War Service Record. – None. Photo – NAO.

Clark, Lloyd David Military: US Army - 7/2/1942 Ft Niagara/Private - Fifth Army, 88th Infantry Division, 338th Artillery Battalion – Truck Driver/Technician 5 - Camp Gruber, OK, Ft Sam Houston, TX /INA - INA - Italy - Rome-Arno, Northern Apennines, Po Valley - NA - 8/23/1944, Firenzoula - NA - NA - INA – American Campaign Medal, Bronze Star For Bravery, Commanders Commendation for Bravery, Purple Heart, Good Conduct Medal, Five Division Citations, Unit Commendation, 3 Battle Stars, European, African, Middle East Theater Medal, World War II Victory Medal, Battalion received the French Croix de Guerre with Palm for its performance in central Italy - Spent over 300 days in combat from 3/04/44 to 5/2/45, the 338th usually supported the 88th Infantry Division, but teamed with 60 other outfits during the Italian campaign. His brother Everett also served during the war. - Lloyds's great grandfather Andrew Clark and great-great grandfather George Clark (father & son) both served in the Civil War with the 104th NY Infantry Civilian: 7/19/1921 Hume, NY - Nathaniel David Clark (1885 NY) & Ida Pauline ? (? NY) - Everett (1922 NY), Margaret (1924 NY), Mildred (1926 NY) - Everett Redman (1873 NY) & Viola A. ? (1872 MD - Addison N. Clark (1853 NY) & Carrie ? (1853 NY) - Fillmore Central - INA - INA - Theda M. Sylor - Leona (James) - 1/13/1981 - Short Tract Cemetery - 1930 Census Hume - None. Photo – NAO.

Clark, Olson Wesley Military: US Army. According to an entry in the NAO in May of 1943, Olson was called by the draft board in Belmont to go to Buffalo for his physical examination. No other information regarding his military service has been located. Civilian: 3/19/1918 Chicago, IL - Lewis A. Clark (1882 MI) & Alice Wright (1886 MI) - Vena M. (1910), Florence L. (1912), Gordon L. (1923), Oderea L. (1922), Reva P. (1925), Mildred (1927) - Brayton Wright (1862 MI) & Elizabeth M. Pierce (1865 MI) - INA - INA - INA - Minister - Lila M. Durling (M 1945, Waldran, Michigan) - Margaret, Patricia, Susan, Sandra - 10/2/2010 Houghton – Mt. Pleasant Cemetery, Houghton - 1930 Federal Census Houghton - None.

Closser, Vernon Albert II Military: US Army - 11/6/1942/Buffalo/Private - Army Service Forces, 2nd Service Command, Service Unit Company 1243 - Clerk/Private - Fort Jay, Governors Island, NY/5 months - NA - NA - NA - NA - NA - NA - 3/25/1943, Albany, NY - American Campaign Medal, World War II Victory Medal. His son Vernon A. Closser III also served during the war. Civilian: 1903 NY - Vernon A. Closser I (1882 NY) & Helen (Nellie) Jane Booth (1882 NY) - INA - Mark H. Booth (1853 NY) & Louise C. Ransom (1853 NY) - John Closser (1850 NY) & Emma ? - Fillmore Central (2 years high school) - Laborer, Steel Industry - INA - Elizabeth M. Gorton (M 3/10/1923) - Vernon III (1923 NY), Katherine (1926 NY) - 4/7/1962, Hamburg, NY - INA - 1910, 1920, 1940 Census Hume - None.

Closser, Vernon Albert III Military: US Air Force - 3/12/1943/Buffalo/Private - 677th Bomb Squadron, 444th Bomb Group - Bomb Sight Mechanic/Corporal - Miami, FL, Lowry Field, Co, Kirkland field, N.M., CRP AAF, Utah, /11 months 3 weeks - 20 months 2 weeks - India, Tinian - India-Burma, Central Burma, Air Offensive Japan, China Defensive, Western Pacific, Air Combat - NA - NA - NA - NA - 11/24/1945, Fort Knox, KY - American Campaign Medal, Asiatic Pacific Theater Medal, Good Conduct Medal, 6 Battle Stars, 2 Distinguished Units Citations – Japan May 10-14, 1945, Japan July 24, 1945, World War II Victory Medal. Father Vernon Albert Closser II also served during the war. Civilian: 7/17/1923/ Rochester, NY - Vernon A. Closser II (1903 NY) & Elizabeth M. Gorton (1905 NY) - Katherine E. (1926 NY) - Fred A. Gorton (1868 NY) & Alice M. Bush (1875 NY) - Vernon A. Closser I (1882 NY) & Helen Booth (1882 NY) - Fillmore Central, Class of 1940 – Laborer, Steel Plant/Welder - INA - Margaret A. Cooney (1/1959 Bayonne, NJ) - INA - 1/22/2000, Burnside, KY - White Chapel Memorial Gardens, Barboursville, WVA. - 1930, 1940 Federal Census, Hume. Photo – Yearbook.

Clute, Everett Frank Military: US Army 1 7/2/1942, Buffalo/Private - Quartermaster Corps, 1959th Quartermaster Truck Company - Truck Driver, Dispatcher Clerk/Sgt - NA - NA - NA - NA - NA - NA – 3/25/1943, Albany, NY - American Campaign Medal, World War II Victory Medal - None. Civilian 5/26/1921 Binghamton, NY - Nathan Louis Clute (1890 NY) & Henrietta B. Fohle (1901 NY) - Violet A. (1924), Geraldine M. (1925), Harry L. (1927), Robert H. (1929), Dorothy J. - William Fohl (1867 NY) & Margaret? (1859 NY) - John Clute (1849 NY) & Ellen? (1854 NY) - FCS, one-year high school - Mechanic, Auto Garage, Stock Clerk, McCullam Hatch, Bronze Co, Buffalo - INA - Edith M.? - Ellery Jon - 7/29/1991, Polk, Florida - INA - 1930,1940 Census Hume - None.

Cockle, Allen William (Sonny) Military: US Army - 3/30/1945 Buffalo/Private - Company C, 62 Signal Battalion - Lineman/Technician 5th Grade - Fort Knox, Fort Ord/8 months - 10/13/1945 to 10//21/1946/12 months - Japan (Kure, Sapporo, Koriyama) - None - NA - NA - NA - NA - 12/7/1946, Fort Dix - Asiatic Pacific Theater Medal, Army of Occupation, Japan - World War II Victory Medal: Civilian: 9/27/1924 NY - Roy Lucas Cockle (1902 NY) & Alice Irene   Buffey (1900 Canada) - Sarah (1921), Irene (1923), Bernice (1927), Olive (1929), Roy N. 1932), Glenn M. (1936 NY), Linda E (1939 NY) - William Buffey, Jr. (1848 Canada) & Elizabeth Chatwell (1862 Canada) - William Cockle (1859 NY) & Malinda Van Luwen (1873 NY) - Fillmore Central - Farmer, Luckey & Sandford Auto - Erie RR, Painter, Town of Hume Transportation Department - Roberta Woodruff - Trudy (stepdaughter), Tammy, Lynn Allen, Kathy - 3/28/1981 - Pine Grove Cemetery, Fillmore, NY - 1930 Federal Census Hume -Sister Olive (Polly) Cockle Miller. Photo – Family.

Colburn, Alfred Loren Jr. (Al) Military: US Army Air Corps - 7/16/1942 Buffalo/Private – 3rd Air Division, Eighth AF – Operations /Staff Sergeant - Miami Beach, FL, Ft. Logan, CO., MacDill Field, FL/12 months - 26 months - England - INA - NA - NA - NA - NA - 9/4/1945 Ft. Dix, NJ - American Campaign Medal, European African Middle East Theater Medal, WW II Victory Medal. Spoke at Rotary Club meeting in Fillmore while on leave 8/45. Brother Robert also served during war. Civilian: 5/23/1910 NY - Alfred L. Colburn (1870 NY) & Martha Mae Sprowl (1884 NY) - Harold (Harry) (1908 NY), Robert D. (1914) – William H. Sprowl (1840 VT) & Martha C. Flanigan (1851 CT) - Loren Colburn ((1822 VT) & Emily A. Buel (1830 CT) - FCS, Cornell University - Principal, Cuba Central School - Principal, Cuba Central School - Isabel Moore - Stephen - March 4, 1981 Cuba, NY – Holland Cemetery, Holland, NY- 1930 Fed Cen Hume - Son Stephen Colburn. Photo – NAO.

Colburn, Robert Delemore (Bob) Military: US Army - 12/11/1942 Rochester/Private - 14th Armored Division, 25th Tank Battalion, 25th Recon Platoon - Infantryman/Sergeant - Camp Chaffee, AR, Nashville, TN, Camp Campbell, KY/36 months - 4 months - France, Germany - Ardennes-Alsace, Rhineland - NA - 12/18/1944, shrapnel to back and left leg during attack on Kapsweyer - NA - NA - 4/2/1947 - Combat Infantry Badge, Bronze Star (1947), Purple Heart, Good Conduct Medal, American Campaign Medal, European African Middle East Theater Medal, WW II Victory Medal, 2 Battle Stars - Was in Halloran Hospital on Staten Island and Northington G.H. in Tuscaloosa, AL for plastic surgery after his return. Brother Alfred also served during war. Civilian: 6/24/1913 Hume, NY - Alfred L. Colburn (1870 NY) & Mae M. Sprowl (1884 NY) - Alfred L. (1910 NY) Harry S. (1908 NY) - William H. Sprowl (1840 VT) & Martha Flanegan (1851 CT) - Loren Colburn (1822 VT) & Emily A. Buel (1830 CT) - FCS, Class of 1932 - Manager, General Store, Hume - Principal, Physical Education Instructor, Wayne County, NY Central School - Elizabeth G. Foley - Loren, David - 9/19/1997 - Wayne County, NY Cemetery - 1930 Federal Census Hume - Sons Loren & David. Photo – NAO.

Cole, Edward Mark Military: US Army - 10/16/1942 Rochester/Private - 4th Infantry Division, Military Police Platoon, Military Policeman, Orderly of the Guard/PFC – Unknown/22 months - 15 months - England, France, Belgium, Luxemburg, Germany - Normandy, Northern France, Rhineland, Ardennes Alsace, Central Europe - NA - NA - NA - NA - November, 1945. (Reenlisted December, 31, 1945 – Discharged 10/10/1962) – American Campaign Medal, 5 Battle Stars, European African Middle East Theater Medal, WW II Victory Medal, Army Occupation Medal, Germany Clasp. Brother George A. also served. Great Grandfather Levi Stanton served with Company K, 7th NY Artillery during Civil War. Levi died and was buried at the infamous prison Andersonville, Ga. Civilian: 5/22/1922 (Caneadea, NY) - Edward L. Cole (1872 PA) & Leah May Stanton (1883 NY) - Mary B. (1912), Onolee I. (1916), George A. (1918) - Mark Stanton (1854 NY) & Ida E. Sheldon (1864 NY) – Lyman Cole (INA) & Martha Hogan (INA) - Nunda Central, FCS - Moulder - Career Military, Army - INA - Edward - 4/25/1983 Monterey, CA - INA - 1940 Federal Census Hume - None.

Cole, George Adelbert Not FCSD. From Nunda. Military: US Army - 1/11/1943/Rochester/Private - Civilian: 1918 - Edward Cole (1872 PA) & Leah M.? (1873 NY) - Mary B. (1912), Onolee I. (1916), Edward M. (1922) - INA - INA - INA - INA - INA - INA - INA - INA - INA -? - None. Brother Edward M. also served. Unlike his brother Edward, George apparently never lived in the FCSD area.

Collopy, John William Military: US Army - 1/26/1944/Rochester/Private - 209th Military Police Company - Military Policeman/Private - INA - 22.5 months served - New Caledonia, Philippines, Japan – Leyte – NA – NA – NA – NA – 12/9/1946 – Asiatic Pacific Theater Medal, World War II Victory Medal, One battle star, Meritorious Unit Commendation, Philippine Presidential Citation, Army of Occupation Medal, Asian Clasp. John's father, also a John Collopy, registered for WW I. Civilian: 10/4/1922, Lockport, NY -John William Collopy & Beatrix E.R. (maybe Rose) - Marion (1921 NY), Nelson (1925 NY) - Maybe William H. Rose (1855 NY) & Sarah? (1855 NY) - John W. Collopy (Canada) & Margaret A.- INA - INA - INA - INA - INA - 2/1/2010, Fillmore - Holy Cross Cemetery. Lived in Centerville post war, died in Fillmore.

Collver, Colin Craig Military: US Army - 12/20/1944(Reenlisted)/ Buffalo/Private - INA – INA/Private (WW II) - Fort Dix, NJ, Camp Blanding, FL, Camp Mead, MD/8 months (during WW II) - Arrived overseas in September, 1945 - (Overseas Post War) Manila, Philippines - None - NA - NA - NA - NA - 7/27/1951 - American Campaign Medal, Asiatic-Pacific Theater Medal, World War II Victory Medal. Civilian: 8/21/1926, Buffalo, NY - Leland Collver (1875 NY) & Clara Belle Webb (1883 NY) - Doris (1907 NY), Muriel (1909 NY), Isabel (1911 NY), Arville (1915 NY), Shirley (1920 NY), Lorne F. (1922 NY) - INA - INA - Pike Central School - Student - Veterinarian John G. Marvin - INA - INA - 2/10/1998 Fulton, NY - INA - NAO, July, 1945. Brother Lorne also served. Colin was a direct descendant of Reverend Jabez Coller, a friend of George Washington who served as a Chaplin during the Revolutionary War.

Collver, Lorne Fayette Military: US Army Air Corps - 3/5/1943/Private - Headquarters and Base Service Squadron, 540th Air Service Group – Member of Service Crew/PFC - Drew Field, FL/7 months - 24 months - North Africa, Italy - INA - NA - NA - NA - NA - 10/30/1945, Drew Field, FL - European African Middle East Theater Medal, World War II Victory Medal. Civilian: 4/13/1922 NY - Leland Collver (1875 NY) & Clara Belle Webb (1883 NY) - Dorris (1907 NY) Muriel (1909 NY), Isabel (1911 NY), Arville (1915 NY), Shirley (1920 NY), Colin C. (1926 NY) – William Wallace Webb (1850 NY & Katherine? (1859 NY) – Carolton Cullver (1846 Canada) & Amarella Ann? (1844 Canada) - Pike Central School - Bakery - Cornell University, Bus Driver, Dryden School System - INA - INA - 3/27/2003 Cortland, NY - Cortland Rural Cemetery - NAO, July, 1945. Brother Colin also served. Lorne was a direct-descendant of Reverend Jabez Coller, a friend of George Washington who served as a Chaplin during the Revolutionary War.

Common, Adair Wells (Wellsie)  Military: US Army Airborne - 2/20/1936/Buffalo/ Private - 101st Army Airborne, 17th Airborne Division, 502nd Parachute Regiment, 513th Parachute Regiment - Unit Commander/1st Lieutenant - FT. Niagara, FT. Bragg, NC, FT. Benning, GA, Fort Jackson, SC/8 years - 8/44 to 1/45 - England, France, Belgium - Ardennes-Alsace Campaign (Battle of the Bulge) - 1/1/1945 Belgium - NA - NA - NA - 1/1/1945 - American Defense Medal, American Campaign Medal, Combat Infantryman Badge, Bronze Star (1947), Purple Heart, One Battle Star, European African Middle East Theater Medal, WW II Victory Medal. His great grandfather Augustus "Jacob" Sartar served with both the 147th Pennsylvania Infantry and the 17th New York Infantry during the Civil War, and participated in numerous Civil War battles. His brother Ralph also served during the WW II. Civilian: 3/19/1916 Fillmore, NY - Bert Luther Common (1893 NY) & Pearl Sartor (1893 NY) - Ralph (1921) - Jacob Sartar (1853 Germany) & Delia B. Beardsley (1857 NY) - Edward N. Common (1862 NY) & Mary E. Luther (1868 NY) - Fillmore Central, Class of 1935 - Student - NA - Velma? (7/22/1943 Phoenix City, AL) - Lauretta Kay, Step Daughter Mryna - 1/1/1945 Belgium, Battle of the Bulge - Pine Grove Cemetery, Fillmore - 1930 Federal Census Fillmore - None. Photo – NAO.

Common, Ralph Luther  Military: US Army Air Corps - 11/3/1942/Staunton, VA/Private - 1505 AAF Base Unit (Assigned to B-29 Squadron) - B-29 Armorer/Tech Sergeant - Richmond, VA, Camp Stockton, CA. Miami Beach, FL/14 months - 22 months - India, China, Tinian – India-Burma, China Defensive, Western Pacific, Air Offensive, Japan, Central Burma - NA - NA - NA - NA - 11/15/1945, Westover AFB, MA - American Campaign Medal, Asiatic Pacific Theater Medal, 5 Battle Stas, WW II Victory Medal. Ralph also served in Korea and Vietnam. His great grandfather Augustus "Jacob" Sartar served with both the 147th Pennsylvania Infantry and the 17th New York Infantry during the Civil War, and participated in numerous Civil War battles. His brother Adair also served during WWE II. Civilian: 3/21/1921 Fillmore, NY - Bert Luther Common (1892 NY) & Pearl Sartor (1890 NY) - Adair Wells (1916 NY) - Jacob Sartar (1853 Germany) & Delia A. Beardsley (1858 NY) - Edward N. Common (1862 NY) & Mary E. Luther (1868 NY) - Fillmore Central, Class of 1939 – Sheet metal worker, Wayne Manufacturing Corp. - Career Military (Air Force) - Helen? - INA - 6/16/1999 Zephyr Hills, FL – Florida National Cemetery, Bushnell, FL - 1930 Federal Census Fillmore - None. Photo – Yearbook.

Conklin, Charles Harley Not FCSD. From Friendship, but see Part XI, The B-29.

Cooley, Clifford Delos  Military: US Navy Air - 7/23/1942/Buffalo/Apprentice Seaman - Naval Air Transport Service, VR Squadron 11 - Pilot/Lieutenant (JG) - Buffalo, Chapel Hill, NC, Corpus Christie, TX, Atlanta, Glenville, IL, Oakland, CA/INA - total service time 39 months - Flew many flights to overseas Pacific bases. (total time involved overseas not available) - Hawaii (Based Pearl Harbor) - Likely Papua, NG - NA - NA - NA - NA - 11/6/1945/ USNPSC, New York City - American Campaign Medal, Asiatic Pacific Theater Medal, WW II Victory Medal. One battle star. Civilian: 3/27/1921 Hume, NY- Cheston F. Cooley (1895 NY) & Melrose Lee (1893 NY) - Velman L. (1918 NY) – Ira Lee (1869 NY) & Mae Curtis (1872 NY) - Cordell D. Cooley & Harriet Bennett (1865 NY) - Fillmore Central, Class of 1937 - Carborundum Co., Niagara Falls, NY - Asst. Operator, Optical Power Production - INA -? (M 11/5/1943) - David - 5/30/2005, Freedom, NY - East Koy Cemetery, Pike, NY - 1930 Federal Census Hume - Son David Cooley. Photo – Family.

Cox, Ralph Herbert Military: US Navy - 6/4/1945/Apprentice Seaman - *USS Fairisle, USS Dixie, USS Orvetta, USS Repose* -? - Seaman First Class - Sampson Naval, Camp Shoemaker, CA, Treasure Island Naval Base /4 months - 10 months - Mariana Islands area, Eniwetok, Okinawa, Philippines, Shanghai, China - None - NA - NA - NA - NA - 8/7/1946/Lido Beach, NY - American Campaign Medal, Asiatic Pacific Theater Medal, WW II Victory Medal, Navy Occupation Medal, Asian Clasp, China Service Medal. 1927 MD -Joseph Herbert Cox (1904 NY) & Olive Josephine Barker (1902 NY) – Mary (1929 NY, Sers (1931 NY), Eva (1932 NY), Eleanor (1934 NY), Philip (1935 NY), John (1937 NY), Joseph (1939 NY), Virginia (1940 NY) – Ernest D. Barker (1877 NY) & Alida P. J. Thompsen (1882 NY) – John H. Cox (1852 NY) & Mary E. Leclair (1865 NY) – Nunda Central School - Student - Owner, NAPA Auto Parts Shop, Fillmore - Rose? - INA - NA - NA - NAO 12/1945 - Photo – NAO.

.

Crandall, John Curtis Jr. (Jack) (Note: He was supposed to be named Curtis John, Jr. after his father. However, the birth physician, Dr. Robert Lyman filled out his birth certificate as John Curtis, Jr.**)** Military: US Navy - 10/4/1942/Buffalo/AS - LCI (L) 430 - Ship Commander/ Lieutenant - Notre Dame University/12 months? - 21 months? - Australia, New Guinea, Philippines - Hollandia, Western New Guinea (Morotai), Manila Bay- Bicolo (Nasugu) Operations - NA - NA - NA - NA - INA - American Campaign Medal, Asiatic Pacific Theater Medal, World War II Victory Medal, 3 Battle Stars, Philippine Liberation Medal. Brother William and half-brother Frederick Houser also served. Civilian: 2/9/1919 NY - Curtis John Crandall (1877 PA) & Louise Clement (1885 NY) - William C. (1921 NY), Half-brother Frederick C. Houser (1911 NY), There may have been another half-brother Joseph A. Kemp (1902 Eng.) who may have been adopted. - Jacob Truman Clement (1840 NY) Eliesa R. Willson (1857 NY) - David E. Crandall (1830 NY) & Kate A. Furch (1857 NY) - Houghton College - Teacher - Teacher, Brockport College - Jill Carlson - Candy, Molly - 7/3/1995 - Chautauqua County, NY - 1930 1940 Federal Census Houghton - None.

Crandall, William Clement (Billy) Military: US Army - 12/5/1942/Buffalo/Private - 357th Infantry Regiment/ 90th Infantry Division – Transportation Dispatcher/Sergeant – Miami, FL/16 months - 23 months - France, Germany, Czechoslovakia - Normandy, Northern France, Ardennes-Alsace, Rhineland, Central Europe - NA - NA - NA - NA – 3/3/1946 - European, African, Middle East Theater Medal, Arrowhead Badge, French Croix de Guerre, World War II Victory Medal - Brother Curtis John Crandall and half-brother Frederic Houser also served. Civilian: 5/5/1921/NY - Curtis John Crandall (1878 PA)) & Louise Clement (1885 - NY) - Gladys L. Crandall (1904 PA), Half-sister - John Curtis, Jr. (1919), Half-brother Frederick C. Houser (1911), There may have been another half-brother named Joseph A. Kemp (1902 Eng) who may have been adopted - Jacob Truman Clement (1840 NY) & Electa R. Willson (1857 NY) - David E. Crandall (1830 NY) & Kate A. Furch (1857 NY) - INA - INA - Owner, Crandall & Son Cemetery Memorial Company - Beulah J. Damon - Curtis W., Connie, Christy, Carol J. - 11/19/2003/Olean, NY - Ulysses, Potter Co., PA - 1930 1940 Federal Census Houghton - None.

Cronk, Charles Allen Jr. Military: US Navy - 8/1/1943/Apprentice Seaman - INA - Pharmacists Mate/3rd Class - Sampson Naval. Naval Hospital, Portsmouth, VA /? - INA - Scotland - INA - NA - NA - NA - NA - INA – American Campaign Medal, European African Middle East Theater Medal, WW II Victory Medal. Civilian: 1926 NY - Charles A. Cronk (1882 NY) & Emma E. ? (1888 NY) - Doris (1906), Alice M. (1910), Clifford (1912), Victor (1915), John (1917), June A. (1921), Betty M. (1923), Wilma J. (1930) - INA - INA - Fillmore Central, Class of 1942 - INA - INA - INA - INA -INA - Alger Cemetery, Hume -1930 1940 Federal census Hume - None. Photo – NAO.

Cronk, Theos Ervin Military: US Army Air Corps - 11/5/1942/Private - INA - Assistant Special  Services Officer/Captain (as of 10/16/1943) - Ft. Dix, NJ, Scott Field, Il, OCS School, Miami Beach, Fl, Lexington, VA, St Louis, MO/41 months - NA - NA - NA - NA - NA- -NA - NA – 4/5/1946 – Good Conduct Medal, American Campaign Medal, WW II Victory Medal. His grandfather, Chester B. Cronk, served with Company D, 64th NY Infantry during the Civil War. His great grandfather, three times removed, Nehemiah Houghton, served as a muster master in the Revolutionary War in the defense of West Point. He was promoted to Captain in 1780. Civilian: 7/21/1911 Fillmore, NY - Marshall C. Cronk (1880 NY) & Julia E. Kunz (1882 NY) - Alton M. 1909), Malcolm A. (1915), Barbara E. (1920) – Julius Kunz (1860 Switzerland) & Barbara Durst (1855 Switzerland) - Chester B. Cronk (1840 NY) & Lillian J. Houghton (1854 NY) - Houghton College, Class of 1932, Princeton Westminster Choir College MA 1936 - Choir Personnel Director/Concert Manager - INA - Margaret Jean Thompson - Daniel T., Jay S. - 8/13/1959 Bardstwon, KY - Arlington, Cemetery, Delaware County, PA. - 1930 Federal Census Houghton - None. Photo – Yearbook.

Cummings, Robert Lincoln Military: US Army - 1/1943/Private -5th Engineer Special Brigade - Bugler, French Interpreter, Guard, Patrolman /PFC - Camp? (Mojave Desert Training Site), Virginia, Boston /? - ? - Scotland, Wales, England, France, Germany - Normandy, Northern France - NA - NA - NA - NA - 1/1946 – American Campaign Medal, European African Middle East Theater Medal, WW II Victory Middle, 2 Battle Stars, Occupation Medal, Germany Clasp, French Normandy Medal (2000) Civilian: 1923 NY - Malcolm P. Cummings (1887 NY) & Charlotte M. Likely Robinson (1890 NY - Arlie F. (1917 NY), Donald M. (1919 NY), Marjorie R. (922 NY), Beverly (1925 NY) - Likely Willard J. Robinson (1858 NY) & Sarah (maybe Kettle) (1857 NY) - Milo Cummings (1861 NY) & Francis Collins (1868 Canada) - INA - Worked in a Defense Plant - Teacher of German, Houghton College - Marion ? - INA - INA - INA - Fillmore History Club, 1945 WW II Book, 12/1945. Photo – NAO.

Curry, William Alton (Bill) Military: US Navy - 3/7/1943/Apprentice Seaman - *USS Guinivere* - Motor  Machinist Mate/Seaman 2nd Class - Sampson Naval Base, Norton Heights, CT, Fargo Receiving Station, Boston, MA/INA - INA - Atlantic Fleet - NA - NA - NA - NA - NA - INA - American Campaign Medal, WW II Victory Medal. Civilian: 8/9/1924 NY - John J. Curry (1895 NY) & Viola B.? (1898 NY) - Lillian G. (1919), Lois E. (1921), Leona M. (1922), Norma F. (1927), Wilma J. (1931), Joan B. (1925), Patricia A. (1937) - INA - INA - Fillmore Central - INA - INA - Dolores B.? - INA - 3/22/2007, Fillmore, NY - Short Tract Cemetery - 1940 Federal Census Granger - Patricia Curry Fenton. Photo – NAO.

Darling, Herbert Tuttle (Herb) Military: US Army - 12/13/1941/Buffalo/Private - Medical Corps,  Veterinary Department - Veterinary Technician/PFC - Washington, DC, Charleston, SC/Total Service 48 months - Did make trips to Europe with animals -Returned from last one 7/3/1945 – European Area - NA - NA - NA - NA - NA - December 15, 1945 – European, African Middle East Theater Medal, American Campaign Medal, WW II Victory Medal. Civilian: 5/5/1919, Marshfield, Oregon - Herbert E. Darling (1872 NE) & Anna Mae Tuttle (1880 NY) – Floyd (1901 OR), Jeanine (1916 OR), Waldo (1917 OR), Ralph (1922 WA) - Cassius M. Tuttle (1858 NY) & Lillie A.? (1859 NY) - William Darling (1850 MA) & Esther Nellie Clough (1853 NY) - Likely attended high school in State of Washington. Had two years of college, Alfred University, NY - Farm Hand, New York State

School of Agriculture, Alfred, NY - Custodian, Robeson Cutlery Co., Castile - Norma Worden (M 10/5/1942, Charleston, SC) – Dee, Donald - 5/8/2009 Warsaw, NY – Short Tract Cemetery. NAO 8/1942 Short Tract – Final Pay Voucher, 1940 Draft Card says he lived in Fillmore. Photo -NAO.

Davis, Gerald Gustavus Military: US Army - 8/25/1941/Buffalo/Private - Headquarters, Headquarters Company, Army Ground Forces - Personal Affairs Consultant/Sergeant - Fort Bragg, NC, Ft. McClellan, AL/38 months - 12 months - Hawaii - None - NA - NA - NA - NA - 11/5/1945 - American Defense Medal, American Campaign Medal, Good Conduct Medal, Asiatic Pacific Theater Medal, World War II Victory Medal. Brother Kermit was KIA during the war. Civilian: 3/10/1914 NY/Centerville, NY - Henry W. Davis (1873 NY) & Irene (Rene) G. Lane (1878 NY) - Kenneth (1904 NY), Alice (1907 NY), Harold (1909 NY), Kermit (1911 NY), Ada (1921 NY) - Gustavus Lane (1848 NY) & Euphemia Day (1852 NY) - Milton Davis (1831 NH) & Betsey Amelia? (1830 MA) - FCS, graduated Bliss High School, Geneseo Normal School - Clerk, Dept. Store - Grade School Teacher, Fillmore & Arcade - NA - NA - 9/27/1993/Silver Lake, NY - Pine Grove Cemetery, Fillmore, NY - 1920, 1940 Federal Census Centerville - None.

Davis, Kermit Adolph Military: US Army - 4/1/1943/Buffalo/Private - Co. C, 275th Combat Engineer Battalion, 75th Infantry Division - Explosive Handler/Tec 5 - Fort Leonard Wood, MO, Louisiana Texas Maneuvers, Camp Breckinridge, KY/18.5 months - 2.5 months - England, France, Holland, Belgium - Ardennes-Alsace,, Rhineland - 12/31/1944 (Died of wounds) - WIA, 12/28/1944, Belgium - NA - NA - 12/31/1944, Belgium - American Campaign Medal, European African Middle East Theater Medal, Purple Heart, World War II Victory Medal, two Battle Stars. Brother Gerald also served during the war. Civilian: 4/20/1910 NY - Henry W. Davis (1874 NY) & Irene? (1878 NY) - Kenneth (1904 NY), Alice (1907 NY), Harold (1909 NY), Gerald (1914 NY), Ada (1921 NY) - INA - Milton Davis (1873 NH) & Betsey Amelia? (MA) - FCS - Loader, Salt Plant - NA - Norma (Hoyle) (name of first husband) (1913 NY) - Step children, Norman Mabel, Joan, Cora Mae - 12/31/1944. Belgium- Hope Cemetery, Castile, NY - 1920, 1940 Federal Census Centerville - None. Photo – Archives.

Denning, Clarence Alvin Military: US Army - 11/14/1942/Buffalo/Private - INA - INA/Sergeant - Camp Van Dorn, MS, Memphis, TN, Ft. Lewis, WA/36 months - NA - NA - NA - NA - NA - NA - NA – 1/31/1946 - American Campaign Medal, World War II Victory Medal. Brother Harold may have served during the war. Civilian: 8/3/1922, Fillmore, NY - Harvey Leroy Denning (1892 NY) & Martha E. Hopkins (1897 NY) - Charles (1914 NY), Lawrence A. (1920 NY), Harold R. (1917 NY), Vesta E. (1926 NY), Burton G. (1928 NY) - Charles R. Hopkins (1863 NY) & Bertha Payne (1874 NY) - Christopher Denning (NY) & Lillian J. Addsit (NY) - FCS - Farm Laborer - Likely Military Career (a Public Directory shows him still in Army living in Memphis in 1951.) - Thelma Louise McDonald – Lori Ann, Janice M., Sandra K., Clarence - 11/10/2005, Buffalo, NY - INA - 1930, 1940 Federal Census Hume - None. Photo – NAO.

Denning, Harold Russell Military: US Army - 4/1942 /Belmont/Private - The NAO reported in April of 1942 that Harold was working for Virgil Wolfer on his farm and had been inducted into the service. A separate item that same month reported that Board No. 535 in Belmont announced that Harold and David P. Richardson, both of Fillmore had been inducted. No other information regarding military service pertaining to Harold has been located. That Nationals Personnel Record Center in St. Louis, MO notified the author that they had been unable to locate any files on Harold. It should be noted that most

US Army files for World War II personnel were destroyed in a fire. However, in almost all cases, a reconstructed file containing the final payroll records for each veteran is available. No such file for Harold has been identified. His brother Clarence did serve during the war. Civilian: 10/12/1915, Poughkeepsie, NY – Harvey Leroy Denning (1892 NY) & Martha (Metta) E. Hopkins (1897 NY) - Charles (1914 NY), Lawrence A. (1920 NY), Clarence (1922 NY), Vesta (1926 NY), Burton G. (1928 NY) - Charles R. Hopkins (1863 NY) & Bertha Payne (1874 NY) - Christopher Denning (NY) & Lillian J. Addsit (NY) - FCS – Farm Laborer, worked for Town of Fillmore - INA – INA (Married 4/3/1941, Angelica) - INA - 2/16/1961 (home of Fred Muir, Hume, NY) - Pine Grove Cemetery, Fillmore, NY - 1930, 1940 Federal Census Hume.

Devaney, Edward – Military: US Army - 2/18/1943/Rochester/Private - INA - INA/PFC - Fort Benning/8 months - 25 months - Trinidad - American Campaign - NA - NA - NA -NA - October, 1945 - American Campaign Medal, WW II Victory Medal. Civilian: NAO, 10/1942 Wiscoy (living with Mrs. Mae Bennett.) NAO, July, 1943. NAO, July 1943 at Fort Benning. NAO October 1945. 11,1945 25 months in Trinidad.

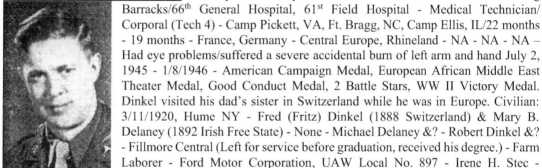

Dinkel, Robert Michael (Bob) Military: US Army - 8/3/1942/Private - 5th Medical Training Barracks/66th General Hospital, 61st Field Hospital - Medical Technician/ Corporal (Tech 4) - Camp Pickett, VA, Ft. Bragg, NC, Camp Ellis, IL/22 months - 19 months - France, Germany - Central Europe, Rhineland - NA - NA - NA – Had eye problems/suffered a severe accidental burn of left arm and hand July 2, 1945 - 1/8/1946 - American Campaign Medal, European African Middle East Theater Medal, Good Conduct Medal, 2 Battle Stars, WW II Victory Medal. Dinkel visited his dad's sister in Switzerland while he was in Europe. Civilian: 3/11/1920, Hume NY - Fred (Fritz) Dinkel (1888 Switzerland) & Mary B. Delaney (1892 Irish Free State) - None - Michael Delaney &? - Robert Dinkel &? - Fillmore Central (Left for service before graduation, received his degree.) - Farm Laborer - Ford Motor Corporation, UAW Local No. 897 - Irene H. Stec - Frederick, Robert - 2/6/1991 – Lakeside Cemetery, Hamburg, NY - 1930, 1940 Federal Census Hume - Sons Fred and Bob. Photo – NAO, Family.

Dunn, Roland Carlyle Military: US Army -11/4/1942/Buffalo/Private - Company A, 794th Military Police Battalion - Military Policeman/Corporal - FT. Riley, KS, Fort Custer, MI/5 months - 2 years,7 months - North Africa, Italy, France - Naples-Foggia, Rome-Arno, Southern France, Rhineland - NA - NA - NA - Suffered from Malaria - 11/4/1945 - Good Conduct Medal, 4 Battle Stars, European African Middle East Theater Medal, WW II Victory Medal. While in Italy he ran into Glenn Williams of Centerville. Civilian: 6/16/1911 NY - Leonard A. Dunn (1882 NY) & Viola J. Morrow (1893 NY) - Lyle A. (1915), Elaine (1921), Margaret L. (1923), Harland S. (1925) - James Morrow (1836 Ireland) & Sarah? (1843 Ireland) - Jones Dunn (1864 NY) & Flora? (1866 NY)- Fillmore Central, Class of 1929 - Farm Hand – Equipment Operator, Erie Railroad - Elsie H. Sonnleitner Holiday - None - 9/19/1976 - Pine Grove Cemetery, Fillmore, NY - 1920, 1930 Federal Census Granger - None. Photo – NAO.

Eldridge, Arnold Harlo (Pat) Military: US Army - 3/1/1943/Private - 242nd Port Company, Army

 Transportation Corps - Winch Operator, Warehouse Supervisor/PFC - FT Niagara, NY, Indiantown Gap, PA, 495th Port Battalion, CA/ nine months - 25 months - Australia, Philippines, New Guinea, Japan - New Guinea, Luzon, Leyte - NA - NA - NA - Malaria, Measles & Dengue Fever - 1/8/1946, FT Dix, NJ - Asiatic-Pacific Theater Medal, Good Conduct Medal, 3 Battle Stars, Philippines Presidential Unit Citation, Army of Occupation, Asian Clasp, WW II Victory Medal - Arnold managed to send home a captured Japanese flag. Civilian: 3/17/1924 Olean, NY - Archie H. Eldridge (1893 NY) & Hazel C. Shaw (1895 NY) - Pauline (1916), Virginia (1918) – Edward D. Shaw (1854 NY) & Carrie Z. Cook (1861 NY) – William F. Eldridge (1869 NY) & Cora Mae Lee (1874 NY) - Fillmore Central, Class of 1941 - Electrician, Lord Electric, NYC - INA - Virginia Tillson (M 9/1/1949 – D 7/8/1963) - Patricia - 9/5/1995 - Pine Grove Cemetery, Fillmore, NY – 1930, 1940 Federal Census Fillmore - Allegany County War Service Record. Photo – NAO.

Eldridge, Eugene Russell Military: US Navy – April 28, 1943/Ensign - *USS Canberra* - INA/Lieutenant

 (jg) (Lt. Commander post war) - Noroton Heights, CT/INA - 13 months - South Pacific/Task Force 58 -Task Force 38 (Operated as part of *USS Yorktown* Carrier Groups & *USS Enterprise* Carrier Group) - Marshall Islands Operations, Asiatic Pacific Raids, Western New Guinea Operations, Bonin's Raids, Marianas Operations, Western Carolinas Operations, Leyte Operations - NA - NA - NA - NA – 12/10/1945 - American Campaign Medal, 7 Battle Stars, Asiatic Pacific Theater Medal, Navy Occupation Medal, Asian Clasp, WW II Victory Medal. Member of the Sons of the American Revolution. Civilian: 12/16/1913 NY - William F. Eldridge (3/2/1863 NY) & Cora M Lee (1873 NY) - Archie (1892 NY), Fern (1894 NY), Russell (1897 NY), Florence L. (1905) – Benjamin Lee (1828 NY) & Mary E. Bentley (1835 NY) - Roswell Eldridge (1819 NY) & Harriet Utter (1835 NY) - Fillmore Central, Class of 1932, George Washington University - Clerk, US Treasury Department - US Treasury Department, US General Accounting Office - Clara Sheppard - None - 3/15/1999 Frederick, MD - Resthaven Memorial Gardens, Frederick, MD - 1930 Federal Census, Granger. Niece Sandy Hodnett Arden. Photo – Yearbook.

Ellis, Leon Robert Military: US Army: 3/21/1944/INA/Private - 13th Armored Division, Hq. Co., 46th

 Tank Battalion - INA/PFC - Fort Dix, NJ, Camp Bowie/INA - INA - France, Germany - Central Europe, Rhineland - NA - NA - NA - NA – 4/21/1946 - American Campaign Medal, European African Middle East Theater Medal, 2 Battle Stars, World War II Victory Medal, French Fourragere Unit Award. Civilian: 5/5/1925/Pike, NY - Raymond Ellis (1903 NY) & Ruth M. Hamer (1903 NY) - Mary (1923 NY), Vivian M. (1928 NY), Donald R. (1930 NY) - Horace E. Hamer (1882 MI) & Grace F. Ackerman (1882 NY) - Earl E. Ellis (1878 MI) & INA (NY) - FCS - Farm Hand for John Cronk – INA - Edwina Sprague/Married 3/10/1946 - INA - Robert - 5/10/2007, Fillmore - Alger Cemetery, Hume - 1930 1940 Federal Census Hume - Son Robert. Photo – NAO.

Emmons, Horace Nason Military: US Army - 5/25/1943/Private - 43rd Infantry Division, 172nd Infantry  Regiment, 2nd Battalion - Rifleman, Supply Sgt/Sergeant - Portland, ME, Camp Wheeler, GA/6 months - two years one month - New Caledonia, New Zealand, New Guinea, Luzon, Leyte, Manila, Philippines, - New Guinea, Luzon, Southern Philippines - NA - NA - NA - NA - 1/8/1946 Camp Beale, CA - Presidential Citation, Asiatic Pacific Theater Medal, WW II Victory Medal, 3 Battle Stars, Good Conduct Medal, Army Occupation Medal, Japan Clasp. Civilian: 7/22/1919/Maine - Alfred E. Emmons ((ME) & Carrie E. Nason (ME) - Myrtle (Day), Lester - Nehemiah J. Nason (1842 ME) & Mariah F. (maybe Wakefield) (1845ME) - Horace P. Emmons (1824 ME) & Harriet R. Tibbetts (1829 ME) -Waterboro High School, ME, Class of 1937 -Leather Worker, Security Guard, Farmer, School Lunch Employee, Bus Driver - Food Service Manager, Gordon College, Houghton College - 1. Mertice Muriel Wentworth (M 4/9/1943 ME), 2. Diane Lynn Lytle (12/26/73 Houghton) - Robert (1946), Virginia (1949), Alfred (1953), Beth (1960) - 12/19/2015, Houghton, NY- Houghton Cemetery - NAO 12/1945 History Society Book - Veteran Horace N. Emmons. Photo – NAO.

Evans, Harland C. Military: US Army - 4/17/1945/Buffalo/Private - INA -? -Private - Camp Clairborne, LA/ 6-7 months - NA - NA - NA - NA - NA - NA - NA - 10/1945 - American Campaign Medal, WW II Victory Medal. Civilian: 1/31/1912 NY - Fred Evans (1879 NY) & Pearl Minerva Davis (NY) - Raymond F. (1905 NY), Gerald V. (1910 NY), Norma R. (1920 NY) - Likely Timothy M. Davis (1860 NY) & Elizabeth? (1856 NY) - FCS (grammar school) - Tractor Driver, Town Highway Dept. - INA - Loretta A. Owens (M 11/2/1934, Limestone, NY) - Harlan C., Jr. (1936 NY), Constance - 5/28/1969, Centerville - Freedom Cemetery, Cattaraugus County - 1940 Federal Census Hume - None.

Eyler, Marvin Howard Military: US Army Air Corps - 8/3/1942/Private - INA - OIC, Physical Training/  Captain - Miami Beach Training Center, FL, Lowry Field, Denver, CO, Fresno, CA, Los Angeles, CA, San Diego, CA/41 months - NA - NA - NA - NA - NA - NA - NA - January, 1946, Lowry AFB, CO - American Campaign Medal, World War II Victory Medal. Civilian: 7/6/1920, Olean NY - Howard E. Eyler (1884 PA) & Bertha E. Schouten (1888 PA) - Kenneth E. (1915 NY), Elizabeth 1916 NY), Doris L. (1923 NY) - Thannal Schouten (1862 NY) & Elizabeth S? (1864 Eng.) - Sylvester Eyler (1859 PA) & Anna Belle? (1857 PA) B.A., Houghton College, Class of 1942, MA & PHD, University of Illinois - Student - Dean, Department of Physical Education, University of Maryland - Catherine Virginia Parks (M 1942) - John, Judith, William - 4/15/2005 - Mt. Pleasant Cemetery, Houghton - 1940 Federal Census Houghton - Wife, Catherine V. Parks Eyler. Photo – Family.

Fairbank, Harry Willard Military: US Army - 12/17/1914 Kansas City, MO/Private, (Following info  for WW II only) - 5th Engineers, Corps of Engineers - Top Sergeant/ Master Sergeant - Camp Breckenridge, KY, Camp Forrest, TN, Army War College, DC /1943-1945 - 22 months - Iceland - NA - NA - NA - NA - NA - First retired 11/30//1945 (Harry reenlisted 1/04/1946 and retired for good 1949) - American Defense Medal, American Campaign Medal, European African Middle East Theater Medal, WW II Victory Medal. (Harry served the US in three wars, Mexican Border War, WW I and WW II. Besides Iceland, he served overseas in the Philippines, Panama Canal Zone, Hawaii, France, and Germany. He participated in five major campaigns in WW I, Chateau Thierry, ST. Mihiel, Vesle Sector, Aisne, Marne, Champaign-Marne and Meuse Argonne. He was wounded 7/15/1918 during the Champaign-Marne battle. In addition to his WW II decorations, Harry earned the Mexican Border Ribbon, the Purple Heart, the WW I Occupation of Germany Ribbon, the WW I Victory Medal with five campaign stars and the Good

Conduct Badge.   His daughter Noreen served in the Army in Korea.) Civilian: 6/16/1890 MD - Frank H. Fairbank (1855 MD) & Sarah E. (Likely Crane) (1858 MD) - Helen (1882 MD), Bernard (1887 MD), Amy R. (1892 MD), Hiram C. (1900 MD) - Likely Philip M. Crane (1817 MD) & Sarah M.? (1820 MD)) - Andrew J. Fairbank (1825 MD & Mary Elizabeth Coram (1825 MD) - Kansas City Schools - Salesman - Retired from Military Service - Bernice Mildred Redanz 12/28/1928, Rossburg, NY - Evelyn C. (1922(Canal Zone), Buddy (Hawaii), Harry, Effie (1937 DC), Noreen - 10/29/1950, Fillmore - Pine Grove Cemetery, Fillmore, NY - NAO 4/1944 - Allegany County War Service Record, Evalyn C. Fairbank Sprowl, Daughter. Family moved to Fillmore in 1941. Photo – NAO.

Fancher, James Elroy Military: US Army - 10/26/1942/Buffalo/ Private - Military Police - Military

Policeman/PFC - Buffalo, Others/39 months - NA - NA - NA - NA - NA - NA - NA - 2/1/1946 - American Campaign Medal, World War II Victory Medal. Brother Lowell also served. Civilian: 10/19/1920 NY - Ralph Dennison Fancher (1883 NY) & Lulu Belle Reed (1887 NY) - Lillis I. (1911 NY), Lester E. (1913 NY), Laura (1926 NY), Lowell (1926 NY) - Earl E. Reed (1865 NY) & Addie L? (1867 NY) - Lucius (Ludlow) H. Fancher (1850 NY) & Mary Esther Rathburn (1856 NY) - Houghton College - Student - Minister, White Rubber Company - 1. Blanche Elizabeth Scott 2. Edna Marie Shiflett 3. Orphie Goldsmith - Miriam Ruth, Grace Elizabeth, Esther Mae, Mary Ann, David Paul, Larry James, Johnny Ray, Pauline - 10/15/2002, Elkins, W.VA - Mountain State Memorial Gardens, Elkins - 1930 Federal Census Houghton – Army Military Police Historian, Fort Leonard Wood, MO. Photo – NAO.

Fancher, Lowell Bernard Military: US Army - 7/24/1944/Private - 167th Field Artillery Battalion, 41st

Infantry Division – Gunner/Driver/? - Camp Roberts, CA/4 months, 2 weeks - 1/11/1945 to 8/2/1946/20 months - Philippines till 9/18/1945; Japan till July, 1946 - Luzon, Southern Philippines campaigns - NA - NA - NA -NA - 8/10/1946 - two Battle Stars, One Arrowhead Device (Palawan), Philippine Presidential Unit Citation Medal, Asiatic Pacific Theater Medal, Army of Occupation Medal, Japan, World War II Victory Medal. Brother James E. Fancher also served. Civilian: 3/22/1926 (NY) - Ralph Dennison Fancher (NY) & Lulu Belle Reed (NY) - Lillis I. (1911 NY), Lester E. (1913 NY), James E. (1920 NY), Laura (1926 N – Lowell's twin sister) - Earl E. Reed (1865 NY) & Addie L.? (1867 NY) - (Ludlow) Lucius H. Fancher (1850 NY) & Mary Esther Rathburn (1856 NY) - Houghton Academy 1942-1944, 1946-47, Houghton College 1947, Bryant and Stratton School of Business 1948 - Milk Handler, Breyer's Ice Cream Factory, Milk Handler - Houghton College Press/ School Bus Driver, Fillmore Central - Lois Irene Gillette (Married 8/27/1949 in Cuba, NY) - Lowell Bernard (1956), Jeffery Emmett (1958),David Maxson (1963), Paul Christian (1965) - 2018 - NA - 1930 Fed Cen Houghton - Veteran Lowell Fancher & Wife Lois. Photo – NAO.

Fancher, Maxwell Lavay   Military: US Army - 11/16/1943/Buffalo/Private - 411th Infantry Regiment
(Anti-Tank Company), 103rd Infantry Division - Radio Operator,/Tec 5 - Camp Howze, TX, Camp Shanks, NY/16 months - 10 months - France, Germany - Central Europe, Rhineland - NA - NA - NA - NA - 2/2/1946 - American Campaign Medal, European African Middle Eastern Theater Medal, WW II Victory Medal, 2 Battle Stars, Army Occupation Medal, Germany Clasp - Civilian: 9/6/1925 Indiana - Willard Lavay Fancher (1887 NY) & Zola M. Kitterman (1896 Indiana) - Gwendolyn (1923 Indiana) - Emmis Kitterman (1865 Indiana) & Phebe A. Wood (1867 Indiana) - Lucius (Will) H. Fancher (1850 NY) & Mary Esther Rathbun) (1856 NY) - Houghton Academy - Student - INA - INA - INA -12/29/1998, Glennallen, Valdez, Alaska - Fort Richardson National Cemetery, Alaska - 1940 Federal Census Houghton - None. Photo – NAO.

Farnsworth, Alma Geraldine (Gerry) Military: US Coast Guard Women's Reserve, SPARS (Sempe Paratos Always Ready) (Sempe Paratos is Latin for Always Ready.) - 6/28/1943/ Apprentice Seaman - Coast Guard Fourth District Headquarters, Philadelphia - Store Keeper/ 2C - Palm Beach, FL, Benjamin Franklin Hotel, Philadelphia/33 months - NA - NA - NA - NA - NA - NA - NA – 2/28/1946 - American Campaign Medal, WW II Victory Medal. Civilian: - 4/3/1923 WI - Gerald B. Farnsworth (1900 NY) & Alma Johnson (1900 WI) - Lucille (1921 ND), Joyce (1930 WI), Katheryn, Roy M. - Likely Ole Johnson Monshougen (1862 Norway) & Agnette C. Helleberg (1867 Norway) - Roy B. Farnsworth (1873 NY) & Martha Lapp (1880 NY) - Fillmore Central School - Student - INA - Leonard Ipri - Jeanne (Fallon) - 10/28/2007 - Saint Joseph Catholic Church, Toms River, NJ - 1940 Federal Census Hume - Sister Lucille Farnsworth Knutson. Photo – NAO.

Farnsworth, Richard Charles (Dick) Military: US Army - 8/13/1941/Private - Battery E, 243rd Coast Artillery Battalion - INA/1st LT. - Ft. Niagara, Ft. Eustis, VA (Battery A, 13th Battalion), Ft. Levett, ME (Battery D – 240th Coast Artillery), Ft. Wetherill, RI, FT. Devens, MA/46 months - NA - NA - NA - NA - NA - NA -Broke leg 12/15/1943, Was in Ft. Devens, MA 12/15/43 to 7/4/44 & 1/04/45 to 4/30/45 - 6/19/1945 Ft. Dix, NJ - American Campaign Medal, WW II Victory Medal. Broken leg was serious. Was in Lowell GH, Ft. Devens, MA. for 11 months. His leg rigged with ropes and pulleys for a couple of months before a cast could be applied. His great grandfather Teron Foster served with Company D, 4th NY Heavy Artillery. Civilian: 12/1/1914/ Fillmore, NY - Alan Earl Farnsworth (1879 NY) & Pearl M. Ballard (1888 NY) - Golda D. (1911 NY) - Jay A. Ballard (1887 NY) & Emma Foster (1867) - Charles Farnsworth (1841 NY) & Drusilla ? (1842 NY) - Fillmore Central, Class of 1932, Houghton College, Class of 1936, Albany State Teachers College, Alfred University - Teacher, Wellsville High School - Math Teacher, Wellsville High School - Vera D. ? (Married 6/25/1941) - Nancy Lee - 11/16/2000 Corpus Christi, TX - Pine Grove Cemetery, Fillmore - 1920,1930 Fed Cen Hume - Allegany County War Ser. Record, None. Photo – NAO.

Ferrin, Albert Eugene (Gene) Military: US Navy - 12/27/43/AC - *PT–307*, Motor Torpedo Boat Squadron 22 - Gunners Mate/S 1-C - Sampson Naval, NY/10 months - 2 months - Africa, Mediterranean Sea - Southern France - 12/8/1944 lost at sea - NA - NA - NA - 12/8/1944 – American Campaign Medal, Africa Middle Eastern Theater Medal, WW II Victory Medal - Eugene's PT boat was on its way from one base to another (on patrol) when a violent storm arose unexpectedly. A huge wave swept Eugene and one of the officers overboard. Crew members reported that both were slammed against the torpedoes and were knocked unconscious before going overboard. The PT boat was damaged by the storm, but still managed to search the area. Two ships and a plane also searched, all without success. Civilian: 1926 NY - Clyde E. Ferrin (1900 NY) & Ruth Margaret Rees (1907 NY) - Rowena M. (1828 NY), Richard C. (1935 NY), Robert L. (1938 NY) - Albert E. Rees (1862 NY) & Margaret E. Williams (1868 NY) - Eugene N. Ferrin (1868 NY) & Jennie McIntosh (1873 NY) - Fillmore Central - Student - NA (Deceased) - Never Married - None - 12/8/1944 - Mediterranean Sea. Remains never found. /Memorial Headstone, Freedom Cemetery, Freedom, NY - 1940 Federal Census Centerville - None. Photo – NAO.

Fiegl, Charles Roy Military: US Navy - 1/18/44/AS - *LCI 867* - Quartermaster/S2C - Sampson,

Solomon, MD, NYC, Lido Beach, LI/12 months - 16 months - Palau Islands - Palau Operations,1945 - NA - NA - NA - NA - 5/6/1946 Lido Beach, LI - American Campaign Medal, Asiatic Pacific Theater Medal. WW II Victory Medal, One Battle Star, Navy Occupation Medal, Asian Clasp. Civilian: 12/13/1925 Centerville - Roy Joseph Fiegl ((1901 NY) & Alma M. Loyster (1908 NY) - Dorothy (1927 NY), Donald (1930 NY) - Louis Loyster (NY) & Lena Green (NY) - Joseph H. Fiegl (1877 NY) & Ida A. Daigler (NY) - Blasdell, NY High School, Class of 1943, Brockport State, NY BS 1953, Brockport State, NY MS 1955) - Student - Physical Education Teacher, Clarence High School, NY - Elizabeth M. Jennejahn (1948 Hilton, NY) - Marc Charles (1949 NY), Barbara Lynn (Schmid) (1952 NY), Dale Elaine (Binggeli) (1955 NY), Lance Christopher (1960 NY) - NA - NA - Born in Centerville - Veteran Charles R. Fiegl. Photo – Veteran, Family.

Fiegl, David Charles Military: US Army - 1/18/1944/Buffalo/Private - 1103rd Army Air Force Base Unit – Radio Operator-Maintenance/Corporal - Scott Field, IL/Morrison Field, FL/26 months - 1 month - North Africa - None - NA - NA - NA - NA 5/16/1946, Fort Dix, NJ - American Campaign Medal, Good Conduct Medal, WW II Victory Medal. - Civilian: 7/28/1920 Centerville, NY - Joseph H. Fiegl (1877 NY) & Ida Anna Daigler (1877 NY) - Roy J. (1901 NY), Ethel (1904 NY), Eugene (1906 NY), Ida (1908 NY), Ellen (1910 NY), Robert (1912 NY), Agnes (1913 NY), Estella (1916 NY), Frieda (1918 NY), Lawrence E. (1923 NY) - Andrew Daigler (1844 NY) & Mary (maybe Wendling) (1852 NY) – Joseph Fiegl (1847 Bavaria) & Magdalena (Hazm?) (1850 NY) - Fillmore Central - Family Laborer (Unpaid), Buffalo Arms Corporation - National Fuel Gas Co. - Lillian R. Runyan - Dennis - 7/3/2013, Dunkirk, NY - Forest Lawn Cemetery, Dunkirk - 1920, 1940 Federal Census Centerville - Niece Claudia Kauffman, Son Dennis Fiegl.

Findlay, Albert Edward (Al) Military: US Army - 1/23/1945/Buffalo/Private - INA -? /Tec 4 - Ft.

Meade, MD/18 months - NA - NA - NA - NA - NA - NA - NA - 8/4/1946 - American Campaign Medal, WW II Victory Medal. Civilian: 4/11//1918 NY - Albert E. Findlay (1874 NY) & Lena Belle Merwin (1880 NY) - Earl (1903 NY), Helen (1907 NY), Agnes (1912 NY), Edna (1915 NY) - Marcus Merwin (1846 NY) & Ester? (1849 NY) - Samuel E. Findlay (1836 NY) & Esther? (1848 NY) - Fillmore Central, Class of 1936 - Laborer, Wyoming County Highway Dept. - INA - Pauline Agnes Roberts (1918 NY) - Paul (1939 NY) - 5/16/1979 - RT 3, Centerville, NY - 1930, 1940 Fed Cen, Centerville, Vesta Wilcox Teeter. Mother Lena B. later married John Fabian.
Photo – Family.

Finnemore, Donald W. (No middle name) Military: US Army - 4/1/1943/Buffalo/Private - 89th Infantry

Division, 355th Infantry Regiment, Company E, 3rd Army, 1st Army - Supply Clerk /PFC - Ft. Leonard Wood, Cedar Rapids, IA, CA, Camp Butner, NC/20 months - 15 months - France, Germany - Rhineland, Central Europe - NA - NA? - NA - NA - 4/5/1946, Fort Dix, NJ - American Campaign Medal, 2 battle stars, European, African Middle Eastern Theater Medal, Good Conduct Medal, World War II Victory Medal, Likely Army Occupation Medal -Germany Clasp, Service Lapel Button. Brother Merton also served. Civilian: 11/11/1918 NY - John N. Finnemore (1873 NY) & Alice P. Whitmore (1881 NY) - Merton (1907), Marie (1909 NY), Clinton (1915 NY), Doris (1917 NY), Marilyn (NY) - Charles Whitemore (1845 NY) & Jennie? (1854 NY) David Fennimore (1823 England) & Harriett (maybe) Eldridge (1831 England) - Fillmore Central, Class of 1936 - Bank Assistant - State Bank of Fillmore - Ernestine C. Gillette - INA - 5/29/1975 Rochester - Pine

Grove Cemetery, Fillmore, NY - NAO 6/1945, NAO 8/1945 - 89th Infantry Div. Assoc. - Sister Marilyn Finnemore (Morse). Photo – NAO.

Finnemore, Merton G. Not FCSD. Military: US Army - Brother Donald W. also served. Civilian: 1906 NY - John Finnemore (1873 NY) & Alice? (1881 NY) - Marie (1909 NY), Clinton (1915 NY), Doris (1917 NY), Donald W. (1918 NY) - INA - INA - INA - INA - INA - INA - INA - INA - INA - INA - None. NAO 1943 pages 120 & 131.

.

Fish, Gerald Burt (Jerry) Military: US Army Air Corps - 11/16/1943 FT. Dix, NJ/Private - NA - B-29 Pilot Training/Air Cadet - Buffalo, Moody Field, GA, Napier Field, AL, Aviation Cadet Center, San Antonia, TX, Perrin Field, Sherman, TX/24 months - NA - NA - NA - NA - NA - NA - NA - 11/2/45 Amarillo, TX - American Campaign Medal, WW II Victory Medal. Civilian: 9/23/1925 Rochester, NY - Leslie R. Fish (1906 Ohio) & Genevieve M.? (1908 NY) - INA - Bert A. Fish (1886 NY) - INA - Durand Eastman, Rochester, Fillmore Central, Presbyterian College, - Mechanic - Car Repair Garage Owner - Norma? (M 6/16/1946 Caneadea, NY) - Jerry - 10/15/2014, Wellsville - Mt. Pleasant Cemetery, Houghton, NY - 1940 Federal Census, Hume - None. Photo – NAO.

Fisher, Almond Edward Military: US Army - 12/17/1934, Brooklyn, NY/Private - 45th Infantry Division, 157th Infantry Regiment, Company E - Infantryman/Platoon Leader/ Major (Lt. Colonel in Reserves) – INA/115.3 months - 17 months - Italy, France - Anzio, Rome Arno, Southern France - NA - Grammont, France 9/13/44 (wounds to both feet) - NA - NA - 9/11/1945 - Medal of Honor, Purple Heart, Arrowhead Badge (Southern France Invasion), Combat Infantryman Badge (1947 Bronze Star), European African Middle East Theater Medal, three battle stars, WW II Victory Medal, French Croix de Guerre (with Palm), 45th Division Unit Award, American Defense Medal, American Campaign Medal - Remained in National Guard for 19 years following almost 11 years of active service. Civilian: 1/28/1913 Hume, NY - John A. Fisher (1886 NY) & Amanda E. Wood (1891 NY) - Gerald (1815 NY), Martha F. (1918 NY), Charles B. (1920 NY), James B. (1922 NY), John A. Jr. (1925 NY), Velma (1927 NY), Alfred (1929), Donald (NY) - John H. Wood (1851 NY) & Frances A. ? (1857 NY) - James S. Fisher (1855 NY) & Martha E? (1853 NY) - Enlisted in Army in 1934 - Veterans Administration Employee, Office Director for 25 years in Jamestown, NY, Buffalo and Town of Tonawanda, Ohio, Director, Lake County Ohio Veterans Service Office - Jeanette Smith (M 7/14/1951) - Gregory, Karen, Patricia, Paula - 1/8/1982 - Arlington National Cemetery (Memorial in Alger Cemetery, Hume.) - NAO 4/1945/Medal of Honor Citation, General Order 32, 4/23/1945 - Nephew David C. Fisher. Building 504, Camp Smith, Peekskill, NY renamed Fisher Hall in his honor, Buffalo Citizen of the Year in 1965, Concord Township, Ohio Citizen of the Year in 1981, A portion of Highway 19 in Hume Township, Allegany County named in his honor. Photo – NAO.

Fleming, Paul Robert Military: US Navy - July, 1944/INA AS - *USS Tyrell (AKA 80)* - Boatswain Mate,

Coxswain 1C - Sampson Naval Base, Norfolk, VA7 months - 16 months - Pearl Harbor, Marshall Islands (Eniwetok, Kwajalein), Caroline Islands (Ulithi), Philippines, Okinawa, Japan - Okinawa Gunto - NA - NA - NA - NA - INA - Asiatic Pacific Theater Medal, WW II Victory Medal, Navy Occupation Medal, Asian Clasp, One Battle Star (Okinawa) . Civilian: 5/17/1922 PA - Timothy Fleming (1897 PA) & Ora V. Clark (1898 PA) - Richard (1919 PA), Edward (1921 PA), Charles (1925 PA), James (1933 PA), Mary (1934 PA), Helen (1939 PA), Catherine Agnes (1918 PA) - Edward P. Clark (1868 PA) & Agnes E. Hope (1874 PA) - Richard Fleming (1862 PA) & Catherine (Katie) ? (1861 Eng.) - Marion Baker - INA - Barber, Fillmore - 12/7/2013, Belfast - Holy Cross Cemetery, Belfast - NA - None - Personal Knowledge. Photo – NAO.

Folts, Stewart Ehman Military: US Army Air Corps - 2/17/1943/Private - 9th Air Force/62nd Troop

Carrier Service - C-47 Pilot/1st Lt. - Syracuse University, Stuttgart Field, AR, Sedalia Field, MO/23 months - 17 months - France, England - Rhineland, Central Europe - NA - NA - NA - NA - 6/29/1946 Ft. Dix, NJ - 2 Battle Stars, American Campaign Medal, European African Middle East Theater Medal, WW II Victory Medal. At end of war transported Allied ex-POWs home, mostly to France. Spent two months at Shrivenham American University near London in the summer of 1945. Civilian: 8/8/1921 NY - Clayton C. Folts (1894 NY) & Irma Ehman (1896 NY) - Keith (1928 NY), Walter (1930 NY), Donna (1932 NY) - Walter G. Ehman (1869 NY) & Eliza Pfeffer (1869 Canada) - Earnest R. Folts (1862 NY) & Carrie Moore? (1878 NY) - Houghton College, American University, London - Student - Instrumental Music Teacher, Fillmore Central (30 years) - Elisabeth Jenkel (M 12/24/1943, West Valley, NY) - Dwight (1947 NY), Kathe (1948 NY), Louise (1949 NY) - 2/24/2002, Geneseo, NY - Mt. Hope Cemetery, West Valley, NY - Fillmore History Club December, 1945 Issue - Son Dwight Folts. Photo – Family.

Ford, Harold Frank Military: US Army - 3/16/1944/New Cumberland, PA/Private - NA (Never assigned to a permanent unit) - Trainee /Private – Field Artillery Replacement Training Center, Ft. Sill, Ok, Ft Leonard Wood, MO, Ft. Dix, NJ /8 months - NA - NA - NA - NA - NA - NA - NA - 11/5/1944 Ft. Dix, NJ - American Campaign Medal (maybe), World War II Victory Medal. Civilian: 10/25/1912 NY - James Ford (1869 England) & Anna E. (Juson?) (1875 England) - James A. (1908 NY), Kathleen R. (1910 NY), Margaret C. (1915 NY), William H. (1917), Robert (1930 NY) - MAYBE William Juson (1852 England) & Sarah? (1855 England) - MAYBE Henry Ford (1843 England) & Margaret Howes (1844 England) - Fillmore Central, One-year college - Farm Laborer - INA - Eva Hamer - INA - 2/18/2007 - Phoenix, AZ - 1920, 1930 Federal Census Centerville - None. Harold's Father James Ford emigrated to the US in 1892 and his Mother Anna in 1907.

Foster, Herbert Robert Military: Not FCSD. Father lived in Fillmore during the early 1940's. US Army - 8/22/1941/Buffalo/Private - Fifth Army, 1st Armored Division - Gunner/Corporal - INA - INA - Italy - INA - INA - INA - INA - INA - INA - American Defense Medal, European Theater Medal, WW II Victory Medal. Civilian: 9/26/1916 MI - Robert L. Foster (1886 NY) & Margaret E.? (1885 MI) - Margarita C. (1911 MI), Norris J. (1922 MI), Doris B. (1927 NY).

Fox, Lowell Burr Military: US Army - 8/27/1943/Private - 1632nd Engineer Base Photomapping Platoon

- Geodetic Computer/Sergeant, Tech 4 - Portland, OR, Camp Upton, NY/7 months - 18 months - Melbourne, Australia, Luzon, Philippines - Luzon Campaign - NA - NA - NA - NA - 9/30/1945 Ft. Dix, NJ - Good Conduct Medal, Philippine Liberation Medal, One Battle Star, Asiatic Pacific Theater Medal, WW II Victory Medal. Civilian: 1/28/1907/ Caneadea, NY - Merton A. Fox ((1880 NY) & Nellie A. Burr (1882 NY) - Hazel I. (1916 NY) - likely George B. Burr (1855 NY) & Lillie E.? (1858 NY) - Willis L. Fox (1850 NY) & Achsa (Axie) L. (maybe Arnold) (1854 NY) -
Teacher, Attica, NY - Teacher, Attica, NY - Dorothy E. Eichhorn (M 6/29/1946, Attica, NY) - Gregory, Sharon, Gwen, Janet - 10/18/1999 Attica, NY - Forest Hill Cemetery, Attica - 1930 Fed Cen Houghton - None. Photo – Yearbook.

Fox, Lynford Sherman Military: US Army - 6/26/1941/Trenton, NJ/Private - INA - INA/Corporal - Camp Lee, VA, Camp San Luis Obispo, CA/INA - INA - INA - NA - NA - NA - NA - 7/31/1945 - American Defense Medal, American Campaign Medal, WW II Victory Medal. Civilian: 3/24/1916 NY - Milton W. Fox (1878 NY) & Amelia V. Sherman (1880 NY) - Marion E. (1907 NY) - Likely William Sherman (1852 NY) & Emma June Vincent (1855 NY) - Willis Fox (1850 NY) & Ascha (likely Arnold) (1854 NY) - INA - Freon Gas Co. - INA - Mary Ella Malady- INA - 11/9/1992 Fillmore - Riverside Cemetery, Belfast - 1920, 1940 Census Houghton – None.

Fox, (Edwards) Mabel Elaine Military: US Army Nurses Corps - 1/15/1942/2nd Lt. - 16th Evacuation Hospital - Orthopedic Surgical Scrub Nurse/1st Lt. - Ft. Dix, NJ/16 - 31 months - England, North Africa, Italy - Naples, North Apennines, Rome Arno - NA - NA - NA - NA - 12/20/1945 - American Campaign Medal, European African Middle Eastern Theater Medal, three Battle Stars, Arrowhead devise for amphibious assault at Salerno, WW II Victory Medal. Mabel served with the Army Reserves from 1945 to 1951 and in Korea from 1951 to 1952. Civilian: 9/24/1911 Cameron, PA - William H. Fox ((1880 PA) & Anna M. (likely) Morse (1884 PA) - Michael R. (1900 PA), William H. (1904 PA), Mary E. (1905 PA), Teresa (1906 PA), James P. (1909 PA), Franklin (1914 PA), Evelyn (1916 PA), Half-Brother Louis Broadbent) NY) - INA - likely William H. Morse (1900 PA) & Almira Giberson (1857 PA) - State Teachers College - Charge Nurse, Maternity Division, St. John's Hospital, Yonkers, NY - INA - ? Edwards - Neal M. - 2/24/1997 - Riverside, CA National Cemetery - NAO 9/44, 2/45 - None. Mabel's Mother Anna's second marriage was to Bernie Broadbent and they lived in Fillmore, which was Mabel's "home" during most of the 1930's and World War II. Likely in college and/or nursing school during most of the 30's. Photo -WIMSA Museum.

Fridley, Ronald Gleave Military: US Army - 1/6/1942/Ft. Niagara/Private - Company B, 234th Engineer Combat Battalion - Alligator Tractor Operator/Corporal (Tech 5) - FT. Niagara, FT Belvoir, VA, Alaska (US territory)/11.5 months - 36 months - England, France, Belgium, Holland, Germany - Normandy, Northern France, Rhineland, Central Europe - NA - NA - NA - NA - 10/18/1945 - American Defense Medal, American Campaign Medal, European, African, Middle East Theater Medal, 4 Battle Stars, Bronze Arrowhead Device, WW II Victory Medal, Bronze Star for Heroic Service, Good Conduct Medal, Army Occupation Medal, Germany Clasp. Civilian: 1/19/1920 NY - Elmer D. Fridley (1893 NY) & Elsie L. Gleave (1894 WI) - Margarita C. (1916 NY), Lucille N. (1917 NY), Shirley M. (1922 NY), Beverly O. (1927 NY) - Wendel A. Gleave (1860 Wis) & Harriet E. Line (1861 NY) - Likely George Friedly (1856 NY) & Elsa Kidd (1858 NY) - Fillmore Central - Farm Laborer - Operating Engineer, Local 832, Rochester - Lillian Cartwright - Daniel, Nancy (Britton), Sandra (Domniffey) - 2/16/1999 Warsaw - Warsaw Cemetery - 1930 1940 Federal Census Granger - Son Daniel. Lived with Alva Barney family in Fillmore.

Fuller, Richard Harlow Military: US Navy - 6/8/1945/AS - *USS Luzon* - Opticians Assistant/Special Artificer/SAO 3-C - Sampson Naval, NY/1.5 Months - 12 months - Saipan, Japan - INA - NA - NA - NA - NA - 7/17/1946 - Asiatic Pacific Theater Medal, Navy Occupation Medal, Asian Clasp, WW II Victory Medal. Dick would likely have been part of the Japan invasion force had it been necessary. Civilian: 1927 NY - Harlan M. Fuller (1894 NY) & Mildred (likely Stewart) (1896 NY) - Betty J. (1925 NY) - likely Edward A. Stewart (1866 NY) & Sarah A. (maybe Slade) (1873 NY) - Charles J. Fuller (1858 NY) & Rennie Mercer (1856 NY) - Syracuse, NY schools - Student - Optometrist, Syracuse, NY - INA - Timothy - NA - NA - The History Club "Northern Allegany County Observes 1945", 2006 - None. Dick and his wife moved to Houghton in 1988.

Gambrel, Vernon Military: US Army - 3/20/1945/Private/Buffalo - INA - INA - INA - INA - INA - NA - NA - NA - NA - 3/31/1946 - World War II Victory Medal, American Campaign Medal. Civilian: 11/20/1924/KY – William McKinley Gambrel (1899 KY) & Pearl Inman (1905 KY) - Lorain (Guthrie) (1935 KY), Della (Peace), Mickie (Smith), Phenton (Thomas) - INA – James Gambrel (1862 KY) & Amanda Jackson (1856 KY) - INA - INA - Career Military - Opal Young (M 8/6/1958, Wise, VA) - None - 12/28/2003, LaFollette, TN - Woodland Cemetery, LaFollette. NAO, March, 1945 – NAO, 3/2945.

Gaus, Clarence Fred Military: US Army - 4/5/1943/Buffalo/Private - Station Complement 4416 - Truck Driver/PFC - Fort Dix, NJ, Camp Forest, TN/20.5 months - NA - NA - NA - NA - NA - NA - Suffered from bad feet - 12/12/1944, Fort Dix, NJ -American Campaign Medal, World War II Victory Medal - Brother Norman also served during the war. Civilian: 7/26/1906 NY - Fred H. Gaus (1878 NY) & Minnie C. Otte (1875 Ger) - Gertrude (1902 NY), Lawrence T. (1908 NY). Norman (1915 NY) - Fred (Heinrich Frederich) Otte (1831 Ger) & Sophia (Sophia Auguste Henriette) Mispelhorn (1842 Ger) - John H. Gaus (1838 Ger) & Kate? (1859 NY) - FCS (Grammar School) - Foreman, NEC - INA - Louise L.? - INA - 4/28/1992, Wellsville – Woodland Cemetery, Wellsville – 1910, 1920 Federal Census Allen, 1925 NYS Census Allen - Cousin Keith Gaus. Photo – Family.

Gaus, Norman Arnold Military: US Army - 4/17/1945/Buffalo/Private - 44th Tank Battalion - Tank Crewman/PFC - Fort Dix, NJ, Fort Knox, KY, Fort Meade, MD/7.5 - 11 months - Japan - None - NA - NA - NA - NA - 11/1/1946/Fort Dix, NJ - Asiatic Pacific Theater Medal, Army of Occupation, Japan Clasp, World War II Victory Medal. Brother Clarence F. also served during the war. Civilian: April 6, 1915, Allen, NY - Fred H. Gaus (1878 NY) & Minnie C. Otte (1875 Ger) - Gertrude (1902 NY), Clarence F. (1906 NY), Lawrence T. (1908 NY) – Fred (Heinrich August) Otte (1831 Ger) & Sophia (Sophia Auguste Henrietta) Mispelhorn (1842 Ger) - John H. Gaus (1838 Ger) & Kate? (1859 NY) - FCS - Farmer - INA – Donna Ruth Kingsley - INA - 12/1985/Wellsville - INA – 1920, 1930 Federal Census Allen, Cousin Keith Gaus. Photo – Family.

Gayford, Gerald Burton (Buss) Military: US Army Air Corps - 11/4/1942/Private - Eighth Air Force,

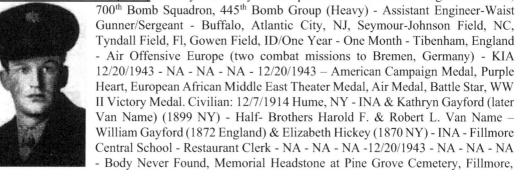

700th Bomb Squadron, 445th Bomb Group (Heavy) - Assistant Engineer-Waist Gunner/Sergeant - Buffalo, Atlantic City, NJ, Seymour-Johnson Field, NC, Tyndall Field, Fl, Gowen Field, ID/One Year - One Month - Tibenham, England - Air Offensive Europe (two combat missions to Bremen, Germany) - KIA 12/20/1943 - NA - NA - NA - 12/20/1943 – American Campaign Medal, Purple Heart, European African Middle East Theater Medal, Air Medal, Battle Star, WW II Victory Medal. Civilian: 12/7/1914 Hume, NY - INA & Kathryn Gayford (later Van Name) (1899 NY) - Half- Brothers Harold F. & Robert L. Van Name – William Gayford (1872 England) & Elizabeth Hickey (1870 NY) - INA - Fillmore Central School - Restaurant Clerk - NA - NA - NA -12/20/1943 - NA - NA - NA - Body Never Found, Memorial Headstone at Pine Grove Cemetery, Fillmore, NY, and Cambridge American Cemetery, Cambridge, England - 1930,1940 Federal Census Hume - None. Photo – NAO, Family.

Gelser, William Calvin Military: US Army - 1/23/1943/Private - Co C, 79th Engineer Combat Construction Battalion - Truck Driver, Light/PFC - Camp Forrest, TN/12 months - 24 months - New Guinea, Philippines - Luzon, New Guinea - NA - NA - NA - NA - 1/12/1946, Fort Knox, KY - Good Conduct Medal, American Campaign Medal, Philippine Liberation Medal, Asiatic Pacific Theater Medal, World War II Victory Medal, 2 Battle Stars (New Guinea, Luzon), Army Occupation Medal, Asian Clasp. Civilian: 12/13/1922 NY - William H. Gelser (1899 NY) & Daisy Evelyn Weaver (1901 NY) - Gladys L. (1926 NY), Thelma (1927 NY), James, Leona, Ira - William Weaver (1858 NY) & Ada V.? (1861 NY) - William J. Gelser (1871 NY) & Anna? (1876 NY) - FCS - INA - INA - Edna Buchholz Fisher (M?) - Judy, Wilma, Keith, Donna; Stepchildren: Donald, Leroy, Robert, Walt, Joan - 12/6/2000 Nunda - Oakland Hill Cemetery, Nunda - 1930 Federal Census Granger - Stepson Donald Fisher.

Gilbert, Forrest Lee Military: US Army - 3/18/1941/Buffalo/Private - INA – INA/Private – INA/Total service time 63 months - INA - INA - INA - NA - INA - INA - INA - 6/20/1947 - American Defense Medal, American Campaign Medal, WW II Victory Medal. Civilian: 5/11/1914 Centerville, NY - Charles H. Gilbert (1882 NY) & Helen Hooper (1892 NY) - Atta (1912 NY), Bernice (1915 NY) - William Hooper (1835 NY) & Helen Campbell (1842 PA) - Albert Gilbert (1854 NY & Clara Van Nocker (1855 NY) - FCS (Grammar School) - Farm Hand - INA - INA - INA - 8/10/1974 - Cadwell Corners Cemetery, Centerville - 1920, 1930, 1940 Federal Census Centerville - None.

Gillette, John Russell (Russ) Military: US Army Air Corps - 11/4/1942/Buffalo/Private - 8th Fighter

Group, 36th Fighter Squadron - Radio Mechanic/Sergeant - Buffalo, Atlantic City, Sioux Falls AFB, SD. Tomah, WI, Jefferson Barracks, MO/12 months - 2 years - Australia, New Guinea, Philippines, Netherlands East Indies, Ie Shima (Okinawa) – Bismarck Archipelago, Papua, New Guinea, Luzon, Leyte, Northern Solomons, Air Offensive Japan, Western Pacific - NA - NA - NA - Bad sunburn, New Guinea - 12/7/1945 Camp Atterbury, IN - Asiatic Pacific Theater Medal, WW II Victory Medal, American Campaign Medal, Good Conduct Medal, Philippine Liberation Medal, 2 Presidential Unit Citations, 7 Battle Stars, Arrowhead Badge (Luzon Invasion). Civilian: 4/28/1919 NY - Robert E. Gillette (1890 NY) & Mabel Maxson (1893 NY) - Anita M. (1914 NY), Robert M. (1916 NY), Althea E. (1926 NY), Lois (1928), Wilma M. (1930 NY) Ronald (1934 NY) – John Maxson - Herbert S. Gillette (1863 NY) & Adeline Reynolds (1863 NY) - Fillmore Central, Class of 1939 - Clerk, Market Basket Stores - INA - Janice Ames - INA - 4/18/1999/Venice, Fl - Venice Memorial Gardens, Venice, FL - 1920 Federal Census Hume - Brother Ronald Gillette. Photo – NAO.

Gleason, Thurlow Heath (Thurlo) Military: US Army Air Corps - 6/17/1938/INA/Private (Reenlisted 11/15/1945 /Rochester) - Likely 341st Bomb Group, 11th Bomb Squadron or 490th Bomb Squadron - Bomb Sight Mechanic (Instrument Repairman)/Master Sgt. - INA/78 months - 10 months - India, Burma, China - India Burma Campaign, Central Burma Campaign - NA - NA - NA - NA - 10/2/1945 - American Defense Medal, American Campaign Medal, Good Conduct Medal, Asiatic Pacific Theater Medal 2 Battle Stars. World War II Victory Medal. Also served in Korea. Civilian: 4/27/1913, Swain, NY - A. Dwight Gleason (1878 NY) & Irma May Heath (1883 NY) - Bessie L. (1904 NY) (McTanaghan) - Mark W. Heath (1842 NY) & Edora D. Clark (1847 NY) - Jerome F. Gleason (1850 NY) & Julia Richardson (1852 NY) - Canaseraga, NY High School, Class of 1931, NY State School of Agriculture, 1934 - Student - Career Military - Caroline K. Powers (M11/1/1941) - David - 4/13/1991 Pasco Co., FL, Cycadia Cemetery, Tarpan Springs, FL - 1930 Federal Census Hume - None.

Graves, Paul Revere Not FCSD. From Wellsville. He was born 9/30/1907 in Genesee, PA. His father was Lewis G. Graves, his mother Lula Haws. Paul was married to Una Wells Graves, the Girls Physical Education teacher at FCS. However, he never lived in the FSCD area. Paul served with the US Army Air Corps from April 1, 1942 until October, 1945. He served in the United States. NAO 1945 pages 24 & 135.

Griggs, Manfred Charles (Manny) Military: US Navy - 3/24/1943/Buffalo/AS - *USS Pentheus* - INA/Seaman 1-C - Sampson Naval, Brooklyn Navy Yard, Great Lakes Naval Training Center, New Orleans, Camp Bradford, Norfolk, VA/15 months - 4 months - Philippines, Aboard Ship - NA- NA - NA - NA - NA - 11/14/1945, Lido Beach NY - American Campaign Medal, Asiatic Pacific Theater Medal, WW II Victory Medal, Navy Occupational Medal, Asian Clasp. The Pentheus was a landing craft repair ship. Civilian: 7/17/1913 NY - Roy O. Griggs (1885 NY) & Emma F.? (1885 WI) - Eleanor M. (1908 NY) Edwin F. (1910 NY), Imogene C. (1911 NY) - INA - Manfred C. Griggs (1858 NY) & Jennie N.? (1858 NY) - INA - Bricklayer - INA – Vrone? (M?) - Joan (1936 NY), June (1939 NY), David? - 3/30/1976 Freedom - Freedom - 1920 Federal Census Hume - None. Photo-NAO.

Harte (Raimondi), Elin Griswold Military: Women's Air Service Pilots (WASPS) - 1/16/1943 - likely, 5th Ferrying Group, ATC/WASP Units, Fort Davis, NC, Ft. Haan, CA - Pilot/WASPs - Hughes Air Field, Houston, TX, Avenger Field, Sweetwater, YX, Love, Field, Dallas, TX, Orlando, FL, Camp Davis Air Field, NC, Ft. Haan, CA/23 months - NA - NA - NA - NA - NA - NA - NA - 12/20/1944 - American Campaign Medal, WW II Victory Medal., WASP Congressional Gold Medal. Order of Finella. Civilian: 1/5/1918, Syracuse, NY -? Harte & Auretta McLeod (1889 NY) - INA - Paul S. McCleod (1847 Canada) & Ellen (Elin?) Ryan (1849 Ireland) - Thomas Hart (1865 Canada) &? - Julia Richmond High School, NYC - Red Cross, Air Traffic Controllers, Columbia Movie Studios - Farming - Adolfo Thomas Raimondi/1946 Ca - Jean (NY), Elin (NY), William (NY) - 3/2/1996 - White Cemetery, Rushford, NY - Per children Jean & William. Photo – Family.

Haskins, Donald Robert (Don) Military: US Army Air Corps: 7/1/1942/Private - 15th Air Force, 746

Bomb Squadron, 456 Bomb Group, Heavy (B-24s) - Armament Chief/Master Sergeant
- Buffalo, Miami, FL, Buckley Field, Denver, Gowan Field, Boise, ID, Bruning AFB,
NB, Camp Kearns, UT, Muroc Air Base, CA /21.2 months - 19 months - Italy – Air
Offensive Europe, Naples-Foggia, Rome-Arno, Normandy, Northern France, Southern
France, North Apennines, Rhineland, Central Europe, Po Valley - NA - NA - NA -
Meningococcal Meningitis at Gowan Field - 9/13/1945 - American Campaign Medal,
Good Conduct Medal, Distinguished Unit Citation (Weiner Neustadt, 5/10/44),
Distinguished Unit Citation (7/2/44 Budapest), European African Middle East Theater
Medal, Presidential Unit Citation with Oak Leaf Cluster, Bronze Star (Meritorious), 10
Battle Stars, WW II Victory Medal. Civilian: 4/24/1921, Centerville, NY - Robert D. Haskins (1901 NY)
& Elizabeth E. Radley (1903 NY) - Arda M. (1923 NY), Jenette G. (1925 NY), June M. (1926 NY),
Earnest (1931 NY), Oline (1933 NY), Roger W. (1935 NY), Arthur J. (1937 NY) - Leonard J. Radley
(1868 NY) & Jeanette Mae Cory (1871 Iowa) - Alfred Haskins (1875 NY) & Grace B. Stull (1878 PA)
- Batavia NY School System - Automobile Mechanic - Transportation Supervisor, Rushford Central
School - Marium Smith - Audean, Dennis, Merle, Alfred - 8/1/2012, Pulaski, TN - White Cemetery,
Rushford, NY - 1940 Federal Census Hume - Veteran Donald R. Haskins.   Photo – NAO.

Hatch, Milford Malary (Sharkey) Military US Army - 5/18/1945/Buffalo/Private - Engineers Corps -

Labor Foreman/ Tech 4 - FT. Leonard Wood, MO/7 months - 6 months - Dutch Guiana
- None - NA - NA - NA - NA - 6/17/1946, Ft. Dix, NJ - American Campaign Medal,
Asiatic Pacific Theater Medal, WW II Victory Medal, Lapel Button. Milford's great
grandfather, Cyrus Hatch, served in the 19th NY Cavalry (1st NY Dragoons) during the
Civil War. He died of small pox during the war. Civilian: 8/27/1915 Hume, NY -
Merton H. Hatch (1891 NY) & Ida M. Beardsley (1889 NY) - Ruby J. (1912 NY),
Alton M. (1915 NY), June J. (1923 NY), Alton G. (1925 NY) - Mallory Beardsley
(1860 NY) & Nancy? (1862 NY) - Adelbert Hatch (1861 NY) & Nettie? (1862 NY) -
FCS - Farmer - INA - Virginia Ivia Covert (M 11/16/1940, Higgins) - Karen (White)
- 6/9/1996 - Freedom Cemetery -1930 1940 Federal Censuses Centerville - None. Milford was in the
Civilian Conservation Corps from 10/14/1935 to 2/11/1936. Photo - NAO

Hatch, Paul Story Military: US Army - 4/8/1943/Ft. Niagara/Private - 37th Infantry Division, Company

A, 129th Infantry Regiment? - Rifleman-Squad Leader/PFC - Buffalo, FT. Leonard
Wood, MO., San Francisco/6 months - 10/1943-3/1944 - Guadalcanal, Bougainville
- Northern Solomon's Campaign - 3/19/1944, Bougainville - NA - NA - NA -
3/19/1944 - One Battle Star, Purple Heart, Silver Star, Pacific Theater of Operations
Medal, WW II Victory Medal. Paul received the Silver Star for saving the life of
wounded soldier Otto J. Boerner on 2/14/1944. He was in charge of a mortar squad
when he was killed by an enemy mine. Civilian: 11/12/1924 Centerville, NY - Story
Palmer Hatch (1887 NY) & Jeanie (Jessie) Webster (1892 NY) - Wellington W.
(1913 NY), Onalee (1919 NY), Harry C. (1931 NY) - Mallory Beardsley (1860 NY)
& Nancy? (1862 NY) - Adelbert Hatch (1861 NY) & Nettie? (1862 NY) - Fillmore
Central School, Class of 1942 - Bookkeeper, Drainage Company - NA - NA - NA - 3/19/1944- Pine
Grove Cemetery, Fillmore (Paul was originally buried in the Military Cemetery on Bougainville) - 1930
1940 Federal Census Centerville, Allegany County War Service Record - None. Paul's great grandfather,
Cyrus Hatch, served in the 19th NY Cavalry (1st NY Dragoons) during the Civil War. He died of small
pox during the war. Photo – NAO.

Hauser, Frederic Clement (Ted) Military: US Army – 5/26/1943 (Entered 6/9/1943)/Buffalo/Private - INA - INA/Corporal - Camp Palacios (previously Hulen), TX/20 months - NA - NA - NA - NA - NA - NA - NA - 1/16/1945 - American Campaign Medal, WW II Victory Medal. Civilian: 9/12/1910 Houghton, NY - Charles A. Hauser, Jr. (NY) & Louise E. Clement (Crandall) (1885 NY) - Gladys (1904 PA), Half Sibs: John Curtis (NY), William Crandall (NY) - INA - Jacob T. Clement (1840 NY) & Electa R. Wilson (1857 NY) - 3 years college - Salesman, cemetery headstones - INA - Elsie Jane Nickerson (M 1/29/1938, Wellsville) – Richard C., Jane Victoria (Colten) - 8/7/1992, Barnstable County, MA - Massachusetts National Cemetery, Bourne, MA - 1930 Federal Census Houghton - None.

Hayes, Willis Harvey Military: US Navy - 2/3/1943/Dartmouth College, NH/AS - Brooklyn Armed Guard Center - Commanding Officer, Armed Guard Unit/Lieutenant - Dartmouth, NH, Princeton, NJ, Naval Training School (Local Defense), Boston, MA, Little Creek, VA/5 months plus - INA - Europe, England - None - NA - NA - NA - NA - 11/16/1945 - American Campaign Medal, European, African, Middle East Theater Medal, WW II Victory Medal. Civilian: 2/13/1915 (Hartford, CT) - Willis L. Hayes (1888 CT) & Agnes Harvey (1889 NY) - Howard W. (1917 CT) - INA - William L. Hayes (1850 CT) & Ida May Emmons (1854 CT) - University of Connecticut - Agricultural Teacher, Rushford Central School, Fillmore Central School - Federal Land Bank, Springfield, MA - Kathryn B.? - Barbara (Tramontana), Elizabeth (Miller) - 8/29/2004 at home, Reeds Landing, Springfield, MA - INA - NAO, 11/1943 - Obituary, Hartford Courant, 9/3/2004. Photo – Yearbook.

Hazlett, Richard William Military: US Army - 4/17/1945/Buffalo/Private - INA - INA - INA/20 months - NA - NA - NA - NA - NA - NA - 12/19/1946 - American Campaign Medal, World War II Victory Medal. Civilian 11/16/1926 - Ray W. Hazlett (1892 NY) & Emma Frances McCord (1903NY) - Mildred (1925 NY), Theodore (1929 NY), Ray F. (1931 NY), Donald P. (1938 NY), Carol J (1937 NY) (Venuto) - William McCord (1868 NY) & Elanora? (1870 NY) - William A. Hazlett (1854 Ohio) & Alice Mary? (1859 NY) - Houghton College -Student - Professor - G. LaDonna Brentlinger - INA - 11/10/2007 Buried Mt. Pleasant, Houghton, NY - 1940 Federal Census. Picture – NAO.

Henry, Robert Albert Not FCSD. His parents were from the area. Robert was born 11/11/1917 and died 11/18/1999. He served in the US Army from 4/11/1941 until 10/5/1945. His parents were Ward B. Henry and Ottilie D. Scharf. Robert was in the second wave of the invasion at Normandy. He was captured in action on July 13, 1944, held at Stalag 3C, it Drewitz Brandenburg, Prussia. He was eventually liberated. NAO 1944 p 90 & 1945 p 24.

Herring, Earl Lewis Military: US Navy - 3/22/1944/Buffalo/AS - *USS Alaska (CB-1)* - INA/S2C - Sampson Naval Base, USS Alaska/6 months - NA - NA - NA - NA - NA – NA - Broken Fingers, Accident aboard ship - 9/5/44, Philadelphia Naval Hospital - World War II Victory Medal, American Campaign Medal. Civilian: 7/14/1926/NY - Roy W. Herring (1903 NY) & Pearl L. Hamilton (1908 NY) - Robert (1929 NY) - Guy E. Hamilton (1881 NY) & Florence Ruth Williams (1884 NY) – Walter B. Herring (1864 NY) & Phebe O. Sipp (1867 NY) - Cuba CS - Student - Farmer - Helen Jean Vaughn - Cindy P. -10/20/2006/West Clarksville, NY/Clarkesville Cemetery, Allegany County - Fillmore History Club WW II Book, 1945 - Son Todd Herring. Photo – Family.

Hodnett, Charles Edward Military: US Army - 11/7/1941/Private - 3rd Army, Transportation Corps - Company Clerk/Sergeant - Ft. Niagara, NY, Camp Lee, VA, Ft, Hamilton, NY/est. 18 months 1 week - est. 28 months 2 weeks - England, France, Germany - possibly Northern France and Rhineland - NA - NA - NA - Ill in base hospital at Ft. Hamilton - 9/30/1945 - American Campaign Medal, European African Middle East Theater Medal, 2 Battle Stars, WW II Victory Medal. While in England, Charles ran into W.W. Hayes, who had been his Agricultural Teacher at Fillmore. Hs brother Russell managed to visit him in France and the two went to Paris together. They had not seen each other in three years. Brother Russell also served during the war. Civilian: 1/9/1920 NY - William H. Hodnett ((1894 NY) & Fern O. (1894 NY) - Russell (1919 NY), Wilma (1923 NY), Keith (1927 NY) - William W. Eldridge ((1868 NY) & Cora Mae Lee (1873 NY) - Herbert Hodnett (1869 NY) & Nellie L. Rice (1893 NY) - Fillmore Central Class of 1939 - INA - INA - INA - Charles Nicholas - 1/20/2005 East Amherst, NY - INA - 1930 Federal Census Hume - None. Photo – NAO.

Hodnett, Forrest Luke Military: US Navy - 7/7/1943, Lorain, OH/AS - *SS Gasper De Portola, SS* *Theodore Parker, SS Josiah B. Grinnell, SS William Brewster* - Navy Armed Guard (Anti-Aircraft)/S1C - Great Lakes Naval Training Base, Armed Guard School, Gulfport, MS, New Orleans Armed Guard Center, Brooklyn Armed Guard Center, Shoemaker, CA, Cleveland/INA - 21 months (assigned to ships above) - INA - INA - NA - NA - NA - Sick, St. Albans Hosp., NT August, 1944 -10/8/1945 , Cleveland, OH - American Campaign Medal, European African Middle Eastern Theater Medal, WW II Victory Medal. Served in the US Coast Guard from 104/1933 to 10/3/1936 in Lorain, OH. Civilian: 9/1/1911 Hume, NY- Henry Richard Hodnett (1873-NY) & Anna Hayes (1874-NY) - Cecilia Frances (1895), Kenneth (1897 NY), Beatrice Anna (1901 NY), Bernice Anastasia (1905 NY), John Garrett (1908 NY), Marion Henry (1909 NY), Marlie James (1912 NY) - Thomas Hayes (1852 IRE) & Margaret Merron (1853 IRE) - Richard Hodnett 1834 (IRE) & Mary Hickey (Hart) 1836 (IRE) - Fillmore Central - Shearman's Helper, American Ship Building Company, Lorain, OH - INA - Virginia Eleanor? (M OH) - None - 5/12/1983 Fillmore - Holy Cross Cemetery, Fillmore, NY - 1920 Fed Cen Hume - Navy Personnel File. Photo – Family.

Hodnett, Marlie James Military: US Army - 6/3/1942/Private - 16th Infantry Regiment, 1st Infantry Division - Rifleman/PFC - Fort Bragg, NC 6/3/42-11/10/42, Camp Butner, NC, Fort Dix, NJ, City College of NY, NY City Post Office, Hospital Troop Train (on detachment from Post Office 6/20/44-10/26/45 - 11/10/42 - 6/20/1944/22 months - 19 months - Tunisia (11/42- 5/43) , Sicily (7/43) - Tunisian & Sicilian Campaigns (Battles, at least nine, including Kasserine Pass, El Guettar, Longstop Hill, Hill 523, Medjez -El-Bab in Tunisia & Gela in Sicily) - NA - Tunisia 3/29/1943,Tunisia, 4/24/1943 (birthday of the author, Marlie's great nephew), Sicily 7/11/1943 - NA - NA - 10/26/1945 - Three Purple Hearts, Distinguished Unit Badge (Sicily), European African Middle Eastern Theater Medal, two Battle Stars, American Campaign Medal, World War II Victory Medal, World War II Service Lapel Button, Arrowhead Badge, Combat Infantryman Badge (1947 Bronze Star). Civilian: 11/16/1912 Hume, NY - Henry Richard Hodnett (1873 NY) & Anna Hayes (1874 NY) - Cecilia Frances (1895 NY), Kenneth (1897 NY), Beatrice Anna (1901 NY), Bernice Anastasia (1905 NY), John Garrett (1908 NY), Marion Henry (1909 NY), Forrest Luke (1911 NY) - Thomas Hayes (1850 IRE) & Margaret Merron (1851 IRE) - Richard Hodnett (1834 IRE) & Mary Hickey (Hart) (1836 IRE) - 3 years, Fillmore Central High - Railroad Track Man - Railroad - Shirley Munn - Craig (1950 NY), Gary (1952 NY) - 8/31/1991 - Pine Grove Cemetery - 1930 Fed Cen Fillmore - Sons Craig & Gary. Photo -NAO.

Hodnett, Russell Clair Military: US S Army - 2/7/1941/Private - 5th Army, 7th Army, 3rd Army, 89th

Ordnance Heavy Maintenance Company - Company Commander/Captain - FT. Niagara, Camp Normoyle, San Antonio, TX, Camp Lee, VA, FT. Warren, WY, FT. Custer, MI, FT. Moultrie, SC, FT. Bragg, NC/ 27 months - 32 months - North Africa, Italy , France, Austria, Germany - Tunisian, Northern Italian, Southern France, Central Germany, Rhineland - NA - NA - NA - Injured, Jeep Accident, France, 11,1944/Had Flu at Camp Normoyle - 1/14/1946, Camp Dix, NJ - American Defense Medal, American Campaign Medal, European African Middle Eastern Theater Medal, Bronze Star for Meritorious Service, 5 Battle Stars, WW II Victory Medal . Brother Charles also served. Civilian: 1/5/1919 Hume, NY - William H. Hodnett (1894 NY) & Fern O. Eldridge (1894 NY) - Charles (1920 NY), Wilma (1923 NY), Keith (1927 NY) - William W. Eldridge ((1868 NY) & Cora Mae Lee (1873 NY) - Herbert Hodnett (1869 NY) & Nellie L. Rice (1893 NY) - Fillmore Central, Class of 1937, Houghton College, Cornell University, Class of 1947 - Student - Asst. Agent, Agricultural Extension Service - Virginia Sheppard   (M 10/13/1945, DC) - Gerald W. (1947 NY), Donald A. (1954 NY), Sandy (Arden) - NA - NA - 1930 Federal Census Hume, Allegany County War Service Record, Veteran Russell C. Hodnett, Daughter Sandy Hodnett Arden. Photo – NAO.

Hoffman, Jr. Jacob Joseph Military: US Army - 12/7/1944 (Reenlisted 12/21/1945 in Ch'ongju,

Korea)/Private - Company C, 17th Infantry Regiment, 7th Infantry Division - Rifleman/Military Policeman Corporal - Camp Blanding, Fl, Portland, OR/6 Months - 20 months - Okinawa, Korea - None - NA - NA - NA - NA - 12/20/1946, Presidio, CA - Army Occupation Medal, Asian Clasp, Asiatic Pacific Theater Medal, WW II Victory Medal. Jacob's unit was scheduled to be in the first invasion wave, if an invasion of Japan had been necessary. Post war was part of the occupation forces in Korea. Civilian: 1926 - Conry J. Hoffman (1890 PA) & Edith M. Crowl (1896 PA) - Howard D. (1921 PA), Eleanor M. (1923 PA) - Likely William A. Crowl (1865 PA) & Stella M? (1876 PA) - William A. Crowl (1865 Austria) & Stella M. Strevy (1876 PA) - INA - INA - INA - Marie - INA - NA - NA. None. Photo – NAO.

Hopkins, Wesley Eugene (Bud) Military: US Army - 11/8/1943/Buffalo/ Private - 26th Infantry

Regiment. 1st Infantry Division - Rifleman/PFC - FT. Benning, GA, Camp Livingston, LA/10 months, 2 weeks - 18 months, 1 week - France, Germany - Ardennes-Alsace, Rhineland, Central Europe - NA - NA - NA - Injured in line of duty February 22. 1945 (2 months in hospital), chopping wood - March 25, 1946, Fort Dix, NJ - American Campaign Medal, European African Middle East Theater Medal, WW II Victory Medal, Good Conduct Medal, Combat Infantry Badge- 1947 Bronze Star, 3 Battle Stars, Army Occupation Medal, Germany Clasp, Belgium Fourragere. Civilian: 6/14/1925 Buffalo, NY - Forrest W. Hopkins (1899 NY) & Josephine Emma Martin (1904 NY) - Richard C. (1935 NY) - William H. Martin (1870 NY) & Abbie A. Mullikin (NY)- Charles M. Hopkins (1863 NY) & Bertha B. Payne (1874 NY) – South Park High School, Buffalo, FCS, Class of 1943, - Curtis Defense Plant, Buffalo – Insurance Manager, Rieman Realty Company – Edna P. Holmes (M 12/14/1946, Buffalo - INA - 5/27/1997 East Aurora, NY – Hillcrest Cemetery & Mausoleum, Hamburg, NY – NAO, 10, 1943 - FCS Graduate 1943 - None.   Photo – NAO.

Howden, Erwin Culver  Military - US Navy - 8/28/1942/Buffalo/AS - *USS Pennsylvania* - Fireman/Machinist Mate 2 C - Great Lakes Naval Training Center, San Francisco/3 months - 1943 to 1945, aboard USS Pennsylvania - Attu, Kiska, Hawaii, Makin Atoll, Butaritari, Kwajalein, Eniwetok, Engebi, Parry Island, New Hebrides Islands, Australia, Saipan, Tinian, Guam, Orote Peninsula, Peleliu, Anguar, Leyte, Luzon, Lingayen Gulf, Okinawa - Operations: Aleutians, Gilbert Islands, Marshall Islands, Marianas, Western Caroline Islands, Leyte, Luzon - NA - NA - NA - NA - 12/1945 - Philippine Liberation Medal, Asiatic Pacific Theater Medal , Navy Unit Commendation Medal, Seven Battle Stars, World War II Victory Medal. Civilian: 9/10/1921 NY - Leon F. Howden (1888 NY) and Ethel Culver (1890 NY) - Virginia (1919 NY), Wendell (1927 NY) - Thomas A. Culver (1863 NY) & Jennie C.? (1870 NY) Allen Howden (1860 NY & Sarah Curtis (1866 (NY) - Fillmore Central, Class of 1939 - Bell Aircraft Plant, Buffalo - Stekl Hardware Store, Fillmore, Carmichael Hardware, Castile, Letchworth State Park - Elizabeth Burr - Cindy (1949 NY) Martin (1954 NY) - 1/18/1994 Rossburg, NY - East Koy Cemetery - 1930 Federal Census Fillmore - Son Martin Howden. Photo NAO.

Howden, Wendell Allen  Military: US Army - 10/22/1945/Private - Battery B, 18th Field Artillery Battalion - Cannoneer/Classification Specialist/Tech 5 - FT. Dix, NJ, FT. Knox, KY, FT Ord, CA, Ft Sill, OK/19 months - NA - NA - NA - NA - NA - NA - NA - 6/1/1947 - American Campaign Medal, WW II Victory Medal. Civilian: 7/3/1927 NY - Leon F. Howden (1888 NY) and Ethel Culver (1890 NY) - Virginia (1919 NY), Erwin (1921 NY) - Thomas A. Culver (1863 NY) & Jennie C.? (1870 NY)- Allen Howden (1860 NY) & Sarah Curtis (1866 (NY) - Fillmore Central, Class of 1945, Alfred State University (Associate Degree), NY - Student - DGCO, General Manager, Martin Oven Co., Owner, Howden's Hardware Store - Mabel Pickett (M2/7/1953) - Alan (1953 NY), Susan (1956 NY), Bruce (1962 NY) - 11/17/1992 Olean, NY - East Koy Cemetery, Pike, NY - 1930 Federal Census Fillmore - Son Bruce Howden. Photo – NAO.

Irish, Clarence Loran (Joker) Military: US Army - 10/3/1042/Buffalo/Private - Troop "A", 2nd Training Regiment - ?/Private - Fort Riley, KS/37 months (plus additional time at the Central Branch, Disciplinary Barracks at Jefferson Barracks, MO. Was confined for being AWOL for the 4th time.) - NA - NA - NA - NA - NA - NA – Feb or Mar, 1944, Injured hand at Fort Riley, in hospital for some time – Dishonorable Discharge11/14/1945 (Date of discharge was suspended until completion of his sentence which was for five years. No information on time served.) - None. Civilian: 5/19/1921 (NY) - Loran B. Irish (1883 NY) & Edna E. Clark (1902 NY) - Lawrence B. (1925 NY), Ruth V. (1929 NY) - Berthal (1931 NY), Francis T. (1933 NY), Betty Jean (1936 NY), Clatham (1938 NY) – Charles V. Clark (1864 NY) & Esther J. Clute (NY) - Perry M. Irish (1853 NY) & Ellen E. Chamberlain (1853 NY) - FCS - Laborer - INA – Ruth G.? - Loren B. - 10/22/1989, Topeka, KS - Rochester Cemetery, Topeka, KS - 1925 Granger - None.

Isham, Allen Leroy (Pat)  Military: US Army - 10/3/1942/Ft. Niagara/Private - 5th Army, 36th Infantry Division, 141st Infantry Regiment - Infantryman/Staff Sergeant - Ft. McClellan, AL, Shenango R.R. Depot, Norfolk, VA./13 months - 12 months - North Africa, Italy – Campaigns - Naples Foggia, Anzio, Rome Arno/ Battles: Salerno, Mount Maggiore, Monte Lungo, San Pietro, Monte Cassino, Anzio, Valletti, Rome, Magliano - KIA, 6/22/1944 - NA - NA - NA - 6/22/1944 - American Campaign Medal, Combat Infantryman's Badge (1947 Bronze Star), Purple Heart, Bronze Star, Silver Star, European Theater of Operations Medal, Arrowhead Badge (Salerno) 3 Campaign Battle Stars, WW II Victory Medal - Silver Star Citation, General Order 230, HQ 36th Infantry Division. Civilian: 3/17/1916 NY - Burton W. Isham (1887 NY) &

Marion L. Johnson (1880 NY) - Richard H. (1899 NY), Mildred (1903 NY), Alberta P. (Mrs. Richard Smith) (1914 NY), - Isaac Johnson (1840 NY) & Mary E.? (1850 NY), Adolph A. Burton (1850 NY) & Jane? (1854 NY) - Rushford Central School, Class of 1934 - Trackman, Pennsylvania Railroad, I.W. Jewell, Inc. - NA - Crystal Marie Burr (M 6/13/1942 Allegany County, NY) - None - 6/22/1944 - Rushford, NY - NAO 11/1944 Houghton - Wife Crystal M. Burr Isham Michel. Photo – Family.

James, Earl Jesse Justin Military: US Army - 6/5/1944/Fort Dix, NJ//Private - Fort Dix, NJ, Basic Training Only - Trainee/Private – Fort Dix, NJ/3 month, 2 weeks - NA - NA - NA - NA - NA - NA - 9/22/1944 - WW II Victory Medal. Brothers Merlin & Francis also served. Civilian: 12/25/1920, NY - Died 5/12/1985 - Leon D. James (1883 NY) & Florence Van Gilder (1888 NY) - Hollis L. (1915 NY), Alvin F. (1917 NY), Lillian P. (1924 NY), Marleah (1926 NY), Evelyn F. (1928 NY) - Francis L. (1910 NY), Merlin (1913 NY), Kenneth G. (1919 NY) - Frank V. Van Gilder (1863 NY) & Esther A. Letson (1867 NY) - George H. James (1859 Canada) & Arabell S. Voss (1862 NY) - Grammar School - Farm Laborer - INA - Ethel J. Gill - Michael, William, John - 5/12/1985 - Short Tract Cemetery, Short Tract, NY - 1940 Federal Census, Short Tract - None.

James, Francis Lyman. Military: US Army - 4/1/1943/Buffalo/Private - INA - INA/Private - Camp Mackall, NC/12 months - NA - NA - NA - NA - NA - Severally injured his foot in February of 1944. - 3/30/1944 - American Campaign Medal, WW II Victory Medal. Bothers Earl and Merlin also served during the war. Civilian: 11/29/1909, NY - Leon D. James (1883 NY) & Florence Van Gilder (1888 NY) - Merlin D. 1913 NY), Hollis L. (1915 NY), Alvin F. (1917 NY), Kenneth (1919 NY), Justine Earl (1921 NY), Marleah (1926 NY), Evylan (1928 NY) - Frank V. Van Gilder (1863 NY) & Esther A. Letson (1867 NY) - George H. James (1859 Canada) & Arabell S. Voss (1862 NY) - Grammar School, probably FCS - Dairy Farmer - INA - Crystal V. Harris - Roger L. - 1/3/1991 Short Tract - Short Tract Cemetery - 1940 Census, Granger - None.

James, Merlin Dee (Tony) Military: US Army - 4/15/1941/Buffalo/Private - Battery G, 9th Coastal Artillery, Headquarters Detachment,1319th Service Command Unit Station Component – Company C, 713th Military Battalion/Policeman/PFC - Ft. Eustis, VA, FT. Andrews, MA, Miami, Fl, Ft. Monroe, VA /28 months - 21 months - Ascension Island, South Atlantic - American Campaign - NA - NA - NA - NA - INA – American Campaign Medal, European, African Middle East Theater Medal, WW II Victory Medal. Brothers Earl & Francis also served during the war. Civilian: 7/18/1912 - Leon D. James (1883 NY) & Florence Van Gilder (1888 NY) - Frances L. (1910 NY), Hollis L. (1915 NY), Alvin F. (1917 NY), Kenneth G. (1919 NY), Earl J. (1920 NY), Lillian P. (1924 NY), Marleah L. (1926 NY), Evelyn F. (1928) - Frank Van Gilder (1863 NY) & Esther Letson (1867 NY) - George H. James (1859 NY) & Arabell S. Voss (1862 NY) - FCS, Grammar School - Farming - INA – Hazel Russell (M 10/9/1945) - INA - 3/18/2006, Richmond, VA – Washington Memorial Parks Mausoleums - NAO 5/45, Short Tract - None. Photo – NAO.

Johannes, Clifford Carl Military: US Army - 5/27/1941/Buffalo/Private - Recalled to Active Service 1/14/1942/Fort Niagara - 396th Engineer Company/Co. C, 713 Military Police Battalion - Military Policeman/PFC - FT. Leonard Wood (396th Engineer Company), MO, Baltimore, MD, Fort Jay, NY/29 months, one week - None - None - NA - NA - NA - NA - Original, November or December, 1941, Last November 30, 1943. Honorable discharge for the convenience of the government by reason of his importance to national health, safety, or interest. Civilian: 10/26/1910, Caneadea NY - Edward C. Johannes (1885 NY) & Winnie L. Archilles (1885 NY) - Clarence E. (1909 NY), Leo H. (1913 NY), Dorothy

W. (1915 NY), Mildred M. (1917 NY), Edith R. (1920 NY) - Henry J. Archilles (1847 Germany) & Dora Walters (1859 Germany) - Fred Johannes (1860 NY) & Caroline (Carrie) Lapp (1859 NY) - Grammar School – Clark E. Walker - Carpenter & Sawmill Operator - Eva Marble - Carmelia, Milford - 1/28/1971 - Riverside Cemetery, Belfast, NY – Discharge Document – Home, Fillmore, NY. Photo – NAO.

Johannes, Edith Rose Military: US Army Nurses Corps - 8/30/1944/2nd Lt. - 201st General Hospital - Nurse/1st Lt. - Atlantic City, NJ/3 months - INA - England, France - Rhineland Campaign - NA - NA - NA - NA - INA – European, African, Middle Eastern Theater Medal, WW II Victory Medal, One Battle Star. Civilian: 4/20/1919 NY - Edward C. Johannes (1886 NY) & Winnie L. Archilles (1885 NY) - Clarence E. (1909 NY), Clifford C. (1911 NY), Leo H. (1913 NY), Dorothy W. (1915 NY), Mildred M. (1919 NY) - Henry J. Archilles (1847 Germany) & Dora Walters (1859 Germany) – Fred Johannes (1861 NY) & Caroline (Carrie) Lapp (1863 NY) - Belfast High School, NY - Student - Professor, Nursing, Alfred University, NY - NA - NA – 3/19/2013, Cabot, PA - Riverside Cemetery, Belfast, NY – 1930 Federal Census Houghton, NAO, 11/1944.

Johannes, Richard Smith Military: US Army - 8/23/1944 Buffalo/Private - Army Services Training Center - INA/PFC - Fort Belvoir/22 months - NA - NA - NA - NA - NA - NA - NA - 6/29/1946 - American Campaign Medal, World War II Victory Medal. Civilian: 7/31/1921/NY - Robert A. Johannes (1890 NY) & Maude C. Smith (1890 NY0 - Lillian (1916 NY) - Frank Smith (1859 NY) & Carrie Phinney (1866 NY) - Andrew Johannes (1837 Germany) & Frederica M. Datus (1850 Germany) - Grammar School - Farm Hand - INA - INA - INA - 7/17/1979, Wellsville - Riverside Cemetery, Belfast - August 1944 NAO, Fillmore.

Jones, John Vannostrand Military: US Army - 1/27/1941/Geneseo/Private - Troop B, 101 NY Cavalry, 199th Army Band - INA/Sergeant - Brooklyn Armory, Brooklyn, NY, Ft. Devens, MA, FT. Meade, MD, Elkins, W VA, FT Bragg, NC, Camp Breckinridge, KY/5 years - NA - NA - NA - NA - NA - NA - NA - 11/1945 - American Defense Medal, American Campaign Medal , Good Conduct Medal, WW II Victory Medal. Civilian: 1917 NY - Clifford B. Jones (1880 NY) & Jeanie L. Van Nostrand (1878 NY) - Clifford Moreau (1907 NY) - John A. Jones (1841 NY) & Frances M. (Minard?) (1844 NY) - Fred Van Nostrand (1857 NY) & Mary I. (Curtis?) - Fillmore Central, Class of 1937 - INA - INA - Geraldine Damon - Suessa Dawn - INA - INA - 1920, 1930 Federal Census Hume - None. Photo – School Yearbook.

Kasznski (Kaszynski), Peter Joseph Military: US Army – 3/2/1942/Buffalo/Private - 178th Coastal Artillery Battalion- Heavy Artillery Crewman/Corporal – Fort Niagara, Fort Bragg/2 months, two week – 42 months - Hawaii, Marshall Islands (Eastern Mandates – Mille, Maloelop Atoll, Wotje Atoll) Mariana Islands (Western Pacific - Saipan & Guam) – 2 Battle Stars - Eastern Mandates, Western Pacific – NA – NA – NA – NA – 11/18/1945, Camp Atterbury, IN – Asiatic Pacific Theater Medal, World War II Victory Medal, Good Conduct Medal, 2 Bronze Stars - (Eastern Mandates, Western Pacific). Civilian: 2/23/917/Buffalo – Anthony Kasznski (Poland) & Stephania Wygmalska (Poland) - Ida (1917 NY), Carrie (1918 NY), Mary (1918 NY), Stanley (1923 NY), Sophia (1927 NY) - INA - INA - FCS - Laborer, building construction - Farmer - Irene Lepsch - Stephanie (Gilbert), Margaret (Hatch), Peter Jr, - 5/18/2012, Canandaigua, NY - Peter & Paul Cemetery, Arcade, NY - 1930, 1940 Census Centerville, Centerville Roll of Honor. Daughter, Stephanie Kasznski. Photo – Family.

Kellogg, Meredith Warburton Military: US Army - 7/16/1942/Buffalo/Private - Headquarters, 236th

Signal Service Battalion - Cable Splicer/Technician 4 - Camp Gruber, OK, St. Norbert College, Camp Crowder, MO/31 months - 15 months - India - None - NA - NA - NA - NA - March 16, 1946, Camp Atterbury, IN - American Campaign Medal, Asiatic Pacific Theater Medal, WW II Victory Medal, Good Conduct Medal, Expert Rifleman, Carbine Sharpshooter. Civilian: 7/19/1921, Berrytown, PA - Frank Kellogg (1895 WI) & Mary Warburton (1898 NY) - Ivan B. (1920 NY) - Merton Warburton (1870 PA) & Carrie B.? (1876 NY) - Charles P. Kellogg (1864 WI) & Julia McKey (1868 IL) - Houghton College (1948), University of Buffalo - Bakery Delivery - Physics Professor, Niagara County Community College - Marjorie Lawrence (10/20/1956) - David, Roger, Sharon, Judy - 3/30/2012, Aurora House, Monroe County - Mt Pleasant Cemetery, Houghton - Fillmore History Club Book, December, 1945 (served as a source of information). Photo – NAO.

Keyes, John Henry Military: US Army - INA - 1202d Army Service Unit Detachment (Armed Forces Mobile Induction Team, Buffalo) - Commanding Officer/ Lt. Colonel - Post Commander, Physical Examination Team, Buffalo/INA - INA - NA -NA - None - NA - NA - NA - NA - INA - American Campaign Medal, WW II Victory Medal - Served in the US Army before and during WW I as both an enlisted man and an officer. Served with famous First Infantry Division. Was eligible to wear the prestigious French Fourragere. Remained in service post war. Served a total of 48 years. Civilian: 10/1892 Kingston, Canada - John Keyes (1869 Canada) & INA - (Maybe: William (1893 Canada), Laurina (1898 Canada), Eugene (likely half-brother, 1900 Canada), (Mary Kuntz (likely step sister 1896 Canada. Daughter of Rachael Law (Kuntz) - INA - INA (Maybe: Patrick Keyes & Mary Nihill) - four years high school – Military, Albany, NY (Caretaker, City Recreation Agency) – Career Military - Amelia C. Schlicht (1896 NY) - Dorothy B. (1928 NY), Stepson: John H. Tesmer (1939 NY) - 2/24/1964 - East Koy Cemetery, Portage, NY - NAO, October, 1944.

Kingsley, Alfred Henry, Jr. Military: Canadian Army - 12/21/1941 at Niagara Falls. Ontario, Canada/

Trooper - Company C, First Royal Canadian Scottish Regiment - Rifleman /PFC - Camp Borden, Ontario Province/4 months - 30 Months - England, France, Netherlands, Germany - Rhineland Campaign - 3/26/1945 - NA - NA - Was in hospital in England in October, 1942, and November, 1943. - 3/26/1945 - Good Conduct Medal, Canadian Volunteer Service Medal and Clasp, Battle Star, France, Battle Star, Germany, War Medal, Canadian Defense Medal, Purple Heart. Civilian: 1/17/1922 NY - Alfred H. Kingsley (1885 NY) & Francis P. Huff (1891 NY) - Charles A. (1913 NY), Ella W. (1915 NY), Evelyn R. (1920 NY), Ruth C. (1920 NY), Frances W. (1925 NY), Grace M. (1932 NY), Caroline V. (1933 NY) - Charles A. Huff &? - ? Kingsley & Catherine? - Fillmore Central School (completed 3 years high school) - Warsaw Button Factory - NA - Was engaged to a Canadian girl from Kilburn, Ontario, Canada (Possibly Maida Vale) - NA - 3/26/1945 - (Was originally buried in Germany) Groesbeek Canadian War Memorial Cemetery, Gelderland, Netherlands - 1940 Federal Census Granger - Canadian Military Records. Photo – NAO.

Kirkpatrick, Richard Robert Military: US Army Air Corps - 7/25/44 Fort Niagara/Private (Reenlisted 12/1/ 1945) - Various - Airplane Engine Mechanic/ PFC - Camp Fannin, TX, FT. Riley, KS, Sheppard Field, TX, Keesler Field, MS/19 months - NA - NA - None - NA - NA - NA - NA - 10/19/1946 - American Campaign Medal, WW II Victory Medal. Civilian: 9/20/1922, York, NY - Robert S. Kirkpatrick (1890 Northern Ireland) & Anna Luness (1890 NY) - Margaret (1918 NY), Betty (1921 NY), Erwin W. Hussong (1934 NY half-brother) - Richard Lynes (1866 Northern Ireland) & Ellen Bennett (1867 Northern Ireland) - William J. Kirkpatrick (1866 Ireland) & Maggie? (1871 Ireland) – One-year high school – Border Builder Company - US Army - Virginia Alexander – Barbara (Orogio), Beberly, Robert - 3/31/2010, Avon, NY - Leicester Cemetery, Leicester, NY - Maybe not a FCSD soldier, but Mother & step Father were living in the area by no later than 3/1945. He attended Allen Rural School 3 -None.

Kleinspehn, Ralph, (NMN) Jr. Military: US Navy - 10/13/1942/AS - Escort aircraft carriers *USS*

Liscome Bay, USS Nehenta Bay, USS Nassau - Athletic Office, Damage Control Officer /Ensign (Remained in the Reserves, Retired from Reserves with rank of Lt. Commander) - Pre-Midshipman School, Asbury Park, NJ, FT. Schuyler, NY, V-12 (OCS) University of North Carolina, NTS Bainbridge, MD/INA - INA - Pacific Fleet - Gilbert Islands, Tarawa, 1943 , Marshall Island 1944, Battle of the Philippine Sea 1944., Marianas - NA - NA - NA - NA - 8/28/1946 - American Campaign Medal, Asiatic Pacific Theater Medal, 3 Battle Stars, China Service Medal, WW II Victory Medal. Ralph survived the sinking of the Liscome Bay on 11/24/1943. He was also present during the Great Marianas Turkey Shoot. Civilian: 3/28/1922 Reading, PA - Ralph Kleinspehn Sr.1901 PA) & Elsie Printz (1902 PA) - John F. Kleinspehn (1863 PA) & Mary J.? (1865 PA) - Henry B. Printz (1867 PA) & Ida M.? (1871 PA) - Frankfurt High School, Philadelphia, Class of 1938, Holand Paten, Class of 1940, Hartwich College 1941, Cortland State University, Class of 1948, University of North Carolina, Cornell University - Student - Physical Education Instructor, Soccer, Basketball, Baseball Coach, English, Social Studies Teacher, Elementary & Vice School Principal - Rose Marie Luppino (M 1951) - Karen, Kim - 3/17/2003 - Holy Cross Cemetery, Fillmore - History Club 1945 WW II Book, p 166 – None. Photo – Family.

Knibloe, Wells Edmund Military: US Army - 2/1/1943 Buffalo/Private - 9301 Technical Service Unit,

Ordnance - Anti-Aircraft Artillery Instructor, Fire Control Repairman Light /Sergeant (Tec 4) - Staten Island, Brooklyn Army Base, Fordham University (Engineering Classes), Ordnance Replacement Center, NYC, Aberdeen, MD, FT. Meade, MD /39.5 months - 3 months - Bikini Atoll (1946) - NA - NA - NA - NA - NA - 8/19/1946 - Good Conduct Medal, American Campaign Medal, WW II Victory Medal. His Aunt, Ada Ruth Mills also served during the war. Civilian: 12/16/1922 Hume, NY - Donald J. Knibloe & Beula M.? (1898 NY) - Keith M. (1025 NY), Elaine A. (1928 NY), Paul C. (1940 NY) - Chesley Mills & Henrietta Buell - William E. Knibloe (1861 NY) & Ida Cox (1861 NY) - Fillmore Central, Class of 1940, University of Buffalo, Houghton College, Fordham University (while in service), University of Buffalo Law School - Student - Attorney in Buffalo- Eileen Cushing - Gale, Wayne, Laurel, Elise - NA - NA - 1940 Federal Census Granger - War Service Record, Sister-in-law Grace Knibloe. Photo – NAO.

Knorr, Earle Closser Military: US Army - 7/24/1944/Buffalo/Private - 9th Infantry Division, Company K, 39th Infantry Regiment - Infantryman/INA - Fort Benning, GA/INA - INA - France, Germany - Rhineland, Central Europe - NA - NA - NA - NA - INA - European African Middle-East Theater Medal, World War II Victory Medal, Army Occupation Medal, Germany Clasp, Combat Infantryman Badge (1947 Bronze Star), 2 Battle Stars. Civilian: 12/6/1924 Brockway, PA - Harry V. Knorr (1883 NY) & Violet F. Closser (1893 NY) - Eleanor (PA) - Frank J. Closser (1864 NY) & Lattie A.? (1879 NY) - Charles Knorr (1864 Germany) & Sophia Sauter (1863 Germany) - Jamestown Community College, NY -Student - Borden Corp., Programming Department - Bernice Woleen - Gregory M. - Cynthia M. - 1/7/2002, Jamestown, NY - Sunset Hill Cemetery, Lakewood, NY - 1940 Federal Census, Allen - None.

Kolakowska, Genevieve D. (MI Only) (Jenny) Military: Women's Army Corps (WAC) - 2/1944/Cadet

- INA - Mail Clerk, Company Clerk, Training Instructor/? - Fort Oglethorpe (1944), George Washington & Lee University, Lexington, VA (1945), Des Moines, IA, Fort Dix, NJ - NA - NA - NA - NA - NA - NA - NA - 8/1945 - Good Conduct Medal, American Campaign Medal, WW II Victory Medal. Women's Army Corps Service Medal. Civilian: 5/27/1921 - Edmund Kolakowski (Poland) & Mary Lipska (Poland) - Stanley & Sofia (1912), Frances (1913), Stella (1915), Roman (1919), Frederick (1922), Richard (1924) - INA - INA - Freedom School, Fillmore Central High School, Cosmology School - Farm Work, Small Machine Shop - Owned & Operated Beauty Parlor - NA - NA – 8/27/2015 – Holy Cross Cemetery, Fillmore, NY - 1940 Federal Census - Veteran Genevieve Kolakowska. Photo – Veteran.

Kolakowski, Roman (NMN) (Ray) Military: US Naval Air - 5/14/1941 2nd Lieutenant - Patrol

Squadron 7 - Pilot/Captain (Post War) - Floyd Bennett Field, NY, Jacksonville, Fl, Glenview Naval Air Station, IL, Lake City, Fl, Beaufort, SC, Quonset Point, RI, Floyd Bennett, NY, Elizabeth City, NJ, Port of Spain, Trinidad, Zanderey Field, Dutch Guinea, Curacao, San Juan, PR - Norfolk, VA, Sanford, ME, Key West, Fl - Foreign assignments listed above - See above - Atlantic Patrols - NA - NA - NA - NA - 7/1/1966 - American Defense Medal, American Campaign Medal, World War II Victory Medal. Civilian: 12/24/1919 Buffalo, NY - Edmund Kolakowski (Poland) & Mary Lipska (Poland) - Stanley & Sofia (1912), Frances (1913), Stella (1915), Genevieve (1921), Frederick (1922), Richard (1924) - INA - INA - Fillmore Central (1937), Cornell University (1941) - Farm Worker - US Navy, Prestige Personnel Agency, AAMCO Dealer – (M 3/11/1946) Margaret J. (Peg) Whittier - James (1948), Ronald (1951), David (?) - INA - INA -? - Son David Kolakowski, Son Ronald Kolakowski, Veteran Roman Kolakowski's autobiography, "This I Remember." Photo – NAO.

Kopler, Frank Joseph (Joe) Military: US Army - 4/15/1942, Richmond, VA/Private – 1256th Engineer

Combat Battalion - Combat Intelligence Staff Officer/Captain - Ft. Meade, MD, Ft. Warren, WY, FT. Belvoir, VA, Camp Shelby, MS, Camp Polk, LA/25 months - 18 months - England, France, Germany - Central Europe, Rhineland - NA - NA - NA - NA - 12/4/1945, Fort Belvoir, VA - American Campaign Medal, European African Middle East Theater Medal, WW II Victory Medal, Army Occupation Medal, Germany Clasp, two battle stars. Served with National Guard until 5/15/1950. Brother Howard served with Merchant Marine during the war. His Great Grandfather, Captain Phipps Lake, was a Company Commander with the 64th NY Infantry during the Civil War. Civilian: 9/23/1910, Cattaraugus County, NY - John Kopler (1887 NY) & Mildred Lake (1888 NY) - Raymond (1913 NY), Mary M. (1926 NY), Wilson L. (1918 NY), Howard E. (1923 Fillmore, NY) - Frank P. Lake (1860 NY) & Carrie S. Johnson (1857 NY) - John Kopler (INA) & Julia? (1864 Germany) - FCS -General Draftsman - Rochester Gas & Electric Co. - Marion? - Julianne (Lazeski) – 3/29/1985 - INA - 1920 1930 Federal Census Hume - None. Photo – NAO.

Kopler, Howard Emerson Military: American Merchant Marine - 8/3/1943 Buffalo/Able Seaman - SS  Frontenac, SS Benjamin D. Wilson, SS Beaver Dam, SS White River, SS Deroche, SS Barren Hill - Maintenance Man, Deck Hand, Coal Passer., Wiper/ Quartermaster - Great Lakes Maritime Commission, Norfolk, VA, San Francisco, CA, New Orleans, LA/3 months - 19 months mostly at sea - Canal Zone, India, Arabia, Ceylon, England, Aruba, Eniwetok, Ulithi, Bahrein Island, Australia, Philippines - Pacific, Atlantic, Mediterranean War Zones - NA - NA - NA - NA - 10/29/1945 (End of last war time assignment) - Merchant Marine Emblem, Atlantic War Zone Bar, Pacific War Zone Bar, Mediterranean Middle East War Zone Bar, Merchant Marine World War II Victory Medal. Brother Frank served with US Army during the war. His Great Grandfather, Captain Phipps Lake, was a Company Commander with the 64th NY Infantry during the Civil War. Civilian: 10/17/1923 Fillmore, NY - John Kopler (1887 NY) & Mildred Lake (1888 NY) - Frank (1910 NY) Raymond (1913 NY), Mary M. (1926 NY), Wilson L. (1918 NY) - Frank P. Lake (1860 NY) & Carrie S. Johnson (1857 NY) - John Kopler (INA) & Julia? (1864 Germany) - Fillmore Central, Class of 1941 - INA - Merchant Marines (as Third Mate) - Never Married - None - INA - Alger Cemetery, Hume, NY - 1920 1930 Federal Census Hume - None. Photo – NAO.

Krause, John Robert (Bob) Military: US Army Air Corps - 11/4/1942 Buffalo/Private - 359th Air Base  Unit, Celestial Navigation Training Unit - Trainer/Staff Sergeant – Niagara Falls, NY, (Basic Training), Chanute Air Field, IL, Alamogordo, NM, Wilmington, DE, - 38 months - NA - NA - NA - NA - NA - NA - NA – 12/21/1945, Rome, NY - American Campaign Medal, WW II Victory Medal. Civilian: 9/8/1920 Olean, NY - John G. Krause (1888 WIS) & Agnes H. Turgerson (1890 WIS) - Dorothy, Marguerite (DeRuiter) – James Torgerson (1858 Wis) & Minnie Larson (1862 Norway) - Gotlieb Krause & Matilda Kuehn (1859 Wis) - Syracuse University Class of 1950 - Farmer - Iowa Highway Division, Richardson & Gordon Consulting Engineers, PA, Bureau of Public Roads, Ohio, Federal Highway Administration, PA - Anita Schraff (Married 1949) - Larry, Vicki (Currie), Adopted Daughter Jackie Thompson - 1/17/2012, Schenectady, NY - Holy Redeemer Cemetery, Schenectady – 1930 Fed Cen Houghton, NAO 8, 1943. Photo - NAO .

Kruppner, Frederick John Military: US Army Air Corps - 8/3/1942/Buffalo/Private - INA - Field  Lighter/PFC - Strother Field, Winfield, KA, Hamilton Field, CA, (others) /INA (at least 25 months) – (at least 12 months) - Hawaii, Johnston Island - NA - NA - NA - NA - NA - 1/29/1946 - American Campaign Medal, Good Conduct Medal, Asiatic Pacific Theater Medal, World War II Victory Medal. Civilian: 3/15/1921, Hume, New York - Frederick Kruppner (1899 Austria) & Anna R. Wilcox (1903 New York) - Pauline (1921 NY), Bernard (1926 NY, Burdett (1926 NY) - John A. Wilcox (1882 NY) & Mildred M. Reynolds (1883 NY) - Alois (Lewis) Kruppner & Tieltier (Delia?) - FCD - INA - INA -Sally Ann? - INA - 12/8/1995, Franklinville, NY - Siloam Cem., Freedom, NY - 1925 Cen Hume - Vesta Wilcox Teeter. Photo – NAO.

Lane Frank Ward Military: US Marines - 5/25/1944/2nd Lieutenant (Had previously served 15 months

in the New York Guard) - Marine Air Warning Squadron 7, Aircraft, Fleet Marine Forces, Pacific - Fighter Director Officer/1st Lieutenant - Quantico, VA, Cherry Point, NC, St. Simons Island, GA, Camp Pendleton, Oceanside, CA (5/44-5/45) - 6/45- 11/45 (6 months) - Okinawa - Okinawa Campaign - NA - NA - NA - NA - Served in reserves until 8/27/1947 - Asiatic Pacific Theater Medal, World War II Victory Medal, American Campaign Medal. Civilian: 3/15/1908 (NY) - Floyd Lane (1878 NY) & Martha Williams (1887 NY) - Elizabeth Ruth (DeYoung) (1906 NY), Bessie Jane (Peterson, Brandel) (1921 NY) - Daniel Williams (NY) & Elizabeth Brain (Bristol, England) - Frank Lane (NY) & Ruth Waite (NY) - Falconer High School, Falconer, NY - Houghton College (BA), St. Bonaventure University (MA-MS) - Almond High School, Dunkirk High School - Professor, Mohawk College, Utica, NY, Sampson College, Geneva, NY, Champlain College, Plattsburgh, NY, Ohio Northern University, Idaho State University - Eileen Mary Loftis 1908 NY) - Mary (1933 - 1933 NY), Joanne Martha (1935 NY), Jeanine Marie (1935 NY), Frank Peter (1939 NY), Daniel Richard (1944 NY) - 2/16/1988 - Holy Cross Cemetery, Fillmore, NY- NAO 11/1945 - Son, Father Frank Lane. Photo – Family.

Leet, Robert Leon Military: US Navy - 10/15/1943/Olean/AS - *USS Lowndes (APA 154)* - Hospital Apprentice/SIC - Sampson Naval Base, Others/16 months - 11 months - Hawaii, Saipan, Iwo Jima, Okinawa, Guam, Japan - Iwo Jima, Okinawa - NA - NA - NA - NA - 1/18/1946 - American Campaign Medal, Asiatic Pacific Theater Medal, 2 Battle Stars, Navy Occupation Medal, Asian Clasp, World War II Victory Medal. Civilian: 10/12/1926/NY - Donald W. Leet (1907 NY) & Evelyn E. Crabtree (1908 NY) - INA - Ralph W. Crabtree (1883 NY & Lillian (likely Lowe) (1888 NY) - Charles Leet (1885 NY) & Ellen Haire (1888 NY) - INA - Student - Cement Finisher - Ester Lou Deveraux - INA - 7/2/1982, Azle, Tarrant County, TX - Blue Bonnet Hills Cemetery, Colleyville, TX - NAO, October, 1943 - None.

Lemonde, Melville Edward (Mel) Military: Canadian Royal Air Corps - 4/16/1943 - Royal Canadian

Air Force,/ RAF Bomber Command, Group 1, 218 Squadron - Air Gunner /Sergeant, Warrant Officer - Hamilton, Alberta, Saskatchewan, Valley Field in Quebec/14.5 months - 14 months - England - Probably Normandy, Ardennes-Alsace, Rhineland, Central Europe - NA - NA - NA - Severely injured his foot, in June, 1943 during training in Alberta - 9/25/1945 - 1939-45 Star, France and Germany Star, Defense Medal, Canadian Volunteer Service Medal with Clasp & War Medal. Civilian: 3/14/1923, Hamilton, Ontario, Canada - Robert Lemonde (1906 Canada) & Myrtle Davis (1898 Canada) - None -? Davis & Lillian? - INA - FCS - Farmer - Gas Station Owner, Fillmore - Camilla Paulsen - Melanie, Larry - 9/10/1997, Venice, FL - NAO, October, 1943 - Son Larry Lemonde. Melville was of Scottish descent. He came to the US (Buffalo) arriving on April 15, 1923, with his Mother Myrtle Davis Lemonde. He was one month old. The family was living in Centerville by the early 1940's. Photo – Family.

Letson, Irving Charles Military: US Army - 10/27/1942/Private - 12th Armored Division, 23rd Tank Battalion, Service Company - Truck Drive/Technical 5 - Fort Campbell, KY, Fort Barkeley, TX/24 months - 14 months - England, France, Germany, Austria -Rhineland, Ardennes-Alsace, Central Europe - NA - NA - NA - NA - 5/16/1946 - American Campaign Medal, Unit Citation, Certificate of Merit, European African Middle East Theater Medal, 3 Battle Stars, WW II Victory Medal. Civilian: 3/10/1919 NY - Unknown & Blanche G. Letson (1899 NY) - Half-sisters: Lillian V. (1922 NY), Virginia R. (1924 NY), Jolene L. (1930 NY) - George Letson (1860 NY) & Mary A.? (1863 ILL) - Unknown - Fillmore Central - Farm Laborer - INA - INA - INA - 12/29/1988, Milton, Santa Rosa County, FL - Barrancas National Cemetery, Pensacola, FL - 1940 Census Wiscoy - None. Photo- NAO.

Lilly, Ray Eugene Military: US Army Air Corps - 4/2/1942/Buffalo/Private- P 38 Squadron - Ground

Crew/Sergeant - INA/4 months - 38 months - England, North Africa, Italy - INA - NA - NA - NA - NA - September 30, 1945 - European African, Middle Eastern Theater Medal, WW II Victory Medal, Battle Stars, Distinguished Unit Citations. Civilian: 1/27/1924, NY - George Lilly (1869 NY) & Mabel Lytle (1893 NY) - Arthur (1900 NY), Clair (1902 NY), Marion (1904 NY), Neil (1907 NY), Robert (1909 NY), Anna (1910 NY), Inez (1912 NY), Carl (1916 NY), Lewis (1917 NY) - Aaron Lilly (1843 Germany) & Cornelia? (1842 NY) - Alexandre Lytle (1845 Ireland) & Fannie? (1850 NY) - Angelica Central - Farm Hand, County Home Farm - Rochester Gas & Electric Company, Fillmore - Winona Alice Bennett (M 11/12/1945 Hume) - Eugene V. (1946 NY), Rayona Ann (1948 NY) - 1/8/1982 Deland, FL. - Short Tract Cemetery - Post War, Worked for RG & E, Fillmore - Wife Winona Bennett (Lilly) (Langley). Photo- NAO.

Lindley, Kenneth Eugene Military: US Navy - 5/17/1944/AS - Navy V-12 Program - Student/S2C -

NTC, Farragut, ID, St. Thomas College, University of MN, St. Paul, MN, University of Wisconsin, Madison/26 months - NA - NA - NA - NA - NA - NA - June 30, 1946 - American Campaign Medal, WW II Victory Medal. Civilian: 3/16/1924 - INA - INA - INA - INA - University of Minnesota, University of Wisconsin - INA - Teacher, Houghton College - Katherine W.? - INA - 2/18/2006 Houghton, NY - Mt Pleasant Cemetery, Houghton, NY - Fillmore History Club 1945 WW II Book - None. Photo – NAO.

Lowe, Frank Austin (Austy) Military: US Navy Air: 7/7/1943/Buffalo/AS - Composite Air Squadron

V95, aboard *USS Croatan, USS Bogue, USS Mission Bay* - Aviation Ordnance Man/Seaman First Class - Sampson Naval Station, Memphis, TN, Hollywood, FL, Norfolk Naval Station, NATTC, Memphis, TN/INA - INA - Atlantic Fleet - Task Group 22.5 (Anti-submarine operations, Atlantic) - NA - NA - NA - NA - 9/14/1946 - American Campaign Medal, One Battle Star, European African Middle Eastern Theater Medal, World War II Victory Medal. Civilian 9/15/1925, Geneseo, NY - Clarence Lowe (1894 NY) & Mary Hinderland (1898 NY) - INA - Henry Hinderland (1867 Germany & Alice? (1873 NY) - Frank Lowe (1856 NY) & Sarah Gray or Swan (1861 NY) - Angelica Central School, Class of 1942 - Student - Shift Supervisor, Corning Glass Works - First, Ruth Richardson (1948), 2nd Marice Holloway (2/18/1995) - Aleyce F., Nancy A., Linda (Moses) (NY 1949), Holly L. - October 13, 2003, Montpelier, Indiana - Fairview Cemetery, Wells County, Indiana - NAO, July, 1943 - Daughter, Linda Lowe (Moses). Photo – NAO.

Luckey, Beverley Alverius (Bev) Military: US Army - 9/22/1944 Buffalo/Private - Co. A, 301st Infantry

Regiment, 94th Infantry Division - Automatic Rifleman/PFC - FT. McClellan, AL/4 months - 12 months - France, Germany, Czechoslovakia - Central Europe, Rhineland - NA - NA - NA - NA - 2/6/1946, Ft. Dix, NJ - Good Conduct Medal, Combat Infantryman Badge (1947 Bronze Star), 2 Battle Stars, Silver Star, European African Middle East Theater Medal, WW II Victory Medal, Army of Occupation-Germany Clasp, Lapel Button. Civilian: 8/20/1920 NY - Alden A. Luckey (1898 NY) & Helen Gayford (1902 NY) - Bonalyn (Weisborn) (1924 NY) - Frederick Gayford (NY) & Dora Damon (England) - William A. Luckey (1873 NY) & Mary (Mame) T. Bentley (1878 NY) - Fillmore Central, Class of 1937/ 2 years college, Houghton - Assembler, Buffalo Forge Co. (Made Air Conditioners) - Assembler, Buffalo Forge Co. - Betty A. \Hurlburt (11/11/1940.

Freedom, NY) - Nancy (1940 NY), Beverly (1942 NY), Gary (1952 NY), Greg (1959 NY) - 11/23/1997 Hume, NY - Freedom Cemetery, Freedom, NY - 1930 Federal Census Hume - Wife Betty Hurlburt Luckey, son Gary, Daughter Nancy. Photo – Family.

Luckey, Gerald Voss Military: US Navy - 2/23/1944/AS - Combat Aircraft Service Unit 36, Santa Rosa, CA - Aviation Ordnanceman /S 1 C - Sampson Naval, NY, Norman, OK, Alameda, CA /24 months - NA - NA - NA - NA - NA - NA - NA - 2/8/1946 - American Campaign Medal, WW II Victory Medal. Father Norris served during WW I. Civilian: 4/25/1921, Granger, NY - Norris F. Luckey (1902 NY) & Lora M. Voss (1906 NY) - Wilma J. (1926 NY), Clair J. (1927 NY) - Thomas Voss & Elizabeth? - William & Mame Bentley - Fillmore Central, Class of 1938 - Inspector, Panel & Final Assembly, Curtis Wright Plant, Buffalo - Foote Blackton & Cement Mixers - Melva Worden (1942, Granger) - Larry, Sandra, Sherrie - NA - NA - 1940 Federal Census Granger - Veteran Gerald V. Luckey. Photo – NAO.

Luckey, Valgeane Cecil Military: US Army - 12/3/1942 Buffalo/Private – 1377th Signal Corps - Mechanic/ Sergeant, T-5 - Jefferson Barracks, MO, Stockton Ordnance Depot, CA, Pinedale Station, Fresno, CA/37 months - 9 months - Australia, India, China - China Offensive - NA - NA - NA - NA – INA - American Campaign Medal, Asiatic Pacific Theater Medal, WW II Victory Medal. Civilian: 11/16/1915 NY - William A. Luckey (1873 NY) & Mary T.? (1878 NY) - Alden (1898 NY), Roosevelt (1899 NY), Wilda (1900 NY), Landis (1902 NY) - INA - Likely James Luckey, Jr. (1849 NY) & Fannie? (1850 NY) - 4 years college - Farm Worker - INA - INA - INA - 2/3/1964 - Pine Grove Cemetery, Fillmore, NY - 1940 Federal Census Hume - None. Photo – NAO.

Lyman, Robert Henry Military: US Army - 7/21/1942 Buffalo/Captain - 35th Station Hospital/195 General Hospital - Chief of Surgery/Lt. Colonel - Camp Holabird, Baltimore, Edgewood Arsenal, Aberdeen, MD, Philadelphia (Army Training), Camp Bryant, IL/32 months - 9 months European Theater/7 months Pacific Theater - France, Belgium, Okinawa, Japan - Rhineland, Ardennes Alsace, Occupation of Japan - NA - NA - NA - NA - 5/6/1946 Camp Dix, NJ - American Campaign Medal, European African Middle East Theater Medal, Asiatic Pacific Theater Medal, Army of Occupation Medal, Japan Clasp, 195th General Hospital Unit Citation, 2 Battle Stars, World War II Victory Medal. Civilian: 3/04/1899 Fillmore, NY - Almond H. Lyman (1861 NY) & Josephine C. Whalen (1875 NY) - Richard C. (1902 NY) - INA - Henry H. Lyman (1826 NY) & Cornelia? (1833 NY) - Fillmore Central, New York Military Academy, Alfred University, University of Pennsylvania, John Hopkins Medical School, Albany - Doctor, Fillmore, NY - Doctor, Fillmore, NY - Leona D. Schaffer (M 1/29/1933 Wellsville, NY) - None - 9/7/1962 - Pine Grove Cemetery, Fillmore, NY - 1930 Federal Census Fillmore - Allegany County War Service Record, NAO Obituary. Photo – NAO.

McCarty, Paul Thomas Military: US Army - 7/11/1943/Buffalo/Private - Department 3, 832nd Signal Service Company, 997th Signal Service Battalion, 4025th Signal Service Group - Radio Repair/Technician 4 - INA - INA - Australia - INA - NA - NA - NA - NA - INA - American Campaign Medal, Asiatic Pacific Theater Medal, World War II Victory Medal. Civilian: 2/17/1914 PA - Lee H, McCarty (1887 PA) & Edith M. Paul (1886 WI) - Gordon P. (1912 PA), Clair B. (1913 PA), Leroy (1915 PA), Bruce C. (1920 PA) - Michael M. Paul (1859 PA) & Phoebe (maybe Letteer (1863 PA) - Thomas W. McCarty (1848 PA) & Mertie Verdellah Grange (1854 PA) - Houghton Academy, Houghton College - Math Science Teacher, Royalton, NY - Math Science Teacher, Royalton, NY - Never Married - None - 6/17/1995, Boynton Beach, FL - Mt Pleasant Cemetery, Houghton, NY. 1920 1930 Censuses Houghton - Sister-in-Law Marion McCarty.

McDonald, John Peter Not FCSD. Parents lived in Fillmore in early 1940's, but apparently, he did not. Lived in Belmont in 1935 and Buffalo in 1940. Entered the US Army Air Corps in November 1942. A November 1942 issue of the NAO reported that he was the son of Mr. & Mrs. John McDonald of Fillmore. It does not appear that John ever lived in the FCSD area. John was a member of the Army Air Corps and served in France. NAO 1942 p 152.

McMaster, Hubert Frederick (Bud) Military: US Army - 1/11/1943 Rochester/Private – Company F, 414th Infantry Regiment, 104th Infantry Division – Infantryman/PFC - Keesler Air Base, MS/INA – Total Service 35 months – Brazil, France, Belgium, Holland, Germany - Northern France, Rhineland, Central Europe - NA - NA - NA - NA - 12/12/1945 - American Campaign Medal, European African Middle East Theater Medal, 3 Battle Stars, Combat Infantryman Badge (1947 Bronze Star), WW II Victory Medal. Civilian: 1924 NY - Hubert H. McMaster (1876 NY) & Harriet B. Democker (1889 NY) - Frances E. (1920 NY), Mary E. (1923) - INA -Hubert McMaster (1835 NY) & Mary E.? (1851 NY) - Fillmore Central, Class of 1940 - INA - Postmaster, Nunda - Lenora Donahue - Douglas, Maureen - 12/18/2009, Nunda - Oakwood Cemetery, Nunda - 1930 1940 Federal Census Hume - Daughter Maureen M. (Sturges). Photo – School.

Mack, Elmer William Military: Army Air Corps - 2/1/1943 Buffalo/Private - Fourth Air Force/460 Air Force Base Unit - Airplane Mechanic/Master Sergeant - Ft. Logan, Co., Oakland Municipal Airport, CA, Bell Aircraft Plant, Niagara Falls, NY, Oakland Municipal Airport, Hamilton Field, CA/36 months - NA - NA - NA - NA - NA - NA - NA - 2/23/1946, Camp Beale, CA - American Campaign Medal, Good Conduct Medal, Combat Crew Wings, WW II Victory Medal Civilian: 3/22/1923 Hume, NY - Warner H. Mack (1895 NY) & Hazel F. Flanegen (1897 NY) - Patricia (1917 NY), Ronald (1929 NY) - INA - Elmer E. Mack (1863 NY) & Jennie A. Poole (1872 NY) - Fillmore Central, Class of 1940 - Dispatcher, Bell Aircraft, Buffalo - INA - Ruth E. Vaugh (M 2/15/1946, San Rafael, CA.) - INA - 9/21/1988 Hume - Pine Grove Cemetery, Fillmore, NY - 1930 Federal Census Fillmore, Allegany County War Service Record - None. Photo – NAO.

Makowski, Walter Donald Military: US Navy - 2/22/1943 Buffalo/AS - *USS Harris* - Gunners Mate(GM)/Seaman 2 Class - Sampson Naval, NY, GM School, San Francisco, CA/8 months - 28 months - Pearl Harbor, Saipan, Peleliu, Kwajalein, Ulithi, Leyte Gulf, Lingayen Gulf, Okinawa, Guam, Tokyo Bay, China - Marianas Operation, Western Caroline Islands Operation, Leyte Operation, Okinawa Gunto Operations, Manila Bay Biscol Operation - NA - NA - NA - NA - 2/10/1946 Sampson Naval Base, NY - American Campaign Medal, Asiatic Pacific Theater Medal, Philippine Liberation Medal, WW II Victory Medal, 5 US Battle Stars (2 Republic of Philippines - Leyte & Lingayen), Occupation Medal with Asian Clasp. Civilian: 4/2/1924 Centerville, NY - Adam A. Makowski (1891 Poland) & Rose M.? (1891 Poland) - Henry (1913 NY), Charles (1914 NY), Helen (1915 NY) Estella (1917 NY), Mary (1918 NY), Chester (1920 NY), Ted (1922 NY), Irene (1928 NY) - INA - INA - INA - Machinist, Curtiss Wright Plant, Buffalo – Dairy Owner, Arcade, NY - Irene? (INA) - Dave - 3/22/2001, Woodburn, Oregon - Zion National Park, Canby, OR - 1940 Federal Census Centerville.

Markham, Burton Hugh Military: US Army - 9/21/1944/Utica, NY/Private - 5th Infantry Division - Infantryman/Private- Fort McClellan, AL/ 3.5 months - 25 months - Scotland, France, Germany- Central Europe - NA - WIA 3/4/45 - MIA-Captured 3/4/1945, (Liberated Easter Sunday, 1945) - Malnutrition as a POW - 3/27/1946 - American Campaign Medal, European, African, Middle Eastern Theater Medal,

WW II Victory Medal, one Battle Star, Army POW Medal, Purple Heart, Combat Infantry Badge (1947 Bronze Star). Spent VE Day in Paris. Civilian: 11/13/1918/NY - Earnest Markham (1886 NY) & Evelyn Wasmuth (1887 NY) - Ernestine (1914 NY), Marian (1916 NY), Robert (1918 NY), Theodore (1922 NY), Janice (1924 NY), William (1925 NY), Shirley (1929) NY) - Theodore Wasmuth (1853 Germany) & Hattie I. Worden (1865 NY) - William Markham (1861 NY) & Laura A. Jones (1860 NY) - 4 years, Cornell University - Farm Credit Administration, Ithaca, NY - Field Representative, Insurance Co. - Melrose Marriott – son Hugh & 3 others - 4/2/1999, New Hartford, Oneida County, NY - INA - NAO, June, 1945 – None.

Marriott, Donald Dwight Military: US Army - 3/25/1944/ Private - Quartermaster Corps - Cook/PFC -

Ft. Dix, NJ, Texarkana, TX/INA - (maybe overseas January, 1945) Total WW II service 21 months – likely 11/12 months – Germany, (maybe Central Europe Campaign) - NA - NA - NA - NA - 1/13/1946 – maybe American Campaign Medal, European, African, Middle East Theater Medal, WWII Victory Medal. Brother Melvin served in the Coast Guard in the 1930s. Donald served again from 1/14/1946 until 4/20/1947. Donald also served in Korea. Civilian: 11/25/1922 Oramel, NY - Frank Beal Marriott ((1881 MI) & Clara Mildred Hammond (1884 NY) - Rowley Thompson (1908 NY), Melvin Russell (1912 NY), Walter (1914 NY), Melrose (1920 NY) - Dwight C. Hammond (1850 NY) & Elizabeth A.? (1853 NY) - Alfred Marriott (1846 England) & Thirza (Theresa) Thompson (1850 Canada) - FCS, 3 years high school - Farm Worker/Machinist - Career Army - 1st Helen? 2nd Margaret - Julia Ann (Mother Helen) (1947), Leanne Marie (Mother Margaret) (1969) - 12/16/1972 Buffalo - Pine Grove Cemetery, Fillmore - 1930, 1940 Census Hume - Niece Marjorie Marriott Sumner, Nephew Charles Sumner. Photo – NAO.

Marsh, Lorenz Harry Military: US Army - 11/13/1942/Buffalo/Private - INA – INA/Corporal - INA – INA/Total service 37.5 months – INA – INA – INA – NA – NA – NA – NA – 12/28/1945, Fort Knox, KY – American Campaign Medal, European, African, Middle East Theater Medal, World War II Victory Medal. Civilian: 3/3/1920 PA - Harry L. Marsh (1890 NY) & Hazel M. Lafferty (1898 NY) - None - Dorr W. Lafferty (1871 NY) & Persie E.? (1874 NY) – Henry Marsh (1867 NY) & Irene C.? (1865 NY) - Grammar School, Belfast, NY - Farmer Laborer - Laborer - Gertrude Aileen Ball (M 5/4/1946) - Thomas Michael - 4/2/1987 S. Mary's, Auglaize, Ohio - Resthaven Memorial Cemetery, St. Mary's - 1940 Census Hume - None.

Metcalf, Walter Roy Called for a physical in March of 1943. No other information located.

Miller, Alvin Paul (Dodd) Military: US Army - 8/11/1941 Buffalo/Private - Company A, 764th

Amphibious Tractor Battalion - Amphibious Tractor Operator/Tec 5 - FT. Knox, KY, Fredericksburg, VA, Ft Ord, CA/52 months - NA - NA - NA - NA - NA - NA - NA - 12/12/1945 - American Defense Medal, American Campaign Medal, Good Conduct Medal, WW II Victory Medal. Civilian: 2/2/1919 (Van Dresser Hotel) Hume, NY - Earl M. Miller (1887 NY) & Lottie M. Webster (1889 NY) - Margaret B. (Cronk) (1906 NY), Harriett M. (Wolfer Thompson) (1909 NY), Melvin (1916 NY), Glenn N. (1932 NY) - Gilman Webster & Harriet? - Nathan Miller (1857 NY) & Mary W.? (1863 NY) - FCS - Farm Worker for Carl Walradt in Freedom, NY - Erie RR, Farm hand for Jerry Cook, Truck Driver & Loader Operator for Town of Hume - Olive K. Cockle (M10/1/1948) - Paul M. (1952 NY), Paula M. (Jones) (1956 NY) - 3/14/2003 - Pine Grove Cemetery - 1940 Census Centerville, Allegany County War Service Record - Wife Olive (Polly) Cockle Miller. Photo – NAO.

Miller, Arthur Claude Military: US Army - 1/8/1941 Buffalo/Private - 371st Engineer Battalion - INA/Sergeant - Pine Camp, NY, Camp Ellis, IL, Camp Patrick Henry, VA/41 months - 18 months - Belgium, France, Germany - Ardennes-Alsace, Rhineland, Central Europe - NA -NA - NA - NA - 11/8/1945 - American Defense Medal, American Campaign Medal, Good Conduct Medal, European Africa Middle East Theater Medal, WW II Victory Medal, 3 Battle Stars, Army of Occupation Medal, Germany Clasp, Meritorious Unit Commendation. Civilian: 7/17/1919 Likely Centerville, NY - Ernest W. Miller (1887 NY) & Ethel R. Hamer (1893 NY) - Harold (1910 NY), Harmon (1912 NY), Albert (1915 NY), Mabel (1917 NY), Maxine (1922 NY) - Bert Hamer 1870 NY & Maggie V. Gardner (1879 NY) - Nathanial W. Miller (1857 NY) & Mary W.? (1863 NY) - FCS & Pike Schools - Laborer - INA - INA - INA – 8/27/1979 Perry, NY - INA - 1920 Federal Census Centerville - None. Photo – NAO.

Miller, Lawrence Ward (Hank) Military: US Navy - 9/15/1943 Buffalo/AS - *USS Matar* (AK 119) - Boatswains Mate/S 2 C - Sampson Naval, NY, Charleston, SC, Jacksonville, FL, Savannah, GA/11 months- 18 months - Pearl Harbor, Palau, Russell Islands, Guadalcanal, Eniwetok, Saipan, Ryukyu Islands (Keramo Retto, Okinawa), Ulithi, Tokyo Harbor, Japan - Western Caroline Islands Operations, Okinawa Gunto Operation - NA - NA - NA - NA - 3/23/1946, Lido Beach, NY - 2 Battle Stars, American Campaign Medal, Asiatic Pacific Theater Medal, WW II Victory Medal, Navy Occupation Medal, Asian Clasp - Visited a number of cities in Japan. Saw total devastation. Civilian: 5/1/1921 NY - Clarence Miller (1900 NY) & Marion Ward (1901 NY) - None – INA – Nathanial W. Miller (1858 NY) & Mable? 1863 NY) - FCS, Class of 1940 - Bell Aircraft Corporation, Buffalo, Rochester Gas & Electric - RG & E Corporation, Fillmore - Frances Powers (M 12/22/1945) – Joseph (1949), Nancy (1947), Daniel (1951), Teresa (1958) - 7/12/1961 - Holy Cross Cemetery, Fillmore, NY - 1930 Federal Census - Son Joseph, Daughter Teresa. Photo – NAO.

Miller, Robert Franklin Military: US Navy - 10/25/1943/Toledo, Ohio/AS - *USS Springfield (CL 66)* - Electrician Mate/S 2 C - Great Lakes Naval Training Center, University of Minnesota/12 months - 29 months - 3rd Fleet, South Pacific, Okinawa, Tokyo Bay, China, Japan, Philippines - Okinawa Gunto, 3rd Fleet Operations Against Japan - NA - NA - NA -NA - 5/23/1946 - American Campaign Medal, Asiatic Pacific Theater Medal, Philippine Liberation Medal, WW II Victory Medal, 2 Battle Stars, Navy Occupation Medal, Asian Clasp, probably China Service Medal - Was in Tokyo Bay for the surrender of the Japanese. Civilian: 1915 NY - Frederick J. Miller (18854NY) & Grace F. Fuller (1885 NY) - Francis N. (1913 NY) E. June (1918 NY), Ruth E. (1919 NY) - Frank M. Fuller (1853 NY) & Chloe E.? (1859 NY) - INA - INA - INA - Houghton College/Ordained Minister - INA - INA - INA - INA - History Club WW II 1945 Book, p 172 - None. Photo - NAO, School Yearbook.

Mills, Ada Ruth Military: Women's Army Corps (WAC) - 2/16/1943Albany, NY/Private - Adjutant
 General Operations Office, War Department General Staff/Convalescent Hospital, FT.
Upton - Administration/2nd Lieutenant - FT. Oglethorpe, GA, FT. Alpine, TX, Ft. Bliss,
TX, FT. Belvoir, VA, FT. Myer, VA (Pentagon), Camp Upton, NY,OCS School, Des
Moines, IA/36 months - NA - NA - NA - NA - NA - NA - NA - July 2, 1946 Ft. Dix,
NY - Good Conduct Medal, Commendation for Meritorious Service/Army
Commendation Ribbon, Certificate of Achievement , American Campaign, WW II
Victory Medal. Civilian: 11/14/1903 Fillmore, NY - Chesley V. MIlls (1871 NY) &
Henrietta M. (1871 NY) - Beula (1898 NY) - Ores Buel (1829 CT) & Ruth Benjamin
(1834 NY) - Volney Mills (1831 NY) & Sarah? (1841 NY) - Fillmore Central School,
Class of 1921, Alfred University, University of Buffalo, Berkshire Summer School of Art - Teacher,
Silver Spring, Cobleskill, Herkimer - INA – Never Married - None - 11/11/1979, Fillmore – Alger
Cemetery, NY - 1930 Federal Census - Allegany County War Service Record. Photo – NAO.

Mills, Bernard Arthur (Bernie) Military: US Army Air Corps - 1/11/1943/Buffalo/Private - 8th Air
Force, 94th Bomb Group,332nd Bomb Squadron - Radio & Radar Countermeasure
Technician/Corporal - Ft. Niagara, Miami Beach, FL., Chicago Radio School, Truax
Field, Madison, WI, Boca Raton, FL, Truax Field, WI, Jefferson Barracks, MO, Boca
Raton, Drew Field, FL/Greensboro, NC, Camp Kilmer, NJ, Staten Island, N/33 months
- 12 months - Bury St. Edmonds, England - Ardennes (Battle of the Bulge), Central
Europe, Rhineland - NA - NA - NA - temporary deafness caused by cold - 11/16/1945
– American Campaign Medal, Good Conduct Medal, European, African, Middle East
Theater Medal, 3 Battle Stars, WW II Victory Medal. Bernard also served in Korea.
Civilian: 12/11/1922 NY - Balfour Dole Mills (1900 NY) & Lenora Marleah Green
(1898 NY) - Lowell B. (1925 NY), Jeanne N. (1928 NY), Stewart S. (1930 NY), Alan W. (1936 NY),
Richard C. (1938 NY) - Arthur R. Mills (1859 NY) & Julia Dole (NY) - Charles Greene (NY) & Abby
Schuknecht (NY) - Fillmore Central, Class of 1940 - Curtiss Wright Plant, Buffalo - Rochester Gas &
Electric, Fillmore (39 years) - Louise Yanda (M 2/1952) - Melissa (1954 NY), James (1956 NY), Lydia
(1966 NY) – 8/19/2016 – Alger Cemetery, Hume NY - 1940 Federal Census Hume - Veteran Bernard
Mills. Photo – NAO.

Mills, Donald Marvin Donald was called to Buffalo for his physical in January of 1943. A report in the
NAO indicated that he expected to be inducted January 4. However, no further evidence of service has
been identified. Civilian: 9/28/1922, Fillmore, NY - Clifford L. Mills (1901 NY) & Harriette Waite (1901
NY) - Majorie (1927 NY) - George D. Waite (1844 NY) & Sarah? (1864 MI) – Charles D. Mills (1842
NY) & Blanche Daily (1864 NY) - FCS, Class of 1941 – Chevrolet Plant, - INA - Betty Lou Howden,
Married 5/29/1946, Hume - INA - 5/21/1985, Fillmore - INA - 1925 NYS Census, Hume, 1930, 1940
Federal Census, Hume – None.

Millspaugh, Clyde Frank Military: US Army - 6/25/1945/Fort Sheridan. IL/Private - Tire Factory,
Detroit - INA/Private - Fort Sill, OK, Detroit, MI/8 months - NA - NA - NA - NA - NA - NA - NA -
10/23/1945. American Campaign Medal, World War II Victory Medal. Great Grandfather Leander
Millspaugh served with Company D, 64th NY Infantry during the Civil War. - Civilian: 10/7/1907 NY -
Frank E. Millspaugh (1884 NY) & Belle Holbrook (1884 NY) - Etta (Sandford) (1906 NY) - INA -
Frederick Millspaugh (1855 NY) & Etta A. Isham (1855 NY) - FCS, Others - INA - INA - 1. Eva
Erickson (5/13/1927/Denver), 2. Lorraine V. Simmons (1/27/1965/L.A.) - INA - 12/6/1979, Los Angeles
- INA – 1920, 1925 Censuses Hume. None .

Mix, Lowell Edward Military: US Army Air Corps - 1938/Buffalo/Private & /10/ 1942/Buffalo/Air

Cadet - 98th Bomb Group, 344th Bomb Squadron - ?/Sergeant, Pilot/Captain - Fort Totten, NY, Greenville, MS, Montgomery, AL, Illinois, Davis Monthan, AS/ months - 10 months - North Africa, Lecce, Italy - Air Offensive Europe, Naples Foggia, Rome Arno - NA - NA - NA - NA - November, 1948/ Tyndall AFB, FL - American Defense Medal, American Campaign Medal, Soldier's Medal for Heroism, European, African Middle East Theater Medal, ? Air Medals, Presidential Unit Citation with Multiple Clusters, Distinguished Flying Cross, WW II Victory Medal. Civilian: 10/29/1919, Hume, NY - Chester V. Mix (1881 NY) & Lettie A.? (1885 NY) - Glenn (1916 NY), Harold (1918 NY), Jane (1923 NY), James (1928 NY), Margaret (1926 NY), Celia (? NY) - INA - Frank Mix (/) & Jennie Washburn (?) - FCS, Friendship High School - Student - Co-Owner, Panama Trailer Sales and Anchorage Mobile Home Park, Panama City, FL - Viola Buzzard (1942, Friendship, NY) - David, Frank, Laura, Mary Lynn - 4/18/2009, Panama City, FL - Kent Forest Lawn Cemetery,
Panama City - 1930, 1940 Federal Census Hume - Wife Viola Buzzard Mix. Photo – NAO.

Molyneaux, Evan Walker Military: US Army - 8/?/1942/Major - XXII Corps, 45th Field Hospital –

Commander, Doctor/Lt. Colonel - INA/22 months - 23 months - England, France, Belgium, Germany, Czechoslovakia - Normandy, Northern France, Ardennes Alsace, Rhineland, Central Europe - NA - NA - NA - NA - 3/?/1946 - Bronze Star, American Campaign Medal, European African Middle Eastern Theater Medal, 5 Battle Stars, WW II Victory Medal . Civilian: 11/11/1907 PA - J. Robert Molyneaux (1874 PA) & Pearl Olivia Ingersoll (1875 NY) - Glenn T. (1898 NY), J. Maxwell (1905 PA), Roberta P. (1907 PA), Charles G. (1910 PA), Silas R. (1916 NY) - INA - Joel Molyneaux (1835 PA) & Alvira M. (likely McCarty) (1845 PA) - Houghton High School, Houghton College, University of Buffalo School of Medicine - Professor of German, Houghton High School, Private Medical Practice,
Buffalo - Private Medical Practice, Hogansville & LaGrange, GA - Kathleen Jane Varley (M 6/7/1940 Buffalo) - Yvonne Suzanne (1941), Roberta Michele (1943), Richard Vahey (1951), Joan Coleller (1962) - 7/30/2000 LaGrange, GA - Molyneaux Estate, Hogansville, GA - 1920 Federal Census Houghton. Daughter Yvonne Molyneaux Bledsoe. The Molyneaux Family can trace its ancestry back to the time of William the Conqueror. The name has also been spelled Molyneux. Photo – Family.

Molyneaux (Grange), Roberta Pearl Military: Women's Army Corps (WAC) - 3/3/1943 (WAAC)

/Buffalo/ Private, 8/27/1943 (WAC)/Buffalo/Private - Air Service Command Depot, England - Administration/Sergeant – Hondo, Texas/7 months - 24 months - England - None - NA - NA - NA - NA - 10/15/1945, Fort Dix, NJ - European African Middle East Theater Medal, Women's Corps Service Medal, Unit Commendation, World War II Victory Medal. Grandfather Bryon T. Ingersoll served with the 184th NY Infantry Regiment during the Civil War. Civilian: 7/22/1906 PA - John Robert Molyneaux (1874 PA) & Pearl Olivia Ingersoll 1875 NY - Glenn T. (1898 NY), J. Maxwell (1905 PA), Evan W. (1907 PA), Charles G. (1910 PA), Silas R. (1916 NY) - Bryon Thomas Ingersol (1844 NY) & Hannah A. Johnson (1844 NY) - Joel Molyneaux (1835 PA) & Alvira M. (likely McCarty) (1845 PA) - Houghton Academy, Houghton College - School Teacher - Teacher -? Grange - None - 7/22/1987,
Tardon Springs, Fl - Mt. Pleasant Cemetery, Houghton, NY - 1920, 1930 Federal Census Houghton – None. Photo WIMSA Museum.

Molyneaux, Silas Robert Military: Army Air Corps -7/6/1942/Binghamton, NY/Private – 2142nd AAF  Base Unit? - Pilot Instructor, Professor of History/Colonel - Shaw AFB, SC, Military Academy at West Point - NA - NA - NA - NA - NA - NA - NA - 1964 - American Campaign Medal, WW II Victory Medal - Brother Evan and Sister Roberta also served during the war. Was a base commander in Korea during the war, and also flew combat missions. Civilian: 4/14/1916 /Houghton, NY - John Robert Molyneaux (1873 PA) & Pearl Oliver Ingersoll (1874 NY) - Glenn T. (1898 NY), J. Maxwell (1905 PA), Roberta P. (1906 PA), Evan W. (1907 PA), Charles G. (1910 PA) - Bryon Thomas Ingersoll (1844 NY) & Hannah A. Johnson (1844 PA) - Joel L. Molyneaux (1835 PA) & Elvira M. (likely McCarty) (1845 PA) - Houghton Academy, Houghton College, Cornell University, Columbia University - High School Teacher, Barker, NY, Student – Career Air Force, Retired 1964, Member of original Air force group which started Air Force Academy, Executive, Buffalo State College, NY - 1. Eleanor Kaltenborn, 2. Marilyn Brauer - Joel, Leslie - 10/27/2012/Lockport, NY - Hartland Central Cemetery, Gasport, NY - 1930 Federal Census, Houghton – Veteran Silas R. Molyneaux. Photo – Obit (He gave me information for the book.)

Morgan, David William Military: US Army - 2/2/1942 Buffalo/Private - 305th Combat Engineer Battalion (80th Infantry Division) - Truck Driver/Corporal -? /17 months - 30 months - England, France, Luxembourg, Germany - Likely Ardennes-Alsace, Northern France, Central Europe - NA - NA - NA - NA - January 8, 1946 - American Campaign Medal, European Africa, Middle East Theater Medal, World War II Victory Medal, US Army Occupation Medal, Germany Clasp - 3 or 4 Battle Stars. Brother Lewis also served during the war. Civilian: 3/30/1917 Centerville, NY - John H. Morgan (1890 NY) & Mary (Mae) J. likely Thomas (1895 PA) - Lewis J. (1918 NY) - Robert J. (1921 NY) - Elizabeth M. (1923 NY) - Howard T. (1925 NY) - Leonard H. (1928 NY) - Lloyd A. 1933 NY) - Leona J. (1936 NY) - David Morgan (1858 NY) & Mary E.? (1863 Wales) - likely William Thomas (1866 Wales) & Jane? (1866 Wales) - FCS, Grammar School - Self-Employed - INA - Marian J. Brown - INA - May 18, 1988 - White Cemetery, Rushford - 1930,1940 Federal Census Centerville - None.

Morgan, Lewis John Military: US Army - 3/7/1942 FT Niagara/ Private - 44th Infantry Division,  Company C, 324th Infantry Regiment, 89th Infantry Division, Company I, 354th Infantry Regiment - Infantryman, Truck Driver/Sergeant - Likely Fort Lewis, WA, Louisiana Maneuvers of 1943, Camp Phillips, KS, Camp Miles, MA/30 months - 16 months - France, German - Northern France, Rhineland, Central Europe - NA - WIA 11/17/1944 - NA - NA - 12/29/45 - American Campaign Medal, European, African Middle Eastern Theater Medal, Purple Heart, Good Conduct Medal, Combat Infantry Badge (1947 Bronze Star), 3 Battle Stars, Meritorious Unit Badge, Army Occupation Medal - Germany, WW II Victory Medal - Brother David also served during the war. Civilian: 3/9/1918 NY - John H. Morgan (1890 NY) & Mary (Mae) J. likely Thomas (1895 PA) - David W. (1917 NY) - Robert J. (1921 NY) - Elizabeth M. (1923 NY) - Howard T. (1925 NY) - Leonard H. (1928 NY) - Lloyd A. 1933 NY) - Leona J. (1936 NY) - David Morgan (1858 NY) & Mary E.? (1863 Wales) - likely William Thomas (1866 Wales) & Jane? (1866 Wales) - FCS, Grammar School - Farmer - INA - Patricia Talor - Gary, Roy, Diana, Donna, Ricky, Mary, John - May 27, 1974 - INA - 1930 1940 Federal Census Centerville - Son Roy, Wife Donna Morgan. Photo – Family.

Morris, Austin Dee (Austy) Military: US Navy - 12/27/1944/Buffalo/AS - 86th Naval Construction

Battalion/125th Naval Construction Battalion (Seabees) – Heavy Equipment
Operator/Motor Machinist Mate/Petty Office 3 C - Sampson Naval, Naval Training
Center, Davisville, R.I., Camp Parks, CA, Naval Hospital, Shoemaker, CA, Personnel
Separation Center, Long, Island, NY/5 months - 13 months - Hawaii, Okinawa - None
- NA - NA - NA - Appendectomy at Shoemaker, CA, March, April, 1945 –
6/28/1946/Long Island, NY – American Campaign Medal, Asiatic Pacific Theater
Medal, Letter of Commendation, WW II Victory Medal. Brothers Douglas F. &
Richard E. also served during the war. Maternal Grandfather George Austin, while
serving with the British Army during WW I, was killed in action at Gallipoli. Civilian:
12/29/1926 NY - Irving C. Morris (1897 NY) & Patricia E. Austin (1901 England) - Douglas F. (1921
NY), Richard E. (1922 NY) - Richard Morris (1855 NY) & Ellen? (1865 NY) - George Austin (1875
England) & Ethel (likely Fry) (1880 England) - Fillmore Central, Class of 1945 - Student - Rochester
Gas & Electric - Louise McNinch - Martin, John, Sally - 8/27/2005, Loudon, TN - INA - 1930 Federal
Census Centerville. Friend, Lt. Col. (Ret) Joel Winchip, Son Marty Morris. Photo – School.

Morris, Douglas Ferdinand Military: Army Air Corps - 1/30/1940 Buffalo/Private - 53rd Pursuit

Group/INA - Navigator/Sergeant - Syracuse University, Greensboro, NC/INA - 26
months - Panama Canal Zone, New Guinea, Southern Philippines, Luzon, Western
Pacific - New Guinea, Southern Philippines, Luzon, Western Pacific - NA - NA -
NA - Malaria 7/14-7/30/1942 (Panama) - 1/14/1946 FT. Knox, KY - American
Defense Medal, American Campaign Medal, Asiatic Pacific Theater Medal, 4 Battle
Stars, Philippine Liberation Medal, Good Conduct Medal, Air Medal (G.O. 2148,
10/27/1945), Distinguished Unit Badge, WW II Victory Medal. Brothers Richard E.
& Austin D. also served during the war. Maternal Grandfather George Austin, while
serving with the British Army during WW I, was killed in action at Gallipoli.
Civilian: 7/4/1921 Centerville, NY - Irving C. Morris (1897 NY) & Patricia Austin (1901 England) -
Richard E. (1922 NY), Austin D. (1926 NY) - Richard Morris (1855 NY & Ellen? (1865 NY) - George
Austin (1875 England) & Ethel (likely Fry) (1880 England) - Fillmore Central, Class of 1938, Houghton
College, Syracuse University, University of Rochester - Clerk, Towner's Department Store - INA - Buela
Wells (M 5/13/1946 Fillmore) - Jeffery Wells – 8/7/1979, Pinellas, FL - INA - 1930 Federal Census
Centerville, Allegany Co, War Service Record - None. Photo – School.

Morris, Francis David (Dave) Military: US Navy - 11/3/1944/AS - *USS San Marcus, PC-574, USS*
Douglas H. Fox - S1C - Sampson Naval Base, Pre-Commissioning Training Newport, RI, California/9
months - 11 months - Japan, Okinawa, Marshall Islands, Caroline Islands, Guam, Saipan, Mariana
Islands, Iwo Jima - None - NA - NA - NA - NA - July 6, 1946, Lido Beach, NY - American Campaign
Medal, WW II Victory Medal, Asiatic Pacific Theater Medal, Navy Occupation Medal, Japan Clasp.
Civilian: 9/24/1927 Centerville, NY - Richard M. Morris (1900 NY) & Irene F. Miller (1903 NY) -
Shirley A. (1921 NY), Jean I. (1924 NY), June A. (1924 NY), Patricia A. (1938 NY), Bonnie (Stenshorn)
- Richard Morris (1855 NY) & Ellen C. Bishop? (1865 NY) - George A. Miller (1868 NY) & Mabel A.
Stickle (1876 NY) - Fillmore Central, Class of 1944 - Laborer, Fillmore Mill - INA – Susan? Elizabeth?
- INA - 1/18/2012, Churchville, NY - St. Vincent de Paul Catholic Church, Churchville, NY - 1940
Federal Census Centerville - None.

Morris, Richard Ellis (Dick) Military: US Navy - 2/1/1943 Buffalo/AS - Navy V-12 Program/*USS*

Champlain (DD 601) - Fire Control Officer/Ensign - Sampson Naval Base, Middlebury College, VT, Dartmouth College, NH, Midshipman School, Asbury Park, NJ, Columbia University, NYC, San Diego, Charleston, SC/42 months - 3.5 months - Okinawa - NA - NA - NA - NA - NA - 11/14/1946 Charleston, SC - American Campaign Medal, Asiatic Pacific Theater Medal, WW II Victory Medal. Brothers Austin D. and Douglas F. also served during the war. Maternal Grandfather George Austin, while serving with the British Army during WW I, was killed in action at Gallipoli. Civilian: 11/27/1922 Hume, NY - Irving C. Morris (1897 NY) & Patricia Austin (1901 England) - Douglas F. (1921 NY), Austin D. (1926 NY) - Richard Morris (1855 NY & Ellen? (1865 NY) – George Austin (1875 England) & Ethel (likely Fry) (1880 England) - Fillmore Central, Class of 1941, Middlebury College, VT, Dartmouth College, NH, Columbia University, NYC, University of Buffalo - Bell Aircraft Co., Buffalo – Engineer, Sylvania TY, Talco - Suzanne Strahan (M 4/13/1946 Fillmore) - Lynne Marie - 3/15/1993 - Pine Grove Cemetery, Fillmore - 1930 Federal Census Centerville - Allegany County War Service Record. Photo – School.

Murray, Edward Charles Not from FCSD. Military: US Army. The NAO reported in July 1944 that Edward Charles Murray of Fillmore had been inducted into the military along with Glenn Ellery Burgess. No evidence has been identified that Murray ever lived or worked in Fillmore or the Fillmore area. His enlistment record indicates he enlisted July 14, 1944 in Rochester, NY. It also indicates he was living in Ontario County and was born in 1925 in Ohio. No information regarding his service has been identified. Civilian: The following information appears to be about Mr. Murray. Born 6/10/1925, Sandusky, Ohio. Some records show 1927 as his birth year with his brother Charles Edward being born in 1925. It is possible that Charles Edward served rather than Edward Charles. - Joseph Edward Murray (1891 NY) & Lillian L. Johnson - Charles Edward (1925 NY), John, Carl - Charles E. Johnson & Nettie Crandall - Edward died 11/22/1985 and is buried in Bay Pines National Cemetery, Pinellas County, FL. - 1930 Census, Phelps, Ontario County, NY, 1940 Census, Bristol, Ontario County as a boarder. NAO 1944 p86.

Naze, (Wilmot) Avis A. Military: US Army 9/27/1943 - US Public Health Service Nursing Cadet at University of Minnesota. No other relevant information. War ended before Avis entered active duty. Civilian: 1926/North Dakota -? Naze (ND) & Ardis J. Mown (1905 MN) - None - John K. Mown (1894 Iowa) & Amy L.? (1878 Iowa) - INA - Student, University of Minnesota - Antique Dealer - Stephen E. Wilmot M?) - INA - NA - NA - Fillmore History Club 1945 WW II Book – None.

Nichols, Colin Stuart (Nick) Military: US Navy Air - 9/29/1942/Buffalo/AS - Headquarters Squadron,

Fleet Air Wing 9, Detachment 1 - Aviation Machinist Mate/Seaman 1 Class - Sampson Naval Base, Naval Training Station, Newport, R/I, Quonset Point, RI, NAS, NY/26.5 months - 10 months - Azores, - Battle of the Atlantic - NA - NA – NA - Chronic Otitis Media (ear infection), Detained in Portugal, a Neutral Country - October 16, 1945, Washington, DC - American Campaign Medal, European, African Middle East Theater Medal. World War II Victory Medal. Civilian: 10/23/1915 - Chester E. Nichols (1877 MI) & Alice M. Fowles (1884 SD) - Clarence A. (1913 SD), Esther R. (1919 SD) - Henry H. Fowles (1857 MA) & Effie M. ? (1861 NY) - Albert M. Nichols (1843 NY) & Lucy Charlotte Dean (1850 MI) - Pike School District, NY - Prospect Garage, Fillmore, Mechanic - Owner Automobile Garage, Belfast, NY - Carmelita Maria Curran - Robert, William - 2/14//1987 Belfast - Holy Cross Cemetery, Belfast, NY - 1940 Federal Census Fillmore - Sons William and Robert. Photo – Family.

Noble, Lester E. Military: US Army - 3/20/1944/Private - Company K, 87th Infantry Division, 347th

Infantry Regiment - Rifleman/Private - Ft. Dix, NJ, Camp Wheeler, GA, FT. Jackson, SC/6 months - 3 months - France - Rhineland Campaign - KIA, 12/16/1944 - NA - NA - NA - 12/16/1944 - American Campaign Medal, Purple Heart, European African Middle East Theater Medal, Combat Infantry Badge (1947 Bronze Star), one battle star, WW II Victory Medal. Civilian: 12/10/1925 NY - Miles G. Noble (1891 NJ) & Rhea M.? (1893 PA) - Alma L. (1916 PA), Richard E. (1919 PA), Roy M. (1921 WVA) - Frank E. Brown (1865 PA) & Lucy F. Hotchkiss (1868 PA) – Harris E. Noble (1866 NJ) & Charlotte A.? (1869 NJ) - Fillmore Central, Class of 1943, Cornell University (Engineering) - Student - NA - NA - NA - NA - 12/16/1944 - Short Tract Cemetery - 1930 Federal Census Granger - None. Photo – NAO.

Noble, Roy Miles Military: US Army - 7/1942 Ft. Niagara/Private - 3467 Ordnance Company,

Quartermaster Corps - Tool Clerk/Technician 5 - FT. Bragg, NC, FT. Jackson, SC/21 months - 20 months - Ceylon, Iran - none - NA - NA - NA - NA – 10/31/1945 - American Campaign Medal, Asiatic Pacific Theater Medal, WW II Victory Medal. Brother Lester also served, KIA. Civilian: 8/19/1920 - Miles G. Noble (1891 NJ) & Rhea M.? (1893 PA) - Alma L. (1916 PA), Richard E. (1919 PA), Lester (1925 NY) - Frank E. Brown (1865 PA) & Lucy F. Hotchkiss (1868 PA) – Harris E. Noble (1866 NJ) & Charlotte A.? (1869 NJ) - Fillmore Central, Class of 1939 - INA - Ernestine Beardsley - James - 4/13/2006, Friendship, NY - Short Tract Cemetery - 1930 Federal Census Granger - None.

Photo – School.

Ortlip, Stephen Jude. Military: US Navy: 3/1943 - US Navy Band, Navy School of Music - Musician,

Instructor/S2C - Washington, DC, Newport, Rhode Island/approx. six years - NA - NA - NA - NA - NA - NA - NA - 1948 - American Campaign Medal, World War II Victory Medal. Civilian: 8/13/1920 New Jersey - Henry Willard Orlip (1886 PA) & Aimee Eschner (1888 PA) - Aileen (1912 PA), Marjorie (1914 PA), Willard (1917 NY), Henry (1919 NY), Ruth (1924 NJ), Paul (1926 NJ) - Luis Eschner (1856 Bohemia) & Emma Israel (1864 Ger.) - William H. Ortlip (1851 Pa) & Carrie E. McCarter (1866 Pa) - Houghton College, NY, Class of 1942, Catholic University, DC - Student – Organist, Conductor, Composer, Decatur Presbyterian Church, others - Doris Armstrong (M 1/22/1946) – Stephanie, Pamela, Benjamin – 8/26/2018, Decatur, GA - INA - NAO, July, 1942 - Mike Bayes, US Navy Band Archivist, Washington, DC, Russ Girsberger, Naval School of Music Library. Photo – Yearbook.

Ostrum, Charles Russell Military: US Army - 7/19/1943 Buffalo/Private - 7th Field Artillery

Observation Battalion - Artillery Observer/Technical 5 Sergeant - Fort Bragg, NC, Camp Shelby, MS, Camp Shanks, NY, Camp Kilmer, NJ, 11 months - 16 months - England, France, Germany, Austria - Normandy, Northern France, Ardennes, Rhineland, Central Europe - NA - NA - NA - NA - 10/24/1945 – American Campaign Medal, Bronze Star, five battle stars, European African Middle Eastern Theater Medal, World War II Victory Medal, Army Occupation Medal, Germany, (Distinguished Service Cross, State of NY) Brother Robert also served during the war. Civilian: 7/2/1920 Hume, NY - Clyde B. Ostrum (1892 PA) & Lucy P. Leet (1894 NY) - Alpha M. (1919 NY), Robert D. (1921 NY) - William R. Leet (1863 NY) & Myra Cornelia Hill (1866 NY) - Isaac Ostrum ((1865 NY) & Maud E. Morrison (1874 PA) - FCS (grade school), Nunda

Central, Class of 1938, Alfred State Agricultural Technical School, Class of 1942 - Coastal Geodetic Agency, DC (Compiled aeronautical charts) - Perry Knitting Mill, Livingston County Infirmary- Marjorie Haines (12/27/1942, Nunda)- None – 10/31/2016 – Oakwood Cemetery, Nunda, NY - 1930 Federal Census Hume - Veteran Charles R. Ostrum. Photo – Nunda Historical Society.

Ostrum, Robert David Military: US Army - 3/15/1943/Rochester, NY/Private – 577th Quartermaster Railroad Company - Pioneer (Combat Engineer)/PFC - Fort Niagara, NY, maybe Fort Breckinridge, KY/Approx. 10-12 months – Approx. 30 months - 10/11/1945 - England, France - None - NA - 3/23/1945, France - NA - Injured aboard LC 507 when it was sunk during Operation Tiger - 12/10/1945 - Purple Heart, European African, Middle East Theater Medal, American Campaign Medal, WW II Victory Medal - Participated in Normandy (Utah Beach) pre-invasion exercise (Operation Tiger) which was a disaster. Served with the NY National Guard (Co. I, 21 Regiment) prior to the war. Brother Charles R. also served during the war. Civilian: 9/3/1921, Hume, NY - Clyde B. Ostrum (1892 PA) & Lucy P. Leet (1894 NY) - Alpha M. (1919 NY), Charles (1920 NY) - William R. Leet (1863 NY) & Myra Cornelia Hill (1866 NY) - Isaac Ostrum (1865 NY) & Maud Morrison (1874 PA) - FCS (Grade School), Nunda Central School, 2 years - INA - INA - Genevieve Hurlburt - Son (1956 NY) - 2/8/2004, Cuba, NY - INA - 1930 Federal Census Hume - Brother Charles R. Ostrum.

Paine, Faith Geraldine Military: Marine Corps Women's Reserve - 11/6/1943/Private/Philadelphia - 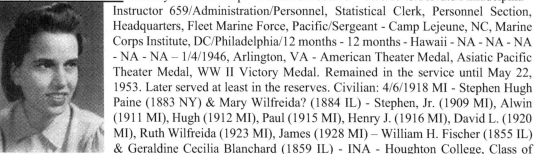 Instructor 659/Administration/Personnel, Statistical Clerk, Personnel Section, Headquarters, Fleet Marine Force, Pacific/Sergeant - Camp Lejeune, NC, Marine Corps Institute, DC/Philadelphia/12 months - 12 months - Hawaii - NA - NA - NA - NA - NA – 1/4/1946, Arlington, VA - American Theater Medal, Asiatic Pacific Theater Medal, WW II Victory Medal. Remained in the service until May 22, 1953. Later served at least in the reserves. Civilian: 4/6/1918 MI - Stephen Hugh Paine (1883 NY) & Mary Wilfreida? (1884 IL) - Stephen, Jr. (1909 MI), Alwin (1911 MI), Hugh (1912 MI), Paul (1915 MI), Henry J. (1916 MI), David L. (1920 MI), Ruth Wilfreida (1923 MI), James (1928 MI) – William H. Fischer (1855 IL) & Geraldine Cecilia Blanchard (1859 IL) - INA - Houghton College, Class of 1940- Financial Assistant, Columbia University Finance Office –Stayed in the service until 1953. Remained in   reserves after leaving active service.) - NA - NA - 2/13/1991 - Mt. Pleasant Cemetery, Houghton, NY - 1940 Federal Census Houghton - None. Photo – Yearbook, Archives.

Papke, Alanson Carl Military: US Navy - 2/8/1943 Buffalo/AS - *USS Pennewill, USS Knudson* - Electrician Mate. S 2 C - Sampson Naval, NY, Purdue University, (Atlantic Fleet Anti-submarine & Escort Service, Trinidad, Brazil, Puerto Rico)/San Diego/30 months - 7 months - Pacific Fleet. Eniwetok, Ulithi, Okinawa, Philippines, Guam - Okinawa Operation, Japan - NA - NA - NA - NA - 3/26/1946 at Sampson Naval. - American Campaign Medal, Asiatic Pacific Theater Medal, Philippine Liberation Medal, Combat Action Ribbon, Navy Occupation Service Medal with Asian Clasp, WW II Victory Medal., One Battle Star, Okinawa. Civilian: 12/20/1922 Hume, NY - Phillip Jesse Papke (1898 NY) & Clara Hildreth (1900 NY) - May I. (1926 NY) - George Hildreth (1872 NY) & Fannie? (1873 NY) - Phillip Papke (1871 NY) & Anna? (1876 NY) - Fillmore Central, Class of 1940 - Lathe Operator, General Motors, Tonawanda, NY - INA - INA - Craig, Valerie (Hubert), Joel - 5/26/2007 Rochester, NY - Marilla, Erie Co., NY - 1930,1940 Federal Census Hume - Allegany Co. War Service Record. Photo – NAO.

Parker, William Burt (Bill) Military: US Army - 6/5/1944/Greensburg, PA/Private - Fifth Army, 92nd

Infantry Division, 473rd Infantry Regiment, Supply Company - Rifleman/PFC/Military Policeman - FT. McClellan, AL, Buffalo/9 months - 10 months - Italy – Likely North Apennines, Po Valley - NA - NA - NA - NA - INA – European, African, Middle East Theater Medal, 2 Battle Stars, WW II Victory Medal. Civilian: 1/31/1925 NY - Theodore Roosevelt Parker (1904 ND) & Bernice Jones (1898 NY) - Betty J. (1927 NY), Anna Mae (1929 NY), Robert W. (1931 NY), Dolores E. (1931 NY) - Burt Jones & Laura Purdy - William A. Parker (1874 NY) & Ada? (1876 NY) - Fillmore Central - Student - Mail Clerk, E Systems (Raytheon) - 1st. Joan? (M St. Petersburg, FL), 2nd Dolores? (M1972 St. Petersburg, FL) - Marlene D., Brenda (Kirkland), Beverly (Gatchel) - 11/8/1980 St. Petersburg, FL - Catholic Cemetery, St. Petersburg - 1940 Federal Census Hume - Sister Dolores Parker Ihrig. Photo – NAO.

Pattison, John B. (MI Only) Military Army Air Corps - 7/27/1942/Rochester/Private – 1386th Air Base Unit, ATC - Crash Boat Operator/Corporal - INA - INA - Meeks Field, Iceland – American Campaign - NA - NA - NA - NA - 8/20/1945 - American Campaign Medal, WW II Victory Medal. Civilian: 7/19/1905, Liverpool, England - John B. Pattison (1881 England) & Annie Walker (1885 England) - Douglas (1912 Canada), Ruby M. (1916 NY) - Joshua Walker (England) - INA - Grammar School, Rochester School System - General Labor for Virgil Wolfer of Hume, Clapp Baby Food Company - INA - Grace? - INA - 9/7/1986, Nunda, NY - Route 3 Cemetery, Centerville, NY - NAO.

Peck, Raymond Irving Military: US Army - 3/11/1943/Buffalo/Private - 3rd Infantry Division, 15th

Infantry Regiment, Anti-Tank Company/Battery A, 216th Anti-Aircraft Artillery Battalion – Infantryman, Truck Driver Light/Corporal - Camp Shelby, MS/5 months, 2 weeks - 26 months 2 weeks - Italy, France, Germany - Anzio, Naples-Foggia, Rome-Arno, Southern France, Rhineland, Central Europe - NA - WIA Italy 2/8/1944, Artillery Shell to face, maybe foot; April,1944, injuries due to slipping, in evacuation hospital 34 days; May 22, 1945, Cellulitis (bacteria skin infection on foot) - NA - NA - 11/19/1945 - Combat Infantry Badge (1947 Bronze Star), Distinguished Unit Badge (1/22 to 2/6/1945), 2 Assault Badges (Anzio, Southern France), French Fourragere (Southern France), Purple Heart, 6 Battle Stars, Good Conduct Medal, European Middle East African Theater Medal, WW II Victory Medal. Civilian: 2/18/1924, Ogden, NY - Lester Peck (1898 NY) & Mabel Elizabeth Erickson (1899 NY) - Cheryl A. (1927 NY), A.C. (1927 NY), Verona (1922 NY), Donald A. (1918 NY) – Elof Erickson (1869 Sweden) and Mary Kilberg (1870 Sweden) – William M. Peck (1863 NY) and May Robinson (1868 Michigan) - Fillmore Central, Class of 1942 - Engine Tester, Curtiss Wright Plant Buffalo - Welder - Mary Louise McQuilkin - Denise, Robert, James, Rita, Sue – 1/1/2009 Batavia, NY - INA - 1940 Federal Census Granger - None. Photo – NAO.

Pero, Deanne Regionald (Dean) Military: Army Air Corps - 3/1/1943/Ft. Niagara/Private - Trainee -

Aircraft Mechanic/Private - Miami Beach, FL, Coral Gables, FL/six months - NA - NA - NA - NA - NA - NA - July, 1943- World War II Victory Medal - None. Civilian: 2/27/1924 Caneadea, NY - Justus F. Pero (1886 NY) & Dollie J.? (1892 NY) - Merton C. (1910 NY), Justa I. (1919 NY) - INA - Calvin Pero (1844 NY) & Mary J. (1846 NY) - Fillmore Central – Carl Oldenburg Gas Station - INA – Elizabeth Miller (M4/6/1946, Syracuse, NY) - Dean - INA - INA - 1940 Federal Census Fillmore - None. Photo – NAO.

Pero, Merton Clute Military: US Army - 8/3/1942/FT/ Niagara/Private - Trainee - NA - INA - NA - NA - NA - NA - NA - NA - NA - NA. Received an Honorable discharge after serving only one full month, 9/1943. Civilian: 11/8/1910, Caneadea, NY - Justus Pero (1886 NY) & Dollie J.? (1892 NY) - Deanne R. (1924 NY), Justa I. (1919 NY) - INA - Calvin Pero (1844 NY) & Mary J. (1846 NY) - Grammar School - Carpenter, Plumbing Co, Allegany Lumber Company - INA - INA - INA - 11/29/1992 Wysox, PA.- INA - 1940 Federal Census Fillmore - None.

Perry, Adelbert Eugene Military: US Navy - 10/1942/AS – San Diego NAS, HedRon, Fleet Air Wing Fourteen – Aviation Ordnanceman/ Maintenance /S 2 C - Great Lakes Naval Training Center, IL, Naval Air Technical Training Center Memphis, Radar Operators School, Naval Air Gunners School, Hollywood, FL, Naval Air Station, San Diego/27 months - NA - NA - NA - NA - NA - NA - NA – 11/21/1944 - American Campaign Medal, WW II Victory Medal. His twin brother Albert also served during the war. Civilian: 1/7/1901 Hume, NY - Benjamin Perry (1873 PA) & Lydia I. Smith (1880 NY) - Albert (1901 NY), Helen M. 1909 NY) - John A. Smith (1819 NY) & Lucinda Wilcox (1822 VT) - Ebenezer Perry (1947 NY) & Eliza Marien (1854 NY) - Fillmore Central - State Trooper - General Motors, Lockport, NY - Elizabeth C. Tennant (M 12/27.1929)/Ruby F. - Albert James, Robert Donald – 9/ 1961, Fillmore, NY - Pine Grove Cemetery, Fillmore, NY - 1910, 1920 Federal Census Hume - Photo – NAO.

Perry, Albert Redman Military: Army Air Corps - 7/17/1942/Ft. Niagara/Private - Provost Marshall Office - INA/Corporal - Keesler Field, MS, Key Field, Meridian, MS/12 months - NA - NA - NA - NA - NA - Ill in hospital at Key Field, MS - INA - American Campaign Medal, WW II Victory Medal. His twin brother Adelbert also served during the war. His wife Elsie Jean Eldridge Perry served with the Women's Auxiliary Army Corps during the war. Civilian: 1/7/1901 NY - Benjamin Perry (1873 PA) & Lydia I. Smith (1880 NY) - Adelbert (1901 NY), Helen M. 1909 NY) - John A. Smith (1819 NY) & Lucinda Wilcox (1822 VT) - Ebenezer Perry (1947 NY) & Eliza Marien (1854 NY) – Fillmore Central - State Trooper - Owner, Store & Gas Station in Rossburg, NY - Elsie Jean Eldridge (M 6/20/1930) - None - 5/22/1966 - Pine Grove Cemetery, Fillmore, NY – 1910, 1920 Federal Census Hume - None. Photo – NAO.

(Perry), Elsie Jean Eldridge Military: Women's Auxiliary Army Corps (WAAC) - 10/1/1942/Ft. Niagara/Private - Aberdeen Proving Grounds, MD, Ballistics Research Laboratory - Radio Television Technician/Corporal - Ft. Niagara, NY, Ft. Des Moines, IA, Kansas City, MO, Ft. Oglethorpe, GA, Aberdeen, MD/ 10 months - NA - NA - NA - NA - NA - NA - NA - 8/1943 - American Campaign Medal, World War II Victory Medal. Her husband Albert Perry also served during the war. Civilian: 11/11/1909 Granger, NY - Everett Eldridge (1885 NY) & Edna? (1885 NY) - Lois M. (1908 NY), Marguerite J. (1915 NY) - INA - Clark Eldridge (1848 NY & Eliza E.? (1859 NY) - Houghton Seminary, Class of 1915, Fillmore Central Training Class, 1916 - Teacher - Electronics Lab, Bell Aircraft, Buffalo, Owner, Store & Gas Station, Postmaster, Geneseo State College - Albert R. Perry (M 6/20/1930) - None - 6/20/2011 - Pine Grove Cemetery, Fillmore, NY - 1910 Federal Census Granger - NAO (Numerous Dates), The New Enterprise, Winter 2001. Photo – NAO.

Perry, Merton Armstrong Not FCSD. Merton apparently never lived in the FCSD area, although he was the manager of the GLF for some time. He was born June 28, 1916 to Earnest Perry (1875 NY) and Mariah Armstrong (1877 NY) in Walton, Delaware County, NY. He lived a number of years in Bliss, Wyoming County, NY, and entered the service from Bliss. On September 4, 1942, he entered the US Army in Buffalo. He died March 31, 1998 in Perryville, AR and is buried in Hope Cemetery in Perryville. NAO 1944 p 10.

Phipps, Carroll Stafford Military: US Army - 12/10/1941/Media, PA/Private - 7th Army, 45th Infantry Division - Rifleman/SGT - Ft. Meade, MD/36 months - 11 months - France, Germany - Rhineland, Ardennes Alsace, Central Europe (liberated Dachau) NA - NA - NA - NA - 11/12/1945, Camp Bowie, TX -European, African, Middle East Theater Medal, American Campaign Medal, World War II Victory Medal, Bronze Star for Meritorious Service, Army Occupation Medal, Germany Clasp. The 45th Infantry Division is recognized as a Liberator Unit by the Holocaust Museum in Washington, DC. As a member of the 45th when it liberated Dachau, Carroll is also recognized as a Liberator. Civilian: 8/11/1917 NY - Raymond S. Phipps (1892 NY) & Mabel A. Havens (1896 NY) - Rowena (1925 NY) - Richmond Havens (1865 NY) & Mary L. Closser (1868 NY) - Fred S. Phipps (1860 NY) & Alice Fisher (1862 NY) – FCS, Monroe County School system - Supply Man, US Gypsum - INA - Billie A. Holley (M 12/28/1946) - INA - 9/7/1980 Sarasota, FL. - INA - 1920 Federal Census Granger - None.

Phipps, Ralph LaRue Military: US Navy - 11/23/1942, entered Active Service 1/17/1943/Geneva, NY/AS - 49th Navy Construction Battalion/134th Naval Construction Battalion - Seabees Construction Mechanic Training Instructor/S 1 C, Coxswain - Camp Endicott, RI, Camp Davis, RI, Camp Parks, CA/INA - NA - Guam- NA - NA - NA - NA - NA - 11/9/1945, Sampson NAS, NY - American Campaign Medal, Asiatic Pacific Theater Medal, WW II Victory Medal. Civilian: 2/28/1910/Fillmore, NY - Frank A. Phipps (1859 NY) & Lena Scott (1872 NY) - Wilbur (1903 NY) -? Scott & Alice? (1843 NY) - Charles Phipps ((1832 NY) & Angelina T.? (1835 NY) - FCS? - Electrical Supplies Salesman/? - INA - 1. Jennie? 2. Norma Martin - Jeffrey, June (Podlech), Louise - 8/29/2011 San Marcos, TX - INA - 1930 Federal Census Fillmore, NAO, November 1943 - None. Photo.

Pierce, Clarence Eugene Military: Not FCSD. Student at Houghton. US Army 2//1943/Private - INA - INA/Staff Sergeant - Camp Kearns, UT/INA - INA - INA - INA - NA - INA -INA - INA - 4/8/1946 - Civilian: 7/21/1916 NY - Henry R. Pierce (1878 NY) & Alice M.? (1893 NY) - Lillian I. (1920), Laura M. (1920), Henry W. (1925 NY), Luann V. (1928) - INA - INA - INA - INA - INA - INA - INA - 4/5/1999 Bainbridge, NY - Linda Vredenburgh Cemetery, Bainbridge - 1940 Federal Census Houghton - None.

Pitt, David Arthur Military: Army Air Corps - 8/13/1941/Erie County, NY/Private – 173rd AAF Base Unit, 139 AAF Base Unit - Synthetic Trainor Instructor/Technical Sergeant - Fort Bragg, NC, Chanute AFB, IL, Shaw Field, NC/52 months - NA - NA - NA - NA - NA - NA - NA - 11/24/1945, Seymour Johnson AFB, SC - American Defense Medal, Good Conduct Medal, American Theater Medal, WW II Victory Medal. David also served with the US Army at Fort Bragg, NC for a short period before transferring to the US Air Corps. Brother Douglas also served during the war. Civilian: 7/13/1913 Ontario, Canada - Joseph R. Pitt (1880 Canada) & Birdie M. Pitts (1878 Canada) (It appears from various records that Joseph's last name was Potts, and that Birdie's maiden name was Pitts. There may have been some mix-up when they emigrated to the US) - Horace (1905 Canada), Winifred M. (1906 Canada), Douglas W. (1919 Canada) - Likely Charles Pitt (1844 Canada) & Clarinda Ann? ((1844 Canada) - Likely John Potts (1845 Canada) &? - Houghton College - Technician - Executive, Gypsum Co, East Aurora, NY- INA - INA - 12/12/1988 - INA - 1930 Federal Census Houghton - None. Family emigrated to the US in May,1921 from Ontario, Canada.

Pitt, Douglas William Military: Army Air Corps - 8/13/1941/Private – 387th Bomb Group, 558th Bomb

Squadron - Pilot/Lieutenant - Ft. Bragg, NC, Ellington Field, TX, Moody Air Force Base, GA, Atlantic City, NJ/30 months, 2 weeks -16 months - England, France - Air Offensive Europe, Normandy Campaign, Northern France, Rhineland Campaign - NA - WIA - NA - NA - (Inactive List 6/7/1945) 6/27/1945 – American Defense Medal, American Campaign Medal, Purple Heart, European African Middle East Theater Medal, WW II Victory Medal, Air Medal with Seven Oak Leaf Clusters, Bronze Star, 4 Battle Stars. Brother David also served during the war. Douglas also served with the US Army at Fort Bragg, NC for a short period before transferring to the US Air Corps. Civilian: 2/28/1919 Ottawa, Canada - Joseph R. Pitt (1880 Canada) & Birlie M. Pitts (1878 Canada) (It appears from various records that Joseph's last name was Potts, and that Birdie's maiden name was Pitts. There may have been some mix-up when they emigrated to the US.) - Horace (1905 Canada), Winifred M. (1906 Canada), David A. (1913 Canada) - Likely Charles Pitt (1844 Canada) & Clarinda Ann? (1844 Canada) - Likely John Potts (1845 Canada) &? - Houghton College - Student - Ford Stamping Plant, East Aurora, NY - Elizabeth (Betty) Douglas (M Epping, Essex, England) - Peter, Susan, Michael, Steven - December 6, 1966, Orchard Park, NY (Car Accident) - Oakwood Cemetery, East Aurora, NY - 1930 Federal Census Houghton – Robert L. Goller, East Aurora, NY Village Historian, Aurora, NY Town Historian. Family emigrated to the US in 1921. Photo – NAO.

Porter, Charles Frederic (Fred) Military: US Army: - 12/18/1940/Olean/Private - 1st Infantry Division, 26th Infantry Regiment, Company M - Rifleman/INA - Plattsburg, NY, Ft. Devens, MA/INA - INA - INA - INA - INA - INA - INA - INA - INA - American Defense Medal - INA. Civilian: 8/2/1916 Richmond, Indiana – (Likely Adopted Parents) Earl Fred Porter (1885 NY) & Myrtle I.? (1892 NY) (Likely Birth parents) John L. Butterworth (1881 Indiana) and Mary Howard (1892 Indiana) - None - INA – (Adopted Paternal Grandparents, Earls parents) - Charles F. Porter (1856 NY) & Anna M. Gillette (1862 NY), (Birth Paternal Grandparents) Charles S. Butterworth (1842 Indiana) & Mary Ellen Parkinson (1851 Indiana) - INA - FCS (3 years HS) - Skilled Mechanic - INA - INA - 9/13/1996 Olean, NY - INA - 1930, 1940 Federal Census Fillmore - None. (Charles was raised in Fillmore by Earl and Myrtle Porter. The 1940 Federal Census says he was their son. However, the 1940 Federal Census also says he was born in Indiana. Further, the Social Security Applications and Claims Index indicates that a Fred C. Porter (Charles Frederic Porter) was born August 21, 1916 in Richmond, Indiana to a John L. Butterworth and a Mary H. Butterworth on August 16, 1916. An Indiana birth certificate shows that a Frederic Howard Butterworth was born August 21, 1916 to a John L. Butterworth and Mary Howard. It appears that Charles Fred Porter was Frederic Howard Butterworth at birth.)

Porter, Donald Carl Military: US Navy - 2/15/44/AS - LST 338 – USS LT 338, USS Marlboro/S1 Class

- Sampson Naval Base, Camp Bradford, VA/approximately 5 months - 23 months total service - European Theater, France - Normandy - NA - NA - NA - NA - 1/19/1946 - American Campaign Medal, European African Middle East Theater Medal, WW II Victory Medal, one battle star. Cousin Charles Frederic Porter of Fillmore also served during the war. Civilian: 5/9/1926 Portageville, NY - John B. Porter (1894 NY) & Edna Mae Gordon (1900 NY) - Joyce C. (1923 NY), Jeanne (1925 NY), Robert R. (1925 NY) - William Gordon (1870 Canada) & Emma Marshall (1878 NY) - Charles F. Porter (1856 NY) & Anna E. Gillette (1862 NY) - Likely Nunda Central, NY – Harts Grocery, Rochester – A&P Grocery Stores, Girls Basketball Coach, Lutheran School, Lockport, NY - Violet Mae Ames (M Feb, 1951, Hume, NY) - Diane (Richard Fox) - 8/5/1993, Niagara Falls, NY - Trinity Lutheran Cemetery, Lockport. NY Donald was born in Portageville, but maybe lived in Fillmore in the 1926-1929 period. Parents were living in Hume in 1925. Also, likely lived there in early 1950's. Was married in Hume in 1951.

Prentice, Lloyd Linford Military: US Army - 8/14/1939/Private - 11th Engineer Combat Regiment,

Panama (likely)/475th Engineer Maintenance Company - Combat Engineer/Tech 4 -
likely Fort Belvoir/2 months - 72 months - Panama Canal Zone (2 years), Iceland (2
years), England, France, Belgium, Germany - Ardennes Alsace, Normandy, Northern
France, Rhineland, Central Europe - NA - NA - NA - NA - INA - American Defense
Medal, European, African, Middle East Theater Medal, WW II Victory Medal, Army
Occupation Medal, Germany Clasp, 5 battle stars. Civilian: 1919 NY - Burton W.
Prentice (1876 PA) & Gussie M. Washburn (1885 NY) - Margaret (1903 NY), Frank V.
(1905 NY), Carl B. (1907 NY), Bertha E. (1909 NY), D.J. (1913 NY), Wilbert R. (1915
NY - Frank Washburn (1858 NY) & Edith Lockwood (1863 NY) - Luther Prentice (1828 NY) &
Catherine? (1842 NY) - FCS - INA - Chief Engineer, Great Lakes Dredge & Dock - Marjorie Mills -
Chip, Michael, Becky, Chris - 1/3/2012 - Evergreen Baptist Church, Sylvester, GA - 1930 Federal Census
Hume - None. Photo – NAO.

Preston, Robert S. (initial only) (Bob) Military: US Navy - 12/22/1943/AS - VPB 100, VPB 17th PBM

Squadron - Radio/ Radar Operator-Waist Gunner/S 1 C - Sampson Naval, Jacksonville,
Fl, Banana River, Fl, San Diego NAS, CA/App. 15 months - App 10 months - Hawaii,
Philippines, Jinsen, Korea, Shanghai Taku, China - Maybe Luzon Operations - NA - NA
- NA - NA - 1/24/1946 - American Campaign Medal, Asiatic Pacific Theater Medal,
WW II Victory Medal, Likely Philippine Liberation Medal with two battle stars, China
Service Medal, Navy Occupation Medal-Asian Clasp (Korea), At least two battle stars
Civilian: 1/22/1921, Hume, NY - Emra N. Preston (1873 NY) & Olive C. Acquard,
Emra's 2nd wife (1887 NY)/1st wife Lena Farnsworth - Stella (1922 NY), Donald (1926
NY), Dorothea (1928 NY) Step Kin: Helen E. (1903 NY, Frank L. (1905 NY), Doris R.
(1907 NY) - INA - Henry Preston (1839 NY) & Adell ? (1839 NY) - Fillmore Central, Class of 1939 -
Construction - Electrician - Helen I. Bennett (M 3/10/1946 Hume) - Gary? - 9/4/1987 - INA - 1930
Federal Census Hume - None. Photo – NAO.

Prinsell, Gustave George Military: US Navy - 10/15/1942/AS - *USS Planter* - Yeoman of the

Ship/Yeoman First Class - Newport RI, Boston, MA, Bureau of Naval Personnel,
Washington, DC/16 months - 24 months - Mediterranean Sea, Southern France,
Pacific Fleet, Okinawa, Japan - Invasion of Southern France - 4/26/1946 -
American Campaign Medal, European African Middle Eastern Theater Medal,
Asiatic Pacific Theater Medal, One Battle Star, Good Conduct Medal, Navy
Occupation Medal, Japan Clasp, WW II Victory Medal. Civilian: 5/26/1922 NY
- Gustave John Prinsell (INA) & Doretta? - INA - INA - INA - Lincoln High,
Jersey City, NJ, Class of 1940, Houghton College, Columbia University Medical
School - Insurance Clerk, 1940-42 - Medical Doctor - Louise Marie Bininger (M
7/27/1946) - 4 sons - NA - NA - Fillmore History Club 1945 WW II Book, 12/45 - Veteran Gustave
Prinsell. Dr. Prinsell's residency and post medical training 1952-1956. He was a Medical Missionary in
Sierra Leone 1957-1964. From 1964 until 1991 he practiced family medicine in Houghton, retiring in
1991. Photo – Family.

Rathbun, Milton Clyde Military: US Army - 1/1942/Ft Niagara/Private - 645th Tank Destroyer Battalion  - INA/Staff Sergeant - Ft. Devens, MA/16 months - 30 months - North Africa, Italy, France, Germany - Naples-Foggia, Anzio, Rome-Arno, Southern France, Ardennes-Alsace, Rhineland, Central Europe - NA - NA - NA - NA – 9/22/1945 - 3 Assault Badges (Arrowhead Devices, Salerno, Anzio, Southern France), 7 Battle Stars, European African, Middle East Theater Medal, American Campaign Medal, Good Conduct Medal, US Army Occupation Medal, Germany Clasp, WW II Victory Medal. Civilian: 4/5/1916 - Clyde V. Rathbun (1882 NY) & Exa Rasey (1891 NY) - Hendrick (1910 NY), Shirley L. (1913 NY), Genevieve L. (1921 NY) - Charles L. Rasey (1852 NY) & Ella M. Lovell (1854 NY) - Lavan Rathbun (1858 NY) & Libbie? (1860 NY) - Fillmore Central, Class of 1935 - Merchant, George Bridge, Pittsford, NY - Owner, Phelps Variety Store - Margaret Wright (M 10/14/1945, Houghton, NY) - Stanley (1946) - 12/31/2000 Leroy, NY - Howard Cemetery, Steuben County, NY - 1930 Federal Census Houghton - Son, Stanley Rathbun. Photo – NAO.

Raybuck, John Stewart Military: US Army Air Corps - 12/2/1942/Buffalo/Private – 110th Army Air Base Unit - Dental Laboratory Technician/Sergeant - Keans Air Base, Kearns, UT, Briggs Field, El Paso, TX , Mitchell Field, NY/ 37 plus months - NA - NA - NA - NA - NA - NA - NA - 1946 - American Campaign Medal, World War II Victory Medal. Civilian: 5/16/1920, PA - Harry S. Raybuck (1887 PA) & Nettie G. Updegraff (1889 PA) - Ida E. (181915 PA), Mary P. (1914 PA) - John M. Updegraff (1853 PA) & Sara M. Gearhart (1856 PA) - Jacob Raybuck (1861 PA) & Anna Mary Bartley (1860 PA) – Houghton Academy, Class of 1939 - INA – Cuba Specialty Manufacturing/Owner, Houghton Gas Service - Olga Lyane Zaveson (M 6/26/1950) - Michael - 1/21/2011, Houghton - Mt. Pleasant Cemetery, Houghton - NAO, January, 1943, Lived Houghton Post War.

Rease, John Stanley Military: US Navy – 2/19/1944/Niagara Falls, NY/AS – Radio Material School, Naval Research Laboratory - Carpenters Mate/S2C - Sampson Naval, NY, Indianhead, MD, Washington, DC/26 months - NA - NA - NA - NA - NA - NA – Operation/Recovery in Bethesda Naval Hospital, 2/20/45 - 4/12/1946 - American Campaign Medal, WW II Victory Medal. Civilian: 5/4/1916, Batavia, NY - John G. Rease (1884 NY) & Beulah? (1886 NY) (1st wife - Lena Barnman (1880 NY)) - Harriet (1923 NY) – Likely Fayette W. Granger (1854 NY) & Estelle M. Nesmith (1858 NY) - John S. Rease (1854 NY) & Emma J. Miller (PA) - FCS, Class of 1935 – Carpenter, E.I. DuPont/DeMemurs Company - Carpenter, Guard – Cleo Ruth Davis - Shirley Jean (1938 NY) - 2/13/1994, Angelica - INA - 1930 Federal Census Hume - None.

Redman, John D. (MI Only) Jr. Military: US Marines - 1/31/1942/Buffalo/Private - Anti-Aircraft Unit, 9th Defense Battalion, FMF (renamed April 1944, Heavy Artillery, Antiaircraft Artillery Group, 9th Defense Battalion, FMF – AAA Machine Gun Crewman/ PFC - Quantico, VA, Norfolk, VA/7 months (3 months in prison for AWOL not included) - 38 months - Cuba, Guadalcanal, (Solomon) New Georgia (Solomons), Rendova (Solomons), Guam (US Territory, Marianas Islands) – Guadalcanal Operations, New Georgia Operations, Guam Operations - NA - NA - NA - NA - 2/11/946 - American Campaign Medal, Asiatic Pacific Theater Medal, 3 Battle Stars, World War II Victory Medal. Brother Robert also served during the war. Civilian: 3/11/1922 Fillmore, NY - John D. Redman (1893 NY) & Dorothy Ellen Burke (1901 NY) - Mary Elizabeth, Dorcas Ann, Robert B., Donald - Tracy Burke (1853 NY) & Elizabeth? (1869 NY) - George A. Redman (1852 NY) & Alice L. Main (1865 NY) - INA - INA - President, John D. Redman Builders - Joan Blasch - John D., Deborah, Gail, Wendy, Pamela, Amy - 1/10/2008 Derby, NY- Short Tract Cemetery - 1925 New York State Census, Allen, Family owned a farm in Allen for decades.

Redman, Robert Burke Military: US Army - 6/17/1941/Buffalo/Private - Battery C, 313th Coast Artillery Balloon Barrage Battalion - INA/Private - Fort Devens, MA/INA - Two Years - Panama Canal Zone - None - NA - NA - NA - Died of non-battle disease - 1944, Fort Devens, MA - American Defense Medal, American Campaign Medal, World War II Victory Medal. Brother John, Jr. also served in the Army during the war. Civilian: 6/26/1923, NY - John D. Redman (1893 NY) & Dorothy E. Burke (1901 NY) - Mary Elizabeth, Dorcas Ann, John, Jr., Donald - Tracy Burke (1853 NY) & Elizabeth? (1869 NY) - George A. Redman (1853 NY) & Alice L. Main (1865 NY) - Kensington High School, Buffalo - Student - NA - None - None - March 31, 1944 Camp Devens MA - Short Tract Cemetery. Family was from Allen but was primarily associated with Fillmore and Short Tract. John's funeral service was held in Fillmore. He played in a family orchestra on a radio program in Buffalo. Photo – NAO.

Redmond, Howard Francis Military: US Army - 6/3/1942/Buffalo/Private – 1714th Signal Service Corps - Truck Driver/Corporal - Ft. Monmouth, NJ, Drew Field, Tampa, FL/25 months - 13 months - Hawaii - NA - NA - NA - NA - NA - 8/3/1945 Ft. Dix, NJ - American Campaign Medal, Asiatic Pacific Theater Medal WW II Victory Medal. Civilian: 6/6/1905 Fillmore, NY - Francis James Redmond (1867 NY) & Eva May Fuller (1870 NY) - None - Oscar Fuller (1849 NY) & Mary Harpes (1844 NY) - Peter Redmond (1834 Ireland) & Catherine Van Middlesworth (1837 NY) - Fillmore Central 3 years - Westbrook Business School, Olean - Walter Adams, Book Keeper, Cooperative Underwriters Insurance Co. - Erma Geraldine Lapp (M 6/19/1929) - Daughter (Stillborn 1933), David (1935 NY) - 6/29/1946, Fillmore - Pine Grove Cemetery, Fillmore, NY - 1940 Federal Census Fillmore - Allegany County War Service Record, Son David Redmond Photo – Yearbook.

Reid, (McCreery), Nancy H. Military: Women's Auxiliary Army Corps (WAAC)/Woman's Army Corps (WAC) - 4/26/1943(enlisted)/7/1/1943(entered)/Buffalo/Private - Pittsburgh Recruiting Office - Administration/Sergeant - Camp Drum, MA, Army Administrative School, Alpine, TX, Camp Pickett, VA, Pittsburgh, PA/31 months - NA - NA - NA - NA - NA - NA - NA - 1/1946, Camp Pickett, VA. - Commendation for Meritorious and Outstanding Service, American Campaign Medal, WW II Victory Medal. Civilian: 4/25/1919/Buffalo, NY - Alexander Reid (1884 Scotland) & Sarah McGarva (1886 Scotland) - Christine (1917 NY), Daisy (1917 NY) - Alexander McGarva (1853 Scotland) & Jemina Brydon (1857 Scotland) - INA - Bennett HS. Buffalo, Buffalo State Teachers College - Homemaking Teacher, Fillmore Central School - Teacher – Husbands: 1. Hubert J. Pederson (M 8/31/1950 L.A.) 2. Fred O. Forsman (M 3/16/1962 L.A.) 3. Bernard L. McCreery (M 3/29/1968)- INA - NA - NA - NAO, 5/1943 - Veteran Nancy Reid McCreery. Father emigrated to US in 1916. Photo – NAO.

Rennicks, George Arnold Military: US Army - 2/11/1938/Niagara Falls, NY/Private (Reenlisted 4/16/1942) -Company E, 28th Infantry Regiment, 111th Training Battalion, Headquarters, ASFTC - Staff Sergeant/Cadre - Camp Butner, NC, Plattsburgh Barracks, NY, Fort Jackson, SC, Fort Bragg, NC, Camp Gordon Johnston, FL/93 months - 10 months – France, Belgium, Germany – Rhineland, Central Europe, possibly Ardennes-Alsace - NA - NA - NA - NA - October 22, 1945, Camp Johnston, FL – American Defense Medal, American Campaign Medal, European African Middle East Theater Medal, World War II Victory Medal, 2 or 3 Battle Stars, Occupation Medal, Germany Clasp. Brother Gerald also served during the war. Civilian: 10/21/1920 Niagara Falls, NY- George Rennicks (1875 PA) & Mary B. McCauliffe (1891 NY) - Maybe Cornelius McCauliffe (1860 NY)

& Mary Obrine (1869 PA) - Maybe Thomas Rennicks (1848 IRE) & Lizzie? (1855 Eng) - Niagara Falls Schools, FCS - Student - INA – Madelaine Webster (M 1952) - INA - 2/23/1968, Leon, FL – Evergreen Memorial Gardens, Bay County, FL - 1935 per 1940 Federal Census. NAO, June 1943 - None. Photo – NAO.

Rennicks, Gerald William (Jerry) Military: US Army - 6/25/1940 /Ft. Niagara/Private - Company A, 28th Infantry Regiment, 8th Infantry Division - Infantryman/Sergeant - Fort Niagara, NY, Fort Leonard Wood, MO. Camp Forest, TN, Camp Kilmer, NJ/39 months - 23 months - England, France, Luxembourg, Germany - Normandy, Northern France, Rhineland, Central Europe - NA - WIA, 2/25/1945, Stockheim, Germany - NA - Operation, March, 1943 at Fort Leonard Wood - 9/8/1945 - American Defense Medal, American Campaign Medal, European, African Middle East Theater Medal, 4 Battle Stars, Purple Heart Medal, Presidential Unit Citation Normandy 9, 27, 1944, 1985 POW Medal, Combat Infantry Badge (1947 Bronze Star), WW II Victory Medal. Brother George also served during the war. Civilian: 4/14/1922, NY - George Rennick (1875 PA) & Mary B. McCauliffe (1891 NY) - George (1920 NY), Genevieve (1912 NY), Marjory (1919 NY) - INA - INA - FCS (the NAO reported in March 1945 that Gerald was a graduate of FCS, but that has not been confirmed.) - Military Service - INA - Ella Evans - Gerald (1944 NY) - 3/3/1991, Ramsonville, NY - North Ridge Cemetery, Ramsonville, NY - 1940 Census, Hume. Photo – NAO.

Rice, Charles Michael Jr. Military: US Army Air Corps - 7/2/1942/Buffalo/Private - 95th Bomb Group/247th Army Air Force Base Unit - Armament Trouble Shooter, Air Gunnery Instructor/Technical Sergeant - Ephrata Air Base, WA, Rapid City Air Base, SD/12 months - 26 Months - England (RAF Framlingham, RAF Horham) - Air Offensive Europe, Normandy, Northern France, Ardennes Alsace, Rhineland, Central Europe - NA - NA - NA - NA - INA. American Campaign Medal, European African Middle East Theater Medal, 3 INA -Presidential Unit Citations, 6 Battle Stars, World War II Victory Medal. Civilian: 4/19/914, NY - Charles Michael Rice (1883 NY) & Clara Isabel (Belle) Sandford (1885 NY) - Monica A. (1909 NY) - William Sandford (1852 NY) & Carrie Snyder (1860 NY) - Garritt S. Rice (1845 NY) & Mary Holland (1845 NY) - FCS - Grocery/Meat Business - Grocery/Meat Business - Vesta D. Steadman - Jackie - 8/30/1979, Fillmore - Holy Cross Cemetery, Fillmore - 1930 Federal Census Fillmore. Photo – NAO.

Richardson, David Plunket Military: US Army - 4/2/1942/Ft. Niagara/Private - Adjutant Generals Office - Attorney/ Captain - FT. McClellan, AL, FT. Washington, MD., Washington, DC/51 months - NA - NA - NA - NA - NA - NA - Pneumonia, May, 1942 during Basic Training - 7/10/1946 Washington, DC - American Campaign Medal, Army Commendation Ribbon, WW II Victory Medal. Brothers Ransom L. & Warren S. also served during the war. Civilian: 8/4/1906 Fillmore, NY - Ransom Lloyd Richardson (1873 NY) & Ruth L. Scott (1886 NY) - Marion S. (1908 NY), Ransom L. (1914 NY), Warren S. (1923 NY) - Sherman S. Scott (1862 NY) & Jennie M. Van Dusen (1863 NY) - David Plunket Richardson (1833 NY) & Julia S. Lloyd (1838 NY) - West High School, Rochester, NY, University of Rochester, Class of 1929 - Attorney - Attorney - Ruth H. Haines (M 8/21/1943) - Gail (1944 NY), Alan (1946 NY) - 1990- Pine Grove Cemetery, Fillmore, NY - 1940 Federal Census Fillmore, Allegany County War Service Record - Son Alan & Daughter Gail. Grandfather David Plunket Richardson was a Member of the House of Representatives from 1879 to 1883. Photo – Family.

Richardson, Ransom Lloyd, Jr. Military: US Army - 8/12/1943/Hartford, CT/Private - Medical Corps,
likely First Army Headquarters, Provost Marshall Section, Headquarters, 12th Army Group, Army Information-Education Staff School - Administration Clerk/Sergeant - Camp Grant, IL/7 months - 20 months - Wales, England, France - Ardennes-Alsace, Central Europe, Normandy, Northern France, Rhineland - NA - NA - NA - NA - 11/24/1945, Ft. Dix, NJ - Good Conduct Medal, European African Middle Eastern Theater Medal, WW II Victory Medal, 5 Battle Stars. Brothers David P. & Warren S. also served during the war. Civilian: 6/21/1914 Fillmore, NY - Ransom Lloyd Richardson (1873 NY) & Ruth L. Scott (1886 NY) - Marion S. (1908 NY), David P. (1906 NY), Warren S. (1923 NY) - Sherman S. Scott (1862 NY) & Jennie M. Van Dusen (1863 NY) - David Plunket Richardson (1833 NY) & Julia S. Lloyd (1838 NY) - West High School, Rochester, NY, Houghton College, Syracuse University - Librarian, Curtis Memorial Library, Meriden, CT. - Librarian - Lois York (M 1939) - David Y. (1943 NY) - 5/10/1989 - Pine Grove Cemetery, Fillmore, NY - Allegany County War Service Record - None. Grandfather David Plunket Richardson was a Member of the House of Representatives from 1879 to 1883. Photo – NAO.

Richardson, Warren Sherman Military: US Navy Air - 12/5/1942/NYC/Cadet - Air Ferry Squadron 4,
Air Ferry Squadron 1, Naval Air Transport Service - Pilot/Ensign - Troy, NY, University of North Carolina, Peru, IN, Pensacola, Fl, Banana River Naval Air Station, FL, Norfolk, VA, Floyd Bennett Field, NY/34 months - NA - NA - NA - NA - NA - NA - NA - 11/15/1945 NYC - American Campaign Medal, WW II Victory Medal. Brothers David P. & Ransom L. also served during the war. Civilian: 12/20/1923 Rochester, NY - Ransom Lloyd Richardson (1873 NY) & Ruth L. Scott (1886 NY) - David P. (1906 NY), Marion S. (1908 NY), Ransom L. (1914 NY) - Sherman S. Scott (1862 NY) & Jennie M. Van Dusen (1863 NY) - David Plunket Richardson (1833 NY) & Julia S. Lloyd (1838 NY) - Fillmore Central School, Class of 1941, University of Rochester - Student - Lawyer, Lobbyist - Nancy? - INA -INA - NA - 1940 Federal Census Fillmore, Allegany County War Service Record - Veteran Warren S. Richardson. Grandfather David Plunket Richardson was a Member of the House of Representatives from 1879 to 1883. Photo – NAO.

Ricketts, Evan Roberts Military: US Army Air Corps - 4/2/1942/Rochester/Private - 15th Air Force, ?
Bomb Group, Technical Services Squadron - Airplane Mechanic/Staff Sergeant - Harding Field, TX/10 months - 31 months - Tunisia, Sicily, Italy - Tunisia, Sicily, Naples-Foggia, Rome-Arno - NA - NA - NA - NA - 9/5/1945 - American Campaign Medal, Unit Meritorious Service Award, Four Battle Stars, European African Middle East Theater Medal, WW II Victory Medal. Civilian: 12/11/1906 NY - Samuel F. Ricketts (1872 NY) & Jennie Smith (1873 NY) - Glenn B. (1897 NY), Ross F. (1899 NY), Frank (1905 NY), Harold C. (1911 NY) - Sardius Smith (1835 NY) & Louisa Bentley (1849 NY) - Frank L. Ricketts (1843 England) & Catherine E. (likely Closser) (1844 NY) - 3 years of college – Teacher Dalton Rural School - Teacher, Dayton Public Schools - None - None - 4/8/1990, Batavia, NY - Hunts Hollow Cemetery, Portage, NY - 1910, 1920, 1930, 1940 Fed Cen Granger - None. Photo – NAO.

Ricketts, Howard Leo (Howie) Military: US Navy - 12/11/1944/Apprentice Seaman - *J. Franklin (APA*
16), Fire Control Man Third Class, Welfare & Recreation Director - Sampson Naval Center, NY, Lake Union, WA, FT. Lauderdale, FL/12 months - 8 months - Okinawa - NA - NA - NA - NA - NA - 7/22/1946 - American Theater Medal, Asiatic-Pacific Theater Medal, World War II Victory Medal. Made extra money on Okinawa as a movie projectionist and a radio repairman. Civilian: 12/13/1926 (NY) - Leslie Ricketts (NY) & Christina Margaret Amore (NY) - Paul L. (Babe) (1929 NY), Calvin R. (1933 NY) - Joseph D. Amore (1877 Italy) & Christina M.? ((1878 Italy) - Fred S. Ricketts

(1860 NY) & Florence? (1856 NY) - Fillmore Central School - Student - Rochester Gas & Electric - 1st, Betty Parker, 2nd Patricia Thomas - March 4/1965 - Todd (1967), Jeffrey (1968), Scott (1970-1990) - 2/29/1979 - Holy Cross Cemetery, Fillmore, NY. Howard helped put flags on veteran's graves after the war. One year he took his son Todd, who was 3, with him. Todd asked Howard if the flags were being put on the graves of the "good guys." Photo – NAO, Lyle Brown.

Ries, Herschel Claude Military: US Army - 10/1/1942/Buffalo/Private - 3163rd Service Signal Company
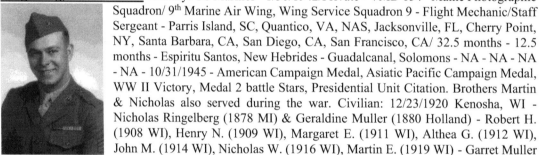
- Radio Repair Frequency Mod Equipment/PFC - University of Nebraska, Lincoln, NB, Monmouth, NJ/ 32 months - NA - NA - NA - NA - NA - NA - NA - 2/21/1946 - American Campaign Medal, WW II Victory Medal. Civilian: 5/6/1923, Seneca Falls, NY - Claude A. Ries (1893 Ohio) & Ruth A. Warbois (1894 NY) - Priscilla (1929 NY) - Charles Warbois (1867 NY) & Addie F. Northrup (1870 NY) - Charles A. Ries (1871 Ohio) & Caroline Ball (1871 Germany) - Student - INA - Houghton College - Technical Services, Head, Maintenance Department - Ruth A. Samuels - David (1949 NY), Deborah, Dan - 12/7/2008, Houghton - Mt. Pleasant Cemetery, Houghton, NY - 1930, 1940 Federal Census Houghton - None. 9. Photo – Military Training Program – University of Nebraska.

Ringelberg, James Gerald Military: US Marines - 1/30/1942/Private - VMD 154th Maine Photographic Squadron/ 9th Marine Air Wing, Wing Service Squadron 9 - Flight Mechanic/Staff Sergeant - Parris Island, SC, Quantico, VA, NAS, Jacksonville, FL, Cherry Point, NY, Santa Barbara, CA, San Diego, CA, San Francisco, CA/ 32.5 months - 12.5 months - Espiritu Santos, New Hebrides - Guadalcanal, Solomons - NA - NA - NA - NA - 10/31/1945 - American Campaign Medal, Asiatic Pacific Campaign Medal, WW II Victory, Medal 2 battle Stars, Presidential Unit Citation. Brothers Martin & Nicholas also served during the war. Civilian: 12/23/1920 Kenosha, WI - Nicholas Ringelberg (1878 MI) & Geraldine Muller (1880 Holland) - Robert H. (1908 WI), Henry N. (1909 WI), Margaret E. (1911 WI), Althea G. (1912 WI), John M. (1914 WI), Nicholas W. (1916 WI), Martin E. (1919 WI) - Garret Muller ((1850 Netherlands) & Henrietta? (1848 Netherlands) - Andrew Ringelberg (1838 Holland) & Greetje E? (1850 Holland) - FCS, Class of 1938, Alfred University - Michigan, Uncle's Company - Iron Worker (Worked on Mt Morris Dam) - Melissa - Melissa (Brady), Lynette (Neuhauer), Joseph, William - 3/25/2002, Tucson, AZ - Tucson, AZ - 1930 Federal Census Granger - Daughter Melissa (Brady). Photo – Family.

Ringelberg, Martin Eugene Military: US Coast Guard - 5/6/1942/Buffalo/AS - INA - Electricians Mate/EM3c(R) - Gulfport, MS, Morgan City, LA/33 months - 5 months sea service (Apparently US based) - NA - NA - NA - NA - NA - NA - 6/7/1945 - American Campaign Medal, World War II Victory Medal. Brothers James and Nicholas also served during the war. Civilian: 9/6/1918 WI - Nicholas Ringelberg (1878 MI) & Geraldine Muller (1881 Holland) - Robert H. (1908 WI), Henry N. (1909 WI), Margaret E. (1911 WI), Athea G. (1912 WI), John M. (1914 WI), Nicholas W. (1916 WI) James G. (1921 WI) - Garret Muller (1850 Netherlands) & Henrietta? (1848 Netherlands) - Andrew Ringelbert (1838 Holland) & Greetje E. (1850 Holland) - INA - INA - INA - INA - INA - 8/25/1981, Canaseraga, NY - Hunts Hollow, Portageville, NY - 1930 Federal Census Granger - None.

Ringelberg, Nicholas William Military: US Army Air Corps - 5/2/1942/Rochester/Private - 27th Air Service Group, 30th Air Service Group, 135th AAFBU, 123rd AAF Base Unit - Airplane Instrument Mechanic/Corporal - Lincoln Army Air Field, Lincoln, NE, Chanute Field, Rantoul, IL, Florida, Millville AAB, New Jersey, Stewart AFB, Georgia, Seymour Johnson AFB, North Carolina/43 months - NA - NA - NA - NA - NA -Tonsillectomy, 1/8/1943, Ear problems 1945 - 11/26/1945 - American Campaign Medal, Good Conduct Medal, World War II Victory Medal. Brothers James and Martin also served during the war. Civilian: 3/20/1916 WI - Nicholas Ringelberg (1878 MI) & Geraldine Mueller (1880 Holland) - Robert H. (1908 WI), Henry N. (1909 WI), Margaret E. (1911 WI), Athea G. (1912 WI), John M. (1914 WI), Martin E. (1919 WI), James G. (1920 WI) - Garret Muller ((1850 Netherlands) & Henrietta? (1848 Netherlands) - Andrew Ringelberg (1838 Holland) &? (1850 Holland) - Nunda, FCS - INA - Machinist, Wheeler Energy Co., Dansville, NY - Betty? (M 3/7/1942 Swain, NY) - Linda (Booth), Nicholas, Jr., Janice (Douglas) - 8/5/2010, Dansville, NY - INA - 1930 Federal Census Granger - None.

Roberts, Floyd Kermit (Curly) Military: US Army - 2/7/1941/Private - 1st Armored Division, Company  A, 58th Armored Field Artillery Battalion - Radio/PFC - Fort Knox, KY, FT. Benning, GA, Greenville, PA./28 months - 6 months - North Africa, Sicily, Normandy, France, Belgium, Luxembourg, Germany - Sicily, Normandy, Northern France, Rhineland, Ardennes-Alsace - KIA 12/22/1944 Belgium - NA - NA - NA - 12/22/1944 - American Defense Medal, American Campaign Medal, Purple Heart, European, African, Middle East Theater Medal, 5 Battle Stars, Arrowhead Device- Assault Normandy, French Croix de Guerre Normandy, WW II Victory Medal. Killed during Battle of the Bulge. Grandfather Albert P. Watson served with Company F, 33rd NY Infantry and Company B, 2nd NY Mounted Rifles, Civil War. Civilian: 8/18/1916 Eagle, NY - Thomas E. Roberts (1860 NY) & Lucia Watson (1877 NY) - Louis (1896 NY), Palmer W. (1898 NY), Grant E. (1900 NY), Elliott (1905 NY), Agnes (1910 NY), Mary (1924 NY) - Albert P. Watson (1830 NY) & Amelia Pratt (1841 NY) - Owen Roberts (1818 Wales) & Jane? (1819 Wales) - Bliss, NY High School – 5 years, Farm Hand for Edwin Minard, Fillmore - NA - NA - NA - 12/22/1944 Belgium - Luxembourg American Cemetery - Allegany County War Ser Record, filed by Florine Minard, wife of last employer. Photo – Hume Museum.

Robinson, Edwin James Military: US Navy - 10/19/1944/Buffalo/AS - NA - NA/AS - Sampson Naval,  NY/3 months - NA - NA - NA - NA - NA - NA - NA - 2/1/1945 - World War II Victory Medal. Civilian: 11/2/1919 NY - Father Unknown. Mother Adeline M. Robinson (1890 NY) - None - Unknown - James E. Robinson (1861 NY) & Harriett E.? (1862 NY) - FCS - Farm Laborer - INA - INA - INA - 2/14/2003, Houghton, NY - East Koy Cemetery, Portageville, NY - 1930 1940 Federal Census Hume – None. Photo – School.

Robinson, Sherman Charles Jr. (Jerry) Military: US Navy - 12/12/1944/ Olean, Buffalo/AS – CASU 5, CASU 32 - S1C/S1C - Sampson Naval, NY, Naval Air Technical Training Center, Norman, OK/12 months (until December, 1945) - - Pacific Fleet (Post War by 12/45 at latest) – None - Sampson NTC, NATTC Norman OK, TADCEN Camp Ellicott, CA, PSC Lido Beach LI. NY, Ordnance Training Unit, San Diego Naval Base/Total Service 19 months, 14 days – Part of service was at sea, amount unknown – At Sea - NA - NA - NA - NA – July 25, 1946. Lido Beach, LI - American Campaign Medal, Asian Pacific theater Medal, World War II Victory Medal. Grandfather Gardner Robinson served with the 160th NY Infantry during the Civil War. Civilian: 10/28/1927 Hume, NY - Sherman C. Robinson (1885 NY) & Jennie E. Morris (1889 NY) - Mary (1918 NY) - Gardner E. Robinson (1836 NY) & Augusta Delia Catlin (2nd Wife) (INA) - Richard Morris (1855 NY) & Ellen likely Bishop (1866 NY) - FCS - Student - INA - INA - 1/25/2001, Osprey, FL - INA - 1930 1940 Federal Census Hume - None.

Rork, Harold David Jr. Military: US Navy - 2/4/1943/Buffalo/AS - Air Transport Squadron 7, VR 7, Hedron Det 1 Fleet Air Wing 11Navy #115, CASU 26 - Aviation Machinist Mate/3c - Sampson Naval, NY, NAS Training Center, Norman, OK, , Falmouth NAS, MA, Miami, FL/30 months - 9 months - San Juan, PR, Guantanamo Bay, Cuba (6 months in 1945) - NA - NA - NA - NA - NA - 3/17/1946, Sampson NAS, NY - American Campaign Medal, Good Conduct Medal, WW II Victory Medal. Civilian: 7/5/1923 Hume, NY - Harold R. Rork, Sr. (1902 NY) & Josephine Bovee (NY) - half-sister Gail (NY) (from Fathers 2nd wife) - John Bovee (1863 NY) & Martha? (1873 Ireland) - Thomas F. Rork (1874 NY) & Esther (Etta) A. Childs (880 MI) - Fillmore Central, Class of 1939 - Foote Company, Nunda, NY, Mechanic - Foote Company, Nunda, NY, Mechanic - Teresa R. Riehe (1950) - Roxanne (1952 NY) - 3/7/1998/Rossburg - Wiscoy Cemetery - 1930 1940 Federal Census Hume - Wife Teresa Riehe Rork. Photo – NAO.

Rose, Herbert Leslie (Herb) Military: US Army - 4/14/1942/Buffalo/Private - Company B, 26 Signal Construction Battalion - Truck Driver/Tech 5 - Fort Monmouth, NJ, Fort Dix, NJ/3 months - 40 months - Iceland, England, France, Germany - Normandy, Northern France, Ardennes-Alsace, Rhineland, Central Europe - NA - NA - NA - NA - 10/28/1945/Fort Dix, NJ - American Campaign Medal, European, African, Middle East Theater Medal, Good Conduct Medal, World War II Victory Medal, 5 Battle Stars, Army of Occupation Medal-Germany Clasp, Motor Vehicle Driver Award. Father registered for WW I. Civilian: 4/28/1917/Caneadea, NY - Simeon H. Rose (1884 NY) & Ruth M. Austin (1893 NY) - Evelyn E. (1912 NY), Wilford A. (1915 NY), Karl M. (1916 NY), Emma A. (1919 NY), Ethel R. (1920 NY), Glenda L. (1921 NY), Norman D. (1923 NY), Junior)1925 NY) - Reuben L. Austin (1855 NY) & Elizabeth A. Snow (1853 NY) - Clark Rose (1847 NY) & Adelia (likely Van Order) (1851 NY) - Rushford Central School - Farmer - Farmer - Ethel Anne Lane - Leslie H., Everett, Haron, Nancy Ann - 8/2/2010, Houghton, NY - Siloam Cemetery, Freedom, NY - Fillmore History Club 1945 Book (Moved to FCSD area in 1974) - None. Photo – NAO.

Roth, Albert Axtell Military: US Army - 9/3/1942/Buffalo/Private - 532nd Coast Artillery Company (renamed 532nd Anti-Aircraft Artillery Automatic Weapons Battalion), 2633rd Service Company - INA/PFC - Fort Bliss, TX/6 months - 31 months - North Africa, Italy - Tunisia, Naples-Foggia, Rome-Arno, North Apennines - NA - NA - NA - NA - 9/1945 - European African Middle East Theater Medal, World War II Victory Medal, 4 Battle Stars - 1940 Federal Census - None. Civilian: 7/5/1911/Ohio - William J. Roth (1869 Ohio) & Clarinda Cole (1871 PA) - Viola (1904 PA), Luella E. (1906 PA), Ida T. (1907 PA), Elmer (1908 PA) - Samuel S. Cole (1821 PA) & Clarinda Axtell (1831 PA) – Maybe Jacob Roth (1846 Ohio) & Barbara (1848 Ohio) - One Year College - Student - INA - INA - INA - Died 10/15/1968, Houghton - Mt. Pleasant Cemetery, Houghton, NY. Photo – Yearbook.

Sandford, Raymond Herbert (Ray) Military: Army Air Corps - 8/19/1942/Private – 565th Army Air Force Base unit India China Wing, Air Transport Command - Airplane Sheet Metal Worker/Sergeant - Reno, NV/13 months - 25 months - India, China - India Burma Campaign, China Defensive Campaign - NA - NA - NA - NA - 10/26/1945 - Presidential Unit Citation, American Campaign Medal, 2 Battle Stars, Asiatic Pacific Theater Medal, WW II Victory Medal. His grandfather, John Wiederight, served with Company F, 104th NY Infantry during the Civil War. Civilian: 2/23/1912 NY - John H. Sandford (1877 NY) & Mary E. Wiederight (1877 NY) - Marion (1914 NY), Bernice (1909 NY) - John Wiederight (1835 NY) & Susan C.

Saylor (1844 NY) - Robert H. Sandford (1849 NY) & Emmaline Francisco (1859 NY) - Fillmore Central, Class of 1931 - Airplane Wing Repairman, Curtiss Wright Plant Buffalo - INA - Lucille Overholt - INA - 6/22/2007, Pike, NY - Alger Cemetery, NY - 1930, 1940 Federal Census Hume - Sandi Howard. Photo – School.

Sandford, William Alton (Bill) Military: US Army - 4/17/1945/Buffalo/Private - Engineer Corps/8th Base Post Office - Supply Clerk/Private First Class - Camp Lee, VA, FT. Belvoir, VA, Ft. Jackson, SC /7 months - 8 months - Iran - NA - NA - NA - NA - NA - 7/8/1946 FT. Dix, NJ - World War II Lapel Button, African Middle East European Theater Medal, WW II Victory Medal. Civilian: 1/5/1916, Hume, NY - Frank E. Sandford (1882 NY) & Margaret A. Wolfer (1883 (NY) - Cleland ((1905 NY), Claude (1910 NY), Barbara R. (1913 NY) - John Wolfer (1850 Germany) & Elizabeth A. Durst (1849 Germany) - Likely William Sandford (1853 NY) & Carrie? (1860 NY) - West Brook Business School - Clerk, F.E. Sandford, Hume - Owner, Sandford & Son, Hume - Bernice Angalee (M 8/29/1939 Caneadea) - INA - 7/27/1987 Hume - INA - 1920, 1930 Federal Census Hume - Allegany County War Service Record, Kent Sandford.

Saunders, Gerald Frank (Jerry) - Military: US Army Air Corps 1/4/1943/Buffalo/Private - 84th Bomb Squadron, 47th Bomb Group - Armorer Gunner/Staff Sergeant - Miami Beach Air Force Base Training Center, Scott Field, IL, Lowry Filed, CO, Fort Myers, FL/26 months, 2 weeks - 12 months - Italy, France - Rome-Arno, North Apennines, Po Valley, Southern France - NA - NA - NA – Dental Issues - 10/11/1945, Seymour Johnson Field, NC - American Campaign Medal, European, African, Middle East Theater Medal, World War II Victory Medal, 4 Battle Stars Good Conduct Medal, 3 Air Medals, Distinguished Unit Citation - Civilian: 6/10/1922, Sherbrook, Canada - Alfred F. Saunders (1899 England) & Irene M. Williams (1879 Wales) - None - Likely John J. Williams (1861 Wales) & Basil ? (1876 Wales) - Likely Benjamin Saunders (1865 England) & Hannah? (1870 England) - Niagara Falls School System - INA - Niagara Mohawk, Mechanic - June M. Haskins (M9/9/1950, Centerville) - INA - 12/26/2005, Orlando, FL - White Cemetery, Rushford, NY – NAO, SSDI, Fillmore, NY. Photo – NAO.

Savory, Paul - Not from the FCSD area. Was visiting relatives in area. Brother Stephen's wife was from Granger. Stephen had served with Fillmore resident Grant Vedder at a Naval Base in Australia. He visited Grants parents when he visited his wife who was with her parents in Granger. Many non-FCSD area WW II personnel were married to local FCSD women and visited the area during the war. NAO 1944 P 115.

Scherer Jr., August (NMN) Military: Army Air Corps - 7/24/1944/Private - 489th Bombardment Group (Very Heavy) B-29 Group - Aerial Gunner/CPL - FT. Myer, FL, Lincoln, NB, Davis-Monthan Air Base, AZ//26 months - NA - NA - American Campaign - NA - NA - NA - NA - 9/21/1946 - American Campaign Medal, WW II Victory Medal. Father August registered for World War I. Civilian: 3/16/1926, Buffalo, NY - August Scherer (1890 NY) & Hazel D. Mcalen (1893 NY) - Lois ((1913 NY), Eugene O. (1915 NY) - Thomas Mcalen (1866 NY) & Alice? (1864 NY) - George Scherer (1861 NY) & Mary? (1857 NY) - Fillmore Central, Class of 1944 - Student - INA - INA - INA - 1/10/2000 Long View, TX - INA - 1940 Federal Census Centerville - None.

Schlicht, William Earnest - Not from FCSD area. Visited his brother Otto who lived in area. He was from the Buffalo/Tonawanda area. Like military personnel such as Paul Savory above who visited his wife's family, other non-FCSD area WW II military personnel visited relatives in the FCSD area during the war. NAO 1943 p36, 1944 p 144, 1945 p 134.

Schmidt, Hilda Louise (Gibbons). Military: US Army Nurses Corps (Cadet) - Admitted to nurse's corps  12/7/1943. Had committed to two years in the Army Nurses Corps following graduation from nursing school, but war ended before she graduated. Terminated from Corps 9/28/1945. Civilian: 10/1924 (NY) - William F. Schmidt (1881 Germany) & Emma L. Haas (1900 NY) - Emma L. (1915 NY), Edna W. (1916 NY), Frieda W. (1920 NY), Mildred E. (1922 NY), Harold E. (1926 NY), Betty M. (1928 NY) George L. (1930 NY), John R. (1933 NY), Martha J. (1936 NY) - Herman Schmidt (Germany) & Augusta Schultz (Germany) - Frederick Haas (1879 Germany) & Emma Mews (1874 Germany) - Fillmore Central, Class of 1941, Craig School of Nursing, Sonyea, NY - Baby Sitter - Nurse, Veteran's Hospital, Northport, NY, School, Portville Central, Portville, NY - John J. Gibbons - James J., Michael J., Patricia A., John P., Anne M. - NA - NA -1930 Federal Census Granger - Hilda Schmidt Gibbons, Son Mike Gibbons. Photo – Family.

Schmidt, Harold Earnest Military: Us Army - Possibly April-May, 1945/Belmont, NY/Private - Field  Artillery, Instrument & Survey Battery - likely Fire Control Instrument Operator/PFC - Fort Bragg, NC, others/estimated 24 months - NA - NA American Campaign - NA - NA - NA - NA - 4/26/1947 - American Campaign Medal, World War II Victory Medal. Civilian: 7/23/1926, NY - William F. Schmidt (1881 Germany & Emma L. Hass (1900 NY) - Emma L. (1915 NY), Edna M. (1919NY), Freda M. (1920 NY), Mildred E. (1922 NY), Hilda L. (1925 NY), Betty M. (1928 NY), George L. (1930 NY), John R. (1939 NY), Martha J. (1936 NY) - Frederick Hass (1877 Germany) & Emma Mews (1871 Germany – Herman Schmidt (Germany) & Augusta Scherer (Germany) - Fillmore Central, Class of 1943 - Student - INA – Alice Lorraine Kellogg – Gary Frederich, Alice Hilda, Lucille Mae, Daniel Louis, Karl Edward – 7/7/1995 - Pine Grove Cemetery, Fillmore - 1930, 1940 Federal Census Granger - Nephew Mike Gibbons. Photo – Family.

Schmidt, Mildred Elizabeth (Millie) Military: US Army Nurses Corps - 1/1945(Reported 2/1/1945)/2nd  Lieutenant - 232nd Hospital Ship Complement/ Hospital Ship "Aleda E. Lutz" - Nurse/First Lieutenant (Captain Post War) - Halloran Hospital, New York City (Early 1945)Charleston, SC/8 months - 12 weeks - 4 trips to Europe to pick up wounded soldiers France & England) - NA - NA - NA - NA - NA - NA - 6/15/1952 (Remained in service/died in airplane accident near Fairbanks, Alaska in 1952) - European African Middle East Theater Medal, American Theater Medal, World War II Victory Medal - Buried with full military honors, including a 21 gun salute. Her sister Hilda was in the Army Nurse Cadet Training Program when the war ended. Civilian: 5/6/1922 (NY) - William F. Schmidt (1881 Germany) & Emma L. Haas (1900 NY) - Emma L. (1915), Edna W. (1916), Frieda W. (1920), Hilda L. (1924), Harold E. (1926), Betty M. (1928), George L., 1930 NY), John R. (1933 NY), Martha J. (1935 NY) - Herman Schmidt (Germany) & Augusta Schultz (Germany) - Frederick Haas & Emma Mews - Fillmore Central, Class of 1940, Craig School of Nursing, Sonyea, NY, Presbyterian Hospital, NYC, University of Colorado, Boulder - Student - Military Nurse - NA - NA - 6/15/1952 Alaska - Pine Grove Cemetery, Fillmore, NY - 1930 Federal Census Granger - Sister Hilda Schmidt Gibbons. Photo – Family.

Schramm, Edward Fredrick Military: US Army Air Corps - 2/1/1943/Buffalo/Private - 390th Bomb Group, 571st Bomb Squadron - Left Waist Gunner/Staff Sergeant -INA/6 months - 26 months - Framlingham, England - Normandy, Rhineland, Central Europe - NA - NA - NA - NA - 10/1/1945 - 3 Battle Stars, Air Medal, European, African, Middle East Theater Medal, WW II Victory Medal. Civilian: 1/6/1924 NY - Herman G. Schramm (1890 NY) & Mary Flynn (Finn) (1888 IRE) - Mary Esther (1915 NY), Herman (1917 NY), Rita (1919 NY), Delores (1925 NY) - Edward Flynn (1862 Ire) & Anna? (1871 Ire) - Gottfried Schramm (1863 NY) & Anna C.? (1863 Sweden) - Rushford Central School - Farm Laborer - INA - Edith A.? (M 11/4/1944) - Corey, Phillipe - 4/15/2000, Boston, NY - INA – 1935 1940 Census, Centerville. Photo – Archives.

Schuknecht, Harry Albert Military: Army Air Corps - 10/27/1942/Buffalo/Private – 11th Air Force - INA/Corporal - St. Petersburg, FL, Kearns, UT, Fort Dix, NJ/4 months - 33 months - Alaska, Aleutian Islands - Aleutians Campaign - NA - NA - NA - NA - 11/9/1945 Ft. Dix, NJ - Asiatic Pacific Theater Medal, one battle star, WW II Victory Medal. Civilian: 10/22/1922, NY - Kenneth H. Schuknecht (1899 NY) & Laura Pike ((1898 NY) - Lorna (1922 NY), Gordon (1933 NY) - Harry S. Pike (1869 NY) & Alice E.? (1871 NY) - Albert T. Schuknecht (1872 NY) & Florence Beardsley (1875 NY) - Fillmore Central, Class of 1940 - Farm Laborer - Over the Road Truck Driver - Myrna J. Lanski - Janine - 11/23/2003, Cattaraugus County, NY - Willow Brook Cemetery, Dunkirk, NY - 1930 1940 Federal Census Hume - None. Photo- NAO.

Schultz, Robert Evert Woodrow Military: US Navy - July 25, 1944/Buffalo/AS - Armed Guard Center, Brooklyn, NY/USS Bland - Armed Guard/Seaman First Class - Sampson Naval Base, Armed Guard School, Norfolk, VA, Armed Guard Center, Brooklyn, NY/INA - INA - Africa, Asia, Europe - None - NA - NA - NA - NA - January 24, 1946 - American Campaign Medal, European African Middle East Theater Medal, World War II Victory Medal. Civilian: 5/13/1919/NY - Earnest Schultz (1892 Alsace) & Edith Sarah Green (1895 NY) - Buelah (1913 NY), Sarah (1915 NY), Bertha (1918 NY), Herbert (1921 NY), Marie (1924 NY, Doris (1926 NY), Ernestine (1929 NY) - William Green (1866 NY) & Matie? (1869 NY) - Julian Schultz (1854 Germany) & Amelia? (1854 Germany) - Buffalo School System - Steelworker - Operating Engineer, Local 17, Buffalo - Betty R. Voss (12/12/1939) - Robert, Donna (Partello), Carol (Boone), Ronald, Betty Lou, Richard - 9/2/2012, Wyoming County Hospital (Residence Fillmore, NY) - Pine Grove Cemetery, Fillmore - Moved to Fillmore area in 1972 for work per Historical Society 1945 NAO Book. Photo – Hume Museum.

Sciera, Charles (NMN) Military: Army Air Corps - 11/2/1942/Ft. Niagara/Private - Army Airways Communication System/111th Squadron Transmitting Station - Communications Specialist/Sergeant - McClelland Field, CA, Portland, OR,, Pocatello, ID, Scott Field, IL, Chicago, Vancouver, WA, Smyrna Air Base, TN/19 months - 18 months (5/44-11/45) - North Africa (Oran, Algiers, Marrakesh, Morocco, Dakar, Senegal) - NA - NA - NA - NA - NA - 11/24/1945 Ft. Dix, NJ - American Campaign Medal, European African Middle East Theater Medal, WW II Victory Medal. Brother Leo served in the Navy during World War II. Civilian: 10/2/1907 Wadowice, Poland - Frank Sciera (1884 Poland) & Anna Gondro (1885 Poland) - Elizabeth (1909 Poland), Martha (1911 Poland), Leo (1913 Poland), Frances (1915 NY), Jenny (1917 NY) -? & Magdalene? (1849 Poland) - INA - Buffalo Public School System - Radio Repair Shop, Fillmore - Self-employed, Radio Repair Store - Clarissa E. Weast

(5/23/1936 Buffalo) - Charles Mark, Susan - 9/2/1997 Sarasota, FL - Memorial Gardens, Sarasota, FL - NAO, 10/1945 - Allegany County War Service Record, son C. Mark Sciera. Photo – NAO.

Shaffer, Florence Mary Military: Not FCSD. Portageville. US Navy WAVES (Women Accepted for Volunteer Emergency Service) - Was sister of Kay Shaffer Vasile who did live in Fillmore.

Shea, John Gerald Whitney Military: Army Air Corps - 9/19/42/2nd Lieutenant - Code & Cipher Section, 75 Army Air Force Base Unit, Staff Officer, 73rd AAC3 Group - Historical Editor, Security Officer-Cryptology/Captain - Miami Beach, FL, Morrison Field, West Palm Beach, FL, Bolling Field, DC/38.5 months - 4.5 months - Caribbean Locations - NA - NA - NA - NA - NA - 4/1/1946, Mitchell field, NY - American Campaign Medal, WW II Victory Medal. Civilian: 7/4/1904 Ontario, Canada - Adam J. Shea (1872 Canada) & Maude M. Whitney (1881 Canada) - Pauline, Grace, George, Alton, Ruth, Lois - Houghton College, Class of 1933 - Associate Professor, Economics & Sociology, Houghton College - Professor, Economics and Sociology, Houghton College - Phoebe Lusk (INA) - Sally A. (1935 NY) - 5/4/1994, Akron, Ohio - Mt. Pleasant Cemetery, Houghton, NY - 1940 Federal Census Houghton - None. Photo – NAO, School.

Slack, Donald Lorren (Don) Military: US Navy - 1/19/1940/Buffalo/AS - *USS Denebola,* Iceland, *USS Lexington, USS Pennsylvania, USS Rocky Mount, USS William R. Biddle, USS Wharton* - Yeoman/S 1 C - Sampson Naval, Norfolk, VA, Boston Naval Yard, California/INA - INA - Iceland, Pacific Fleet - Tawara Island, Wake Island Raids, Gilbert Islands (Makim, Atoll, Bataroian Island), Marshall Island Operations (Kwajalein), Mariana Islands (Saipan, Guam, Tinian), Leyte Assault (Philippines) - NA - NA - NA - NA - Career Navy - American Defense Medal, American Campaign Medal, WW II Victory Medal, Asiatic Pacific Campaign Medal, Navy Occupation Medal, Japan Clasp, 6 Battle Stars. Civilian: 10/23/1920 NY - Lorron W. Slack (1900 NY) & Eunice V. Bray (1895 NY) - Vernon W. (1926 NY), Robert C. (1928 NY), Lyle (1935 NY) - William Bray (1857 NY) & Lena R. Worden (1867 NY) - Burton D. Slack (1873 NY) & Ada (Addie) L. (maybe Caryl) (1876 NY) - Scio, NY Central - Student - Career Navy - 1. INA (3/18/1943), 2. Marilyn Schroeder (M 9/18/1946) - Donald Edward (NY), Donna Lynn (1949 NY) - 3/29/2002, Cattaraugus Co, NY - INA - NAO 5/1943, (Family was living in Fillmore by 1940. He lived there in late 1930's.) - None. Photo – NAO.

Slack, Vernon Beredette Military: US Navy - 7/1944/AS - Torpedo Testing Range, Montauk, LI, Hoboken, NJ*, USS Wickes* - INA/S 1C - Sampson Naval, NY, Naval Torpedo Testing Range, Montauk, Long Island, Hoboken, NJ/12 months - 5 months - Hawaii - None - NA - NA - NA - NA - INA - American Campaign Medal, Asiatic Pacific Theater Medal, WW II Victory Medal. (Above information is through the end of the war. Vernon served beyond the war, and later served on LST 761, and LST 904) Civilian: 8/12/1926 NY - Lorron W. Slack (1900 NY) & Eunice V. Bray (1895 NY) - Donald L. (1920 NY), Robert C. (1928 NY), Lyle (1935 NY) - William Bray (1857 NY) & Lena R. Worden (1867 NY) - Burton D. Slack (1873 NY) & Ada (Addie) I. (maybe Caryl) (1876 NY) - Fillmore Central - Student - INA - INA - Bernard - 2/12/2007, Belfast - Riverside Cemetery, Belfast, NY - 1940 Federal Census Fillmore - Son Bernard Slack.

 **Slocum, Melvin L** Military: Army Air Force - 12/10/1942/Buffalo/Private - 486th Bomb Squadron, 340th Bomb Group, 12th Air Force, 340th Bomb Group, 486th Bomb Squadron - Radio Operator, Gunner/Technical Sergeant - Sioux Falls, SD, Las Vegas, NV, Wisconsin/20 months - 12 months - Tunisia, Italy, Corsica - Air Offensive Europe, Rome-Arno, Po Valley, Southern France - NA - WIA (Flax to Wrist) - NA - NA - 8/1945 - American Campaign Medal, Purple Heart, 9/23 Group Distinguished Unit Citation, European, African, Middle East, Theater of Operations Medal, WW II Victory Medal, 4 Battle Stars. Civilian - 3/26/1921 NY- Howard Blaire Slocum (1893 NY) & Lois S.? (1897 NY) - Dana B. (1907 PA) - Willard J. Slocum (1854 NY) & Arabelle E. Chaffee (1859 NY) - INA - INA - INA - Computer Technician, Pa RR - Maxine E.? - Gordon, Gerald, Carol (Ormsby) - 8/12/2011, Winter Haven, FL - Florida National Cemetery, Bushnell, FL - NAO 10/1943 Centerville - None. Wife Maxine, son Gordon lived in Hume during war. Photo – NAO.

Smith, Albert S. or E. Military: US Army - The April, 1941 entry in the NAO, page 37-38 in the History Club WW II series, year 1941, is the only information that has been identified that indicates Albert may have served during the war. No other information, including enlistment records for Albert have been located. Brother Lyman served during the war. Civilian: 2/7/1909, Allen, NY - Edward C. Smith (1868 NY) & Lillian J. Lamb (1869 MI) - Glenn W. (1892 NY), Lottie A. (1893 NY), Flora D. (1895 NY), Stewart L. (1899 NY), Gordon E. (1905 NY), William (1906 NY), Lyman E. (1914 NY) - Stewart Lamb (1828 NY) & Hannah Thomas (1831 NY) - William Smith (1819 Eng) & Hannah? (1826 Eng.) - Likely FCS school system - Farmer - INA - INA - INA – INA - INA – 1920, 1930 Federal Census Allen, 1940 Federal Census Wellsville. April, 1941 NAO, page 37 states: Albert Smith left for Fort Niagara.

 **Smith, Allen Richard** Military: US Navy – Initial enlistment 6/23/42/AS/Plattsburg, NY/Commissioned 6/27/44/Ensign - *USS Minotaur* - Communications Officer, Navigator, Chief Censor/Lt (JG)- Naval Reserve Midshipman School, Plattsburg, NY, Amphibious Training Base, Camp Bradford, VA, Mobile, Al, New Orleans/35 months 2 weeks - 12 months - Pearl Harbor, Eniwetok, Ulithi, Okinawa, Iwo Jima, Chichi Jima, Bonin Islands) - Okinawa Campaign - NA - NA - NA - NA - June 8, 1946 - American Campaign Medal, Asiatic Pacific Theater Medal, One Battle Star, WW II Victory Medal, Navy Occupation Medal, Asian Clasp. Civilian: 8/25/1921 Houghton, NY - Henry R. Smith, Jr. (1880 Ohio) & Lois Burtnett Osborn (1882 Ohio) - Willard Garfield (1911 NY), Florence Belle (1913 NY) - Allen C. Osborn (1842 NY) & Melissa Burtnett (1850 Ohio) - Henry Reed Smith, Sr. (1847 Ohio) & Celia Lenora Potter (1855 Ohio) - Houghton College, Class of 1939 – Linotype Operator and Assistant Manager, Houghton College - Manager, Houghton Print Shop - Esther E. Fulton (M 6/30/1944 Houghton) - Audrey, Richard, Connie, Charles, Norva, Janet - 12/30/2011, Houghton - Mount Pleasant Cemetery, Houghton - 1930 Federal Census Houghton - Lois Ann Smith Thomas Niece, Daughter Audrey (Pocock). Photo – Family.

 **Smith, Clare James** Military: US Navy - 6/5/1944/AS - V-12 Program - Student/AS - University of Michigan, University of Rochester, V-12 Program/18 months - NA - NA - NA - NA - NA - NA - NA - 11/1945 - American Campaign Medal, World War II Victory Medal. Brother Robert Q. also served during the war. Civilian: 11/10/1924 NY - Quincy J. Smith (1888 NY) & Blanche C. Eisaman (1888 NY) - Robert Q. (1918 NY), Roland (1923 NY) - John G. Eisaman (1859 NY) & Vienne M.? (1858 NY) - Albert W. Smith (1861 NY) & Emily F.? (1869 NY) - Fillmore Central, Class of 1942, University of Michigan, University of Rochester - Student - Dentist - Mary Ellen? - INA - 2/19/1997

Honeoye Falls, NY - North Bloomfield Cemetery, Ontario County, NY - 1930 Federal Census Hume - Photo – School.

Smith, Clark Otis Military: US Marines - 3/1943/Private - 1st Marine Division/Marine Air Warning  Squadron 7 - Communications/Radar Technician/Sergeant - Parris Island, Jacksonville, FL, Quantico, VA - Miramar, CA/27 months - 16 months (1/45-4/46) - Okinawa, Peking, China - Okinawa - NA - NA - NA - NA - 6/1946 – American Campaign Medal, One Battle Star, Asiatic Pacific Theater Medal, WW II Victory Medal. Civilian: 8/9/1924 NY - Otis C. Smith (1868 NY) & Mildred R. Hussong (1892 NY) - David William (1929 NY) - Floyd L. Hussong (1876 NY & Effie Eldridge (1877 NY) - William A. Smith (1864 NY) & Israeli Brown (1864 - NY) - Fillmore Central, Class of 1941, Alfred Welding School (Ships), 1942, Alfred Agriculture Tech (1946-1948 - Radio Trouble Shooter, Colonial Radio, Buffalo (1943) - IBM Field Engineer (Trouble Shooting Computers) - Josephine M. Honkala (M 4/16, 1956, Fairport, Ohio) - Kim Andrea (1957), Lani Ann (1958), Todd Aaron ((1959), Kelly Lehua (1960), Scott Adam (1966) - NA - NA - 1940 Federal Census Granger - Veteran Clark O. Smith. Clark's great grandfather's brother William Hussong was killed July 4, 1863 at the Battle of Gettysburg during the Civil war. William served with Company F, 104th NY Infantry. Photo – NAO.

Smith, Donald Burdette Military: US Army - 3/3/1941/Buffalo/Private - 62nd Coast Artillery, Anti-Aircraft Artillery - INA/First Sergeant - Fort Totten, LI, Camp Campbell, KY, Camp  Stewart, GA, Camp Wheeler, GA/39 months - 16 months (8/1942-12/1943) - England, Algiers, Tunisia, Sicily - Algiers, Tunisia, Sicily - NA - NA - NA - NA - 9/29/1945 - American Defense Medal, American Campaign Medal, African Middle East European Theater Medal, WW II Victory Medal. Donald also served in the Army 1/8/1948 until 1/7/1951. Civilian: 8/22/1910, Houghton, NY - Bert A. Smith (1882 NY) & Anna B.?(1885 NY) - Pauline (1908 NY), Marion (1914 NY) - INA - Maybe Benjamin W. Smith (1834 NY) & Amelia? (1848 NY) - FCS - Farm Laborer, E.W. Hall - INA - INA - INA - 11/21/82, Portage, NY - INA - 1930 Federal Census Hume - None. Photo – NAO.

Smith, Lawrence Manning Military: US Army - 8/23/1944/Buffalo/Private - 3466th Signal Equipment Detachment - INA/Private - Washington, DC, Camp Chowder, MO, Upper Darby, PA, Presque Isle, ME/16 months - NA - NA - NA - NA - NA - NA - NA - 11/4/1945 - American Campaign Medal, WW II Victory Medal. Civilian: 6/30/1919, Wiscoy, NY - Charles M. Smith (1885 NY) & Florence I (likely Gleason) (1893 NY) - Mildred (1914 NY), Bernice J. (1924 NY), Gordon D. (1929 NY) - (Maybe Jerome Gleason 1854 NY & Julia? 1852 NY) - Lawrence Smith (1854 NY & Isabella (Bell) Granger (1850 NY) - FCS – William J. Danz - INA - Ellen M. Berry – Larry Robert - 4/21/1961, Castile, NY - East Koy Cemetery, Pike, NY - 1940 Federal Census Hume - None. Photo – NAO.

Smith, Lyman Edward - Military: US Army - 3/19/1941/Buffalo/Private - Fifth Army - INA/Staff

Sergeant - Camp Lee, NJ, Fort Jackson, SC, Camp Gordon, GA/20 months - 30 months - Italy - INA - NA - NA – NA - NA - 6/4/1945, Fort Dix, NJ - American Defense Medal, American Campaign Medal, European African Middle East Theater Medal, World War II Victory Medal, two battle stars. Civilian: 9/22/1914 NY, Allen Township - Edward C. Smith (1868 NY) & Lillian J. Lamb (1870 MI) - William S. (1906 NY), Albert S. (1909 NY), Glenn (1892 NY), Lottie (1893 NY), (1895 NY), Stewart (1899 MI) - Stewart Lamb (1828 MI) & Hannah Thomas (1831 NY) - William Smith (1819 Eng) & Hannah ? (1826 Eng) - FCS, Class of 1934 - Farmer - INA - INA - INA - 1/23/1997, Wayne County, NY - INA - 1920, 1930 Federal Censuses, Allen - None. Photo – School.

Smith, Robert Quincy Military: US Navy Air – 11/15/1943/Ensign - Navy Air Ferry Squadron 1 (VRF-

1), Naval Air Ferrying Service - Pilot/ Lt. (JG) - Corpus Christi, TX, Dallas, TX, Floyd Bennett Field, LI/34 months - NA - NA - NA - NA - NA - NA - NA - 8/12/1946- American Campaign Medal, World War II Victory Medal. Bob served as a civilian flight instructor for the Navy in Ithaca, NY during 1942 and 1943. He served with the Navy Reserve after the war. Brother Clare J. also served during the war. Civilian: 12/9/1918 NY - Quincy J. Smith (1888 NY) & Blanche Eisaman (1888 NY) - Ronald (1923 NY, Clare J. (1925 NY) - John G. Eisaman (1859 NY) & Vienne M.? (1858 NY) - Albert W. Smith (1861 NY) & Emily F.? (1964 NY) - Fillmore Central, Class of 1937, Houghton College, Cornell University - Student/Civilian

Flight Instructor - Dairy Farmer - Farmer, US Navy Reserve - Craig - 8/15/1987 Fillmore - INA - 1930 Federal Census Hume - Son Craig. Authors first ride in an airplane was with Mr. Smith in his Piper Cub in the late 1940s. Photo – NAO.

Smith, Ronald Vittellius Son of Quincy James Smith and Blanche Clark Eisaman, of Hume, was born November 28, 1922. The NAO reported in March, 1943 that Ronald had been called for his Army induction physical examination on April 1, 1943. No other documentation regarding his military service has been located.

Smith, Sanford Irving Military: US Army - 6/3/1941/Ft. Niagara/Private - 5th Armored Division Band - INA/PFC - Ft. Knox. KY/36 months - 22 months - England, France, Belgium, Luxembourg, Germany - Normandy, Northern France, Rhineland, Ardennes-Alsace, Central Europe - NA - NA - NA - NA - 10/9/1945, Fort Dix, NJ - American Defense Medal, American Campaign Medal, European African, Middle East, Theater Medal, World War II Victory Medal, five battle stars. Civilian: 5/21/1917, Caton, NY - Samuel I. Smith (1884 Ohio) & Charlotte M. Davis (1890 NY) - Ellabyne (1912 NY), Bernard (1919 NY) - Henry H. Davis (1863 NY) & Mary Bray (1858 Canada) - Eli Smith (1861 Ohio) & Myra F. Roberts (TN) - Houghton College, Georgetown University - Farmer, Post Office Clerk - USAF Motion Picture Film Depository - Paula Genevieve Sayers - None - 11/14/2009 - Seaside Memorial Park, Corpus Christi, TX - (1935) 1940 Federal Census Houghton - None.

Speicher, Robert Homer Military: US Marines - 7/23/1942/Private - Co. A, 4th Pioneer Battalion, 20th

Marines (Combat Engineer) 4th Marine Division - Demolition Expert/Staff Sergeant - Parris Island, NC, Camp Lejeune, NC,, Camp Pendleton, CA, San Diego, CA , Bainbridge, MD/17 months - 19 months - Kwajalein Atoll (Marshall Islands), Saipan (Mariana Islands), Tinian (Mariana Islands), Iwo Jima (Volcano Islands) - Occupation of Kwajalein Atoll, Capture and Occupation of Saipan, Capture of Tinian, Assault and Occupation of Iwo Jima - NA - NA - NA - NA - 11/1/1945 - 4 Battle Stars, Bronze Star for Meritorious Service, Gold Star for Heroism (in lieu of a 2nd Bronze Star), American Campaign Medal, Asiatic Pacific Theater Medal, WW II Victory Medal, 2 Naval & Marine Corps Presidential Unit Citations, one Navy Unit Commendation - Sent his wife a Japanese silk flag and paper money from Tinian. Civilian: 8/27/1921 Johnston, PA - Robert H. Speicher, Sr. (1875 PA) and Jessie E. Wagner (1898 PA) - Geraldine L. (1923 PA), DeVaughn (1932 NY), Step sisters - Vonnell E. (1917 PA), Viola Moore (1900 PA) Irene L.1908 PA), Step brother Ardell (1920 NY), Burley (1920 NY), Ernest Roy (1903 PA) - Peter Speicher (1852 PA) & Rebecca J.? (1854 PA) - Amos Wagner (1856 PA) & Rachael Ann Shuman (1860 PA) - Rushford Central School, Class of 1936 - Machinist, General Motors Plant, Buffalo - Fisher Price Company, Farmer, Fillmore, NY - Norma Carol Evans (M 12/28/1942 NY) - Robert H. III (1943 NY), Joyce K. (1944 NY), Candace (1947 NY), James Lynn (1949 NY)- 5/8/1980 Warsaw, NY - Alger Cemetery, Hume, NY- NAO - Son Robert III & Daughter Joyce K. Photo – NAO.

Stevens, Robert Warren (Bob) Military: US Army Air Corps -10/3/1942/Buffalo/Private - 448th

Headquarters and Base Service Squadron - Teletype Operator/Corporal - Salt Lake City, Utah/3 months - 34 months - England - Air Offensive Europe, Normandy, Northern France, Ardennes Alsace, Rhineland, Central Europe - NA - NA - NA - Suffered back problems which took him off flight status per son - 11/1/1945 - European African Middle East Theater Medal, World War II Victory Medal, 6 Battle Stars. Civilian: 3/19/1922/ Hume, NY - Arthur B. Stevens (1895 NY) & Yolande Hanks (1899 NY) - None - Lynn Hanks (1870 NY) & Myrtle? (1874 NY) - William J. Stevens (1870 NY) & Mabel E. Bennett (1879 NY) - FCS, Class of 1940 - Student - INA - Mae? - James, Allison - 2/13/1985/Hume - Pine Gove Cemetery, Fillmore - 1930 Census, Fillmore - Son James. Photo – NAO.

Stickle, Francis Norman Military: US Army Air Corps - 8/1943/Private - Army Air Transport

Command - Flight Instructor, Pilot/Flight Officer - Endicott, NY, Louisiana, Greenville, MS, Blytheville, AR, Wilmington, DE, New Castle, DE, Romulus, MI, Nashville, TN/47 months - NA - NA - NA - NA - NA - NA - NA - 10/23/1945 - American Campaign Medal, World War II Victory Medal. His brother William also served in the military and was killed in flight accident in Hawaii. His paternal great grandfather, Judson Stickle served with Co. F, 19th NY Cavalry (1st NY dragoons) during the Civil War. His maternal great grandfather, Andrew Means, served with Co. A, 154th NY Infantry. Civilian:1/20/1921 NY - Howard Stickle (1894 NY) & Nellie E. Ackerman (1893 NY) - Ellen M. (1916 NY), William J. (1918 NY), Margaret L. (1923 NY) - Mark M. Ackerman (1867 NY) & Betty L. Mearns (1868 NY) - Chilon Stickle (1871 NY) & Elllen N.? (1871 NY) - Fillmore Central, Class of 1937 - Instructor, Lafayette School of Aeronautics - INA - Mildred - INA - 7/25/1988 - Grace Cemetery, Castile, NY - 1930 Federal Census Centerville - None. Photo – NAO.

Stickle, William Judson Military: Army Air Corps - 1/1941Private - 371st Bomb Squadron, 307th Bomb  Group – Navigator/2nd Lieutenant - Ft. Bragg, NC, Hemet Field, Sacramento, CA, Ephrata, Washington, Sioux City, Iowa, Hamilton Field, CA/20 months - 3 months - Hawaii, Southwester Pacific - None- Died in a plane crash, on duty, but not in battle - 12/16/1942 - NA - NA - NA - American Campaign Medal, Purple Heart, American Defense Medal, Asiatic Pacific Theater Medal, WW II Victory Medal. His brother Francis Norman also served during the war. His paternal great grandfather, Judson Stickle, served with Co. F, 19th NY Cavalry during the Civil War. His maternal great grandfather, Andrew Means, served with Co. A, 154th NY Infantry. Civilian: 10/16/1917, Allegany County, NY - Howard Stickle (1892 NY) & Nellie L. Ackerman (1893 NY) - Ellen M. (1916 NY), Francis Norman (1921 NY), Margaret L. (1923 NY) - Mark O. Ackerman (1867 NY) & Betty L. Mearns (1868 NY) - Chilon Stickle (1871 NY) & Ellen N.? (1871 NY) - Fillmore Central, Class of 1935 – Aluminum Cooking Company, Rochester, NY Sales - NA -Buelah Wells (M 6/1942) - None - 12/16/1942 - National Cemetery, Hawaii (Memorial Headstone, Bates Cemetery, Centerville, NY) - 1930 Federal Census Centerville - None. Photo – NAO.

Strait, Royal Seymour (Roy) Military: Army Air Corps - 1/6/1942 (Reenlisted as an officer 1/7/1944) - 15th Air Force, 2nd Bombardment Group, 49th Bomb Squadron (Heavy) - Co-Pilot, Navigator/1st Lieutenant - INA - 41 months total service - Italy, flew 35 combat missions over European targets - Rome Arno, North Apennines, Southern France, Rhineland, Northern France, Normandy - NA - NA - NA - NA - 5/30/1945 - American Campaign Medal, 6 Battle Stars, European African Middle East Theater Medal, WW II Victory Medal, Air Medal with 2 Oak Leaf Clusters - Civilian: 6/29/1920 NY - Seymour C. Strait (1873 NY) & Luia B. (Belle) (Nellie) Metcalf (1882 NY) - Winifred (1900 NY), Clarence 1906 NY, Ellen 1909 NY) - INA - Henry H. Strait (1845 NY & Adelaide Carpenter (1855 NY) - FCS/Cuba HS (3 years HS) - INA - INA - Maybe 1.Dorothy Longwell (M 12/27/1945, Cuba), 2. Mary Antoinette Storey - Leslie David, Mahlon Lynn - Columbus, MS - 4/8/1960 - Forest Cemetery, Pickens County, Alabama - 1930 Federal Census Fillmore - 2nd Bombardment Group Association.

Stroud, Harry Lynford Jr. Military: US Navy - 7/6//1942/Buffalo/AS - *USS Nightingale (AP 70), USS Capps (DD 550)* - INA/S1C - Newport, RL. Norfolk, VA/3 months - NA - NA - NA - NA - NA - NA – NA – 11/30/1943. Harry received a Bad Conduct discharge. Civilian: 10/26/1924 Pike, NY - Harry Howden. Stroud (1897 NY) & Edna L. Coombs (1903 NY) - Janice (1931 NY), Dean R. (1935 NY) - INA & Emma Coombs (1887 PA) - Samuel Stroud (1856 England) & Ella M. (likely Waite) (1864 NY) - INA - Farm Labor - Transportation Dept. - Town of Pike - Dorothy E. Swain - Charlotte (Buckley), David, Daniel, Delores, Dennis, Glenda, Charlene, Dale, Greg, Glenn - 6/19/2011, Pike, NY - Pike Cemetery - NAO 8/1942 - Daughter Charlene Stroud Buckley. Harry Senior's name was Henry according to the 1900 Federal Census. If correct, then Junior was also likely Henry. Harry, Sr. lived in Genesee Falls in 1900 with his parents Samuel and Ella.

Swales, Burt (NMN) Military: Army Air Corps - March 1943/Tioga Co., PA/Private - Basic Training  Unit, Keesler Air Base - Recruit/Private - Keesler Air Base, Biloxi, MS/2 months - NA - NA - NA - NA - NA - NA - NA - 5/19/1943, Keesler Air Base, Biloxi, MS - WW II Victory Medal. Civilian: 2/18/1921 Blackburn, England - William Swales (1882 England) & Eleanor Horn (1882 England) - Stanley (1914 NY), Elsie (1917 NY) - William Horn (1859 England) & Mary Jane? (1862 England) - William G. Swales (1847 England) & Eliza Jane Milner (1852 England) - Houghton College - Student - Guidance Officer, Fillmore Central - Esther Hagburg - Sharon, David, Jeffrey, Laurie - 5/17/2011 Fillmore - Pine Grove Cemetery, Fillmore, NY - Senior Class president at Houghton College. - Post war 50 plus year Fillmore resident - None. Photo – School.

 **Swales, Stanley (NMN)** Military: US Army - 4/9/41/PA/Private – Detachment, Veterans Administration Facility, Fort Hood - INA/Sergeant – Fort Niagara, NY, Camp Edwards, MA, Camp Hood, TX/10 months – 44 months, one week - Iceland – American Campaign - NA - NA - NA - NA – 11/15/1945 - American Campaign Medal, WW II Victory Medal. Civilian: 6/2/1913 NY - William Swales (1882 England) & Eleanor Horn (1882 England) - Stanley (1914 NY), Elsie (1917 NY) - William Horn (1859 England) & Mary Jane? (1862 England) - William G. Swales (1847 England) & Eliza Jane Milner (1852 England) - INA - INA - INA - Pearl G. Blewett (M 7/14/1943) - INA - 3/10/1993 Fillmore - Pine Grove, Fillmore - NAO, January, 1942, p 152 Fillmore, Lived & Died Post War Fillmore - None. Photo – NAO.

 **Swanson. Evar George (Benk)** Military: US Navy - 10/13/1942/Warrant Officer – Brooklyn Naval Yard - Planning Officer, Construction/ Lt. Commander - Brooklyn Naval Yard, Norfolk, VA/32.2 months – 5 months? - Pacific Fleet, Guam - None - NA - NA - NA - NA – 11/28/1945 -Letter of Commendation, Brooklyn Naval Yard, American Campaign Medal, Asiatic Pacific Theater Medal, WW II Victory Medal. Civilian: 4/23/1905 Ludlow, PA - Emil Swanson (1875 Sweden) & Charlotte Hogman (1877 Sweden) - Helena (1901 PA), Carl (1903 PA), Linnea (1903 PA), Emma (1915 PA), Edith (1915 PA) - Sven Swanson (1853 Sweden) & Johanna Gustafspotter (1839 Sweden) - Sven Swanson (1853 Swenden) & Emma Eliaspotter (1855 Sweden) - Ludlaw, PA School System - Rochester Gas & Electric Fillmore, Line Foreman - Rochester Gas & Electric Company, General District Engineering Supervisor - Doris M. Gilbert (M 8/1/1930) - None - 11/4/1972 - Sodus Rural Cemetery, Sodus, NY - 1940 Federal Census Fillmore - Sister-in-law, Frances Gilbert Wiles - Retired Officers Association, Masons, Rotary, National Wildlife Association, Audubon Society. Was Scout Master in Fillmore for a time in the 1930s, and was active with the Fire department post war. He was skilled in both metal and wood working. Photo – NAO.

 **Swartout, Leon Herbert** Military: US Army - 9/24/1943, Binghamton, NY/Private - Medical Detachment, 665th Field Artillery Battalion - Surgical Technician/PFC - Beaufort General Hospital, El Paso, TX/26 months - 3 months, one week - France, Germany - Rhineland - NA - NA - NA - NA - 2/7/1946, Fort Dix, NJ - American Campaign Medal, European African Middle East Theater Medal, World War II Victory Medal, Good Conduct Medal, one Battle Star. Son's Dale and Gary both served during the Vietnam War. Gary was killed in an auto accident in Fayetteville, NC while serving as an officer in the US Army. Civilian: 5/4/1922, NY - Herbert L. Swartout (1896 NY) & Florence L. Sanders (1901 NY) - Marion (1922 NY), Corrine (1929 NY) - Milford D. Sanders (1876 NY) & Edith M.? (1884 PA) - Selah Swartout (1867 NY) & Mary Swayze (1868 PA) - Houghton College - Medical Student -FCS Science Teacher, FCS Principal - Lois J. Taylor - Dale (1945 NY), Gary (1946 NY) - 11/16/1999, Houghton - Mt. Pleasant Cemetery, Houghton, NY - Resident for over 50 years – Son Dale. Photo – Family.

Sweet, Bernard (NMN) Military: US Army Air Corps - 5/15/1942/Buffalo/Aviation Cadet - 406th
Fighter Group, 514th Fighter Squadron - P-47 Thunderbolt Pilot/Captain - Governors
Island, NY, Nashville, TN, Maxwell Field, AL, Jackson Field, TN, Newport, AR,
Napier Field, AL, Dale Mabry Field, FL, Perry Field, FL, Congaree, Field, SC, Camp
Shanks, NY/22 months - 12 months - England, France, Belgium, - Air Offensive
Europe, Air Offensive-Europe, Normandy, Rhineland, Northern France, Central
Europe - March 25, 1945, Asch Air Strip, Belgium, Killed in Crash Landing - NA -
NA - NA - 3/25/1945 - Distinguished Flying Cross, Air Medal with 13 Oak Leaf
Clusters, Purple Heart, Presidential Unit Citation , European African Middle Eastern
Theater Medal, American Campaign Medal, 5 Battle Stars, WW II Victory Medal.
Brother Lawrence Sweet also served during the war. Civilian: 10/25/1919 NY - Merton Sweet (1882
NY) & Ethel Snyder (1898 NY) - Madeline (1922 NY), Laurence (1924 NY) - Frank Snyder (1873 NY)
& Bertha T. Bliss (1870 NY) – Lowell Sweet (1855 NY) & Jennie Clark (1859 NY) - Rushford Central
School - Student (Farm Laborer) - NA - NA - NA - 3/25/1945, Asch, Belgium - US Military Cemetery,
Margraten Holland – 1925 State Census Centerville - Nieces Linda Biel Armison & Donna Van Name.
Photo – Family.

Sweet, Laurence Arnold (Larry) Military: US Navy -9/15/1943/AS - USS Bennington (CV 20) -
Pharmacist Mate 3c - Sampson, NY, /11 months - 1/8/1945 to 11/7/1945 - Fleet
Operations, Western Pacific - Iwo Jima, Okinawa, Air Operations, Japan - NA - NA
- NA - NA - 4/17/1950 - American Campaign Medal, Asiatic Pacific Campaign
Medal, WW II Victory Medal, Navy Occupation Medal, Asian Clasp, 3 Battle Stars.
Civilian: 1/8/1924 NY - Merton Sweet (1882 NY) & Ethel Snyder (1898 NY) -
Madeline (NY 1922), Bernard (1919 NY) - Frank Snyder (1873 NY) & Bertha Bliss
(1870 NY) - Lowell Sweet (1855 NY) & Jennie Clark (1859 NY) - Rushford Central
School, Class of 1941, Corcoran School of Art, Washington, DC - Farm Laborer -
Artist, (Washington Evening Star), Aetna Insurance Company - Aurelia Honeycutt
(M INA) - Patricia (Curry), Wayne, Aaron - 6/14/2009 at Vero Beach, FL - Hill Crest Royal Gardens,
Ft. Fierce, FL - (1925 NY State Census Centerville (Rushford), 1940 Federal Census Centerville - Nieces
Linda Biel Armison & Donna Van Name. Photo – Family.

Sylor, Alton Adelbert (Al) Military: US Navy - 9/27/43/Buffalo/AS - *LST 1029* - Electrician Mate/S 2
C - Sampson Naval, Camp Bradford, VA, Boston, MA, Galveston, TX, St. Albans,
LI/13 months - 18 months - Philippines, Okinawa, Japan - Luzon, Okinawa - NA - NA
- NA – Broke his ankle, tripped over a hose - 6/1/1946, Lido Beach, LI - American
Campaign Medal, Asiatic Pacific Theater Medal 2 Battle Stars, Philippine Liberation
Medal 1 Star, WW II Victory Medal, Navy Occupation Medal - Asian Clasp, Philippine
Presidential Unit Citation. Civilian: 12/1/1925/Allen NY - Kenneth J. Sylor (1898 NY)
& Miona L Bennett (1897 NY) - INA - INA - Fillmore Central - Student - Owner,
Electrical Business/Politician - Bonnie Nevinger (M INA) - Vaun, Gretchen, Victor,
Bridgett - 1/30/2000 Short Tract - Short Tract Cemetery - Fillmore Central School - Son Victor Sylor.
Photo – NAO.

Sylor, Norbert Frank (Norb)  Military: US Army - 3/20/1945/Fort Dix, NJ/Private - Field Artillery Battalion/ Antic-Aircraft Battalion - Analyst/PFC - Camp Blanding, Fort Bragg, NC, Fort Bliss, TX/18 months - NA - NA - NA - NA - NA - NA - Severe Damage to Knee - 10/28/1946 - American Theater Medal, WW II Victory Medal. Civilian: 9/7/1926 Granger, NY - Wayne C. Sylor (1903 NY) & Gladys L. Smith (1902 NY) - Wayne, Jr. (1923 NY), Bernice L. (1928 NY), Adelbert (1935 NY) - Frank C. Smith (1876 NY) & May Belle Phinney (1876 NY) - Adelbert Sylor (1873 NY) & Pearl Cox (1879 NY) - Fillmore Central, Class of 1945 - Student - Driver, C. J. Winchip, Ground Superintendent/ Director, United Methodist Church Camp Asbury, Silver Lake, Perry, NY – Wilma Jeanne Steadman (M 12/24/1945 Washington, DC) - Claudia, Karen, Audrey, Kathleen - NA - NA - 1930 Federal Census Granger - Veteran Norbert F. Sylor, Niece Rondus Miller. Photo – NAO.

Sylor, Wayne Cox Jr.  Military: Army Air Force - 3/10/1943/Private - INA - Aircraft Engine Mechanic /Master Sergeant - Miami Beach, FL, Kansas City, MO, Detroit, MI (Packard Company), Kelly Field, TX/INA - INA - Hawaii - American Campaign - NA - NA - NA - NA - 2/18/1946.- American Campaign Medal, World War II Victory Medal. Civilian: 9/13/1923 NY - Wayne C. Sylor (1903 NY) & Gladys L. Smith (1902 NY) - Norbert F. (1926 NY), Bernice L. (1928 NY), Adelbert (1935 NY) - Frank C. Smith (1876 NY) & May Belle Phinney (1876 NY) - Adelbert Sylor (1873 NY) & Pearly E. Cox (1879 NY) - Fillmore Central, Class of 1941 - Curtiss Wright Plant, Buffalo, Experimental Development Section - Mechanical Engineer - Gloria Smith – Mark, Eric - 6/24/2007 Lake County, OH - Short Tract Cemetery - 1930 Federal Census Granger - Son Eric Sylor, Niece Rondus Miller. Photo – NAO.

Thayer, Harold Edgar  Military: US Army - 6/3/1941/Buffalo/Private - 9th Armored Division. 2nd Tank Battalion - Tank Mechanic/Sergeant - Pine Camp, NC, FT. Knox, KY, Pine Camp, NC, FT. Riley, KS, Louisiana/39 months - 4 months - England, France, Luxembourg - Rhineland, Ardennes-Alsace - KIA 12/18/1944 Luxembourg - NA - NA - NA - 12/18/1944 - American Defense Medal, American Campaign Medal, Presidential Unit Citation, 2 Battle Stars, European African Middle Eastern Theater Medal, Purple Heart, Bronze Star, WW II Victory Medal, Distinguished Unit Citation. Brothers Herbert, Leroy, & Richard also served during the war. Civilian: 6/21/1918 Olean, NY - Edgar W. Thayer (1893 NY) & Anna V. Taft (1896 NY) - Herbert H. (1920 NY), Richard A. (1922 NY), Leroy W. (1923 NY), Gerald V. (1925 NY), Milton Robert (1928 NY) - Frank B. Taft (1871 NY) & Edith N. Losey (1875 NY) - Herbert Horace Thayer (1857 NY) & Mary E. Dickson (1867 NY) - Fillmore Central - Road Construction - NA – Anna Virginia? - NA - 12/18/1944 Luxembourg - Ardennes American Cemetery (Memorial headstone - Mt. Pleasant Cemetery, Houghton, NY) – WW II Young Men's Draft says he was living in Fillmore in 1940, NAO 1/1942 - None. Photo – NAO.

Thayer, Herbert Horace (Herb) Military: Army Air Corp - 7/2/1942/Buffalo/Private - 6th Technical

Squadron - Truck Driver, light/Corporal/INA - INA - New Guinea, Australia, Philippines - Bismarck Archipelago, Papua, New Guinea, Luzon, Southern Philippines - NA - NA - NA - NA - 10/13/1945 -Asiatic Pacific Theater Medal, 4 battle stars, World War II Victory Medal. Civilian: 8/13/1920 NY - Edgar W. Thayer (1893 NY) & Anna V. Taft (1896 NY) - Harold E. (1919 NY), Richard A. (1922 NY), Leroy W. (1923 NY), Gerald V. (1925 NY), Milton Robert (1928 NY) - Frank B. Taft (1871 NY) & Edith N. Losey (1875 NY) - Herbert Horace Thayer (1857 NY) & Mary E. Dickson (1867 NY) - Fillmore Central, Grammar School – Farm Laborer - INA - Edna Bennett - Kenneth, Wayne, Maxine - 12/5/2007, Hume - Alger Cemetery, Hume, NY - NAO 11/1943, Post-War, Fillmore - None. Photo – NAO.

Thayer, Leroy Warren (Roy) Military: US Navy - 4/1/43/Buffalo/AS - *USS Dionne/USS Piedmont* -

Machinist Mate/S 2 C - Sampson Naval/approximately 8 month - 25 months - Hawaii (Pearl Harbor), Gilbert Islands (at sea), Marshall Islands (Eniwetok/Kwajalein), Caroline Islands (Ulithi), Admiralty Islands (Manus), Philippines (Lingayen Gulf), Tokyo Bay - Gilbert Island Operations, Marshall Islands Operation - NA - NA - NA - NA - 2/5/1946 - 2 battle stars, Asiatic Pacific Theater Medal, WW II Victory Medal, Naval Occupation Medal -Asian Clasp. Civilian: 3/6/1923 NY - Edgar W. Thayer (1893 NY) & Anna V. Taft (1896 NY) - Harold E. (1919 NY), Richard A. (1921 NY), Herbert H. (1920 NY), Gerald V. (1925 NY), Milton Robert (1928 NY) - Frank B. Taft (1871 NY) & Edith N. Losey (1875 NY) - Herbert Horace Thayer (1857 NY) & Mary E. Dickson (1867 NY) - Fillmore Central, Class of 1941 - INA - Commercial Construction Worker - Donna Lee Bunnell (Married 11/20/1970/Fillmore) - Vickie, David, Mark, Lisa, Beth, Kevin - 3/24/2007, Temple, TX - Mt. Pleasant Cemetery, Houghton - NAO 3/1943 - None. Photo – NAO.

Thayer, Richard Albert Military: US Army - 10/12/1942/Buffalo/Private - Medical Corps – INA/PFC

- Nashville, TN/12 months 1 weeks – 19 months, 2 weeks - INA - INA - NA - NA - NA - NA - 10/29/1945 - American Campaign Medal, Likely European, African Middle East Theater Medal, , World War II Victory Medal. Civilian: 11/18/1021 Franklinville, NY - Edgar W. Thayer (1893 NY) & Anna V. Taft (1896 NY) - Harold E. (1919 NY), Leroy W. (1923 NY), Herbert H. (1920 NY), Gerald V. (1925 NY), Milton Robert (1928 NY) - Frank B. Taft (1871 NY) & Edith N. Losey (1875 NY) - Herbert Horace Thayer (1857 NY) & Mary E. Dickson (1867 NY) - Fillmore Central, Grammar School - Farm Laborer - Machinist - Dorothy A. Ralston - Robert - 6/23/2007, St. Petersburg, FL - Memorial Park Cemetery, St. Petersburg, FL - NAO 3/1943 - None. Photo – NAO.

Thomas, Gerald Frederick (Gatie) Military: US Army - 2/17/1941/Ft Niagara/Private - 2nd Armored

Division, 66th Armored Regiment/599th MTR (Ambulance) - Automotive Mechanic/Sergeant - Ft. Benning, GA, Ft. Knox. KY/20 months - 33 months - North Africa, Sicily, Corsica, France, Germany - Algeria-French Morocco, Tunisia, Sicily, Southern France, Central Europe, Rhineland - NA - NA - NA - Hospitalized one & ½ months 9/10/1943 - 7/11/1945 FT. Dix, NJ - Good Conduct Medal, American Defense Medal. American Campaign Medal, European African Middle East Theater Medal, 2 Arrowhead Devices French Morocco, Casablanca, Sicily), 6 Battle Stars, WW II Victory Medal, Distinguished Unit Award, 11/18-28/1944, Belgian Fourragere (9/2/44 & 12/21-28/44. Likely Army Occupation Medal, Germany Clasp. Brother Roland also served during the war. Met Roland in North Africa after not seeing him for two years. Civilian: 7/3/1912 Hume, NY - Ralph E. Thomas (1887 NY) & Catherine E. Wilklow (1891 NY) - Norman (1915

NY), Roland J. (1917 NY) - George Wilklow (1853 NY) & Desdamona Lasell (1851 NY) - Fernando L. Thomas (1860 NY) & Emma? (1868 NY) - Fillmore Central – Luckey & Sandford Automobile Mechanic - Automobile Mechanic- Never Married - None - 6/10/1981 Hume, NY - INA - 1930 Federal Census Hume - Janet Gayford Thomas. Gerald was a direct descendant of William Brewster of Plymouth Colony who came to the United States aboard the Mayflower. Photo – Family.

Thomas, John Louis (Dude) Military: US Navy - 9/23/1943/Buffalo/AS - Merchant Ship SS David G. Farragut, Merchant Ship SS Dilworth, Merchant Ship SS Franklin K. Lane, USS Shannon (DM 25) - Armed Guard, Gunner's Mate/GM3C - Sampson Naval Training Facility, Armed Guard Training School, Norfolk, VA. Armed Guard Center, Brooklyn, NY, Camp Perry, Williamsburg, VA, Charleston, SC/20 months - 20 months - Italy, France, Dutch East Indies, New Guinea, Philippines - Southern France, Leyte - NA - NA - NA - 2/15/46, Bethesda Naval Hospital, Cut Hand, 10/12/1946 Charleston Naval Hospital - 3/1/1947, Charleston, SC Receiving Station - American Campaign Medal, European African Middle East Theater Medal, Good Conduct Medal, Asiatic Pacific Theater Medal, Philippine Liberation Medal, (Likely two Battle Stars),World War II Victory Medal. Uncle Dee Victor Thomas was killed in battle in World War I. Civilian: 1/23/1926 Fillmore, NY - Lawrence G. Thomas (1895 NY) & Leah A. Wolfer (1897 NY) - Robert L. (1924 NY), Jean A. (1928 NY), Clair L. (1931 NY), Clarice A. (1931 NY), Janice M. (1927), Patricia (NY) - John Wolfer (1874 NY) & Julia B. McIntosh (1877 NY) - Lewis Fernando Thomas (1860 NY) & Emma Hopper (1868 NY) - Fillmore Central - Farm Hand/Student - INA - Ethel Richardson - None - 1/19/1988, Houghton, NY - Mt. Pleasant Cem., Houghton, NY - Sister Patricia (Ricketts). Photo – NAO.

Thomas, Roland James (Rod) Military US Army - 3/3/1941/Buffalo/Private - Battery D, 62 Coast Artillery, Company C, 242nd Infantry Regiment, 42nd Infantry Division (Transferred to 242nd Regiment 1/19/1945) - Artillery Gun Crewman, Infantryman/Corporal - Ft. Totten, LI/20 months - 33 months - England, Scotland, French Morocco, Tunisia, , Sicily, Italy, France, Germany - Algeria-French Morocco, Tunisia, Rome-Arno, Southern France, Rhineland, Central Europe - NA - WIA 1944 France - NA - In hospital with arm & hand infection (1/1942) - 7/5/1945 - American Defense Medal, American Campaign Medal, Good Conduct Medal with Clasp, Purple Heart , European African Middle East Theater Medal, WW II Victory Medal, Combat Infantryman Badge, (Bronze Star 1947), 7 Battle Stars. Brother Gerald also served during the war. Met his brother Gerald in North Africa after not seeing him for two years. Civilian: 8/8/1917, Hume, NY - Ralph E. Thomas (1887 NY) & Catherine E. Wilklow (1891 NY) - Gerald (1913 NY), Norman (1915 NY) - George Wilklow (6/18/1853 NY) & Desdamona Lasel (2/1851 NY) - Fernando L. Thomas (1860 NY) & Emma? ((1868 NY) - Fillmore Central, 2 years high school – Roy Colburn, Plumber Apprentice - INA – Mary M. Berry (2/23/1946, Eagle, NY) - Diane (Sullivan) - 8/9/1985 - Holy Cross Cemetery, Fillmore, NY - 1930 Federal Census Hume - None. Roland was a direct descendant of William Brewster of Plymouth Colony who came to the United States aboard the Mayflower. Photo -NAO.

Tillinghast, Roy George Military: US Army - 8/3/1942, Buffalo, Private - Co. C, 46th Engineer Construction Battalion - INA/Tech 5 -INA - Total service 36 months – Papua, New Guinea, Leyte, Luzon - NA - NA - NA- NA - 7/28/1945 - American Theater Medal, Asiatic Pacific Theater Medal, WW II Victory Medal, Arrowhead Assault Badge (Leyte), 2 Meritorious Unit Citations, Philippine Presidential Unit Citation, 3 Battle Stars. Father George registered for WW I. Civilian: 10/19/1921/NY - George Roy Tillinghast (1890 NY) & Grace F. (likely Jenkins) (1900 NY) - Hazel (1916 NY), Howard (1920 NY), Rosa (1924 NY), Mabel (1928 NY), Betty (1935 NY), George (1937 NY), (Donald (1939 NY), Otto (NY) - Likely William Jenkins (1859 NY) & Unice T.? (1856 NY) - Sigmund Tillinghast (1860 NY) &

Rosa B.? (1868 MI) - Grammar School - Farm Laborer/Carpenter - INA - NA. - NA - 6/27/1947 Wiscoy (drowned) - Sardinia Rural Cemetery. NAO July, 1942. Mother Grace, who applied for the headstone for his grave, likely lived at RFD, Fillmore as late as 1949.

Tisdale, George William Military: US Army - 12/16/1943/Buffalo/Private - 822nd Tank Destroyer Battalion/PFC - Fort Hood, TX, Camp Bowie, TX 13 months - 7 months - France, Germany - Rhineland, Central Europe - NA - INA - NA - INA – Likely August/September 1945 - American Campaign Medal, European African Middle East Theater Medal, World War II Victory Medal, Army Occupation Medal, Germany Clasp, 2 Battle Stars. Good Conduct Medal. Father Archie and Grandfather George both registered for WW I. Civilian: - 5/2/1925 NY - Archie W. Tisdale (1894 NY) & Bessie Laura Farrar (1903 NY) - Emma F. (1921 NY), Emmagene L. (1921 NY), Howard M. (1923 NY), Forrest J. (1928 NY), Pearl I. (1930 NY) - INA - George H. Tisdale (1876 NY) & Flora E. (?Likely Clement) (1877 NY) - FCS - Farm Hand – Forklift Operator, Fitzpatrick & Weller - Mabel Butler - Shirley A., Ruby, Josephine, Sylvia, Nancy, Lloyd, Francis - 2/23/2003 - Tisdale Family farm, Kill Buck, Cattaraugus County, NY, Calvary Cemetery - 1920 1930, 1940 Federal Census Centerville - None.

Treusdell (Truesdale), Lawrence Lynn (Larry) Military: US Army - 2/1/1941/Buffalo/Private - 198th Infantry Regiment, 27th Infantry Division - Infantry Trainee/Private - Fort McClellan, AL/3.5 months - NA - NA -NA - NA - NA - NA - injured in line of duty while in training - 5/19/1941 - American Defense Medal, World War II Victory Medal. Lawrence's father Jefferson registered for World War I. Civilian: 2/1/1915/NY - Jefferson Charles Treusdell (1887 NY) & Elizabeth B. (Libby) Ackerman (1889 NY) - Gordon R. (1912 NY), Kenneth R. (1923 NY) - Lafayette J. Ackerman (1833 NY) & Josephine Harwood (1833 NY) - Bebe Burt Treusdell (1851 NY) & Frances A. Halsey (1850 NY) - One year high school - Laborer, Works Progress Administration - INA - Justa Pero (INA) - Lawrence (1937) - 6/13/1983, Wellsville - Bellville Cemetery, Bellville, NY - 1940 Federal Census, Fillmore. (The 1940 Census spelled Lawrence last name Truesdale.)

Turnstrom, Carl Oscar Military: US Army: 8/4/1942/Buffalo/Private - 791st Technical School Squadron - Airplane Mechanic/PFC - Ft. Niagara, NY, Atlantic City, NJ, Marianna, FL, Seymour Johnson, NC/10 months - NA - NA - American Campaign - NA - NA - NA - Severe Asthma - 5/25/1943 - American Campaign Medal, WW II Victory Medal. Was discharged due to his asthma. Civilian: 4/1/1915 Hubbard Wood. IL - Carl Frederick Turnstrom (Sweden) & Nanette (Nannie) Pearson (Sweden) - Hildur (Kratt), Robert W. (1925 NY), Dorothy (White) (1927 NY) - INA - INA - Pike High School - Gas Station Attendant, Oldenburg's Kendall Station, Fillmore, Self Employed Auto Mechanic, Community Garage, Fillmore - Anna Lester married 6/24/1945 Angelica, NY - None - 1/25/1962 Batavia, NY - Pine Grove Cemetery, Fillmore, NY - NAO, 6/1943 - Wife Anna Lester Turnstrom. Photo – Family.

Tuthill, Irwin Kneeland Military: US Army - 2/23/42/Buffalo/Private - 1st Army, 3rd Army, 7th Army, 4th Infantry Division, 8th Infantry Regiment, Medical Detachment - Medical Technician/T 3 - Fort Niagara, Camp Croft, SC, Camp Gordon, GA, Ft. Dix, NJ, Augusta, GA, Carrabelle, FL, Camp Butner, NC/23 months - 19 months - England, France, Belgium, Germany - Normandy, Northern France - Central Europe, Ardennes - Rhineland - NA - NA - NA - NA - 10/5/1945, Camp Butner, SC – American Campaign Medal, Invasion Arrowhead, Normandy (Utah Beach), European, African, Middle East Theater Medal, 5 Battle Stars, Bronze Star for Heroism, Presidential Unit Citation Badge, Silver Medical Combat Badge, Good Conduct Medal, WW II Victory Medal. Civilian: 10/16/1919 Fillmore, NY - Frank L. Tuthill (1883 NY) & Edna Viola Cartwright (1881 NY)

- Leon (1915 NY), Harlan (1919 NY) - Carlos F. Cartwright (1849 NY) & Elnora Bentley (1851 NY)) - George L. Tuthill (1850 NY) & Margaret A. Carrick (1850 NY) - Fillmore High School, Class of 1937, Houghton College, Class of 1941 - Working in Finance - INA - INA - INA - INA - INA - 1930 Federal Census Fillmore - Allegany County War Service Record. Photo- Family, NAO.

Van Buskirk, Hugh Herbert Military: US Navy - 4/26/44/Buffalo/AS - *USS Natoma Bay/USS Edsall* – On-the-Job Trainee - Seagoing Janitor (Jack of all trades)/S1C - Sampson Naval Base/8 months - 16 months – Hawaii, Admiralty Islands, Philippines, Iwo Jima, Okinawa - Leyte, Luzon, Iwo Jima, Okinawa - NA - NA - NA - NA - 5/18/1946 - American Campaign Medal, Asiatic Pacific Campaign Medal, WW II Victory Medal, 4 battle Stars, Presidential Unit Citation, Philippine Liberation Medal with two Bronze Stars. Served with the US Air Force during the Korean War. Civilian: 4/15/1927/Caneadea, New York - James B. Van Buskirk (1886 Ohio) & Josephine B. Patterson (1900 NY) - Charles (1919 NY), Lorna (1921 NY), James, Jr. (1929 NY) - Leroy Patterson (1869 NY) & Belle Addie Hotchkiss (1871 NY) - Charles H. Van Buskirk & May J. Edwards - Belfast CS – Student/Laundryman, - Construction Engineer, Cold Springs Construction - June Patterson - Gregory, Sharon (Dahlen), Sierra (Gower), Kelly, Shelly (Swanson) - 7/20/2004/Sarasota, FL - Cremated, Ashes spread in Gulf of Mexico - 1930 Federal Census Allen, 1977NAO Hume, Obituary, sister Lorna (Harrington).

Van Name, Harold Francis Post WW II soldier. His brother Robert L. Van Name served during the war. His half-brother, Gerald B. Gayford served and died in action during the war. Civilian: 1/19/1924, Hume, NY - Jesse M. Van Name (1897 NY) & Katherine Gayford (1899 NY) - Robert L. (1922 NY), Dorothy (NY), Half Brother, Gerald B. Gayford (1914 NY) - William H. Van Name (1866 NY) & Lyde? (1872 NY) - William Earnest Gayford (1872 England) & Elizabeth Hickey (1870 NY) - Fillmore Central - INA - Patter Dewitt Construction Co., Town of Grove Road Superintendent - Jessie? (?) - Jesse R., Sue Ann Van Name; Step Daughter Linda (Youngman), Step Sons Larry Hendryx, Harold & Michael Mitchell - 2/21/1993 Dalton, NY - Dalton - 1930 Federal Census Hume - Son Jesse R. Van Name.

Van Name, Percy J. Military: US Army - 6/5/1944/Private - Army Transportation Corps, Port Battalion - Military Policeman, Quay foreman/T 4 - Watertown, NY, Camp Pine, NC, Ft. Riley, KS, Ft. Meade, Maryland/12.5 months - 11.5 months - Calcutta, India - None - NA - NA - NA - NA - 5/31/1946 Ft. Dix, NJ - American Campaign Medal, Medal, Good Conduct Medal, Asian Pacific Theater Medal, WW II Victory Medal. He also served for a period as a military policeman. Percy reenlisted 6/10/1946 and served a second tour in the Army. Civilian: 9/13/1919, Fillmore, NY - Harry Van Name (1880 NY) & Maude Sweetland (1882 NY) - Jeanette (1912 NY) - Byron Van Name (1838 NY) & Emeline? (1842 NY) - Fillmore Central - Trackman, Pennsylvania RR - Borden County Maintenance Department, Nichols Discount City, Herkimer, NY - 1. Madeline Ruth Sweet (M 8/15/1940, Fillmore), 2. Kit ?, 3. Elsie Becraft - (Madeline Sweet - Donna (1941 NY), Ronald (1944 NY)) (Kit ? - Frances, Nancy, Diane, James) One other. - 1970, Ilion, NY - Hurricane Cemetery, Gray, NY - 1930 Federal Census Fillmore - Allegany County War Service Record, Daughter Donna Van Name. Photo – Family.

Van Name, Robert Lowell Military: US Army Air Corps- 9/12/1942/Rochester/Private - 15th Air Force,

456th Bomb Group - Airplane Mechanic/Corporal - Seymour Johnson AB, NC, Chanute Field, IL/INA - 19 months - Italy - Air Offensive Europe, Rome-Arno, Naples-Foggia, Normandy, Northern France, Southern France, North Apennines, Rhineland, Central Europe, Po Valley - NA -NA - NA – Medical Treatments, 9//44, 3/45, 6/45 – 9/30/1945, Fort dix, NJ - American Campaign Medal, Good Conduct Medal, Distinguished Unit Citation (Weiner Neustadt, 5/10/44), Distinguished Unit Citation (7/2/44 Budapest), European African Middle East Theater Medal, Presidential Unit Citation with Oak Leaf Cluster, 10 Battle Stars, WW II Victory Medal. His brother Harold F. also served after the war. His half-brother, Gerald B. Gayford served and died in action during the war. Civilian: 5/31/1922, Hume, NY - Jesse Merlon Van Name (1896 NY) & Katherine Gayford (1898 NY) - Harold F. (1924 NY), Half Brother, Gerald B. Gayford (1914 NY) - William H. Van Name (1866 NY) & Eliza M. (Lyde)? (1872 NY) - William Earnest Gayford (1872 England) & Elizabeth Hickey (1870 NY) - Fillmore Central - Farm Laborer - Postman - Helen Webber (M 2/9/1946 Burns, NY) - INA – 2/16/2014, Crystal River, FL – Fountains Memorial Park, Citrus County, FL - 1930 Federal Census Hume. None. Photo- NAO.

Vasile, Anthony Richard (Tony) Military: US Army - 4/24/1941Buffalo/Private - Company B, 171st

Tank Destroyer Battalion - Automotive Parts Clerk/Tech 5 - Fort Ethan Allen, VT, Fort Bragg, NC, Fort Devens, MA, Camp Edwards, MA, A. P. Hill Reservation, VA, Pine Hill, NY, Camp Hood, TX, Fort Dix, NJ, Camp Shanks, NY/30 months - 25 months - England, Wales, France, Belgium, Holland, Germany - Rhineland, Central Europe - NA - NA - NA - NA - 12/2/1945, Ft. Dix, NJ - American Defense Medal, American Campaign Medal, European, African, Middle East Theater Medal, Good Conduct Medal, Presidential Unit Citation, Army of Occupation, Germany Clasp. World War II Victory Medal, 2 Battle Stars. Civilian: 10/7, 1919 - Samuel Vasile (1884 Italy) & Leonarda Gennaro (1896 Italy) - Rose (1915 NY), Mary (1917 NY), Joseph (1918 NY), Thomas (1920) - INA - INA - Nunda Central School - Truck Hand, Knitting Mill - Executive, Rochester Gas & Electric Co., Fillmore - Catherine Shaffer - Kathy Ann - INA - INA. - 1940 Federal Census - Daughter Kathy Ann Vasile Vetter. Photo – Family.

Vedder, Grant Albert Military: US Navy - 12/29/1936 (reenlisted 12/19/1940)/AS - *USS*

Richmond/USS Grampus - Torpedoman Mate/ S 1 C - Newport, RI, San Diego, CA, New London, CT/ INA - INA - Atlantic Fleet, Pacific Fleet, Australia , at sea Solomon Islands, Guadalcanal area, Philippines (Luzon & Mindoro areas) Kwajalein Atoll area , Wotje Atoll area - INA - KIA, 3/5/1943 Blackett Strait near Solomon Islands - NA - NA - Scarlett Fever, New London, CT, 10/1941 - 3/5/1943 - Submarine Combat Patrol Insignia with Commendation, American Defense Medal, Asiatic Pacific Theater Medal, Purple Heart, 3 Battle Stars (1st , 4th & 5th Patrols), WW II Victory Medal. Civilian: 11/22/1918 Hume, NY - Clyde H. Vedder (1892 NY) & Winifred E. Jones (1895 NY) - None - Grant A. Jones (1872 NY) & Emma I.? (1873 NY) - Albert Vedder (1865 NY) & Grace J.? (1872 NY) - Fillmore Central, Class of 1936 - Student - None - None - None - 3/5/1943 - At Sea, Blackett Straits, Solomon Islands - 1930 Federal Census Fillmore None. Photo – NAO.

Voss, Everett Edwin (Jack)   Military: US Army - 1/11/1943/Ft. Niagara/Private - Company L, 475th

Quartermaster Truck Regiment/90th Field Artillery Battalion - Light Truck Driver, Mechanic, Infantryman /Tech 5 - Fort Dix, NJ, Camp Blanding, FL, Maryland, Boston, Texas, California/31 months - 6 months - Philippines (Luzon), Japan - Defense of the Americas - NA - NA - NA - Hernia (1943) - 2/16/1946, Fort Dix, NJ - American Campaign Medal, Good Conduct Medal, Asiatic Pacific Campaign Medal, Army of Occupation, Japan Clasp, WW II Victory Medal - Received a letter from President Truman thanking him for his service. Brother Lawrence W. also served. Grandfather Isaac Van Nostrand served with the 19th NY Cavalry (1st NY Dragoons) during the Civil War. His great-great grandfather, also named Isaac Van Nostrand, served in the Revolutionary War. Civilian: 3/11/1923 - Morris A. Voss (1890 NY) & Ruth Jane Van Duser (1891 NY) - Murray L. (1909 NY), Grace M. (1911 NY), Melrose C. (1914 NY), Lawrence W. (1916 NY), Melva G. (1925 NY), Alvin M. (1929 NY), Bonita R. (1933 NY) - Dwight Van Duser (1894 NY) & Armanda Wood (1850 NY) - Harry S. Voss ((1880 NY) & Florence Belle Van Nostrand (1860 NY) - FCS, District 1, Granger - Granger Highway Department - Granger Highway Department (Heavy Equipment Operator) - Anne Higby Remsen   (NY 1926) (M 5/10/1946) - Rebecca Anne (Turinia) (NY 1947), Jane Marie (Koerner) (NY 1951), Randy Mark (NY 1949) - 11/22/2008 Short Tract - Short Tract Cemetery, Short Tract, NY - 1930 Federal Census Granger - Wife Anne Voss, Daughters Jane Koerner.& Rebecca Turinic. Photo – NAO.

Voss, Gerald James   Military: US Army - 12/10/1942/Ft Niagara/Private - 3rd Army, Company C, 449th Anti-Aircraft Automatic Weapons Battalion - INA/Sergeant - Camp Eustice, VA, Camp Edwards, MA/16 months - INA - England, France, Luxemburg, Germany, Czechoslovakia - Normandy, Northern France, Rhineland, Ardennes-Alsace, Central Europe - NA - NA - NA - NA - INA - European, African, Middle East Theater Medal, American Campaign Medal, Good Conduct Medal, 5 Battle Stars, Army Occupation Medal, Germany Clasp, WW II Victory Medal . Civilian: 4/3/1919 NY - Harold E. Voss (1897 NY) & Marjorie Piatt (1895 NY) - Helen P. (1918 NY), Leo H. (1922 NY), Betty M. (1926 NY), Marjorie E. (1930 NY) - Fred R. Piatt (1862 NY) & Lizzie M. Closser (1865 NY) - Richard W. Voss & Sarah J. Elliott (1868 Ireland) - Fillmore Central 3 years high school - Paper Factory - Accountant, Kee Lox Manufacturing Co. Bernadette M. Sullivan - Cynthia, Linda, Heida, Stephen, Tracy - 7/20/1964, Rochester, NY - Riverside Cemetery, Rochester - 1930 Federal Census, Granger - Rondus Perry Miller. Photo – NAO.

Voss, Howard Ladette – Howard, of Granger (1930 census) and Fillmore (1940 census), was called for his final physical in February of 1943. A problem apparently was identified since there is no evidence that he served during the war.

Voss, Lawrence Wayne (Bing) Military: Army Air Force - 9/3/1942/Private – 268th AAF Base Unit - Aircraft Mechanic, B-17, B-29/Sergeant - Miami Beach, FL, Amarillo Field, TX, Boeing Plant, Seattle, WA. Alexandria Army Air Field, LA, Peterson Field, CO /36 months - 4.5 months - Cuba (Caribbean Theater of Operations) - NA - NA - NA - Yellow Fever - 2/1944, Cholera - 8/1944 - 1/31/1946, Lowery Field, CO - Good Conduct Medal, American Campaign Medal, WW II Victory Medal. Brother Everett C. also served. Grandfather Isaac Van Nostrand served with the 19th NY Cavalry (1st NY Dragoons) during the Civil War. His great-great grandfather, also an Isaac Van Nostrand, served in the Revolutionary War. Civilian: 7/18/1916 NY - Morris A. Voss (1890 NY) & Ruth J. Van Duser (1891 NY) - Murray L. (19109 NY), Grace M. (1911 NY), Melrose E. (1914 NY), Everett E. (1923 NY), Melva G. (1925 NY), Alvin M. (1929 NY), Bonita R. (1933 NY) - Dwight Van Duser (1844 NY) & Armanda Wood (1850 NY) - Harry S. Voss ((1880 NY) & Florence Belle Van Nostrand (1860 NY) - FCS - Slossom Lumber Mill, Dalton, NY - Slossom Lumber Mill - Thelma ? - Douglas - 7/13/1976/Short Tract - Short Tract Cemetery, NY - 1930 Federal Census Granger - Son Douglas, Sister Bonita (Rissinger). Photo – NAO, Family.

Wagner, Carl Max Not FCSD. Army Air Corps. Wagner was a student at Houghton College. Born in Michigan, he and his family lived in Charlotte, Chautauqua County, NY. He was training as an aviation cadet when he was killed in a trainer crash at the basic flying school at Cochran Field, Macon, Georgia. Several students from Houghton College, who were not local, served during the war, and are not included in this book.

Wakefield, Lewis Amos Military: US Army - 7/2/1943/Buffalo/Private - INA - Chemical Warfare/Captain - INA -Total Service 28 months 3 weeks - INA - INA - NA - NA - NA - NA - 11/21/1945 - American Campaign Medal, World War II Victory Medal. Civilian: 10/9/1920, Portville, NY - Raymond W. Wakefield (1895 NY) & Clara C. Griffin (1895 NY) - None – Henry Griffin (1844 NY) & Harriet Jobe (1863 NY) - Orson M. Wakefield (1872 NY) & Clara I. Colby (1871 NY) - Houghton College (Chemistry Major) - Student - Owner, Windham, NY Pharmacy - Gwendolyn Yager - Sharon, Marcia, Melanie, John, Debra - 3/23/1987/Palm Beach, FL - Pleasant Valley Cemetery, Windham, NY- 1940 Federal Census, Houghton - None. Family moved to Friendship by 1930 and to Houghton by 1935. Photo – Yearbook.

Wallace, David Dodge Military: Army Air Corps - 8/23/1941/Private - 453rd Bomb Group, 733rd Squadron - B-26H Liberator Co-Pilot/1st Lieutenant - Camp Stewart, GA, Kessler Field, MS, Maxwell Field, AL, March Field, CA/27 months - 3 months - England - Air Offensive Europe - KIA 3/6/1944 (Berlin Mission, bailed Out, Froze in North Sea) - NA - NA - NA - 3/6/1944 - American Defense Medal, American Theater Medal, European African Middle Eastern Theater Medal, One Battle Star, Purple Heart, WW II Victory Medal. Participated in first American Bomber Raid on Berlin. Served with the New York National Guard (Battery G, 209th Coast Artillery) from 12/26/1940 until enlisting in the Army in 1941. Civilian: 1/7/1919 Caneadea, NY - William H. Wallace (1881 NY) & Eva C. Sears (1885 NY) - Lyle (1908 NY), Neil 1914 NY), Flora (1906 NY), William (1915 NY) – Charles E. Sears (1851 NY) & Helen A. Morehouse (1856 NY) – John Wallace (1855 Michigan) & Mary E. Powers (1868 NY) - Warsaw High School, Class of 1936 - Farm Hand - NA - NA - NA - 3/6/1944 - Body lost in North Sea – NA – NA – NA - NAO, January, 1945 - None. (Sister Flora graduated from FCS in 1923.) Photo – NAO.

Ward, Alwin Jay Military: Army Air Corps - Inducted 8/25/42, Entered into active service 4/7/1943/Ft.

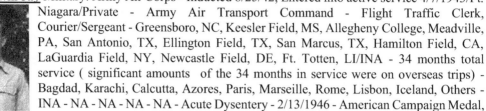

Niagara/Private - Army Air Transport Command - Flight Traffic Clerk, Courier/Sergeant - Greensboro, NC, Keesler Field, MS, Allegheny College, Meadville, PA, San Antonio, TX, Ellington Field, TX, San Marcus, TX, Hamilton Field, CA, LaGuardia Field, NY, Newcastle Field, DE, Ft. Totten, LI/INA - 34 months total service (significant amounts of the 34 months in service were on overseas trips) - Bagdad, Karachi, Calcutta, Azores, Paris, Marseille, Rome, Lisbon, Iceland, Others - INA - NA - NA - NA - NA - Acute Dysentery - 2/13/1946 - American Campaign Medal, Good Conduct Medal, European African Middle East Theater Medal, WW II Victory Medal. On return trips from overseas helped care for wounded soldiers being transported back to states.   Civilian: 7/27/1920 NY - Lester J. Ward (1895 NY) & Vesta L. Cole (1895 NY) - Lynette A. Ward (Witter) (1922 NY) - Frank Cole (1866 NY) & Mary Holland (1865 NY) - Harvey Ward (1857 NY) & Laura (Etta) Monroe (1873 NY) - Fillmore Central, Class of 1938, Cornell University, Class of 1942 - Father's Drug Store/Student - Pillsbury Company, Hadco Storage Company - Sophia Wagner (M 12/30/1946 Minnesota - Mary, Jeff, David, Nancy, Susan, Elizabeth - 2/4/2009, St. Joseph, MO - Mount Olivet Cemetery, Saint Joseph, MO - 1930 1940 Federal Census Fillmore - Wife Sophia Wagner Ward, Son Jeff. Photo – NAO.

Washbon, Leslie Clarence. Not FCSD area. US Navy. His family moved to Fillmore by at least 1935, when Leslie was 25. They were living there during the war, as was his wife. Leslie entered the service in 1933, and served until at least 1949. He served on several ships, including the aircraft carrier *USS Wasp* from 1943 to 1945. He earned eight battle stars during the war. He lived in both Rushford and Caneadea prior to the war. There were several instances of families moving to Fillmore without children who served during the war but who never lived in Fillmore themselves.

Washburn, Llewellyn Max Military: US Army: 3/1/1944/Fort Dix, NJ/Private – 893rd Anti-Aircraft Automatic Weapons Battalion - INA/Private - Camp Blanding, FL, Fort Meade, MD/7 months - 19 months - England, France, Germany - Central Europe, Rhineland - NA - NA - NA - NA - 5/1/1946 - American Campaign Medal, European African Middle East Theater Medal, World War II Victory Medal, two battle stars, Army Occupation Medal, Germany Clasp. Brother Mark also served. Llewellyn's great grandfather Andrew Mearns Jr. served with Company A, 154 NY Infantry during the Civil War. Civilian: 1/24/1920, Centerville, NY - Leslie G. Washburn (1897 NY) & Nina E. Ackerman (1896 NY) - Mark (1922 NY), Edith (1924 NY), Lettie (1927 NY), Carol (1884 NY) - Mark M. Ackerman (1868 NY) & Maplet Louisa (Letty) Mearns (1869 NY) - Frank Washburn (1858 NY) & Edith Huff (1863 NY) - Fillmore Central – Farm Laborer - INA - 1. Margaret Mix, 2. Victoria Bachelor - Suzanne (Eubanks) - 2/4/2005 Osceola, FL - INA - 1930 Federal Census Hume - Daughter Suzanne Eubanks.

Washburn, Mark Kendall Military: US Army - 10/5/1942/Buffalo/Private – Battery C, 237th Anti-Aircraft Artillery Searchlight Battalion - Radar Operator/ Sergeant - Camp Edwards, MA, Radar School, FL/25 months 2 weeks – 13 months 2weeks - New Britain, New Guinea, Philippines - Bismarck Archipelago Island, New Guinea, Leyte, Southern Philippines - NA - NA - NA - NA - 1/4/1946/Fort Dix, NJ - American Campaign Medal, Army Good Conduct Medal, Asiatic Pacific Campaign Medal, World War II Victory, Philippine Liberation Medal with Bronze Star Medal, 3 Battle Stars. Brother Llewellyn also served during the war. Civilian : 1/30/1922 NY (Centerville) - Leslie G. Washburn (1897 NY) & Nina E. Ackerman (1896 NY) - LLewellyn (1920 NY), Edith (1924 NY), Lettie (1927 NY), Carol (1884 NY) - Mark M. Ackerman (1868 NY) & Maplet Louisa (Letty) Mearns (1869 NY) - Frank Washburn (1858 NY) & Edith Huff (1863 NY) - FCS/Castile - Farm Laborer/Folding Machine Operator - General Foreman, Kittinger Furniture & Holstery Company - Jane Mix - Kenneth, James S., Stephen, Richard, Edith, Letty, Carol - 8/23/2013 – Grace Cemetery, Castile, NY - 1930 Census Centerville – None.

Wass, Harold Wesley Military: US Navy - 8/25/1943/Buffalo/AS - *USS Fidelity (AM 96), USS PC 1600*

(same ship). Originally a minesweeper, re-designated as a submarine chaser - Soundman, 2C - Sampson Naval Base, Casco Bay, Maine, Treasure Island, CA/19 months - 18 months - Pacific Fleet, Hawaii, Eniwetok, Marshall Islands, Hollandia, New Guinea, New Britain, Manus, Guadalcanal, Russell Islands, Palau, Guam- Leyte Operation, Luzon Operation - NA - NA - NA - NA - 3/2/1946 - American Campaign Medal, Asiatic Pacific Theater Medal, WW II Victory Medal, Philippine Liberation Medal with Battle Star, 2 US Battle Stars, Navy Occupation Service Medal, Asian Clasp. -Also served in Navy 10/24/1949 to 1/8/1953 Civilian: 7/13/1926 NY - Harold Wass (1887 England) & Mildred M. Easton (1900 NY) - Anna M (1924 NY), Jessie E. (1928 NY), Eric F. (1931 NY) - William R. (1933 NY) - Milo B. Easton (1868 NY) & Bertha I Lewis (1878 NY) - Thomas E. Wass (1861 England) & Sabina (likely Close) (1864 England) - Fillmore Central - Student – Remained in service post war, later lived in Hammondsport, NY - Esther R. Perry - INA - 4/5/1989, Hammondsport, NY - Pleasant Valley Cemetery, Hammondsport - 1940 Federal Census, Fillmore - None. Photo – Yearbook.

Weaver, Kent Miles Military: US Army - 3/21/1944/FT. Dix, NJ/Private - 5th Army, 34th Infantry

Division, 133rd Infantry Regiment, 1st Battalion, Company D/88th Infantry Division, 349th Infantry Regiment - Infantryman, Squad Leader/Sergeant - Camp Wheeler, Ft Meade, MD/8 months - 15 months - Scotland, France, Italy - North Apennines, Po Valley - NA - NA - NA - Several weeks in hospital in Italy, Yellow Jaundice - 2/13/1946 Ft. Dix - Combat Infantry Badge, (Bronze Star 1947), Good Conduct Medal, European African Middle East Theater Medal, 2 Battle Stars, World War II Victory Medal. Brother Kent served as a Naval Cadet at Annapolis during the war. Civilian: 9/13/1923 (NY) - Harrison W. Weaver (1888 NY) & Fairolia Christiana Babbitt (1890 NY) - Roy (1921 NY) - Miles W. Weaver (1836 NY) & Mary Wing (1850 NY) - Benjamin Franklin Babbitt (1854 NY) & Mary Fairolia Stephens (1858 NY) - Fillmore Central, Class of 1940, Cornell College of Agriculture, University of Florence, Italy - Student - INA - Marcella Bennett (Married 5/12/1946 Centerville, NY) - Dennis, Marilyn, Harrison II - 7/25/2006, Rushford, NY – Podonque Cemetery, Rushford - 1940 Federal Census Fillmore - Allegany County War Service Record, Babbitt Family History from Virginia Aspell Babbitt. Photo – NAO.

Weaver, Roy Babbitt Military: US Navy - 8/5/1942/ Annapolis, MD/Midshipman - US Naval

Academy/*USS Los Angeles* - Midshipman/Ensign - Annapolis/4 years - one year - Atlantic Fleet, Pacific Fleet, Hawaii - None - NA - NA - NA - NA - Asiatic Pacific Theater Medal, American Campaign Medal, WW II Victory Medal. Brother Kent also served during the war. Marched with the Midshipmen in the funeral parade for President Roosevelt. Spent 5 months in Fleet Training Center in Hawaii following graduation and while aboard the Los Angeles. Civilian: 11/22/1921 Fillmore, NY - Harrison W. Weaver (1888 NY) & Fairolia Christiana Babbitt (1890 NY) - Kent M. (1923 NY) - Miles W. Weaver (1836 NY) & Mary Wing (1850 NY) - Benjamin Franklin Babbitt (1854 NY) & Mary Fairolia Stephens (1858 NY) - Fillmore Central, Class of 1937, Houghton College, Class of 1941, US Naval Academy, Class of 1945) - Civilian Instructor in radio, Scott Field, IL - Naval Officer - Alice Taylor (? MD) - INA - 10/21/2000, Burlington, NJ- Nelson Bay Cemetery, Sea Level, NC -1940 Federal Census, Fillmore 1940 - Allegany County War Service Record, Babbitt Family History from Virginia Aspell Babbitt. Photo – NAO.

Wells, George Robert Military: US Navy - (1/1942/Enlisted Houghton) Entered Summer 1943/AS - 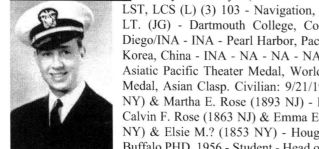LST, LCS (L) (3) 103 - Navigation, Deck Officer, Executive. Gunnery Officer/ LT. (JG) - Dartmouth College, Columbia University, Coronado Island, San Diego/INA - INA - Pearl Harbor, Pacific Fleet, Saipan, Tinian, Guam, Iwo Jima, Korea, China - INA - NA - NA - NA - NA - 8/1946 - Letter of Commendation, Asiatic Pacific Theater Medal, World War II Victory Medal, Navy Occupation Medal, Asian Clasp. Civilian: 9/21/1921/Connecticut - Howard A. Wells (1885 NY) & Martha E. Rose (1893 NJ) - Horace J. (1925 NY), John E. (1929 NY) - Calvin F. Rose (1863 NJ) & Emma E.? (1864 NJ) - Addison Joshua Wells (1849 NY) & Elsie M.? (1853 NY) - Houghton College, Class of 1942, University of Buffalo PHD, 1956 - Student - Head of Physical Education, Houghton College, 38 years - Doris Driscoll (M 8/19/1945 PA) - G. Robert, Laura Lee, Delores, Darlene, David - 10/15/2009 Houghton, NY - MT. Pleasant Cemetery, Houghton - Fillmore History Club 1945 WW II Book - None. Photo – NAO.

Whalen, Donald Leo Military: US Army - 7/28/1944/Private (Reenlisted 12/5/1945) - 292nd Combat Engineer Battalion - Driver/PFC - FT. Dix, NJ, FT. Belvoir, VA, Texas, FT. Meade, MD/7 months - 11 months - England, Holland, Germany – Rhineland, Central Europe - NA - NA - NA - NA - 1948 - Letter of Commendation, American Campaign Medal, Two Battle Stars, European African Middle East Theater Medal, WW II Victory Medal, Army Occupation Medal - Germany Clasp. (Don reenlisted and stayed in the Army until 1948. However, the above information and his write-up only covers the period of WW II, from his entering in July of 1944, until he arrived back in the US January 2, 1946. There is also an indication that he may have spent some time in the Navy during early 1943.) Civilian: 11/25/1925, Hume, NY - Leo T. Whalen (1896 NY) & Beatrice Anna Hodnett (1901 NY) - Carmelita (1920 NY), Evelyn (1923 NY) - Henry Richard Hodnett (1873 NY) & Anna Hayes (1874 NY) - John Henry Whalen (1862 NY) & Anatasia B. Powers (1872 NY) - Fillmore Central, Friendship Central, one-year high school - Truck Driver, Liberty Motor Freight, Buffalo - Self Employed Truck Driver - 1. Elsie I. Kingsley (M 2/9/1945 Fillmore) 2. Dora Mary Wiltberger - Donna Lee (1948 NY), Michael Calvin (1949 NY), Kathleen Sue (1951 NY) - 12/23/1994 Haines City, FL - Florida National Cemetery, Bushnell, FL - 1930 Federal Census Hume - First wife Elsie Kingsley Babbitt.

Wilcox, Howard June (Nick) Military. US Navy - 6/8/1943/Buffalo/AS - *USS Rich, USS Maumee, USS* *Bogue* - Quartermaster/S2C - Sampson Naval Base, NY, Norfolk Naval Base, VA. Brooklyn Naval Yard, Boston Naval Yard/25 months? (12 of these months unaccounted for) - nine months? - Atlantic Fleet (Northern Ireland), Pacific Fleet (Guam, Alaska?) - None - NA - NA - NA - NA - April 16, 1946/Shelton, VA - American Campaign Medal, European African Middle Eastern Theater Medal, Asiatic Pacific Theater Medal, WW II Victory Medal, - Brothers Virgil, Lyle and Lowell also served during the war. Civilian. 6/19/1911 Wirt, NY - John Aaron Wilcox (1880 NY) & Mildred Mae Reynolds (1881 NY) - Anna R. (1902 NY), Leon J. (1903 NY), Joyce W. (1905 NY), Homer L. (1907NY), Virgil E. (1908 NY), Alvira (1910 NY), Hartley W. (1913 NY), Kenneth H. (1914 NY), Lowell J. (1918 NY), Lyle (1918 NY), Opal M. (1921 NY), Violet M. (1922 NY) -? Reynolds &? Pierce - Wilson Greene Wilcox (1841 NY) & Anna Wescott (1842 NY) - Self-Employed - Heavy Equipment Operator, Local 832, Rochester, NY - 1. Alta Travis (M 12/25/1934), 2. Hazel M. Gardner (M1943), 3. Dorothy Hosfield (M 1/11/1990) - June (1936 NY), Joy (1939 NY), Judy (1958 NY) - 8/17/1996, Newfane, Niagara County, NY - West Ridgeway Cemetery, Medina, NY - 1915, 1925 NYS Census Centerville, 1920 Federal Census Centerville - Daughter Joy Wilcox, Niece Karla Wilcox, Niece Karen Sonnleitner Lucas. Photo – Family.

Wilcox, Lyle A (NMN) (Mike) Military. US Army - 12/10/1940/Olean/Private - First Infantry Division,  26th Infantry Regiment - Infantryman/Private - Camp Devens, MA/11 months - NA - NA - NA - NA - NA - NA - NA - 11/1941 (Honorable, Medical) - American Defense Medal. Brothers Howard, Virgil and twin brother Lowell also served during the war. Civilian: 7/19/1918 NY, Centerville, NY - John Aaron Wilcox (1880 NY) & Mildred Mae Reynolds (1881 NY) - Anna R. (1902 NY), Leon J. (1903 NY), Joyce W. (1905 NY), Homer L. (1907 NY), Virgil E. (1908 NY), Alvira (1910 NY), Howard (1911 NY), Hartley W. (1913 NY), Kenneth H. (1914 NY), Lowell J. (1918 NY), Opal M. (1921 NY), Violet M. (1922 NY) -? Reynolds &? Pierce - Wilson Greene Wilcox (1841 NY) & Anna Wescott (1842 NY) - FCS - Farm Hand - Union Operating Engineer, Rochester, NY - Mildred Marie Clark (M 7/19/1944) - Wanda Lee (1945-2012 NY), Alana Jane (1948 NY), Kim Andrea (1957 NY) - 1/31/2009 Warsaw, NY - Alger Cemetery, Hume, NY - 1920, 1930 Federal Census Centerville - Niece Karla Wilcox, Niece Karen Sonnleitner Lucas. Photo – Family.

Wilcox, Lowell J (NMN) (Ike) Military: US Army - 12/10/1940/Olean/ Private - First Infantry Division,  26th Infantry Regiment - Rifleman, Armorer-Artificer, Supply/Staff Sergeant - Ft. Devens, MA, Camp Blanding, FL, Ft. Benning, GA, Indiantown Gap Military Reservation, PA, New York Port/20 months - 37 months - England, North Africa, Sicily, France, Germany, Czechoslovakia - Algeria-French Morocco, Tunisia, Sicily, Normandy, Northern France, Rhineland, Ardennes-Alsace, Central Europe- NA - WIA shrapnel in back, North Africa - NA - NA - 9/8/1945 - American Defense Medal, American Campaign Medal, European, African, Middle East, Theater Medal, Bronze Star for Meritorious Service, WW II Victory Medal, Purple Heart, 7 Battle Stars, Combat Infantryman Badge (1947 Bronze Star), 3 Arrowhead (assault) Badges (North Africa, Sicily, Normandy, Omaha Beach), French Croix de Guerre with Palm (Kasserine), French Croix de Guerre with Palm (Normandy), French Fourragere Aux Coulers Du Ruban de la Medaille Militaire, Order of the Day Belgian Army (Action at Eupen-Malmedy), one more? Brothers Howard and Virgil and twin brother Lyle also served during the war. Civilian: 7/19/1918 Centerville, NY - John Aaron Wilcox (1880 NY) & Mildred Mae Reynolds (1882 NY) - Anna R. (1902 NY), Leon J. (1903 NY), Joyce W. (1905 NY), Homer L. (1907 NY), Virgil E. (1908 NY), Alvira (1910 NY), Howard (1911 NY), Hartley W. (1913 NY), Kenneth H. (1914 NY), Lyle A. (1918 NY), Opal M. (1921 NY), Violet M. (1922 NY) -? Reynolds &? Pierce - Wilson Greene Wilcox (1841 NY) & Anna Wescott (1842 NY) - FCS - Dairy Farm Hand - Heavy Equipment Operator, Road Construction, Bartender, 3-H Restaurant, Dansville, NY - Jean Adabella Brant (M 5/29, 1947) - Karla Jane (1946 NY), Jay Dee (1948 NY), John Shanton (1952 NY), Aaron Lowell (1955 NY) - 9/2/1980, Bath, NY - Greenmount Cemetery, Dansville, NY - 1920, 1930 Federal Census Centerville - Daughter Karla Wilcox, Niece Karen Sonnleitner Lucas. Photo – NAO.

Wilcox, Virgil Eugene (Doc) Military: US Army - 11/12/1942/Private - Coast Artillery/Headquarters &  Headquarters Battery - Field Lineman, Second Class Gunner/Corporal - Fort Hancock, NY, Ft. Wadsworth, Staten Island, NY/33 months - NA - NA - NA - NA - NA - NA - NA - 10/3/1945- American Campaign Medal, WW II Victory Medal. Brothers Howard, Lyle and Lowell also served during the war. Civilian: 8/2/1908 Wirt, NY - John Aaron Wilcox (1880 NY) & Mildred Mae Reynolds (1881 NY) - Anna R. (1902 NY), Leon J. (1903 NY), Joyce W. (1905 NY), Homer L. (1907 NY), Alvira (1910 NY), Howard (1911 NY), Hartley W. (1913 NY), Kenneth H. (1914 NY), Lyle A. (1918 NY), Lowell J. (1918 NY), Opal M. (1921 NY), Violet M. (1922 NY) -? Reynolds &? Pierce - Wilson Greene Wilcox (1841 NY) & Anna Wescott (1842 NY) -Fillmore Central - Farm Laborer - Construction Engineer - Emily I. Jackson - None -

11/7/1970 Los Angeles, CA - Augur Cemetery, Hume, NY - 1920 Federal Census Centerville - Niece Karla Wilcox, Niece Karen Sonnleitner Lucas., Niece Vesta Wilcox Teeter. Photo – NAO.

Wilday, Alfred Carter Military: US Navy - 2/13/1935 (Reenlisted February, 1939), (Reenlisted

5/8/1941), (Reenlisted 11/1943 per NAO)/Buffalo//AS - *USS Melville, USS Detroit, USS Antaeus* (later renamed USS Rescue,), *USS Bushnell* - Torpedoman/1 C - New London, CT, Mare Island, CA/INA - INA - Guam - NA - NA - NA - NA - INA - American Defense Medal, American Campaign Medal, Asiatic Pacific Theater Medal, Navy Occupation Medal - Asian Clasp, WW II Victory Medal. Brothers Oliver and Glenn also served. Oliver was killed in action. Civilian: 12/28/1911 MD - Harold F. Wilday (1888 NY) & Mary E. Carter (1888 NY) - Oliver Paul (1915 NY), Edward Allen (1918 NY), Glenn C. (1921 NY) - Edward A. Carter (1855 VA) & Anna C.? (1864 Norway) - William Henry Wilday (1859 NY) & Sara E.? (1855 NY)
- Fillmore Central School, Class of 1928, Training Class of 1929 - Farm Laborer for Dad - INA - INA - INA - 1/31/1997 - Rose Hills Memorial Cemetery, Whittier, CA - 1930, 1940 Federal Census Centerville. Photo – School.

Wilday, Burdette Forrest Military: Army Air Corps 10/3/1942/Buffalo/Private - INA - Radio

Mechanic/ Sergeant - Atlantic City, NJ, Richmond, VA, Chicago, IL, Bradley Field, CT/INA - INA - India - INA - NA - NA - NA - NA - INA - American Campaign Medal, Asiatic Pacific Theater Medal, WW II Victory Medal. Civilian: 1/9/1922 Perry, NY - Forrest S. Wilday (1886 NY) & Mabel McDougal (1884 PA) - Velma (1908 NY), Myrtle (1913 NY), Olive (1915 NY) - Likely Fred McDougal (1857 NY) & Florence? (1863 PA) - William H. Wilday (1859 NY) & Sara E.? (1855 NY) - Fillmore Central, Class of 1938 – Erie Railroad, Belmont - INA - Clare Thomas - Sandra - 10/1984 Sheffield Lake, Ohio - INA - 1930 Federal Census Hume - None. Photo – NAO.

Wilday, Glenn Charles Military: US Army - 12/12/1942/Buffalo/Private - 29th Infantry Division, 116th

Infantry Regiment - Radio Operator/Staff Sergeant - FT. Meade, MD/5 months - 24 months - Scotland, England, France (Normandy, 6/6/1944, 2nd wave), Germany - Normandy, Northern France, Rhineland, Central Europe - NA - NA - NA - developed severe daily headaches near end of war - 4/1945 - 4 Distinguished Unit Citations (Division), Croix de Guerre Avec Palme from France, (Division for Normandy D Day), Assault Badge (Normandy/Omaha Beach), 4 Battle Stars, European Theater Medal, WW II Victory Medal . Glenn was in second wave at Omaha Beach on June 6, 1944. Brothers Oliver and Alfred also served. Oliver was in first wave on Utah Beach on June 6, 1944, and was killed in action on June 20, 1944. Civilian: 9/9/1921 NY - Harold F. Wilday (1888 NY) & Mary E. Carter (1888 ND) - Alfred Carter (1911 NY), Oliver Paul (1915 NY), Edward Allen (1918 NY) - Edward A. Carter & Anna C.? (1864 Norway) - William Henry Wilday (1859 NY) & Sara E.? (1855 NY) - Fillmore Central, Class of 1938 - Farm Laborer (working for Dad) - Printer Shop Bindery Man, Case-Hoyt, Rochester, NY - Margaret Stickle - Cassandra (NY), Daphne (NY), Dana (NY), Marcia (NY), William (NY) - 11/9/1995, Centerville - Bates Cemetery, Centerville - 1930, 1940 Federal Census Centerville - Son Dana Wilday. Photo – School.

Wilday, Oliver Paul Military: US Army 10/6/1943/Philadelphia/Private - 4th Infantry Division, 8th

Infantry Regiment – Infantryman-Armorer-Artificer/PFC - Camp Blanding, FL/8 months - one month - England, France - Normandy - KIA 6/20/1944 Cherbourg - NA - NA - NA - 6/20/1944 Cherbourg, France - European African Middle East Theater Medal, World War II Victory Medal, Distinguished Unit Citation for Normandy, Arrowhead Device, Purple Heart, One Battle Star, Combat Infantryman Badge, (1947 Bronze Star). Brothers Glenn and Alfred also served. Glenn was in second wave at Omaha Beach. Civilian: 11/13/1915 IN - Harold F. Wilday (1888 NY) & Mary E. Carter (1888 NY) - Alfred Carter (1911 NY), Glenn Charles (1921 NY), Edward Allen (1918 NY) - Edward A. Carter & Anna C.? (1864 Norway) - William Henry Wilday -Steel Co. Delaware - None - None - None - 6/20/1944 Cherbourg, France - Normandy American Cemetery and Memorial, St. Laurent, Sur -Mer, France - 1930 Federal Census Centerville. Photo – NAO.

Wiles, Elon Curtis. Military: Army Air Corps - 10/15/1942/Buffalo/1st Lieutenant - INA/US Army

Dental Corps - Dentist/Major - Miami Beach, FL, Salt Lake City, UT, Geiger Field, Spokane, WA/43 months - NA - NA - NA - NA - NA - NA - NA - 5/23/1946 Mitchell Field, LI - American Campaign Medal, WW II Victory Medal. Brother Maurice also served during the war. Civilian: 7/25/1909 Ripley, NY - Arthur R. Wiles (1881 NY) & Olive Curtis (1877 NY) - Verena (1913 NY). Maurice (1918 NY) - Lewis S. Curtis (1836 NY) & Clarissa Rowley (1840 NY) - Linus E. Wiles (1850 NY) & Mary A. Robinson (1855 NY) - Fillmore Central, Class of 1928, Houghton College, Western Reserve University. BS 1934, DDA 1936 - Dentist, Fillmore - Dentist, Fillmore - Frances A. Arnold (M 8/22/1934, Tully, NY) - Alan R., Nancy E. - 9/1972 - Cremated/Pine Grove Cemetery, Fillmore - 1930 Federal Census Fillmore - Allegany County War Service Record, Daughter Nancy, Son Alan. Photo – NAO.

Wiles, Maurice Robinson Military: US Navy - 2/23/1944/Apprentice Seaman - Galveston Receiving

Station, TX - Mailman/Mailman Second Class - Sampson Naval Training Station, NY, New Orleans Naval Station (4 weeks), New Orleans Receiving Station (2 weeks) Galveston Receiving Station, TX, 2/23/44 to 2/6/1946 - NA - NA - NA - NA - NA - NA - NA - February 6, 1946 - American Theater Medal, World War II Victory Medal. Civilian: Civilian: March 8, 1918, Ripley, NY - Arthur R. Wiles (1881 NY) & Olive Curtis (1877 NY) - Elon (1910-1977)), Verona (1912-1999) - Lewis S. Curtis (1836 NY) & Clarissa Rowley (1840 NY) - Linus E. Wiles (1850 NY) & Mary A. Robinson (1855 NY) - Fillmore Central School, Class of 1937, Parks Air College (1937-38) - Rural Mail Carrier, Fillmore - Rural Mail Carrier, Fillmore (1942 - 1976) - Frances V. Gilbert (Genesee, PA, Married 9/6/1938) - Robin G. (1939-2009), Jeffrey C. (1947) - NA -NA - 1930 Federal Census Fillmore - Veteran Maurice Wiles, Allegany County War Service Record. In 2013, Maurice and Frances celebrated their 75th wedding anniversary. Photo – Troy, NY Weekly Paper. Provided by family.

Williams, Albert Military: US Army - 2/2/1942/Ft. Niagara/Private - 45th Infantry Division, 179th

Infantry Regiment, Cannon Company - INA/Private - Alabama/16 months - 30 months - North Africa, Sicily, France, Germany - Anzio, Ardennes-Alsace, Central Europe, Naples-Foggia, Rhineland, Rome-Arno, Sicily, Southern France - NA - NA - NA - NA - 12/3/1945 - American Campaign Medal, European, African, Middle Eastern Theater Medal, 7 Battle Stars, 4 Assault Badges, Army Occupation Medal, Germany, WW II Victory Medal. Brother Fred also served during the war. Civilian: 12/18/1915 Oklahoma - John W. Williams (1872 NY) & Sarah E. (maybe Miller) (1884 PA) - Fred (1917 OK), Mamie (1921 OK), Blanche (1926 OK), Helen (1928 TX) - (Maybe George Miller (1862 NY & Rachel L.? (1862 NY)) - John R. Williams (1850 NY & Mary? (1850 NY) - Grammar School - Farm Laborer - Pennsylvania Railroad, Fillmore - Myrtle I.? - INA - 10/7/1958, Fillmore - Pine Grove Cemetery, Fillmore, NY - 1940 Federal Census Hume - Photo – NAO.

Williams, Clair Norman Military: US Army - 3/04/1941/Buffalo/Private - Battery D, 7th Coastal Artillery Battalion/HQ Battery, 38th Coastal Artillery Battalion/? - INA/Corporal - Fort Tilden, NY, Fort Jackson, SC/Total service 59 months - INA – Possibly Okinawa – Possibly Okinawa - NA - NA - NA - NA - 11/11/1945 – American Defense Medal, American Campaign Medal, Asiatic Pacific Theater Medal, Possibly Okinawa, World War II Victory Medal - Brother Kenneth also served during the war. Grandfather James Williams served with Company E, 19th NY Cavalry (1st NY Dragoons) during the Civil War. Civilian: 12/9/1916 Centerville, NY - Thomas J. Williams (1879 NY) & Myrtle M. Patterson (1884 NY) - Leslie T. (1906 NY), Edith A. (1908 NY), Kenneth A. (1911 NY), Beulah M. (1914 NY) - Lewis W. Patterson (1844 NY) & Bertie Belle Eckert (1886 NY) - James Williams (1844 NY) & Hannah Jane Jones (1849 NY) - Grammar School, FCS - Farm Hand, Thomas J. Williams - Ford Motor Corporation - Gladys M. Pixley - Susan - 4/24/2001, Delevan, NY - Delevan Cemetery - 1930 1940 Federal Census Centerville - Daughter Susan.

Williams, Fred (NMN) Military: US Army - 3/21/1944/Ft. Dix, NJ/Private – Company B, 1280th

Engineer Combat Battalion – Light Tank Crewman/Private – Ft. Dix, NJ, FT. Knox, KY, Camp Gruber, OK/10 months - 4 months, 3 weeks - England - None - NA - NA - NA – Dermatitis, Generalized, teeth problems, Sabies - 7/3/1945 (Medical - Walter Reed Hospital, DC) - European, African, Middle East Theater Medal. WW II Victory Medal, was formally considered for Good Conduct, discharged before awarded. Brother Albert also served during the war. Civilian: 12/13/1917 Shamrock, Oklahoma - John W. Williams (1872 NY) & Sarah Lavina (maybe Miller) (1884 PA) - Albert (1915 OK), Mamie (1921 OK), Blanche (1926 OK), Helen (1928 TX) - Maybe George Miller (1862 TN) & Rachael (Keller?) (1862 TN)) - John R. Williams (1850 NY) & Mary D. (maybe Miller) (1850 England) – FCS, One-year high school - Dairy Farmer - INA - INA - INA - 11/25/1979, Fillmore, NY - Pine Grove Cemetery, Fillmore, NY - 1940 Federal Census Hume - None. Photo – NAO.

Williams, Glenn Floyd Military: US Army - 2/2/1942/Ft. Niagara/Private - 5th Army, 3rd "Marne" Infantry Division, Co. I, 30th Infantry Regiment - Infantryman/Staff Sergeant - Alabama, Framingham, MA, New Eastern Hotel, Machias, ME, FT. Redman, MA /22 months - 21 months - England, Italy, France, Germany - Naples-Foggia, Rome-Arno, Southern France, Rhineland, Central Europe - NA - WIA 4 times - 2/1944, 8/20/1944, ?, 11/21/44 - Leg Infection (Probably from 11/21 wound) - NA - 10/14/1945, Fort Dix, NJ – 5 Battle Stars, 4 Purple Hearts (Discharge documents only cites 2), Silver Star, Good Conduct Medal, American Campaign Medal, European African, Middle Eastern Theater Medal , Arrowhead Badge

(Southern France), 2 Presidential (Distinguished) Unit Citations (Besander, Colmar Pocket), Combat Infantryman Badge (1947 Bronze Star), NY State Conspicuous Service Cross with devise, French Croix-de-Guerre Medal with palm (Colmar Pocket), WW II Victory Medal. Glenn's grandfather, James Williams, served with Company E, 1ˢᵗ NY Dragoons (19ᵗʰ NY Cavalry) during the Civil War. Civilian: 11/4/1914 NY - Frederick D. Williams (1883 NY) & Maud C. Wood (1877 NY) - Evelyn (1905 NY), Howard (1911 NY), Genevieve (1913 NY), Catherine (1919 NY) - Edwin O. Wood (1850 PA) & Mary? (1848 NY) - James Williams (1842 (Wales) & Hannah Jane Jones (1849 NY) - Fillmore Central - Punch Press Operator - Heavy Equipment Operator, Local 12, Buffalo - Eunice Wolfer Flynn - Step-children Michael Flynn, Patricia (Engh), Sharon (Wilson) - March 7, 1998, Wellsville Memorial Hos - White Cem., Rushford - 1930 Fed Cen Centerville - Darlene Williams Mowers, Patricia Flynn (Engh). Photo – NAO.

Williams, Kenneth Arthur Military: US Army - 11/17/1942/Buffalo/Private - INA - Military Policeman/PFC - INA - INA - Italy - INA - NA - NA - NA - NA - 11/1945 – American Campaign Medal, European African Middle East Theater Medal, WW II Victory Medal. Brother Clair also served during the war. Grandfather James Williams served with Company E, 19ᵗʰ NY Cavalry (1ˢᵗ NY Dragoons) during the Civil War). Civilian: 10/3/1910, NY - Thomas J. Williams (1879 NY) & Myrtle M. Patterson Eckert (1883 NY) - Leslie T. (1906 NY), Edith A. (1908 NY), Beulah M. (1914 NY), Clair (1916 NY) - Lewis W. Patterson (1871 NY) & Bertie Belle Eckert (1886 NY) - James Williams (1844 NY) & Hannah Jane Jones (1849 NY) - FCS – Farm Laborer - INA – Freida Bagley - INA -2/18/1982, Ocala, FL - Forest Lawn Memory Garden Cemetery, Ocala, FL - 1930, 1940 Federal Census Centerville - None.

Wilmot Stephen Edward (Ed) Military: US Coast Guard - 7/16/1942 Buffalo/AS - INA - Beach Patrol, Yeoman Striker, Aviation Radio Technician/S2C - Curtis Bay, Baltimore MD, DCGO, Fifth Naval District, Wallops Beach L.B.S., Berkley Rec. Station, CA, Chincoteague Station, Norfolk, VA, Naval Training School, Chicago, IL, Texas A & M University, TX, Ward Island, Corpus Christie, TX, CG Air Station, Salem, MA/41 months - NA - NA - NA - NA - NA - NA - 10/31/1945 Brooklyn, NY - Good Conduct Medal, American Campaign Medal, WW II Victory Medal. Wife Avis was a Cadet Nurse with the Army Nurses Corps. Civilian: 2/11/1921 NY - Stephen E. Wilmot (1859 NY) & Mary E. Gordon (1875 NY) - Clarence P. (1901 NY), Alice (1906), Obed Gordon (1909 NY), William B. (1912 NY) - INA - William Wilmot (1815 England) & Jane? (1822 England) - Rushford Central School, Class of 1938, Cornell University (3 years pre-war, one-year post), University of Minnesota - Student - Agriculture Teacher, Fillmore 33 years, Retired 1978 - Avis Naze - INA - 12/3/1998 Portageville, NY - White Cemetery, Rushford, NY - Fillmore History Club 1945 WW II Book, December, 1945 - None. Photo – NAO.

Wilson, Richard J. Military: US Navy - 2/7/1943/AS - *LST 653, LST 729* - Watertender/S2C - Sampson Naval, NY/INA - 30 months - Pacific Fleet-SW Pacific, China - INA - NA - NA - NA - NA - June 1, 1946 - Asiatic Pacific Theater Medal, American Campaign Medal, WW II Victory Medal, Naval Occupational Medal, Asian Clasp. Civilian: 8/1/1924 Caneadea, NY - Volney C. Wilson (1888 NY) & Emma M. Taft (1893 NY) - Ruth E. (Damon) (1927 NY) - Henry TM. Taft (1865 NY) & Delina (Delila) (likely Stone) (1871 NY)- James A. Wilson (1865 NY) & Ruth Couch (1857 NY) - Belfast Central - Student – Game Warden - Jean E. Thomas —-Larry, Stephen, Jay - 5/9/2010 - Mt. Pleasant Cemetery, Houghton, NY - NAO, 5/1944 Fillmore – Houghton per Obituary. Photo – NAO.

Winchip, Frederic Seward (Fred/Rick) Military: US Navy - 12/27/1944/AS - 86th Naval Construction
Battalion/146 Naval Construction Battalion/96th Naval Construction Battalion
(Seabees) - Heavy Equipment Driver, Machinist Mate/3C - Sampson Naval, NY,
Naval Training Center, Davisville, R.I., Camp Parks, CA / 5 months - 14 months -
Hawaii, Okinawa, China - None - NA - NA - NA - NA – 7/18/1946, Lido Beach,
NY - American Campaign Medal, Asiatic Pacific Theater Medal, China Service
Medal, WW II Victory Medal. Fred operated heavy construction equipment during
his tour, on Okinawa. Was on Okinawa when Typhoon Louise hit. Had winds of 104
miles per hour. Father Claire served in Europe with Co. K, 312 Infantry Regiment
during World War I. Civilian: 1/15/1927 NY - Claire J. Winchip (1894 NY) &
Elizabeth Elsey (1901 NY) - David (1928 NY), Joel (1935 NY) - Earnest E. Elsey (1870 NY) & Mabel
F. Peacock (1877 NY) - Joel Harvey Winchip (1863 NY) & Margaret Moot (1870 NY) - Fillmore
Central, Class of 1945, Rochester Business Institute - Student - Owner, Oil Distribution Company,
Fillmore - Chachita Loux - Rick, John, Candy, Debbie, Philip- 5/13/1994, Indianatown, FL - Pine Grove
Cemetery, Fillmore, NY - 1930, 1940 Federal Census Fillmore - Brother Lt. Col. (Retd) Joel Winchip.
Photo – School.

Witter, Ray Charles Military: US Navy - 6/18/1942/New York/Seaman First Class - Motor Torpedo
Boat Flotilla I, Panama Canal Zone, Chapel Hill, NC Pre-Flight School
- Radio Operator, Educational Therapy/Lieutenant - Norfolk, VA,
Chapel Hill, NC/27 months - 12 months - Panama - American Campaign
- NA - NA - NA - NA - 9/28/1945 – American Campaign Medal, WWII
Victory Medal. Witter also served in the Navy during WW I. He
remained in the service after WW II, and rose to the rank of Commander
before retiring in 1958. Civilian: 2/19/1896 NY - Volney Spalding
Witter (1842 NY) & Mary Mckee (1868 Ireland) - Robert E. (1898 NY)
- INA - Ebenezer Witter (1813 NY) & Eliza? (1817 NY) - Warsaw,
Class of 1915, Syracuse University, Alfred University, Graduate work
in New York, Cambridge, Colorado, Cornell, Panama, & Mexico -
Principal, Silver Creek, Fillmore, Bolivar, Little Valley, Castile, & Little Falls NY High Schools -
Military Service - 1. Violet Hoffman (M 9/6/1926, Bolivar) 2. Ruth A. Cowden (M 7/10/1951) - Jean
(1927 NY) - 8/4/1983 - LaGrange Cemetery, Wyoming County, NY.\ - NAO March, 1942 - Played
professional football & semi-pro baseball. Various internet sites. According to the June, 1942 NAO
Witter served as Principal of FCS from 1921 to 1923. Photo – Passport.

Wolfe, Frank William Jr. Military: US Army - 10/24/1942/Buffalo/Private – Hq Battery, 470th Anti-
Aircraft Artillery Automatic Weapons Battalion - General Clerk/Sergeant - Fort
Eustis, VA/12 months - 25 months – Australia, Bismarck Archipelago, New Guinea,
Philippines - Bismarck Archipelago, New Guinea, Southern Philippines, Luzon - NA
– 11/1943 (Shrapnel wound-right wrist) - NA- NA - 10/29/1945, Fort Dix, NJ -
American Campaign Medal, Asiatic Pacific Theater Campaign Medal, Good Conduct
Medal, Purple Heart, Philippine Liberation Medal, Philippine Presidential Unit
Citation, four Battle Stars, World War II Victory Medal. Civilian: 1/19/1014, NY -
Frank W. Wolfe (1872 NY) & Minnie R. Lynch (1880 NY) - Thelma D. (1910 NY),
Ethel B. (1913 NY), Alice L. (1915 NY) - Laurence F. Lynch (1844 NY) & Mary A.?
(1843 NY) - John Wolfe (1841 Prussia) & Dorothea P.? (1849 Germany) – Niagara County NY School
System – Stock Clerk, Almaine Company - INA - Pauline Smith - Nancy, Patricia - 1/22/1997, Niagara
Falls, NY - INA - Family lived in FCSD post war. Daughter Nancy a 1951 FCS graduate. Daughter
Patricia was a member of the Class of 1955. His wife Pauline was from the FCSD area, the village of
Wiscoy. Photo – NAO.

Wolfer, Robert B. (MI Only) Military: US Army - 2/2/1943/Buffalo/Private - 551st Anti-Aircraft Artillery Automatic Weapons Battalion, Battery B - Truck Driver/Technician 5 - Likely Fort Edwards, MA, Camp Butner, NC, participation in maneuvers in Tennessee twice and South Carolina/12 months - 19 months - England, France, Germany, Austria - Normandy, Northern France, Ardennes Alsace, Rhineland, Central Europe -NA - NA - NA - NA - 8/16/1945 - American Campaign Medal, European, African, Middle Eastern Theater Medal, Good Conduct Medal*, 5 Battle Stars, World War II Victory Medal, Army of Occupation Medal, Germany Clasp. Civilian: 4/6/1923 NY - William F. Wolfer (1876 NY) & Nellie E. Billings (1880 NY) - Frederick (1902 NY), Carl (1904 NY), Mildred (1907 NY), Donald R. (1912 NY) - Parson Billings (1833 NY) & Sarah? (1843 NY) - John Wolfer (1850 Germany) & Elizabeth Alice Durst (1849 Switzerland) - Grammar School, FCS - Farm Worker - INA – Theo M. – Sheila (Germack), Daniel, Duane - 4/14/2005, Portville, NY - Chestnut Hill Cemetery, Portville, NY - 1925, 1930 Federal Census Centerville - None. (*Per General Order 3, dated 2/18/1944 awarding Wolfer the Good Conduct Medal, he had no middle name.) 1925 NY State Census shows a middle initial of B.

Wood, Leonard Arthur (Jug) Military: Army Air Corps - 2/1/1943/Buffalo/Private - 1878th Aviation Engineer Battalion - Service Company, Ambulance Driver/PFC - Missouri, Dyersburg, TN, Brookley Field, Mobile, AL/23 months - Total Service 12 months - Hawaii, Saipan, Okinawa - Okinawa, Western Pacific - NA - NA - NA - Appendectomy at Brookley Field, Al 8/1943 - 12/30/1945 - American Campaign Medal, Asiatic Pacific Theater Medal, WW II Victory Medal, Good Conduct Medal, Meritorious Unit Award, Two Battle Stars, Army Occupation Medal with Asian Clasp, Korea. Civilian: 12/12/1923 NY - Walter J. Wood (1904 NY) &Cora D. Snyder (1905 NY) - Lois Elizabeth (1925 NY) - Stanton Adelbert Snyder (1866 NY) & Cora T. Pifer (1881 NY) - John H. Wood (1851 NY) & Frances Ana Robinson (1851 NY) - Fillmore Central, one-year high school - W.K. Folger, Rossburg - INA - INA - 11/27/1988, Warsaw - INA - 1930 Federal Census Hume - None. Photo – NAO.

Woolsey, Warren Morris Military: Army Air Corps - 2/1943/Air Cadet - 15th Air Force, 47th Bomb Wing, 449th Bomb Group (H), 717th Bomb Squadron - Bombardier/1st Lieutenant - Atlantic City, NJ, Norwich, VT, Nashville, TN, Las Vegas, NV, Deming, NM, Tucson, AZ/12 months - 20 months - Italy - Southern France, North Apennines, Rhineland, Central Europe, Po Valley - NA - NA - NA - Hospitalized, Nashville, TN - 10/14/1945 - Good Conduct Medal, American Campaign Medal, Air Medal, European African Middle East Theater Medal, 5 Battle Stars, WW II Victory Medal. Father Pierce E. Woolsey served in Europe in WW I with the 332nd Infantry Regiment. Civilian: 4/2/922 Indiana - Pierce Edgar Woolsey (1895 Ohio) & Mildred Morris (1896 Ohio) - Martha C. (1924 Ohio) - Joseph Morris (? Ohio) & Cora E. Shales (1868 Ohio) - Westley D. Woolsey (Ohio) & Minnie E. Pierce (Ohio) - Houghton College, Class of 1943, Seminary, NJ - College Student - Missionary Educator, Sierra Leone, Teacher, Houghton College - Ella Phelps (M 8/23/1946) - Stephen, Daniel, Matthew, Ruth – December 24, 2017, Houghton, NY -Mt. Pleasant Cemetery, Houghton - 1930 Federal Census Houghton - Fillmore History Club, Mark Coffee, 449th Bomb Group Historian. Photo – NAO.

Wright, Kenneth Watson Military: US Army - 8/12/1942/Captain – Army Medical Corps, Company
D, 113th Medical Battalion, 38th Infantry Division - Doctor/Captain – INA/19 months, one week - 25 months - New Guinea, Philippines, Japan - New Guinea, Southern Philippines, Luzon - NA - NA - NA - NA - 4/22/1946, Camp Atterbury, IN - American Campaign Medal, Asiatic Pacific Theater Medal, WW II Victory Medal 3 Battle Stars, Philippine Liberation Medal with a battle star, Distinguished Unit Citation. Civilian: 6/13/1912, West Chazy, NY - Stanley W. Wright (1886 PA) & Edna M. Bedford (1888 NY) - Florence E. (1914 NY), Margaret E. (1917 SC), Ruth E. (1922 PA), Alice L. (1926 PA) - Sylvester Bedford (1849 PA) & Elizabeth A. (1852 NY) - Watson R. Wright (1843 PA) & Ellen E. Parade (1848 PA) - Houghton College, Syracuse University, College of Medicine, - Physician, Berea College, Berea, KY, Teacher, Houghton College - Physician - Lois Laura Hope Shea - Nancy, Janet, Geoffrey - 2/16/2003, Syracuse, NY - Mt. Pleasant Cemetery, Houghton - 1930 Federal Census Houghton - None. Photo.

Yanda, William Martin Military: Army Air Corps - 12/20/1943/Buffalo/Private – 2135th AAF Base
Unit, Tyndall, FL - Aerial Gunner, Airplane & Engine Mechanic, Butcher's Assistant/Sergeant - Ypsilanti, MI, Nashville, TN, Tyndall Field, Fl/28 months - NA - NA - NA - NA - NA - NA - NA - 4/20/1946, Ft. Dix, NJ - American Campaign Medal, WW II Victory Medal. Civilian: 1/12/1923 Centerville, NY - Charles Lewis Yanda (1900 MN) & Christina E. Van Name (1903 NY) - Charles L. (1925 NY), Louise J. (1930 NY), John R. (1933 NY, Richard W. (1939 NY) - William H. Van Name (1866 NY) & Eliza M.? (1872 NY) - Martin Yanda (1861 Bohemia) & Shinark? (1868 Bohemia) -Rushford Central School, Class of 1940 - Dispatcher, Bell Aircraft, Buffalo, Auto Company - Service Station Owner, Houghton & Belfast - Annie Sue Johnson (M, TN)- Allen (NY) - 10/21/2009, Houghton - Mt. Pleasant Cemetery, Houghton, NY - 1930 Fed Cen Centerville - Brother Charles Yanda, Son Allen Yanda. Photo – NAO.

Young, Ansel Gay (Skip) Military: US Navy Air - 4/18//1942/Chapel Hill, NC/Aviation Cadet - Navy
Air Transport Service, Squadron VR 2 - First Pilot/Lieutenant - Pre-Flight Chapel Hill, NC, Primary, Dallas, TX, Basic, Pensacola, FL, Instrument Training, Atlanta, GA, NAS, Alameda, CA, NASD, Alemeda, CA/ 46 months – 4 months (Approximate (Flew missions from Alameda, CA to Hawaii and other locations in the Pacific) - Hawaii - NA - NA - NA - NA - 7/13/1946, San Francisco - American Campaign Medal, Asian Pacific Theater Medal, WW II Victory Medal. Brother Norman also served during the war. Received a civilian pilot's license in 1942. His wife Janet said that Ansel really enjoyed being a Naval Aviator. Civilian: 10/19/920 NY - Hollis G. Young (1893 NY) & Bernice B. Doud (1899 NY) - Norman (1925 NY), Wilson (1930 NY) - Menzer J. Doud (1882 NY) & Belle R.? (1867 NY) - Wilson L. Young (1856 NY) & Emma D. Meineke (1866 NY) - Fillmore Central, Class of 1938, University of Pennsylvania, Class of 1942 - Student - Rochester Gas & Electric, Stockbroker, Gannett, Brighton Securities - 1. Nancy Hayden (M 1944 Wyoming, NY), 2. Janet M. Moffat (M 1957, Rochester, NY, B Scotland) - Emily, Hayden, Robert, Rebecca - 11/4/1994/Rochester - Pine Grove Cemetery, Fillmore, NY - 1930 Federal Census Fillmore - Wife Janet Moffat Young. Ansel had a column "Rambling" in the Perry, NY Herald newspaper for a long time. He wrote on various subjects (rambling), everything from the economy to the origins and problems of Silver Lake. Photo – Family.

Young, James Alexander Jr. Military: US Army - 8/1941/INA - 40th Infantry Division, 108th Infantry Regiment - Infantryman/Captain - FT. McClellan, AL, Ft. Ord, CA, Camp Stoneman, CA, Ft. Dix, NJ/13 months - 36 months - Hawaii, Guadalcanal, New Britain, Philippines, Korea - Bismarck (New Britain), Luzon, Leyte, Southern Philippines - NA - NA - NA - NA - 9/7/1945 - Expert Infantryman's Badge, American Campaign Medal, 4 Battle Stars, Asiatic Pacific Theater Medal, WW II Victory Medal, Philippines Presidential Unit Citation. Civilian: 1/31/1918/NY - James A. Young, Sr. (1885 NY) & Adelaide Burdick (1891 NY) - Janet (1916 NY), Milo (1913 NY) - Milo F. Burdick (1864 NY) & Mary C. Hotchkiss (1863 NY) - Walter G. Young (1863 NY) & Jennie Gillies (1864 NY) - Angelica High School, Class of 1936, Cornell University, class of 1940 - Agricultural Teacher, FCS - Farmer, Allegany County Highway Superintendent - Mary (Cohen) - William J., James A., Richard A. - 12/12/1993 in Clermont, FL - Until the Dawn, Angelica, NY - NAO 2/1942, son James. Photo – NAO.

Young, Norman Leonard Military: US Army - 3/1/1943/Buffalo/Private - 703rd, 394th, 1242nd Military Police BN's - Military Policeman/Sergeant - Ft. Meyer, VA, Fitzsimmons General Hospital, Denver. Co, Letterman General Hospital, San Francisco, CA, Camp Sibert, AL, Cleveland, OH/38 months - NA - NA - NA - NA - NA - NA -NA - 4/26/1946 Ft. Dix, NJ - American Campaign Medal, WW II Victory Medal. Except for three months in training as a Dental Medical Technician, spent entire service career as a MP. Was assigned to passenger train guard duty in Cleveland at one time. Civilian: 6/17/1924 Fillmore, NY - Hollis G. Young (1893 NY) & Bernice B. Doud (1899 NY) - Ansel G. (1921 NY), Wilson (1930 NY) - Menzer J. Doud (1882 NY) & Belle R.? - 1867 NY) - Wilson L. Young (1856 NY) & Emma D. Meineke (1866 NY) - Fillmore Central, Class of 1942, Cornell University, Rochester Business Institute - Student - INA - Judith? - David - 5/7/1992 /Jamestown, NY - Pine Grove Cemetery, Fillmore, NY - 1930 Federal Census Fillmore - Allegany County War Service Record. Photo – NAO.

EPILOGUE

These FCSD men and women were part of what was called the Greatest Generation by NBC Newscaster Tom Brokaw. While Brokaw apparently based his honorary designation on the generation's performance in facing up to and winning the Second World War, I would take it a step further. Mostly these men and women were born in the 1910's and 1920's and came of age during the 1930's and early 40's. They faced not only the usual problem of achieving adulthood, but also coming of age during the worst depression in American History. Despite these challenges they became productive adults and helped face down the Depression. In fact, just as the country was about to fully emerge from the depression along came World War II. To my knowledge no other generation in American history has ever had to address two events of the magnitude of the Great Depression and World War II. They won both battles. Some certainly led trying lives. All were not always the paragons of virtue and behavior we expect and wish for from our heroes. But as said elsewhere, they did not see themselves as supermen and heroes. As with all lives, fairness requires that judgement must be rendered by the overall, not just a part. By that standard of fairness, they were an exceptionally strong and determined generation of men and women. Calling them the Greatest may be an understatement. We can only wish and hope that every generation could be as strong, as patriotic, as dedicated to the ideas and principles of the United States as the World War II generation.

I believe a hallmark of World War II veterans was their reluctance to even mention much less discuss their experiences during the war. That reluctance is historical and has been mentioned several times in this book. Those of us who were not there see such reluctance as commendable and honorable for reasons we believe justify it. Being no difference from others, I highly respect their reluctance. I believe it is the result of those experiences. Why would a veteran want to discuss the horror and slaughter of war, to which they personally had contributed; the dying of close friends of only a few months who were closer to them then life-long friends; the incredible destruction of what was called civilization. Who would want to remember, but be unable to forget, and certainly not discuss, the last visit to a lost buddy, whose remains were now in pieces. Who could possibly forget the stench of concentration camps and the parts of unburned bodies still visible in the camps ovens. They may not have wanted to discuss the war, and they had many reasons for their reluctance, but it would be wrong to think they ever forgot any of it.

SOURCES

Besides the sources listed below, many individual sources are listed in part XIV of the book in the section for each veteran for whom an individual or entity provided information, and/or in the write-up in the book on that veteran's service.

Air Force Historical Agency, Maxwell AFB, AL

Allegany County War Service Records

BIRLS Files

Cemetery Records and Headstone Information

Department of Veteran Affairs BIRLS Death Files – 1850-2010

Fillmore Central School Senior Class Pictures, 1920-1940
Fillmore, NY History Club

Historical Society, Belfast, NY
Historical Society, East Aurora, NY
Historical Society, Lyons, NY
Historical Society, Nunda, NY
Historical Society, Warsaw, NY
Historical Society, Wyoming County, NY

Internet Sites (Unit Histories, Obituaries, Unit Associations, WW II Battles, Unit Historical Sites, US Naval Ships)

Library – Belfast, NY
Library – Cuba, NY
Library, Fillmore, NY

National Archives and Records Administration (NARA), College Park, MD – WW II Unit Files (Histories, Journals, After-Action Reports, General Orders, Air Corps Combat Missions, Navy Ship Deck Logs, Navy Ship War Diaries, Armed Guards Reports, Navy/Marine Corps Muster Rolls, etc.)

National Archives and Records Administration, St. Louis, MO – Military Personnel Records – WW II Personnel Files, Discharge Records, Final Pay Records, Medical Records.

Northern Allegany County Observer 1940 – 1945, (All NAO citations in this book refer to the WW II NAO books, 1941 to 1945, as produced by the Fillmore History Club)

Nunda NY Veterans Project

Pennsylvania Veterans Compensation Application Files, WW II, 1950-1966

Registry – World War II Memorial, Washington, DC

Roll of Honor, WW II - Centerville, NY
Roll of Honor, WW II – Hume, NY
Roll of Honor, WW II - Fillmore, NY

Social Security Death Index (SSDI)
Social Security Applications and Claims Index

Town of Hume, NY Museum, Rondus Miller, Historian

US Army World War II Enlistment Records 1938

US Federal Censuses (1850 to 1940)

US World War II Draft Registration Cards, 1942
US World War II Draft Cards Young Men 1940 – 1947
US World War Hospital Admission Card File 1942 - 1954
US Holocaust Museum

Veterans Unit Associations - Internet
        2nd Bomb Group Association
        449th Bomb Group Association

Veterans History Project, Library of Congress

Women's Air Service Pilots WW II Museum, Avenger Field, Texas
Women in Military Service to America Museum, Washington, DC

BOOKS

Atkinson, Rick, *An Army at Dawn,* Henry Holt
Atkinson, Rick, *The Guns at Last Light – The War in Western Europe, 1944 -1945*, Picador

Balkoski, Joseph, *Omaha Beach D-Day, June 6, 1944*, Stackpole Books

Bradley, James, *Fly Boys,* Random House

Coffey, Thomas M., *HAP,* Viking

Department of the Army, *Unit Citation and Campaign Participation Credit Register*

Hastings, Max, *Inferno,* Knofp

Hillenbrand, Laura, *Unbroken,* Random House

Hoegh, Leo A. (Editor), Doyle, Howard J. (Associate Editor), *Timberwolf Tracks 104 Infantry Division,* Infantry Journal, Inc.

Hodgson, Godfrey, *The Colonel - The Life and Wars of Henry Stimson 1867 – 1950*

Klingaman, William K., *1941 Our Lives in a World on the Edge*

Manchester, William & Reid, Paul, *The Last Lion Winston Spenser Churchill Defender of the Realm 1940-1965,* Little, Brown

Maurer, Maurer (Editor) *World War II Combat Squadrons of the United States Air Force*, Smithmark

Morrison, Wilbur H., F*ortress Without a Roof,* St. Martin's Press

Monahan, Evelyn M. & Neidel-Greenlee, Rosemary, *And If I Perish,* Knopf

Mosley, Leonard, *Marshall,* Hearst

Pogue, Forrest C., *George C. Marshall Ordeal and Hope 1939-1942,* Viking
Pogue, Forrest C., *George C. Marshall, Organizer of Victory 1943-1945,* Viking

Prange, Gordon W., *At Dawn We Slept – The Untold Story of Pearl Harbor*, McGraw
Prange, Gordon W. (Goldstein, Donald M. and Dillon, Katherine V.), *Pearl Harbor - The Verdict of History*, McGraw
Prange, Gordon W. (Goldstein, Donald M. and Dillon, Katherine V.) *Miracle at Midway,* McGraw

Smith, Jean Edward, *FDR,* Random House

Speer, Albert, *Inside the Third Reich Memoirs,* Macmillan

Stafford, Edward P. Commander U.S.N., *The Big E - The Story of the USS Enterprise*, Random House

Starusbaugh, John, *Victory City,* Twelve

Taylor, Theodore, *The Magnificent Mitscher,* Norton

Tibbetts, Paul W. (Clair Stebbins & Harry Franken), *The Tibbetts Story*, Stein, and Day

Thomas, Gordon & Morgan Witts, Max, *Enola Gay,* Stein, and Day

MAGAZINES

Eighth Air Force Historical Society, various issues

World War II – Volume 33, No. 6 April 2019

ABBREVIATIONS

AAA	- Anti-Aircraft Artillery
AAFB	- Army Air Force Base
AFRTC	- Armed Forces Replacement Training Center
AGF	- Army Ground Forces
AGO	- Attorney General's Office
AK	- Alaska
AL	- Alabama
AMM	- Aviation Machinist Mate
APTO	- Asiatic Pacific Theater of Operations
AR	- Arkansas
ASF	- Army Service Forces
ASTP	- Army Specialized Training Program
AT	- Air Transport
AVP	- Seaplane Tender
AWBN	- Automatic Weapons Battalion
AWOL	- Away Without Leave
B -17	- Bomber built by Boeing Aircraft Company
BIRLS	- Beneficiary Identification Records Locator System
CA	- California
CAG	- Construction Mechanic
CASU	- Carrier Air Service Unit
CB	- Construction Battalion (Navy Seabees)
C/B	- Chemical/Biological
CCD	- Certificate of Disability
CIB	- Combat Infantry Badge
CM	- Construction Mechanic
CO	- Colorado
CO	- County
ATC	- Calvary Replacement Training Center
CT	- Connecticut
CVE	- Escort Aircraft Carrier
CWS	- Chemical Welfare Service

DE	- Delaware
EAME	- European African Middle East Theater Medal
ERC	- Enlisted Reserve Corps
ETO	- European Theater of Operations
FARTC	- Field Artillery Replacement Training Center
FAW	- Fleet Air Wing
FCS	- Fillmore Central School
FCSD	- Fillmore Central School District
FL	- Florida
FMF	- Fleet Marine Force
FO	- Field Order
FW – 190	- German fighter plane built by Focke Wulf Company
F4F- F	- Fighter aircraft/4-4th version, nicknamed Wildcat/F-built by Grumman Corporation
F6F- F	-stands for Fighter, 6- sixth version, F- built by Gruman Corporation. The F6F's nickname was Hellcat. It replaced the F4F and was the dominant aircraft carrier fighter in the Pacific.
F4U-	F-Fighter aircraft/4-4th version/U-built by chance Vaught Corporation
GE	- Georgia
G.I.	- General Issue
GMC	- Gun Motor Carriage (A self-propelled artillery vehicle)
GO	- General Order
HEDRON	- Headquarters Squadron
HI	- Hawaii
HMS	- His/Her Majesty's Ship
HQ	- Headquarters
ID	- Idaho

IL	- Illinois	OCS	- Officer's Candidate School
IN	- Indiana		
IO	- Iowa	OH	- Ohio
		OK	- Oklahoma
KIA	- Killed in Action	OR	- Oregon
KS	- Kansas	OTU	- Operational Training Unit
KY	- Kentucky		
		PA	- Pennsylvania
LA	- Louisiana	PBM	- PB-Patrol Bomber/-Built by Glenn L. Martin Company
LCI	- Landing Ship Infantry		
LOD	- Line of Duty		
LST	- Landing Ship Tank	PBY	- Patrol bomber built by Consolidated Aircraft Company
LVT	- Landing Vehicle Tracker		
MA	- Massachusetts	POW	- Prisoner of War
ME	- Maine	PR	- Puerto Rico
MD	- Maryland	PT	- Patrol Torpedo plane
ME – 109	- German fighter built by Messerschmitt Corporation	PV	- Patrol bomber built by Lockheed Corporation for anti-submarine work
MI	- Michigan		
MN	- Minnesota		
NMN	- No Middle Name	PB4Y-1	- Converted Army B-26 Liberator used by Navy for anti-submarine work
MO	- Missouri		
MOS	- Military OccupationSpecialty		
MS	- Mississippi	QC	- Quartermaster Corps
MT	- Montana	QSMV	- Quadruple Screw Motor Vehicle
MTB	- Motor Torpedo Boat		
MTO	- Mediterranean Theater of Operations		
		RAF	- Royal Air Force
NAF	- Naval Air Facility	RCAF	- Royal Canadian Air Force
NAO	- Northern Allegany Observer	RG&E	- Rochester Gas & Electric Company
NAS	- Naval Air Station	RI	- Rhode Island
NATTC	- Naval Air Technical Training Center	RMIC	- Radio Man First Class
		RMMV	- Royal Mail Motor Vessel
NB	- Nebraska	RMS	- Royal Mail Ship
NC	- North Carolina	RON	- Squadron
ND	- North Dakota	ROTC	- Reserve Officers Training Corps
NH	- New Hampshire		
NILOD	- Not in Line of Duty	R&R	- Rest and Recuperation
NJ	- New Jersey		
NM	- New Mexico	SBD	- Scout Bomber, built by Douglas Aircraft
NTC	- Naval Training Center		
NV	- Nevada	SC	- South Carolina
NY	- New York	SCTC	- Submarine Chaser Training School
NYC	- New York City		
		SD	- South Dakota

SEABEES	- Navy Construction Battalions (From CB, Construction Battalions)
SPARS	- Semper Paratus (Latin for Always Ready)
SOS	- (Not an abbreviation - does not stand for anything), just a distress signal
SS	- Steamship
SSDI	- Social Security Death Index

SS Troops - German Schutzstaffel (Cadre of combat troops whose specialty was killing Innocent people -originally Hitler's personal body guard.

TADCEN	- Naval Training &Distribution Center
TBF	- Torpedo Bomber Reconnaissance
TBM	- Torpedo Bomber built by General Motors
TN	- Tennessee
TNT	- Trinitrotoluene - an explosive
TX	- Texas

U-Boat	- Undersea Boat
US	- United States
USAFBI	- United States Forces in the British Isles
USAFE	- United States Air Forces Europe
USAFET	- United States Army Forces European Theater
USAHS	- United States Army Hospital Ship
USS	- United States Ship
UT	- Utah

VC – 9	- V-heavier than air/C-composite squadron 9 (or other numbers)
VF	- V-heavier than air/F-fighter
VFA	- V-heavier than air-fixed wings/F-fighter/A-attack

VF7	- V-heavier than air/R-transport/7-7th of type
VFR	- Air Ferrying Squadron
VI	- Virginia
VMD	- V-heavier than air/M-marine/D-photographic
VN	- Training Plane
VPB	- V-heavier than air/P-patrol/B-Bomber
VR	- V-heavier than air/R-transport
VT	- Vermont
V1	- V- "Vergeltungswaffen" in German/retribution weapon/in English a long-range missile.
V2-	Same as above – First liquid propellant rocket.

WA	- Washington
WAAC	- Women's Auxiliary Army Corps
WAC	- Women's Army Reserve Corps
WASPS	- Women's Air Service Pilots
WAVE	- Women Accepted for Volunteer Emergency Service
WV	- West Virginia
WY	- Wyoming

INDEX
The Men and Women Who Served